Lecture Notes in Computer Science 3541

Commenced Publication in 1973
Founding and Former Series Editors:
Gerhard Goos, Juris Hartmanis, and Jan van Leeuwen

Nikunj C. Oza Robi Polikar
Josef Kittler Fabio Roli (Eds.)

Multiple
Classifier Systems

6th International Workshop, MCS 2005
Seaside, CA, USA, June 13-15, 2005
Proceedings

Volume Editors

Nikunj C. Oza
NASA Ames Research Center
Mail Stop 269-3, Moffett Field, CA 94035-1000, USA
E-mail: oza@email.arc.nasa.gov

Robi Polikar
Rowan University, Electrical and Computer Engineering
136 Rowan Hall, 201 Mullica Hill Road, Glassboro, NJ 08028, USA
E-mail: polikar@rowan.edu

Josef Kittler
University of Surrey, Center for Vision, Speech and Signal Processing
Guildford, Surrey GU2 7XH, UK
E-mail: j.kittler@eim.surrey.ac.uk

Fabio Roli
University of Cagliari, Department of Electrical and Electronic Engineering
Piazza D'Armi, 09123 Cagliari, Italy
E-mail: roli@diee.unica.it

Library of Congress Control Number: 2005927319

CR Subject Classification (1998): I.5, I.4, I.2.10, I.2, F.1

ISSN   0302-9743
ISBN-10   3-540-26306-3 Springer Berlin Heidelberg New York
ISBN-13   978-3-540-26306-7 Springer Berlin Heidelberg New York

Springer is a part of Springer Science+Business Media

springeronline.com

© Springer-Verlag Berlin Heidelberg 2005
Printed in Germany

Typesetting: Camera-ready by author, data conversion by Scientific Publishing Services, Chennai, India
Printed on acid-free paper.   SPIN: 11494683   06/3142   5 4 3 2 1 0

Preface

The belief that a committee of people make better decisions than any individual is widely held and appreciated. We also understand that, for this to be true, the members of the committee have to be simultaneously competent and complementary. This intuitive notion holds true for committees of data sources (such as sensors) and models (such as classifiers). The substantial current research in the areas of data fusion and model fusion focuses on ensuring that the different sources provide useful information but nevertheless complement one another to yield better results than any source would on its own. During the 1990s, a variety of schemes in classifier fusion, which is the focus of this workshop, were developed under many names in different scientific communities such as machine learning, pattern recognition, neural networks, and statistics. The previous five workshops on Multiple Classifier Systems (MCS) were themselves exercises in information fusion, with the goal of bringing the different scientific communities together, providing each other with different perspectives on this fascinating topic, and aiding cross-fertilization of ideas. These five workshops achieved this goal, demonstrating significant advances in the theory, algorithms, and applications of multiple classifier systems.

Following its five predecessors published by Springer, this volume contains the proceedings of the 6th International Workshop on Multiple Classifier Systems (MCS 2005) held at the Embassy Suites in Seaside, California, USA, June 13–15, 2005. Forty-two papers were selected by the Scientific Committee, and they were organized into the following sessions: Boosting, Combination Methods, Design of Ensembles, Performance Analysis, and Applications. The workshop program was enriched by an invited talk given by Leo Breiman (University of California, Berkeley, USA).

The workshop was organized by the NASA Ames Research Center (USA), Rowan University (USA), and PureSense Environmental (USA). It was sponsored by the International Association for Pattern Recognition through its Technical Committee TC1: Statistical Techniques in Pattern Recognition. We also wish to express our gratitude to all who helped to organize MCS 2005. We thank the authors of all the submissions for their hard work and efforts toward making this workshop a true exercise in information fusion. We also thank the members of the Scientific Committee and many other reviewers for performing the difficult task of selecting the best papers from a large number of high-quality submissions. Special thanks to Terry Windeatt (University of Surrey, UK), Darren Galaviz (NASA), John Williamson (PureSense), Christopher Peri (PureSense), and Giorgio Fumera (University of Cagliari, Italy) for their substantial contributions to local organization and website management.

June 2005   Nikunj C. Oza, Robi Polikar, Josef Kittler, and Fabio Roli

Organization

Workshop Chairs

N.C. Oza (NASA Ames Research Center, USA)
R. Polikar (Rowan University, USA)
J. Kittler (University of Surrey, UK)
F. Roli (University of Cagliari, Italy)

Scientific Committee

J.A. Benediktsson (Iceland)
H. Bunke (Switzerland)
L.P. Cordella (Italy)
B.V. Dasarathy (USA)
R.P.W. Duin (The Netherlands)
C. Furlanello (Italy)
J. Ghosh (USA)
V. Govindaraju (USA)
T.K. Ho (USA)
S. Impedovo (Italy)
N. Intrator (Israel)
A.K. Jain (USA)
M. Kamel (Canada)
L.I. Kuncheva (UK)
D. Partridge (UK)
A.J.C. Sharkey (UK)
C.Y. Suen (Canada)
K. Tumer (USA)
G. Vernazza (Italy)

Organizing Committee

T. Windeatt (University of Surrey, UK)
G. Fumera (University of Cagliari, Italy)
D. Galaviz (NASA Ames Research Center, USA)
J. Williamson (Puresense Environmental, USA)
C. Peri (Puresense Environmental, USA)

Sponsoring Institutions

Intelligent Systems Division, NASA Ames Research Center
Department of Electrical and Computer Engineering, Rowan University
Puresense Environmental
International Association for Pattern Recognition
IAPR Technical Committee TC1

Table of Contents

Future Directions

Boosting

Combination Methods

Design Methods

Performance Analysis

Applications

Semi-supervised Multiple Classifier Systems: Background and Research Directions

Fabio Roli

Dept. of Electrical and Electronic Engineering, University of Cagliari,
Piazza d'Armi, 09123 Cagliari, Italy
roli@diee.unica.it

Abstract. Multiple classifier systems have been originally proposed for supervised classification tasks. In the five editions of MCS workshop, most of the papers have dealt with design methods and applications of supervised multiple classifier systems. Recently, the use of multiple classifier systems has been extended to unsupervised classification tasks. Despite its practical relevance, semi-supervised classification has not received much attention. Few works on semi-supervised multiple classifiers appeared in the machine learning literature. This paper's goal is to review the background results that can be exploited to promote research on semi-supervised multiple classifier systems, and to outline some future research directions.

1 Introduction

During the 1990's, several classifier fusion schemes, especially the ones that operate at the so-called decision-level, have emerged under a plethora of names within various scientific communities, including information fusion, machine learning, neural networks, pattern recognition, and statistics. The initial works on multiple classifier systems (MCS) dealt almost exclusively with supervised classification, and this trend continued over the years. In the five editions of MCS workshop [1], most papers have dealt with design methods and applications of supervised multiple classifier systems. Only recently, the multiple classifiers approach has been extended to unsupervised classification, and some methods have been proposed to combine multiple clustering algorithms [2,3]. Although past MCS research was focused on supervised classification, many pattern recognition applications cannot be addressed effectively under the pure supervised approach. In fact, there are applications that are characterized by two contrasting factors: the need for large quantities of labelled data to design classifiers with high accuracy, and the difficulty of collecting such data. For example, in text classification, the common end-user is not available to manually label a large amount of data necessary to achieve reasonable classification accuracy [4]. In remote-sensing image classification, Jackson and Landgrebe pointed out that the large number of spectral bands of modern sensors and the large number of land-cover classes of interest, require a number of training examples that are too expensive or tedious to acquire [5]. Similar scenarios occur in face recognition, medical

N.C. Oza et al. (Eds.): MCS 2005, LNCS 3541, pp. 1–11, 2005.
© Springer-Verlag Berlin Heidelberg 2005

imaging, and intrusion detection in computer networks [6,7,8]. On the other hand, in these applications, collecting unlabelled data is often easy and inexpensive. In many text classification applications (e.g., web page categorization), unlabelled examples are freely and abundantly available. In remote sensing, thanks to the high spatial resolution of modern sensors, a large number of unlabelled examples become available when new images are captured. It is easy to see that such applications demand classification methods that achieve high accuracy using only a few labelled but many unlabelled examples. Semi-supervised classification deals with the design of classifiers using both labelled (possibly few) and unlabelled training examples. Various approaches to semi-supervised classification have been proposed [9].

Despite the theoretical and practical relevance of semi-supervised classification, the proposed approaches so far dealt with only single classifiers, and, in particular, no work was clearly devoted to this topic within the MCS literature. To the best of our knowledge, few works on semi-supervised multiple classifiers have appeared in the machine learning literature [7,10,11,12,13].

This paper is aimed at reviewing the background results that can be exploited to promote research on semi-supervised multiple classifier systems, and to outline some future research directions. Section 2 provides the basic concepts and briefly reviews the main approaches to semi-supervised classification. Section 3 reviews the few works which dealt with semi-supervised multiple classifiers, and attempts to give a systematic definition of semi-supervised MCS. Some directions for future research are outlined in Section 4.

2 Semi-supervised Classification

Given a set D_l (usually, small) of labelled data, and a set D_u (usually, large) of unlabelled data, semi-supervised classification methods aim to design classifiers using both sets. In this section, we first review briefly the main methods proposed for semi-supervised classification, with a particular attention paid to the co-training method due to its strong connection to MCS. Our review is biased due to its restricted focus on MCS, and consequently is not exhaustive. We refer the reader to [9] for a broader overview on semi-supervised classification methods. Finally, we briefly review the main arguments on the usefulness of unlabelled data in increasing the classification accuracy.

2.1 Methods for Semi-supervised Classification

Decision-Directed Methods
It is easy to see that a most straightforward approach to semi-supervised classification should be based on exploiting the available labeled examples in automatically assigning class labels to unlabeled data. The basic approach works as follows. An initial classifier is designed using the labeled data set D_l. This classifier is then used to assign class labels to examples in D_u. Then the classifier is re-trained using $D_l \cup D_u$. As the convergence of this simple algorithm can not be guaranteed in general, the last two steps are usually repeated for a given number of times or until some heuristic

convergence criterion is satisfied. It is worth noting that, while traditional pattern recognition systems are "open-loop" systems, this approach corresponds to the implementation of simple "closed-loop" systems [15,16]. Although encouraging results have been reported in real applications [14], it is easy to see that the performance of this approach strongly depends on the accuracy of the classifiers used to assign the "pseudo-labels". The classification accuracy can improve over the iterations only if the initial and subsequent classifiers correctly label most of the data. Unfortunately, the issue of labelling accuracy needed to guarantee low generalization error is nearly impossible to address [15]. In practical applications, unreliable class labels are disregarded using measures of classification confidence in order to limit the number of labelling errors.

This simple approach to semi-supervised classification and its related methods, have been referred under various names by different communities: self-learning methods [9,15], self-corrective recognition [15,16], adaptive methods, naïve labelling approach [17], and decision-directed methods [18]. We choose the last name to refer to this paragraph since it reflects well the fundamental mechanism of this approach and it is used in statistical parameter estimation and signal processing areas.

Expectation-Maximization Methods

Expectation-maximization (EM) is a well known class of iterative algorithms for maximum-likelihood or maximum a posteriori estimation in problems with incomplete data [19,20]. In the case of semi-supervised classification, the unlabeled data are considered incomplete because they do not have class labels. The basic EM approach first designs a probabilistic classifier (e.g., a Gaussian classifier) with the available data set D_l. Then, such classifier is used to assign probabilistically-weighted class labels to unlabeled examples by calculating the expectation of the missing class labels. Then a new classifier is trained using both the original labelled data and the formerly unlabelled data, and the process is repeated.

The main advantage of EM approach is that it allows exploiting, in a theoretically well grounded way, both labelled and unlabelled data. Therefore, it meets the main requirement of semi-supervised classification in a natural way. In addition, it is quite general, and it has been used with different probabilistic models of classifiers [10,20].

Results on different classification tasks showed that EM methods allow exploiting unlabelled data effectively. For example, Nigam et al. show that unlabelled data used with EM methods in a document categorization problem can reduce classification error by up to 30% [20]. On the other hand, Cohen et al. recently showed that EM methods can increase the classification accuracy only if the assumed probabilistic model of the classifier matches well with data distribution; otherwise, the use of unlabelled data can become counter productive [6].

Co-training

A co-training approach to semi-supervised classification was proposed by Blum and Mitchell in 1998 [21]. The basic idea can be illustrated with the web-page classification example originally used by the authors. Web pages can be characterized by two distinct types of features: features characterizing the text appearing in the web page, and features characterizing the hyperlinks pointing to the page. The key idea is to design two independent classifiers using the text and hyperlink features separately. These two classifiers are trained with the initial, small, labelled data set D_l, and it is assumed that the classifiers will exhibit a low, but better than random, accuracy (it is worth noting that this definition closely resembles the concept of "weak" classifier used in the MCS field). Each classifier is then applied to the unlabeled examples. For each classifier, the unlabelled examples that received the highest confidence by this classifier are added to labelled data, so that the two classifiers contribute to increase the data set. Both the classifiers are re-trained with this augmented data set, and the process is repeated a specified number of times. When the co-training process finishes, the two resulting classifiers can be combined by the product of the outputs. However, it is worth noting that the basic co-training algorithm does not contain this combination phase. In fact, the main goal of this approach is to increase the accuracy of the two individual classifiers by co-training. But the reported results have shown that the combination can further increase the classification accuracy.

Intuitively, co-training is expected to work because the two classifiers are assumed to be "complementary", thanks to the use of disparate features. In particular, a classifier may assign correct labels to certain examples while it may be difficult for the other classifier to do so. Therefore, each classifier can increase the training set to be used by the other classifier. It should be also noted that co-training is expected to increase the size of the training set more quickly than what each individual classifier could do using a decision-directed, self-learning, mechanism.

Several authors reported experimental results which show the effectiveness of co-training [9,22,28]. Blum and Mitchell provided some theoretical support for co-training within the PAC learning framework [21]. However, the fundamental issue about the conditions under which, and the extent at which, the use of unlabeled data with co-training can increase classification accuracy is basically unsolved.

Although, to the best of our knowledge, co-training has always been used with just two classifiers, Blum and Mitchell pointed out that this approach can be used with a larger ensemble of classifiers, particularly if are "independent". It is easy to see that this makes co-training a good candidate for the development of semi-supervised MCS. However, it should be noted that co-training was not originally meant as a method to create and combine classifiers; in fact, the basic co-training algorithm does not contain any classifier combination. Therefore, a lot of work remains to be done about the use of co-training to create good classifier ensembles, and, in particular, about the combination techniques when the independence assumption is likely to be violated.

Active Learning
This approach assumes the availability of an external "oracle" to assign class labels [9]. Basically, unlabeled examples are repeatedly selected, and the oracle (e.g., a human expert) is asked to assign class labels to such data. The goal of active learning is to select the most informative unlabeled examples, in order to effectively train the classifier with the minimum number of calls to the oracle. To this end, different selection strategies have been proposed [9]. For the purpose of this paper, the so-

called *query by committee* selection strategy is worth pointing out; an ensemble of classifiers is first designed, and then the examples which cause the maximum disagreement among these classifiers are selected as the most informative [13].

2.2 The Added Value of Unlabelled Data

It is easy to see that the fundamental issues for semi-supervised classification concern the conditions and the extent to which the use of unlabeled data can increase the classification accuracy reached with a limited set of labelled examples. Experimental evidence on the usefulness of unlabeled data is in fact controversial. Some works based on current semi-supervised methods support the claim that unlabeled data can increase classification accuracy [20,22]. On the other hand, there are experimental results showing that unlabeled data can degrade the classification accuracy [6]. The few theoretical analyses on the added value of unlabeled data do not yet provide clear answers. Some researchers provided qualitative arguments in favour of the usefulness of unlabeled data. For example, Nigam et al. suggested that unlabeled data can provide information on correlations among features [20]. Castelli and Cover showed that unlabeled data are asymptotically useful for classification [23]. Recently, Cohen et al. showed that unlabeled data increase classification accuracy of EM methods when the probabilistic model assumed for the classifier matches the data generating distribution [6]. Despite these valuable works, the conditions and the extent to which the use of unlabeled data can increase classification accuracy are not clear for many current semi-supervised methods. In particular, clear conditions are not available to indicate when the use of unlabeled data is likely to be counter productive, and what is the right trade-off between labeled and unlabeled data. However, we already have some experimental evidences and theoretical supports on the usefulness of the semi-supervised methods that we reviewed in the previous section.

3 Semi-supervised Multiple Classifier Systems

3.1 Background

In the past editions of MCS workshop, no work was clearly devoted to semi-supervised classification. In this section, we review the few works on semi-supervised multiple classifiers which, to the best of our knowledge, have appeared in the literature so far.

Miller and Uyar proposed a mixture-of-expert classifier model which allows the use both labelled and unlabelled data [10]. The authors assume that the data is well modelled by a mixture density, and propose a generalized mixture model where the class labels are viewed as random quantities depending on the mixture components. This classifier model can be regarded as a mixture-of-experts, because the class posterior probabilities have a "mixture" structure where the "gating units" are the probabilities of mixture components [31]. The mixture is trained by maximising the data likelihood over both the labelled and unlabelled examples using EM algorithms. Although the authors have not stressed the aspects specifically related to MCS, this work points out that EM methods can be easily used to design semi-supervised probabilistic mixtures of experts. In addition, the authors appropriately stressed an important point for extending the range of application of semi-supervised MCS, namely, the possibility of regarding the unknown test data as unlabeled, and performing a semi-supervision cycle before classifying a new batch of test data. This is an important point for the use of semi-supervised MCS in non stationary pattern recognition applications [29].

To the best of our knowledge, one of the first works clearly devoted to semi-supervised MCS is by d'Alchè-Buc et al. [11], which is an extension of one authors' previous work. In fact, the goal is to generalize Boosting to semi-supervised classification. To this end, they adopt MarginBoost, a version of AdaBoost based on the minimisation of an explicit cost functional. Such functional is defined for any scalar decreasing function of the margin. As the usual definition of margin cannot be used for unlabeled data, the authors extend the margin notion to unlabeled data. In practice, the margin is estimated using the MarginBoost classification output. Then, they reformulate the cost function of MarginBoost to accommodate both the labelled and unlabelled data. A mixture model is used as a base classifier because it is well suited to the use of unlabeled data by EM algorithms. Reported results show that semi-supervised MarginBoost clearly outperforms the classical AdaBoost only when very few labelled data are available (5% labelled vs. 95% unlabeled data).

Bennet et al. proposed an interesting semi-supervised MCS, named ASSEMBLE, which iteratively constructs classifier ensembles using both labelled and unlabelled data. It is worth noting that ASSEMBLE is explicitly aimed at overcoming some limitations of MarginBoost [12]. For example, while MarginBoost requires the base classifier to be an algorithm well suited to semi-supervision with EM (e.g., a mixture model), ASSEMBLE can be used with any cost-sensitive base classifier. ASSEMBLE operation alternates between assigning pseudo-classes to the unlabelled data using the current ensemble and constructing the next base classifier using both the labelled and pseudo-labelled data. ASSEMBLE is shown to work very well in practice, and it won the NIPS 2001 unlabeled data competition using decision trees as base classifiers.

Martinez and Fuentes described an interesting application of semi-supervised MCS to face recognition [7]. They reported experiments with MCS made up of five strong classifiers (i.e., three k-nearest neighbour classifiers, one multi-layer perceptron, one locally weighted linear regression classifier) using a simple decision-directed semi-supervision method. The classifier ensemble is first trained with a small set of labelled data. Then, this ensemble is used to assign pseudo-class labels to unlabelled data. These two steps are repeated until the number of available unlabeled data becomes lower than the number of pseudo-labelled examples. Their results appear to be preliminary, and a more extensive experimentation would be necessary to draw final conclusions. However, this work points out the relevance that semi-supervised MCS could have for face recognition.

Melville and Mooney deal with active learning by the *query by committee* selection strategy [13]. They propose an algorithm, named ACTIVE-DECORATE (basically, a version of the authors' DECORATE algorithm devoted to active learning), which uses ensembles created by the DECORATE algorithm to select the most informative examples. Experimental results show that this active learning method leads to more effective sample selection than query by Bagging and query by Boosting.

Finally, it is worth mentioning the recent work of Agogino dealing with an agent based method to combine different clustering algorithms [32]. Agogino's ensemble method is quite different from traditional classifier combining techniques, as it is based on the COIN (COllective INtelligence) framework introduced by Wolpert and Tumer [33]. Although it was originally meant for unsupervised classification tasks, its use for semi-supervised classification could be investigated. In fact, clustering of unlabelled data, followed by the assignment of pseudo-class labels to identified clusters by a classifier previously trained with available labeled data, is a possible approach to semi-supervised classification [9].

3.2 A Definition of Semi-supervised Multiple Classifier System

Current supervised MCS can be characterized by:

- **Architecture:** Also called the topology, the architecture could be parallel, serial, dynamic, or a combination thereof. Different taxonomies of MCS architectures can be found in [24];
- **Ensemble of Classifiers:** A single type of base classifiers can be used (e.g.., decision tree), such as in Bagging or AdaBoost, or different classification algorithms can be combined. The ensemble can be further decomposed into subsets in the case of non parallel architectures;
  Combination Function: Two main types of functions are currently used: the so-called fusers wherein all classifiers contribute to the final classification, and the selectors wherein for each pattern a single or subset of classifiers contributes to the final classification. It should be noted that some complex MCS architectures can have various combinations of the types [24].

In most of the supervised MCS, labelled data are used to design and train base classifiers and, if necessary, to implement the combination function. The so-called "fixed" combination functions, such as majority voting, average and product of classifier outputs, do not require training. On the other hand, there are trainable combination functions, such the Behaviour Knowledge Space combiner, which need a large and independent set of labelled data. The architecture, however, is usually fixed in these cases.

Therefore, a simple definition of semi-supervised MCS can be given as follows:

Semi-supervised MCS is an MCS where the labelled and unlabelled data are jointly used to design and train the classifier ensemble, and/or the combination function, and/or the architecture.

The works reviewed in Section 3.1 fit well within the above definition. MarginBoost and the semi-supervised mixtures of experts are examples of MCS which jointly use labelled and unlabelled data to train the classifier ensemble [10,11]. But this definition suggests further uses of unlabeled data in MCS. For example, it is well known that the effective use of trainable combiners is seriously limited by the requirement of a large, independent set of labelled examples. As pointed by Raudys [25], such examples should be independent of the data set used to train the base classifiers. But this requirement is difficult to satisfy in practical applications. For some trainable combiners, simple decision-directed and self-corrective algorithms using unlabelled data could be investigated to reduce the generalization error.

4 Research Directions

On the basis of background presented in Section 3.1, the author thinks that the following three research directions should be considered. The following list is not obviously exhaustive, and it only outlines three possible directions, without discussing in detail the various activities which could be carried out within each direction. The main aim is to stimulate research on this challenging topic and to promote discussion and activities within the MCS community.

1. Using unlabelled data in current MCS design

This research direction should investigate the benefits of using unlabelled data within the current MCS design methods.

As pointed out in section 3.2, unlabelled data could be exploited to improve the design of trainable combiners, which often needs a lot of training examples. To this end, the use of the decision-directed approach illustrated in Section 2.1 could be investigated. A multiple classifier system could be initially created using the available set of labelled data. Then, such system could be used to assign class labels to unlabelled data, disregarding unreliable class labels on the basis of some classification confidence measure. Then base classifiers could be re-trained with the data set augmented with the pseudo-labelled data. The last two steps could be iterated for a given number of times.

Unlabelled data could be also exploited in the creation of classifier ensembles. In fact, there are methods for the creation of classifier ensembles which could benefit by increased data sets. For example, methods based on training data manipulation, such as data splitting belong to this category.

2. Semi-supervised MCS

The goal of this research direction should be the development of new semi-supervised MCS.

Some of the current MCS could be extended to semi-supervised classification in simple ways. For example, a first attempt to the development of a semi-supervised version of Bagging could be done using a decision-directed algorithm. The same approach could be used with other coverage optimisation methods, such as the random subspace method [27].

As outlined in Section 2.1, the co-training approach can be naturally exploited to develop semi-supervised MCS, because, in principle, it can be used with more than two classifiers. So far co-training was mainly used when a natural feature subdivision exists, that is, when patterns can be characterized by distinct sets of features. This is the case for the web-page classification task considered in the original work of Blum and Mitchell [21], and also for some multi-sensor, multi-modal classification tasks (e.g., multi-modal biometric recognition). However, when a natural feature subdivision does not exist, other techniques could be investigated to split features and use co-training. For example, the random subspace method could be used for feature splitting [27]. In addition, Goldman and Zhou showed that co-training can be also used with different classifiers using the same features [28]. Their work was limited to two classifiers, but the use of larger ensembles could be investigated.

Finally, it should be noted that several methods to create and combine multiple classifiers have been developed by the MCS community. On the other hand, various approaches to semi-supervised classification have been developed in other communities. The development of new semi-supervised MCS should be based on the integration of both these bodies of work.

3. Applications of semi-supervised MCS

As discussed in the introduction, there are many pattern recognition applications which demand semi-supervised approaches, because they are suited for handling the scarcity of labelled data, and unlabelled examples are available freely and in abundance. On the other hand, it is easy to see that some of these applications could also benefit from the use of multiple classifiers (e.g., multi-source remote-sensing classification and face recognition [7,30]). Finally, in many applications, a lot of unlabelled data are acquired online during the course of operation of a pattern recognition system. This suggests the use of semi-supervised methods to design adaptive MCS which can improve with use. This could be a promising research direction for non stationary pattern recognition applications [29].

Acknowledgments

The author wishes to thank the anonymous reviewers for helpful comments and suggestions. A special thank goes to Nina Hathaway and Nagi Rao for their friendly and precious help with the editing and revision of this manuscript.

References

[1] *Multiple Classifier Systems*, Springer Verlag, Lecture Notes in Computer Science, Vols. 1857 (2000), 2096 (2001), 2364 (2002), 2709 (2003), 3077 (2004).
[2] Fred A., Finding consistent clusters in data partitions, *2nd Int. Workshop on Multiple Classifier Systems* (J.Kittler, F.Roli Eds.), Springer Verlag, Lecture Notes in Computer Science, Vol. 2096, 2001,pp. 309-318.
[3] Ghosh J., Multiclassifier systems: back to the future, *3rd Int. Workshop on Multiple Classifier Systems* (F.Roli, J.Kittler Eds.), Springer Verlag, Lecture Notes in Computer Science, Vol. 2364, 2002,pp. 1-15.
[4] Lang K., Newsweeder: learning to filter netnews, *Machine Learning: Proceeding of the Twelfth International Conference (ICML '95)*, 1995, pp. 331-339

[5] Jackson Q. and Landgrebe D., An adaptive classifier design for high-dimensional data analysis with a limited training data set, *IEEE Trans. On Geoscience and Remote Sensing*, Vol. 39, No. 12, Dec. 2001, pp. 2664-2679.

[6] Cohen I., Cozman F.G., Sebe N., Cirelo M.C., Huang T., Semi-supervised learning of classifiers: theory, algorithms and their applications to human-computer interaction, *IEEE Trans. On Pattern Analysis and Machine Intelligence*, Vol. 26, No. 12, Dec. 2004, pp. 1553-1567.

[7] Martinez C., Fuentes O., Face recognition using unlabeled data, *Computacion y Sistems, Iberoamerican Journal of Computer Science Research*, Vol. 7. no. 2, 2003, pp. 123-129.

[8] Stolfo S.J., Wenke L., Chan P.K., Fan W., Eskin E., Data mining-based intrusion detectors: an overview of the Columbia IDS project, *SIGMOD Record*, Vol. 30, No. 4, Dec. 2001, pp. 5-14.

[9] Seeger M., Learning with labeled and unlabeled data, *Technical Report, University of Edinburgh, Institute for Adaptive and Neural Computation*, Dec. 2002, pp. 1-62.

[10] Miller D. J., Uyar H.S., A mixture of experts classifier with learning based on both labeled and unlabeled data, *Neural Information Processing Systems Foundation, NIPS 1997*, 1997.

[11] d'Alchè-Buc F., Grandvalet Y., Ambroise C., Semi-supervised marginboost, *Neural Information Processing Systems Foundation, NIPS 2002*, 2002.

[12] Bennet K., Demiriz A., Maclin R., Exploiting unlabeled data in ensemble methods, *Proc. 8th ACM SIGKDD Int. Conf. On Knowledge Discovery and Data Mining*, 2002, pp. 289-296.

[13] Melville P., Mooney R., Diverse ensembles for active learning, *21th Int. Conf. On Machine Learning*, Article no. 74, Canada, July 2004.

[14] Kemp T., Waibel A., Unsupervised Training of a Speech Recognizer: Recent Experiments, *Proc. Eurospeech*, vol. 6, 1999, pp. 2725- 2728.

[15] Nagy G., Shelton G.L., Self-corrective character recognition systems, *IEEE Trans. On Information Theory*, IT-12, no. 2, April 1966, pp. 215-222.

[16] G. Nagy, Classifiers that improve with use, *Proc. Conference on Pattern Recognition and Multimedia*, IEICE, Tokyo, February 2004, pp. 79-86.

[17] Inoue M., Ueda N., Exploitation of unlabeled sequences in hidden markov models, *IEEE Trans. On Pattern Analysis and Machine Intelligence*, Vol. 25, No. 12, Dec. 2003, pp. 1570-1581.

[18] Young T.Y., Farjo A., On decision directed estimation and stochastic approximation, *IEEE Trans. On Information Theory*, Sept. 1972, pp. 671-673.

[19] Dempster A.P., Laird N.M., Rubin D.B., Maximum likelihood from incomplete data via the EM algorithm, *Journal of the Royal Statistical Society, Series B*, 39(1), 1977, pp. 1-38.

[20] Nigam K., McCallum A.K., Thrun S., Mitchell T., Text classification from labeled and unlabeled documents using EM, *Machine Learning*, 39, 2000, pp. 103-134.

[21] Blum A., Mitchell T., Combining labeled and unlabeled data with co-training, *Proc. of the Workshop on Computational Learning Theory*, 1998, pp. 92-100.

[22] Nigam K, Ghani R., Analyzing the effectiveness and applicability of co-training, *Proc. 5th Int. Conf. On Information and Knowledge Management*, 2000, pp. 86-93.

[23] Castelli V., Cover T.M., On the exponential value of labeled samples, Pattern Recognition Letters, 16, 1995, pp. 105-111.

[24] Kuncheva L.I., *Combining Pattern Classifiers: Methods and Algorithms*, John Wiley&Sons Pub., 2004.

[25] Raudys S., Experts' boasting in trainable fusion rules, *IEEE Trans. on Pattern Analysis and Machine Intelligence*, Vol. 25, no. 9, Sept. 2003, pp. 1178-1182.

[26] Raudys S., Roli F., The Behaviour Knowledge Space Fusion Method: Analysis of Generalization Error and Strategies for Performance Improvement, *4th Int. Workshop on Multiple Classifier Systems*, T. Windeatt and F. Roli Eds., Springer, LNCS 2709, 2003, pp. 55-64.

[27] Ho T.K., The Random Subspace Method for Constructing Decision Forests, *IEEE Trans. on Pattern Analysis and Machine Intelligence*, 20, 8, Aug. 1998, pp. 832-844.

[28] Goldman S., Zhou Y., Enhancing supervised learning with unlabeled data, *Proc. Of the 7th Int. Con. On Machine Learning, ICML 2000*, 2000, pp. 327-334.

[29] L.I. Kuncheva, Classifier ensembles for changing environments, *5th Int. Workshop on Multiple Classifier Systems* (F.Roli, J.Kittler, T.Windeatt Eds.), Springer Verlag, Lecture Notes in Computer Science, Vol. 3077, 2004, pp. 1-15.

[30] Briem G.J., Benediktsson J.A, Sveinsson J.R., Boosting, bagging, and consensus based classification of multisource remote sensing data, *2nd Int. Workshop on Multiple Classifier Systems* (J.Kittler, F.Roli Eds.), Springer Verlag, Lecture Notes in Computer Science, Vol. 2096, 2001,pp. 279-288.

[31] Jordan M.I., Jacobs R.A, Hierarchical mixtures of experts and the EM algorithm, *Neural Computation*, 6, 1994, pp. 181-214.

[32] Agogino A.K.,Design and control of large collections of learning agents, PhD thesis, The University of Texas at Austin, 2003.

[33] D. H. Wolpert D.H., Tumer K., Optimal payoff functions for members of collectives, *Advances in Complex Systems*, 4(2/3), pp. 265–279, 2001.

Boosting GMM and Its Two Applications

Fei Wang[1], Changshui Zhang[1], and Naijiang Lu[2]

[1] State Key Laboratory of Intelligent Technology and Systems,
Department of Automation, Tsinghua University,
Beijing 100084, P.R.China
feiwang03@mails.tsinghua.edu.cn
zcs@mail.tsinghua.edu.cn
[2] Shanghai Cogent Biometrics Identification Technology Co. Ltd., China
lunj@cbitech.com

Abstract. Boosting is an effecient method to improve the classification performance. Recent theoretical work has shown that the boosting technique can be viewed as a gradient descent search for a good fit in function space. Several authors have applied such viewpoint to solve the density estimation problems. In this paper we generalize such framework to a specific density model – Gaussian Mixture Model (GMM) and propose our boosting GMM algorithm. We will illustrate the applications of our algorithm to cluster ensemble and short-term traffic flow forecasting problems. Experimental results are presented showing the effectiveness of our approach.

Keywords: boosting, GMM, cluster ensemble, short-term traffic flow forecasting.

1 Introduction

Boosting [1] is one of the most important developments in classification methodology. It can reduce the variance of the unstable classifiers and improve the classification performance [2]. Some theoretical work suggests that the effectiveness of this method can be attributed to its tendency to produce large margin classifiers [3]. Mason et al [4] generalized this margin-based idea and derived boosting algorithms as gradient descent algorithms. They proved that the weights in every iteration of the boosting algorithms correspond to the gradient of some margin cost function at "current" fit. In a recent paper, Rosset et al [5] showed that the gradient-based boosting methodology can be applied to density estimation problems and proposed a general boosting density estimation framework. They also illustrated the potential of their framework by experiments with boosting Bayesian networks to learn density models.

Gaussian Mixture Model (GMM) [6] is a popular parametric density model that can approximate any arbitrary probability density functions. Usually we use Maximum Likelihood Estimation (MLE) to estimate the parameters in a GMM when data is available. The Expectation-Maximization (EM) algorithm

N.C. Oza et al. (Eds.): MCS 2005, LNCS 3541, pp. 12–21, 2005.
© Springer-Verlag Berlin Heidelberg 2005

is an effective method to carry out this procedure. But the main problem EM faces is that it is sensitive to the initial parameters, which makes it easily get trapped in a local maximum.

This paper generalizes the work in [5] and proposes a novel approach that combines boosting and GMM together to make the estimated density model more accurate. We use the negative log likelihood of the data as our object function and apply the gradient-based boosting methodology to reduce it gradually until the termination condition is met. Theoretical analysis of our algorithm guarantees its feasibility.

We also illustrate two aspects of applications of our algorithm. One is applying it to solve the cluster ensemble problems. The other is using it to improve the prediction precision of the short-term traffic flow forecasting system. Experimental results are presented showing the effectiveness of our approach.

This paper is organized as follows: we formally present our Boosting GMM algorithm in Section 2. Section 3 and section 4 show the applications of our algorithm in cluster ensemble and short-term traffic flow forecasting respectively, followed by the conclusions and discussions in section 5.

2   Boosting GMM

Assume that we observe a dataset X which is composed of N i.i.d. d-dimensional data objects $\{x_1, x_2, \cdots, x_N\}$ drawn from some unknown distribution $f(x)$. The goal of density estimation is to produce a density function $\hat{f}(x)$ from the dataset to approximate $f(x)$. The theory of MLE tells us to assess the estimation quality by maximizing the expected data log-likelihood

$$L(\hat{f}) = E_x \log \hat{f}(x) = \int f(x) \log \hat{f}(x) dx \qquad (1)$$

where the integral is performed over the whole sample space. Since we don't know the true $f(x)$, we can approximate $L(\hat{f})$ by Monte Carlo integration

$$L(\hat{f}) \approx \hat{L}(\hat{f}) = \frac{1}{N} \sum_{k=1}^{N} \log(\hat{f}(x_k)) \qquad (2)$$

where the expected data log-likelihood is estimated by its empirical value.

As we mentioned in section 1, boosting can be applied to minimize the negative data log-likelihood $-\hat{L}(\hat{f})$ gradually. We choose the GMM method as our initialization method because it can guarantee the negative data log-likelihood converge to a local minimum. The boosting procedure will be performed afterwards to mix new components, which offer the largest decrease in the object function at each step, with the current model sequentially to minimize $-\hat{L}(\hat{f})$. We assume the component added in each boosting iteration is also a GMM.

More precisely, assume at each boosting step t, the density function estimated so far is $\hat{G}_{t-1}$. Now we want to add a new component g to $\hat{G}_{t-1}$ with a small coefficient ε, that is $\hat{G}_t = \hat{G}_{t-1} + \varepsilon g$. Our objective is to minimize $-\hat{L}(\hat{G}_t)$. We can write $-\hat{L}(\hat{G}_t)$ in a Taylor series around $\hat{G}_{t-1}$ as follows.

$$-\hat{L}(\hat{G}_t) = \sum_{i=1}^{N} -\log(\hat{G}_t(x_i)) = \sum_{i=1}^{N} -\log(\hat{G}_{t-1}(x_i) + \varepsilon g(x_i))$$

$$= \sum_{i=1}^{N} -\log(\hat{G}_{t-1}(x_i)) - \varepsilon \sum_{i=1}^{N} \frac{1}{\hat{G}_{t-1}(x_i)} g(x_i) + O(\varepsilon^2) \qquad (3)$$

Because ε is small, we can ignore the second order term of ε, and choose g to maximize

$$\hat{l}(g) = \sum_i \frac{1}{\hat{G}_{t-1}(x_i)} g(x_i) \qquad (4)$$

Since $\hat{G}_t$ must also be a probability distribution, we can not simply augment $\hat{G}_{t-1}$ to $\hat{G}_t = \hat{G}_{t-1} + \varepsilon g$. Instead we introduce a "forgetting factor" $\eta \in [0, 1]$, and let $\hat{G}_t = (1 - \eta)\hat{G}_{t-1} + \eta g$. Then we normalize the term $\frac{1}{\hat{G}_{t-1}(x_i)}$ in equation (4), and let

$$W_t(x_i) = \frac{1}{\hat{G}_{t-1}(x_i)Z} \qquad (5)$$

where $Z = \sum_i \frac{1}{\hat{G}_{t-1}(x_i)}$ is the normalization factor. W_t can be viewed as the sample distribution in boosting iteration t.

In this way, our algorithm will adjust the sampling distribution (weights) of the dataset at each step according to the current model, and keep on increasing the total data likelihood until the termination condition has been met. The detailed description of our algorithm is shown in Table 1.

There is still a problem remain unanswered which is how to determine the size of a GMM. We choose the Bayesian Information Criterion (BIC) [7] to solve the problem. BIC is a model selection criterion derived from the Laplace approximation [8]. The BIC value of a GMM can be defined as follows :

Table 1. Boosting GMM

BoostingGMM

Input: Dataset $X = \{x_1, x_2, \cdots, x_N\}$, Iteration number T;
Output: GMM $\hat{G}_T$

1. Set $\hat{G}_0 = 0$.
2. For t=1:T
   (a) Set $W_t(x_i) = \frac{1}{\hat{G}_{t-1}(x_i)Z}$, $Z = \sum_{i=1}^{N} \frac{1}{\hat{G}_{t-1}(x_i)}$
   (b) Sample the original dataset according to W_t and do GMM estimation on the sampled dataset, then output the result g_t
   (c) Let $\hat{G}_t = (1 - \eta_t)\hat{G}_{t-1} + \eta_t g_t$, $\eta_t = \arg\min_\eta \sum_i -\log((1-\eta)\hat{G}_{t-1}(x_i) + \eta g_t(x_i))$
       If $\hat{L}(\hat{G}_t) < \hat{L}(\hat{G}_{t-1})$, break;
3. Output $\hat{G}_T$

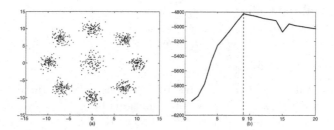

Fig. 1. Data set and the corresponding BIC value curve

$$BIC(G|X) = \log P(X|\hat{G}) - \frac{d}{2}\log N \qquad (6)$$

The first term of (6) is the log-likelihood term, where $\hat{G}$ represent the GMM with the ML parameter configuration. The second term is the model complexity penalty term where d represents the number of parameters in G and N is the size of the dataset. BIC selects the best GMM corresponding to the largest BIC value by trading off these two terms. Our experiments show that the BIC criterion can discover the true GMM size effectively. For example, Fig. 1(a) is a dataset generated from a GMM composed of nine Gaussian kernels; Fig. 1(b) is the BIC curve corresponding to the GMM model size.

3   Application in Cluster Ensemble

3.1   Related Work

Clustering is an old data analysis problem that seeks to construct homogeneous groups of data objects. A recent advance of clustering techniques is the development of cluster ensemble methods, which can increase the robustness and rationality of the clustering solution through combining several individual clustering results [9]. Previously resampling methods have been successfully applied to this domain. But these methods are mostly based on the bagging technique [10], which first randomly sample the original dataset with replacement (which is called "bootstrap"), and then clustering these sampled subsets. Finally the algorithm integrate all the clustering results based on some criterion [11][12][13].

For example, *bagged clustering* proposed by Friedrich et al [11] is one of the earliest papers that used the bagging technique to solve the cluster ensemble problem. It works as follows:

1. Bootstrap the dataset B times and get datasets$\{X_1, X_2, \cdots X_B\}$;
2. Do K-means clustering on each X_i and get the cluster center set $\{c_{11}, \cdots c_{1K}, c_{21} \cdots, c_{2K}, \cdots c_{BK}\}$;
3. Run an agglomerative clustering algorithm on the center set using Euclidean distance.
4. Assign each data to the cluster which corresponding to the closest center.

Experimental results in [11] showed that "bagged clustering" could perform better than K-means.

3.2   Boosted Clustering

As it is known that GMM can also be treated as a "soft assignment clustering" method [14]. It first estimates the density function of the dataset as we mentioned in section 1, and then assigns the data objects to the Gaussian kernel of the result GMM under which their probability is the highest. This algorithm is computationally efficient and yields good results if the clusters are compact, hyper-ellipsoidal in shape. However, usually we do not know the shape of the clusters in a real world dataset. So we propose our boosted clustering algorithm based on the *Boosting GMM* algorithm presented in section 2. The algorithm is summarized below.

Table 2. Boosted Clustering

Boosted Clustering

Input: Dataset $X = \{x_1, x_2, \cdots, x_N\}$, Iteration number T, Cutting threshold s.
Output: Clusters $C = \{c_1, c_2, \cdots, c_K\}$
1. Run *boosting GMM* on the dataset and get the final GMM G with M Gaussian kernels.
2. Assign each data object to the Gaussian component in G under which its probability is the highest.
3. Cut the Gaussian kernels whose data objects number is less than s
4. For i = 1 : (M − 1)
   (a) For each pair of components g_i, g_j, which contain N_i, N_j samples respectively, compute $S_{ij} = \sum_{x_u \in g_j} g_i(x_u) + \sum_{x_v \in g_i} g_j(x_v)$
   (b) Find $S_{ij}^* = \max_{g_i, g_j} S_{ij}$, merge g_i, g_j as $G_{ij} = \frac{N_i}{N_i + N_j} g_i + \frac{N_j}{N_i + N_j} g_j$.
   (c) Delete g_i, g_j from G. Treat G_{ij} as a new component in G. Calculate all the probabilities the data under it.
5. Select the number K and output the resulting K clusters

Step 4 is the agglomerative cluster ensemble procedure. We do not adopt the merging method in [11] based on Euclidean distance, because it is not suitable for merging GMMs (which we can see from our experiments below).

3.3   Experimental Results

We tested our algorithm on several datasets. Some of the results are shown in Fig. 2. Fig. 3(a) shows us that the data likelihood of the dataset "4-clusters" corresponding to Fig. 2(a) keeps on increasing with the boosting iterations. The cluster number K can be decided by merging the clusters achieved from step 3 continuously and choosing the number of which the maximum similarity S_{ij}^* approaching zero. Fig. 3(b) is the S_{ij}^* curve of the dataset "4-clusters" versus

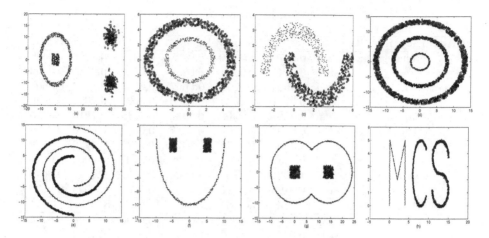

Fig. 2. Some cluster results on synthetic datasets

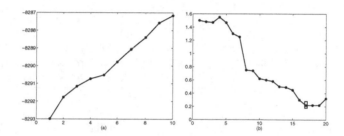

Fig. 3. Data likelihood and maximum similarity of the dataset in Fig. 2(a)

Table 3. Basic information of the datasets

Name	Size	Dimension	PCA	Clusters
4-clusters	1400	2	N	900,100,200,200
2-circles	1500	2	N	500,1000
Banana	1000	2	N	531,469
Breast-cancer	683	10	2	444,239
Diabetes	768	8	2	500,268

the merging iterations. We also compared the results of our algorithm to 5 other methods on five datasets. In all the experiments we set the cutting threshold s=10 empirically. Table 3 is some basic information of these datasets including three artificial datasets (the first 3) corresponding to Fig. 2(a), (b), (c) and two UCI datasets (the last 2) .We do PCA on the last two datasets and reduce the dimensionalities of them to two.

We use Accuracy [11] and Normalized Mutual Information (NMI) [9] to measure the quality of the final clustering solutions. The results are shown in table 4,

Table 4. Experimental Results

Accuracy Results		BoGMM	BaGMM	BeGMM	BaKMN	KMeans	GMM
4-cluster	Mean	0.9970	**1.0000**	0.9223	0.8976	0.8486	0.8429
	std	0.0141	0.0000	0.0294	0.0580	0.0713	0.0703
2-circles	Mean	**0.9957**	0.9294	0.6667	0.6667	0.6667	0.6667
	std	0.0191	0.1028	0.0000	0.0000	0.0000	0.0000
banana	Mean	**1.0000**	1.0000	0.7332	0.7210	0.7210	0.8270
	std	0.0000	0.0000	0.0587	0.0000	0.0000	0.0000
Breast-cancer	Mean	**0.9758**	0.9573	0.9729	0.9722	0.9722	0.9122
	std	0.0037	0.0405	0.0029	0.0000	0.0000	0.0000
Diabetes	Mean	**0.6822**	0.6734	0.6690	0.6654	0.6626	0.6510
	std	0.0196	0.0211	0.0202	0.0000	0.0099	0.0000
NMI Results		BoGMM	BaGMM	BeGMM	BaKMN	KMeans	GMM
4-cluster	Mean	0.9892	**1.0000**	0.7298	0.6636	0.5996	0.6275
	std	0.0495	0.0000	0.0372	0.0845	0.1166	0.0881
2-circles	Mean	**0.9767**	0.7729	0.0047	0.0001	0.0002	0.0001
	std	0.0769	0.3053	0.0064	0.0000	0.0001	0.0001
banana	Mean	**1.0000**	1.0000	0.2218	0.1448	0.1448	0.3447
	std	0.0000	0.0000	0.1376	0.0000	0.0000	0.0000
Breast-cancer	Mean	**0.8422**	0.7582	0.8303	0.8067	0.8067	0.6424
	std	0.0145	0.1053	0.0115	0.0000	0.0000	0.0000
Diabetes	Mean	**0.0668**	0.0616	0.0588	0.0556	0.0523	0.0510
	std	0.0287	0.0253	0.0143	0.0000	0.0280	0.0000

Table 5. Time Comparison for BoGMM and BaGMM (in seconds)

	4-cluster	2-circles	banana	Breast-Cancer	Diabetes
Boosted_clustering	25.2974	56.9510	37.0515	26.9239	27.3372
Bagged_clustering	41.4971	62.2454	51.5625	34.1023	37.3554

where "BoGMM" represents our *boosted clustering* method; "BaGMM" represents the *bagged GMM* method which sequentially do GMM clustering on the bootstrapped datasets, and combine all the result Gaussian kernels using our merging criterion (step 4 in table 2); "BeGMM" is the method that first do *boosting GMM* on the original dataset, then do agglomerative merging of the Gaussian kernels based on the Euclidean distance of their means as in [11]; "BaKMN" is the *bagged K-means* method in [11]; "KMeans" and "GMM" refer to the conventional K-means and GMM clustering respectively. Each entry in table 4 is the result of 100 independent runnings. For each experiment the iteration steps of our *boosting GMM* method (parameter T in Table 1) is 5.

From table 4 we can see that mostly the results of "BoGMM" and "BaGMM" are better than other methods. But our boosting GMM method costs much less time, which can be seen in table 5. Each entry in table 5 is the mean CPU time of the 100 independent experiments.

4   Application in Short-Term Traffic Flow Forecasting

4.1   Related Work

Intelligent Transportation Systems (ITS) is a young research area that has achieved great developments in recent years. Short-term traffic flow forecasting [15], which is to determine the traffic volume in the next interval usually in the range of five minutes to half an hour, is one of the most important problems of ITS. Zhang et al [15] proposed to use the Bayesian network to model the casual relationship of time series of traffic flows among a chosen link and its adjacent links in a road network. Then the GMM method is applied to approximate the joint probability distribution of all nodes in the constructed Bayesian network. Finally, traffic flow forecasting of the current link is performed under the rule of Minimum Mean Square Error (MMSE). They showed experimentally the effectiveness of their method. But as we mentioned above, the GMM method may easily get trapped in a local maximum. So we propose to use our boosting GMM algorithm to improve the precision of the forecasting results.

4.2   Overview of Our Method

The flow chart of our approach can be described as follows:

1. Construct the Bayesian network model between input (cause nodes, which include the historical traffic flow values of the effect node and the adjacent links)and output (effect node) for a chosen road link;

2. Approximate the joint probability distribution of all nodes in the constructed network by *boosting GMM*.

3. Perform the estimation of traffic flow of the current link as in [15].

4.3   Experimental Results

The experimental data is the vehicle flow rates of discrete time series recorded every 15 minutes on many road links by the UTC/SCOOT system in Traffic Management Bureau of Beijing, whose unit is vehicles per hour (vph). The data is from Mar.1 to Mar.25, 2002 and 2400 data points totally. Fig. 4(a) is one patch of the traffic map. Circle nodes denote road links, arrows show the directions of the traffic flows of the corresponding road links. Fig. 4(b) is the original vehicle flow of road link K_a.

The forecasting orders from the current link and from the adjacent links are respectively taken as 4 and 5 as in [15] (for example, if we want to predict the current traffic flow of K_a, then $K_a(t)$ is the effect node, $K_a(t-1)\cdots K_a(t-4), H_i(t-1)\cdots H_i(t-5), H_l(t-1)\cdots H_l(t-5)$, are the cause nodes). We employ PCA to reduce the input (cause nodes) data dimension to 2. Fig. 5(a) shows the results for the last 395 data points of K_a where the curve is the original curve and the star curve refers to our predicted curve. Fig. 5(b) gives the Root Mean Square Error (RMSE) curve corresponding to the boosting iterations, from which we can see that the forecasting results can be more accurate when the boosting

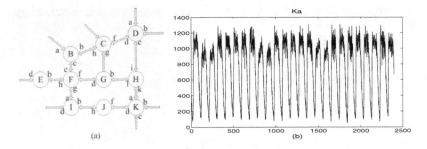

Fig. 4. Traffic map patch and traffic flow of Ka

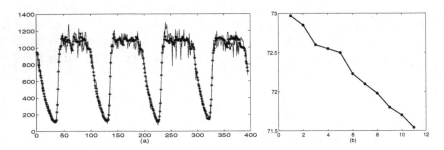

Fig. 5. Forecasting results of Ka

Table 6. RMSE Comparison for simple GMM and *boosting GMM*

	Bb	Ch	Dd	Fe	Gb	Ka	Hi	Dc
boosting GMM	77.5625	66.1572	61.7221	125.8233	83.2050	72.6480	87.4343	82.6639
simple GMM	77.6683	66.1659	61.7230	126.6164	84.3554	72.9788	87.5836	83.5509

iteration increases. Table 6 is the RMSE comparison for the last 395 data points of the simple GMM method and our *boosting GMM* method after 3 iterations (T=3 in table 1).

5   Conclusion and Discussion

In this paper we generalize the boosting framework to the GMM models and present our *boosting GMM* algorithm. We show the applications of our algorithm in cluster ensemble and short-term traffic flow forecasting problems. Theoretical analysis and experimental results show the advantages of our approach.

Because we use GMMs as our "weak models", our method may be limited when the size of the dataset is small but the dimensionality of it is high although we can preprocess the dataset with PCA. The application of the boosting technique to other density models seems like a promising avenue for future research.

Acknowledgements

This work is supported by the project (60475001) of the National Natural Science Foundation.

References

1. Y. Freund, R. Schapire. Experiments With a New Boosting Algorithm. Proc. of the 13th ICML. (1996)
2. L. Brieman. Arcing Classifiers. The Annals of Statistics, 26(3): 801-849. (1998)
3. R. E. Schapire, Y. Freund. Boosting the Margin: A New Explanation for the Effectiveness of Voting Methods. The Annals of Statistics, 26(5): 1651-1686. (1998)
4. L. Mason, J. Baxter, P. Bartlett, M. Frean. Boosting Algorithms as Gradient Descent. Proc. NIPS99. (1999)
5. S. Rosset, E. Segal. Boosting Density Estimation. Proc. NIPS02. (2002)
6. J. A. Bilms. A Gentle Tutorial of the EM Algorithm and its Application to Parameter Estimation for Gaussian Mixture and Hidden Markov Models. International Computer Science Institute, Berkeley CA. Technical Report. (1998)
7. G. Schwarz. Estimating the dimension of a model. Annuals of Statistics, 6. (1978)
8. D. Heckerman, D. Geiger, D. M. Chickering. A Tutorial on Learning with Bayesian Networks. Machine Learning 20, 197-143. (1995)
9. A. Strehl, J. Ghosh. Cluster Ensembles– A Knowledge Reuse Framework for Combining Multiple Partitions. JLMR 3, 583-617. (2002)
10. L. Breiman. Bagging Predictors. Technical Report. 421, Department of Statistics, University of California, Berkeley. (1994)
11. L. Friedrich. Bagged Clustering. Working papers SFB "Adaptive Information Systems and Modeling in Economics and Management Science", no.51. (1999)
12. B. Minaei-Bidgoli, A. Topchy, W. Punch. Ensembles of Partitions via Data Resampling, in Proc. ITCC04. (2004)
13. B. Minaei-Bidgoli, A. Topchy, W. Punch. A Comparison of Resampling Methods for Clustering Ensembles, Intl. Conf. on Machine Learning; Models, Technologies and Applications, (MLMTA04), Las Vegas, Nevada. (2004)
14. M. Kearns, Y. Mansour, A. Y. Ng. An information-theoretic analysis of hard and soft assignment methods for clustering. In Proc. of UAI. AAAI. (1997)
15. C. Zhang, S. Sun, G. Yu. A Bayesian Network Approach to Time Series Forecasting of Short-Term Traffic Flows. IEEE ITS04. (2004)

Boosting Soft-Margin SVM with Feature Selection for Pedestrian Detection

Kenji Nishida and Takio Kurita

Neuroscience Research Institute,
National Institute of Advanced Industrial Science and Technology (AIST),
Central 2, 1-1-1 Umezono, Tsukuba, Ibaraki 305-8568 Japan
kenji.nishida@aist.go.jp

Abstract. We present an example-based algorithm for detecting objects in images by integrating component-based classifiers, which automaticaly select the best feature for each classifier and are combined according to the *AdaBoost* algorithm. The system employs a soft-margin SVM for the base learner, which is trained for all features and the optimal feature is selected at each stage of boosting. We employed two features such as a histogram-equalization and an edge feature in our experiment. The proposed method was applied to the MIT CBCL pedestrian image database, and 100 sub-regions were extracted from each image as local-features. The experimental results showed fairly good classification ratio with selecting sub-regions, while some improvement attained by combining the two features, histogram-equalization and edge. However, the combination of features could to select *good* local-features for base learners.

1 Introduction

In this paper, we present an example-based algorithm for detecting objects in images by integrating component-based classifiers, which **automatically** select the best local-feature for each classifier and are combined according to the *AdaBoost*[1] algorithm. Our method can be applied to any object composed of distinct identifiable parts that are arranged in a well-defined configuration, such as cars and faces. However, we focused on the pedestrian detection in images, which could be used in driver assistance systems and video surveillance systems. Pedestrian detection is more challenging than detecting other objects such as cars and faces, since people take a variety of shapes and it is nontrivial to define a single model that captures all of these possibilities.

Gavrila[3] employed hierarchical template matching to find pedestrian candidates from incoming images. His method provide multiple templates in advance that were outline edge images of typical pedestrians, and dissimilarities (or similarities) between the edge feature of incoming images were measured by the chamfer distance. The variety of shapes of pedestrians was accommodated with the variety of templates, which bound system performance.

N.C. Oza et al. (Eds.): MCS 2005, LNCS 3541, pp. 22–31, 2005.

Viola et al.[4] presented a pedestrian detection system that integrated image intensity information with motion information. Their detection algorithm scaned a detector over two consecutive frames of a video sequence, and the detector was trained using *AdaBoost* to take advantage of both motion and appearance information. They achieved a high detection speed (about four frames/second) and a very low false positive rate, while combining two different modalities of information in one detector.

Although they showed the advantage of integrating motion information, it is still difficult to apply their algorithm to an on-board pedestrian detection system, since canceling out the movement of the camera only from visual information is difficult. Therefore, we focused on pedestrian detection from static images to achieve our example-based object detection method.

Mohan et al.[2] applied an Adaptive Combination of Classifiers (ACC) to pedestrian detection. Their system consisted of two stage hierarchical classifiers. The first stage was structured with four distinct example-based classifiers, which were separately trained to detect different component of pedestrians, such as the head, legs, right arm, and left arm. The second stage had an example-based classifier which combined the results for the component detectors in the first stage to classify the pattern as either a "person" or a "non-person". A Support Vector Machine (SVM)[5][6][7] is employed for each classifier. Their results indicated that combination of component-based detectors performed better than a full-body person detector. The components in their system were determined in advance and they were not exactly optimal to classify the examples.

We employed a feature-selection algorithm in the training phase of each component-based classifier, so that the classifier could automatically select the optimal component to classify the examples. Mohan et al.[2] pre-defined the number of the component-based classifiers as four; however, our proposed method combines a larger number of component-based classifiers with the *AdaBoost* algorithm.

Our experimental results show that the proposed method achieves a fairly good classification ratio by selecting a sub-region of the input image, while a slightly greater improvement is achieved by selecting the optimal feature from histogram-equalization images and edge images of inputs.

We describe our object detection method in the next section, and the experimental results are presented in the final section.

2   System Configuration

Our key-idea is introducing feature selection and the soft-margin SVM into *AdaBoost* to enhance the generalization ability of a strong learner by automatically selecting the best feature for base learners at each boosting step. We describe our boosting algorithm with feature selection and outline the soft-margin SVM in this section. We also describe the sample images and experimental conditions we used for our experiments.

2.1   Algorithm

Figure 1 presents the overall algorithm for our pedestrian detection system, which introduces a feature selection algorithm into each step of *AdaBoost*. We define a local-feature as the combination of a feature (a characteric extracted from an input image such as an edge feature) and a sub-region of an input image. Our feature selection method selects the best local-feature (with the lowest error ratio) at each boosting step.

---

1. Let N be the number of samples, M be the number of boosting steps, L be the number of sub-regions, and K be the number of features. Thus, $K \times L$ is the total number of local-features in the local-feature pool.
2. Generate a local-feature pool for all local-features from input samples $\boldsymbol{x}$, such as $\boldsymbol{x} \rightarrow \boldsymbol{x}^{11}, \ldots, \boldsymbol{x}^{1L}, \boldsymbol{x}^{21}, \ldots, \boldsymbol{x}^{kl}, \ldots, \boldsymbol{x}^{KL}$.
3. Initialize the observation weights $w_i = 1/N$, $i = 1, 2, \ldots, N$.
4. For $m = 1$, to M:
   (a) For $k = 1$ to K, for $l = 1$ to L
       i. Fit classifier $G_m^{kl}(x^{kl})$ to the training samples of local-feature x^{kl} which are randomly selected depending on weights w_i from all the training samples
       ii. Compute $err_m^{kl} = \dfrac{\sum_{i-1}^{N} w_i I(y_i \neq G_m(x_i^{kl}))}{\sum_{i=1}^{N} W_i}$.
   (b) Set err_m with the smallest err_m^{kl}, $l = 1, 2, \ldots, L, k = 1, 2, \ldots, K$.
   (c) Set $G_m(x) \leftarrow G_m^{kl}(x^{kl})$ with k and l in the above step.
   (d) Compute $\alpha_m = \log((1 - err_m)/err_m)$.
   (e) Set $w_i \leftarrow w_i \cdot \exp[\alpha_m \cdot I(y_i \neq G_m(x_i))]$, $i = 1, 2, \ldots, N$.
5. Output $G(x) = \text{sign}[\sum_{m=1}^{M} \alpha_m G_m(x)]$.

Fig. 1. *AdaBoost* with Feature Selection

Initially, features (in our experiment, histogram-equalizaton and edge features are employed) are extracted from input images and a pre-defined number (in our experiment: 100) of sub-region images for each feature are generated as a local-feature pool (Fig. 2) with equal sample weight. In the ith boosting step, the ith base learner is trained under the sample weights determined by the $i-1$th base learner for all local-features in the local-feature pool, and it selects the best local-feature for ith base learner. The sample weights for the next boosting step and significance of the base learner are computed according to the error ratio. Variations in features and sub-regions are determined by a trade-off in the feasible CPU time and desired precision.

2.2   Boosting Soft-Margin SVM

We employed a soft-margin SVM for the base learner. We will first describe a SVM briefly followed by a description of the soft-margin SVM.

The classification function is given as

$$y = \text{sign}(\boldsymbol{w}^T \boldsymbol{x} - h), \tag{1}$$

where $\boldsymbol{x}$ stands for the input vector, $\boldsymbol{w}$ stands for the weight vector of input, and h stands for the threshold. Function $\text{sign}(u)$ is a sign function, which outputs 1 when $u > 0$ and outputs -1 when $u \leq 0$. The SVM determines the separating hyperplane with a maximal margin (distance), which is the distance between the separating hyperplane and the nearest sample. If the hyperplane is determined, there exists a parameter to satisfy

$$t_i(\boldsymbol{w}^T \boldsymbol{x_i}) \geq 1, \ \ i = 1, \ldots, N, \tag{2}$$

where t_i stands for the correct class label for input vector x_i. This means that the samples are separated by two hyperplanes of H1: $\boldsymbol{w}^T \boldsymbol{x}_i - h = 1$ and H2: $\boldsymbol{w}^T \boldsymbol{x}_i - h = -1$, and no samples exist between them. The distance between the separating hyperplane and H1 (or H2) is defined as $1/\|\boldsymbol{w}\|$. Determining parameters $\boldsymbol{w}$ and h that give a maximal margin is defined as an optimization problem for the following evaluation function

$$L(\boldsymbol{w}) = \frac{1}{2}\|\boldsymbol{w}\|^2 \tag{3}$$

under constraint

$$t_i(\boldsymbol{w}^T \boldsymbol{x}_i - h) \geq 1, \ \ i = 1, \ldots, N. \tag{4}$$

A soft-margin SVM allows some training samples to violate hyperplanes H1 and H2. When the distance from H1 (or H2) is defined as $\xi_i/\|\boldsymbol{w}\|$ for the violating samples, the sum

$$\sum_{i=1}^{N} \frac{\xi_i}{\|\boldsymbol{w}\|} \tag{5}$$

should be minimized. Therefore, a soft-margin SVM is defined as an optimization problem for the following evaluation function

$$L(\boldsymbol{w}, \boldsymbol{\xi}) = \frac{1}{2}\|\boldsymbol{w}\|^2 + C \sum_{i=1}^{N} \xi_i \tag{6}$$

under constraint

$$\xi_i \geq 0, \ \ t_i(\boldsymbol{w}^T \boldsymbol{x}_i - h) \geq 1 - \xi_i, \ \ i = 1, \ldots, N \tag{7}$$

where C stands for the **cost** parameter for violating hyperplane H1 (or H2). Solving this problem with optimal solution $\boldsymbol{\alpha}^*$, the classification function can be redefined as

$$\begin{aligned} y &= \text{sign}(\boldsymbol{w}^{*T} \boldsymbol{x} - h^*) \\ &= \text{sign}(\sum_{i \in S} \alpha_i^* t_i \boldsymbol{x}_i^T \boldsymbol{x} - h^*). \end{aligned} \tag{8}$$

The samples are grouped with α_i^*; sample x_i is classified correctly when $\alpha_i^* = 0$, when $0 < \alpha_i^* < C$, sample x_i is also classfied correctly and is located on the hyperplane H1 (or H2) as a support-vector. If $\alpha_i^* = C$, sample x_i becomes a support-vector but is located between H1 and H2 with $\xi \neq 0$.

The kernel-trick, which drastically improved the performance of the SVM, can also be applied to the soft-margin SVM. In Kernel-Trick, the input vectors are transformed by non-linear projection $\phi(x)$ and linearly classified in the projected space. Since SVM depends on the product of two input vectors, the product of the input vectors in projected space can be used instead of computing the non-linear projection of the each input vector, such as

$$\phi(x_1)^T \phi(x_2) = K(x_1, x_2). \tag{9}$$

K is called a *Kernel Function* and is usually selected as a simple function, a Gaussian function

$$K(x_1, x_2) = \exp\left(\frac{-||x_1 - x_2||^2}{2\sigma^2}\right) \tag{10}$$

for instance. The classification function can be redefined by replacing input vectors with kernel functions, as follows

$$\begin{aligned} y &= \text{sign}(w^{*T}\phi(x) - h^*) \\ &= \text{sign}(\sum_{i \in S} \alpha_i^* t_i \phi(x_i)^T \phi(x) - h^*) \\ &= \text{sign}(\sum_{i \in S} \alpha_i^* t_i K(x_i, x) - h^*). \end{aligned} \tag{11}$$

Introducing cost parameter C, we could have two choices to achieve sample weighing with *AdaBoost*, the first is building the SVM by defining a cost parameter as the weight of each sample, the second is re-sampling according to the sample weights. Schwenk et al.[8] showed that defining a pseudo-loss function and re-sampling had similar effects with *AdaBoost*. We therefore selected re-sampling so that we could use LIBSVM[9] for our evaluation. One thousand images were re-sampled from 1,400 in the training samples.

2.3   Sample Images and Local Features

We employed the MIT CBCL database for the sample data, which contained 926 pedestrian images with 128×64 pixels, and we collected 2,000 random non-pedestrian images. We reduced the resolution of all the samples to 64×32 before we applied them to our system. We extracted histogram-equalization and edge features from the input images, and local-features were extracted as adequate sub-regions of the featured images. We selected 100 sub-regions for our evaluation; extracting small sub-regions from input images with a variety of region sizes such as 4×8 pixels ranging to the whole image.

Figure 2 shows the original image, extracted features, and local features. We selected 700 pedestrian and 700 non-pedestrian images for training, and 200 pedestrian and 200 non-pedestrian images to test the generalization error.

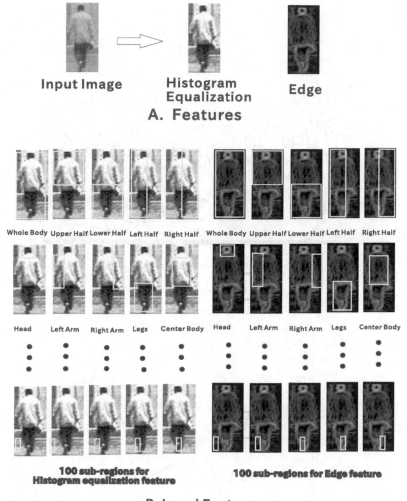

Fig. 2. Sample Images and Local Features

3   Results

We first examined the effect of SVM cost parameter C by using a raw input image with ten sub-regions, such as the whole body, upper half, lower half, right half, left half, right arm, left arm, head, legs, and center body. Figure 3 plots error ratio against the number of boosting steps with cost parameter C for 0.1, 0.7, and 100. Ten local features are almost evenly selected at each boosting step. After 100 boosting steps, test error reaches 4% with C=0.7, 4.5% with C=100, and 5.25% with C=0.1. Figure 4 plots test error against cost parameter C after 50 boosting steps. Test error records a minimal value of 4% at c=0.7. This indicates

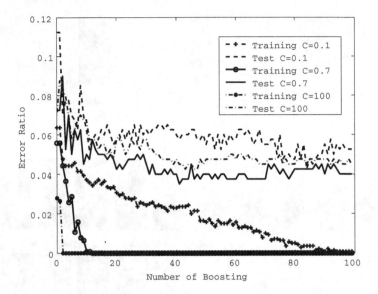

Fig. 3. Error Ratio for Ten Local-Features

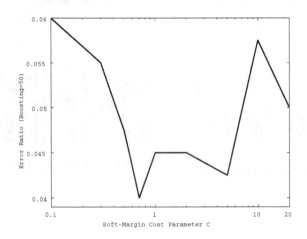

Fig. 4. Error Ratio against Cost Parameter C

that the soft-margin SVM advantageous to usual hard-margin (or firm-margin) SVM for boosting; however, there exists an optimal value for cost parameter C.

Figure 5 plots error ratio against the number of boosting steps with cost parameter C for 0.7, accorcding to the previous results. The experimantal results were averaged over three trials.

The training error converges to zero at boosting step 5 for histogram-equalization, and at boosting step 10 for Edge features. This indicates the histogram-equalization tends to have lower training error than edge features.

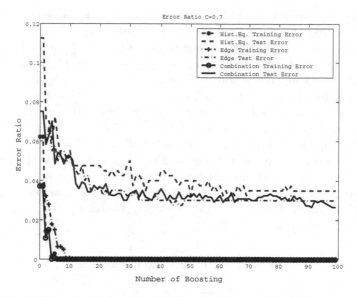

Fig. 5. Error Ratio for 100 (200 for Combination) Local-Features

Athough histogram-equalization has the lower training error, edge features has the lower test error after 100 boosting steps, 3% for edge features and 3.5% for histogram-equalization.

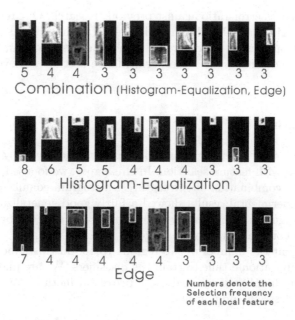

Fig. 6. Example of Selected Local Features

Selecting the best local feature from the combination of histogram-equalization and edge features, test error reached 2.7% after 100 boosting steps. Eighty-four boosting steps selected histogram-equalization for their base-learners, and 16 steps selected edge features. This indicates that the test error is improved by only 16 classifiers selecting edge features, since test error for histogram-equalization tends to be higher than that of edge feature.

Although we provided 100 sub-regions, only about 50 sub-regions were selected. Figure 6 shows examples of selected local features. This indicates that pedestrian components are automatically selected by our local-feature selection. Small sub-regions, which are not meaningful as pedestrian components, tend to be selected with one feature (such as histogram-equalization or edge), while large sub-regions, which can be meaningful as pedestrian components, are selected with a combination of the two features. Therefore, the combination of features selects *good* local-features.

Table 1. The Error Ratio Comparison

	Error Ratio
Gavrila	10-40%*
Mohan	1-2%
Viola	10%
Our Result	2.7-3%

* For first stage

Table 1 compares error ratio against previous research. Our results achieved a better error ratio than Gavrila and Viola et al., while it was a little worse than Mohan's. Considering the difference in non-pedestrian data, we concluded that our result had almost the same performance as that achieved by Mohan et al.

4   Conclusion

We presented an object detection method that was achieved by boosting the soft-margin SVM with feature selection. In this paper, we focused on pedestrian detection using a combination of two features, histogram-equalization and edge features. The experimental results showed a fairly good generalization error ratio of 2.7%. The good components were automatically selected by local-feature selection by the combining the two features.

We had to limit the number of sub-regions to 100 in this paper, because we had limited computational time to train the classifiers. We are planning to evaluate with a larger number of sub-regions to prove our method can automatically extract good pedestrian components.

References

1. T. Hastie, R. Tibshirani, and J. Friedman, *The Elements of Statistical Learning - Data Mining, Inference, and Prediction*, Springer-Verlag, USA, 2001.
2. A. Mohan, C. P. Papageorgiou, and T. Poggio, "Example-Based Object Detection in Images by Components," IEEE Trans. on Pattern Analysis and Machine Intelligence, Vol. 23, No. 4, pp. 349-361, 2001.
3. D. M. Gavlira, "Pedestrian Detection from a Moving Vehicle", *Proc. of European Conference on Computer Vision*, pp. 37-49, 2000.
4. P. Viola, M. J. Jones and D. Snow, "Detecting Pedestrians Using Patterns of Motion and Appearance", *Proc. of Int'l Conf. on Computer Vision*, pp. 734-741, 2003.
5. V.N.Vapnik, *Statistical Learning Theory*, John Wiley & Sons, USA, (1998).
6. B. Scholkopf, C. J. C. Burges, and A.J.Smola, *Advances in Kernel Methods - Support Vector Learning*, The MIT Press, USA, 1999.
7. N. Cristianini and J. S. Taylor, *An Introduction to Support Vector Machines and Other Kernel-based Learning Methods*, Cambridge University Press, 2000.
8. H. Schwenk and Y. Benjio, "Boosting Neural Networks", *Neural Computation*, Vol. 12, pp. 1869-1887, 2000.
9. C. C. Chung and C. J. Lin, "LIBSVM: a libraly for support vector machines", *Software available at* http://www.csie.ntu.edu.tw/, 2001.
10. R. E. Schapire, "The Boosting Approach to Machine Learning: An OverView", *MSRI Workshop on Nonlinear Estimation and Classification*, 2002.

Observations on Boosting Feature Selection

D.B. Redpath and K. Lebart

ECE, School of EPS, Heriot-Watt University,
Edinburgh, EH14 4AS, UK
{dr2, K.Lebart}@hw.ac.uk

Abstract. This paper presents a study of the Boosting Feature Selection (BFS) algorithm [1], a method which incorporates feature selection into Adaboost. Such an algorithm is interesting as it combines the methods studied by Boosting and ensemble feature selection researchers.

Observations are made on generalisation, weighted error and error diversity to compare the algorithms performance to Adaboost while using a nearest mean base learner. Ensemble feature prominence is proposed as a stop criterion for ensemble construction. Its quality assessed using the former performance measures. BFS is found to compete with Adaboost in terms of performance, despite the reduced feature description for each base classifer. This is explained using weighted error and error diversity. Results show the proposed stop criterion to be useful for trading ensemble performance and complexity.

1   Introduction

Adaboost first proposed by Freund and Schapire [2] has emerged as one of the most successful ensembling algorithms in recent years. A number of variations and improvements on the original implementation have since been proposed.

In its simplest form Adaboost, know generally as Boosting drives down the ensemble error rate by concentrating on points that are particularly difficult to classify. At each iteration Boosting updates the weighting on the training patterns emphasizing those that are incorrectly classified. The base learner is then retrained using the reweighted training patterns. The resulting ensemble is a linear combination of each base learners decision. The final decision is an approximate large margin as Boosting concentrates the final decision on the class boundary. Later extensions and study have confirmed this more rigorously [3].

Another active area of ensemble research in recent years has been ensemble feature selection which involves building ensembles using different feature sets for each base learner [4,5,6,7,8,9,10]. Separate from the dimensionality reduction aspect of feature selection, the main theme of much of the research in this area has been error decorrelation or specifically *error diversity*. Feature selection provides a additional way of promoting error diversity in comparison to reweighting or partitioning of training patterns [11].

The first suggestions of combining Boosting and ensemble feature selection were indirectly made for *Decision Stumps* [12] and *Domain-Partitioning* for

N.C. Oza et al. (Eds.): MCS 2005, LNCS 3541, pp. 32–41, 2005.

Boosting [13]. In both cases the motivation was to improve base classifer behaviour to that of a *weak learner*. Later, *Boosting Feature Selection* [1] explicitly performed feature selection as a means to extract relevant features for ensemble classification. However, these authors did not refer to the implications of combining the two areas toward improving error diversity, and no analysis of this type was conducted.

Here Boosting feature selection is studied. Observations on generalisation, weighted error and error diversity are used to comment on the properties of the algorithm. In particular, we propose using ensemble feature prominence, a measure representing the ensemble feature exploitation, as a stopping criterion for building the ensemble. The paper is organized as follows. Section 2 introduces the Boosting feature selection algorithm. Section 3 presents the measures we use to analyse the behaviour of the algorithm. Section 3.2 introduces feature prominence. Section 4 presents experimental results and discussions based on a number of benchmark datasets. Section 5 concludes the paper.

2   Boosting Feature Selection

2.1   Ensemble Feature Selection

Building ensembles using features has been studied by a number of researchers. Several methods based around improvements of the Random Subspace Method (RSM) [4] have been proposed. Refinement of RSM accuracy [5, 6] can be used to improve ensemble accuracy. Whereas genetic search starts with a randomisation stage on which feature populations are refined [7]. These can create good ensembles, but do not explicitly perform feature selection to remove redundancy and irrelevance. Alternatively, methods using sequential feature selection [8, 9] have also been proposed but require a careful choice of selection criteria to prevent overfitting. In each of these methods the principal objective is to use different feature subsets for training base learners, as a means of decorrelating errors between them.

2.2   Boosting Feature Selection

The Boosting Feature Selection (BFS) algorithm proposed by Tieu and Viola [1] was first to explicitly combine Adaboost and ensemble feature selection together. The BFS algorithm shown in Fig. 1 differs for Adaboost only by the way the weights are initialised and that each base hypothesis h_t, is trained on and classifies only one feature. The feature is selected on the basis of lowest weighted error ϵ_t for the given weighting w_t. As the weighting changes, different features are selected for the current hypothesis h_t which best reduce ϵ_t. Using different features this way provides an additional means of error decorrelation for Boosting (Sect. 3.1).

In this study, a weighted Nearest Mean (NM) classifier is used. Typically, when Boosting all the features the NM classifier performs poorly for two reasons. Firstly, the classifier complexity is limited to linear descison hyperplanes

---

Input: Training set $S = \{(\mathbf{x}_1, y_1), ..., \mathbf{x}_M, y_M)\}$, Number of Iterations T.
Initialize: Sample weights $w_{1,m} = \frac{1}{2M^-}, \frac{1}{2M^+}$ for $y_m = -1, 1$, $m = 1, ..., M$, where M^- and M^+ are the number of negatives and positives respectively.
Do for t=1,...,T

1. **Train:** Find N hypotheses h_n, by training the base learner on each feature x_n of the given training set, using current weighting $w_{t,m}$.
   Calculate: the weighted training error for each hypothesis h_n

$$\epsilon_n = \sum_{m=1}^{M} w_{t,m} \mathbf{I}(y_m \neq h_n(\mathbf{x}_{m,n})). \tag{1}$$

2. **Select:** hypothesis h_n with the lowest ϵ_n, set $h_t = h_n$ and $\epsilon_t = \epsilon_n$.
3. **if** $\epsilon_t = 0$ or $\epsilon_t \geq 0.5$, reset to initial weights $w_{t,m} = w_{1,m}$, **goto** 1.
4. **Calculate:** hypothesis coefficient

$$\alpha_t = \frac{1}{2} \ln \left(\frac{1 - \epsilon_t}{\epsilon_t} \right).$$

5. **Update:** sample weights

$$w_{t+1,m} = \frac{1}{Z_t} w_{t,m} \exp(-\alpha_t y_m h_t(\mathbf{x}_m)),$$

where Z_t is a normalisation coefficient such that $\sum_m (w_{t+1,m}) = 1$.
Output: Final hypothesis

$$\mathcal{H}_T(\mathbf{x}) = \text{sign} \left(\sum_{t=1}^{T} \alpha_t h_t(\mathbf{x}) \right).$$

Fig. 1. Boosting feature selection as proposed by Tieu and Viola [1]

uncommon in many problems. Secondly, reweighting the training set does not invoke a significant decision change, compared to an unstable classifer such as a neural network. However, Boosting one dimension at a time demands less complex decisions and is optimal as long as the data is unimodal. Therefore, the NM classifier is suitable for BFS.

3   Indicators of Performance

3.1   Error Diversity

Over using a single classifier, one of the benefits of an ensemble comes from combining base learners that make different mistakes on different parts of the problem space. The ideal condition would be to have base learners as accurate and diverse as possible, such a condition is termed *error diversity*. The previously mentioned ensemble feature selection methods promote decision diversity through resampling the training set features. In a recent review [11] this was regarded as the most effective way of creating an ensemble of diverse decisions. The extent to which accuracy and diversity should be traded in an ensemble is a difficult issue. In a regression context the role of accuracy and diversity can be clearly explained using the *bias-variance* decomposition. However, no analogy has yet been found for classification involving non-ordinal outputs. This difficulty has resulted in a number of qualitative definitions of error diversity and there is no unique choice for measuring it. The literature has proposed numerous ways of measuring error diversity which can be broadly split into pairwise and non pairwise measures [14]. Here the non-pairwise measure of *inter-rater* agreement or kappa statistic is used [15]. It is defined as follows.

A set of classifiers in an ensemble have the decisions $\mathcal{D} = \{D_1, ..., D_L\}$, trained using labelled dataset $\mathbf{S} = [\mathbf{s}_1, ..., \mathbf{s}_M]$, where $\mathbf{s}_m$ is the training pair $(\mathbf{x}_m, y_m)$ and $\mathbf{x}_m \in \mathbb{R}^N$. The Kappa statistic can then be defined as

$$\kappa = 1 - \frac{\frac{1}{L}\sum_{m=1}^{M} l(\mathbf{s}_m)(L - l(\mathbf{s}_m))}{M(L-1)\bar{p}(1-\bar{p})}. \tag{2}$$

where $\bar{p}$ denotes the average individual classification accuracy in the ensemble and $l(\mathbf{s}_m)$ is the number of classifiers from $\mathcal{D}$ that correctly recognise $\mathbf{s}_m$. The kappa statistic measures the degree of similarity between classifiers while compensating for the probability that a similarity occurs by chance. κ is equal to zero when classifier agreement equals that expected by chance (but can be negative) and is equal to 1 when the classifiers agree on every example. It has also been shown to be related to Kohavi-Wolpert variance and the disagreement measures of diversity [14].

3.2 Ensemble Feature Prominence

The implementation of BFS used allowed features to be reselected during construction. At any time an ensemble of size T will consist of the equivalent number of features T. Some of these features will be unique selections denoted $\mathbf{F}_{\text{unique}}$, the remainder are replicated selections. The replicated selections may not necessarily be redundant as they may offer additional information based on the sample weighting. The unique selections $\mathbf{F}_{\text{unique}}$ normalised by the ensemble size T can be used to find the Ensemble Feature Unicity (EFU), defined as

$$\text{EFU} = \frac{\mathbf{F}_{\text{unique}}}{T} \tag{3}$$

which is unity when only unique selections are present and decreases as redundant features are included into the ensemble. At some point, no new selections will be made and the EFU continues to fall at rate of c/T, where c is the maximum number of informative features and perhaps the total number N.

As the number of replicate selections by BFS rises, the effective feature information to the ensemble begins to reach a limit. The remaining features can then be considered irrelevant for classification purposes. The unique selections $\mathbf{F}_{unique}$ in terms of the total number of features available for selection $|\mathbf{F}|$ can be used to determine the Ensemble Feature Exploitation (EFE), defined as

$$\text{EFE} = \frac{\mathbf{F}_{unique}}{|\mathbf{F}|} \tag{4}$$

where a unity EFE indicates that all features have been used once and no feature redundancy is present. Depending on how many irrelevant features are present, a point might be reached when the EFE tends towards a constant rate $f/|\mathbf{F}|$, where f is the number of informative features.

The number of features and intrinsic feature relevance is problem dependant. A suitable ensemble size should be selected so that the ensemble includes all the relevant features from the dataset without including too much redundancy. We propose to combine the two previous measures of ensemble feature unicity and feature exploitation to allow a way of observing how well the current ensemble size has exploited the total number of features in the dataset. Combining (3) and (4) leads to the following, termed Ensemble Feature Prominence (EFP) and defined

$$\text{EFP} = \frac{\mathbf{F}_{unique}^2}{T|\mathbf{F}|}. \tag{5}$$

The falling EFU and rising EFE combine to make a function that peaks distinctly. This behaviour can be used as a stop criterion for building a BFS ensemble. As an illustrative example, the EFU, EFE and EFP plots against T are shown in figure 2 for the Wdbc dataset described in Sect. 4. The EFU is seen to reach a distinct peak when $T = 21$, meaning not all of the 30 features available for selection have been useful to the ensemble. On average only 15 unique selections have been made in $T = 21$ iterations. Therefore when $T > 21$, the number of repeated selections increases and the plots of EFU and EFE begin to fall and rise respectively at the fore mentioned rates. These then combine to make the observed peak in EFP.

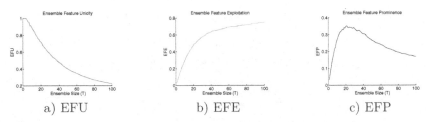

a) EFU   b) EFE   c) EFP

Fig. 2. Ensemble feature unicity, exploitation and resulting prominence for the Wdbc dataset

4   Comparison of BFS Against Adaboost

The ensembling quality of BFS and Adaboost were compared on a NM classifer. Performance was assessed using four benchmark datasets from the UCI repository [16]. The binary learning datasets Wdbc, Sonar and Musk were selected for experimentation. Additionally, the multiclass dataset Multiple Features (Mfeat) was used. We re-formulate it as a binary learning problem of classifying the numbers 0-4 from 5-9. All the features were used in this dataset except the profile correlation and pixel averages. All data was used in the case of Wdbc and Sonar, but the Musk and Mfeat were reduced in size (for computational reasons) to 600 training samples using stratified random sampling. The datasets were pre-processed by rejecting 3% of outlying samples furthest from the global mean. Features were then normalised to zero mean and unit variance.

The performance of each method was estimated on the benchmark datasets using the following measures: Training and test error were used to measure generalisation, weighted error (1) to check the bounds of the base learner. The kappa statistic (2) was measured over base learner outputs using training and test data to assess error decorrelation of the ensemble. Finally, feature prominence (5) was estimated for the BFS ensembles to assess feature exploitation. Adaboost was prevented from stopping when $\epsilon_t \geq 0.5$ by resetting sample weightings to initial conditions [17]. This was necessary to keep the two types of ensembles consistent in size for comparison. BFS and Adaboost were run for $T = 1 \rightarrow 1.5N$ iterations and observations made over this range. The mean of each performance measure was found for 10 runs of 2-fold cross validation. The results are shown in Figs. 3-6.

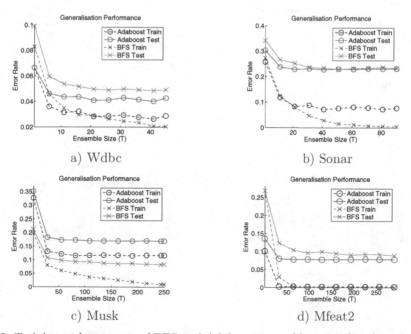

Fig. 3. Training and test error of BFS and Adaboost ensembles using benchmark data

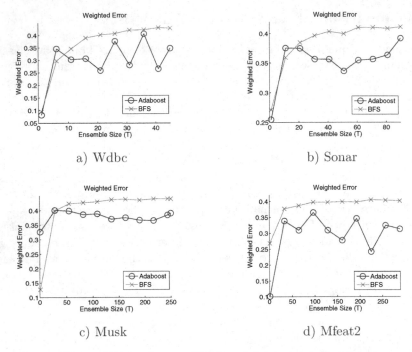

a) Wdbc

b) Sonar

c) Musk

d) Mfeat2

Fig. 4. Weighted error of BFS and Adaboost ensembles

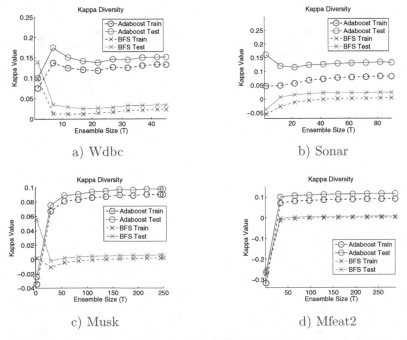

a) Wdbc

b) Sonar

c) Musk

d) Mfeat2

Fig. 5. Kappa error diversity (↓) of BFS and Adaboost ensembles

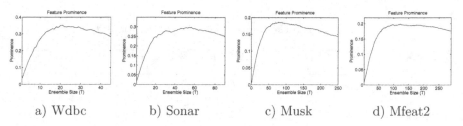

a) Wdbc   b) Sonar   c) Musk   d) Mfeat2

Fig. 6. Feature prominence for BFS ensembles

4.1   Discussion

Using the observations on generalisation, weighted error, kappa diversity and feature prominence the following differences between Adaboost and BFS were observed.

Training error was lower overall for BFS than for Adaboost (Fig. 3). Test error of BFS was lower than Adaboost for the Musk dataset, comparable for the Sonar and Mfeat2 datasets but higher for Wdbc. The poorer performance of Adaboost on the Musk dataset was caused by features containing multimodal data which the linear classifier could not correctly fit using all dimensions. These results show that Boosting features can compete with Adaboost despite the lower dimensional description when using only one feature. Feature selection can provide a better match between data and classifier than using the entire feature description. Two explanations for this behaviour are presented based on weighted error and error diversity.

Adaboost had a lower weighted error than BFS (Fig. 4), as frequently $\epsilon_t \geq 0.5$ causing the weights to be reset to initial conditions (Fig. 1). Although BFS using the NM classifer has a high weighted error, it has kept within the weighted error bounds required for Boosting $0 \leq \epsilon_t \leq 0.5$ [18, 19]. Hence Boosting continues to provide an incremental reduction in training and test error. Adaboost using the NM classifer has less Boosting effect. Cases where $et \geq 0.5$ reflect that the linear NM classifer has been unable to represent the complexity of the mult-dimensional decision surface. Despite resetting to initial weighting to continue, this has not provided any improvement in performance as confirmed by the minimum test and training error shown in (Fig. 3).

Decision diversity was consistently higher (lower kappa) for BFS than Adaboost (Fig. 5). This was consistent for both training and test data, though the latter was slightly less diverse. As already stated in Sect. 2, training Adaboost using different features has provided a better method of error decorrelation. This provides an additional method than relying on the reweighted training set alone. However, the increased diversity cannot be shown to correlate with improved performance in these experiments.

Final observations are on EFP, our proposed ensemble construction stop criterion based on ensemble feature exploitation. Examining (Fig. 6), BFS gives a strong peak for each dataset which is below that of the dataset dimensionality $|\mathbf{F}|_{EFP} < N$. The peak in feature prominence does not correspond to the

Table 1. Summary of the unique selections $|\mathbf{F}|$ present at peak ensemble feature prominence $T = \mathrm{EFP_{max}}$, compared to the complete number of iterations $T = 1.5N$

Dataset Name	$|\mathbf{F}|_{\mathbf{N}}$	$|\mathbf{F}|, \mathrm{EFP_{max}}$	Error	$|\mathbf{F}|_{\mathbf{T,1.5N}}$	Error
Wdbc	30	14	0.049±0.013	19	0.049±0.014
Sonar	60	31	0.236±0.036	36	0.232±0.032
Musk	167	49	0.095±0.015	77	0.083±0.016
Mfeat2	193	68	0.098±0.019	99	0.088±0.019

lowest achievable error rates (Fig. 3), but indicates that most of the reduction in error has occurred. Table 1 summarises the number of unique features selected at maximum feature prominence and at $T = 1.5N$ along with the test set error rate for each benchmark dataset. Boosting beyond feature prominence continues to include more features. However, these features provide only small improvements and might not justify the cost of feature extraction and a larger classifier ensemble. Similar conclusion can be made for diversity (Fig. 5). After peak prominence there are no improvements in diversity. Only a slow decrease as replicate features are added to the ensemble.

5   Conclusion

In conclusion, a number of observations have been made on BFS which have not been previously studied. We have shown BFS to be suitable for Boosting a low complexity NM classifier on which Adaboost performs more poorly.

Despite the reduced complexity, BFS has been shown to have a competitive error rate to Adaboost. This of course depends of the fitting of the selected base classifer to the source data, as with all classification problems. Improvements in error decorrelation have been illustrated Boosting on different features, unfortunately this was not correlated with low error rate in all cases. Ensemble feature prominence has been presented as an ensemble construction stop criterion and displayed as a means of trading feature exploitation and redundancy. Such a condition is particularly important for problems involving high dimensional feature representation.

References

1. Tieu, K., Viola, P.: Boosting image retrieval. IEEE Conf. on Computer Vision and Pattern Recognition (2000) 228–235
2. Freund, Y., Schapire, R.: Experiments with a new boosting algorithm. In Proc. 13th International Conference on Machine Learning (1996) 148–156
3. Rätsch, G., Warmuth, M.: Maximizing the margin with boosting. In Proceedings of the 15th Annual Conference on Computational Learning Theory (2002) 334–350

4. Ho, T.: The random subspace method for constructing decision forests. IEEE Transactions on Pattern Analysis and Machine Intelligence **20** (1998) 832–844
5. Cunningham, P., Carney, J.: Diversity versus quality in classification ensembles based on feature selection. 11th European Conference on machine learning (ECML2000), lecture notes in artificial intelligence (2000) 109–116
6. R. Bryll, R. Gutierrez-Osuna, F.Q.: Attribute bagging: improving accuracy of classifier ensembles by using random feature subsets. Pattern Recognition **36** (2003) 1291–1302
7. Guerra-Salcedo, C., Whitley, D.: Feature selection mechanisms for ensemble creation: a genetic search perspective. AAAI-99 (1999)
8. Tsymbal, A., Pechenizkiy, M., Cunningham, P.: Diversity in search strategies for ensemble feature selection. Information Fusion **6** (2005) 83–98
9. Günter, S., Bunke, H.: Feature selection algorithms for the generation of multiple classifier systems and their application to handwritten word recognition. Pattern Recognition Letters **25** (2004) 1323–1336
10. Oza, N., Tumer, K.: Input decimation ensembles: Decorrelation through dimensionality reduction. In Proc. of 2nd International Workshop on Multiple Classifier Systems, Cambridge, UK. (2001) 238–247
11. Brown, G., Wyatt, J., Harris, R., Yao, X.: Diversity creation methods: A survey and categorisation. Information Fusion **6** (2005) 5–20
12. Quinlan, J.R.: Bagging, boosting and c4.5. In Proceedings of the Thirteenth National Conference on Artificial Intelligence (1996) 725–730
13. Schapire, R., Singer, Y.: Improved boosting algorithms using confidence-rated predictions. Machine Learning **37** (1999) 297–336
14. Kuncheva, L., Whitaker, C.: Measures of diversity in classifier ensembles. Machine Learning **51** (2003) 181–207
15. Feiss, J.: Statistical methods for rates and proportions (1981)
16. Blake, C., Merz, C.: UCI repository of machine learning databases (1998)
17. M. Skurichina, L.I. Kuncheva, R.D.: Bagging and boosting for the nearest mean classifier: Effects on sample size diversity and accuracy. MCS 2002, Lecture Notes in Computer Science **2365** (2002) 62–71
18. Freund, Y., Schapire, R.: A decision-theoretic generalization of on-line learning and an application to boosting. Journal of Computer and System Sciences (1997) 119–139
19. Schapire, R., Freund, Y., Bartlett, P., Lee, W.: Boosting the margin: A new explanation for the effectiveness of voting methods. The Annuals of Statistics (1998) 1651–1686

Boosting Multiple Classifiers Constructed by Hybrid Discriminant Analysis

Qi Tian[1], Jie Yu[1], and Thomas S. Huang[2]

[1] Department of Computer Science,
University of Texas at San Antonio, TX 78249,
{qitian, jyu}@cs.utsa.edu
[2] Beckman Institute,
University of Illinois at Urbana-Champaign,
Urbana, IL 61801
huang@ifp.uiuc.edu

Abstract. In this paper, a set of hybrid dimension reduction schemes is constructed by unifying principal component analysis (PCA) and linear discriminant analysis (LDA) in a single framework. PCA compensates LDA for singular scatter matrix caused by small set of training samples and increases the effective dimension of the projected subspace. Generalization of hybrid analysis is extended to other discriminant analysis such as multiple discriminant analysis (MDA), and the recent biased discriminant analysis (BDA), and other hybrid pairs. In order to reduce the search time to find the best single classifier, a boosted hybrid analysis is proposed. Our scheme boosts both the individual features as well as a set of weak classifiers. Extensive tests on benchmark and real image databases have shown the superior performance of the boosted hybrid analysis.

1 Introduction

Dimension reduction is an important problem in machine learning and also arises in many other fields such as information processing, data compression, scientific visualization and pattern recognition. The aim of dimension reduction is to obtain compact representation of data which captures desired information without loss of too much information.

Dimension reduction techniques can be categorized into two major classes: linear and non-linear techniques. The linear methods include Principal Component Analysis (PCA), Factor Analysis, and Independent Component Analysis (ICA). The nonlinear methods include Multidimensional Scaling (MDS), Self-Organizing Map (SOM), and Neural Network, etc.

The classical techniques, PCA [1] and MDS [2], are simple to implement, efficiently computable, and guaranteed to discover the true structure of data lying on or near a linear subspace of the high-dimensional input space. PCA finds a low-dimensional embedding of the data points that best preserves their variance as measured in the high-dimensional input space. Classical MDS finds an embedding that

N.C. Oza et al. (Eds.): MCS 2005, LNCS 3541, pp. 42–52, 2005.
© Springer-Verlag Berlin Heidelberg 2005

preserves the interpoint distances, equivalent to PCA when those distances are Euclidean. However, many data sets contain essential nonlinear structures that are invisible to PCA and MDS. Tenenbaum et al. [3] proposed a nonlinear dimension reduction technique, Isomap, which combines the major algorithmic features of PCA and MDS – computational efficiency, global optimality, and asymptotic convergence guarantees – with the flexibility to learn a broad class of nonlinear manifolds. Their approach builds on classical MDS but seeks to preserve the intrinsic geometry of the data, as captured in the *geodesic* manifold distances between all pairs of data points. Given sufficient data, Isomap is guaranteed asymptotically to recover the true dimensionality and geometric structure of a nonlinear manifold.

Isomap has been successfully applied to many problems in nonlinear dimensionality reduction. Isomap's embeddings, however, are optimized to preserve geodesic distances between general pairs of data points, which can only be estimated by computing shortest paths through large sublattices of data. Recently, Roweis and Saul [4] introduced locally linear embedding (LLE). The basic idea of LLE is that each data point and its neighbors lie on or close to a locally linear patch of the manifold and therefore the local geometry is characterized by linear coefficients that can reconstruct each data point from its neighbors. Different from Isomap, LLE eliminates the need to estimate pairwise distances between widely separated data points. It thus avoids the need to solve large dynamic programming problems, and it also tends to accumulate very sparse matrices, whose structure can be exploited for savings in time and space. Many other popular nonlinear dimensionality reduction algorithms do not share the favorable properties of LLE. Iterative hill-climbing methods such as autoencoder Neural Network, Self-Organizing Maps, and latent variable models do not have the same guarantees of global optimality or convergence; they also tend to involve many more free parameters, such as learning rates, convergence criteria, and architectural specifications.

We should add that nonlinear dimensionality reduction (NLDR) by itself is a very large area of research. In our scenario dimension reduction is the first step for indexing or classification in similarity search from very large databases such as content-based image retrieval and biometrics-based person recognition. Real-time implementation is very desirable. Use of iterative NLDR techniques such as Isomap, LLE, Laplacian Eigenmaps [5] is usually prohibited by the need to perform real-time and repeatable projections or closed-form computation.

Linear discriminant analysis (LDA) [6] is a simple and efficient algorithm that is used for both dimension reduction and classification. LDA plays a key role in many research areas in science and engineering such as face recognition, image retrieval, and bio-informatics. Compared to PCA, LDA constructs the *most discriminant* features while PCA constructs the *most descriptive* features in the sense of packing most "energy". LDA attempts to minimize the Bayes error by selecting the feature vectors w which maximize $\frac{|w^T S_B w|}{|w^T S_W w|}$, where S_B measures the variance between the class means, and S_W measures the variance of the samples in the same class.

In pattern classification community, when comparing LDA with PCA, there is a tendency to prefer LDA over PCA, because, as intuition would suggest, the former deals directly with discrimination between classes, whereas the latter deals without paying particular attention to the underlying class structure. However, an interesting result is reported by Martinez ad Kak [7] that PCA might outperform LDA when the number of samples per class is small or when the training data non-uniformly sample the underlying distribution.

PCA and LDA are often used alone without combining other types of analysis. It would be interesting to investigate the possibility of combining these two techniques. In this paper, a novel hybrid dimension reduction scheme is proposed to unify LDA and PCA in a single framework. This hybrid analysis can be generalized to combine other discriminant analysis.

The rest of paper is organized as follows. Section 2 describes the hybrid discriminant analysis. Section 3 shows the experimental results on image databases. AdaBoost is applied in Section 4 to construct a more powerful classifier from a set of weak classifiers. Conclusions and discussions are given in Section 5.

2   Hybrid Discriminant Analysis

2.1   Linear Discriminant Analysis

It is common practice to preprocess data by extracting linear and non-linear features. What one would like to obtain is a feature, which is as invariant as possible while still covering as much of the information necessary for describing the data's properties of interest. A classical and well-known technique that solves this type of problem is the maximization of the *Rayleigh* coefficient [6].

$$J(W) = \frac{|W^T S_1 W|}{|W^T S_2 W|} \tag{1}$$

Here, W denotes the weight vector of a linear feature extractor (i.e., for an example $\mathbf{x}$, the feature is given by the projections ($W^T \cdot \mathbf{x}$) and S_1 and S_2 are symmetric matrices designed such that they measure the desired information and the undesired noise along the direction W. The ratio in equation (1) is maximized when one covers as much as possible of the desired information while avoiding the undesired.

If we look for discriminating directions for classification, we can choose S_1 to measure the between-class variance S_B, and S_2 to measure the within-class variance S_W. In this case, we recover the Fisher discriminant analysis (FDA) [6], where S_B and S_W are given by:

$$S_B = \sum_{j=1}^{C} N_j \cdot (m_j - m)(m_j - m)^T \tag{2}$$

$$S_W = \sum_{j=1}^{C} \sum_{i=1}^{N_j} (x_i^{(j)} - m_j)(x_i^{(j)} - m_j)^T \tag{3}$$

We use $\{x_i^{(j)}, i = 1, \ldots, N_j\}, j = 1, \ldots, C$ ($C = 2$ for FDA) to denote the feature vectors of samples. C is the number of classes, N_j is the size of the jth class, $x_i^{(j)}$ is the ith

sample of the jth class, m_j is mean vector of the jth class, and m is grand mean of all samples.

Multiple discriminant analysis (MDA) is a natural generalization of Fisher's linear discriminative analysis for multiple classes [6]. If S_W is nonsingular matrix then the ratio in Eq. (1) is maximized when the column vectors of the projection matrix, W, are the eigenvectors of $S_W^{-1}S_B$. It should be noted that W maps the original d_1-dimensional data space X to a d_2-dimensional space Δ (where $d_2 \leq C-1$, C is the number of classes). Because FDA and MDA are linear techniques, they are called LDA.

2.2 Biased Discriminant Analysis

Contrary to FDA and MDA which treats every class symmetrically when finding the optimal projection subspace, Zhou and Huang [8] modified MDA and proposed biased discriminant analysis (BDA) and applied it in content-based image retrieval (CBIR). The intuition behind the BDA is that *"all positive examples are alike, and each negative example is negative in its own way"*. Compared with the state-of-the-art methods such as Support Vector Machine (SVM), kernel BDA outperforms SVM when the size of the negative example is small (<20).

BDA differs from MDA in the computation of between-class scatter matrix S_B and within-class scatter matrix S_W. They are substituted by $S_{N \to P}$ and S_P, respectively.

$$S_{N \to P} = \sum_{i=1}^{N_y} (\mathbf{y}_i - m_x)(\mathbf{y}_i - m_x)^T \tag{4}$$

$$S_P = \sum_{i=1}^{N_x} (\mathbf{x}_i - m_x)(\mathbf{x}_i - m_x)^T \tag{5}$$

where $\{\mathbf{x}_i, i=1,\cdots,N_x\}$ denotes the positive examples and $\{\mathbf{y}_i, i=1,\cdots,N_y\}$ denotes the negative examples, m_x is the mean vector of the sets $\{\mathbf{x}_i\}$, respectively. $S_{N \to P}$ is the scatter matrix between the negative examples and the centroid of the positive examples, and S_P is the scatter matrix within the positive examples. $N \to P$ indicates the asymmetric approach, which means the user's biased opinion towards the positive class [8].

2.3 Hybrid PCA and LDA analysis

If S_1 in equation (1) is the covariance matrix S_Σ of all the samples, and S_2 identity matrix, we recover standard principal component analysis (PCA) [1]. If S_1 is the data covariance and S_2 the noise covariance, we obtain *oriented* PCA (OPCA) [1], which aims at finding a direction that describes most variance in the data while avoiding known noise as much as possible.

If we design our optimal function as

$$W_{opt} = \arg\max_{W} \frac{|W^T[(1-\lambda)\cdot S_B + \lambda\cdot S_\Sigma]W|}{|W^T[(1-\eta)\cdot S_W + \eta\cdot I]W|} \tag{6}$$

where λ, η are two parameters in the range of $(0,0)$ to $(1,1)$, S_Σ is the covariance matrix of all the training samples, and I is the identity matrix.

With different (λ,η) values, the equation (6) provides a set of alternatives to PCA and LDA: $(\lambda=0,\eta=0)$ reduces to the full LDA; $(\lambda=1,\eta=1)$ recovers the full PCA; $(\lambda=0,\eta=1)$ gives a subspace that is mainly defined by maximizing the scatters among all the classes with minimal effort on clustering each class; $(\lambda=1,\eta=0)$ gives a subspace that mainly preserves the most energy while minimizing the scatter matrices of within-classes; $(\lambda=\frac{1}{2},\eta=\frac{1}{2})$ gives a subspace that is a trade-off between LDA and PCA. With continuous (λ,η) values, more alternatives beyond PCA and LDA, which haven't been studied before, can be easily obtained.

The difference of the hybrid analysis from the existing formulae for LDA is subtle, but critical. Two points are worth mentioning: *regularization*; and *effective dimension*.

Regularization. It is well known that sample-based plug-in estimates of the scatter matrices based on equations (2-5) will be severely biased for small number of training samples. If the number of the feature dimensions is large compared to the number of training examples, the problem becomes ill-posed, i.e., $|W^T S_W W| = 0$ in equation (1). A compensation or regularization can be simply done by adding quantities to the diagonal of the scatter matrices [9]. It is denoted as simple regularization scheme. It has been shown in [10] that even simple regularization scheme can significantly improve the classification accuracy in average by 15% ~ 40%.

If we examine the denominator of equation (6), adding the matrix $\eta\cdot I$ achieves simple regularization. But the difference from simple regularization is that we also consider preserving the descriptive features in the nominator of equation (6).

Effective Dimension. In LDA, the maximum dimension of the projected subspace is $C-1$, where C is the number of the classes [6], while in PCA there is no such limitation. Due to the full rank of the matrix $(1-\eta)\cdot S_W + \eta\cdot I$, the hybrid PCA-LDA analysis has *effective dimension* up to d_1, while for FDA it is only 1 and for MDA it is at most $C-1$ ($d_1 >> C$ usually). This gives the hybrid approach significantly higher capacity for informative density modeling, for which FDA has virtually none.

2.4 Hybrid MDA and BDA Analysis

The main difference of MDA and BDA is their symmetric/asymmetric treatment to the positive and negative examples. They can also be unified. Similarly to equation (6), we design our optimal function as

$$W_{opt} = \arg\max_{W} \frac{|W^T[(1-\lambda)\cdot S_{N\rightarrow P} + \lambda\cdot S_{P\rightarrow N}]W|}{|W^T[(1-\eta)\cdot S_P + \eta\cdot S_N]W|} \tag{7}$$

where $S_{N \to P}$ (or $S_{P \to N}$) is the between-class scatter matrix from the negative (or positive) examples to the centroid of the positive (or negative) examples, and S_P (or S_N) is the within-class scatter matrix for the positive (or negative) examples, respectively.

Similar to the PCA-LDA analysis, both BDA and MDA become the special cases in the unified framework, and a rich set of the discriminant analysis beyond BDA and MDA can be obtained by setting parameters (λ, η).

It is our expectation that these new alternatives could boost the classification performance since they compensate each other but overcome their drawbacks.

3 Experiments and Analysis

3.1 Comparison of PCA, LDA and Hybrid Analysis

In the first experiment, several benchmark[1] data sets are used. It contains three different data sets: Hearts, Breast-Cancer and Banana. The data dimensions of these three data sets are 13, 9, and 2, respectively. The sizes of the training sets are 170, 200, 400, and the sizes of the testing data sets are 100, 77, and 4900, respectively.

The original data is first projected to the lower subspace and expectation-maximization (EM) algorithm [6] is applied on the projected data for classification. The distribution of the labeled samples, i.e., training data set, is learned and the unlabeled test samples will be classified with the learned distribution. Empirical observations suggest that the transformed image data often approximates a Gaussian in the lower subspace, and so in our implementation, we use low-order Gaussian mixture to model the transformed data.

Figure 1 shows the classification error rate using PCA, LDA and hybrid PCA-LDA analysis. For Heart data, the error rate is 20.7% for PCA, 18.8% for LDA, and 16.1% for the hybrid PCA-LDA analysis for the best pair $(\lambda = 0.4, \eta = 0)$. For Breast-Cancer data, the error rate is 26.4% for PCA, 28.5% for LDA, and 25.4% for the hybrid PCA-LDA analysis for the best pair $(\lambda = 0.4, \eta = 0.2)$.

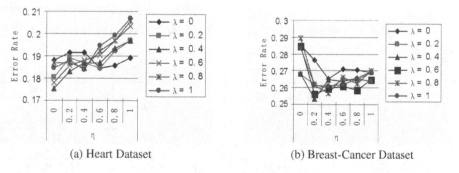

(a) Heart Dataset   (b) Breast-Cancer Dataset

Fig. 1. Comparison of PCA, LDA, and hybrid PCA-LDA analysis PCA: $(\lambda = 1, \eta = 1)$, LDA: $(\lambda = 0, \eta = 0)$, best hybrid pair: $(\lambda = 0.4, \eta = 0)$ for Heart Dataset; $(\lambda = 0.4, \eta = 0.2)$ for Breast-Cancer Dataset

---

[1] The benchmark data sets are obtained from http://mlg.anu.edu.au/~raetsch/

Table 1. Comparison of PCA, LDA, and hybrid PCA-LDA analysis on the Heart dataset

Error Rate (%)	Projected Subspace Dimension			
	1	2	4	8
LDA	18.8	18.3	21.0	24.5
PCA	20.7	21.2	20.8	21.5
Best PCA-LDA pair (λ^*, η^*)	16.1 (0.4, 0)	17.9 (0.2, 0.2)	18.7 (0.4, 0.2)	20.5 (0.4, 0)

Table 1 shows the error rates for different dimensions of the projected subspace. It is obvious that the hybrid PCA-LDA analysis performs best among three techniques.

3.2   Comparison to State-of-the-Art

In the second experiment, hybrid PCA-LDA analysis combined with semi-supervised learning through the EM algorithm is compared to state-of-the-art classification techniques, which include a single Radial Basis Function (RBF) classifier, a support vector machine (SVM), AdaBoost, and the Kernel Fisher discriminant (KFD), and DEM and its kernel version (KDEM) [12] on the benchmark dataset [11]. RBF kernels are used in all kernel-based algorithms.

Besides the hybrid PCA-LDA analysis, we also consider the hybrid oriented PCA (OPCA) and BDA analysis. Oriented PCA has the property of maximizing Signal-to-Noise Ratio (SNR) of a given signal. The formulation of hybrid OPCA-BDA analysis is similar to equations (6) and (7).

Table 2 shows the classification error and their standard deviation for various classification methods. The hybrid analysis is well comparable to state-of-the-art kernel-based methods except for the Banana data (the original dimension is 3, the gain by all linear projections is limited), even though for the former methods only linear transformations are performed.

Table 2. Benchmark test: The average error rate (%) and standard deviation

Error rate (%) and standard deviation	Benchmark		
	Heart	Breast-Cancer	Banana
RBF	17.6±0.33	27.6±0.47	10.8±0.06
AdaBoost	20.3±0.34	30.4±0.47	12.3±0.07
SVM	16.0±0.33	26.0±0.47	11.5±0.07
KFD	16.1±0.34	25.8±0.48	10.8±0.05
DEM	19.42±1.43	28.57±1.37	38.43±2.5
KDEM	16.5±0.85	27.4±1.53	11.03±0.26
PCA–LDA (λ^*, η^*)	17.6±0.71 (0.4, 0)	25.4±1.69 (0.4, 0.2)	43.16±1.69 (0.4, 0)
OPCA–BDA (λ^*, η^*)	16.3±0.82 (0.2, 0.2)	27.01±1.42 (0.2, 0)	38.79±3.12 (0.4, 0)

3.3 Comparison to Variants of Discriminant Analysis

In the third experiment, we compare our hybrid analysis with discriminant-EM algorithm (DEM) and kernel DEM (KDEM) [12], BDA, and kernel BDA (KBDA) [8].

The data sets used are the MIT facial image dataset (2358 images) and non-face images (2958 images) from Corel database. All the face and non-face images are scaled down to 16×16 gray images and normalized feature vector of dimension 256 is used to represent the image. The size of the training set is 100, 200, 400, and 800, respectively. Compared with the feature vector dimension of 256, the training sample size is set from relatively small to relatively large.

Table 3. Comparison of DEM, BDA, KDEM, KBDA, and the hybrid pairs

Error Rate (%)	Size of Training Set			
	100	200	400	800
DEM	10.5	19.3	15.0	9.0
BDA	34.7	25.4	18.5	19.3
KDEM	6.93	1.43	0.7	0.5
KBDA	3.04	2.89	2.58	1.44
PCA-LDA (λ^*, η^*)	1.73 (0.4, 0.2)	2.2 (0.2, 0)	1.5 (0.2, 0)	0.73 (0.2, 0.2)
OPCA-BDA (λ^*, η^*)	4.0 (0.2, 0)	3.2 (0.2, 0)	1.3 (0.2, 0.2)	1.2 (0.2, 0)
MDA-BDA (λ^*, η^*)	4.2 (0.2, 0)	1.9 (0.4, 0.2)	1.7 (0.2, 0.2)	1.6 (0.2, 0.2)
OPCA-MDA (λ^*, η^*)	2.3 (0.4, 0.2)	1.9 (0.4, 0.2)	1.8 (0.2, 0)	1.3 (0.4, 0)

Several conclusions can be drawn from results in Table 3. (i) When compared with DEM or BDA, the PCA-LDA pair performs much better. (iii) When compared with KDEM and KBDA, the PCA-LDA pair performs better than KBDA, and comparable to KDEM. It should be noted only linear transformation is used in the hybrid analysis. The performances of other hybrid pairs are very comparable to KDEM and KBDA. These results show the robust performance of the hybrid analysis.

4 Boosting Hybrid Analysis

Hybrid PCA-LDA analysis has shown promising performance in Section 3. However the optimal classifier often lies between PCA and LDA in the parametric space of (λ, η). We have to search the whole parametric space to find the best pair (λ^*, η^*). This will result in extra computational complexity. It is also true that the best pair we found for one particular dataset is often different from that of another dataset and therefore this cannot lead to a generalization.

AdaBoost [13] developed in the computational machine learning area has strong justification in terms of bounds on the generalization error, and connection to additive models in statistics. The basic idea of boosting is to iteratively re-weight the training examples based on the outputs of some weak learners, with difficult-to-learn points receiving higher weights to enter the next iteration. The final learner is a weighted combination of the weaker learners. Therefore AdaBoost provides a general way of combining and enhancing a set of PCA-LDA classifiers in the parametric space.

Unlike most of the existing approaches that boost individual features to form a composite classifier, our scheme boosts both the individual features as well as a set of weak classifiers. Our algorithm is shown below:

Algorithm **AdaBoost with PCA-LDA as weak learner**
Given: Training Sample set X and corresponding label Y
            K PCA-LDA classifiers with different (λ, η)
Initialization: weight $w_{k,t=1}(x) = 1/|X|$

Adaboost:
For $t = 1, \ldots, T$
    For each classifier $k = 1, \ldots, K$ do

- Train the classifier on weighted mean and weighted scatter matrices in the following way. Note that $\sum_{x \in X} w_{k,t}(x) = 1$.

    (i)   Update weighted mean μ_{all}, μ_p, and μ_n

    $$\mu_{all} = \sum w_{k,t}(x) \cdot x / \sum w_{k,t}(x)$$
    $$\mu_p = \sum_{x \in p} w_{k,t}(x) \cdot x / \sum_{x \in p} w_{k,t}(x) \text{ and } \mu_n = \sum_{x \in n} w_{k,t}(x) \cdot x / \sum_{x \in n} w_{k,t}(x)$$

    (ii) Update within-class and between-class scatter matrices and co-variance matrix
    $$S_w = \sum_{x \in p}(x - \mu_p)w_{k,t}(x)(x - \mu_p)^T / \sum_{x \in p} w_{k,t}(x) + \sum_{x \in n}(x - \mu_n)w_{k,t}(x)(x - \mu_n)^T / \sum_{x \in n} w_{k,t}(x)$$
    $$S_b = (\mu_p - \mu_{all}) \cdot (\mu_p - \mu_{all})^T \cdot \sum_{x \in p} w_{k,t}(x) + (\mu_n - \mu_{all}) \cdot (\mu_n - \mu_{all})^T \cdot \sum_{x \in n} w_{k,t}(x)$$
    $$S_\Sigma = \sum_{x \in X}(x - \mu_{all})w_{k,t}(x)(x - \mu_{all})^T / \sum_{x \in X} w_{k,t}(x)$$

- Get the confidence-rated prediction on each sample $h_{k,t}(x) \in (-1,1)$

    If $P(x \in positive) \geq P(x \in negative)$

    $$h(x) = \frac{P(x \in postive)}{P(x \in postive) + P(x \in negative)}$$

    else

    $$h(x) = \frac{-P(x \in negative)}{P(x \in postive) + P(x \in negative)}$$

- Compute the weight of on classifier based on its classification error rate $\varepsilon_{k,t}$

    $$\alpha_{k,t} = \frac{1}{2} \ln(\frac{1 - \varepsilon_{k,t}}{\varepsilon_{k,t}})$$

- Update the weight of each sample
    $$w_{k,t+1}(x) = w_{k,t}(x) \exp(-\alpha_{k,t} \cdot h_{k,t}(x) \cdot y)$$
    End for each classifier
End for t
The final prediction $H(x) = sign(\sum_k \alpha_{k,T} \cdot h_{k,T}(x))$

As a comparison, we also boost individual features for a single classifier of PCA, LDA, and the best pair $(\lambda*,\eta*)$ classifier found in the parametric space, respectively. Figure 2 shows the results. Clearly as iteration goes on, the error rate decreases for all boosted algorithms. Boosted PCA-LDA starts with a set of weak classifiers (compared to the best pair $(\lambda*,\eta*)$ classifier), but after one iteration, the boosted PCA-LDA outperforms the single best classifier $(\lambda* = 0.4, \eta* = 0)$. This is because not only individual features are boosted but also a set of weak classifiers are combined into a strong one.

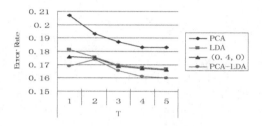

Fig. 2. AdaBoost on Heart benchmark data set

For simply searching the parametric space, the larger the searched space, the better is the performance of the best single classifier. However, the exhaustive search means more computational costs. Table 4 shows the boosted PCA-LDA classifier and the best single classifier of PCA-LDA analysis in the different search spaces. The searching step size of λ and η is 0.25, 0.2, 0.167, and 0.1 resulting in the searching space size 16, 25, 36, and 100, respectively. The boosted PCA-LDA classifier is not sensitive to the size of the search space, e.g., the boosted PCA-LDA classifier from a weak set of 16 single classifiers achieves the better performance (i.e., 16.45%) than the best single classifier (i.e., 16.95%) of search space size 100 after three iterations. Therefore, instead of exhaustive search, the boosted PCA-LDA classifier provides a more efficient way to combine a small set of weak classifiers into a more powerful one.

Table 4. Comparison of the boosted PCA-LDA classifier and best single classifier of PCA-LDA pair on Heart dataset

Search space size	Error rate (%) of the best single classifier $(\lambda*, \eta*)$	Boosted PCA-LDA		
		$T = 1$	$T=3$	$T = 5$
16	17.85 (0.33, 0)	17.03	16.45	16.45
25	17.2 (0.5, 0.25)	16.95	16.6	16.5
36	17.6 (0.4, 0)	16.9	16.55	16.0
100	16.95 (0.5, 0.1)	17.05	16.37	15.9

5 Conclusions and Discussions

Curse of dimensionality is an impediment for any computer vision applications. To address this issue, we propose a novel hybrid feature dimension reduction scheme for classification. In order to reduce the computational complexity and combine a set of weak classifiers into a powerful one, the boosted hybrid analysis is applied. The weighted training scheme in AdaBoost adds indirect non-linearity and adaptivity to the linear methods and thus enhances it by iterations.

Many interesting issues are worth investigating in the future. (i) The first is the fusion of PCA and LDA. (ii) The second is to investigate the variants of standard AdaBoost to remove the outliers in the boosting. (iii) The third is to apply the hybrid analysis to other classification problems in bioinformatics and biometrics.

References

1. T. Jolliffe, *Principal Component Analysis.* 2nd edition, New York: Springer-Verlag, 2002.
2. W. S. Torgerson, *Psychometrika.* 17:401-419, 1952.
3. J. Tenenbaum, V. D. Silva, and J. C. Langford, "A global geometric framework for nonlinear dimensionality reduction," *Science*, 290(5500):2319-2323, 2000.
4. S. Roweis, and L. Saul, "Nonlinear dimensionality reduction by locally linear embedding," *Science*, 290(5500):2323-2326, 2000.
5. Belkin and P. Niyogi, "Laplacian eigenmaps for dimensionality reduction and data representation," *Neural Computation*, 15 (6):1373-1396, 2003.
6. R. Duda, P. Hart, and D. Stork, *Pattern Classification*, John Wiley & Sons, Inc., 2001.
7. M. Martinez and A. C. Kak, "PCA versus LDA," *IEEE Trans. on Pattern Analysis and Machine Intelligence,* vol. 23, no. 2, pp. 228-233, February 2001.
8. X. Zhou, and T.S. Huang, "Small sample learning during multimedia retrieval using bias-Map," *Proc. of IEEE Conf. Computer Vision and Pattern Recognition*, December 2001.
9. J. Friedman, "Regularized discriminant analysis," *Journal of American Statistical Association*, vol. 84, no. 405, pp. 165-175, 1989.
10. Q. Tian, J. Yu, T. Rui, and T.S., Huang, "Parameterized discriminant analysis for image classification," *Proc. IEEE Int'l Conf. on Multimedia and Expo*, Taiwan, 2004.
11. S. Mika, G. Rätsch, J. Weston, B. Schölkopf, A. Smola, and K. Müller, "Fisher discriminant analysis with kernels," *IEEE Workshop on Neural Networks for Signal Proc.*, 1999.
12. Q. Tian, Y. Wu, J. Yu, and T.S. Huang, "Self-supervised learning based on discriminative nonlinear features for image classification," *Pattern Recognition,* vol. 38, no. 6, 2005.
13. Y. Freund, "Boosting a weak learning algorithm by majority," *Information and Computation*, 121(2):256-285, 1995.

Decoding Rules for Error Correcting Output Code Ensembles

R.S. Smith and T. Windeatt

Centre for Vision, Speech and Signal Processing, University of Surrey,
Guildford, Surrey GU2 7XH, UK
{R.S.Smith, T.Windeatt}@surrey.ac.uk

Abstract. The ECOC technique for solving multi-class pattern recognition problems can be broken down into two distinct stages - encoding and decoding. Given a pattern vector of unknown class, the encoding stage consists in constructing a corresponding output code vector by applying to it each of the base classifiers in the ensemble. The decoding stage consists in making a classification decision based on the value of the output code. This paper focuses on the latter stage. Firstly, three different approaches to decoding rule design are reviewed and a new algorithm is presented. This new algorithm is then compared experimentally with two common decoding rules and evidence is presented that the new rule has some advantages in the form of slightly improved classification accuracy and reduced sensitivity to optimal training.

1 Introduction

Many real-world statistical pattern recognition applications call for the ability to discriminate between a multiplicity of classes. For example, in character recognition a minimum requirement is to distinguish between the 26 letters of the alphabet, whilst a face-recognition database may contain images of hundreds of different people. In contrast to this, most of the established pattern recognition techniques, such as the Multi-Layer Perceptron (MLP) and Support Vector Machine (SVM), work best when applied to problems with just two distinct target classes.

There is thus a mismatch between the capabilities of the basic approaches to pattern recognition and the needs of modern practical applications. A fruitful approach to overcoming this problem has been to recast multi-class problems as sets of 2-class problems. This enables the 2-class problems to be solved using well-established techniques and the results then integrated so as to provide a solution to the original multi-class problem. The 2-class classifiers are referred to as *base classifiers* and the group of base classifiers is called an *ensemble*.

A number of possible architectures for the decomposition of multi-class problems into 2-class problems have been studied [1, 3, 9]. These include One-Against-All, Pairwise Classifier, Binary Hierarchical Classifier and Error-Correcting Output Code (ECOC) ensembles. These architectures differ in how the 2-class problems are selected from the $2^{N-1} - 1$ distinct possibilities, where N is the total

N.C. Oza et al. (Eds.): MCS 2005, LNCS 3541, pp. 53–63, 2005.
© Springer-Verlag Berlin Heidelberg 2005

number of classes to be distinguished. A unified framework for treating all such architectures is presented in [1].

This paper is concerned with the ECOC approach to constructing ensembles. ECOC was introduced by Dietterich and Bakiri [2, 3] and was inspired by error-correcting code transmission techniques from communications theory. The basis of the method is to repeatedly partition the complete set of classes into pairs of super-classes and, for each pair, to train a base classifier to distinguish between these two super-classes. When the partitions are chosen correctly an overall classification decision can be made by examining the outputs from each of the individual base classifiers.

The choice of partitions of the complete set of classes Ω into L super-class pairs is represented by an $N \times L$ binary *coding matrix* $\mathbf{Z}$. The rows $\mathbf{Z}_i$ are unique *codewords* that are associated with the individual target classes ω_i and the columns $\mathbf{Z}^j$ represent the different super-class partitions. Denoting the jth super-class pair by S^j and $\overline{S^j}$, element Z_{ij} of the coding matrix is set to 1 or 0 [1] depending on whether class ω_i has been put into S^j or its complement. This is illustrated in Table 1 which shows a possible coding matrix for a 4-class problem.

Table 1. A possible coding matrix for a 4-class problem. This code is known as an *exhaustive code* because *all* non-trivial partitions are included

Class	Partition Number						
	1	2	3	4	5	6	7
ω_1	1	1	1	1	1	1	1
ω_2	0	1	0	0	0	1	1
ω_3	0	0	1	0	1	0	1
ω_4	0	0	0	1	1	1	0

Given an input pattern vector $\mathbf{x}$ whose true class $y(\mathbf{x}) \in \Omega$ is unknown, let the soft output from the jth base classifier be $s_j(\mathbf{x}) \in [0, 1]$. We assume that the base classifiers are constructed in such a way that this value can be interpreted as an approximate measure of the probability that the pattern should be classified as belonging to S^j, that is

$$s_j(\mathbf{x}) \cong P\left(y(\mathbf{x}) \in S^j\right) . \tag{1}$$

The set of outputs from all the classifiers can be assembled into a vector $\mathbf{s}(\mathbf{x}) = [s_1(\mathbf{x}), \ldots, s_L(\mathbf{x})]^{\mathrm{T}} \in [0, 1]^L$ called the *output code* for $\mathbf{x}$.

The principle of the ECOC technique is to obtain an estimate $\hat{y}(\mathbf{x}) \in \Omega$ of the class label for $\mathbf{x}$ from a knowledge of the output code $\mathbf{s}(\mathbf{x})$. The ECOC algorithm can thus be broken down into two distinct stages - the *encoding* stage and the *decoding* stage. The encoding stage consists in applying the base classifiers

---

[1] Alternatively, the values +1 and -1 are often used.

to the input pattern $\mathbf{x}$ so as to construct the output code $\mathbf{s}(\mathbf{x})$, whilst the decoding stage consists in applying some *decoding rule* so as to make an estimate of the class label $\hat{y}(\mathbf{x})$ which should optimally be assigned to $\mathbf{x}$. A decoding rule involves the application of some *decision function* $d : [0,1]^L \rightarrow \Omega$ so that $\hat{y}(\mathbf{x}) = d(\mathbf{s}(\mathbf{x}))$.

This paper is concerned with the second of these two stages. Sections 2, 3 and 4 review some of the decoding rules which have been discussed in the literature. A new rule, dubbed the *likelihood* decoding rule, is introduced in section 3.1. Finally, section 5 presents experimental evidence which suggests that the likelihood decoding rule has a slight advantage over at least two popular alternatives.

2 Decoding Rules Based on Distance

The simplest ECOC decoding methods, and those originally proposed by Dietterich and Bakiri [2,3], are based on measuring the distance between the output code and the codewords associated with each of the target classes. In this scheme the codewords $\mathbf{Z}_i$, which always occur at the corners of a unit hyper-cube in the L-dimensional output space of the ensemble, are taken to be ideal points which represent the target classes ω_i in that space. Here the term 'ideal' refers to the fact that a hypothetical perfectly accurate ECOC ensemble would always map an input pattern to the appropriate one of these points.

The ensemble decision is to assign $\mathbf{x}$ to the class whose codeword is nearest to the output code $\mathbf{s}(\mathbf{x})$ using a suitable metric. That is

$$d(\mathbf{s}(\mathbf{x})) = \arg\min_{\omega_i} \Delta(\mathbf{s}(\mathbf{x}), \mathbf{Z}_i) \tag{2}$$

where Δ is the metric being used. Two possible metrics are the Hamming metric and the L^1 metric. These give rise to the *Hamming* decoding rule and the L^1 decoding rule respectively.

For the Hamming metric the soft outputs $s_i(\mathbf{x})$ from the individual classifiers are first hardened into decisions by rounding them to the nearest integer, 0 or 1. This converts $\mathbf{s}(\mathbf{x})$ into a *binary* output code and the Hamming distance $\Delta_{Hamming}(\mathbf{s}(\mathbf{x}), \mathbf{Z}_i)$ is obtained by counting the number of bit positions at which this output code differs from $\mathbf{Z}_i$. Application of this decoding rule can be viewed as a process of correcting bit errors in the output code and thus gives the ECOC technique its name.

The L^1 metric measures the L^1 distance between $\mathbf{s}(\mathbf{x})$ and $\mathbf{Z}_i$ so that

$$\Delta_{L^1}(\mathbf{s}(\mathbf{x}), \mathbf{Z}_i) = \sum_{j=1}^{L} |s_j(\mathbf{x}) - Z_{ij}| . \tag{3}$$

3   Decoding Rules Based on Probability Estimation

A second approach to decoding rule design is based on using the soft output code $\mathbf{s}(\mathbf{x})$ to obtain an estimate of the posterior probabilities $q_i(\mathbf{x}) = P(\omega_i \mid \mathbf{x})$. The classification decision is then made by assigning to $\mathbf{x}$ the class with maximum posterior probability:

$$d(\mathbf{s}(\mathbf{x})) = \arg \max_{\omega_i} q_i(\mathbf{x}) \ . \tag{4}$$

The *least squares* decoding rule [4, 6, 11] is based on finding the vector $\hat{\mathbf{q}}$ which leads to the smallest value of $\epsilon^T \epsilon$ in the equation

$$\mathbf{s}(\mathbf{x}) = \mathbf{Z}\mathbf{q} + \epsilon \ . \tag{5}$$

Here ϵ is an unknown error term which must be included because the probabilities in 1 are only approximate. It can be shown that such an optimal assignment of class posterior probabilities is given by

$$\hat{\mathbf{q}} = \left(\mathbf{Z}\mathbf{Z}^T\right)^{-1} \mathbf{Z}\mathbf{s}(\mathbf{x}) \tag{6}$$

provided $\mathbf{Z}\mathbf{Z}^T$ is non-singular. This latter requirement imposes some restrictions on the form of $\mathbf{Z}$ and in particular requires that the columns of $\mathbf{Z}$ be distinct. It may not always be possible to satisfy this latter condition, for example when using a random coding matrix or when constructing a large ensemble where the number of base classifiers exceeds the number of possible column values.

The generalisation accuracy of the least squares decoding rule has been shown to be comparable with with that of the L^1 metric [11]. An advantage of this rule is that, when the avoidance of mis-classification errors is paramount, it allows the possibility of taking the *reject option* (i.e. not committing to a classification decision) when the maximum class posterior probability is below a pre-defined threshold. Another benefit is that it allows cost functions other than the 0-1 cost function to be applied.

3.1   The Likelihood Decoding Rule

We now introduce a new ECOC decoding rule called the *likelihood* decoding rule. Like the least squares rule it starts from Eq. 1 which assumes that $s_j(\mathbf{x})$ can be interpreted as an approximate measure of the probability[2] of membership of S^j; it also takes $1 - s_j(\mathbf{x})$ as an approximate measure of the probability that $\mathbf{x}$ belongs to the complementary super-class $\overline{S^j}$. Within a super-class (or its complement) the constituent target classes are mutually exclusive and together form a partition of the super-class (or complement). We assume that they are

---

[2] It is in recognition of the fact that $s_j(\mathbf{x})$ is not, in general, an accurate probability measure, that the term *likelihood*, rather than probability, is used in the name of the decision rule .

equally likely and compute class membership probabilities from the jth classifier for each target class ω_i as follows:

$$\hat{P}_j\left(\omega_i \mid \mathbf{x}\right) = \begin{cases} \frac{s_j(\mathbf{x})}{|S^j|} & \text{if } \omega_i \in S^j \\ \frac{1-s_j(\mathbf{x})}{|\overline{S^j}|} & \text{if } \omega_i \in \overline{S^j} \end{cases} \tag{7}$$

These are then combined by averaging to produce an overall estimate

$$\hat{q}_i = \frac{1}{L} \sum_{j=1}^{L} \hat{P}_j\left(\omega_i \mid \mathbf{x}\right) \tag{8}$$

which, when substituted into Eq. 4, allows a classification decision to be made.

Another way to look at this decoding rule is as a weighting scheme. When $|S_j|$ is large (i.e. the super-class contains many target classes) membership of S_j conveys less information than when $|S_j|$ is small. This is factored into the decoding rule by, in effect, weighting each classifier and target class by $1/|S_j|$ or $1/|\overline{S_j}|$ as appropriate.

The approach described here is somewhat akin to the the loss-based decoding method of Allwein and Schapire [1]. The latter method, however, weights each base classifier equally and thus does not adjust for the size of each super-class or complement.

Note that 2-class problems allow only one non-trivial decomposition into super-classes; in this case $|S_j| = |\overline{S_j}| = 1$ for all classifiers and the likelihood decoding rule is equivalent to the L^1 rule. For multi-class problems, however, the two decoding rules do differ and the difference is likely to be larger when the coding matrix shows a large disparity between $|S_j|$ and $|\overline{S_j}|$ for some of the classifiers.

4   Decoding Rules Based on Pattern Space Transformation

A third type of decoding rule is based on the view that the encoding stage of ECOC is a means of transforming from the original pattern space, in which the target classes are represented by overlapping probability distributions, into a new space in which the target classes, though still overlapping, are much more cleanly separated. This approach does not attach any special significance to the codewords as points in the output space; instead attention is focused on the clusters of training set output codes for each class. An unknown pattern vector $\mathbf{x}$ is classified by applying the ECOC transformation to it and then finding the cluster which is nearest to its output code $\mathbf{s}\left(\mathbf{x}\right)$, that is

$$d(\mathbf{s}\left(\mathbf{x}\right)) = \arg\min_{\omega_i} \Delta\left(\mathbf{s}\left(\mathbf{x}\right), Y_\mathbf{i}\right) \tag{9}$$

where Y_i is the set of points in the ECOC output space to which the sets of training patterns X_i for class ω_i are transformed.

The distance between $\mathbf{s}(\mathbf{x})$ and the cluster Y_i can be defined in different ways. In the *centroid* decoding rule [4] Y_i is represented by the centroid $\mathbf{c}_i \in [0,1]^L$ obtained by taking the mean or median over Y_i. The distance $\Delta_{Centroid}(\mathbf{s}(\mathbf{x}), Y_i)$ is then calculated as the L^2 distance between $\mathbf{s}(\mathbf{x})$ and $\mathbf{c}_i$.

When the number of training samples is small the class centroids are unreliable. A better alternative in this situation is to use the *first order Minkowski* decoding rule [5]. This uses the mean L^1 distance between $\mathbf{s}(\mathbf{x})$ and *each* of the training set image points:

$$\Delta_{Minkowski}(\mathbf{s}(\mathbf{x}), Y_i) = \frac{1}{|Y_i|} \sum_{\mathbf{x}_j \in X_i} \sum_{k=1}^{L} |s_k(\mathbf{x}) - s_k(\mathbf{x}_j)| \ . \qquad (10)$$

The L^1 metric is employed here rather than L^2 because it is less sensitive to outliers in the training data.

5   Experiments

In this section we present an experimental comparison of the accuracy of three of the above decoding rules, namely Hamming, L^1 and likelihood. The experiments consisted in training ECOC ensembles to solve a variety of classification problems and then measuring the generalisation error which resulted when each of these decoding rules was used.

As summarised in table 2, the experiments were performed on seven natural data sets and one artificial data set. The natural data sets were taken from the UCI[7] and Proben1[8] repositories.

Table 2. Test data sets

Name	Number of samples	Number of classes	Number of features (inputs)	Missing data?	Categorical data?	Source
diabetes	768	2	8	N	N	UCI
glass	214	6	10	N	N	UCI
iris	150	3	4	N	N	UCI
letter	20,000	26	16	N	N	UCI
segment	2,310	7	19	N	N	UCI
soybean	683	19	35 (82)	Y	Y	Proben1
synthetic	2,250	4	2	N	N	manufactured
vowel	990	11	10	N	N	UCI

The artificial data set, SYNTHETIC, was based on that described in [10] and consisted of samples drawn from four overlapping Gaussian distributions in 2 dimensions:

Class 1: $N\left[\begin{pmatrix} 0 \\ 0 \end{pmatrix}, \begin{pmatrix} 0.1 & 0 \\ 0 & 0.1 \end{pmatrix}\right]$

Class 2: $N\left[\begin{pmatrix} 0.8 \\ 0 \end{pmatrix}, \begin{pmatrix} 0.1 & 0 \\ 0 & 0.1 \end{pmatrix}\right]$

Class 3: $N\left[\begin{pmatrix} 0 \\ 0 \end{pmatrix}, \begin{pmatrix} 0.1 & 0 \\ 0 & 2 \end{pmatrix}\right]$

Class 4: $N\left[\begin{pmatrix} 0.8 \\ 0 \end{pmatrix}, \begin{pmatrix} 0.01 & 0 \\ 0 & 0.01 \end{pmatrix}\right]$

The Bayes decision boundaries for SYNTHETIC are illustrated in Fig. 1. The theoretical Bayes error for the distribution was evaluated numerically over a grid of 20,000 by 20,000 points covering the area $-5 \leq x \leq 5, -5 \leq y \leq 5$ and was found to be 22.53%. The Bayes misclassification error for the particular SYNTHETIC data sample used was 23.05%.

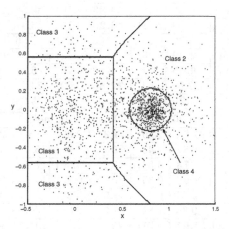

Fig. 1. Bayes decision boundaries for SYNTHETIC

In these experiments a 50/50 training/test set split was used in general. The exception to this was LETTER where the split was 20/80. The training sets were constructed in a random but stratified manner, with the number of representatives of each class being proportional to the number of samples of that class in the data set as a whole. The recommendations in [8] were followed when representing categorical data, missing values etc.

The ECOC coding matrices were randomly generated as described in [4]. In each experiment 100 base classifiers were trained, so the length of the rows of the coding matrices was 100. The base classifiers consisted of identical MLP neural networks that were comprised of an input layer which was fully connected to a layer of hidden neurons which in turn was fully connected to a single output neuron.

In order to obtain a spread of training and complexity levels, each experiment was run with combinations of 1, 2, 4, 8, 16 and 32 training epochs and 1, 2, 4, 8 and 16 hidden neurons. Each of these 30 combinations of experimental parameters was run ten times with different random seeds. Hence 300 runs were performed in all per data set. Many of the data sets did not exhibit any significant degree of over-training even at the highest number of epochs and hidden neurons. To determine the impact of over-training therefore, the experiments were re-run with 20% added classification noise.

Table 3. Percentage generalisation error (standard deviation) for different ECOC decision rules measured at the best-case combination of epochs and hidden nodes. Lowest values shown in **bold**

Dataset	likelihood	L^1	Hamming
With no added classification noise			
diabetes	**23.33** (1.80)	**23.33** (1.80)	23.41 (1.61)
glass	29.52 (3.56)	**29.33** (3.56)	30.38 (2.99)
iris	3.33 (2.11)	**3.20** (2.10)	3.47 (2.01)
letter	**7.29** (0.26)	7.35 (0.25)	7.96 (0.31)
segment	**2.69** (0.36)	2.74 (0.42)	2.81 (0.44)
soybean	**6.65** (0.74)	6.85 (0.76)	6.94 (0.81)
synthetic	22.82 (0.62)	**22.80** (0.60)	23.25 (0.62)
vowel	**5.25** (1.47)	5.54 (1.52)	5.98 (1.94)
With 20% added classification noise			
diabetes	**25.31** (2.39)	**25.31** (2.39)	25.44 (2.54)
glass	**33.81** (4.43)	35.14 (4.68)	35.43 (4.79)
iris	**7.73** (3.54)	8.27 (4.06)	7.87 (4.81)
letter	**9.98** (0.35)	10.03 (0.33)	11.16 (0.35)
segment	4.94 (0.55)	**4.90** (0.50)	5.04 (0.61)
soybean	9.85 (1.81)	**9.74** (2.08)	10.50 (1.65)
synthetic	**23.67** (0.71)	23.75 (1.06)	24.42 (1.50)
vowel	**19.96** (1.61)	20.02 (1.63)	21.45 (1.62)

Table 3 shows the lowest generalisation error observed over all 30 combinations of training epochs and hidden layer sizes. It can be seen that the likelihood decoding rule produced a slightly better performance than the L^1 rule, which in-turn was better than the Hamming rule. Indeed, in all experiments likelihood out-performed Hamming and in all experiments but one (i.e. IRIS with 20% added noise) L^1 out-performed Hamming.

Table 4. Summary of differences in generalisation performance for each pair of decoding rules. Figures show the mean *relative* improvement in performance, taken over all experiments, of the first-named rule over the second. Also shown is the number of experiments which were favourable to the first-named rule (with the 2-class problem DIABETES being omitted when comparing likelihood with L^1)

Added noise	Best-case error over all epochs and hidden nodes		Mean error over all epochs and hidden nodes	
	Favourable experiments	Mean % improvement	Favourable experiments	Mean % improvement
likelihood over L^1				
None	4/7	0.85	5/7	1.91
20%	5/7	1.33	7/7	2.53
likelihood over Hamming				
None	8/8	4.76	7/8	4.62
20%	8/8	4.42	7/8	3.97
L^1 over Hamming				
None	8/8	4.04	6/8	3.02
20%	7/8	3.23	6/8	1.79

On the SYNTHETIC data set, the misclassifcation error for all three decoding rules was close to the Bayes rate of 23.05%, with likelihood and L^1 being slightly lower and Hamming slightly higher than this value.

A summary of the relative differences in generalisation performance for each pair of decoding rules is shown in Table 4. This compares the performance measured at the optimal training and complexity levels and also the mean performance taken over all training and complexity levels examined. This table indicates that the likelihood decoding rule has a greater advantage over L^1 when the mean is taken over all training conditions and suggests that the likelihood rule is less sensitive to the ensemble being optimally trained. This is borne out by the fact that the likelihood decoding rule also performs somewhat better than L^1 when 20% noise is added so that the classifiers are more susceptible to overtraining. Such a reduced sensitivity to optimal training is a desirable property of any decoding rule as statistical variation between data samples implies that even optimal tuning for a given training set may not translate into optimal tuning for the underlying class conditional probability distributions.

6   Discussion and Conclusions

This paper has examined six ECOC decoding rules and has categorised such rules into three types, namely those which are based on distance measurements between the output code and the target codewords, those which are based on estimating the class membership probabilities and those which are based on transforming the pattern space.

A new decoding rule, named likelihood, was presented which falls into the second of these three categories. This was compared experimentally with two of the ECOC decoding rules, namely those based on distance measurements using the L^1 and Hamming metrics. Evidence was presented that the likelihood decoding rule demonstrates a small advantage over the L^1 rule which in turn is generally superior to the Hamming rule. The evidence also indicated that the likelihood rule has the additional properties that it is less sensitive to optimal tuning of the base classifiers and that it performs relatively better than the other rules when the data set is susceptible to over-training.

This work could usefully be extended by exploring whether the class membership probability estimates from the likelihood rule are reliable. If so then this method could provide the means of obtaining the advantages of the least squares decoding rule, but at a lower computational cost and without imposing restrictions on the form of the coding matrix. A further refinement which may lead to greater accuracy when the class prior probabilities are known, would be to subdivide the base classifier soft outputs in proportion to those prior probabilities, rather than subdividing them into equal parts as in Eq. 7. Finally, it would be worthwhile to extend the experimental work to compare the effectiveness of likelihood decoding with that of other approaches, such as the pattern space transformation methods of section 4 and the loss-based decoding scheme described in [1].

References

1. Allwein EL, Schapire RE, Singer Y. Reducing multiclass to binary: A unifying approach for margin classifiers. *Proc. 17th International Conf. on Machine Learning*, pages 9-16. Morgan Kaufmann, San Francisco, CA, 2000.
2. Dietterich TG, Bakiri G. Error-correcting output codes: A general method for improving multiclass inductive learning programs. *Proceedings of the Ninth National Conference on Artificial Intelligence* (AAAI-91) (pp. 572-577). Anaheim, CA: AAAI Press, 1991.
3. Dietterich TG, Bakiri G. Solving Multiclass Learning Problems via Error-Correcting Output Codes. *Journal of Artificial Intelligence Research* 2: 263-286, 1995.
4. James G. Majority Vote Classifiers: Theory and Applications. PhD Dissertation, Stanford University, 1998.
5. Kittler J, Ghaderi R, Windeatt T, Matas J. Face identification and verification via ECOC, *Third Int. Conf. Audio- and Video-Based Biometric Person Authentication*, Halmstad, pp 1-13, June 2001.
6. Kong EB, Dietterich TG. Probability estimation using error-correcting output coding. *IASTED International Conference: Artificial Intelligence and Soft Computing*, Banff, Canada, 1997.
7. Merz CJ, Murphy PM. UCI Repository of Machine Learning Databases. 1998. http://www.ics.uci.edu/~mlearn/MLRepository.html.
8. Prechelt L. PROBEN1 - A Set of Neural Network Benchmark Problems and Benchmarking Rules. Technical Report 21/94, Fakultat fur Informatik, Universitat Karslruhe, 1994.

9. Rajan S, Ghosh J. An Empirical Comparison of Hierarchical vs. Two-Level Approaches to Multiclass Problems. In F. Roli, J. Kittler and T. Windeatt editors, *Multiple Classifier Systems 2004*, LNCS 3077, Springer, pp. 283-292, 2004.
10. Ueda N. Optimal Linear Combination of Neural Networks for Improving Classification Performance. *IEEE Transactions on Pattern Analysis and Machine Intelligence*, Vol 22 No. 2, February 2000.
11. Windeatt T, Ghaderi R. Least Squares and Estimation Measures via Error Correcting Output Codes. 2nd. int. Workshop *Multiple Classifier Systems*, Lecture Notes in Computer Science, Springer-Verlag, pages 148-157, 2001.

A Probability Model for Combining Ranks

Ofer Melnik, Yehuda Vardi, and Cun-Hui Zhang

Rutgers University, Piscataway NJ, USA
melnik@dimacs.rutgers.edu, {vardi, czhang}@stat.rutgers.edu

Abstract. Mixed Group Ranks is a parametric method for combining
rank based classifiers that is effective for many-class problems. Its parametric structure combines qualities of voting methods with best rank
approaches. In [1] the parameters of MGR were estimated using a logistic loss function. In this paper we describe how MGR can be cast as a
probability model. In particular we show that using an exponential probability model, an algorithm for efficient maximum likelihood estimation
of its parameters can be devised. While casting MGR as an exponential
probability model offers provable asymptotic properties (consistency),
the interpretability of probabilities allows for flexiblity and natural integration of MGR mixture models.

1 MGR as a Score Function

Many rank combination approaches can be cast as the problem of assigning scores
to classes based on the ranks they receive from multiple consituent classifiers.
Once assigned, then classes can be ordered based on their scores, generating a
combined ranking.

We use the following notation. There are K target classes $t_1, \ldots, t_K$ and a
collection of J component classifier algorithms $a_1, \ldots, a_J$. For any particular
query, the output of algorithm a_j is $r^{(j)} \equiv \left(r^{(j)}(1), \ldots, r^{(j)}(K) \right)$, with $r^{(j)}(k)$
being the rank assigned by algorithm a_j to class t_k. A score function, for each
class maps the rankings to a scalar

$$S\left(\theta\right) \equiv f_\theta \left(r^{(1)}, \ldots, r^{(J)} \right)$$

where θ is a class in $t_1, \ldots, t_K$. As score functions are ultimately used to generate
new rankings, they have the important property of being invarient to monotonic
transformations.

$$R^*(k) \leq R^*(k') \Leftrightarrow S(k) \geq S(k') \Leftrightarrow g(S(k)) \geq g(S(k')) \tag{1}$$

where g is monotonically increasing, and R^* denotes the combined ranking derived from the class scores.

Some example score functions are the Borda count, Linear Score and the
Best Rank [2]. The Borda count is a voting method, which assigns the (neg-
ative) sum of ranks as a score, $S_{Borda}(\theta) = -\sum_{j=1}^{J} r^{(j)}(\theta)$. The Linear Score

N.C. Oza et al. (Eds.): MCS 2005, LNCS 3541, pp. 64–73, 2005.

generalizes the Borda count by assigning a weight to each classifier, $S_{Linear}(\theta) = -\sum_{j=1}^{J} w_j r^{(j)}(\theta)$. The Best Rank score selects the best rank a class receives as its score, $S_{Best}(\theta) = -\min_{j \in 1...J} r^{(j)}(\theta)$.

In [1] we proposed the Mixed Group Ranks (MGR) score function which generalizes the Best Rank and Linear scores. It is a weighted linear sum of the minimum rank of all subsets of classifiers

$$S_{MGR}(\theta) = - \sum_{A \subseteq \{1...J\}} w_A \min_{j \in A} r^{(j)}(\theta)$$

The MGR score function combines the democratic voting aspect of the Linear and Borda Scores with the emphasis on confident rankings of the Best Rank score. In [1] we describe the general category of score functions that embody these characteristics; Score functions that are both monotonic and quasiconvex (in the ranks assigned to a class) prefer lower ranks to bigger ranks and assign greater influence to smaller ranks. With non-negative weights, $w_A \geq 0, \forall A$, MGR is both monotonic and quasiconvex, embodying these score properties.

2   Probabilistic Framework for Rank Combination

In this section we reformulate combination of rank classifiers as a problem of estimating maximum likelihood (ML) and Bayes rules.

Unlike a black-box score function approach which does not model the process used to generate the constituent rankings, in the probabilistic setting we consider the rankings generated by the constituent classifiers as coming from a stochastic process, where

$$p_\theta \left(r^{(1)}, \ldots, r^{(J)} \right) \equiv p \left(r^{(1)}, \ldots, r^{(J)} | \theta \right) \tag{2}$$

is the conditional joint distribution of $R^{(j)} \equiv \left(R^{(j)}(1), \ldots, R^{(j)}(K) \right)$, $j \leq J$, as J random vectors, with $R^{(j)}(k)$ being the rank assigned by algorithm a_j to class t_k, when the actual class is t_θ, $\theta \in 1 \ldots K$. This formulation is the key to a probabilistic combination approach, considering each combination of ranks as having a distinct conditional probability that implicitly captures the biases and interactions in the rank combinations.

The likelihood function of the probability, $L(\theta) \equiv p_\theta \left(R^{(1)}, \ldots, R^{(J)} \right)$, can form the basis for statistical combination procedures. In particular, the *ideal* Maximum Likelihood combination method would assign combined ranks, $R^*(k)$, to each class t_k that satisfy

$$R^*(k) \leq R^*(k') \Leftrightarrow L(k) \geq L(k') \tag{3}$$

according to the likelihood function $L(\cdot)$. This rule estimates θ, the index of the true class by $\widehat{\theta} \equiv \arg\max_{1 \leq \theta \leq K} L(\theta)$. It is an idealized algorithm in the sense that it requires full knowledge of the probability densities in (2), which are never available in practice.

The ideal ML rule becomes the Bayes rule when q is a random query with the uniform distribution $P\{q \sim t_k\} = 1/K$. In general, if the class has a prior distribution $g(k) = P\{q \sim t_k\}$, then the ideal Bayes algorithm would rank the classes according to the posterior distribution $p\left(\theta | R^{(1)}, \ldots, R^{(J)}\right) \propto g(\theta)L(\theta)$. We observe that the ideal Bayes rule, R^*, generates optimal rankings for all monotone loss functions in terms of the rank of the true identity. In other words, if $P_g\{q \sim t_k\} = g(k)$ and $\xi(k)$ is any rank combination function of the outputs of the component classifiers, then $E_g h(R^*(\theta)) \leq E_g h(\xi(\theta))$ for all nondecreasing loss functions h, where E_g is the expectation under P_g and θ is the index of the true identity of the random query q, i.e. $q \sim t_\theta$.

3   MGR as an Exponential Probability Model

Implementing the ideal Bayes rules requires full knowledge of the probability vectors p_θ in (2) and the prior probabilities for all possible values of θ, the classes. In reality p_θ is unkown and has to be estimated. This poses a serious dimensionality problem as the estimation (training) data is usually of smaller order than the K^J dimensionality of the domain of p_θ. This suggests that directly applying non-parametric frequency estimation for the probability vectors p_θ might be ineffective, (we will return to this question in a later section on mixture models), whereas a parametric model would not suffer from this dimensionality curse. In this paper we develop a parametric probability model based on the MGR structure.

Remember that score functions are invarient to monotonic transformations (see equation (1)). In particular, applying a montonically increasing function to the output of MGR does not change how it ranks. The problem is to find a monotonic transformation of MGR functions which form a mathematically and computationally tractable family of parameteric distributions. A solution we develop is the following exponential family with MGR scores as basis functions:

$$p_\theta(x) = h(s(x)) = \frac{\exp(s(x))}{C} = \frac{1}{C}\exp\left(-\sum_{A \subseteq \{1...J\}} w_A min\{x_j : j \in A\}\right) \quad (4)$$

where C is an appropriate normalization constant.

The advantage of using an exponential family are the well behaved properties of such distributions. The likelihood of a distribution function in the exponential family is convex and therefore has the property of having at most one maxima, where this maxima is the unique MLE [3]. Moreover estimates of the MLE have the property of being typically asymptotically efficient w.r.t the quantity of estimation data.

3.1   Calculating the Normalization Factor

In the case of combining 2 classifiers, surprisingly there is an analytical solution for the model parameters (which is beyond the scope of this paper). In the general case estimation of the parameters of (4) requires a way of computing the constant, C. Having C gives an explicit formula for (4) and allows the parameters to be estimated using convex programming techniques [4] (cite). We provide here a derivation and procedure for calculating C.

Let $\mathcal{A}_J = \{A \,|\, A \subseteq \{1, \ldots J\}, A \neq \emptyset\}$ be the set of non-empty subsets, and let $\vec{\beta} = \{\beta_1, \beta_2, \beta_{12}, \beta_3, \beta_{13}, \ldots\} = \{\beta_A \,|\, \forall A \in \mathcal{A}_J\}$ be the set of all coefficients. The probability distribution (4) can be written as

$$f(x_1, \ldots, x_J) = \frac{\exp\left(-\sum_{A \in \mathcal{A}_J} \beta_A \min_{j \in A} x_j\right)}{T_J\left(\vec{\beta}\right)} \tag{5}$$

where

$$T_J\left(\vec{\beta}\right) = \sum_{y_1=1}^{\infty} \sum_{y_2=1}^{\infty} \cdots \sum_{y_J=1}^{\infty} \exp\left(-\sum_{A \in \mathcal{A}_J} \beta_A \min_{j \in A} y_j\right) \tag{6}$$

If we write $y_* = \min(y_1 \ldots y_J)$ then we can rewrite (6) as

$$T_J\left(\vec{\beta}\right) = \sum_{\substack{B \in \mathcal{A}_J}} \sum_{\substack{y_1 \cdots y_J \\ B = \{j \,|\, y_j = y_*\}}} \exp\left(-\sum_{A \in \mathcal{A}_J} \beta_A \min_{j \in A} y_j\right), \tag{7}$$

where the inner sum runs over all vectors of $(y_1 \cdots y_J)$ where the y_j, $j \in B$, are the minimal elements, i.e. $y_j = y_*$. Thus, the outer sum picks which y's will be the minimal elements, and the inner sum goes over all values of the y's where that holds.

Defining $\beta_* = \sum_{A \in \mathcal{A}_J} \beta_A = 1^T \vec{\beta}$ and using the notation $\vec{\beta}^C$ as the restriction of $\vec{\beta}$ on the subset C, the inner sum of (7) can be rewritten as

$$\sum_{\substack{y_1 \cdots y_J \\ B = \{j \,|\, y_j = y_*\}}} \exp\left(-\sum_{A \in \mathcal{A}_J} \beta_A \min_{j \in A} y_j\right)$$

$$= \sum_{\substack{y_1 \cdots y_J \\ B = \{j \,|\, y_j = y_*\}}} \exp\left(-\beta_* y_* - \sum_{A \in \mathcal{A}_J} \beta_A \min_{j \in A}(y_j - y_*)\right)$$

$$= \sum_{y_*=1}^{\infty} \sum_{\substack{y_j > y_* \\ j \in B^c}} \exp\left(-\beta_* y_*\right) \exp\left(-\sum_{\substack{A \in \mathcal{A}_J \\ A \subset B^c}} \beta_A \min_{j \in A}(y_j - y_*)\right)$$

Algorithm 1 A Dynamic-Programming algorithm for computing $T_j\left(\overrightarrow{\beta}\right)$

$T(B)$ corresponds to $T_{|B|}\left(\overrightarrow{\beta}^B\right)$

for $i = 1 \ldots J$ **do**
  for all
  $B \in \mathcal{A}_J, |B| = i$ **do**
    $T(B) \leftarrow 1$
    for all
    $C \subset B, C \neq \emptyset$ **do**
      $(*)\ T(B) \leftarrow T(B) + T(C)$
    end for
    $T(B) \leftarrow \dfrac{e^{-\overrightarrow{\beta}^B_*}}{1 - e^{-\overrightarrow{\beta}^B_*}} T(B) + T(C)$
  end for
end for

$$= \sum_{y_*=1}^{\infty} \exp\left(-\beta_* y_*\right) \sum_{\substack{y_j - y_* = 1 \\ j \in B^c}}^{\infty} \exp\left(- \sum_{\substack{A \in \mathcal{A}_J \\ A \subset B^c}} \beta_A \min_{j \in A}\left(y_j - y_*\right)\right)$$

$$= \sum_{y_*=1}^{\infty} \exp\left(-\beta_* y_*\right) T_{|B^c|}\left(\overrightarrow{\beta}^{B^c}\right) \tag{8}$$

Thus equation (7) can be written using the recursive relationship

$$T_J\left(\overrightarrow{\beta}\right) = \sum_{y_*=1}^{\infty} \exp\left(-\beta_* y_*\right) \sum_{B \in \mathcal{A}_J} T_{|B^c|}\left(\overrightarrow{\beta}^{B^c}\right)$$

$$= \frac{e^{-\beta_*}}{1 - e^{-\beta_*}} \sum_{B \in \mathcal{A}_J} T_{|B^c|}\left(\overrightarrow{\beta}^{B^c}\right)$$

with $T_0\left(\overrightarrow{\beta}^\emptyset\right) = 1$. This relationship says that $T_j\left(\overrightarrow{\beta}\right)$ can be calculated by recursively summing over all subsets. This type of structure lends itself to a dynamic programming type algorithm [5] that caches values of smaller subgroups.

The complexity of Algorithm 1 is dependent on the number of times that statement $(*)$ is executed. There are $\binom{J}{i}$ subsets of size i, each of which has $2^i - 2$ relevant subsets (not including itself and the empty set). Thus summing over subsets of different sizes we get

$$\sum_{i=2}^{J} \binom{J}{i}\left(2^i - 2\right) < (2+1)^J = 3^J$$

executions of statement (∗). Therefore calculating $T_j\left(\vec{\beta}\right)$ of the probability distribution (4) with n coefficients is $O\left(n^{1.59}\right)$, where $n = 2^J$ and $1.59 > \log(3)/\log(2)$.

3.2   Parameter Estimation

Given an efficient algorithm for calculating the MGR probability distribution function (5), the parameters of this function can be estimated using a maximum likelihood approach. The MLE solution is the set of parameters that maximize the log likelihood,

$$\log \prod_{i=1}^{n} \frac{\exp\left(-\sum_{A\in\mathcal{A}_J} \beta_A \min_{j\in A} x_{ji}\right)}{T_J\left(\vec{\beta}\right)} \tag{9}$$

where the product is over all sample data and subject to $\beta_A \geq 0$ for the monotnicity and quasiconvexity of the MGR function and $\beta_A > 0$ for $|A| = 1$ to maintain the feasibility of $T_J\left(\vec{\beta}\right)$.

This is a convex optimization problem, as the maximization criteria (9) is concave being the likelihood of an exponential family, and the constraints are linear. There are standard algorithms for optimizing nonlinear programming problems of this sort (e.g., primal-dual interior point algorithms [4]). In the experiments we present in this paper we used the MATLAB optimization toolbox for simplicity. Note that there are many alternative packages avaialble, see http://www.ece.northwestern.edu/OTC/ for more information.

4   Mixture Models

A probability model for ranks offers a consistent mechanism for integration with other probability models. The advantage of using a parametric probability model, such as the probabilistic MGR is its ability to handle and generalize from relatively sparse data. However, it seems that data in combination datasets are typically not uniformly sparse. Since the classifiers that are combined already posses significant accuracy, we expect that many of the rank vectors for the correct class will contain ranks of 1. In effect, what we see in many datasets is that a small minority of rank vectors repeat while the majority do not. In table 1 we see this for the combination dataset generated by two different face recognition algorithms run on a face recognition dataset. This table shows for each rank vector (that appears more than once) the number of times it appears as the correct class in the combination training set. For the remaining rank vectors (not shown), 98 appear only once and the rest never appear as the correct class in the training set.

In presenting the MGR model we stated that the purpose of using a parametric model was to handle the datas' sparseness. While this is true in general, a

Table 1. The frequency of rank vectors in a combination training dataset that was generated applying the UMD and USC classifiers on the dup I dataset, shows a non-uniform distribution. The remaining 98 unlisted rank vectors appear only once in the dataset

Rank Vector	(1,1)	(1,2)	(2,1)	(3,1)	(1,3)	(2,2)	(1,6)
# appearances	252	12	9	5	5	4	4
Rank Vector	(1,4)	(4,1)	(1,5)	(17,1)	(33,1)	(1,14)	(1,18)
# appearances	3	3	3	2	2	2	2

small subset of rank vectors have denser coverage. This suggests that the probability of the rank vectors can be estimated more accurately by a nonparametric method, cell frequency estimation. Having the flexibility of a probabilistic interpretation of rank generation, allows us to combine these two different approaches. In particular, we can construct a mixture model that uses cell frequency estimation for the dense rank vectors while using an exponential MGR model for other rank vectors.

Let χ be the set of dense rank vectors. We define the mixture model as

$$
p(x) = \begin{cases} P_\chi(x) & x \in \chi \\ \left(1 - \sum_{x \in \chi} P_\chi(x)\right) \dfrac{\exp\left(-\sum_{A \in \mathcal{A}_J} \beta_A \min_{j \in A} x_j\right)}{T_J\left(\vec{\beta}\right) - D} & x \notin \chi \end{cases} \tag{10}
$$

where $D = \sum_{x \in \chi} \exp\left(-\sum_{A \in \mathcal{A}_J} \beta_A \min_{j \in A} x_j\right)$. This model is estimated as

$$
\widehat{p}(x) = \begin{cases} \dfrac{\#\{x \in I\}}{|I|} & x \in \chi \\ \lambda \dfrac{\exp\left(-\sum_{A \in \mathcal{A}_J} \beta_A \min_{j \in A} x_j\right)}{T_J\left(\vec{\beta}\right) - D} & x \notin \chi \end{cases}
$$

where $\lambda = 1 - |I|^{-1} \sum_{x \in \chi} \#\{x \in I\}$, $\#\{x \in I\}$ indicates the number of times that rank vector x appeared as the correct class in a combination training set I and $|I|$ is the number of correct class rank vectors in the combination training set. The β_A parameters are estimated as before, except that we have a different denominator term and we only estimate the parametric model using the rank vectors that are not in χ.

4.1 Mixing Frequencies

The mixture model (10) requires the preselection of the rank vectors that will be estimated using cell frequencies. A natural question is which vectors to use. A heuristic criteria is to select those rank vectors that have sufficient data to warrant direct estimation. It is beneficial to examine this question empirically. Figure 1 shows how a variation in the composition of the χ set affects test

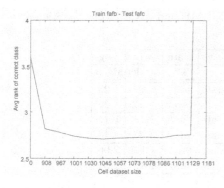
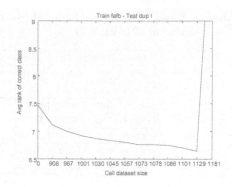

Fig. 1. These graphs show how varying the size of Cell datasets and thus controlling the proportions in the mixture model affects performance as emasured by the average rank of the correct class. They represent combination datasets generated using the ANM and USC classifiers on the the the fafb dataset (described in section 5). The x-axis shows the number of rank vectors used in the cell frequency estimation. The first tick represents including the most frequent rank vectors for frequency estimation (1,1), the second tick represents including the first and second most frequent rank vectors and so on until all rank vectors are used for cell frequency estimation

performance. These graphs are typical of our experimental results. The x-axis represents different sizes of χ, the leftmost is a pure MGR exponential model, the rightmost represents a pure cell frequency model, while the intermediate positions are mixture models. For each mixture the average rank of the correct class (w.r.t. the test dataset) is shown, where ranks greater than 50 are truncated to diminish the noise effects of high ranks. As can be seen, estimating the denser rank vectors with cell frequencies improves performance almost consisitently. This implies that in selelcting the cutoff point for inclusion in χ we can allow sparse vectors to be included as long as the truely sparse rank vectors are estimated by probabilistic MGR.

5 Experimental Results

FERET [6] was a government sponsored program for the evaluation of face recognition algorithms. In this program commercial and academic algorithms were evaluated on their ability to differentiate between 1,196 individuals. The test consisted of different datasets of varying difficulty, for a total of 3,816 different images. The datasets in order of perceived difficulty are: the *fafb* dataset of 1,195 images which consists of pictures taken the same day with different facial expressions; the *fafc* dataset of 194 images that contains pictures taken with different cameras and lighting conditions; the *dup I* dataset of 488 images that has duplicate pictures taken within a year of the initial photo; and the most difficult, the *dup II* dataset of 234 images which contains duplicate pictures taken more than a year later. Note that in our experiments we separate the images of dup II

Table 2. Average rank in combining the USC, UMD and ANM face recognition algorithms with a cutoff at rank 50

test set	train set	Mix Model	Log MGR	test set	train set	Mix Model	Log MGR
dup i	dup ii	**8.58**	9.08	fafb	dup i	**1.21**	1.23
dup i	fafb	8.90	**8.44**	fafb	dup ii	**1.22**	1.26
dup i	fafc	**9.35**	9.37	fafb	fafc	1.18	**1.15**
dup ii	dup i	**10.59**	11.11	fafc	dup i	**2.31**	2.43
dup ii	fafb	**10.47**	10.92	fafc	dup ii	**1.86**	2.06
dup ii	fafc	**10.08**	10.68	fafc	fafb	2.12	**1.92**

from the dup I dataset, unlike the FERET study where dup II was also a subset of dup I.

The FERET study evaluated 10 baseline and proprietary face recognition algorithms. The baseline algorithms consisted of a correlation based method and a number of eigenfaces (Principle Components) methods that differ in the internal metric they use. Of the 10 algorithms we selected three dominant algorithms. From the baseline algorithms we choose to use the *ANM* algorithm which uses a Mahalanobis distance variation on angular distances for eigenfaces [7]. Within the class of baseline algorithms this algorithm was strong. Moreover, in accuracy w.r.t. average rank of the correct class on the dup I dataset it demonstrated superior performance to all other algorithms. The other two algorithms we used were the University of Maryland's 1997 test submission (UMD) and the University of Southern California's 1997 test submission (USC). These algorithms clearly outperformed the other algorithms. UMD is based on a discriminant analysis of eigenfaces [8], and USC is an elastic bunch graph matching approach [9].

The outputs of these 3 face recognizers on the four FERET datasets, fafb, fafc, dup I and dup II were the data for the experiments. Thus, we never had access to the actual classifiers, only to data on how they ranked the different faces in these datasets. In each experiment one of the FERET datasets was selected as a training set and another dataset was selected for testing. This gave 12 experiments (not including training and testing on the same dataset) per group of face recognizers, where we get combinations of training on easy datasets and testing on hard datasets, training on hard and testing on easy datasets, and training and testing on hard datasets.

We compare the mixture model with the original MGR, estimated using a logistic error function. In [1], we already demonstrated that the original MGR is superior to traditional score function approaches in overall performance. In this mixture model rank vectors with more than 2% of the training data were estimated by cell frequency, while the sparser rank vectors were captured by the MGR probability model. For each combiner the average rank of the correct class (across the test dataset) is shown, where ranks greater than 50 are truncated to diminish the noise effects of high ranks. As these results show the mixture model is comparable and at times superior to the logistic estimation of MGR.

6   Conclusion

We present a new probabilistic framework for for the combination of rank generating classifiers. In this framework rank vectors are interpreted as coming from a conditional probability distribution given the correct class. The MGR model is translated into this framework by casting it as an exponential distribution. We give an algorithm for efficiently calculating probabilities from this distribution and use it to calculate maximum likelihood estimates of its parameters. One advantage of having a probability model is that we can naturally combine it with a direct cell frequency estimation model. Thus, we form a mixture combination model where denser vectors are estimated using cell frequencies and sparser ones with the MGR model. While, we would not expect the MLE method to outperform the logistic estimation the MGR model in all instances, we do see that the mixture model offers comparable and at times superior performance on combination of FERET algorithms.

In conclusion, in this paper we show how a probability approach to rank combination, offers the advantages of interpretability, asymptotic estimation consistency of parameters and flexibility in how it is applied.

References

1. Melnik, O., Vardi, Y., Zhang, C.H.: Mixed group ranks: Preference and confidence in classifier combination. IEEE Pattern Analysis and Machine Intelligence 26 (2004) 973–981
2. Ho, T.K., Hull, J.J., Srihari, S.N.: Combination of decisions by multiple classifiers. In Baird, H.S., Bunke, H., (Eds.), K.Y., eds.: Structured Document Image Analysis. Springer-Verlag, Heidelberg (1992) 188–202
3. Bickel, P., Doksum, K.: Mathematical Statistics: Basic Ideas and Selected Topics. Prentice Hall, Englewood Cliffs, NJ (1977)
4. Boyd, S., Vandenberghe, L.: Convex Optimization. Cambridge University Press (2004)
5. Bellman, R.: Dynamic Programming. Princeton University Press, Princeton, NJ (1957)
6. Phillips, P., Moon, H., Rizvi, S., Rauss, P.: The feret evaluation methodology for face-recognition algorithms. IEEE Trans. on Pattern Analysis and Machine Intelligence 22 (2000)
7. Moon, H., Phillips, P.: Computational and performance aspects of pca-based face-recognition algorithms. Perception 30 (2001) 303–321
8. Zhao, W., Krishnaswamy, A., Chellappa, R., Swets, D., Weng, J.: Discriminant Analysis of Principal Components. In: Face Recognition: From Theory to Applications. Springer-Verlag, Berling (1998) 73–86
9. Wiskott, L., Fellous, J.M., Kruger, N., von der Masburg, C.: Face recognition by elastic bunch graph matching. IEEE Transactions on Pattern Analysis and Machine Intelligence 17 (1997) 775–779

EER of Fixed and Trainable Fusion Classifiers: A Theoretical Study with Application to Biometric Authentication Tasks

Norman Poh and Samy Bengio

IDIAP Research Institute, Rue du Simplon 4,
CH-1920 Martigny, Switzerland
norman@idiap.ch, bengio@idiap.ch

Abstract. Biometric authentication is a process of verifying an identity claim using a person's behavioural and physiological characteristics. Due to the vulnerability of the system to environmental noise and variation caused by the user, fusion of several biometric-enabled systems is identified as a promising solution. In the literature, various fixed rules (e.g. min, max, median, mean) and trainable classifiers (e.g. linear combination of scores or weighted sum) are used to combine the scores of several base-systems. How *exactly* do correlation and imbalance nature of base-system performance affect the fixed rules and trainable classifiers? We study these *joint* aspects using the commonly used error measurement in biometric authentication, namely Equal Error Rate (EER). Similar to several previous studies in the literature, the central assumption used here is that the class-dependent scores of a biometric system are approximately normally distributed. However, different from them, the novelty of this study is to make a *direct link* between the EER measure and the fusion schemes mentioned. Both synthetic and real experiments (with as many as 256 fusion experiments carried out on the XM2VTS benchmark score-level fusion data sets) verify our *proposed theoretical modeling of EER* of the two families of combination scheme. In particular, it is found that weighted sum can provide the best generalisation performance when its weights are estimated correctly. It also has the additional advantage that score normalisation prior to fusion is not needed, contrary to the rest of fixed fusion rules.

1 Introduction

There exists a vast literature study that proposes to model theoretical classification errors for fusion, e.g., [1, 2, 3]. However, to the best of our knowledge, a direct modeling of Equal Error Rate (EER), i.e., an evaluation error commonly used in biometric authentication tasks, has not been attempted. This is partly because of the unknown decision threshold which prevents further analysis. Analysis of EER is cumbersome without making any assumption about the distribution of the classifier scores, e.g., using a non-parametric approach. We tackle this problem by assuming that the class-dependent scores are normally distributed. With a very large number of independent experiments, our previous work [4] shows that although the class-dependent scores are often not normally distributed, the estimated EER is *fairly robust* to deviation from such assumption.

N.C. Oza et al. (Eds.): MCS 2005, LNCS 3541, pp. 74–85, 2005.

In [1], the theoretical classification error of six classifiers are thoroughly studied for a two-class problem. This study assumes that the base classifier scores are probabilities $\in [0, 1]$. Hence probability of one class is one minus the probability of the other class and the optimal threshold is always set to 0.5. It also assumes that all baseline classifier scores are drawn from a common distribution. Gaussian and uniform distributions are studied. The first assumption is not always applicable to biometric authentication. This is because the output of a biometric system is often not necessarily a probability but a distance measure, a similarity or a log-likelihood ratio. Moreover, decisions are often taken by comparing a classifier score with a threshold. The second assumption, in practice, is also unrealistic in most situations, particularly in multimodal fusion. This is because the (class-dependent) score distributions are often *different* across different classifiers. The proposed EER model is also different from the one presented in [2, 3] in terms of application, assumption and methodology (see Section 3).

The goal of this paper is thus to study the EER of fixed and trainable fusion classifiers with respect to the correlation and the imbalance performance nature of baseline systems. Section 2 briefly discusses the general theoretical EER framework and how it can be applied to study several commonly used fusion classifiers. Section 3 discusses the important assumptions made and draws differences between EER and current theoretical model to explaining why fusion works. Sections 4 and 5 present experimental results on synthetic and real data. These are followed by conclusions in Section 6.

2   Theoretical EER

The fundamental problem of biometric authentication can be viewed as a classification task to decide if person x is a client or an impostor. In a statistical framework, the probability that x is a client after a classifier f_θ observes his/her biometric trait can be written as:

$$y \equiv f_\theta(f_e(s(x))), \tag{1}$$

where, s is a sensor, f_e is a feature extractor, θ is a set of classifier parameters associated to the classifier f_θ.

Note that there exists several types of classifiers in biometric authentication, all of which can be represented by Eqn. (1). They can be categorized by their output y, i.e., probability (within the range $[0, 1]$), distance metric (more than or equal to zero), or log-likelihood ratio (a real number). the context of multimodal BA, y is associated to the subscript i, which takes on different meanings in different context of fusion, as follows:

$$y_i(x) = \begin{cases} f_\theta(f_e(s(x_i))) & \text{if multi-sample} \\ f_\theta(f_e(s_i(x))) & \text{if multimodal} \\ f_\theta(f_{e,i}(s(x))) & \text{if multi-feature} \\ f_{\theta,i}(f_e(s(x))) & \text{if multi-classifier} \end{cases} \tag{2}$$

Note that i is the index to the i-th sample in the context of multi-sample fusion. i can also mean the i-th biometric modality in multimodal fusion, etc. In a general context, we refer to $y_i(x)$ as the i-th *response* and there are altogether N responses ($i = 1, \ldots, N$). It is important to note that all $y_i(x)$ belong to the *same* access. We write y_i instead of $y_i(x)$ for simplicity, while bearing in mind that y_i is always dependent on x.

To decide if an access should be granted or not, all $y_i|\forall_i$ have to be combined to form a single output. This can be expressed as: $y_{COM} = f_{COM}(y_1, \ldots, y_N)$. Several types of combination strategies are used in the literature, e.g., min, max, median, mean (or sum), weighted sum, product and weighted product. They are defined as follow:

$$y_{min} = \min_i(y_i), \qquad y_{max} = \max_i(y_i) \qquad y_{med} = \text{median}_i(y_i),$$
$$y_{wsum} = \sum_{i=1}^{N} w_i y_i, \qquad \text{and} \qquad y_{wprod} = \prod_{i=1}^{N} y_i^{w_i}, \qquad (3)$$

where $w_i|\forall_i$ are parameters that need to be estimated. The mean operator is a special case of weighted sum with $w_i = \frac{1}{N}$. Similarly, the product operator is a special case of weighted product with $w_i = 1$.

The decision function based on the score y (for any y after fusion $\{y_{COM}|COM \in \{min, max, mean, median, wsum, prod, wprod\}$ or any y_i prior to fusion; both cases are refered to simply as y) is defined as:

$$\text{decision} = \begin{cases} \text{accept} & \text{if } y > \Delta \\ \text{reject} & \text{otherwise.} \end{cases} \qquad (4)$$

Because of the binary nature of decision, the system commits two types of error called False Acceptance (FA) and False Rejection (FR) errors, as a function of the threshold Δ. FA is committed when x belongs to an impostor and is wrongly accepted by the system (as a client) whereas FR is committed when x belongs to a client and is wrongly rejected by the system. They can be quantified by False Acceptance Rate (FAR) and False Rejection Rate (FRR) as follow:

$$\text{FAR}(\Delta) = \frac{\text{FA}(\Delta)}{NI} \qquad \text{and} \qquad \text{FRR}(\Delta) = \frac{\text{FR}(\Delta)}{NC}, \qquad (5)$$

where $\text{FA}(\Delta)$ counts the number of FA, $\text{FR}(\Delta)$ counts the number of FR, NI is the total number of impostor accesses and NC is the total number of client accesses.

At this point, it is convenient to introduce two conditional variables, $Y^k \equiv Y|k$, for each k being client or impostor, respectively i.e., $k \in \{C, I\}$. Hence, $y^k \sim Y^k$ is the score y when person x is $k \in \{C, I\}$. Let $p(Y^k)$ be the probabilistic density function (*pdf*) of Y^k. Eqns. (5) can then be re-expressed by:

$$\text{FAR}(\Delta) = 1 - p(Y^I > \Delta) \qquad \text{and} \qquad \text{FRR}(\Delta) = p(Y^C > \Delta). \qquad (6)$$

Because of Eqn. (4), it is implicitly assumed that $E[Y^C] > E[Y^I]$, where $E[z]$ is the expectation of z. When $p(Y^k)$ for both $k \in \{C, I\}$ are assumed to be Gaussian (normally distributed), they take on the following parametric forms (see [4]):

$$\text{FAR}(\Delta) = \frac{1}{2} - \frac{1}{2}\text{erf}\left(\frac{\Delta - \mu^I}{\sigma^I \sqrt{2}}\right) \qquad \text{and} \qquad \text{FRR}(\Delta) = \frac{1}{2} + \frac{1}{2}\text{erf}\left(\frac{\Delta - \mu^C}{\sigma^C \sqrt{2}}\right) \qquad (7)$$

where μ^k and σ^k are mean and standard deviation of Y^k, and the erf function is defined as follows:

$$\text{erf}(z) = \frac{2}{\sqrt{\pi}} \int_0^z \exp\left[-t^2\right] dt. \qquad (8)$$

At Equal Error Rate (EER), FAR=FRR. Solving this constraint yields (see [4]):

$$\text{EER} = \frac{1}{2} - \frac{1}{2}\text{erf}\left(\frac{\text{F-ratio}}{\sqrt{2}}\right) \equiv \text{eer(F-ratio)} \qquad \text{where} \qquad \text{F-ratio} = \frac{\mu^C - \mu^I}{\sigma^C + \sigma^I}. \qquad (9)$$

Table 1. Summary of theoretical EER based on the assumption that class-independent scores are normally distributed

Fusion methods	EER	where
average baseline[1]	$\text{EER}_{AV} = \text{eer}\left(\frac{\mu_{AV}^C - \mu_{AV}^I}{\sigma_{AV}^C + \sigma_{AV}^I}\right)$	$\mu_{AV}^k = \frac{1}{N}\sum_i \mu_i^k$ $\left(\sigma_{AV}^k\right)^2 = \frac{1}{N}\sum_i \left(\sigma_i^k\right)^2$
single-best classifier	$\text{EER}_{best} = \text{eer}\left(\max_i\left(\frac{\mu_i^C - \mu_i^I}{\sigma_i^C + \sigma_i^I}\right)\right)$	–
mean rule	$\text{EER}_{mean} = \text{eer}\left(\frac{\mu_{mean}^C - \mu_{mean}^I}{\sigma_{mean}^C + \sigma_{mean}^I}\right)$	$\mu_{mean}^k = \frac{1}{N}\sum_i \mu_i^k$ $\left(\sigma_{mean}^k\right)^2 = \frac{1}{N^2}\sum_{i,j} \Sigma_{i,j}^k$
weighted sum[3]	$\text{EER}_{wsum} = \text{eer}\left(\frac{\mu_{wsum}^C - \mu_{wsum}^I}{\sigma_{wsum}^C + \sigma_{wsum}^I}\right)$	$\mu_{wsum}^k = \sum_i \omega_i \mu_i^k$ $\left(\sigma_{wsum}^k\right)^2 = \sum_{i,j} \omega_i \omega_j \Sigma_{i,j}^k$
OS combiners[2]	$\text{EER}_{OS} = \text{eer}\left(\frac{\mu_{OS}^C - \mu_{OS}^I}{\sigma_{OS}^C + \sigma_{OS}^I}\right)$	$\mu_{OS}^k = \mu^k + \gamma_1 \sigma^k$ $\left(\sigma_{OS}^k\right)^2 = \gamma_2 \left(\sigma^k\right)^2$

Remark 1: This is not a classifier but the average performance of baselines when used independently of each other. By its definiton, scores are assumed independent as classifiers function independently of each other. **Remark** 2: OS classifiers assume that scores *across classifiers* are i.i.d. The reduction factor γ is listed in Table 2. The mean and weighted sum classifiers *do not* assume that scores are i.i.d. **Remark** 3: the weighted product (respectively product) takes the same form as weighted sum (respectively sum), except that log-normal distribution is assumed instead.

The function eer is introduced here to simplify the EER expression as a function of F-ratio because eer will be used frequently in this paper. Note that the threshold Δ is omitted since there is only one unique point that satisfies the EER criterion.

2.1   Theoretical EER of Fusion Classifier

We now derive several parametric forms of fused scores using different types of classifiers, namely the single-best classifier, mean, weighted sum, product rule and Order Statistics (OS)-combiners such as min, max and median. The OS-combiners are further discussed in Section 2.2.

The analysis in this section is possible due to the simple expression of F-ratio, which is a function of four parameters: $\{\mu^k, \sigma^k | \forall_{k=\{C,I\}}\}$ as shown in Eqn. (9). Suppose that the i-th response is y_i^k sampled from $p(Y_i^k)$ and there are N classifiers, i.e., $i = 1, \ldots, N$. The *average baseline* performance of classifiers, considering that each of them works independently of the other, is shown in the first row of Table 1. The (class-dependent) average variance, σ_{AV}^k, is defined as the average over all the variances of classifier. This is in fact not a fusion classifier but the *average performance* of classifiers measured in EER. The single-best classifier in the second row chooses the baseline classifier that maximises the F-ratio. This is the same as choosing the one with minimum EER because F-ratio is inversely proportional to EER, as implied by the left part of Eqn. (9).

The derivation of EER of weighted sum (as well as mean) fusion can be found in [5]. The central idea consists of projecting the N dimensional score onto a one dimensional score via the fourth equation in Eqns. (3). Suppose that the class conditional scores (prior to fusion) are modeled by a multivariate Gaussian with mean $(\mu^k)^T = \mu_1^k, \ldots, \mu_N^k$ and covariance Σ^k of N-by-N dimensions. Let $\Sigma_{i,j}^k$ be the i-th row and

j-th column of covariance matrix Σ^k for $k = \{C, I\}$. $E[\cdot]$ is the expectation operator (over samples) and W_i^k is the noise variable associated to classifier i for all k. The linear projection from N dimensions of score to one dimension of score has the same effect on the Gaussian distribution: from N multivariate Gaussian distribution to a single Gaussian distribution with mean μ_{wsum}^k and variance $(\sigma_{wsum})^2$ defined in the fourth row of Table 1 for each class k. The mean operator is derived similarly with $w_i = \frac{1}{N} \forall i$. Note that the weight w_i affects both the mean and variance of fused scores. In [4], it was shown mathematically that the EER of mean, EER_{mean}, is always smaller than or equal to the EER of the average baseline performance (EER_{AV}). This is closely related to the ambiguity decomposition [6] often used in the regression context (as opposed to classification as done in [4]). However, there is no evidence that $\text{EER}_{mean} \leq \text{EER}_{best}$, i.e., the EER of the best-classifier. In [7], it was shown that $\sigma_{wsum}^k \leq \sigma_{mean}^k$, supposing that the $w_i \forall_i$ are optimal. In [3], when the correlation among classifiers is assumed to be zero, $w_i \propto (\text{EER}_i)^{-1}$. As a result, this implies that $\text{EER}_{wsum} \leq \text{EER}_{mean}$. The finding in [7] is more general than that of [3] because the underlying correlation among baseline classifiers is captured by the covariance matrix. Hence, fusion using weighted sum can, in theory, have better performance than the mean rule, assuming that the weights are tuned optimally. A brief discussion of weight-tuning procedures are discussed in Section 5.2. Although there exists several methods to tune the weights in the literature, to the best of our knowledge, no standard algorithm *directly* optimises EER (hence requiring further investigation which cannnot be dealt here).

For the product operator, it is necessary to bound Y to be within the range $[0, 1]$, otherwise the multiplication is not applicable. Consider the following case: two instances of classifier score can take on any real value. The decision function Eqn. (4) is used with optimal threshold being zero. With an impostor access, both classifier scores will be negative if correctly classified. Their product, on the other hand, will be positive. This is clearly undesirable.

The weighted product (and hence product) at first seems slightly cumbersome to obtain. However, one can apply the following logarithmic transform instead: $\log(Y_{wprod}^k) = \sum_i w_i \log(Y_i^k)$, for any y_i^k sampled from $p(Y_i^k)$. This turns out to take the same form as weighted sum. Assuming that Y_i^k is log-normally distributed, we can proceed the analysis in a similar way as the weighted sum case (and hence the mean rule).

2.2   Theoretical EER of Order Statistics Combiners

To implement fixed rule *order statistics* (OS) such as the maximum, minimum and median combiners, scores must be comparable. Unfortunately, attempting to analyse analytically the EER values as done in the previous section is difficult without making (very) constraining assumptions.

The first assumption is that the instance of scores must be *comparable*. If scores of various types of classifiers are involved for fusion, their range may not be comparable. Hence, score normalisation is imperative while this pre-processing step is *unnecessary* in the previous section. The second assumption assumes that scores are i.i.d. In this case, there exists a very simple analytical model[1]. Although this model seems too con-

---

[1] This assumption will be *removed* during experimentation with synthetic data.

Table 2. Reduction factor γ_2 of variance (2 for the second moment) with respect to the standard normal distribution due to fusion with min, max (the second column) and median (third column) OS combiners for the first five samples according to [8]. The fourth column is the *maximum* reduction factor due to mean (at zero correlation), with minimum reduction factor being 1 (at perfect correlation). The fifth and sixth columns show the shift factor γ_1 (for the first moment) as a result of applying min and max for the first five samples. These values also exist in tabulated forms but here they are obtained by simulation. For median, γ_1 is relatively small (in the order of 10^{-4}) beyond 2 samples and hence not shown here. It approaches zero as N is large

N	γ_2 values			γ_1 values	
	OS combiners		mean	OS combiners	
	min, max,	median	($\frac{1}{N}$)	min	max
1	1.000	1.000	1.000	0.00	0.00
2	0.682	0.682	0.500	-0.56	0.56
3	0.560	0.449	0.333	-0.85	0.85
4	0.492	0.361	0.250	-1.03	1.03
5	0.448	0.287	0.200	-1.16	1.16

straining, it is at least applicable to fusion with multiple samples which satisfies some of the assumptions stated here: scores are comparable; and they are *identically distributed* but unfortunately not necessarily *independently* sampled.

All OS combiners will be collectively studied. The subscript OS can be replaced by min, max and median. Supposing that $y_i^k \sim Y_i^k$ is an instance of i-th response knowing that the associated access claim belongs to class k. y^i has the following model: $y_i^k = \mu_i^k + \omega_i^k$, where μ_i^k is a deterministic component and ω_i^k is a noise component. Note that in the previous section ω_i^k is assumed to be normally distributed with zero mean. The fused scores by OS can be written as: $y_{OS}^k = OS(y_i^k) = \mu^k + OS(\omega_i^k)$, where i denotes the i-th sample (and not the i-th classifier output as done in the previous section). Note that μ^k is constant across i and it is *not affected* by the OS combiner. The expectation of y_{OS}^k as well as its variance are shown in the last row of Table 1, where γ_2 is a reduction factor and γ_1 is a shift factor, such that $\gamma_2(\sigma^k)^2$ is the variance of $OS(\omega_i^k)$ and $\gamma_1\sigma^k$ is the expected value of $OS(\omega_i^k)$. Both γ's can be found in tabulated form for various noise distributions [8]. A similar line of analysis can be found in [2] except that class-independent noise is assumed. The reduction factors of combining the first five samples, assuming Gaussian distribution, are shown in Table 2. The smaller γ_2 is, the smaller the associated EER. The fourth column of Table 2 shows the reduction factor due to mean (as compared to the second and third columns). It can be seen that mean is overall superior.

3   General Discussion

We gather here a list of assumptions made that will be used in simulating a theoretical comparison of fixed and trainable fusion classifiers listed in Table 1. For each assumption, we discuss its relevance and acceptability in practice.

1. **Class-dependent gaussianity assumption.** Perhaps this is the most severe assumption as this does not necessarily hold in reality. In [4], 1186 data sets of scores

were used to verify this assumption using the Kolmogorov-Smirnov statistics. Only about a quarter of the data sets supported the gaussianity assumption. However, to much surprise, the theoretical EER (estimated using the Gaussian assumption) matches closely its empirical counterpart (obtained by directly estimating the EER from scores). Hence, the theoretical EER employed here is somewhat robust to deviation from such assumption. This in part may be due to the fact that the classifier scores are unimodal but not necessarily Gaussian. The Gaussianity assumption is used mainly because of its easy interpretation. A mixture of Gaussian components could have been used in place of a single Gaussian. However, this subject requires a dedicated study which cannot be adequately dealt in the present context.

2. **Score comparability assumption.** This assumption is *only necessary* for OS combiners because of their nature that requires comparison relation "$\geq$". Scores can be made comparable by using score normalisation techniques. We use here the zero-mean unit-variance normalisation (or z-score), where a score is subtracted from its global mean and divided by its standard deviation, both of which are calculated from a training set. For the product rule which naturally assumes classifier outputs are probabilistic (in the range $[0, 1]$), the min-max normalisation is used. This is done by subtracting the score from its smallest value and divided by its range (maximum minus minimum value), all of which calculated from a training set

3. **Class-dependent correlation assumption.** Under such assumption, one assumes that the correlation of client and impostor distributions are correlated, i.e., $\rho^I \propto \rho^C$. This means that knowing the covariance of impostor joint distribution, one can actually estimate the covariance of the client joint distribution. A series of 70 intramodal and multimodal fusion experiments taken from the BANCA database were analysed in [4] and it was shown that the correlation between ρ^I and ρ^C is rather strong, i.e., 0.8.

Different from studies in [1, 2], we do not assume identical distribution across different classifiers. In fact, for OS combiners, the analytical EER expression that does not commit such assumption is cumbersome to be evaluated. Hence, we propose to resolve to simulations, which are relatively easier to carry out and reflect *better* the fusion tasks in biometric authentication.

Note that we do not make the independence assumption in the sense that correlation across different classifiers is non-zero. In fact, the correlation among classifier scores is captured by the covariance matrix via the definition of correlation, as follows: $\rho^k_{i,j} \equiv \frac{\Sigma^k_{i,j}}{\sigma^k_i \sigma^k_j}$. This indicates that if one uses a multivariate Gaussian, the correlation is automatically taken care of by the model.

Our theoretical analysis is different from [2, 3] in several aspects. In [2, 3], two types of errors are introduced, namely Bayes (inherent) error and added error. The former is due to unbiased classifier whose class posterior estimates correspond to the true posteriors. The latter is due to biased classifiers which result in wrongly estimated class posteriors. The EER used here is commonly found in binary classification problems while the error (sum of bayes error and added error) applies to any number of classes. It is tempting to conclude that EER is equivalent to the Bayes error for a two-class problem. There are, however, important differences. In [2, 3] (the former), the bayes error is due to additive error in the feature space near the decision boundary. In EER (the latter), the input measurement is not a set of features but a set of scores of one or more base-classifiers. The output posteriors between the two classes in the former are enforced by linear approximation, whereas in the latter, they are assumed to be (integral of) Gaussian. The local continuity at the boundary is hence implicitly assumed. Furthermore, the Bayes error cannot be reduced (the added error can) but EER can [4].

4   Experiments with Synthetic Data

We designed a series of 110 synthetic experiment settings. Each experiment setting consists of a fusion task of *two* classifier outputs. All three assumptions mentioned in Section 3 are used here, i.e., (1) the 2D scores will be sampled from a multivariate Gaussian distribution for each class (client and impostor); (2) scores are comparable, i.e., the mean of client and impostor distributions are fixed to 0 and 1, respectively. However, for the product rule, scores are further normalised into the range $[0, 1]$ by the min-max normalisation; and finally, (3) the *same* covariance matrix is used for the client and impostor distributions.

In order to evaluate classifier performance, Half Total Error Rate (HTER) is commonly used for biometric authentication. It is defined as: HTER $= \frac{1}{2}$(FAR(Δ) + FRR(Δ)), where the threshold Δ is chosen to minimise the Weighted Error Rate (WER) at a given pre-defined $\alpha \in [0, 1]$ which balances between FAR and FRR. WER is defined as:

$$\text{WER}(\alpha) = \alpha\text{FAR}(\Delta) + (1 - \alpha)\text{FRR}(\Delta). \tag{10}$$

To optimise the EER criterion, instead of WER, $\alpha = 0.5$ is used. We further define a performance gain variable called β_{min}, as follows: $\beta_{min} = \frac{\text{HTER}_{best}}{\text{HTER}_{COM}}$ where COM is any one of the fusion classifiers/rules under study. When $\beta_{min} > 1$, the particular fusion classifier is better than the best underlying system.

The first classifier, designed as the *better* classifier of the two, has a (class-dependent) variance of 0.5 and is kept constant across all synthetic data sets, whereas the second classifier has a variance that varies with a ratio between 1 to 4 (or absolute variance value between 0.5 to 2). This causes the first expert to have a HTER between 5.3% and 6.2%, with a mean of 5.8% and the second expert between 5.4% and 22% of HTER with a mean of 15% at the EER point. Furthermore, the correlation value is varied between 0 and 1, at a step of 0.1 increment.

The simulation results are shown in Figure 1. For figures (a)-(e), the plane with $\beta_{min} = 1$ indicates the best single classifier, i.e., the baseline performance. As can be seen, the weighted sum classifier achieves the best overall gain. In fact, its $\beta_{min} > 1$ across all variance ratios and across all correlation values. The mean rule shows that the performance gain is more than 1 only when the variance ratio is 3 at correlation=0. As correlation increases, to maintain a positive gain, the variance ratio has to be decreased. This behaviour has been theoretically verified in [4]. The min and max rules follow the same trend as mean and weighted sum except that their gain is much smaller. There is no significant difference between the min and max rules. This is somewhat expected following their theoretical EER models presented in Table 1.

We further examined the weight attributed to the second (weaker) classifier by the weighted sum classifier to see how the weights evolve with various variance ratios and

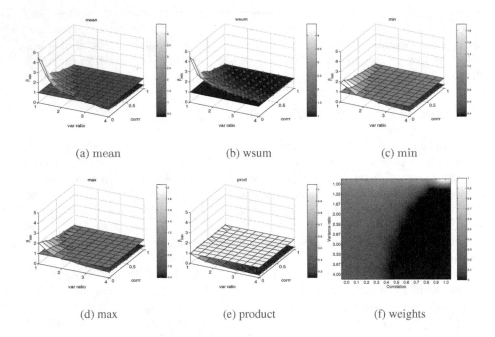

(a) mean   (b) wsum   (c) min

(d) max   (e) product   (f) weights

Fig. 1. Performance gain of HTER, at EER criterion, with respect to the best underlying classifier, β_{min}, (the Z-axis) across different variance ratios (of two experts) from 1 to 4 (the X-axis) and different correlation values from 0 to 1 (the Y-axis), as a result of fusing synthetic scores of two expert systems (classifiers) assuming class-dependent scores are normally distributed. The scores are combined using (a) mean, (b) weighted sum, (c) min, (d) max and (e) product fusion classifiers. (f): the weight of the *weaker* expert found in the weighted sum after training. This can be thought of as the degree of "reliance on the weaker expert"

correlations. This weight can be interpreted as "reliance on the weaker system". This is shown in Figure 1(f). On this Cartesian coordinate system (X is correlation and Y is variance ratio), the point (1,1) implies that the two classifiers have exactly the same performance. Hence, the weight attributed to classifier 1 or 2 makes no difference. However, at exact correlation (=1), the weight attributed to classifier 2 (the weaker one) immediately becomes zero as the variance ratio increases. Furthermore, there is absolutely no improvement for this case (see in Figure 1(b)). On the other hand, at zero-correlation, the weaker classifier *contributes* to fusion (i.e., the weights are not zero). The corresponding performance gain *always increases* with decreasing variance ratio (increasingly stronger weak classifier). The product rule only has performance as good as the single-best classifier at variance ratio=1 while does not match the rest of the fusion classifiers. Its performance does not evolve with the correlation. One plausible explanation of such suboptimal performance comes from [9], stating that the product rule is more sensitive to error as compared to the sum (or mean) rule. Despite their difference, all fusion classifiers except the product rule show that low correlation and low variance ratio increase the fusion performance. Note that no generalisation performance is involved here. In real applications, where there is a mismatch between training and test data sets, generalisation performance becomes an important concern. This is treated in the next section with real data.

5   Experiments with Real Data

5.1   Database Settings and Evaluation

The publicly available[2] XM2VTS benchmark database for score-level fusion [10] is used. There are altogether 32 fusion data sets and each data set contains a fusion task of two experts. These fusion tasks contain multimodal and intramodal fusion based on face and speaker authentication tasks. For each data set, there are two sets of scores, from the *development* and the *evaluation* sets. The development set is used *uniquely* to train the fusion classifier parameters, including the threshold (bias) parameter, whereas the evaluation set is used uniquely to evaluate the generalisation performance. They are in accordance to the two originally defined Lausanne Protocols [11]. The 32 fusion experiments have 400 (client accesses) $\times$ 32 (data sets)= 12,800 client accesses and 111,800 (impostor accesses) $\times$ 32 (data sets) = 3,577,600 impostor accesses.

The most commonly used performance visualising tool in the literature is the Decision Error Trade-off (DET) curve. It has been pointed out [12] that two DET curves resulting from two systems are not comparable because such comparison does not take into account how the thresholds are selected. It was argued [12] that such threshold should be chosen *a priori* as well, based on a given criterion. This is because when a biometric system is operational, the threshold parameter has to be fixed *a priori*. As a result, the Expected Performance Curve (EPC) [12] was proposed. This curve is constructed as follows: for various values of α in Eqn. (10) between 0 and 1, select the optimal threshold Δ on a development (training) set, apply it on the evaluation (test) set and compute the HTER on the evaluation set. This HTER is then plotted with respect to α. The EPC curve can be interpreted similarly to the DET curve, i.e., the lower the curve, the better the generalisation performance. In this study, the *pooled* version of EPC is used to visualise the performance. The idea is to plot a single EPC curve instead of 32 EPC curves for each of the 32 fusion experiments. This is done by calculating the *global* false acceptance and false rejection errors over the 32 experiments for *each* of the α values. The pooled EPC curve and its implementation can be found in [10].

5.2   Experimental Results and Discussion

Figure 2 shows the pooled EPC curves of several fusion classifiers/rules under study, each over the 32 XM2VTS fusion data sets. As can be observed, the weighted sum gives the best generalisation performance. The mean rule follows closely. As expected, both min and max rules have improved generalisation performance *after* score-normalisation. For the normalised case (see figure (b)), max turns out to outperform min significantly for a large of α, according to HTER significance test at 90% of confidence [13].

---

[2] Accessible at http://www.idiap.ch/~norman/fusion

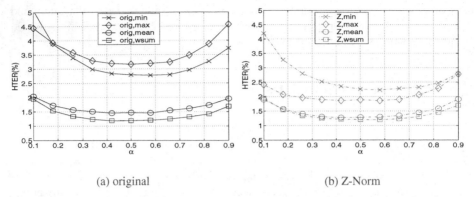

(a) original   (b) Z-Norm

Fig. 2. Pooled EPC curves, each derived from 32 fusion data sets, as a result of applying min, max, mean and weighted sum fusion, with (a) unnormalised orignal scores, (b) margintransformed scores, (c) z-scores and (d) F-ratio transformed scores

The weight parameters in the weighted sum are optimised using a 1D search procedure with a constant step-size of 0.05 within the bound $[0, 1]$ since only two classifier outputs are involved. This strategy has been employed by [14] for user-specific weighting. The advantage of this technique over the technique assuming zero-correlation, such as [3] or Fisher-ratio [7–Sec. 3.6] is that no assumption is made about the underlying class-dependent distribution. Support Vector machines with linear kernel could also have been used instead since it too does not make this assumption. We actually carried out the two control experiments using the two techniques mentioned and found that their generalisation performance are significantly inferior to our line search or SVM approach (not shown here). This is a probable reason why the empirical study conducted here is somewhat different from [15], where the authors did not find weighted sum significantly outperforms the mean rule, although the *same* database was used.

6   Conclusions

In this study, the theoretical and empirical aspects of fixed and trainable fusion classifiers are studied using the EER. Although this subject is well studied [1, 2, 3], the effects of correlation on Order Statistics (OS) combiners, e.g, min, max, and median, are largely unknown or rarely discussed due to intractable analysis. We studied the *joint effect* of correlation and base-classifier imbalance performance on EER by simulation. This simulation is based on three major assumptions: class-dependent Gaussianity assumption, score comparability assumption and class-dependent correlation assumption. Each assumption is adequately addressed (see Section 3). In particular, for the second assumption, several score normalisation techniques are discussed. Based on 4 fusion classifiers $\times$ 2 normalisation techniques (and) $\times$ 32 data sets = 256 fusion experiments, we show that weighted sum, when weights are tuned correctly, can achieve the best generalisation performance, with the additional advantage that no score normalisation is needed.

Acknowledgment

This work was supported in part by the IST Program of the European Community, under the PASCAL Network of Excellence, IST-2002-506778, funded in part by the Swiss Federal Office for Education and Science (OFES) and the Swiss NSF through the NCCR on IM2. This publication only reflects the authors' view.

References

1. L.I. Kuncheva, "A Theoretical Study on Six Classifier Fusion Strategies," *IEEE Trans. Pattern Analysis and Machine Intelligence*, vol. 24(2), pp. 281–286, February 2002.
2. K. Tumer and J. Ghosh, "Robust Combining of Disparate Classifiers through Order Statistics," *Pattern Analysis and Applications*, vol. 5, pp. 189–200, 2002.
3. G. Fumera and F. Roli, "Analysis of Linear and Order Statistics Combiners for Fusion of Imbalanced Classifiers," in *LNCS 2364, Proc. 3rd Int'l Workshop on Multiple Classifier Systems (MCS 2002)*, Cagliari, 2002, pp. 252–261.
4. N. Poh and S. Bengio, "How Do Correlation and Variance of Base Classifiers Affect Fusion in Biometric Authentication Tasks?," Research Report 04-18, IDIAP, Martigny, Switzerland, 2004, accepted for publication in *IEEE Trans. Signal Processing*, 2005.
5. N. Poh and S. Bengio, "Towards Predicting Optimal Subsets of Base-Experts in Biometric Authentication Task," in *IDIAP Research Report 04-17, Martigny, Switzerland*, Accepted for publication in *Joint AMI/PASCAL/IM2/M4 Workshop on Multimodal Interaction and Related Machine Learning Algorithms*, 2004.
6. A. Krogh and J. Vedelsby, "Neural Network Ensembles, Cross-Validation and Active-Learning," *Advances in Neural Information Processing Systems*, vol. 7, 1995.
7. C. Bishop, *Neural Networks for Pattern Recognition*, Oxford University Press, 1999.
8. B.C. Arnold, N. Balakrishnan, and H.N. Nagaraja, *A First Course in Order Statistics*, Wiley, New York, 1992.
9. J. Kittler, M. Hatef, R. P.W. Duin, and J. Matas, "On Combining Classifiers," *IEEE Trans. Pattern Analysis and Machine Intelligence*, vol. 20, no. 3, pp. 226–239, 1998.
10. N. Poh and S. Bengio, "Database, Protocol and Tools for Evaluating Score-Level Fusion Algorithms in Biometric Authentication," Research Report 04-44, IDIAP, Martigny, Switzerland, 2004, Accepted for publication in *AVBPA 2005*.
11. J. Matas, M. Hamouz, J. Kittler, Y. Li, C. Kotropoulos, A. Tefas, I. Pitas, T. Tan, H. Yan, F. Smeraldi, J. Begun, N. Capdevielle, W. Gerstner, S. Ben-Yacoub, Y. Abdeljaoued, and E. Mayoraz, "Comparison of Face Verification Results on the XM2VTS Database," in *Proc. 15th Int'l Conf. Pattern Recognition*, Barcelona, 2000, vol. 4, pp. 858–863.
12. S. Bengio and J. Mariéthoz, "The Expected Performance Curve: a New Assessment Measure for Person Authentication," in *The Speaker and Language Recognition Workshop (Odyssey)*, Toledo, 2004, pp. 279–284.
13. S. Bengio and J. Mariéthoz, "A Statistical Significance Test for Person Authentication," in *The Speaker and Language Recognition Workshop (Odyssey)*, Toledo, 2004, pp. 237–244.
14. A. Jain, K. Nandakumar, and A. Ross, "Score Normalisation in Multimodal Biometric Systems," *Pattern Recognition (to appear)*, 2005.
15. F. Roli, G. Fumera, and J. Kittler, "Fixed and Trained Combiners for Fusion of Imbalanced Pattern Classifiers," in *Proc. 5th Int'l Conf. on Information Fusion*, 2002, pp. 278–284.

Mixture of Gaussian Processes for Combining Multiple Modalities

Ashish Kapoor, Hyungil Ahn, and Rosalind W. Picard

MIT Media Lab, Cambridge MA 02139, USA,
{kapoor, hiahn, picard}@media.mit.edu,
http://affect.media.mit.edu

Abstract. This paper describes a unified approach, based on Gaussian Processes, for achieving sensor fusion under the problematic conditions of missing channels and noisy labels. Under the proposed approach, Gaussian Processes generate separate class labels corresponding to each individual modality. The final classification is based upon a hidden random variable, which probabilistically combines the sensors. Given both labeled and test data, the inference on unknown variables, parameters and class labels for the test data is performed using the variational bound and Expectation Propagation. We apply this method to the challenge of classifying a student's interest level using observations from the face and postures, together with information from the task the students are performing. Classification with the proposed new approach achieves accuracy of over 83%, significantly outperforming the classification using individual modalities and other common classifier combination schemes.

1   Introduction

There are a growing number of scenarios in pattern recognition where multi-modal information is used, and where information from multiple sensors needs to be fused to recover the variable of interest. Multi-sensor classification is a problem that has been addressed previously by using either data-level fusion or classifier combination schemes. In the former, a single classifier is trained on joint features; however, when the data has even one missing channel, a frequent problem, then usually all the data is ignored for that time block, resulting in a significant reduction in the total amount of data for training. One way to address this problem is by training a classifier for each modality that is present, and then combining these for a final decision.

The problem becomes even more challenging when there is labeling noise; that is, some data points have incorrect labels. In many computer vision and HCI applications like emotion recognition, there is always an uncertainty about the true labels of the data; thus, requiring a principled approach to handle any labeling noise in the data.

The highly challenging problem we address in this paper combines the three problems described above: there is multi-sensory data, channels are frequently missing and there might be labeling errors in the data.

N.C. Oza et al. (Eds.): MCS 2005, LNCS 3541, pp. 86–96, 2005.

We address this challenging problem in a Bayesian framework using a combination of Expectation Propagation [9] and variational approximate inference [1]. The framework utilizes a mixture of Gaussian Processes, where the classification using each channel is learned via Expectation Propagation, a technique for approximate Bayesian inference. The resulting posterior over each classification function is a product of Gaussians and can be updated very quickly. We evaluate the multi-sensor classification scheme on the task of detecting the affective state of interest in children trying to solve a puzzle, combining sensory information from the face, the postures and the state of the puzzle task, to infer the student's state. The proposed unified approach achieves a significantly better recognition accuracy than classification based on individual channels and the standard classifier combination methods. Also, on the affect data set we found that the standard classifier combination rules, which are justified using the probability theory, work better when the individual classifiers are probabilistic (as in the Gaussian Process classification) as opposed to the SVM.

1.1   Previous Work

There are many methods, including Boosting [12] and Bagging [2], which generate an ensemble of classifiers by choosing different samples from the training set. These methods require a common set of training data, which is a set of joint vectors formed by stacking the features extracted from all the modalities into one big vector. As mentioned earlier, often in multi-sensor fusion problems the training data has missing channels and labels; thus most of the data cannot be used to form a common set of training data. Similarly, most of the data remains unused in "feature-level fusion," where a single classifier is trained on joint features.

Kittler et al. [7] have described a common framework for combining classifiers and provided theoretical justification for using simple operators such as majority vote, sum, product, maximum and minimum. Hong and Jain [4] have used a similar framework to fuse multiple modalities for personal identification. Similarly, Han and Bhanu [3] also perform rule-based fusion for gait-based human recognition. One problem with these fixed rules is that, it is difficult to predict which rule would perform best. Then there are methods, such as layered HMMs proposed by Oliver et al. [10], which perform decision fusion and sensor selection depending upon utility functions and stacked classifiers. One main disadvantage of using stacked based classification is that these methods require a large amount of labeled training data. There are other mixture-of-experts [5] and critic-driven approaches [8] where base-level classifiers (experts) are combined using second level classifiers (critics or gating functions) that predict how well an expert is going to perform on the current input. To make a classifier selection, the critic can either look at the current input or base its decision upon some other contextual features as well. For example, Toyama and Horvitz [13] demonstrate a head tracking system based on multiple algorithms, that uses contextual features as reliability indicators for the different tracking algorithms. The framework described by us in this paper is also based on sensor-selection and is most similar to Tresp [14], where the mixture of Gaussian Processes is described. The key differences include classification based on Gaussian Process rather than regression; also, we use Expectation Propagation for Gaussian Process classification and our classification likelihood is robust to labeling errors and noise. Our framework is also capable of quickly re-learning the classification given updated label associations. Further, we provide a complete Bayesian treatment of the problem rather than using a maximum-likelihood training.

2   Our Approach

Figure 1 shows the model we follow to solve the problem. In the figure, the data $\mathbf{x}^p$ from P different sensors generate soft class labels y. The switching variable λ, determines modalities that finally decide the hard class label $t \in \{1, -1\}$. In section 2.1, we first review classification using Gaussian Process (GP). Section 2.2 then extends the idea to a Mixture of Gaussian Processes and describes how to handle multiple modalities in the same Bayesian framework.

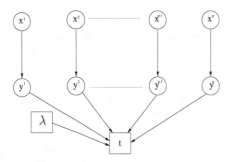

2.1   Gaussian Process Classification

Assume we are given a set of labeled data points $\mathbf{X} = \{\mathbf{x}_1, .., \mathbf{x}_n\}$, with class labels $\mathbf{t} = \{t_1, .., t_n\}$. For two-way classification, the labels are, $t \in \{-1, 1\}$. Under the Bayesian framework, given an unlabeled point $\mathbf{x}^*$, we are interested in the distribution $p(t^*|\mathbf{X}, \mathbf{t}, \mathbf{x}^*)$. Here t^* is a random variable denoting the class label for the point $\mathbf{x}^*$. Although, in this paper we only describe how to classify one new point, all

Fig. 1. A mixture of Gaussian Processes for p sensors

the machinery described applies as well to a set of new points without any additional computational overhead.

The idea behind GP classification is that the hard labels $\mathbf{t}$ depend upon hidden soft-labels $\mathbf{y} = \{y_1, ..., y_n\}$. These hidden soft-labels arise due to application of a function f directly on the input data points (i.e. $y_i = f(x_i) \; \forall i \in [1..n]$). Further, we assume a Gaussian Process prior on the function f; thus, the results $\mathbf{y}$ of the evaluation of the function f on any number of input data points $\mathbf{x}$ are jointly Gaussian. Further, the covariance between two outputs y_i and y_j can be specified using a kernel function applied to $\mathbf{x}_i$ and $\mathbf{x}_j$. Formally, $\{y_1, .., y_n\} \sim N(0, K)$ where K is a n-by-n kernel matrix with $K_{ij} = K(\mathbf{x}_i, \mathbf{x}_j)$.

The observed labels $\mathbf{t}$ are assumed to be conditionally independent given the soft labels $\mathbf{y}$ and each t_i depends upon y_i through the conditional distribution:

$$p(t_i|y_i) = \epsilon + (1 - 2\epsilon)\Phi(y_i \cdot t_i)$$

Here, ϵ is the labeling error rate and $\Phi(z) = \int_{-\infty}^{z} N(z; 0, 1)$. Very similar likelihoods have been previously used for Gaussian Process classification [11] and Bayes-point machines [9]. The above described likelihood explicitly models the labeling error rate; thus, the model should be more robust to label noise.

Our task is then to infer $p(t^*|D)$, where $D = \{\mathbf{X}, \mathbf{t}, \mathbf{x}^*\}$. Specifically:

$$p(t^*|D) = p(t^*|\mathbf{X}, \mathbf{t}, \mathbf{x}^*) \propto \int_{\mathbf{y}, y^*} p(t^*|\mathbf{y}, y^*)p(\mathbf{y}, y^*|\mathbf{X}, \mathbf{t}, \mathbf{x}^*) \qquad (1)$$

Where the posterior $p(\mathbf{y}, y^*|\mathbf{X}, \mathbf{t}, \mathbf{x}^*)$ can be written as:

$$p(\mathbf{y}, y^*|\mathbf{X}, \mathbf{t}, \mathbf{x}^*) = p(\mathbf{y}, y^*|D) \propto p(\mathbf{y}, y^*|\mathbf{X}, \mathbf{x}^*)p(\mathbf{t}|\mathbf{y})$$

The term $p(\mathbf{y}, y^*|\mathbf{X}, \mathbf{x}^*) \sim N(0, K)$ is the GP prior and it enforces a smoothness constraint. The second term, $p(\mathbf{t}|\mathbf{y})$ incorporates information provided in the labels. In the frameworks described here, $p(\mathbf{y}, y^*|D)$ is approximated as a Gaussian distribution using Expectation Propagation (EP), a technique for approximate Bayesian inference [9]. Assuming conditional independence of labels given the soft-labels, $p(\mathbf{t}|\mathbf{y})$ can be written as:

$$p(\mathbf{t}|\mathbf{y}) = \prod_{i=1}^{n} p(t_i|y_i) = \prod_{i=1}^{n} [\epsilon + (1 - 2\epsilon)\Phi(y_i \cdot t_i)]$$

The idea behind using EP is to approximate $P(\mathbf{y}, y^*|D)$ as a Gaussian. Although the prior $p(\mathbf{y}, y^*|\mathbf{X}, \mathbf{x}^*)$ is a Gaussian distribution, the exact posterior is not a Gaussian due to the form of $p(\mathbf{t}|\mathbf{y})$. Nonetheless, we can use EP to approximate the posterior as a Gaussian. Specifically, the method approximates the terms $p(t_i|y_i)$ as:

$$p(t_i|y_i) \approx \tilde{t}_i = s_i \exp(-\frac{1}{2v_i}(y_i \cdot t_i - m_i)^2) \qquad (2)$$

EP starts with the GP prior N(0,K) and incorporates all the approximate terms $\tilde{t}_i$ to approximate the posterior $p(\mathbf{y}, y^*|D) = N(\mathbf{M}, \mathbf{V})$ as a Gaussian. For details readers are encouraged to look at [9]. To classify the test point $\mathbf{x}^*$, the approximate distribution $p(y^*|D) \approx N(M^*, V^*)$ can be obtained by marginalizing $p(\mathbf{y}, y^*|D)$ and then equation 1 can be used:

$$p(t^*|D) \propto \int_{y^*} p(t^*|y^*)N(M^*, V^*) = \epsilon + (1 - 2\epsilon)\Phi(\frac{M^* \cdot t^*}{\sqrt{(1 + V^*)}}) \qquad (3)$$

2.2   Mixture of Gaussian Processes for Sensor Fusion

Given n data points $\bar{\mathbf{x}}_1, .., \bar{\mathbf{x}}_n$, obtained from P different sensors, our approach follows a mixture of Gaussian Processes model described in figure 1. Let every i^{th} data point be represented as $\bar{\mathbf{x}}_i = \{\mathbf{x}_i^{(1)}, .., \mathbf{x}_i^{(P)}\}$, and the soft labels as $\bar{\mathbf{y}}_i = \{y_i^{(1)}, .., y_i^{(P)}\}$. Given $\lambda_i \in \{1, .., P\}$, the random variable that determines the combination of the channels for the final classification, the classification likelihood can be written as:

$$P(t_i|\bar{\mathbf{y}}_i, \lambda_i = j) = P(t_i|y_i^{(j)}) = \epsilon + (1 - 2\epsilon)\Phi(t_i \cdot y_i^{(j)})$$

Given $\{\bar{\mathbf{X}}, \mathbf{t}\}$ and $\bar{\mathbf{x}}^*$

Step 1: Initialization
-For all the labeled points $i = 1$ to n do
    · Initialize $Q(\lambda_i)$ using uniform distribution
-For all the modalities $p = 1$ to P do
    · Incorporate all the labeled data points to obtain a Gaussian posterior for the soft labels:
    $$p^0(\mathbf{y}^{(p)}) = N(\mathbf{y}^{(p)}; \mathbf{M}_{\mathbf{y}^{(p)}}, \mathbf{V}_{\mathbf{y}^{(p)}})$$
    · Initialize: $Q(\mathbf{y}^{(p)}) = p^0(\mathbf{y}^{(p)})$

Step 2: Variational Updates
-Repeat until change in posteriors is less than some small threshold
    · Update $Q(\mathbf{\Lambda})$ using equation 6.
    · Update $Q(\bar{\mathbf{Y}})$ using equation 7.

Step 3: Classifying Test Data
-Compute $\hat{\mathbf{\Lambda}} = \arg\max_{\mathbf{\Lambda}} Q(\mathbf{\Lambda})$
-Use P-way classification to get the posterior $Q(\lambda^*)$
-Estimate $p(t^*|\bar{\mathbf{X}}, \mathbf{t})$ using equation 9

Fig. 2. Summary of the algorithm to classify the test data point using a mixture of Gaussian Processes. This algorithm can be readily extended to more than one test points without any computational overhead

Given a test point $\bar{\mathbf{x}}^*$, let $\bar{\mathbf{X}} = \{\bar{\mathbf{x}}_1, .., \bar{\mathbf{x}}_n, \bar{\mathbf{x}}^*\}$ denote all the training and the test points. Further, let $\bar{\mathbf{Y}} = \{\mathbf{y}^{(1)}, .., \mathbf{y}^{(P)}\}$, denote the hidden soft labels corresponding to each channel of all the data including the test point. Let, $Q(\bar{\mathbf{Y}}) = \prod_{p=1}^{P} Q(\mathbf{y}^{(p)})$ and $Q(\mathbf{\Lambda}) = \prod_{i=1}^{n} Q(\lambda_i)$, denote the approximate posterior over the hidden variables $\bar{\mathbf{Y}}$ and $\mathbf{\Lambda}$, where $\mathbf{\Lambda} = \{\lambda_1, .., \lambda_n\}$ are the switches corresponding only to the n labeled data points. Let $p(\bar{\mathbf{Y}})$ and $p(\mathbf{\Lambda})$ be the priors with $p(\bar{\mathbf{Y}}) = \prod_{p=1}^{P} p(\mathbf{y}^{(p)})$, the product of GP priors and $p(\mathbf{\Lambda})$ uniform. Given $\bar{\mathbf{X}}$ and the labels $\mathbf{t}$, our algorithm iteratively optimizes the variational bound:

$$F = \int_{\bar{\mathbf{Y}}, \mathbf{\Lambda}} Q(\bar{\mathbf{Y}}) Q(\mathbf{\Lambda}) \log\left(\frac{p(\bar{\mathbf{Y}}) p(\mathbf{\Lambda}) p(\mathbf{t}|\bar{\mathbf{X}}, \bar{\mathbf{Y}}, \mathbf{\Lambda})}{Q(\bar{\mathbf{Y}}) Q(\mathbf{\Lambda})}\right) \tag{4}$$

The classification using EP is required only once, irrespective of the number of iterations. In each iteration to optimize the bound given in equation 4, the classification rules are updated using the Gaussian approximations provided by EP. The algorithm is shown in figure 2 and can be divided into 3 steps: initialization, optimization and classification, which are described below.

Step 1: Initialization: In the first step, the approximate posterior $Q(\bar{\mathbf{Y}})Q(\mathbf{\Lambda})$ $= \prod_{p=1}^{P} Q(\mathbf{y}^{(p)}) \prod_{i=1}^{n} Q(\lambda_i)$ is initialized. Here, $Q(\lambda_i)$ are multinomial distributions and are initialized randomly using a uniform distribution. $Q(\mathbf{y}^{(p)})$ are normal distributions and to initialize them, we first use EP as described in section 2.1, considering all the data points irrespective of the state of the switches. EP results in the approximate Gaussian posteriors $p^0(\mathbf{y}^{(p)}) = N(\mathbf{y}^{(p)}; \mathbf{M}_{\mathbf{y}^{(p)}}, \mathbf{V}_{\mathbf{y}^{(p)}})$ for all $p \in \{1, .., P\}$, which are used to initialize $Q(\mathbf{y}^{(p)})$. A very useful biproduct of EP is the Gaussian approximations of the likelihoods, which would later be used to update our classification during the variational iterations in step 2.

Step 2: Optimization: The bound given in equation 4 is optimized by iteratively updating $Q(\bar{\mathbf{Y}})$ and $Q(\mathbf{\Lambda})$. Given the approximations $Q^k(\mathbf{\Lambda})$ and $Q^k(\bar{\mathbf{Y}})$ from the kth iteration, $Q^{k+1}(\mathbf{\Lambda})$ and $Q^{k+1}(\bar{\mathbf{Y}})$ can be updated using variational updated rules [1]. Specifically, update rules for $Q(\lambda_i)$ and $Q(\mathbf{y}^{(p)})$ are as follows:

$$Q^{k+1}(\lambda_i) \propto \exp\{\int_{\bar{\mathbf{Y}}} Q^k(\bar{\mathbf{Y}}) \log p(t_i|\bar{\mathbf{Y}}, \lambda_i)\}$$

$$Q^{k+1}(\mathbf{y}^{(p)}) \propto \exp\{\int_{\mathbf{\Lambda}} Q^k(\mathbf{\Lambda}) \log p(\mathbf{y}^{(p)})p(\mathbf{t}|\mathbf{y}^{(p)}, \mathbf{\Lambda})\}$$

The update for $Q(\lambda_i = p)$ can be written as:

$$Q^{k+1}(\lambda_i = p) \propto \exp\{\int_{y_i^{(p)}} Q^k(y_i^{(p)}) \log p(t_i|y_i^{(p)})\} \tag{5}$$

$$= \exp\{\int_{y_i^{(p)}} Q^k(y_i^{(p)}) \log(\epsilon + (1 - 2\epsilon)\Phi(t_i y_i^{(p)}))\} \tag{6}$$

Equation 6 is intractable but can be computed efficiently by importance sampling using the 1-D Gaussian $Q^k(y_i^p)$ as a proposal distribution. Further, we have the Gaussian approximations from EP for the likelihood term $p(t_i|y_i^{(p)}) \approx s_i^{(p)} \exp(-\frac{1}{2v_i^{(p)}}(y_i^{(p)} \cdot t_i - m_i^{(p)})^2)$. It can be shown that the update rule for $Q(\mathbf{y}^{(p)})$ reduces down to:

$$Q^{k+1}(\mathbf{y}^{(p)}) \propto p(\mathbf{y}^{(p)}) \prod_{i=1}^{n} N(y_i^{(p)}; m_i^{(p)} \cdot t_i, \frac{v_i^{(p)}}{Q^k(\lambda_i)}) \tag{7}$$

This is just a product of Gaussian terms; thus, there is no need to rerun the EP to estimate the new posterior over soft classifications. Further, note that $Q(\lambda_i)$ divides the variance, hence controlling the contribution of each labeled data point for different channels.

Step 3: Classification: In the final step, given the posterior over the switches, $Q(\lambda_i) \; \forall i \in [1..n]$, we first infer the switches for the test data $\bar{\mathbf{x}}^*$. For this, we do a P-way classification using the GP algorithm described in 2.1 with $\hat{\mathbf{\Lambda}} = \arg\max_{\mathbf{\Lambda}} Q(\mathbf{\Lambda})$ as labels. Specifically, for an unlabeled point $\bar{\mathbf{x}}^*$, P different classifications are done where each classification provides us with q_r^*, where $r \in \{1, .., P\}$, and equals to the probability that channel r was chosen to classify $\bar{\mathbf{x}}^*$. The posterior $Q(\lambda^* = r)$ is then set to $\frac{q_r^*}{\sum_{p=1}^{P} q_p^*}$. In our experiments, for each of these P classifications, we clubbed all the channels together using -1 as observations for the modalities that were missing. Note, that we are not limited to using all the channels clubbed together; but, various combinations of the modalities can be used including other indicator and contextual variables.

Once we have the posterior over the switch for the test data, $Q(\lambda^*)$, we can infer class probability of an unlabeled data point $\bar{\mathbf{x}}^*$ using:

$$p(t^*|\bar{\mathbf{X}},\mathbf{t}) = \int_{\bar{\mathbf{Y}},\lambda^*} p(t^*|\bar{\mathbf{Y}},\lambda^*)Q(\lambda^*)Q(\bar{\mathbf{Y}}) \tag{8}$$

$$= \sum_{p=1}^{P} Q(\lambda^* = p)(\epsilon + (1-2\epsilon)\Phi(\frac{M_{y^{(p)}}^* \cdot t^*}{\sqrt{1+V_{y^{(p)}}^*}})) \tag{9}$$

Here, $M_{y^{(p)}}^*$ and $V_{y^{(p)}}^*$ are the mean and the variance of the marginal Gaussian approximation for p^{th} channel corresponding to the hidden soft label $\bar{\mathbf{y}}^*$.

3   Experiments and Results

We first demonstrate the features of the approach on a toy dataset and then apply it to the task of affect recognition using multiple modalities. We also evaluate the performance of other classifier combination schemes by training SVMs and the GP classifiers on the complete data. These standard classifier combination schemes are shown in Table 1.

Toy Dataset: A toy dataset is shown in figure 3(a), which has been previously introduced by Zhou et al. [15]. The top and the bottom half moon correspond to two different classes. The example shown in the figure has 15 labeled points from each class (30 total) and 100 test points (200 total). First, we perform two GP classifications using the method described in 2.1; one classifies the test points by just using the X-modality (dimension) and the other just using the Y-modality (dimension). Figures 3(b) & (c) show the results of these classifications using each individual modality, which is fairly poor. Figure 3(d) & (e) show classification using the sum and the product rule applied using the result of X and the Y classification. Finally, figure 3(f) shows successful classification using the mixture of GP framework. In figure 3(f) the data points drawn as triangles were classified with a greater weight on the Y modality and the data points drawn as circles with a greater weight on the X-modality. We can see from the

Table 2. Average recognition rates (standard deviation in parenthesis) for 24 runs on affect data

Table 1. Classifier Combination Methods

Rule	Criteria
Sum	$p(t=1|\mathbf{x}^{(1)}..\mathbf{x}^{(P)}) \propto \sum_{p=1}^{P} p(t=1|\mathbf{x}^{(p)})$
Product	$p(t=1|\mathbf{x}^{(1)}..\mathbf{x}^{(P)}) \propto \prod_{p=1}^{P} p(t=1|\mathbf{x}^{(p)})$
Max	$p(t=1|\mathbf{x}^{(1)}..\mathbf{x}^{(P)}) \propto \max_p p(t=1|\mathbf{x}^{(p)})$
Min	$p(t=1|\mathbf{x}^{(1)}..\mathbf{x}^{(P)}) \propto \min_p p(t=1|\mathbf{x}^{(p)})$
Vote	$p(t=1|\mathbf{x}^{(1)}..\mathbf{x}^{(P)}) \propto$ $\{\begin{matrix}1 & \text{if } \sum_{p=1}^{P}\lceil p(t=1|\mathbf{x}^{(p)})\rceil \geq \lceil\frac{P}{2}\rceil \\ 0 & \text{otherwise}\end{matrix}$

	SVM	GP
Face	52.66%(1.4)	52.78%(0.7)
Posture	82.99%(0.6)	82.02%(0.9)
Puzzle	60.82%(1.5)	60.54%(0.9)
Sum	63.63%(0.9)	81.34%(1.2)
Prod	63.76%(0.9)	81.34%(1.2)
Max	71.94%(1.5)	81.34%(1.0)
Min	71.94%(1.5)	81.37%(1.0)
Vote	62.35%(1.2)	60.90%(0.6)
Mix of GP	NA	**83.55%(1.2)**

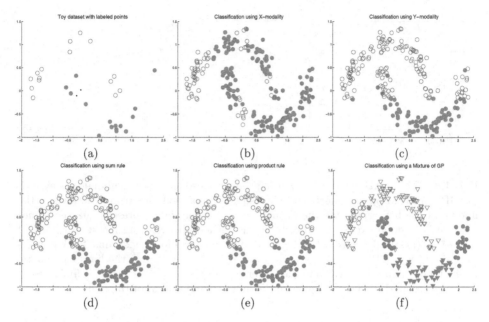

Fig. 3. (a) Toy dataset with the labeled points highlighted, and classification results using (b) X-modality only, (c) Y-modality only, (d) sum rule, (e) product rule and (f) the mixture of GP. The circles in (f) represent points classified with a greater weight on the X-modality and the triangles with a greater weight on the Y-modality

figure, that the final classification decision adapts itself according to the input space; thus, demonstrating the capability to perform sensor selection.

Recognizing Affect: We applied the mixture of GP framework to the problem of machine recognition of affect using multiple modalities. We look at the problem of detecting the affective state of interest in a child who is solving a puzzle on the computer. The training and the testing data consists of observations from three different channels: the face, posture and the puzzle activity. Every feature vector corresponding to a datapoint encodes the facial activity, posture activity and game information for a time segment of 8 secs [6]. The database includes 8 children and consists of 61 samples of high-interest, 59 samples of low-interest and 16 samples of refreshing. Only 49 samples had all three channels present. The other 87 samples had the face channel missing. In this paper, we only look at the binary problem of detecting the state of high-interest (61 samples) versus the states of low-interest and refreshing (75 samples).

We trained GP classifiers for each of the three channels using an RBF kernel to compute the similarity matrices for the GP priors with the kernel-width hyper-parameter σ fixed to 0.81, 7.47 and 5.90 for the face, the posture and the puzzle channel respectively. The value of ϵ was fixed at 0.42 for face, 0.0 for posture and 0.37 for the puzzle modality. These parameters were choosen using evidence maximization a standard approach within the Bayesian framework. We

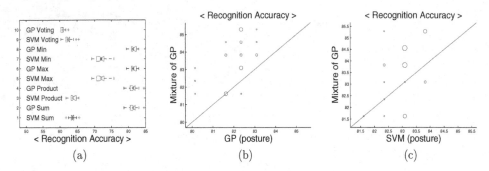

Fig. 4. (a) MATLAB boxplots comparing the standard classifier combination methods for GP and SVM on the affect data. The squares represent the mean, the lines in the middle of the box represents the median, the bounding box represent quartile values and the '+' symbols represent the statistical outliers. (b) Recognition rates of mix of GP vs. GP(posture) and (c) Mix of GP vs. SVM(posture) for the 24 runs. Each point is (accuracy SVM/GP (posture), accuracy mix of GP). Points over the lines correspond to the trials when mix of GP had the better recognition rate. The circle radii represent repeating results; the larger the circle the more the repetition of the points

randomly selected 87.5% of the points as training data and computed the hyperparamters using evidence maximization. This process was repeated 10 times and the mean values of the hyperparameters were used in our experiments. The P-way classification for estimating the posterior over λ^* was also performed using an RBF kernel with kernel width set to 10.38.

We also evaluate the performance of SVM on this dataset. The SVMs were trained using an RBF kernel and the leave-one-out validation procedure was applied for selecting the penalty parameter C and the kernel width σ. The validation procedure was performed ten times, where each time 87.5% of datapoints were randomly choosen as training data. The mean of the resulting 10 parameters (σ, C) were finally choosen and were equal to (10.48, 1.49), (11.47, 1.33) and (10.66, 2.24) for the face, the posture and the puzzle modality respectively.

We performed 8-fold cross-validation to report the results. In every round the dataset was equally split into 8 parts. The algorithms were tested on every part with the other 7 parts (87.5% of data) used as the training set. Each of these rounds was repeated 24 times to report the results.

First, we compare the performance of standard classifier combination methods for GP based classification and SVMs. The GP classification provides class probabilities for the datapoints, which can directly be used in the standard classifier combination methods (table 1). The sigmoid function can be used to map an SVM output to a value between 0 and 1 and can be used to combine classifiers using the standard rules. There have been many other approaches suggested to convert the SVM output to a probability value and we leave the comparison of those as future work. Figure 4 shows the MATLAB boxplots and compares the performance of the different fixed classifier combination approaches for GP and SVM. The figure plots the mean, the median and quartile values. The figure shows that the GP based classifier combinations outperform the classifier combinations based on the probabilistic interpretation of the SVM output.

Further, table 2 shows the recognition results for each individual modality and many classifier combination rules. Among the individual modalities, the posture channel achieves the highest recognition both with the GP classification and the SVM. Further, it can be easily seen that the classification based on the posture modality outperforms the standard classifier combination rules. Since most of the discriminating information is contained in the posture channel, the standard classifier combination methods don't work well as they assign equal importance to all the channels. The mixture of GP approach on the other hand is sensitive to this kind of information and thus can adapt to whichever channel works well. The scatter plots shown in the figures 4 (b) and (c) compares the performance of every single trial among the 24 runs of the mixture of GP approach vs SVM/GP classifiers trained on the posture modality. It can be seen clearly that the mixture of GP based approach outperforms the posture modality both when using SVM and GP classification and with table 2 we can see that it outperforms the standard classifier combination methods.

4   Conclusions and Future Work

In this paper, we proposed a unified approach using a mixture of Gaussian Processes for achieving sensor fusion under the challenging conditions of missing channels and noisy labels. We provide a Bayesian algorithm designed with a fast update of classification decisions based on variational and Gaussian approximations. On both a toy example, and on the task of classifying affective state of interest using information from face, postures and task information, the mixture of GP method outperforms several standard classifier combination schemes. Future work includes incorporation of active learning and application of this framework to other challenging problems with limited labeled data.

Acknowledgments

Thanks to Yuan (Alan) Qi for helpful comments. This research was supported by NSF ITR grant 0325428.

References

1. M. J. Beal, Variational Algorithms for Approximate Bayesian Inference, Ph.D. Thesis, University College London, 2003.
2. L. Breiman, Bagging Predictors, *Machine Learning*, Vol. 26(2), 1996.
3. J. Han, B. Bhanu, Statistical Feature Fusion for Gait-based Human Recognition, *CVPR*, 2004.
4. L. Hong, and A. K. Jain, Integrating Faces and Fingerprints for Personal Identification, *PAMI*, Vol. 20(1), 1998.

5. R. A. Jacobs, M. I. Jordan, S. J. Nowlan and G .E. Hinton, Adaptive Mixtures of Local Experts, *Neural Computation,* Vol. 3, pp. 79-87, 1991.
6. A. Kapoor, R. W. Picard and Y. Ivanov, Probabilistic Combination of Classifiers to Detect Interest, *ICPR,* 2004.
7. J. Kittler, M. Hatef, R. P. W. Duin and J. Matas, On Combining Classifiers, *PAMI,* Vol. 20(3), 1998.
8. D. J. Miller and L. Yan, Critic-Driven Ensemble Classification, *Signal Processing,* Vol. 47(10), 1999.
9. T. Minka, Expectation Propagation for Approximate Bayesian Inference, *UAI,* 2001.
10. N. Oliver, A. Garg and E. Horvitz, Layered Representations for Learning and Inferring Office Activity from Multiple Sensory Channels, *ICMI,* 2002.
11. M. Opper and O. Winther, Mean field methods for Classification with Gaussian Processes, *NIPS,* Vol. 11, 1999.
12. R. Schapire, A Brief Introduction to Boosting, *International Conference on Algorithmic Learning Theory,* 1999.
13. K. Toyama and E. Horvitz, Bayesian Modality Fusion: Probabilistic Integration of Multiple Vision Algorithms for Head Tracking, *ACCV,* 2000.
14. V. Tresp, Mixture of Gaussian Processes, *NIPS,* Vol. 13, 2001.
15. D. Zhou, O. Bousquet, T. N. Lal, J. Weston and B. Scholkopf, Learning with Local and Global Consistency, *NIPS,* Vol. 16, 2004.

Dynamic Classifier Integration Method

E. Kim[1] and J. Ko[2]

[1] National Computerization Agency,
NCA Bldg, 77, Mugyo-dong, Jung-gu, Seoul 100-775, Korea
outframe@nca.go.kr
[2] Dept. of CE, Kumoh National Institute of Technology,
1 Yangho-dong, Gumi, Gyeongbuk 730-701, Korea
nonezero@kumoh.ac.kr

Abstract. The diversity of application domains of pattern recognition makes it difficult to find a highly reliable classification algorithm for sufficiently interesting tasks. In this paper we propose a new combining method, which harness the local confidence of each classifier in the combining process. Our method is at the confluence of two main streams of combining multiple classifiers: classifier fusion and classifier selection. This method learns the local confidence of each classifier using training data and if an unknown data is given, the learned knowledge is used to evaluate the outputs of individual classifiers. An empirical evaluation using five real data sets has shown that this method achieves a promising performance and outperforms the best single classifiers and other known combining methods we tried.

1 Introduction

In the field of character recognition, multiple classifier systems based on classifier fusion (or combination) methods have been proposed as an approach to develop a high performance recognition system [1,2,3,4,5]. At this point, it is well known that a combination of many different classification algorithms can improve classification accuracy. This is because classification algorithms based on different methodologies and/or using different input features have complementary characteristics. Classifiers based on different architectures and different feature sets do not necessarily have the same recognition error, which may be regarded as error independent [6]. By exploiting the complementary characteristics, combination mechanisms can take advantage of the strengths of the individual classifiers, avoid their weaknesses, and improve their classification accuracy. As described above, it is generally easier to apply several error independent classifiers to the same recognition task and use their error independence to improve recognition performance of a combined system than to invent a new architecture or a feature extractor to achieve the same accuracy. Despite promising results reported in the literature, performances of a multiple classifier system greatly depend on the assumption that classifiers exhibit a sufficiently large uncorrelation in their classification errors [7]. Some researchers clearly showed an increase in classification accuracy of combination scheme is possible only if the assumption is satisfied [7]. In real pattern recognition problem, this assumption of independent

N.C. Oza et al. (Eds.): MCS 2005, LNCS 3541, pp. 97–107, 2005.

classification error is very difficult to keep. To design and train independent classifiers is difficult, even if each classifier is based on different methodologies or feature sets. This significantly limits their applicability.

In this paper, we present a new ensemble method called dynamic fusion. This method exploits the advantages of both of classifier fusion system and selection system.

2 Previous Works

Generally, combining method of multiple classifiers can be divided into two types: classifier fusion and classifier selection. The conventional approaches belonging to the classifier fusion method generally calculate the weight of each classifier by estimating its average error over the entire range of training data. This averaging activity causes the combining algorithm to become insensitive to differences in the local performance of base classifiers. As a result, it is unable to take into account the local expertise of each classifier for a final decision. When a new instance is difficult to classify, then the average classifier will give an erroneous prediction, and the majority vote will probably result in a wrong prediction. The problem may consist in discarding base classifiers (by assigning small weights through averaging process) that are highly accurate in a restricted region of the instance space because this accuracy is swamped by their inaccuracy elsewhere. It may also consist in the use of classifiers that are accurate in most of the space but still unnecessarily confuse the entire classification committee in some regions of the space.

Classifier selection has the merit of considering the locality. This method divides the entire feature space into partitions and nominates the best classifier for each partition during the training time. The classifier selection method has two main problems: The first problem is owing to the selection of best classifier. If a classifier pairs with a partition of feature space, some classifiers might be never selected and never have a chance to take part in the combining scheme afterwards. This is because the number of classifiers is not necessarily equal to the number of regions K. When a new instance is difficult to classify, then the selected classifier will give a wrong prediction. The problem may consist in discarding the classifiers with a highest accuracy over the whole feature space and can give complementary information to cover the mistake of the selective classifier. For highly noisy data, this method is less desirable than the classifier fusion method since the decision is compromised by a single large error. In short, the weakening of a group consensus strategy is one drawback of the classifier selection approach. Generally, Classifier selection method partitions a space into separate regions with a one-to-one mapping to classifiers and trains each classifier as a local expert [8,9,10,11,12]. Such mapping information is used as a gating function for expert selection for a given unknown pattern. One of the most representative methods of classifier selection is Mixture of Experts (MoE) [8,9].

Recently, some works addressed problems produced by the "divide-and-conquer" strategy. Different classifiers will tend to make errors in different ways because of their varying architecture or their differing measurements extracted from the pattern. For the same reasons, the skilled regions of one classifier can also be distinct from those of other classifiers. Dynamic integration of classifiers is based on the assumption that each committee member is best inside certain sub areas of the whole feature space. A common point of most works belonging to this category is that they estimate each classifier's accuracy in local regions of feature space surrounding an unknown test sample, and then use the decision of the most locally accurate classifier [8,9,10]. For implementation, the local regions are frequently defined in terms of the K-nearest neighbors located in the vicinity of a given test sample in the training data.

A dynamic meta-classification framework consisting of two levels was proposed by [10]. The first level contains base classifiers, while the second level contains a combining algorithm that predicts the local classification errors for each of the base classifiers through several cross-validation runs. In the training phase, the information is collected about the local errors of the base classifiers for each training instance. The weighted nearest neighbor prediction (WNN) is used to predict classification error of each base classifier in the application phase. Woods et al. [13] proposed a method that estimates local accuracy of each classifier instead of dividing the whole feature space. The basic idea is to estimate each classifier's accuracy in local regions of feature space surrounding an unknown test sample, and then uses the decision of the most locally accurate classifier. They define the local regions in terms of the K-nearest neighbors of input instance in the training data.

A dynamic integration system can be regarded as a sort of classifier selection approach in that it selects the best classifier from multiple base classifiers. However, it differs from the classifier selection approach in that it is not concerned about how each base classifier is generated. Instead, it concentrates on learning the local region in which each classifier is expert.

As mentioned above, dynamic integration methods generally perform a "lazy selection" in the application phase by employing "lazy learning" method such as K-nearest neighbor algorithm to estimate the local accuracy of each base classifier and select of best classifier [16]. Lazy classifier selection method based on lazy learning defers the definition of local area until each new instance is encountered, in the application phase. They divide the whole input space into two regions in view of a new input instance (local region near to new instance and the remaining long-distance region). Their region segmentation method and segmentation time differ from the traditional classifier selection method, which divides the entire feature space into several sub regions during training phase. Fig.1 illustrates those two types of region segmentation.

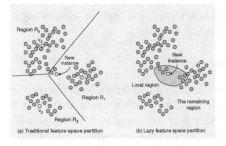

Fig. 1. Comparison between eager and lazy partition

In this paper, we introduce a new combining algorithm belonging to the dynamic integration approach, but use a sort of "eager learning" method rather than "lazy learning" method to speed up the processing time of evaluating the local accuracy of each base classifier. Our method is at the confluence of two main streams: classifier fusion and classifier selection.

3   Dynamic Classifier Integration

Here, we propose a framework of the classifier integration method based on local confidence. Our system consists of three parts: base classifiers, an aggregation network and a weight-adapting network as shown in Fig. 2.

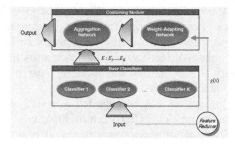

Fig. 2. Combination framework based on local confidence

An aggregation network and a weight-adapting network are closely connected to each other, since the outputs of the weight-adapting network are used as weights of the aggregation network. Without the weight-adapting network, this framework can be regarded as a sort of classifier fusion system with a linear combination methodology. The weight-adapting network introduces dynamic characteristics to this fusion system. It learns the degree of expertise of each classifier in local area and informs aggregation network of the learned knowledge. The training process only occurs in the weight-adapting network and the aggregation network merely exploits the learned knowledge of weight-adapting network by using outputs of the weight-adapting network as its weight values.

The concept of local confidence and process of training and test will be discussed in more detail in the next sub sections.

3.1   Local Confidence

Different classifiers will tend to make errors in different ways because of their varying architecture or their different measurement extracted from the pattern. For the same reasons, the skilled regions of one classifier can also be distinct from other classifiers. The conventional approaches to combining multiple classifiers with weight calculate the weight of each classifier by estimating the average error on the whole training data. Because of the diversity of the ways in which individual classifiers make a mistake as described above, a more elaborate weighting scheme is needed.

Definition 1. The **Local Confidence** LC_k of classifier k is a *degree of expertise* of classifier k in a local region of feature space.

In the literature of dynamic integration system, several ways exist to estimate the local confidence. Woods et al. [13] simply defines local region in terms of K-nearest neighbor during the application phase and suggests two methods for calculating local accuracy. One is simply the percentage of training samples in the region that are correctly classified. Another possibility is to estimate local accuracy with respect to some output class. We can determine the percentage of the local training samples assigned to class C_i by a classifier k that has been correctly labeled.

In this paper, we evaluate three functions estimating local confidence, derived from the predicted error of each classifier with respect to the given input as follows:

$$LC_k(x) = \frac{1 - \sum_{i=1}^{M} |d_i(x) - m_{ik}|}{M} \tag{1}$$

$$LC_{ik}(x) = 1 - |d_i(x) - m_{ik}| \tag{2}$$

$$LC_k(x) = \begin{cases} 1, & if \ \ d(x) = E_k(x) \\ 0, & otherwise \end{cases} \tag{3}$$

where $LC_k(x)$ means the local confidence of classifier k on give input x, $LC_{ik}(x)$ is a confidence value of classifier k on the class i, $d(x)$ is a target class of the given input x, $d_i(x)$ is a desired output value for class i on given input x, and m_{ik} is a measurement value of classifier k, meaning the possibility assigning input x to class i.

3.2 Training

In our implementation, the local confidence vector $LC_k = (w_{1k}, w_{2k}, ..., w_{Mk})$ of classifier k is a M-dimensional vector which contains the measurement values on local expertise of the kth classifier with respect to each class and w_{ik} is a local confidence value of classifier k with respect to class i. To learn the local confidence of each classifier, the training data set should be generated from the predictions of base classifiers and the transformed vector of the input.

Training data are generated through two parallel steps: the base classifier prediction and the feature transformation (or reduction). The prediction results of base classifiers and transformed feature values are merged as a training data set for weight-adapting network. Various transformation functions can be used for this purpose. For example, Clustering algorithm such as K-means or Self Organizing Map (SOM), Principle Component Analysis (PCA), and other statistical methods able to reduce feature dimensions can be used. An identity function without reducing feature dimensions can be also used.

$$r\_vec = g(x) \tag{4}$$

where $r\_vec = (r\_vec_1, r\_vec_2, ..., r\_vec_r)$ is a reduced feature vector, r_vec_i is a ith value of r_vec, g is a selected transformation function, and $x = (x_1, x_2, ..., x_n)$ is an original feature vector.

The weight-adapting network can be single- or multi-layered perceptrons. In this paper, we construct the weight-adapting network with a multi-layered perceptrons. Note that the weights of a classifier can be different from each other identical for all classes according to the selection of a confidence function $LC_k(x)$.

The error function $E(x)$ of weight-adapting network is defined by:

$$E(x) = \frac{1}{KM} \sum_{k=1}^{K} \sum_{i=1}^{M} (LC_{ik}(x) - WNet_{ik}(r\_vec))^2 \tag{5}$$

where K is the number of base classifiers, M is the number of classes, $WNet_{ik}(x)$ is the output of weight-adapting network for classifier k with respect to class i. The standard back-propagation (BP) algorithm has been used for weight adjustments in the mode of pattern-by-pattern updating [17].

Our training algorithm can be summarized as follows:

Training Process of Dynamic Fusion based on Local Confidence

T_W: weight-adapting network training set
$WNet$: weight-adapting network
LC_k: Local Confidence vector of classifier k

1. Design the individual classifiers E_1, ..., E_K using the labeled data set T.

2. For each data x in T, estimate the local accuracy of E_i with respect to class s. To accomplish this, take measurement values offered for x by classifier E_i, $i=1$, ..., L, and calculate the errors by comparing the measurement values with class label of x. Estimate the local confidence with respect to each class with those errors.

3. Construct weight-adapting network training set T_w using all x in T and the local confidence obtained for x.

4. Train weight-adapting network $WNet$ with T_w to approximate the local confidence vector LC_k with respect to each classifier for every x in T.

5. Return trained weight-adapting network WNet.

3.3 Operation

The aggregation network takes E_1, ..., E_K, as input, where $E_k = (m_{1k}, m_{2k}, ..., m_{Mk})$ is a M-dimensional vector containing the measurement values the kth classifier produces for the given pattern. The output of the aggregation network is the final decision. Let $O = (o_1, ..., o_M)$ be the final decision vector. If we consider a single-layered perceptions without bias as an aggregation network and the linear transfer function as activation function, the output o_i for class i is the weighted summation of the measurement values. This can be shown as:

$$o_i = \sum_{k=1}^{K} w_{ik} m_{ik} \tag{6}$$

The weight w_{ik} denotes the degree of importance of the kth classifier for class i and implies the estimation of how important the kth classifier is for the classification of the class i compared to other classifiers.

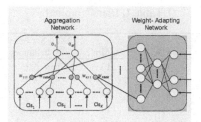

Fig. 3. Inner architecture of the combining module

Fig.3 shows the relation between the aggregation network and weight-adapting network. As shown in the figure, the outputs of the weight-adapting network are exploited as a weight of aggregation network. Therefore, the number of nodes in the output layer in the weight-adapting network equals the total number of weights in aggregation network. This architecture gives our method the ability to dynamically estimate the local expertise of individual classifiers.

The outputs of weight-adapting network can be organized as the matrix W:

$$
W = \begin{bmatrix} w_{11} & w_{21} & \cdots & w_{M1} \\ w_{12} & w_{22} & \cdots & w_{M2} \\ \vdots & \vdots & & \vdots \\ w_{1K} & w_{2K} & \cdots & w_{MK} \end{bmatrix} = \begin{bmatrix} w_1 & w_2 & \cdots & w_K \end{bmatrix} \tag{7}
$$

The kth row of W is the estimated LC_k meaning the local expertness of classifier k for each class.

4 Experimental Results

Five real datasets from *University of California, Irvine* (UCI) *Repository of Machine Learning Database* [18] were used in the experiment for our combining approach. The properties of the datasets are shown in Table 1. We used fifteen base classifiers for this experiment: three neural networks trained by a general backpropagation algorithm (NN1, NN2, and NN3), another three decor related neural networks (DCNN1, DCNN2, and DCNN3) [2], five K-nearest neighbor classifiers using different number of K: $K=3$, 7, 11, 15, 21 (KNN1, KNN2, KNN3, KNN4, and KNN5) and four support vector machines with different kernel functions: linear, RBF, polynomial with degree 2, and polynomial with degree 3 (SVM1, SVM2, SVM3, and SVM4). All neural networks are different from each other in the number of hidden units and initial weights.

Table 2, 3, 4 and 5 show the experimental results on those four groups, respectively. In the table 4, the improvement from LCCOMB was relatively small. We assume this is because K-nearest neighbor classifiers are 'stable' and therefore don't benefit as much from combining as 'unstable' classifiers such as neural networks.

Table 5 shows the comparison between combining algorithms. For the experiment, results from all classifiers (NN1, NN2, NN3, DCNN1, DCNN2, DCNN3, DCNN4, KNN1, KNN2, KNN3, KNN4, KNN5, SVM1, SVM2, SVM3, and SVM4) were combined.

Table 1. Dataset properties

| Data Set | Data Set Properties | | | |
	# Cls.	# Attr.	# Instances	Test
Australian Credit	2	14	690	(10-fold CV)
Image Segment	7	19	2,310	(10-fold CV)
Satellite Image	6	36	6,435	2,000
Vehicle	4	18	846	(9-fold CV)
Pima Indian	2	8	768	(10-fold CV)

Table 2. Classification errors of the three neural networks and our proposed method on them

| | Classifier | Data Set | | | | |
		Australian Credit	Image Segment	Satellite image	Vehicle	Pima Indian
	NN1	14.78	5.15	17.65	19.51	24.48
	NN 2	14.49	5.24	18.30	19.27	24.48
Error Rate (%)	NN 3	14.78	5.15	17.65	19.27	24.48
	LCCOMB(ORG)	**13.91**	**4.02**	15.30	18.21	23.08
	LCCOMB(KM)	14.49	4.98	13.64	**16.44**	23.61
	LCCOMB(PCA)	**13.35**	5.02	**12.30**	18.79	**22.16**

Table 3. Classification errors of three decorrelated neural networks and our method on them

| | Classifier | Data Set | | | | |
		Australian Credit	Image Segment	Satellite image	Vehicle	Pima Indian
	DCNN1	15.51	4.07	12.60	17.84	23.42
	DCNN 2	14.78	4.50	11.73	16.19	23.71
Error Rate (%)	DCNN 3	15.51	4.28	11.25	17.96	24.00
	LCCOMB(ORG)	**14.64**	3.25	11.00	15.13	21.71
	LCCOMB(KM)	15.22	3.25	**10.70**	15.13	20.00
	LCCOMB(PCA)	14.93	**3.20**	11.35	**15.01**	**18.42**

Table 4. Classification errors of the five K-neaneighbor classifiers and our method on them

| | Classifier | Data Set | | | | |
		Australian Credit	Image Segment	Satellite image	Vehicle	Pima Indian
	KNN 1	15.94	4.94	10.75	31.21	25.66
	KNN 2	15.07	5.24	10.75	29.43	25.66
	KNN 3	15.36	5.41	10.90	31.32	26.05
Error Rate (%)	KNN 4	14.64	5.50	12.25	30.73	25.00
	KNN5	14.06	6.10	11.90	32.03	25.13
	LCCOMB(ORG)	14.93	4.33	10.55	28.72	24.74
	LCCOMB(KM)	14.64	4.50	10.70	29.31	24.21
	LCCOMB(PCA)	14.49	4.33	10.65	28.96	24.74

Table 5. Classification errors of the four support vector machines and our method on them

	Classifier	Data Set				
		Australian Credit	Image Segment	Satellite image	Vehicle	Pima Indian
	SVM1	14.49	6.80	17.85	22.23	24.74
	SVM2	14.49	6.71	16.80	20.57	26.58
Error	SVM3	14.50	6.58	16.20	21.09	24.47
Rate	SVM4	14.86	6.45	16.35	22.00	24.82
(%)	LCCOMB(ORG)	14.49	6.57	15.78	**19.24**	24.34
	LCCOMB(KM)	**14.35**	6.32	**15.06**	20.09	24.34
	LCCOMB(PCA)	14.49	**5.26**	15.78	19.83	**23.86**

Table 6. Classification errors of combining algorithms

	Classifier	Data Set				
		Australian Credit	Image Segment	Satellite image	Vehicle	Pima Indian
	Majority Vote	14.05	4.72	16.95	17.69	24.10
Error	ProductRule	13.98	4.58	16.34	18.62	23.96
Rate	LCCOMB(ORG)	12.96	3.60	11.64	**16.83**	22.37
(%)	LCCOMB(KM)	13.24	**3.12**	11.82	16.98	22.93
	LCCOMB(PCA)	**11.94**	**3.12**	**10.09**	16.98	**20.00**

To implement our method, we use three different transformation functions: original data (ORG), reduced feature by K-means algorithm (KM), reduced feature by PCA (PCA). The error rate of every table is the average of 10-fold (or 9-fold) cross-validation runs except the satellite image dataset. For the aggregation network, a single-layered feedforward neural network was used and for the weight-adapting network, a multi-layered feedforward neural network was used. The weight-adapting network was trained with a gradient-descendent method with a momentum. The proposed method shows a better performance than any individual classifiers on all the dataset we tried.

5 Conclusions

We have proposed a multiple classifier combining method based on local confidence. Our main idea is based on the fact that different classifiers potentially offer complementary information about the patterns to be classified. Specifically, if we can consider the local expertise of each classifier into the combining process, the performance will be improved. The proposed method combines the advantages of classifier fusion and classifier selection, which are the two main categories of traditional combining algorithms. This method reflects the opinions of all classifiers like in classifier fusion approach and the weight of each classifier's opinion (the importance of individual classifier) is recalculated dynamically according to the given input as in the classifier selection approach.

The contributions of our proposed method can be summarized as follows. In the view of accuracy, we attempt to obtain more accuracy than the classifier fusion method by using the local accuracy of each classifier. We also try to improve on the classifier selection method by strengthening the aspect of "group consensus." From the viewpoint of efficiency, we choose "eager learning" rather than "lazy learning" to learn the local accuracy of each classifier, compared with the work of Woods et al. We believe that this choice makes our method more effective than that of Woods.

We used the five real data sets from UCI data repository in the experimental evaluation. The results show that the proposed combining method outperforms the other combining methods as well as any individual classifiers. Based on these encouraging results, we can expect that the proposed combining method can be successfully applied to the classification task in the real world case with more accuracy than traditional data mining approaches.

References

1. Gader D., Hepp D., Forester B., Peurach T., and Mitchell T.: Pipelined systems for recognition of handwritten digits in USPS ZIP codes, Proc. of U.S. Postal Service Advanced Technology Conference, (1990) 539-548.
2. Kimura F., Shridhar M.: Handwritten Numeral Recognition Based on Multiple Algorithms, Pattern Recognition, 24 (10) (1991) 969-983.
3. Matsui T., Noumi T., Yamashita I., Wakahara T., and Yoshimuro M.: State of the Art of Handwritten Numeral Recognition in japan-The results of the First IPTP Character Recognition Competition, Proc. of the 2nd ICDAR, (1993) 391-396.
4. Noumi T. et al: Result of Second IPTP Character Recognition Competition and Studies on Multi-Expert Handwritten Numeral Recognition, Proc. of 4th IWFHR, (1994) 338-346.
5. Xu L., Krzyzak A., and Suen Y.: Method of Combining Multiple Classifiers and Their Application to Handwritten Numeral Recognition, IEEE Trans. on Systems, Man and Cybernetics, 22 (3) (1992) 418-435.
6. Tumer K., and Ghosh J.: Linear and order statistics combiners for pattern classification, In A.J.C. Sharkey, editor, Combining Artificial Neural Nets, (1999) 127-161.
7. Tumer K., and Gosh J.: Error correlation and error reduction in ensemble classifiers, Tech. Report, Dept. of ECE, University of Texas, (1996) July 11.
8. M. I. Jordan and R. A. Jacobs: Hierarchical Mixtures of Experts and the EM Algorithm, Neural Computation, 6, (1994) 181-214.
9. M. I. Jordan and R. A. Jacobs: Modular and Hierarchical Learning Systems, In M.A.Arbib, ed., The Handbook of Brain Theory and Neural Networks, (1995).
10. Ran Avnimelech and Nathan Intrator: Boosted Mixture of Experts: An Ensemble Learning Scheme, Neural Computation, 11(2), (1999) 483-497.
11. Bin Tang, Malcolm I. Heywood, and Michael Shepherd: Input partitioning to mixture of experts, International Joint Conference on Neural Networks, (2002) 227-232.
12. Henry Stern: Improving on the mixture of experts algorithm, CSCI 6508: Fundamentals of Computational Neuroscience project, Dalhousie University, Halifax, NS, Canada, (2003).
13. Woods K.: Combination of Multiple Classifiers Using Local Accuracy Estimates, IEEE Trans. on Pattern Analysis and Machine Intelligence, 19(4) 405-410.
14. Mitiche M., Thomas D., and Nagy G.: Classifier Combination for Handprinted Digit Recognition, Proc. of 2nd Int'l Conf. on DAR, (1993) 163-166.

15. Tsymbal A.:Decision Committee Learning with Dynamic Integration of Classifier, Lecture Notes in Computer Science, (2000).
16. Mitchell T.: Machine Learning, Mcgraw Hill, (1997).
17. Rumelhard E., Hinton E., and Williams J.: Learning internal representations by error propagation, Parallel Distributed Processing: Explorations in the Microstructures of Cognition, MIT Press, Cambridge MA, (1996).
18. Blake C., Keogh E., and Merz J.: UCI repository of Machine Learning databases, (1999) http://www.ics.uci.edu/~mlearn/MLRepository.html.

Using Dempster-Shafer Theory in MCF Systems to Reject Samples

Christian Thiel, Friedhelm Schwenker, and Günther Palm

Department of Neural Information Processing,
Universität Ulm, 89069 Ulm, Germany
{cthiel, fschwenker, palm}@neuro.informatik.uni-ulm.de

Abstract. In this paper the Dempster-Shafer theory of evidence is utilised in multiple classifier systems to define rejection criteria for samples presented for classification. The DS theory offers the possibility to derive a measure of contradiction between the classifier decisions to be fused. Moreover, assigning positive belief mass to the universal hypothesis Θ in the basic probability assignments produced by the classifiers, allows to quantify the belief in their correctness. Both criteria have been evaluated by numerical simulations on two different benchmark data sets. The results are compared to standard static classifier combination schemes and basic classifiers. It is shown that DS classifier fusion can boost the combined classifier accuracy to 100% on the set of accepted data points ($\sim 70\%$). This behaviour could be of interest in applications with high costs for a *miss*, e.g. in medical screening tests.

1 Introduction

The Dempster-Shafer (DS) theory of evidence, also known as the theory of belief functions, is a tool for representing and combining evidence. Being a generalisation of Bayesian reasoning, it does not require probabilities for each question of interest, but the belief in a hypothesis can be based on the probabilities of related questions. Contributing to its success is the fact that the belief and the ignorance or uncertainty concerning a question can be modelled independently.

Here, Dempster-Shafer theory has been chosen over probability theory [1], possibility theory [2] and fuzzy theory [3, 4] because of its straightforward application to the problem, and experimental results [5] showing that it performs well in the area of classifier fusion. The above mentioned theories are categorised with respect to their behaviour and the information they depend on in [6].

The Dempster-Shafer theory was brought forward by Dempster [7] and Shafer [8], then came to the attention of artificial intelligence researchers in the early 1980s as an approach to adopt probability theory to expert systems [9] and is still applied in this field [10, 11]. We will use the theory in the context of the fusion of multiple classifiers in order to define rejection criteria, exploiting its features to model uncertainty and conflict of final decisions. This allows to boost the accuracy on the accepted data, which is desired in situations where

N.C. Oza et al. (Eds.): MCS 2005, LNCS 3541, pp. 118–127, 2005.
© Springer-Verlag Berlin Heidelberg 2005

a missclassification is very expensive or must not happen. As a possibility to evaluate the doubt in a decision, *certainty measures* are used.

In the next section, the basic concepts of the Dempster-Shafer theory and some special aspects needed for our purpose will be presented; Section 3 briefly describes how in related works the sensor answers are converted into measures suitable for the DS theory. The experiment setup and results are presented in Section 4 and evaluated in Section 5.

2   Introduction into the Basic Concepts of the Dempster-Shafer Theory

The Dempster-Shafer theory starts by assuming a universe of discourse, or *frame of discernment*, consisting of a finite set of mutually exclusive atomic hypotheses $\Theta = \{\theta_1, ..., \theta_q\}$. Let 2^Θ denote the set of all subsets of Θ. Then a function $m : 2^\Theta \to [0, 1]$ is called a *basic probability assignment (bpa)* if it satisfies

$$m(\emptyset) = 0 \quad \text{and} \quad \sum_{A \subseteq \Theta} m(A) = 1 \ . \tag{1}$$

So, according to the conditions above, *belief* can not only assigned to an atomic hypothesis, but some set $A = \{a_1, ...a_n\} \subset \Theta$. Hence, our belief in $m(A)$ represents our ignorance, which can not be subdivided among the subsets of A. Each element B with $m(B) > 0$ is called a *focal element*. Now with a bpa m, the *belief function* $bel : 2^\Theta \to [0, 1]$ is defined as

$$bel(B) = \sum_{A \subseteq B} m(A) \ . \tag{2}$$

It represents the minimum trust we can have in B because of the supporting subsets A. Looking at the definition, it can be noticed that $bel(\{\theta_k\}) = m(\{\theta_k\}) \ \forall \ k = 1 \ldots n$. Furthermore, if every focal element is an atomic hypothesis, we find ourselves in the situation of standard probability theory. To get an intuitive understanding, one can consider a basic probability assignment a generalisation of a probability density function and a belief function a generalisation of a probability function [12].

The most interesting part of the theory is the possibility to combine two bpas m_1 and m_2 on Θ with the *orthogonal sum* $m_{12} = m_1 \oplus m_2$ which is defined as

$$m_{12}(C) = K \sum_{A,B:A \cap B = C} m_1(A) \cdot m_2(B) \tag{3}$$

where

$$K^{-1} = 1 - \sum_{A,B:A \cap B = \emptyset} m_1(A) \cdot m_2(B) = \sum_{A,B:A \cap B \neq \emptyset} m_1(A) \cdot m_2(B) \ . \tag{4}$$

The factor K is a measure of contradition between m_1 and m_2, with $\log(K)$ being called the *weight of conflict*. The orthogonal sum $m_1 \oplus m_2$ exists iff $K^{-1} \neq 0$, elsewise the sources are said to be *total contradictory*. Combining multiple bpas can easily be realised, as the orthogonal sum is commutative and associative.

In the following, two aspects of the Dempster-Shafer framework will be presented that allow us to reject samples.

2.1   Assigning Belief to Θ (Doubt)

Any belief mass assigned to Θ, the universal hypothesis or proposition [13], represents the belief that the assignment of masses to other focal elements may be based on evidence that is not legitimate. Hence, $m(\Theta) > 0$ constitutes the doubt into the correctness of the bpas, and can be used to reject a sample to be classified. Except for [14], this rejection criterion possibility is not yet widely exploited in the literature.

Assigning belief to Θ can be effectuated by the sensor producing the bpas to be combined [15], or by the technique of discount factors.

The *discount factors* are an idea that dates back to Shafer's initial work [8] and have later been justified [16] in the context of the *transferable belief model*. Assuming a certainty measure C concerning the output of a classifier is given (in our case, $0 \leq C \leq 1$, where $C = 1$ indicates a very certain classifier). Then the bpa m induced by the output are scaled, or discounted, with C:

$$m_d(A_i) = C \cdot m(A_i), \quad m_d(\Theta) = 1 - C \cdot (1 - m(\Theta)) \tag{5}$$

The advantage is that the doubt, represented by $m_d(\Theta)$, inferred by the certainty measures, is taken into account automatically when now combining sensors with the orthogonal sum. But basically, the combined $m_d(\Theta)$ is based on the product of the inverted certainty measures, meaning that its value will decrease with each combination. This has to be taken into consideration when comparing doubt values, preferably restricting this to bpas that have been calculated over the same number of classifier combination steps.

Discounting can be done at different stages of the fusion process, for example for each classifier or even each class of each classifier, giving ample opportunity to incorporate expert knowledge.

2.2   Assigning Belief to $\emptyset$ (Conflict)

The combination via the orthogonal sum is not without problems. When bpas are combined, the result does not allow for any conclusions if there had been a conflict between the sources. In fact, Zadeh [17] constructed an example where the resulting bpas are equal, regardless if the sources were totally agreeing or quite contradictory. To get around this, it was suggested [18] to show a measure of conflict with each combination of two bpas m_1 and m_2:

$$conflict(m_1, m_2) = -\log(1 - K) \tag{6}$$

Here K is the conflict as defined earlier in Eq. 4.

But there is an even better way to preserve information about the conflicts of the merged sources: Using the orthogonal sum without its normalising denominator. The idea was brought up by Smets in the framework of the *transferable belief model*, which is based on the work of Dempster-Shafer. As explained in [19], the distribution of the probability mass missing to the sum of 1 among the remaining bpas A_i with $m(A_i) > 0$ is not good, inter alia, because *plausibility*(A_i) is defined as the maximal degree of support that can be assigned to A_i, and must not be increased by the combination. Instead, the missing mass should be assigned to some contradictory state, which is shown to be the empty set $\emptyset$. Thus, the belief $m(\emptyset)$ is a measure for the *conflict* or *disagreement* between all the sources that have been combined using the orthogonal sum without normalisation. Again, setting a threshold value for the conflict and rejecting samples that induced a higher conflict allows to boost the rate of correct classification.

Note that the combination of the two methods, hence unnormalised sum and using certainty factors to discount, does not work. The certainty factors alter the answers of each classifier, so that the conflict is not a viable measure any more.

3   How to Produce the Basic Probability Assignments - A Look at the Literature

As early as 1988, Mandler and Schürmann [20] developed a method to make use of the Dempster-Shafer theory in the process of multiple classifier fusion. Applied to on-line script recognition, they used a prototype based classification system. Each classifier, termed *expert*, produced a bpa that was calculated as the likelihood ratio of the intra-class-distance model to the inter-class-distance model, a measure that is also motivated by DS theory.

In their influential 1992 paper on methods of combining multiple classifiers [13], Xu, Krzyzak and Suen also tackled the issue. They used crisp classifiers, whose answer is a vote for exactly one class or rejection of the sample. On a test set, they estimated the recognition rate ϵ_r^k and substitution rate ϵ_s^k for each of the K classifiers. Out of those, a bpa function was constructed by basically defining

$$m_k(\theta_c) = \epsilon_r^k, \quad m_k(\neg\theta_c) = \epsilon_s^k, \quad m_k(\Theta) = 1 - \epsilon_r^k - \epsilon_s^k \tag{7}$$

with $\theta_c \in frame\ of\ discernment$ referring to one of the C possible classes. The introduction of $m_k(\Theta)$ was necessary to account for the rejection rate.

Rogova [12] applied the DS concept to the combination of multiple classifiers with fuzzy, not crisp, outputs. She built a bpa for each class c for each classifier, then combined the bpas per class with the orthogonal sum. The final decision was made for the class c with the highest pro-c evidence. The interesting twist is that the information concerning the other $\neg c$ classes was used in the construction of the first per-class-per-classifier bpas. Kuncheva, Bezdek and Duin included this approach in their experimental comparison [5] of the decision templates (DT) fusion technique with other, established methods. They came to the conclusion that the method "rated comparatively high on both data sets. It had a little lower final rank than the best DT techniques, and can be put basically in the same group."

Al-Ani and Deriche came up with a new variant in 2002 [21]. Their idea was to improve on the way Rogova calculated the bpas for each classifier and class. In her work, it was based on the distance between the classification of an input vector and a reference vector, which was calculated as the mean classification output on training data for the class. Now, the reference vectors are adopted so that the mean square error between the final output per class and the training vectors is minimised.

A somewhat similar approach has been taken by Denoeux [14] in 2000. However, his aim was to build a single classifier which produces a bpa. He uses protoypes with fuzzy memberships and adapts them using a neural network (MLP) to optimise a performance criterion. The Dempster-Shafer theory is employed to merge the information provided by each of the prototypes.

The papers by Milisavljevic and Bloch [15] and Le Hégarat-Mascle et al. [22] use expert knowledge about the domain of application, the detection of anti-personnel mines and the combination of multi-scale satellite data respectively, to produce the bpas. Because of this they are, unlike the other approaches, able to assign belief not only to atomic but also to compound hypotheses.

4   Experiments

The experiments were performed on two datasets, the images of *fruits* and of handwritten *numerals*. The first data set comes from a robotic environment. In the camera image, regions of interest are detected, and the task is to classify the fruit contained [23]. The dataset employed has 840 samples from 7 different classes (apples, oranges, plums...). Four features are extracted from each image: three histograms based on different parts of the greyscale image (left/middle/right) using the Sobel edge detector [24], representing the form of the three dimensional object, and the mean colour values of the image after it has been converted to the HSV colour space representation [25]. In our framework, the features are each classified with a Gaussian RBF network [26], the 10 and 7 prototypes per class for which have been calculated using the K-Means algorithm (details see [27]). Results are calculated using 5-fold cross validation.

The handwritten numerals data set consists of 10000 samples which are labeled according to their class 0 - 9 [28], each sample being originally represented by a 16x16 matrix containing greyscale values of 8 bit resolution. Three features have been used: The data projected onto the first 8 principal components of the training data, extracted by means of a Karhunen-Loève transformation (PCA) [29, 30], the sums over the rows and columns of the picture, with it being rotated ten times in the process (forming a big feature vector with a dimension of 320), and the picture matrix simply flattened to a 256-dimensional vector. The first two features were classified using the same procedure as described above, the last one using a Fuzzy K-Nearest-Neighbour algorithm [31]. Results are calculated using 10-fold cross validation on this set.

For the purpose of this paper, a straightforward method is used to construct the bpas: for a sample, the output of each classifier is normalised to sum up to one, and thus forms the bpa that will be fused with the belief assignments of the other classifiers using the orthogonal sum. The final classifying answer is extracted from the combined bpa using the maximum rule.

4.1   Rejection due to High Conflict

As described in Section 2.2, the not normalised orthogonal sum can be used to preserve knowledge about conflicting answers from the combined classifiers. If the conflict was above a certain threshold, meaning the allocation of belief mass above a certain threshold to $\emptyset$, the sample will be rejected (see Figure 1). The experiments (see Figure 2) showed that the accuracy on the accepted samples can be increased significantly. Accuracy of about 100% can be achieved on both data sets while discarding only about 34% of the presented data.

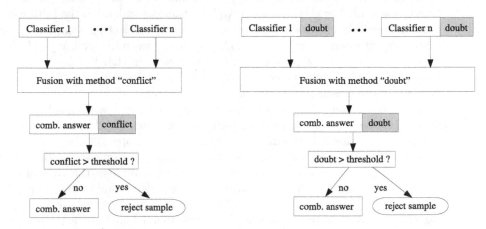

Fig. 1. Architecture of the two combination schemes. Classifier answers are fused, and a sample is rejected if the associated conflict or doubt is too high (meaning above a set threshold)

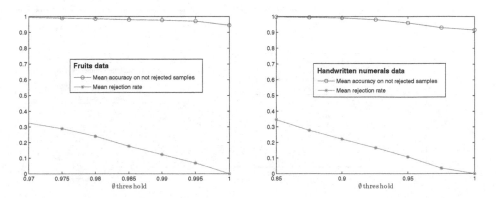

Fig. 2. Accuracy with not normalised DS fusion on the fruits and handwritten numerals data. Samples rejected if $m(\emptyset)$ above threshold (conflict)

4.2   Rejection due to High Doubt

The belief in Θ, the universal hypothesis, represents the doubt that the combined bpa is correct. The assignment of belief mass to Θ can, as mentioned in Section 2.1, be done by each classifier or sensor, or by using the technique of discount factors. As classifiers producing bpas on the fruits data set, we used the software published by Denoeux, which implements his algorithm described in [14]. As explained above, it is based on prototypes with fuzzy memberships, which are adapted using a neural network (MLP) to optimise a performance criterion. The output is a bpa which assigns masses only to atomic hypotheses but also Θ, which is why it was employed instead of our own framework. The software was run with the standard settings, mandating 5 prototypes per class and fuzzy memberships for them, also running the optimisation part. Each feature of the fruits data was classified separately, the results then fused using the standard orthogonal sum. The classifier seems to be rather dependent on the initialisation, the combined classification performance when not rejecting samples having a rather high standard deviation of 2.02, varying between an accuracy of 90% and 95%. The experiment was successful (see Figure 3) in that the accuracy can be increased by rejecting data points, for example a rejection rate of 0.3 yields an increase in the classification rate of 3 percent points.

For the assignment of belief to Θ in the experiment with the handwritten numerals data set, the discounting technique was employed. The certainty factor used was gained by calculating the Shannon entropy [32] for each classifier answer, normalising by $\log_2(\#classes)$, and subsequent inversion. The final factor is in the range between 0 and 1, with its maximum in the case of a crisp answer. Our assumption that the basic classifiers would tend to answer less fuzzy if they are sure and correct turned out to be true on the test data sets. The mean certainty factor of answers to samples a classifier labeled correctly was higher than for those samples on which the classifier was wrong. This resulted in a very successful setup, an accuracy of 100% being possible while rejecting only 13.7%

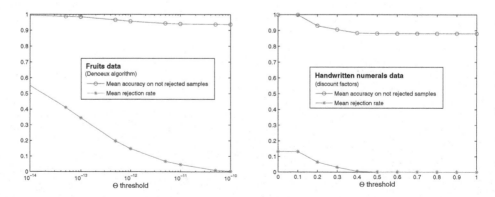

Fig. 3. Accuracy with DS fusion on the fruits (Denoeux algorithm) and handwritten numerals (discounting) data. Samples rejected if $m(\Theta)$ above threshold (doubt)

of the samples. For the performance on other data sets and techniques to even improve on that result, see [27].

5   Discussion

The main question was how much accuracy we can achieve by allowing a percentage of the samples to be rejected[1]. Thus we compared (Table 1) our Dempster-Shafer approaches to the basic classifiers we employed as well as the two static combination techniques *probabilistic product* and *median*, which had a generally good accuracy on our example data sets. It turns out that the combined classifiers always have a higher accuracy then any single classifier, with only the exception of the one operating on the picture feature which gives astonishingly clear answers. When rejecting samples, it is always one of our Dempster-Shafer

Table 1. Accuracy (in %) of different classifiers when rejecting at most the percentage of samples given in the first row. In the first half, accuracies are given for single classifiers working on only one feature, in the second half, accuracies for combined answers

Numerals	0	5	10	20	50	Fruits	0	5	10	20	50
PCA	87.6	90.7	92.1	94.9	98.8	histo_left	80.5	83.7	84.6	89.1	94.9
sums	**92.0**	**94.4**	96.2	97.8	99.6	histo_middle	**83.3**	85.6	**88.0**	**90.4**	96.1
picture	88.0	91.9	**99.0**	**99.9**	**99.9**	histo_right	82.4	**84.4**	86.7	90.2	94.4
						HSV	80.8	83.9	85.2	89.1	**96.2**
product	91.6	93.4	94.1	94.3	92.6	product	**95.4**	95.5	95.3	95.3	95.1
median	**92.1**	93.6	95.4	96.8	96.8	median	94.1	93.7	93.5	93.4	92.6
DS conflict	91.6	**94.9**	96.0	99.2	**100**	DS conflict	93.6	**98.0**	**98.0**	**98.8**	**100**
DS doubt	88.0	92.0	**97.4**	**100**	**100**	DS doubt	91.6	92.7	93.5	95.9	99.7

rejection methods who has the highest accuracy, being significantly better than the other basic combination schemes. While employing methods like Decision Templates [5, 35] or BKS [36] that incorporate further statistical information calculated by the classifiers on the training set will yield a higher accuracy, it is by using one of the Dempster-Shafer approaches and rejection that an accuracy of 100% can be achieved. This is useful in applications like medical screening tests where a false-negative is very expensive or must not happen, but rejected samples can just be reevaluated, decided using new data, or simply passed on to a human for review.

---

[1] On the basic classifiers, the RAD criterion [33] (the normalised distance to the nearest hard target vector) was used as basis for the rejection, the DIF criterion not yielding significantly different results. For the combined classifiers, the inverted *integral pairwise coincidence J5* from [34] was employed on the answers concerning the winning class, with no different outcome if the normalised variance was chosen instead. The rejection thresholds were raised from 0 to 1 with a step width of 0.01, for the DS combined fruits data the threshold range was 1e-18 to 1e-10.

References

1. Pearl, J.: Probabilistic Reasoning in Intelligent Systems: Networks of Plausible Inference. Morgan Kaufmann (1988)
2. Dubois, D., Prade, H.: Combination of information in the framework of possibility theory. In Abidi, M.A., Gonzalez, R.C., eds.: Data Fusion in Robotics and Machine Intelligence. Academic Press (1992) 481–505
3. Zadeh, L.A.: Fuzzy sets. Information and Control **8** (1965) 338–353
4. Zadeh, L.A.: Fuzzy sets as a basis for a theory of possibility. Fuzzy Sets and Systems **1** (1978) 3–28
5. Kuncheva, L.I., Bezdek, J.C., Duin, R.P.W.: Decision templates for multiple classifier fusion: An experimental comparison. Pattern Recognition **34** (2001) 299–314
6. Bloch, I.: Information combination operators for data fusion: A comparative review with classification. IEEE Transactions on Systems, Man and Cybernetics, Part A **26** (1996) 52–67
7. Dempster, A.P.: A generalization of Bayesian inference. Journal of the Royal Statistical Society **30** (1968) 205–247
8. Shafer, G.: A Mathematical Theory of Evidence. University Press, Princeton (1976)
9. Shafer, G.: Dempster-Shafer Theory. http://www.glennshafer.com/assets/downloads/article48.pdf (∼2002)
10. Grzymala-Busse, J.W.: Managing Uncertainty in Expert Systems. Kluwer Academic Publishers, Boston (1991)
11. Pomykalski, J.J., Truszkowski, W.F., Brown, D.E.: Expert systems. In Webster, J., ed.: Wiley Encyclopedia of Electronic and Electrical Engineering. (1999)
12. Rogova, G.: Combining the results of several neural network classifiers. Neural Networks **7** (1994) 777–781
13. Xu, L., Krzyzak, A., Suen, C.Y.: Methods of combining multiple classifiers and their applications to handwriting recognition. IEEE Transactions on Systems, Man, and Cybernetics **22** (1992) 418–435
14. Thierry Denoeux: A Neural Network Classifier Based on Dempster-Shafer Theory. IEEE Transactions on Systems, Man and Cybernetics, Part A **30** (2000) 131–150
15. Milisavljevic, N., Bloch, I.: Sensor fusion in anti-personnel mine detection using a two-level belief function model. IEEE Transactions on Systems, Man and Cybernetics, Part C **33** (2003) 269–283
16. Smets, P.: Belief functions: The disjunctive rule of combination and the generalized Bayesian theorem. International Journal of Approximate Reasoning **9** (1993) 1–35
17. Zadeh, L.A.: Book review: A mathematical theory of evidence. AI Magazine **5** (1984) 81–83
18. Heinsohn, J., Socher-Ambrosius, R.: Wissensverarbeitung. Eine Einführung. Spektrum Akademischer Verlag (1999)
19. Smets, P.: The nature of the unnormalized beliefs encountered in the transferable belief model. In: Proceedings of the 8th Conference on Uncertainty in Artificial Intelligence, San Mateo, California, Morgan Kaufmann (1992) 292–297
20. Mandler, E., Schürmann, J.: Combining the classification results of independent classifiers based on the Dempster/Shafer theory of evidence. Pattern Recognition and Artificial Intelligence (1988) 381–393
21. Al-Ani, A., Deriche, M.: A new technique for combining multiple classifiers using the Dempster-Shafer theory of evidence. Journal of Artificial Intelligence Research **17** (2002) 333–361

22. Le Hegarat-Mascle, S., Richard, D., Ottle, C.:   Multi-scale data fusion using Dempster-Shafer evidence theory.   Integrated Computer-Aided Engineering **10** (2003) 9–22
23. Fay, R., Kaufmann, U., Schwenker, F., Palm, G.: Learning Object Recognition in a NeuroBotic System. In Groß, H.M., Debes, K., Böhme, H.J., eds.: 3rd Workshop on SelfOrganization of AdaptiVE Behavior SOAVE 2004. Number 743 in Fortschritt-Berichte VDI, Reihe 10. VDI (2004) 198–209
24. Gonzales, R.C., Woods, R.E.: Digital Image Processing. 2nd edn. Addison-Wesley (1992)
25. Smith, A.R.: Color gamut transform pairs. In: Proceedings of the 5th Annual Conference on Computer Graphics and Interactive Techniques. Volume 12. (1978) 12–19
26. Schwenker, F., Kestler, H.A., Palm, G.: Three learning phases for radial-basis-function networks. Neural Networks **14** (2001) 439–458
27. Thiel, C.: Multiple Classifier Fusion Incorporating Certainty Factors. Master's thesis, University of Ulm, Germany (2004)
28. Michie, D., Spiegelhalter, D.J., Taylor, C.C., eds.: Machine Learning, Neural and Statistical Classification. Ellis Horwood, New York (1994)
29. Karhuhnen, K.: Zur Spektraltheorie stochastischer Prozesse. Annales Academiae Scientiarum Fennicae **34** (1946)
30. Loève, M.M.: Probability Theory. Van Nostrand, Princeton (1955)
31. Fukunaga, K.: Introduction to Statistical Pattern Recognition. 2nd edn. Academic Press, New York (1990)
32. Shannon, C.: A mathematical theory of communication. Bell System Technical Journal **27** (1948) 379–423
33. Schürmann, J.: Pattern Classification, a unified view of statistical and neural approaches. John Wiley & Sons (1996)
34. Kuncheva, L.I.: Using degree of consensus in two-level fuzzy pattern recognition. European Journal of Operational Research **80** (1995) 365–370
35. Dietrich, C., Palm, G., Schwenker, F.: Decision Templates for the Classification of Time Series. International Journal of Information Fusion **4** (2003)
36. Huang, Y.S., Suen, C.Y.: A method of combining multiple experts for the recognition of unconstrained handwritten numerals. IEEE Transactions on Pattern Analysis and Machine Intelligence **17** (1995) 90–94

Multiple Classifier Fusion Performance in Networked Stochastic Vector Quantisers

R. Patenall, D. Windridge, and J. Kittler

Centre for Vision, Speech and Signal Processing,
Dept. of Electronic & Electrical Engineering, University of Surrey,
Guildford, GU2 5XH Surrey, United Kingdom

Abstract. We detail an exploratory experiment aimed at determining the performance of stochastic vector quantisation as a purely fusion methodology, in contrast to its performance as a composite classification/fusion mechanism. To achieve this we obtain an initial pattern space for which a simulated PDF is generated: a well-factored SVQ classifier then acts as a composite classifier/classifier fusion system in order to provide an overall representation rate. This performance is then contrasted with that of the individual classifiers (constituted by the factored code-vectors) acting in combination via conventional combination mechanisms. In this way, we isolate the performance of networked-SVQs as a *purely* combinatory mechanism for the base classifiers.

1 Introduction

1.1 The Networked SVQ Methodology

We explore a variant on the stochastic vector-quantisation (SVQ) technique [1-3] that acts to integrate aspects of independent component analysis within standard vector-quantisation [5]. It achieves this by maximising the error resilience of bandwidth-limited transmissions of pattern-vector information sampled stochastically from a code-book, thereby providing a natural mechanism for imposing an appropriate coordinatization and topology on the training vectors. This contrasts with the *a priori* impositions that must be made within a conventional topographic feature-mapping environment [4] (to which behaviour networked-SVQs essentially default in the presence of unambiguously non-manifold pattern-data).

In more specific terms, stochastic vector-quantisation utilises a 'folded' Markov chain topology to statistically relate input and output vectors conceived as occupying the same vector space via the minimisation of a positional reconstruction error measure.

Hence, for an input vector denoted x, we minimise the aggregate Euclidean reconstruction distance:

$$D \equiv \int dx \, Pr(x) \sum_{y_1=1}^{M} \sum_{y_1=2}^{M} \cdots \sum_{y_n=1}^{M} Pr(y|x) \int dx' Pr(x'|y)||x - x'||^2 \qquad (1)$$

N.C. Oza et al. (Eds.): MCS 2005, LNCS 3541, pp. 128–135, 2005.

where x' is the output vector, and $y = (y_1, y_2, \ldots y_n) : 1 \leq y \leq M$ the code-index vector encoding of x.

This is soluble non-parametrically for certain theoretical cases. However, in practise, a number of constraints are required to achieve this minimisation [3], the most significant of which for the present purposes being the limitation of $Pr(y|x)$ to a sigmoid form:

$$Pr(y|x) = \frac{Q(y|x)}{\sum_{y'=1}^{M} Q(y'|x)} \qquad (2)$$

where

$$Q(y|x) \equiv \frac{1}{1 + \exp(-\omega(y).x - b(y))} \qquad (3)$$

b here represents a bias offset in the input space; ω represents a weight vector with behaviour characteristics familiar from the study of artificial neural networks (although the normalisation factor can considerably modify the intrinsic sigmoid morphology).

It is also possible, within the SVQ theoretical framework, to concatenate chains of individual SVQs together to form a multistage network with the previous code-vector space becoming the input space of the sub sequent SVQ, in which case the objective function defaults to a weighted sum of the reconstruction errors of each stage in the chain. Networked SVQs can thus act in a supervised, as well as an unsupervised manner.

What makes stochastic vector quantisers interesting from the classifier fusion perspective, however, is their capacity to spontaneously factor code-vector posterior PDFs in relation to the input data, thereby achieving a maximally compact representation of strongly manifold-like pattern-data. Bundles of orthonormal code-vectors can therefore act as individually independent classifiers, with the folded Markov chain topology serving to combine classifier outputs in order to provide an overall estimate of the reconstruction vector (which has associated with it a unique probability density value).

1.2 Objective

We shall, in this paper, set out an exploratory experiment aimed at determining the performance of the networked stochastic vector quantisation technique as a purely fusion methodology, in relation to its performance as a composite classification/fusion system.

Achieving this will require that we generate a simulated PDF such that a well-factored two-stage SVQ classifier may act as a composite classifier/classifier fusion system, providing an overall representation rate.

This performance is then contrasted with that of the *individually* factored classifiers (formed by the collinear code-vector bundles) acting in isolation, with outputs combined via a pair of a conventional combination mechanisms.

In this way we aim to isolate the performance of the SVQ methodology as a *purely* combinatory mechanism for the base classifiers, with respect to the two benchmark fusion mechanisms.

2   Testing the Networked-SVQ Methodology's Abilities as a Classifier Combiner

We have argued that the behavioural qualities of the networked SVQ methodology as a factorising classifier bear many comparisons to classical multiple classier fusion. A strongly factorised SVQ essentially divides the input space into orthogonal manifolds with stochastic outputs that are independent to the degree that they represent true independence within the training data (it is here tacitly assumed that factorisation will only take place when so indicated by the data). The folded aspect of the Markov-chain topology that defines the SVQ architecture then *combines* these outputs to derive a (probabilistically distributed) vector in the input space. This comes about because both the final vector and the individual reconstruction vectors are associated with the orthogonal sigmoid bundles correlated with a particular probabilistic output for the original ground-truth training-vector distribution. There is hence a strong sense in which the orthogonal weight-vector bundles may be regarded as individual classifiers with a corresponding probability output, and the final reconstruction vector regarded as a combined classifier output.

Without specific constraints (such as partitioning) on the SVQ, this combination is of an inherently complex and non-linear type. However, it is broadly expected to equate to a *vector* summation of the individual weight reconstruction vectors. Were this analogy with classifier combination exact, we would anticipate the output of the SVQ to be, rather than a combination of component vectors *associated* with probability values, instead of a combination of *probability values* associated with the vectors. Thus we see, by virtue of the explicit *co-ordination* of vector components, that SVQs have an intrinsic advantage over convectional classifier/classifier combiner systems.

It therefore seems appropriate, in assessing the performance of the networked SVQ methodology as a classifier *combiner* (that is to say, as distinct from a classifier), to benchmark it against other combination systems which utilise as common base classifiers those sub-classifiers formed by the orthogonal sigmoid bundles.

To do this we need an appropriate simulated ground truth distribution, with an absolute probability value associated with each vector of the input space: we therefore opt, in the following, for variants on the toroid distribution.

The most appropriate combining schemes against which to benchmark the networked-SVQ systems are the Sum and Product Rules, since they collectively represent opposing poles in the gamut of possibilities (Kittler *et al* [6] have demonstrated all other combining systems to be reducible to one or other of them in terms of broad functionality).

In the following experiment, we shall thus seek to benchmark the accuracy (mean-square deviation) of the final probability values arising from the networked-SVQ reconstruction of test vectors sampled from the simulated toroid PDF. That is, we shall seek to compare the ground-truth PDF value at a range of randomly-sampled test vectors with those defined by:

- **1.** The networked-SVQ reconstruction vector.
- **2.** The *sum* of the probabilities associated with the reconstruction vectors of the orthogonal spaces defined by collinear sigmoid bundles.
- **3.** The *product* of the probabilities associated with the reconstruction vectors of the orthogonal spaces defined by collinear sigmoid bundles.

Hence, we compare the the probabilistic output errors of the SVQ, sum rule and product rule combination mechanisms, respectively.

Specifically, we set about this as follows:

2.1   Experimental Approach

First, a set of training data is prepared that derives from a specific and defined probability density function (see below). This is then presented to a networked-SVQ classifier for training using simulated annealing to try to force the classifier to form a factorial set of codes. These codes are then split into the collinear sets (as specified via an angular-deviation threshold) to form a set of new classifiers.

A new set of training data conforming to the original probability density function is created, and the reconstruction vectors for all of the code-bundles in the factorially-separated classifiers are found.

The probability density function function is then evaluated at these points via the simulated PDF function, as well at the points specified by the original data. The probabilities that result from the networked-SVQ classifier directly, and from the sum and product of the probabilities associated with the multiple sub-classifiers are then compared to that of the simulated PDF in order to evaluate how well the differing mechanisms (SVQ, Sum Rule and Product Rule) combine.

As pseudocode, the experimental approach may thus be written;

1. Initialisation
   i) Generate prospective polynomial ground truth PDF.
   ii) Generate training set from prospective ground truth PDF.
   iii) Create SVQ from training data.
   iv) Test for factorial SVQ behaviour via angular collinearity criterion.
      GOTO 1. until test satisfied

2. Evaluate Sum, Product Rule Performances
   2a. (Generation of Sub-Classifier Outputs)
      i) Separate SVQ code vectors into N factorised subsets.
      ii) Generate training set from ground truth PDF.
      iii) Generate N reconstruction vectors from training set.
      iv) Associate probabilities with reconstruction vectors via ground truth PDF.

   2b. (Compute Linear Combiner Performance)
      i) Combine probabilities via Sum and Product Rules.
      ii) Calculate RMS deviations from ground truth PDF.

3. Evaluate SVQ Performance
3a. (Generate SVQ Classifier Output)
i) Generate reconstruction vectors from training set for full set of SVQ code-vectors.
ii) Associate probabilities with reconstruction vectors via ground truth PDF.

3b. (Compute Composite SVQ Classifier/Combiner Performance)
i) Calculate RMS deviation of SVQ probabilities from ground truth PDF.

2.2   Experimental Findings

A two-toroid embedded in four-dimensional space with random Gaussian-sampled radial perturbations was selected as the ground truth probability density function most appropriate to the problem. With a mean inner radius of 1.0 and a standard deviation of 3.0 this provides a reasonably diffuse object, but with a definite manifold aspect. Two distinct toroids displaced by 1.5 × the inner radius are employed to *represent* a two-class classification scenario. Hence, although we require stochastic vector quantisation to provide independent factorisations of the distinct classifiers (each with an independent reference PDF), we do not explicitly determine classification rates at any stage; we are primarily interested in the deviation of the combined classifier output from that of the model.

After sparse (50 vector) sampling and presentation to the networked-SVQ for training, this pattern-data factorised effectively, producing the set of codes depicted in figures 1 and 2. Processing the factorised classifier outputs via the various combinatory mechanisms (SVQ, Sum-rule and Product-rule), and computing the RMS deviation of the combined output probability from that of the reference two-toroidal PDF, provides the following aggregate results:

Fig. 1. Individual code posterior PDFs for the perturbed toroid manifold, classifier 1 (depicted in 2-dimensional internal manifold coordinates, wrapping around on the horizontal and vertical axes)

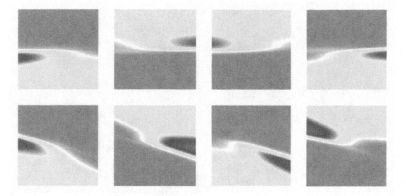

Fig. 2. Individual code posterior PDFs for the perturbed toroid manifold, classifier 2 (depicted in 2-dimensional internal manifold coordinates, wrapping around on the horizontal and vertical axes)

	SVQ	Sum rule	Product rule
RMS error	0.218559	0.188461	0.2724854

This result, giving second placing to the networked-SVQ, is perhaps counter-intuitive since the mechanism has inherently more free-parameters to deploy in the combination. A possible explanation, however, is presented by the arbitrary symmetry of the training data, and the associated possibility of over-parameterisation. A second toroid probability density function was hence created in which a relative deviation component of 1.2 in dimensions 3 and 4 with respect to dimensions 1 and 2 was permitted.

This does not factorise into orthonormality to the degree that the previous data set does, but still forms a factorial classifier within our angular-threshold-based definition of the term (and as can be seen in figures 3 and 4), the threshold being set to within $\pm 5°$ of collinearity. Processing these classifiers in the previous manner provided the following results:

	SVQ	Sum rule	Product rule
RMS error	0.203262	0.181961	0.317731

These are substantially the same as those of the previous case, and we would therefore tend to the view that they represent a real trend with respect to the experimental assumptions. If this is so, we then have a respective hierarchy of classifier-combinatory abilities of, from best to worst; Sum Rule, SVQ, Product Rule, with the networked-SVQ and the Sum Rule having relatively similar combinatory abilities.

This would tend to correlate with the view that the Sum Rule is the most robust mechanism for error-cancellation available. However, the Product Rule is

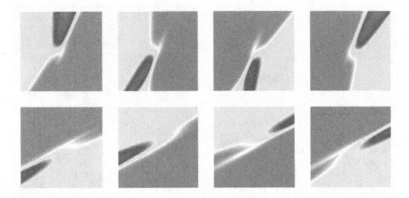

Fig. 3. Individual code posterior PDFs for the elliptically-deviated toroid, classifier 1 (depicted in 2-dimensional internal manifold coordinates, wrapping around on the horizontal and vertical axes)

Fig. 4. Individual code posterior PDFs for the elliptically-deviated toroid, classifier 2 (depicted in 2-dimensional internal manifold coordinates, wrapping around on the horizontal and vertical axes)

the most geometrically conservative *linear* mechanism for calculating underlying composite PDFs from marginal distributions, despite its tendency for multiplication of error magnitudes. Stochastic vector quantisation, being in effect a complex non-linear combination mechanism for factorial components, has a still greater capacity for geometric information conservation. We may therefore expect that more complex morphologies will tend to bring out this aspect of networked-SVQs more fully. For the present, the near Sum-Rule levels of error-robustness are a promising indication that networked-SVQs represents a stable platform for both classification and classifier combination (particularly when the latter arises as a spontaneous consequence of the former).

3   Conclusions

We have sought to provide an exploratory quantification of the networked stochastic vector quantiser's ability to act a purely combinatorial mechanism for factorised classifiers via an experimental benchmarking against existing linear methods.

It was determined that, for the chosen test data set, stochastic vector quantisation combines near Sum-rule levels of error-robustness with an adaptable non-linear mechanism for geometric combination of factorial components. Further testing on simulated and empirical data is required to establish this conclusion fully convincingly; this shall be the endeavour of future research. However, this preliminary result is suggestive in its own right.

Beyond the performance issues, we have found that the method potentially represents a stable and useful classification platform for general pattern classification, the unique strength of SVQs being to spontaneously characterise the *dimensionality* of an input manifold, forming classifiers and combination mechanisms as the data demands, without any inherent necessity for external parameter fixing.

Acknowledgement

The authors would like to gratefully acknowledge the support and assistance of Dr Stephen P. Luttrell in the compilation of this paper. The research itself was carried out at the University of Surrey, UK, supported by, and within the framework of, QinetiQ sub-contract number CU016-013391.

References

1. **Luttrell S P**, Self-organised modular neural networks for encoding data, in Combining Artificial Neural Nets: Ensemble and Modular Multi-Net Systems, 1997, pp. 235-263, Springer-Verlag, ed. Sharkey A J C.
2. **Luttrell S P**, A Bayesian analysis of self-organizing maps, Neural Computing 6 (1994) 767-794.
3. **Luttrell S P**, A usesr's guide to stochastic encoder/decoders. DERA Technical Report, DERA/S&P/SPI/TR990290 (1999)
4. **Kohonen T**, "Self organisation and associative memory", 1994, Springer-Verlag.
5. **Linde T, Buzo A and Gray R M**, An algorithm for vector quantiser design, IEEE Trans. COM, 1980, **28**, pp 84-95
6. **J. Kittler, M. Hatef, R.P.W. Duin, and J. Matas**, "On combining classifiers", IEEE Transactions on Pattern Analysis and Machine Intelligence, vol. 20, no. 3, 1998, 226-239

On Deriving the Second-Stage Training Set for Trainable Combiners

Pavel Paclík, Thomas C.W. Landgrebe, David M.J. Tax,
and Robert P.W. Duin

Information and Communication Theory Group,
TU Delft, The Netherlands
{P.Paclik, T.C.W.Landgrebe, D.M.J.Tax, R.P.W.Duin}@ewi.tudelft.nl

Abstract. Unlike fixed combining rules, the trainable combiner is applicable to ensembles of diverse base classifier architectures with incomparable outputs. The trainable combiner, however, requires the additional step of deriving a second-stage training dataset from the base classifier outputs. Although several strategies have been devised, it is thus far unclear which is superior for a given situation. In this paper we investigate three principal training techniques, namely the re-use of the training dataset for both stages, an independent validation set, and the stacked generalization. On experiments with several datasets we have observed that the stacked generalization outperforms the other techniques in most situations, with the exception of very small sample sizes, in which the re-using strategy behaves better. We illustrate that the stacked generalization introduces additional noise to the second-stage training dataset, and should therefore be bundled with simple combiners that are insensitive to the noise. We propose an extension of the stacked generalization approach which significantly improves the combiner robustness.

1 Introduction

When designing pattern recognitions systems, it is often the case that multiple types of data representation and classifiers may be exploited. Instead of selecting the best single algorithm for a given problem, multiple classification systems combine a number of base algorithms to provide (in some cases) more accurate and robust solutions [6]. A second stage combiner is used to assimilate and process the outputs of the base classifier. Two types of combination strategies are typically considered - fixed and trainable combiners. While the fixed combiners operate directly on the outputs of the base classifiers, the trainable ones use the outputs of base classifier as a new feature representation.

Fixed combining rules assume that the responses of the base classifiers are comparable. This assumption does not necessarily hold if different classifier architectures are combined, such as Fisher Linear Discriminant (FLD), Support vector machines or neural networks. The trainable combiners are capable of overcoming this problem by learning the pattern in the outcomes of base classifiers.

N.C. Oza et al. (Eds.): MCS 2005, LNCS 3541, pp. 136–146, 2005.

Although benefits of trainable combiners have been demonstrated in number of studies [4, 2, 11, 5, 1, 9], it is still unclear which training strategy results in the best performance to suit a particular situation. Thus far, several strategies have been utilized. The first uses the same training set for both training of the base classifiers and (after processing by the trained base classifiers) also for the training of the combiner. Using the same set of examples for both stages, however, inevitably leads to a biased combiner. In order to remedy this situation, Raudys proposed to estimate the bias of the base classifier and correct for it [8]. This solution is, however, applicable only in the special case of linear base classifiers. A practical general recommendation, given by Duin in [2], is to train the base classifiers in a weak fashion. The combiner may then still have the flexibility to correct for their weakness as the bias is almost avoided.

Another training strategy avoids the biased dataset for training of the combiner by the use of a validation set. The available training data is split into two independent subsets. The first is utilized for training of the base classifiers. The second set, processed by the trained base classifiers, serves to train the combiner. The shortcoming of this approach is that the data available for training of each of the stages is typically severely limited, and thus leading to poorer overall performance. A compromise solution may be the construction of partially overlapping training and validation sets [1]. This observation might suggest that trainable combining rules are applicable only for large datasets [11, 9].

In this paper, we focus on an alternative approach which has a potential to improve the applicability of trainable combiners to smaller sample size problems, called *stacked generalization*, first introduced by Wolpert [13]. This is a general technique for construction of multi-level learning systems. In the context of classifier combination, it yields unbiased, full-size training sets for the trainable combiner in the following way:

- For each base classifier, an internal rotation-based cross-validation is performed such that all the fold test sets constitute the full original dataset.
- A classifier, trained in one of the internal folds, is applied to the respective fold test set and its outputs (such as class posteriori probability estimates or confidences) are stored.
- By collating the outputs of all the classifiers produced by the internal cross-validation, a full-size dataset consisting of the classifier outputs is constructed to be used for the second-stage training. Since each of these training examples was processed by the base classifier trained on an independent data set, the base classifier outputs in the resulting dataset are unbiased.

Stacked generalization therefore alleviates both of the aforementioned problems by providing the unbiased training set for the combiner, without sacrificing any of the available training examples.

Stacked generalization was discussed in a classifier combining context by Ting and Witten [12]. In their study, it outperformed both the model selection based on cross-validation, and the majority voting combiner. From a regression viewpoint, LeBlanc and Tibshirani [7] investigated the stacked generalizing combiner in a small artificial example using a linear classifier and the nearest neighbor rule. The existing studies on trainable combining using the stacked generalization focus on the selection of base classifiers and their outputs or viable combiner models. To our knowledge, the analysis of the relation between the performance of stacked combiners and training sizes has not been performed.

In this paper we investigate the behaviour of trainable combiners based on stacked generalization in comparison to two other primary approaches, namely re-using of the full training set (denoted the *re-use method*) by both stages, and the strategy based on the validation set (the *validation method*). We compare the behaviour of the three strategies across varying training set sizes in an attempt to understand their strengths and weaknesses.

In Section 2, the derivation of the combiner training set for the different approaches is formally introduced. We also discuss derivation of the base classifiers used in the stacked system and propose an alternative method increasing their robustness. In Section 3, we describe a set of experiments on several datasets and discuss our main findings. The final conclusions are given in Section 4.

2   Derivation of Training Set for the Trainable Combiner

We assume a training dataset X, with N examples $x_i \in R^D$, $i = 1, ..., N$ each assigned into one of C classes and a set of B untrained base classifiers A_b, $b = 1, ..., B$. The base classifiers are trained according to the fusion strategy used. Note, that if independent feature representations are available, the base classifier A_b will be trained on the corresponding dataset X_b. In the following, we denote such a trained classifier by $\hat{A}_b(X_b)$. By reapplying the trained classifier $\hat{A}_b(X_b)$ to the input set X_b, a dataset Y_b with C classifier outputs is created. The procedure, repeated for each of the base classifiers, yields a set Y, with N examples and BC features. The combiner A_{comb} is trained on this second-stage dataset Y. This procedure coincides with the *re-use method* for both the base classifiers and the combiner.

A new incoming observation $z \in R^D$ is assigned into one of the C classes using the trained combiner $\hat{A}_{comb}(Y)$ in the following way: First, the observation is subjected to each of B trained base classifiers $\hat{A}_b(X_b)$ using appropriate feature representations. The resulting outputs of the base classifiers are concatenated to form a feature vector in BC-dimensional space, and then finally the trainable combiner $\hat{A}_{comb}(Y)$ is applied.

The second approach (the *validation method*), investigated in this paper uses an independent validation set, in order to reduce the bias of the trainable combiner. The input dataset X is split into the training part Tr, and the mutually exclusive validation set V. The output dataset Y is composed of outputs of the trained classifiers $\hat{A}_b(Tr_b)$, obtained on the respective validation sets V_b, $b = 1, ..., B$. Note that both, base classifiers and and combiner, are trained on subsets of the original input datasets.

The application of *the stacked generalization* technique is illustrated in Figure 1, focusing on a single base classifier A_b. The dataset X_b is split into F

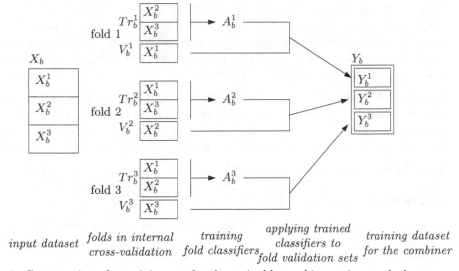

Fig. 1. Construction of a training set for the trainable combiner using stacked generalization, shown for the base classifier A_b

mutually exclusive parts X_b^f, $f = 1, ..., F$ of almost equal sizes. In an internal F-fold cross-validation procedure, trained classifiers $\hat{A}_b^f(Tr_b)$ are constructed using the per-fold training subsets $Tr_b^f = \cup_{j=1, j \neq f}^F X_b^j$. Each of the F trained fold classifiers are applied to the independent validation subset $V_b^f \equiv X_b^f$, yielding an output set Y_b^f. The full output set, specific to b-th base classifier is then constructed by concatenation $Y_b = \cup_{f=1}^F Y_b^f$. The process is concluded by re-training the base classifier on the full set X_b, i.e. by producing $\hat{A}_b(X_b)$ [12,1].

Because the internal cross-validation derived F versions $\hat{A}_b^f(Tr_b^f), f = 1, ..., F$ for each base classifier A_b, we propose to use their fixed combination $\hat{A}_b^*(Tr_b)$ as the final base classifier, instead of a single re-trained one. Our motivation is to leverage the slight variations in the existing per-fold classifiers for the sake of increasing the robustness of the whole classification system. Because we assume a similar distribution of noise in the cross-validated training subsets, we propose to use the mean combiner [2].

3   Experiments

3.1   Experimental Setup

In this section the results of a number of experiments are shown, comparing the different approaches to deriving the training dataset for trainable combiners. The experiments were performed on the following datasets:

Handwritten Digits. The handwritten digits dataset (UCI repository[1]) contains 2000 objects from ten digit classes (200 objects per class). The dataset is composed of four different feature representations using the Fourier descriptors (76 features), Karhunen-Loeve coefficients (64 features), Zernike moments (47 features) and raw pixel values (240 features).

Spectra. A set of 988 measurements of fluorescent spectra in oral cavity labeled into two classes (856 healthy and 132 diseased tissue examples) [10]. Each measurement consists of six independent spectra measured in different locations in the oral cavity. Each spectrum is represented by of 199 wavelengths.

Waveform. An artificial dataset with three classes of waves each derived as a combination of two of three "base" waves (UCI repository). The dataset has in total 5000 examples and 21 features.

Sonar. A two-class real-world dataset with 208 data samples (111 examples of metal, and 97 examples of rock) and 60 continuous features (UCI repository).

The handwritten digits and spectra datasets contain different feature representations for each measurement. Therefore, we use a single type of a base classifier which is applied in different feature spaces. The waveform and sonar datasets are examples of problems with a single feature representation. Hence, we combine different base models in a single feature space.

In order to understand the behaviour of combiners utilizing different strategies for the construction of the second-stage training set, we estimate the learning curves in the following way. A training set of a desired size and an independent test set are drawn from the input dataset. On the training set, the base classifiers are trained and the second-stage dataset is constructed by the procedures described in Section 2. This dataset is then used for training of the combiner. The trained combiner is executed on the test set, and the mean classification error over the test examples is estimated. Note that all steps required for building the combiner, including the internal cross-validation of the stacked generalization, are performed on the training set only. For a given training set size, this procedure is repeated 10 times and the results are averaged. For the handwritten digits, spectra and waveform datasets the training set sizes vary from 5 to 100

Table 1. Experimental configurations

dataset	base classifiers	test set size (per class)
handwritten digits	FLD	50
spectra	FLD	30
waveform	FLD,Parzen,1-NN	500
sonar	FLD,Parzen,1-NN,NMC	40

---

[1] http://www.ics.uci.edu/~mlearn/MLRepository.html

examples per class, for the sonar dataset from 5 to 50 examples per class. The base algorithms and test set sizes used are summarized in Table 1.

The outputs of the Parzen base classifier consists of posterior probability estimates. The outputs of the non-density based classifiers (distances to a decision boundary or a distance to the closest prototype) were normalized to a $< 0; 1 >$ range by a sigmoid function [3]. We have considered three different types of trainable combiners, ranging from simple to complex models, namely the decision templates (DT) [5] (effectively the nearest mean classifier), the Fisher linear discriminant (FLD), and the 1st nearest neighbor rule (1-NN). Note that while the FLD internally scales its inputs, the DT and 1-NN combiners require the proper scaling as explained above.

The experiments compare the three combiner training strategies, namely the *re-use method*, *validation method* (50/50% split), and *stacked generalization* using 10-fold internal cross-validation. For stacked generalization, we distinguish two approaches for construction of the trained base classifiers, as described in Section 2. We refer to the case when base classifiers are re-trained on the complete training dataset as "method I" [12, 1]. The second method, denoted "method II", uses a mean combiner over the set of 10 classifiers, trained during stacked generalization process.

3.2   Results and Discussion

The handwritten digit results are presented in Figure 2, subfigures (a),(c), and (e). This subfigures (b), (d), and (f) correspond to the spectral dataset. The rows of the Figure 2 refer to FLD, DT, and 1-NN training combiners, respectively.

In the subfigure 2 (a), we can observe that the combiner re-using the training set (thin solid line) exhibits a drastic error increase between 10 and 50 examples per class. This is caused by superimposing the error peaks of the base FLD classifiers occurring when the sample size matches the feature space dimensionality. The combiner using the validation set (thin dashed line, circular markers) delivers significantly better results. The stacked generalizer using method I (thick dash-dotted line) significantly improves over these two traditional techniques for more than 10 examples per class. For the smallest training sample size, it is surprisingly outperformed by the re-use method. The proposed stacked generalizer using method II is the best of all remaining combiners even for the smallest training sample size. The dotted line represents a learning curve of a single FLD classifier directly applied to the full dataset. It illustrates that combining of different feature representation is beneficial. Employing the Parzen base classifier instead of FLD lead to analogous results (experiments not shown here).

For large sample sizes, the methods become comparable. This is understandable because a large training set diminishes the effects of bias when the training dataset is re-used and, at the same time, is sufficiently large for splitting into training and validation subsets.

The results obtained on the spectral dataset depict the significant performance deterioration occurring for larger sample sizes. It is the result of a peaking effect where for 200 training examples a linear classifier is built in a 199 dimen-

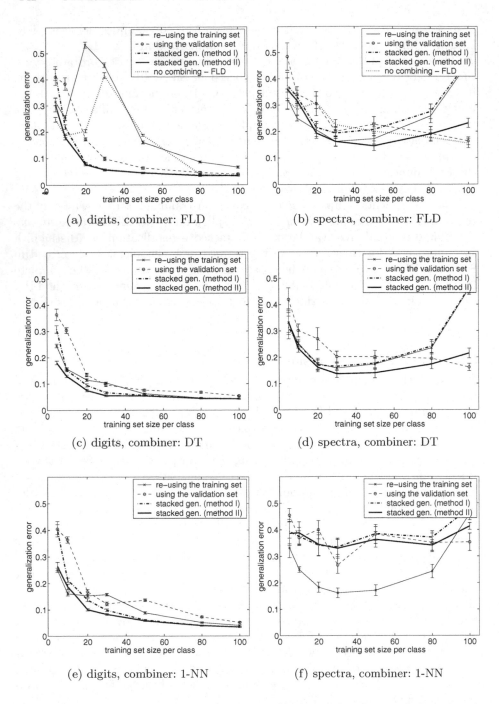

(a) digits, combiner: FLD

(b) spectra, combiner: FLD

(c) digits, combiner: DT

(d) spectra, combiner: DT

(e) digits, combiner: 1-NN

(f) spectra, combiner: 1-NN

Fig. 2. Handwritten digit datasets (left column) and spectral dataset (right column). In all cases the FLD was used a base classifier

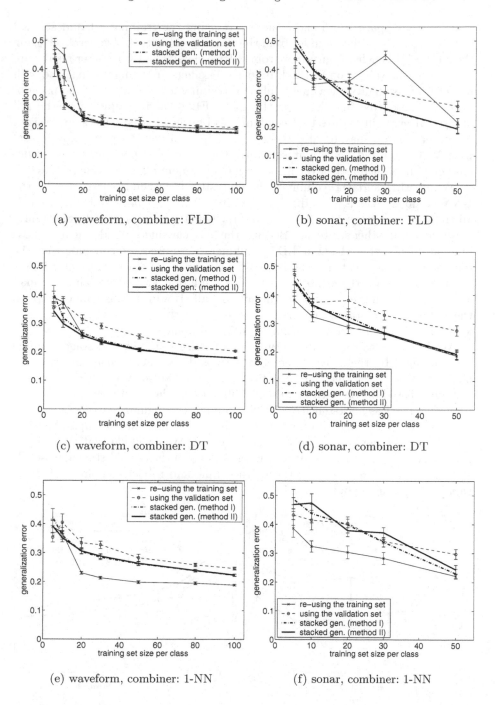

(a) waveform, combiner: FLD

(b) sonar, combiner: FLD

(c) waveform, combiner: DT

(d) sonar, combiner: DT

(e) waveform, combiner: 1-NN

(f) sonar, combiner: 1-NN

Fig. 3. Experiments with waveform and sonar datasets. The base classifiers are indicated in Table 1

sional feature space. Both the combiner re-using the training set and stacked generalizer with method I suffer from the peaking. The stacked generalizer using the method II benefits from a more robust base classifiers. Even better results are reached by the validation method. Its base classifiers are trained in a space with higher dimensionality then the number of training examples, using the pseudo-inverse. The dotted line denoting the single FLD classifier applied to the full dataset. It again illustrates that combining is beneficial for smaller sample sizes.

Similar trends may be also observed in Figure 3 depicting the experiments with Waveform and Sonar datasets and in additional experiments with other base classifiers such as nearest mean or Parzen we omit for the sake of brevity.

While FLD and DT combiners exhibit similar learning curve trends, the 1-NN combiner yields very different results. The most profound difference is apparent in subfigures 2 (f), 3 (e) and 3 (f), where the re-use method significantly outperforms all other strategies. Because the base classifiers are identical to those in experiments where FLD and DT combiners were used, we conclude that the inferior results are related to the 1st nearest neighbor combiner. This behaviour is understandable for the combiner using the validation set because already small amount of training examples is still cut in half. However, this cannot explain the failure of the stacked generalizers employing the second-stage datasets of identical size to the well-performing re-using approach.

We hypothesize that it is the presence of noise in the second-stage training set generated by the stacked generalization and the subsequent failure of the noise-sensitive 1-NN rule. We have performed an additional experiment with a combiner based on the 5-th nearest neighbor rule. The results are presented in Figure 4. The less noise-sensitive 5-NN combiner (triangular markers) results in a significant improvement eventually reaching the performance comparable with the 1-NN combiner trained on a re-used dataset. We conclude that the stacked generalization introduces additional level of noise in the second-stage dataset. It should be, therefore, used together with simple and robust combiners that are capable of averaging out this noise.

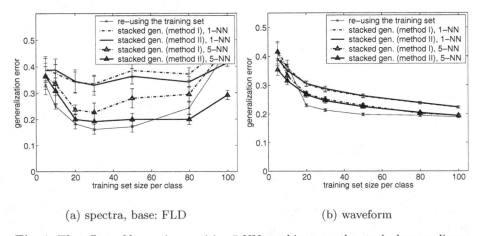

(a) spectra, base: FLD   (b) waveform

Fig. 4. The effect of less noise sensitive 5-NN combiners on the stacked generalizers

4   Conclusions

In this paper, we have compared three principal methodologies for the construction of the second-stage training sets for trainable combiners. Apart of the commonly employed re-using of the available training set by both stages and the validation set, we also investigate the stacked generalization technique which yields full-size unbiased second-stage training sets. However, the stacked generalization, inevitably introduces additional noise into the second-stage datasets.

Our experiments demonstrate that trainable combiners, derived using the stacked generalization exhibit significant performance improvements over the other two currently used methods for moderate training set sizes. For very small sample sizes, the best strategy is the re-use of a complete training set for both stages. Any split strategy sacrifices the scarce training data and should be, therefore, avoided. For a large number of training samples, the studied approaches to derivation of the second-stage training set do not differ and the re-using strategy may be again recommended as the simplest solution.

For the moderate training set sizes, the stacked generalization appears to significantly outperform the other two approaches. Commonly used combiners based on stacked generalization train the final base classifiers on the full training set. We have proposed to construct the base classifier from the available fold classifiers by a fixed mean combiner. This solution appears to bring additional robustness and should be preferred in applications where evaluation of all the fold classifiers for each new example does not pose a excessive speed burden.

We have noticed the performance drop of the stacked generalizers using the 1-NN combiner. We have shown that the stacked generalization introduces additional noise into the second-stage training dataset and therefore requires simple and robust combiners such as FLD or DT for a good performance. We conclude our study noting that the stack generalization provides a combiner training strategy superior to the validation set approach and for larger than very small sample sizes systematically outperforms the re-using approach.

Acknowledgements. This research is/was supported by the Technology Foundation STW, applied science division of NWO and the technology program of the Ministry of Economic Affairs.

References

1. C. Dietrich, G. Palm, and F. Schwenker. Decision templates for the classification of bioacustic time series. *Information Fusion*, 4:101–109, 2003.
2. R.P.W. Duin. The combining classifiers: to train or not to train? In *Proc. of 16th Int.Conf. on Pattern Recognition (Quebec City), vol. II*, pages 765–770, 2002.
3. R.P.W. Duin, P. Juszczak, D. de Ridder, P. Paclík, E. Pekalska, and D. M. J. Tax. PR-Tools 4.0, a Matlab toolbox for pattern recognition. Technical report, ICT Group, TU Delft, The Netherlands, January 2004. http://www.prtools.org.

4. R.P.W. Duin and D.M.J. Tax. Experiments with classifier combining rules (invited paper). In *Proc. of Multiple Classifier Systems MCS 2000*, volume LNCS, vol.1857, pages 16–29, 2000.
5. L.I. Kuncheva, J.C. Bezdek, and R.P.W. Duin. Decision templates for multiple classifier fusion: an experimental comparison. *Pattern Recog.*, 34(2):299–314, 2001.
6. Ludmila I. Kuncheva. *Combining Pattern Classifiers*. Wiley & Sons, 2004.
7. Michael LeBlanc and Robert Tibshirani. Combining estimates in regression and classification. *Journal of the American Statistical Association*, 91(436), 1996.
8. S. Raudys and A. Janeliunas. Reduction a boasting bias of linear experts. In *Proc. of Multiple Classifier Systems MCS 2002*, volume LNCS vol.2364, 2002.
9. F. Roli, S. Raudys, and G. L. Marcialis. An experimental comparison of fixed and trained fusion rules for crisp classifier outputs. In *Proc. of Multiple Classifier Systems MCS 2002*, volume LNCS vol.2364, pages 232–241, 2002.
10. M. Skurichina, P. Paclik, R.P.W. Duin, D.C.G. de Veld, H.J.C.M. Sterenborg, M.J.H. Witjes, and J.L.N. Roodenburg. Selection/extraction of spectral regions for autofluorescence spectra measured in the oral cavity. In *Proc.of SSSPR 2004*, volume vol. 3138 LNCS, Springer, Berlin, pages 1096–1104, 2004.
11. Ching Y. Suen and Louisa Lam. Multiple classifier combination methodologies for different output levels. In *Proc. of Multiple Classifier Systems MCS 2000*, volume LNCS, vol. 1857, Springer, Berlin, 2000.
12. Kai Ming Ting and Ian H. Witten. Issues in stacked generalization. *Journal of Artificial Intelligence Research*, 10:271–289, 1999.
13. D.H. Wolpert. Stacked generalization. *Neural Networks*, 5:241–259, 1992.

Using Independence Assumption to Improve Multimodal Biometric Fusion

Sergey Tulyakov and Venu Govindaraju

SUNY at Buffalo, Buffalo NY 14228, USA

Abstract. There is an increased interest in the combination of biometric matchers for person verification. Matchers of different modalities can be considered as independent 2-class classifiers. This work tries to answer the question of whether assumption of the classifier independence could be used to improve the combination method. The combination added error was introduced and used to evaluate performance of various combination methods. The results show that using independence assumption for score density estimation indeed improves combination performance. At the same time it is likely that a generic classifier like SVM will still perform better. The magnitudes of experimentally evaluated combination added errors are relatively small, which means that choice of the combination method is not really important.

1   Introduction

Use of multiple biometric identification devices requires robust combination algorithms to increase their effectiveness. Though a plethora of possible combination algorithms are described in scientific literature, there seems to be no consensus on which is the best. Hence a practitioner is forced to try different combination strategies in order to see which algorithm works best for the task at hand.

In this paper we shall deal with the combination of independent classifiers. We assume that classifiers output a set of scores reflecting the confidences of input belonging to corresponding class. It is safe to assume that matching scores for biometrics of different modalities (e.g. fingerprint and face) are independent random variables. The matchers or classifiers possessing this property are independent classifiers. This assumption is fairly restrictive for the field of classifier combination since combined classifiers usually operate on the same input. Though frequently using completely different features for different classifiers still results in dependent scores. For example, features can be dependent, image quality characteristic can influence scores of combined classifiers, and input may have an inherent low match to stored class templates giving low scores for all matchers. In certain situation even classifiers operating on different inputs will have dependent scores, as in the case of using two fingers for identification (fingers will likely be both moist, both dirty or both applying same pressure to the sensor). In the case of multimodal biometrics the inputs to different sensors are independent (for example, no connection of fingerprint features to face features

N.C. Oza et al. (Eds.): MCS 2005, LNCS 3541, pp. 147–155, 2005.

have been noticed so far). Hence matching scores will also be independent. We will use this property in our work.

Much of the effort in the classifier combination field has been devoted to dependent classifiers and most of the algorithms do not make any assumptions about classifier independence. The main purpose of this work is to see if independence assumption can be effectively used to improve the combination results. We will use the property that the joint density of the classifiers' scores is the product of the densities of the scores of individual classifiers.

We choose the magnitude of added error as a measure of combination goodness. It is the difference between an error of optimal Bayesian combination and current combination algorithm. In order to calculate this error we make a hypothesis on the true score distribution, and produce training and testing samples using these hypothesized distributions. This technique could be used to estimate added error in real-world classifier combinations. The main purpose of using this technique is to provide some confidence in combination results. This would enable us to say: "'The total combination error in this particular combination is 5% and added error due to combination algorithm is likely to be less than 1%"'.

2   Previous Work

The added error introduced by Tumer and Ghosh[1] was under much consideration lately [2, 3, 4, 5]. The definition of this added error requires assumption that combined classifiers operate in the same feature space and class samples are random points in this space with some fixed distributions. The Bayes error is determined by the distributions in the feature space and added error is the difference of the combination error of trained classifiers and Bayes error.

This framework does not work for combinations of biometric classifiers since these classifiers do not have the same feature space. For our task we will be treating classifiers as black boxes outputting matching scores. Scores are random variables in the score space defined by some fixed score distributions and the combination algorithm is a classifier operating in the score space. The Baeys error, or rather minimum Bayes cost, of the combination is determined by the score distributions. And we define combination added error, or combination added cost, as a difference between total error(cost) and this Bayes error(cost). The difference with the previous definition is that we use distributions of scores in score space and not distributions of feature vectors in feature vector space for definition of Bayes error. Thus our combination added error in contrast to previously defined added error[1] will not depend on the added errors of individual classifiers but will depend only on the combination algorithm. See section 3.2 for formal definition of combination added error.

To further explain the difference between two types of added error, let us have an example of few imperfect classifiers operating in the same feature space. Suppose that we have optimal combination based on Bayesian classifier operating on scores in score space (assuming the score distribution are known). In this case added error in Tumer and Ghosh's framework will be some non-zero number reflecting the errors made by classifiers. In our setting the added error is 0, since the combination algorithm is perfect and did not add any errors to the classification results.

Another assumption made in Tumer and Ghosh's added error framework is that the outputs of the classifiers approximate posterior class probabilities $s_i = P(c_i|x)$. Since in that framework all classifiers use same feature vector x, this implies that output scores of classifiers are very strongly correlated. If we think about score space $s_1, \ldots, s_n$, the outputs of these classifiers would be near the diagonal $s_1 = \cdots = s_n$. Decision boundary of combination algorithm can be represented as a hypersurface in score space and combination decision is roughly equivalent to hypersurface intersecting diagonal at same place. So this added error is mostly concerned with what happens locally near diagonal of the score space and how combination algorithm hypersurfaces intersect it. In this situation, any fixed combination rule will produce approximately the same total recognition error, since their hypersurfaces will be able to intersect the diagonal in some optimal place.

In our case we consider a more general case of output scores not approximating posterior class probabilities and present anywhere in the score space. This is a frequent situation with biometric scores which usually represent some internal matching distance. In this situation, the total error would greatly depend on the used combination rule and score densities. So any combination method which has limited number of trainable parameters will be considered suboptimal in this situation. For example, weighted sum rule will have hyperplanes as decision boundaries and would fail to properly separate classes with normally distributed scores and with hyperquadric decision surface.

It would make little sense to define combination added error for such methods and perform its analysis. Indeed, if optimal decision surface is of the form supported by such combination, the added error will be very close to 0 (limited number of parameters, large number of training samples), and its comparison to any other method will be unfair. On the other hand, if optimal decision surface is different from the ones supported by combination algorithm, there will always be some fixed minimum added error, which this combination method would not be able to improve no matter how many training samples we have.

For these reasons we consider only combination algorithms able to approximate any decision functions given a sufficient number of training samples. In particular, we consider combination methods based on non-parametric density estimation, neural networks and support vector machines. We are interested in seeing what magnitude of combination added error they make with respect to different parameters of combination: number of training samples, total error, number of combined classifiers.

3   Combination Methods

In this work we shall deal with 2-class classifiers. As we mentioned earlier, the main motivation for this work is the combination of biometric matchers. The combination problem in this area is usually split into two tasks: verification and identification. The verification problem asks if a person's identity coincides with the claimed one, and the identification problem asks to which person among k enrolled persons the given biometric readings belong. We investigate the verification problem and assume that there are two classes of events: the claimed identity coincides with the person's identity and claimed identity is different from the person's identity.

Though two classes are considered, only one score for each matcher is usually available - matching score between input biometric and stored biometric of the claimed identity. Consequently, we will assume that the output of the 2-class classifiers is 1-dimensional. For example, samples of one class might produce output scores close to 0, and samples of the other class produce scores close to 1. The set of output scores originating from n classifiers can be represented by a point in n-dimensional score space. Assuming that for all classifiers samples of class 1 have scores close to 0, and scores of class 2 are close to 1, the score vectors in combined n-dimensional space for two classes will be close to points $\{0, ..., 0\}$ and $\{1, ..., 1\}$. Any generic pattern classification algorithm can be used in this n-dimensional space as a combination algorithm.

Note that this is somewhat different from the usual framework of k-class classifier combination, where k-dimensional score vectors are used and, for example, samples of class i are close to vector $\{0, ..., 1, ..., 0\}$ with only 1 at ith place. In this case the scores for n classifiers will be located in nk-dimensional space and the classification problem will be more difficult. This framework will be suitable for a biometric identification problem, and should be addressed in the future work.

Since we assume that we combine independent classifiers, is it possible to use this information to design better combination than generic 2-class n-dimensional classifier? The idea is that it might be possible to better estimate joint score density of n classifiers as a product of n separately estimated score densities of each classifier. Effectively, an n-dimensional (for 2 classes) combination problem will be reduced to n 1-dimensional density estimation problems. The question is will this combination based on density products perform better than generic pattern classifiers?

3.1   Combination Using Products of Density Functions

Consider a combination problem with n independent 2-class classifiers. Denote the density function of scores produced by j-th classifier for elements of class i as $p_{ij}(x_j)$, the joint density of scores of all classifiers for elements of class i as $p_i(\mathbf{x})$, and the prior probability of class i as P_i. Denote the region of n-dimensional score space being classified by combination algorithm as elements of class i as R_i, and the cost associated with misclassifying elements of class i as λ_i. Then the total cost of misclassification in this problem is defined as $c = \lambda_1 P_1 \int_{R_2} p_1(\mathbf{x})d\mathbf{x} + \lambda_2 P_2 \int_{R_1} p_2(\mathbf{x})d\mathbf{x}$.

Since R_1 and R_2 cover whole score space, $\int_{R_1} p_1(\mathbf{x})d\mathbf{x} + \int_{R_2} p_1(\mathbf{x})d\mathbf{x} = 1$. Thus

$$c = \lambda_1 P_1 \left(1 - \int_{R_1} p_1(\mathbf{x})dx \right) + \lambda_2 P_2 \int_{R_1} p_2(\mathbf{x})dx$$

$$= \lambda_1 P_1 + \int_{R_1} \left(\lambda_2 P_2 p_2(\mathbf{x}) - \lambda_1 P_1 p_1(\mathbf{x}) \right) dx$$

To minimize cost c the region R_1 should be exactly the set of points $\mathbf{x}$ for which $\lambda_2 P_2 p_2(\mathbf{x}) - \lambda_1 P_1 p_1(\mathbf{x}) < 0$. Since we have independent classifiers, $p_i(\mathbf{x}) = \prod_j p_{ij}(x_j)$ and decision surfaces are described by the equation

$$f(\lambda_1, \lambda_2, \mathbf{x}) = \lambda_2 P_2 p_2(\mathbf{x}) - \lambda_1 P_1 p_1(\mathbf{x})$$

$$= \lambda_2 P_2 \prod_{j=1}^{n} p_{2j}(x_j) - \lambda_1 P_1 \prod_{j=1}^{n} p_{1j}(x_j) = 0 \quad (1)$$

To use equation 1 for combining classifiers we need to learn $2n$ 1-dimensional probability density functions $p_{ij}(x_j)$ from training samples.

3.2 Combination Added Error

Learning 1-dimensional probability density function $p_{ij}(x_j)$ from training samples will result in their approximations $p'_{ij}(x_j)$. Using equation 1 with these approximations will result in decision regions R'_i which ordinarily will not coincide with optimal Bayesian decision regions R_i. The combination added cost(AC) will be defined as a difference between cost of using trained regions R'_i and optimal regions R_i for combination:

$$AC = \lambda_1 P_1 \int_{R'_2} p_1(\mathbf{x})dx + \lambda_2 P_2 \int_{R'_1} p_2(\mathbf{x})dx$$

$$- \lambda_1 P_1 \int_{R_2} p_1(\mathbf{x})dx - \lambda_2 P_2 \int_{R_1} p_2(\mathbf{x})dx \quad (2)$$

Using set properties such as $R'_1 = (R'_1 \cap R_1) \cup (R'_1 \cap R_2)$, we get

$$AC = \int_{R'_2 \cap R_1} \left(\lambda_1 P_1 p_1(\mathbf{x}) - \lambda_2 P_2 p_2(\mathbf{x}) \right) dx$$

$$+ \int_{R'_1 \cap R_2} \left(\lambda_2 P_2 p_2(\mathbf{x}) - \lambda_1 P_1 p_1(\mathbf{x}) \right) dx \quad (3)$$

For generic classifiers we define R'_i as the region in which samples are classified as belonging to class i. The combination added error is defined in the same way.

In the following experiments we will assume that prior costs and probabilities of classes are equal, and use term 'error' instead of 'cost'. We also will be using relative combination added error, which will be defined as combination added error divided by the Bayesian error, and this number will be used in tables. For example, number 0.1 will indicate that combination added error is 10 times smaller than Bayesian error.

4   Experiments

The experiments were performed for two normally distributed classes with means at (0,0) and (1,1) and different variance values (same for both classes). It was also assumed that costs and prior probabilities of both classes are equal. The Bayesian decision boundary in this situation is a straight line $x + y = 1$. Note that both sum and product combination rules have this line as a decision surface, and combinations using these rules would give no combination added error. This is the situation where specific distributions would favor particular fixed combination rules, and this is why we eliminated these rules from our experiments.

The product of densities method described in previous section is denoted here as DP. The kernel density estimation method with normal kernel densities [6] was used for estimating one-dimensional score densities. We chose least-square cross-validation method for finding a smoothing parameter. Arguably, the choice of normal kernel would favor this combination method given underlying normal distributions. We employed kernel density estimation Matlab toolbox [7] for implementation of this method.

For comparison we used generic classifiers provided in PRTools[8] toolbox. SVM is a support vector machine with second order polynomial kernels, Parzen is is a density estimation Parzen classifier, and NN is back-propagation trained feed-forward neural net classifier with one hidden layer of 3 nodes.

Each experiment would simulate sampling score distributions to get training data, training classifiers with this training data and evaluating classifier performance. Since score distributions are available, it is possible to generate arbitrarily large testing set, but instead we simply used formula 3 to numerically get added error. For each setting we average results of 100 simulation runs and take it as average added error. These average added errors are reported in the tables.

In the first experiment (table 1) we tried to see what added errors different methods of classifier combination have relative to the properties of score distributions. Thus we varied the standard deviation of the score distributions (STD) which varied the minimum Bayesian error of classifiers. All classifiers in this experiment were trained on 300 training samples.

Table 1. Dependence of combination added error on the variance of score distributions

STD	Bayesian error	DP	SVM	Parzen	NN
0.2	0.0002	1.0933	0.2019	1.2554	3.1569
0.3	0.0092	0.1399	0.0513	0.1743	0.1415
0.4	0.0385	0.0642	0.0294	0.0794	0.0648
0.5	0.0786	0.0200	0.0213	0.0515	0.0967

Table 2. Dependence of combination added error on the training size

Number of training samples	DP	SVM	Parzen	NN
30	0.2158	0.1203	0.2053	0.1971
100	0.0621	0.0486	0.0788	0.0548
300	0.0200	0.0213	0.0515	0.0967

Table 3. Dependence of combination added error on the number of classifiers

Number of classifiers	Bayes error	DP	SVM	Parzen	NN
2	0.0385	0.2812	0.1645	0.2842	0.2669
3	0.0004	0.8544	0.7882	0.6684	0.8747

The first observation is that smaller standard deviations result in larger relative added errors. This is expected in the case of density based classifiers because of the inherent difficulty of estimating density in the tails of distributions. Small standard deviation means that optimal decision boundary will be at the ends of both class distributions, and a density based method will work poorly there. Interestingly, SVM and NN classifiers also showed similar behavior. Another observation is that SVM showed better performance than all other methods, especially for low Bayesian error cases. Only for $STD = .5$ DP method was able to get similar performance.

In the second experiment (table 1) we wanted to see the dependency of combination added error on the size of the training data. We fixed the standard deviation to be 0.5 and performed training/error evaluating simulations for 30, 100 and 300 training samples.

As expected, the added error diminishes with increased training data size. It seems that the DP method gets better faster with increased training data size, but it is not certain. Interestingly, the magnitude of added error is relatively small for all methods. Note that we did not experiment with the number of hidden units of neural network, which might explain why its performance did not improve much with the increased number of training samples.

For the third experiment (table 3) we attempted to see how added error changes if we combine 3 classifiers instead of 2. We take normally distributed scores with standard deviations of .4 and the size of the training data as 30. Though additional classifier makes relative combination added error bigger, the dramatic decrease of Bayesian error would be much more important for total error. Also note that result for 3 classifiers and results of first two rows of table 1 have comparable Bayesian errors, with SVM method not performing as well as for two classifiers.

5   Conclusion

In this paper we presented the results of evaluating combination added error. We experimentally showed that this error is relatively small for all combination methods. So it does not really matter which combination method is used to combine results of classifiers. By using a larger number of training samples an inferior combinator will easily outperform superior combinator. Thus it is more important what minimum Bayesian error combination has, which is determined by classifiers' performances and their interdependence (assuming that trainable generic classifier is used as combinator and not fixed combination rules, like sum or product rule). The choice of combination algorithm becomes more important when classifiers have small Bayesian errors.

The presented method for combining independent classifiers by means of multiplying one-dimensional densities showed slightly better performance than comparable Parzen classifier. Thus using independence information can be beneficial for density based classifiers. At the same time DP method was still not as good as SVM. It seems that if more training samples were used and more classifiers are combined, DP might be better than SVM.

Though only one type of density functions was used in our experiments, the technique can be easily expanded to other density functions. Clearly, performance of presented methods can be different if other density functions are used. In real-life applications it would make sense to set a hypotheses on available biometric score densities, and perform similar type of experiments in order to find the best combination method.

Still, even if such experiments are performed, and best combination method is found, it is not guaranteed that the combination method will be the best for a particular available training sample. Note that figures in presented tables are averages of added errors over different training sets. In fact there were many simulation cases, where inferior combination algorithm outperformed all other algorithms for a particular training set.

The main motivation of this paper was to find a possibly best combination method for multimodal biometric matchers. Though presented techniques will help to choose a reasonably well performing combination method, other factors should also be taken into consideration. For example, if costs of incorrect classification or prior probabilities of classes change, the SVM or neural network method will require retraining. Also, if output of combination confidence is required for system operation, these methods might be a bad choice. The ability of density based methods to output posterior class probability can be a decisive factor for their adoption.

References

1. Tumer, K., Ghosh, J.: Linear and order statistics combiners for pattern classification. In Sharkey, A.J., ed.: Combining Artificial Neural Nets: Ensembles and Multi-Net Systems. Springer-Verlag, London (1999) 127–162
2. Kuncheva, L.: A theoretical study on six classifier fusion strategies. Pattern Analysis and Machine Intelligence, IEEE Transactions on **24** (2002) 281–286
3. Fumera, G., Roli, F.: Performance analysis and comparison of linear combiners for classifier fusion. In: SSPR/SPR. (2002) 424–432

4. Fumera, G., Roli, F.: Analysis of error-reject trade-off in linearly combined multiple classifiers. Pattern Recognition **37** (2004) 1245–1265
5. Alexandre, L.A., Campilho, A.C., Kamel, M.: On combining classifiers using sum and product rules. Pattern Recognition Letters **22** (2001) 1283–1289
6. Silverman, B.W.: Density estimation for statistics and data analysis. Chapman and Hall, London (1986)
7. Beardah, C.C., Baxter, M.: The archaeological use of kernel density estimates. Internet Archaeology (1996)
8. Duin, R., Juszczak, P., Paclik, P., Pekalska, E., Ridder, D.d., Tax, D.: Prtools4, a matlab toolbox for pattern recognition (2004)

Half-Against-Half Multi-class Support Vector Machines

Hansheng Lei and Venu Govindaraju

CUBS, Center for Biometrics and Sensors,
Computer Science and Engineering Department,
State University of New York at Buffalo, Amherst NY 14228, USA
{hlei, govind}@buffalo.edu

Abstract. A Half-Against-Half (HAH) multi-class SVM is proposed in this paper. Unlike the commonly used One-Against-All (OVA) and One-Against-One (OVO) implementation methods, HAH is built via recursively dividing the training dataset of K classes into two subsets of classes. The structure of HAH is same as a decision tree with each node as a binary SVM classifier that tells a testing sample belongs to one group of classes or the other. The trained HAH classifier model consists of at most K binary SVMs. For each classification testing, HAH requires at most K binary SVM evaluations. Both theoretical estimation and experimental results show that HAH has advantages over OVA and OVO based methods in the evaluation speed as well as the size of the classifier model while maintaining comparable accuracy.

1 Introduction

Support Vector Machine (SVM) has been proved to be a fruitful learning machine, especially for classification. Since it was originally designed for binary classification [1], it is not a straightforward issue to extend binary SVM to multi-class problem. Constructing K-class SVMs ($K \gg 2$) is an on-going research issue [2].

Basically, there are two types of approaches for multi-class SVM. One is considering all data in one optimization [3]. The other is decomposing multi-class into a series of binary SVMs, such as "One-Against-All" (OVA) [4], "One-Against-One" (OVO) [5], and DAG [6]. Although more sophisticated approaches for multi-class SVM exist, extensive experiments have shown that OVA, OVO and DAG are among the most suitable methods for practical use [7, 8].

OVA is probably the earliest approach for multi-class SVM. For K-class problem, it constructs K binary SVMs. The ith SVM is trained with all the samples from the ith class against all the samples from the rest classes. Given a sample x to classify, all the K SVMs are evaluated and the label of the class that has the largest value of the decision function is chosen:

$$class \ of \ x = argmax_{i=1,2,...,K}(\mathbf{w}_i \cdot x + b_i), \tag{1}$$

where $\mathbf{w}_i$ and b_i depict the hyperplane of the ith SVM.

OVO is constructed by training binary SVMs between pairwise classes. Thus, OVO model consists of $\frac{K(K-1)}{2}$ binary SVMs for K-class problem. Each of the $\frac{K(K-1)}{2}$

N.C. Oza et al. (Eds.): MCS 2005, LNCS 3541, pp. 156–164, 2005.

SVMs casts one vote for its favored class, and finally the class with most votes wins [5]. DAG does the same training as OVO. During testing, DAG uses a Directed Acyclic Graph (DAG) architecture to make a decision. The idea of DAG is easy to implement. Create a list of class labels $L = (1, 2, \cdots, K)$ (the order of the labels actually does not matter). When a testing sample is given for testing, DAG first evaluates this sample with the binary SVM that corresponds to the first and last element in list L. If the classifier prefers one of the two classes, the other one is eliminated from the list. Each time, a class label is excluded. Thus, after $K - 1$ binary SVM evaluations, the last label remaining in the list is the answer.

None of the three implementation methods above, OVA, OVO or DAG, significantly outperforms the others in term of classification accuracy [7, 8]. The difference mainly lies in the training time, evaluation speed and the size of the trained classifier model. Although OVA only requires K binary SVM, its training is most computationally expensive because each binary SVM is optimized on all the N training samples (suppose the training dataset has N samples altogether). OVO or DAG has $\frac{K(K-1)}{2}$ binary SVMs to train, which sounds much more than what OVA needs. However, each SVM is trained on $\frac{2N}{K}$ samples. The overall training speed is significantly faster than OVA. For testing, DAG is fastest in that it needs only $K - 1$ binary SVM evaluation and every SVM is much smaller than those trained by OVA. As for the total size of classifier model, OVO is the most compact one since it has much less total number of support vectors than OVA has. DAG needs extra data structure to index the binary SVMs, thus, it is a little bit larger than OVO.

Our motivation here is whether there potentially lurks different but competitive multi-class SVM implementation method? Fortunately, OVA, OVO and DAG are not the end of the story. In this paper, we propose a Half-Against-Half (HAH) multi-class SVM method. We compare it with OVA, OVO and DAG in several aspects, especially evaluation speed, the compactness of the classifier model and the accuracy of classification.

The rest of this paper is organized as follows. In section 2, we describe the implementation of HAH. In section 3, we discuss related works and compare HAH with OVA, OVO and DAG via theoretical analysis and empirical estimation. Then, experiments are designed and discussed in section 4. Finally, conclusion is drawn in section 5.

2 Half-Against-Half Multi-class SVM

Our motivation came from when we dealt with the classification problem of the Synthetic Control Chart (Scc) sequences [9]. Scc was synthetically generated to test the accuracy of time series classification algorithms. It has six different classes of control charts with 100 instances each class. Fig.1 shows examples of the Scc sequences.

The existing multi-class SVMs all try to match one class against one another. This leads to OVA, OVO or DAG implementation method. Now, since the sequences in the last three classes are some kind of similar to each other, as shown in Fig.1 D-F, can we group them together as a bigger category {D,E,F} and match it against {A,B,C}? After a test sample is decided to lie in {D,E,F}, we can go further to see which class it should be labeled exactly. In this way, we have a recursive binary classification problem, which of course can be implemented by regular SVM. The structure of the classifier is same as

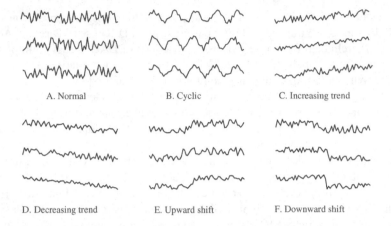

A. Normal   B. Cyclic   C. Increasing trend

D. Decreasing trend   E. Upward shift   F. Downward shift

Fig. 1. Examples of the Scc sequences. There all 6 classes together. Class D,E and F have some kind similarity to each other

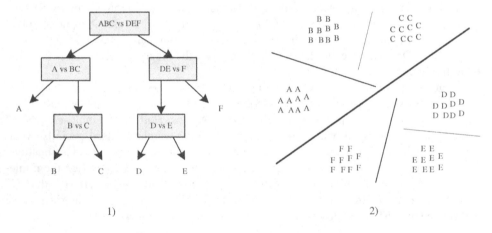

Fig. 2. A possible decision tree for classifying the Scc samples. 1) Each node is a binary SVM that evaluates one group of classes against another group. 2) Half-Against-Half divisions of the six classes

a decision tree with each node as binary SVM. The classification procedure goes from root to the leaf guided by the binary SVMs, same as traveling a decision tree. Fig. 2 shows a possible SVM decision tree for the Scc data and the intuitive divisions of the 6 classes by Half-Against-Half. In the input space, two groups of classes might be non-separable, but in the feature space, SVM can achieve good separation by kernel tricks.

For datasets with small number of classes, we can divide them into groups from coarse to fine manually with prior knowledge. Similar or close classes can be grouped together. Given a large K-class problem, its preferred to define groups automatically. Straightforwardly, we can recursively divide the K classes into two groups by random. The problem here is the separability between the arbitrary two groups might be not high,

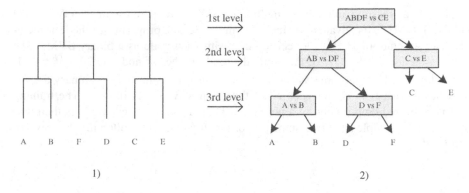

Fig. 3. The decision tree of HAH can follows the structure of the hierarchy clustering of the classes. 1) The hierarchy structure of the Scc dataset based on the mean distance between classes. 2)The corresponding decision tree of HAH

thus, the accuracy of classification is not reliable. The most desirable choice is to find the optimum two groups that lead to minimum expected error. With binary SVM, the expected error is $E(error) = \frac{nSV}{N}$, where nSV is the number of support vectors (SV) and N is the number of training samples. Thus, the problem is equivalent to dividing classes into two halves with which the trained SVM has the minimum number of SVs. For K classes, there are $\binom{K}{\lfloor K/2 \rfloor}$ possible divisions. Training a binary SVM on each possible division and choosing the one with minimum nSV is not feasible.

Unlike "One-Against-One" and "One-Against-All", the dividing method is actually "Half-Against-Half". The biggest challenge is to determine the optimum divisions. While keeping the optimal division as an open problem, we found hierarchy clustering of classes is a suboptimal choice. Each class is considered as an element. The distance between two elements is defined as the mean distance between the training samples from the two classes. In this way, a hierarchy clustering structure for the K classes can be built. Then, the HAH model can be trained accordingly. Fig. 3 shows an example on the Scc dataset. The hierarchy of the 6 classes has $\lceil log_2(6) \rceil = 3$ levels. Therefore, the corresponding decision tree of HAH has 3 levels.

3   Related Works and Discussion

A multistage SVM (MSVM) for multi-class problem was proposed in [10]. It uses Support Vector Clustering (SVC) [11] to divide the training data into two parts and then a binary SVM is trained. For each part, the same procedure recursively takes place until the binary SVM gives a exact label of class. The unsolved problem for MSVM is how to control the SVC to divide the training dataset into exact two parts. The two parameters, q (the scale of the Gaussian kernel) and C (the soft margin constant) could be adjusted to achieve this goal. However, this procedure is painful and unfeasible, especially for large datasets. The training set from one class could lie in both clusters. Moreover, there is no guarantee that exact two clusters can be found by varying p or C.

HAH is an feasible solution for multi-class SVM. Compared with the OVA, OVO and DAG, HAH as its advantages. Table 1 summarizes the properties of the four methods. The structure of HAH is a decision tree with each node as a binary SVMs. The depth of the tree is $\lceil log_2(K) \rceil$, therefore, the total number of nodes is $2^{\lceil log_2(K) \rceil} - 1$. The training of DAG is same as OVO and both need to train $\frac{K(K-1)}{2}$ binary SVMs. OVA has a binary SVMs for each class, thus, it has K SVMs in total. The training time is estimated empirically by a power law [12]: $T \approx \alpha N^2$, where N is the number of training samples and α is some proportionality constant. Following this law, the estimated training time for OVA is:

$$T_{OVA} \approx K\alpha N^2 \tag{2}$$

Without loss of generality, let's assume the each of the K classes has the same number of training samples. Thus, each binary SVM of OVO only requires $\frac{2N}{K}$ samples. The training time for OVO is:

$$T_{OVO} \approx \alpha \frac{K(K-1)}{2}(\frac{2N}{K})^2 \approx 2\alpha N^2 \tag{3}$$

The training time for DAG is same as OVO.

As for HAH, the training time is summed over all the nodes in the $\lceil log_2(K) \rceil$ levels . In the ith level, there are 2^{i-1} nodes and each node uses $\frac{N}{2^{i-1}}$ training samples. Hence, the total training time is:

$$T_{HAH} \approx \sum_{i=1}^{\lceil log_2(K) \rceil} \alpha 2^{i-1}(\frac{N}{2^{i-1}})^2 \approx \sum_{i=1}^{\lceil log_2(K) \rceil} \alpha \frac{N^2}{2^{i-1}} \approx 2\alpha N^2 \tag{4}$$

Here, we have to notice that T_{HAH} does not include the time to build the hierarchy structure of the K classes, since doing so won't consume much time and the quadratic optimization time dominates the total SVM training time.

According the empirical estimation above, we can see that the training speed of HAH is comparable with OVA, OVO and DAG. In testing, DAG is faster than OVO and OVA, since it requires only $K - 1$ binary SVM evaluations. HAH is even faster than DAG because the depth of the HAH decision tree is $\lceil log_2(K) \rceil$ at most, which is superior to $K - 1$ especially when $K \gg 2$. Although the total number of SVs that do inner product with the testing sample contribute a major part of the evaluation time, the number of binary SVMs also counts. Our experiments also show that HAH has less kernel evaluations than DAG.

The size of the trained classifier model is also an important concern in practical applications. The classifier model usually stay in the memory. Large model consumes a great portion of computing resources. The fifth column in Table 1 is a coarse estimation of the size of model. Assume for each binary SVM, a portion of β of the training samples will become SVs. Since the number of SVs dominates the size, we can estimate the size of HAH is:

$$S_{HAH} \approx \sum_{i=1}^{\lceil log_2(K) \rceil} 2^{i-1}(\beta \frac{N}{2^{i-1}}) \approx \sum_{i=1}^{\lceil log_2(K) \rceil} \beta N = \lceil log_2(K) \rceil \beta N \tag{5}$$

Table 1. The properties of HAH, OVO, DAG and OVA in training and testing

Method	Training		Testing	
	# of SVMs	Estimated Time	# of SVMs	Size of Model
HAH	$K-1$	$2\alpha N^2$	$\lceil log_2(K) \rceil$	$\lceil log_2(K) \rceil \beta N$
DAG	$K(K-1)/2$	$2\alpha N^2$	$K-1$	$(K-1)\beta N$
OVO	$K(K-1)/2$	$2\alpha N^2$	$K(K-1)/2$	$(K-1)\beta N$
OVA	K	$K\alpha N^2$	K	$K\beta N$

The size of OVO is:

$$S_{OVO} \approx \frac{K(K-1)}{2}\beta\frac{2N}{K} = (K-1)\beta N \tag{6}$$

The size of DAG is similar as OVO besides some extra data structure for easy indexing. Similarly, the size of OVA is estimated as $K\beta N$.

According to the estimation above, HAH has the minimum size of classifier model among the four methods. Of course, real experiments are needed to testify the estimation.

4 Experiments

According to the empirical estimation, HAH is superior to OVO, DAG and OVA in testing time and the size of classifier model. Experiments were conducted to firm this. Another very important concern is the classification accuracy. HAH was evaluated on multi-class datasets to compare its accuracy with that of OVO, DAG and OVA. The four datasets we used in experiments are: the Iris, the Scc,the PenDigits and the Isolet, all of which are from the UCI machine learning repository [9]. The description of the datasets are summarized in Table 2. The Iris is one of the most classical datasets for testing classification. It has 150 instances (50 in each of three classes). The Scc dataset has 600 instances together (100 in each class). For both Iris and Scc, 70% were used as training samples, and the left 30% for testing. The PenDigits and Isolet were originally divided into training and testing subsets by the data donators. So, no change was made.

On each dataset, we trained HAH, OVO, DAG and OVA based on the software LIBSVM [13] with some modification and adjustment. The kernel we chose was the RBF_kernel. The regularizing parameters C and σ were determined via cross validation

Table 2. Description of the multi-class datasets used in the experiments

Name	# of Training Samples	# of Testing Samples	# of Classes	# of Attributes
Iris	105	35	3	4
Scc	420	180	6	60
PenDigits	7493	3497	10	16
Isolet	6238	1559	26	617

Table 3. Experimental results by C-SVM

	σ	C	# of Kernel Evaluations	Size of Classifier Model (KByte)	Classification Accuracy
Iris					
HAH	200	500	**12**	**2.2**	**100%**
OVO	200	500	17	2.7	100%
DAG	200	500	13	2.7	100%
OVA	200	500	45	3.4	100%
Scc					
HAH	10^4	5	**66**	**78.1**	**99.44%**
OVO	10^4	10	168	87.7	99.44%
DAG	10^4	10	85	93.8	99.44%
OVA	10^4	5	493	98.5	99.44%
PenDigits					
HAH	2	10	**399**	**183.9**	**98.37%**
OVO	2	5	913	300.0	98.48%
DAG	2	5	439	305.0	98.43%
OVA	2	5	1927	223.1	97.74%
Isolet					
HAH	200	5	**935**	**14,027**	**95.64%**
OVO	200	10	3359	17,254	96.60%
DAG	200	10	1413	17,607	96.73%
OVA	200	5	6370	21,508	94.23%

on the training set. The validation performance was measured by training on 70% of the training set and testing on the left 30%. The C and σ that lead to best accuracy were selected. We also tried the ν-SVM for each method [14]. Similarly, a pair of ν and σ were chosen according to the best validation performance. We did not scale the original samples to range [-1,1], because we found that doing so did not help much.

HAH was trained according to the hierarchy structure of the classes. Each class was considered as whole and the mean distance between two classes was used to build the hierarchy structure. OVO was implemented by the LIBSVM directly and thus we did not do any change. The DAG and OVA were also quite simple in implementation by modifying the LIBSVM source codes. The experimental results are summarized in Table 3 and 4 by C-SVM and ν-SVM respectively.

To compare HAH with OVO, DAG and OVA, three measures were recorded: i)Number of kernel evaluations, ii)Size of trained classifier model and iii)Classification accuracy. The number of kernel evaluations is the total number of support vectors that do kernel dot product with a single test sample. For OVO and OVA, all the support vectors need to do kernel evaluations with a given test sample. For HAH and DAG, different test samples may travel different pathes through the decision tree. So, we averaged the number of kernel evaluations over all testing samples. The number of kernel evaluations indicates the total testing CPU time. We used the kernel evaluations instead of the real testing CPU time because of implementation bias, i.e., the source codes on the same algorithm vary across different programmers. The size of trained classifier model is a good measure how the classifier machine consumes computing resources. In real

Table 4. Experimental results by ν-SVM

	σ	ν	# of Kernel Evaluations	Size of Classifier Model (KByte)	Classification Accuracy
Iris					
HAH	200	0.05	**9**	**1.9**	**100%**
OVO	200	0.05	8	2.3	100%
DAG	200	0.05	7	2.3	100%
OVA	200	0.10	35	3.0	100%
Scc					
HAH	10^3	0.015	**103**	**75.9**	**99.44%**
OVO	10^3	0.05	254	132.4	99.44%
DAG	10^3	0.05	204	146.0	99.44%
OVA	10^3	0.015	1270	184.2	98.33%
PenDigits					
HAH	2	0.01	**311**	**152.5**	**98.17%**
OVO	2	0.05	1464	480.8	97.91%
DAG	2	0.01	353	489.7	97.31%
OVA	2	0.015	2631	300.6	97.37%
Isolet					
HAH	200	0.01	**658**	**9,997**	**95.25%**
OVO	200	0.10	3520	18,082	96.54%
DAG	200	0.01	760	18,591	92.69%
OVA	200	0.01	5075	25,105	93.97%

application with limited memory, such as online handwriting recognition in Personal Digital Assistants (PDAs), compact classifier model is desired. Accuracy, of course, is also very important for a classifier.

Experimental results in both Table 3 and 4 show that HAH has much less number of kernel evaluations than OVO and OVA. Since kernel evaluations dominates the testing time, HAH is much faster than OVO and OVA. As indicated by the number of kernel evaluations in both Table 3 and 4, HAH is between a factor of 2 to 5.3 times faster than OVO on the datasets PenDigits and Isolet, and 4 to 7.7 times faster than OVA. HAH is also faster than DAG, though not that significantly. HAH also has advantages over other methods in the compactness of the classifier model. The size of trained HAH model is around 1.7 to 3 times smaller than OVO and DAG, and about 2 to 2.7 times smaller than OVA. The datasets Iris and Scc are too small to show the advantages of HAH in both the testing speed and the compactness of model. However, they show that HAH can reach the same accuracy as OVO, DAG and OVA do. The accuracies on all the four datasets show that HAH is competitive with OVO, DAG and OVA. On dataset Isolet, the accuracy of HAH is about 1% lower than OVO but over 1% higher than DAG and OVA, as indicated by Table 4. Considering HAH is 5.3 (3520/658) times faster than OVO in testing speed and 1.8 (18,082/9,997) times smaller in the size of model, the sacrifice of 1% accuracy is worthy. The reason why HAH is about 1% lower in accuracy over datasets with large number of categories like Isolet deserve further exploratory research. Dividing the classes into two groups optimally remains as an open problem.

5   Conclusions

A Half-Against-Half multi-class SVM is proposed and studied in this paper. HAH has its advantages over commonly-used methods like OVO, DAG and OVA in the testing speed and the compactness of classifier model. The accuracy of HAH is also comparable with OVO, DAG and OVA. Further research on recursively dividing the classes into two groups optimally might improve the accuracy.

References

1. Boser, B., I.Guyon, Vapnik, V.: A training algorithm for optimal margin classifiers. In Haussler, D., ed.: 5th Annual ACM Workshop on COLT. (1992) 144–152
2. Bredensteiner, E., Bennet, K.: Multicategory classification by support vector machines. In: Computational Optimizations and Applications. Volume 12. (1999) 53–79
3. Crammer, K., Singer, Y.: On the algorithmic implementation of multiclass kernel-based vector machines. Journal of Machine Learning Research **vol. 2** (2001) 265–292
4. Vapnik, V.: Statistical Learning Theory. Wiley, New York (1998)
5. Kreßel, U.: Pairwise classification and support vector machines. In: Advances in Kernel Methods: Support Vector Learnings, Cambridge, MA, MIT Press (1999) 255–268
6. Platt, J., Cristianini, N., Shawe-Taylor, J.: Large margin DAGs for multiclass classification. In: Advances in Neural Information Processing Systems. Volume 12. (2000) 547–553
7. Hsu, C., Lin, C.: A comparison of methods for multi-class support vector machines. IEEE Transactions on Neural Networks **13** (2002) 415–425
8. Rifin, R., Klautau, A.: In defense of one vs-all-classification. Journal of Machine Learning Research **vol. 5** (2004) 101–141
9. Hettich, S., Bay, S.: The UCI KDD archive. (1999)
10. Liu, X., Xing, H., Wang, X.: A multistage support vector machine. In: The 2nd International Conference on Machine Learning and Cybernetics. (2003) 1305–1308
11. Ben-Hur, A., Horn, D., Siegelmann, H., Vapnik, V.: Support vector clustering. Journal of Machine Learning Research **vol. 2** (2001) 125–137
12. Platt, J.: Fast training of support vector machines using sequential minimal optimization. In: Advances in Kernel Methods - Support Vector Learning, Cambridge, MA, MIT Press (1999) 185–208
13. C.Chang, Lin, C.: Libsvm: a library for support vector machines. (2001)
14. Schölkopf, B., Smola, A., Williamson, R., Bartlett, P.: New support vector algorithms. Neural Computation **12** (2000) 1207C1245

Combining Feature Subsets in Feature Selection

Marina Skurichina and Robert P.W. Duin

Information and Communication Theory Group, Faculty of Electrical Engineering,
Mathematics and Computer Science, Delft University of Technology,
P.O. Box 5031, 2600GA Delft, The Netherlands
m.skurichina@ewi.tudelft.nl
r.p.w.duin@ewi.tudelft.nl

Abstract. In feature selection, a part of the features is chosen as a new feature subset, while the rest of the features is ignored. The neglected features still, however, may contain useful information for discriminating the data classes. To make use of this information, the combined classifier approach can be used. In our paper we study the efficiency of combining applied on top of feature selection/extraction. As well, we analyze conditions when combining classifiers on multiple feature subsets is more beneficial than exploiting a single selected feature set.

1 Introduction

In many medical applications it is very difficult to collect a large number of observations (for instance, patients with a certain disease). Usually the number of measurements is limited. On the other hand, such measurements can have a large number of attributes (features). By this, we face the small sample size problem: the number of measurements is smaller than or comparable with the data dimensionality. In such conditions, it is difficult (or even impossible) to construct a good classification rule [1]. One has to reduce the data dimensionality. This can be done by applying feature selection or extraction procedures to the dataset.

When using feature extraction techniques (for instance, PCA [2]), all features contribute in new extracted features. So, one may expect that all (or the most) information useful for discrimination between data classes is taken into account and reflected in an extracted feature set. However, when the feature selection approach (like forward or backward feature selection, for instance) is used, only a subset of features is chosen as a new feature set. While the rest of features (that may still be discriminative) is ignored. Useful information hidden in these features is not taken into consideration. This may result in a poor performance on the selected feature subset.

To benefit from the information presented in the neglected features in feature selection, we suggest to use the combining approach. Instead of constructing a single classifier on one selected feature set, we propose to use the combined decision of classifiers constructed on sequentially selected sets of features. First, an optimal feature set (subspace) is selected. Then on the rest of features, we select the second best feature

N.C. Oza et al. (Eds.): MCS 2005, LNCS 3541, pp. 165–175, 2005.

set etc., until all features are included in a particular feature set. By this, we have a number of optimal feature subsets and may construct a classifier on each of them. By combining decisions of these classifiers, we use all information represented in the original feature space that may improve the performance achieved on a single subset of features.

In order to demonstrate the advantage of combining multiple feature subsets and to study conditions when combining applied on top of feature selection is beneficial, we have selected four real datasets: autofluorescence spectra measured in the oral cavity, images of handwritten digits, sonar and ionosphere datasets. All datasets introduce a 2-class problem. The data are described in section 2. The description of our combined approach applied to feature selection/extraction and the results of our simulation study are presented in section 3. Conclusions can be found in section 4.

2 Data

We perform our study on the following four examples.

The first dataset represents autofluorescence spectra measured in the oral cavity. The data consist of the autofluorescence spectra acquired from healthy and diseased mucosa in the oral cavity. The measurements were performed at the Department of Oral and Maxillofacial Surgery of the University Hospital of Groningen [3]. The measurements were taken at 11 different anatomical locations with excitation wavelength equal to 365 nm. Autofluorescence spectra were collected from 70 volunteers with no clinically observable lesions of the oral mucosa and 155 patients having lesions in the oral cavity. Some patients suffered from multiple lesions, so that a total of 172 unique lesions could be measured. However, a number of measurement sessions had to be left out of the analysis for different reasons: 1) because an accurate diagnosis was not available for the lesion at the time of measurement, 2) because it was not insured that the probe had been located at the correct position because the lesion was hardly visible or very small, 3) because the patient had already been receiving therapy, or 4) because the diagnosis for some benign lesions was overly clear. In total, 581 spectra representing healthy tissue and 123 spectra representing diseased tissue (of which 95 were benign, 11 dysplastic and 17 cancerous) were obtained. After preprocessing [3], each spectrum consists of 199 bins (pixels/wavelengths).

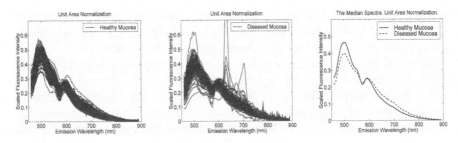

Fig. 1. Normalized autofluorescence spectra for healthy and diseased mucosa in oral cavity

In order to get rid of a large deviation in the spectral intensity within each data class, we normalized spectra by the Unit Area (UA)

$$a_i^{UA} = \frac{a_i}{U}, \quad U = \sum_{j=1}^{199} a_j, \quad i = 1, ..., 199, \tag{1}$$

where a_i is an intensity of a spectrum $A=\{a_1, ..., a_{199}\}$ at bin i, $i=1,...,199$. Normalized autofluorescence spectra representing healthy and diseased tissues and their median spectra are illustrated in Fig. 1.

The second dataset is handwritten digit "mfeat" dataset from [4]. Originally the data contain 10 digit classes with 200 samples per class and six different feature sets. For our study we have chosen the feature set of pixel averages consisting of 240 attributes (features). As well, we restricted ourselves to two-class problem selecting classes which represent digits 3 and 8. The example of these data classes are presented in Fig. 2.

The third dataset is "sonar" dataset from UCI Repository [4]. The task of the sonar dataset is to discriminate between sonar signals bounced off a metal cylinder and those bounced off a roughly cylindrical rock. Thus the dataset consists of two data classes. The first data class contains 111 objects obtained by bouncing sonar signals off a metal cylinder at various angles and under various conditions. The second class contains 97 objects obtained from rocks under similar conditions. Each object is a set of 60 numbers in the range 0.0 to 1.0. Thus, the data are 60-dimensional. Each number (feature) represents the energy within a particular frequency band, integrated over a certain period of time.

The last dataset is also taken from the UCI Repository [4]. It is the "ionosphere" dataset. These radar data were collected by a system consisted of 16 high-frequency antennas with a total transmitted power of about 6.4kW in Goose Bay, Labrador. The targets were free electrons in the ionosphere. "Good" radar returns are those showing evidence of structure in the ionosphere. "Bad" returns are those that do not return anything: Their signals pass through the ionosphere. The data are described by 34 features that introduce two attributes for 17 pulse numbers corresponding to the complex values returned by the function resulting from the complex electromagnetic signal. This dataset consists of 351 objects in total, belonging to two data classes: 225 objects belong to "good" class and 126 objects belong to "bad" class.

Fig. 2. The example of handwritten digits "3" and "8"

For our simulation study, training datasets with 20 (for handwritten digits dataset), 50 (for spectral dataset), 15 (for sonar dataset) and 10 (for ionosphere dataset) samples per class are chosen randomly from the total set. The remaining data are used for testing. The prior class probabilities are set to be equal. To evaluate the classification performance when the combined approach applied to feature selection and standard feature selection/extraction methods are used, we have chosen for Linear Discriminant Analysis (LDA) [2] which was the best performing classifier for these applications at the given sample size. In particular, we apply the linear classifier which constructs a linear discriminant function assuming normal class distributions and using a joint class covariance matrix for both data classes. All experiments are repeated 50 times on independent training sample sets for forward feature selection, random feature selection and PCA. Additionally, for the random feature selection we repeat the random permutation and split of the feature set into the subsets 10 times. In all figures the averaged results over 50 trials (500 trials for the random feature selection) are presented and we do not mention that anymore. The standard deviation of the reported mean generalization errors (the mean per two data classes) is approximately 0.01 for each considered case.

3   Combining Feature Subsets in Forward and Random Feature Selection and in PCA

When the number of available observations is limited and smaller than the data dimensionality, one is forced to apply feature selection/extraction techniques in order to construct a reliable classifier to solve the problem. One of the main differences between feature selection and feature extraction approaches is in the amount of useful information they are capable to retrieve from the data representation in the feature space. In general, feature extraction techniques make use of all original data features when creating new features. The new extracted features are a combination of the original ones. By this, the new extracted feature set may contain all (or almost all, we believe) useful information for classifying the data stored in a multidimensional data representation. However, feature extraction is an operation in the high dimensional space and for small sample sizes (which may be the reason to perform feature reduction) it may suffer from overtraining. As well, it may happen that feature extraction fails due to very complex class distributions in the high dimensional feature space. In this case, feature selection may be an alternative.

Feature selection is a special case of feature extraction. In feature selection, only a part of the original features is chosen as a new feature subset. The rest of features is ignored. Sometimes (depending on data representation in the feature space), this approach works good when a few features provide a good separation between data classes and the rest of features introduces noise. However, in the case when all data features are informative without a clear preference to each other, feature selection approach may be harmful. Useful information stored in neglected features is not taken into account. The selected feature subset is not optimal. That may cause a poor performance of the classifier on this feature subset. As well, some feature selection procedures (for instance, the forward or backward feature selection) have another drawback: the selection of features is performed sequentially one by one. The union of the first best feature selected with the second best one does not necessarily represent the best discriminative pair of features. By this, the selected feature subset might be not the most advantageous one. In addition, the efficiency of feature selection may suffer from the curse of dimensionality. When selecting features, the performance is judged by the class separability provided by these features. The separability of data classes is evaluated by some criterion. Such a criterion can be the performance of a particular classifier. However, the performance of almost all classifiers depends on the relation between the training sample size and the data dimensionality. For a finite size of the training set and an increasing feature space dimensionality, one observes that first the generalization error of a classifier decreases to its minimum and then starts to increase (see Fig. 3). The latter increase of the classification error is caused by the growing complexity of the classification rule that cannot be properly trained due to a lack of training data. In feature selection, a feature subset corresponding to a minimum classification error is chosen as the best one. It is indeed optimal by the feature size related to the available training sample size. But it is not necessary the optimal one in general. The rest of features can be still informative to discriminate the data classes. But they are not taken into consideration due to a shortage of data to construct a reliable classifier in the feature subspace of a higher dimensionality.

To overcome the drawbacks of a standard feature selection technique (say, the forward feature selection) and to make use of all information present in the original feature space when performing feature selection, we suggest to apply the classifiers combining approach on top of feature selection. Previously it has been demonstrated that combining performs well when it is applied to the data described by the different types of representations [5] or when the random subspaces of the data feature set are used [6]. Therefore, we expect that combining classifiers in selected feature spaces (on the selected subsets of features) will be also beneficial.

In our study we consider two examples of feature selection: the forward feature selection and the random feature selection. We choose the forward feature selection for our study because it is a standard well-known and relatively fast approach. On the other hand, forward selection has a number of drawbacks mentioned above. Due to them, the

Fig. 3. The behaviour of generalization error for finite training sample size and increasing data dimensionality

selected feature subsets may be far from optimal. So, the random feature subsets may be as good as the specially selected subsets and they (the random subsets) do not require extensive calculations to be obtained. By this reason, we decided to consider random feature selection as well and compare its performance with the forward technique when single and sequential multiple trials of feature selection are performed. The performance of both considered feature selection techniques is also compared with the performance of the most popular feature extraction technique - Principal Component Analysis.

In the forward feature selection, we sequentially select a number of optimal feature subsets having the same size s. First, we perform feature selection on the entire feature set (which consists of p features) obtaining the first feature subset. Then, on the rest of features $(p-s)$ (excluding already selected features) we find the next optimal feature subset. We again omit the selected features from consideration and apply the forward feature selection to the remaining $(p-2s)$ features getting the third optimal feature subset and so on, until all features are assigned to one of the selected feature subsets. All obtained feature subsets have the same dimensionality s with an exception of the last one, which consists of the remaining $p - t \times s$ features after $t = \lfloor p/s \rfloor$ previously performed feature selection trials. On each of the $t+1$ selected feature subsets, the linear classifier is constructed. The decisions of these are aggregated by three different combining rules: the weighted majority voting [7], the mean rule and the decision templates (DT) [8].

For random feature selection we first randomly permute features in the original feature set and then we split the feature set into $t+1$ subsets (so, each feature is included only in one feature subset and does not appear in other subsets). By this, all obtained random feature subspaces (subsets) have the same dimensionality s besides the last one with dimensionality equal to $p - t \times s$. On each of the selected random subspaces, we construct a linear classifier. Then $t+1$ obtained classifiers are combined by the weighted majority rule, the mean rule and the DT combining rule. Let us note that the random feature selection performed by us is different from the Random Subspace Method (RSM) [6]. In both, in random feature selection and in the RSM, features are selected randomly. However, the drawback of the RSM is that it is not guarantied that all features (and therefore all useful information) are taken into consideration at the end (each time one selects a random feature subset from the total set of features but not from the rest after previous selections). Hence, some features may be multiply represented in feature subsets and some may not be taken into consideration at all (especially when a limited number of small random subspaces is used). In our study it is important that all features are used once when we apply combining on top of feature selection. The RSM does not satisfy this requirement. For this reason, we do not include this technique in our study.

When applying the combining technique on top of PCA, we split the set of principal components into subspaces as following. The first feature subset consists of the first s principal components, the second one contains the next s principal components and so on. Similar to the previous cases, the weighted majority, the mean rule and the DT combining rule are used to aggregate classifiers constructed on the subsets of principal components.

The performance of the linear classifier on a single selected feature subset and the combined decision of linear classifiers on multiply selected feature subsets for forward and random feature selection are illustrated in Fig. 4 on the examples of the spectral and digit datasets and in Fig. 5 for the sonar and ionosphere datasets. We see that the benefit of the combining approach applied on top of feature selection depends on the data distribution, on the type of feature selection and on the size of feature subsets used. In the majority of cases, the better performance is achieved by combining feature subsets than by exploiting a single selected/extracted feature subset. Combining is more effective when it is applied on top of a "weak" feature selection technique (random and forward feature selection) than on top of a "strong" feature selection/extraction technique (in our case PCA). The most improvement in performance is gained on the feature subset sizes that are approximately more than twice smaller than the training sample size.

However, no large difference is noticed between random and forward feature selection when combining is applied to multiple feature subsets. It might be explained by the fact that in both cases all original features participate in the combined decision. The random selection approach seems to be more attractive than the forward feature selection technique by two reasons. First, it might be more successful in selecting independent feature subsets than the forward feature selection, for instance for datasets with many correlated features like spectral data. Then, we may obtain independent classifiers on the feature subsets, which for combining are more beneficial than combining correlated classifiers [9]. Secondly, the random feature selection is very fast and does not need any sophisticated algorithm for finding an optimal feature subset.

In our examples, the feature extraction approach (PCA) performs better (with exception of very small sizes of exploited feature subsets) than a single trial of forward or random feature selection (see Fig. 4 and 5), because the extracted features contain more information for discrimination between data classes than a single selected feature set. What concerns the combining approach applied on top of PCA, its' success merely depends on the data distribution and on the size of feature subsets used. Exercising the classifiers combining on principal components may be advantageous only for small feature subset sizes (that are approximately twice smaller than the training sample size) when the subset of the first few extracted principal components is too small and does not preserve enough useful information to discriminate between data classes. For some datasets (for instance, for the spectral and digit data, see Fig. 4) PCA succeeds in extracting good features. In these cases, the combining approach is useless: a single classifier constructed on a sufficient number of the first principal components performs better than combining of sequential subsets of principal components. However, for other datasets (e.g., the sonar and ionosphere data, see Fig. 5) combining applied on top of PCA and performed on small feature subsets is very effective: it improves the best performance achieved by PCA using a single feature subset. Interestingly, for datasets like sonar and ionosphere (see Fig. 5), using combining on top of random feature selection is even more beneficial than PCA (with or without applying the combining approach to subsets of principal components) when small feature subspaces are considered.

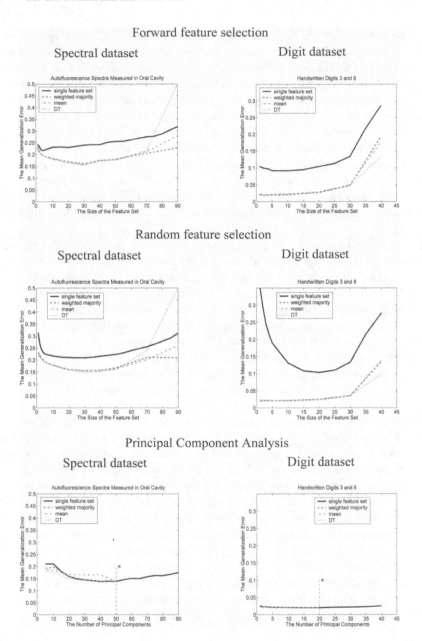

Fig. 4. The mean generalization error (GE) of a single and combined LDA for the forward feature selection (top plots), the random feature selection (middle plots) and PCA (bottom plots) for the spectral (50+50 training objects) and digit (20+20 training objects) datasets. *)For PCA, 100 and 40 principal components are possible to retrieve, because training sample size equals to 100 and 40 objects for spectral and digit dataset, respectively. Hence, the classifiers combining on principal components is performed only up to the feature set size is equal to 50 for spectral dataset and to 20 for digit dataset

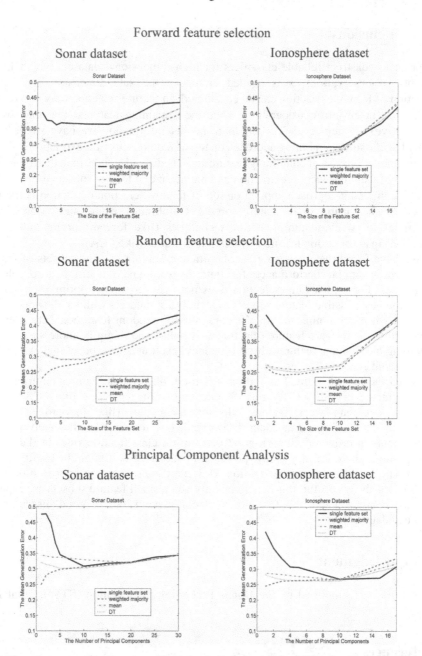

Fig. 5. The mean generalization error (GE) of a single and combined LDA for the forward feature selection (top plots), the random feature selection (middle plots) and PCA (bottom plots) for the sonar (15+15 training objects) and ionosphere (10+10 training objects) datasets. For PCA, 30 and 20 principal components are possible to retrieve, because training sample size equals to 30 and 20 objects for sonar and ionosphere dataset, respectively. Hence, the classifiers combining is performed only up to the feature set size is equal to 30 for sonar dataset and to 20 for ionosphere dataset

4   Conclusions

In order to construct reliable classifiers for high dimensional datasets with a limited number of observations, it is needed to reduce the data dimensionality. Feature selection or feature extraction can be considered. In feature selection only a part of the features is taken into consideration, while the remaining features (that may be still informative) are neglected. To benefit from this information we have suggested to apply the classifier combining approach on top of feature selection/extraction. We have found that the success of combining feature subsets depends on the data distribution, on the type of feature selection/extraction and on the size of feature subsets used.

The combining approach applied on top of feature selection/extraction is the most effective when using small feature subsets. Combining feature subspaces is more beneficial for weak feature selection techniques (like forward or random feature selection) than for strong feature extraction techniques (like PCA).

We have found that exercising the classifiers combining on the subsets of features results in a similar performance for both forward and random feature selection techniques. Forward feature selection does not seem to be the optimal approach to select the best possible feature subsets especially for datasets with small sample sizes. By this, when combining multiple feature subsets, random feature selection may be preferred to the forward feature selection as it is fast and might be more successful in obtaining independent feature subsets (that may result in a more beneficial ensemble of independent classifiers).

When the feature extraction approach is used, all original features contribute in a new extracted feature set. By this, feature extraction technique like PCA is more advantageous than weak feature selection techniques (like forward or random selection). Depending on the data distribution, one may need quite many principal components in order to obtain a good performing classification rule. In the case of small sample sizes, it is not always possible. In such a case, it might be useful to apply combining on top of feature extraction. However, the combining approach on top of PCA is not always useful. It is beneficial only when small feature subsets are exploited and for datasets where the first principal components fail in good discrimination between data classes.

Acknowledgment

This work was supported by the Dutch Technology Foundation (STW), grant RRN 5316.

References

1. Jain, A.K., Chandrasekaran, B.: Dimensionality and Sample Size Considerations in Pattern Recognition Practice. In: Krishnaiah, P.R., Kanal, L.N. (eds.): Handbook of Statistics, Vol. 2. North-Holland, Amsterdam (1987) 835-855
2. Fukunaga, K.: Introduction to Statistical Pattern Recognition. Academic Press (1990) 400-407

3. De Veld, D.C.G., Skurichina, M., Witjes, M.J.H., et.al. Autofluorescence and Diffuse Reflectance Spectroscopy for Oral Oncology. Accepted in Lasers in Surgery and Medicine (2005)
4. Blake, C.L., and Merz, C.J.: UCI repository of machine learning databases (1998). http://www.ics.uci.edu/~mlearn/MLRepository.html
5. Tax, D.M.J., van Breukelen, M., Duin, R.P.W. and Kittler, J.: Combining Multiple Classifiers by Averaging or Multiplying? Pattern Recognition, Vol. 33(**9**) (2000) 1475-1485
6. Ho, T.K.: The Random Subspace Method for Constructing Decision Forests. IEEE Transactions on Pattern Analysis and Machine Intelligence, Vol. 20(**8**) (1998) 832-844
7. Freund, Y., and Shapire, R.E.: Experiments with a New Boosting Algorithm. Proceedings of the 13th International Conference on Machine Learning (1996) 148-156
8. Kuncheva, L.I., Bezdek, J.C., and Duin, R.P.W.: Decision Templates for Multiple Classifier Fusion: An Experimental Comparison. Pattern Recognition, Vol. 34(**2**) (2001) 299-314
9. Kuncheva, L.I.: Combining Pattern Classifiers. Methods and Algorithms. Wiley (2004)

ACE: Adaptive Classifiers-Ensemble System for Concept-Drifting Environments

Kyosuke Nishida, Koichiro Yamauchi, and Takashi Omori

Graduate School of Information Science and Technology, Hokkaido University,
Kita 14 Nishi 9, Kita, Sapporo, 060-0814, Japan
{knishida, yamauchi, omori}@complex.eng.hokudai.ac.jp

Abstract. Most machine learning algorithms assume stationary environments, require a large number of training examples in advance, and begin the learning from scratch. In contrast, humans learn in changing environments with sequential training examples and leverage prior knowledge in new situations. To deal with real-world problems in changing environments, the ability to make human-like quick responses must be developed in machines.

Many researchers have presented learning systems that assume the presence of hidden context and concept drift. In particular, several systems have been proposed that use ensembles of classifiers on sequential chunks of training examples. These systems can respond to gradual changes in large-scale data streams but have problems responding to sudden changes and leveraging prior knowledge of recurring contexts. Moreover, these are not pure online learning systems.

We propose an online learning system that uses an ensemble of classifiers suited to recent training examples. We use experiments to show that this system can leverage prior knowledge of recurring contexts and is robust against various noise levels and types of drift.

1 Introduction

Many real-world problems have a hidden context, which is not given explicitly in input variables and makes the problems very difficult. Changes in the hidden context often cause changes in the target concept, and this is generally known as concept drift [14, 15, 12]. Effective methods for handling concept drift are required in many fields, and studies that assume the presence of a hidden context and concept drift are growing in number. Early systems capable of handling concept drift are STAGGER [10], IB3 [1], and FLORA [15]. Many systems have been proposed to handle a large variety of data (e.g., data on flight simulators [5], Web page access [7], credit card fraud [13], spam mail filtering [2, 4], etc.).

Generally, distinguishing between real concept drift and noise in sequential training examples is very difficult. An effective classifier must be able to respond to both sudden and gradual changes and recognize recurring contexts for lossless learning; however, good strategies for building such an effective classifier depend

N.C. Oza et al. (Eds.): MCS 2005, LNCS 3541, pp. 176–185, 2005.

on the types of the changes, so creating an ideal classifier in various concept-drifting environments is difficult [8, 12].

Several systems have been proposed that use ensembles of classifiers on sequential chunks of training examples for large-scale data streams. The streaming ensemble algorithm (SEA) proposed by Street and Kim [11] uses a simple majority vote of classifiers on sequential chunks and responds to concept drift by replacing an unnecessary classifier with a new classifier. However, if sudden changes occur, the classifiers for old concepts remain voting members for a while after the changes, so their incorrect outputs affect the performance of the system for new concepts. Wang et al. proposed a system similar to SEA for mining concept-drifting data streams [13]. This system uses a weighted average to combine the outputs of classifiers, and the weight of each classifier is a value that is inversely proportional to the mean square error of the classifier on the current chunk. Therefore, the weights of old classifiers often reduce their contributions to the system output; however, we cannot reduce the interference that arises from sudden changes unless we set a small chunk size. The small chunks, however, worsen the performance of each classifier and whole system. Moreover, this approach uses the same weights until the next chunk is given, so a large chunk size extends the period that system cannot respond to new concepts. Furthermore, these two systems replace temporarily unnecessary classifiers with new classifiers, so they often cannot respond to recurring contexts quickly even if they have learned the contexts already.

To overcome these drawbacks, we propose an online learning system that uses an ensemble of classifiers suited to recent training examples. The system includes one online learner and a drift detection mechanism for quick responses to sudden changes, uses the *suitability* of classifiers in a weighted majority vote to avoid the interference of classifiers for old concepts, and leverages prior knowledge in recurring contexts.

The rest of this paper is organized as follows. In Section 2, we outline the proposed adaptive classifiers-ensemble system, ACE. Experimental results are given in Section 3, followed by the conclusion in Section 4. Finally, we append the ACE algorithm in Section A.

2   ACE System

First, we outline the adaptive classifiers-ensemble system, ACE. Then, we describe the system components: one online learner, many batch learners, and a drift detection mechanism. Finally, we show how the final hypothesis of ACE comes from the outputs of classifiers suited to recent training examples.

2.1   Outline

The basic concept of ACE is shown in Figure 1. This system consists of one online learner, many batch learners, and a drift detection mechanism. The outputs of hypotheses from the online learner and the batch learners are integrated by a weighted majority vote using a suitability measure. The system behaves as follows:

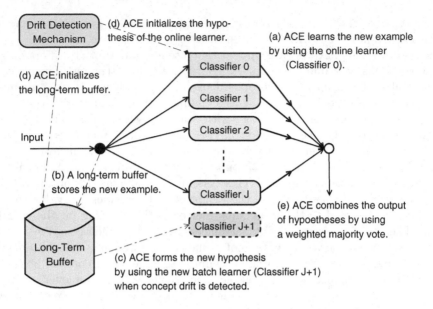

Fig. 1. Basic concept of ACE

1. Let $(\boldsymbol{x}_n \in X, y_n \in Y)$ be a new training example at time n. (a) The system learns $(\boldsymbol{x}_n, y_n)$ and updates the hypothesis $H_0 : X \to Y$ by using the online learner. (b) A long-term buffer, $\boldsymbol{B}_l$, stores $(\boldsymbol{x}_n, y_n)$.
2. When concept drift is detected (or the number of examples in $\boldsymbol{B}_l$ exceeds the chunk size, S_c), (c) Using the new batch learner, the system forms the new hypothesis $H_{J+1} : X \to Y$ from stored training examples in $\boldsymbol{B}_l$, where $J + 1$ is the current number of hypotheses (including H_0). Then, (d) the system initializes H_0 and clears $\boldsymbol{B}_l$ to prepare the online learner for the next training examples.
3. (e) The system forms a final hypothesis by using a weighted majority vote of hypotheses $\{H_j\}_{j=0}^{J}$. The suitability of the jth hypothesis H_j at time n for the most recent S_a examples, $A_{j,n}$, is used to detect drift and make the final hypothesis.

2.2 Online Learner

If sudden changes occur, systems that use only ensembles of classifiers on sequential chunks of training examples delay the response to the changes until the next chunk is given. This interferes with flexible learning, so we include the online learner in the system. We can use any learning algorithm as the online learner of ACE. Some representative algorithms are neural networks, Naive Bayes, and k-Nearest Neighbor [3]. Using window, forgetting, and retraining mechanisms with the online learner proved very effective.

We used the simple k-Nearest Neighbor in the experiments described below.

2.3   Batch Learners

ACE forms a new hypothesis by using the new batch learner from stored training examples in the long-term buffer when concept drift is detected (or when the number of examples in the long-term buffer exceeds the chunk size). We can use any learning algorithm as each batch learner of the system as long as it has high performance. However, ACE does not stop growing and does not use a pruning method to deal with recurring contexts, so simple learning algorithms are better.

Retraining a classifier from scratch to combat concept drift has an effect on sudden changes, but it is not effective for gradual changes. ACE does not retrain the batch learners.

We used C4.5 [9] in the experiments described below.

2.4   Drift Detection Mechanism

The suitability of the jth hypothesis at time n for the most recent S_a examples is

$$A_{j,n} = \textstyle\sum_{s=n-S_a+1}^{n} \mathrm{CR}_{j,s}/S_a, \qquad (1)$$

where $\mathrm{CR}_{j,n} = [\![H_j(\boldsymbol{x}_n) = y_n]\!]$ is the classification result of the jth hypothesis at time n, and $[\![\cdot]\!]$ is 1 if the predicate is true and 0 otherwise. That is, the magnitude of the suitability of each hypothesis can be interpreted as a measure of its accuracy for recent examples. Here, the classification result of the online learner, $\mathrm{CR}_{0,n}$, is the result before the online learner learns the newest example, $(\boldsymbol{x}_n, y_n)$.

We attempted to detect concept drift by using confidence intervals for proportions. First, the upper endpoint, $A_{j,n}^u$, and the lower endpoint, $A_{j,n}^l$, of $100(1 - \alpha)\%$ confidence intervals for the suitability, $A_{j,n}$ (sample proportion), are given by

$$A_{j,n}^l = \frac{S_a}{S_a + z_{\alpha/2}^2} \left(A_{j,n} + \frac{z_{\alpha/2}^2}{2S_a} - z_{\alpha/2}\sqrt{\frac{A_{j,n}(1 - A_{j,n})}{S_a} + \frac{z_{\alpha/2}^2}{4S_a^2}} \right), \qquad (2)$$

$$A_{j,n}^u = \frac{S_a}{S_a + z_{\alpha/2}^2} \left(A_{j,n} + \frac{z_{\alpha/2}^2}{2S_a} + z_{\alpha/2}\sqrt{\frac{A_{j,n}(1 - A_{j,n})}{S_a} + \frac{z_{\alpha/2}^2}{4S_a^2}} \right), \qquad (3)$$

where S_a is the number of samples and $z_{\alpha/2}$ is the upper $(100\alpha/2)$th percentile of the standard normal distribution [6].

Here, $\{H_j\}_{j=1}^{J}$ is not updated after the creation of each hypothesis, so if $A_{j,n}$ is greater than $A_{j,n-S_a}^u$ or less than $A_{j,n-S_a}^l$, concept drift is suspected; however, the online learner continues learning at all times, so we cannot use this method for $A_{0,n}$ and $[A_{0,n-S_a}^l, A_{0,n-S_a}^u]$.

The index of the best suitable hypothesis at time n for the most recent S_a examples is

$$j' = \arg\max_{j:1\sim J} \textstyle\sum_{s=n-S_a+1}^{n} A_{j,s}, \qquad (4)$$

and if

$$A_{j',n} < A^l_{j',n-S_a} \text{ or } A_{j',n} > A^u_{j',n-S_a} \tag{5}$$

is satisfied[1], the system assumes that concept drift occurred, and it forms the new hypothesis $H_{J+1} : X \rightarrow Y$ by using the new batch learner.

Furthermore, when the number of examples in B_l exceeds S_c, the system forms the new hypothesis using the new batch learner to enhance the effect of the classifiers ensemble even if there is no suspicion of concept drift.

2.5   Final Hypothesis

The system forms the final hypothesis by using a weighted majority vote of hypotheses $\{H_j\}_{j=0}^J$. The final hypothesis of the system is

$$H_f(\boldsymbol{x}_n) = \arg\max_{y \in Y} \sum_{j=0}^J \left(\frac{1}{1 - A_{j,n}} \right)^\mu [\![H_j(\boldsymbol{x}_n) = y]\!], \tag{6}$$

where μ is an adjustment factor of the ensemble. The weight of each hypothesis is proportional to its suitability, and it grows exponentially as suitability increases.

By using the suitability of each hypothesis in this weighted majority vote, the system avoids interference from old classifiers and leverages prior knowledge of recurring contexts. Here, a larger μ improves the degree of selection of the hypothesis best suited to recent examples, whereas a smaller μ improves the degree of the ensemble. We think that μ should be chosen based on the complexity of the problem and noise level.

The details of the ACE algorithm are given in Appendix A.

3   Experimental Results: Recurring Context Data

We used recurring context data, which was showed in FLORA [15], and checked the robustness of ACE against various noise levels and types of drift.

In a universe defined by six boolean attributes, $\{a_1, ..., a_6\}$, we defined concepts $A \Leftrightarrow y = a_1 \wedge a_2$ and $B \Leftrightarrow y = (a_3 \wedge a_4) \vee (a_5 \wedge a_6)$, and the two concepts changed by turns. Figure 2 shows $\beta(n)$, the probability that the current context belonged to concept A. Concept A was fully in effect when $\beta(n) = 1$, and concept B had completely taken over when $\beta(n) = 0$. The number of training examples during stable periods, when $\beta(n) = 1$ or $\beta(n) = 0$, and during unstable periods, when $\beta(n) \neq 1$ and $\beta(n) \neq 0$, was given by N and ΔN.

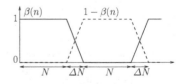

Fig. 2. Function $\beta(n)$

---

[1] Strictly speaking, the j'th hypothesis must be given more than $2S_a$ examples from created time, and the number of examples in B_l must exceeds S_a in addition to Eq. (5) being satisfied.

The total number of training examples was $10 \times 2 \times (N + \Delta N)$, and noise was introduced by switching the labels of $100\eta\%$ of the examples, where η was the noise level.

The systems compared with ACE were 9-Nearest Neighbor (200) and Naive Bayes (200), which use windows of size 200; a streaming ensemble algorithm (SEA) proposed by Street and Kim [11]; Wang et al.'s classifier ensemble approach (WCEA) [13]; BCS, which is a version of ACE that uses the best classifier selection; and Ideal Machine, which knows $\beta(n)$ in advance and assumes concept A if $\beta(n) \geq 0.5$ and concept B otherwise. Here, BCS only differs from ACE in the final hypothesis (Eq. (6)), and the final hypothesis of BCS is

$$H_f(\boldsymbol{x}_n) = H_{\arg\max_j A_{j,n}}(\boldsymbol{x}_n). \tag{7}$$

Note that FLORA also uses the best candidate for the current description to deal with recurring contexts [15]. We used BCS instead of FLORA to see the effect of the best classifier selection.

Table 1. Error counts in recurring context data

N	ΔN	η	period	9-NN	NB	SEA	WCEA	BCS	ACE	IM
			first 1000	74.7	110.0	87.2	47.8	**46.3**	46.8	0
500	0	0	last 1000	104.2	141.5	97.1	39.3	20.8	**14.8**	0
			entire 10000	1018.7	1390.7	953.6	324.6	230.6	**179.2**	0
			first 1000	116.0	145.0	137.2	96.9	**90.6**	90.6	47.0
300	200	0	last 1000	113.0	144.4	118.7	72.4	62.4	**51.7**	46.8
			entire 10000	1126.9	1461.1	1195.6	662.1	646.9	**560.5**	469.4
			first 1000	178.6	194.1	201.5	177.6	174.4	**173.4**	118.5
0	500	0	last 1000	166.7	187.7	178.5	156.0	153.5	**129.5**	116.5
			entire 10000	1685.9	1878.9	1812.6	1484.1	1540.3	**1352.7**	1177.7
			first 1000	175.3	195.4	187.9	164.1	**157.4**	160.5	101.6
500	0	0.1	last 1000	197.1	220.0	192.7	141.4	140.7	**111.6**	98.6
			entire 10000	1967.2	2189.3	1925.7	1346.4	1392.2	**1180.3**	999.0
			first 1000	207.7	224.6	224.7	203.7	195.2	**194.5**	137.2
300	200	0.1	last 1000	205.4	222.6	211.5	170.8	175.9	**142.9**	136.3
			entire 10000	2063.8	2239.6	2130.1	1659.2	1744.1	**1502.5**	1374.1
			first 1000	259.9	265.0	274.9	275.1	264.8	**258.3**	193.5
0	500	0.1	last 1000	246.5	255.4	257.0	231.4	244.8	**207.9**	191.5
			entire 10000	2494.3	2568.8	2586.1	2335.8	2475.0	**2172.6**	1932.8

Notes: 9-NN and NB are 9-Nearest Neighbor and Naive Bayes which uses windows of size 200, and IM is Ideal Machine. All results are averaged over 100 trials.

The parameters for ACE and BCS were $S_a = 30$, $S_c = 200$, $\alpha = 0.01$, and $\mu = 3.0$. The online learner was simple 9-Nearest Neighbor, which does not use a window, and each batch learner was C4.5 [9]. Each classifier of SEA and WCEA also used C4.5. The chunk size and the capacity of classifiers of SEA were 20 and 5, and those of WCEA were 30 and 100. We tuned the parameters of SEA

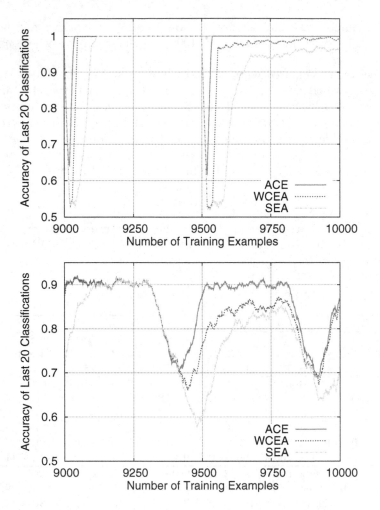

Fig. 3. Accuracy of last 20 classifications of SEA, WCEA, and ACE in last 1000 recurring context data. The upper figure is the case that $(N, \Delta N, \eta) = (500, 0, 0)$, and the lower figure is the case that $(N, \Delta N, \eta) = (300, 200, 0.1)$

and WCEA to respond to sudden changes. SEA and WCEA classify input data randomly when the number of classifiers is 0.

The error counts of each system at various types of drift $((N, \Delta N) = (500, 0)$, $(300, 200)$, and $(0, 500))$ and noise levels $(\eta = 0$ and $0.1)$ are shown in Table 1. All results are averaged over 100 trials. The standard errors in each period are omitted because of space limitations; but the standard errors in the first 1000 and last 1000 examples did not exceed 2.0, and those in the entire 10,000 examples did not exceed 6.5.

9-Nearest Neighbor (200) was worked relatively well when $(N, \Delta N) = (0, 500)$, but it worked poorly when $(N, \Delta N) = (500, 0)$, as shown in Table 1, because systems that use windows cannot easily respond sudden changes. The performance of 9-Nearest Neighbor (200) was not improved even when we used a smaller window, especially in noisy environments. SEA outperformed 9-Nearest Neighbor (200) when $(N, \Delta N) = (500, 0)$ because we tuned the parameters of SEA to respond to sudden changes; in contrast, SEA worked poorly in conditions other than 9-Nearest Neighbor (200), especially when $(N, \Delta N) = (0, 500)$. SEA's performance was not improved even when we enlarged the chunk size or the capacity of classifiers because of the interference of classifiers for old concepts. That is, systems that use a simple majority vote cannot easily deal with various types of concept drift. WCEA worked fairly well in all conditions because it uses a weighted average to combine the outputs of classifiers. However, WCEA cannot perform well unless we set its chunk size small. The small chunk size worsens the performance of each classifier, so the system performance was slightly poor during periods when the current context belonged to concept B because the complexity of concept B was higher than that of concept A (Fig. 3). Moreover, replacing temporarily unnecessary classifiers with new classifiers worsens the performance in recurring contexts.

ACE was more robust against various noise levels and types of drift than WCEA. We can see that ACE achieved about the same high accuracy as Ideal Machine in the final phase of the learning. Furthermore, using ACE, the chunk size need not be small to respond to sudden changes because the drift detection mechanism and the online learner deal with sudden changes. As a result, each classifier's performance in ACE is better than those of WCEA. Because of this property, we believe that ACE can respond to more difficult problems than WCEA can. Finally, BCS worked reasonably well, but it did not work as well as ACE, especially in noisy conditions. We think that systems that use the best classifier selection, such as FLORA, are very simple and reasonable methods for noiseless and uncomplicated problems; however, classifiers ensemble methods are necessary for noisy and complex problems.

4   Conclusion

We proposed a new online learning system, ACE, and checked that it was robust against various noise levels and types of drift in the recurring context data. ACE performed better than other systems that use only ensemble of classifiers on sequential chunks of training examples in all conditions by using a drift detection mechanism and one online learner.

Our future work will be automating the choices of short-term memory size, chunk size, and the adjustment factor of ensemble during learning. The parameter tuning of ACE is not so difficult, but we would like to achieve more human-like learning. Furthermore, we have not implemented a pruning method because conventional methods of pruning classifiers usually worsen performances for recurring contexts; however, we plan to implement a lossless pruning method in the future. Finally, we will investigate applications of ACE to real-world problems.

A   Algorithm of ACE System

The algorithm of ACE is given in Figure 4.

Algorithm ACE
Parameters:
short-term memory size S_a, chunk size S_c ($> S_a$)
confidence level $100(1 - \alpha)\%$, adjustment factor of ensemble μ
Initialize $J = 0$, $\boldsymbol{B}_l = \{\}$, $N_0 = 0$.
for each $(\boldsymbol{x}_n, y_n)$ where $\boldsymbol{x}_n \in X$, $y_n \in Y$, $n : 1 \sim$

Output the final hypothesis $H_f(\boldsymbol{x}_n) = \arg\max_{y \in Y} \sum_{j=0}^{J} \left(\dfrac{1}{1 - A_{j,n-1}} \right)^{\mu} [\![H_j(\boldsymbol{x}_n) = y]\!]$.

for each $j : 0 \sim J$
Set $\mathrm{CR}_{j,n} = [\![H_j(\boldsymbol{x}_n) = y_n]\!]$,
$$
A_{j,n} = \begin{cases} \sum_{s=\max[n-S_a+1, N_0+1]}^{n} \mathrm{CR}_{j,s} / \min[n - N_0 + 1, S_a] & \text{if } j = 0 \\ \sum_{s=n-S_a+1}^{n} \mathrm{CR}_{j,s} / S_a & \text{otherwise} \end{cases}.
$$
Compute $100(1 - \alpha)\%$ confidence intervals for proportions $[A_{j,n}^l, A_{j,n}^u]$.
endfor

Call **Online Learner** $(\boldsymbol{x}_n, y_n)$; Update hypothesis $H_0 : X \to Y$.
Add $(\boldsymbol{x}_n, y_n)$ to $\boldsymbol{B}_l$.

Set AcqFlag = false, $j' = \arg\max_{j:1 \sim J} \sum_{s=n-S_a+1}^{n} A_{j,s}$.
if $\{ A_{j',n} < A_{j',n-S_a}^l$ or $A_{j',n} > A_{j',n-S_a}^u \}$ and $n - N_0 \geq S_a$ and $n - N_{j'} \geq 2S_a$ **then**
Set AcqFlag = true.
endif
if $n - N_0 \geq S_c$ **then** Set AcqFlag = true. **endif**

if AcqFlag = true **then**

Call **Batch Learer** $(\boldsymbol{B}_l)$; Get hypothesis $H_{J+1} : X \to Y$ with error
$$
E_{J+1} = \frac{\sum_{(\boldsymbol{x}_i, y_i) \in \boldsymbol{B}_l} [\![H_{J+1}(\boldsymbol{x}_i) \neq y_i]\!]}{|\boldsymbol{B}_l|}.
$$

if $E_{J+1} \geq 1/|Y|$ **then** Discard H_{J+1}.
else
for each $m : (n - S_a + 1) \sim n$
Set $\mathrm{CR}_{J+1,m} = \mathrm{CR}_{0,m}$,
    $A_{J+1,m} = A_{0,m}$, $A_{J+1,m}^l = A_{0,m}^l$, $A_{J+1,m}^u = A_{0,m}^u$.
endfor

Set $N_{J+1} = n$, $J = J + 1$.
endif
Initialize H_0; Set $\boldsymbol{B}_l = \{\}$, $N_0 = n$.

endif
endfor

Fig. 4. ACE algorithm

References

1. D.W. Aha, D. Kibler, and M.K. Albert, "Instance-based learning algorithms," *Machine Learning*, 6, pp. 37–66, 1991.
2. P. Cunningham, N. Nowlan, S.J. Delany, M. Haahr, "A case-based approach to spam filtering that can track concept drift," *ICCBR'03 Workshop on Long-Lived CBR Systems*, Trondheim, Norway, Jun. 2003.
3. R.O. Duda, P.E. Hart, and D.G. Stork, "Pattern Classification," Wiley-Interscience, 2nd edition, 2000.
4. S.J. Delany, P. Cunningham, A. Tsymbal, and L. Coyle, "A case-based technique for tracking concept drift in spam filtering," Technical Report TCD-CS-2004-30, Department of Computer Science, Trinity College Dublin, Aug. 2004.
5. M.B. Harries, C. Sammut, and K. Horn, "Extracting hidden context," *Machine Learning*, 32, pp. 101–126, 1998.
6. R.V. Hogg and E.A. Tanis, "Probability and Statistical Inference," Prentice Hall, 5th edition, 1997.
7. G. Hulten, L. Spencer, and P. Domingos, "Mining time-changing data streams," *Proc. of the 7th ACM SIGKDD Int. Conference on Knowledge Discovery and Data Mining*, pp. 97–106, 2001.
8. L.I. Kuncheva, "Classifier ensembles for changing environments," *Proc. 5th Int. Workshop on Multiple Classifier Systems (MCS 2004)*, Springer-Verlag, LNCS 3077, pp. 1–15, Cagliari, Italy, 2004.
9. J.R. Quinlan, "C4.5: programs for machine learning," Morgan Kaufmann, 1993.
10. J. Schlimmer and R.H. Granger, "Incremental learning from noisy data," *Machine Learning*, 1(3), pp. 317–354, 1986.
11. W.N. Street and Y.S. Kim, "A streaming ensemble algorithm (SEA) for large-scale classification," *Proc. of the 7th ACM SIGKDD Int. Conference on Knowledge Discovery and Data Mining*, pp. 377–382, 2001.
12. A. Tsymbal, "The problem of concept drift: definitions and related work," Technical Report TCD-CS-2004-15, Department of Computer Science, Trinity College Dublin, Apr. 2004.
13. H. Wang, W. Fan, P.S. Yu, and J. Han, "Mining concept-drifting data streams using ensemble classifiers," *Proc. of the 9th ACM SIGKDD Int. Conference on Knowledge Discovery and Data Mining*, pp. 226–235, 2003.
14. G. Widmer and M. Kubat, "Effective learning in dynamic environments by explicit concept tracking," *Proc. of the Sixth European Conference on Machine Learning*, Springer-Verlag, pp. 227–243, 1993.
15. G. Widmer and M. Kubat, "Learning in the presence of concept drift and hidden contexts", *Machine Learning*, 23, pp. 69–101, 1996.

Using Decision Tree Models and Diversity Measures in the Selection of Ensemble Classification Models

Mordechai Gal-Or[1], Jerrold H. May[2], and William E. Spangler[1]

[1] School of Business Administration, Duquesne University,
Pittsburgh, Pennsylvania 15282 USA
{Galor, Spangler}@duq.edu
[2] Katz Graduate School of Business, University of Pittsburgh,
Pittsburgh, Pennsylvania 15260 USA
jerrymay@katz.pitt.edu

Abstract. This paper describes a contingency-based approach to ensemble classification. Motivated by a business marketing problem, we explore the use of decision tree models, along with diversity measures and other elements of the task domain, to identify highly-performing ensemble classification models. Working from generated data sets, we found that 1) decision tree models can significantly improve the identification of highly-performing ensembles, and 2) the input parameters for a decision tree are dependent on the characteristics and demands of the decision problem, as well as the objectives of the decision maker.

1 Introduction

With the rise of personal video recorders (PVRs) and the corresponding ability of television viewers to minimize or eliminate traditional in-stream television advertising, businesses are increasingly motivated to discover new methods for delivering advertising to viewers. Toward that end, our research seeks to use the data-collection capabilities of the PVR along with statistical modeling techniques to identify the demographic characteristics of viewers based on their viewing patterns: i.e., the programs they watch and when they tend to watch them. While we have found that television viewing data can be used to profile viewers, we also have found that different data segments (e.g., weekend vs. weekday viewing) and different data mining algorithms (e.g., neural networks, logistic regression and linear discriminant analysis) generate different sets of predictions. [8] The sense that no single model in this application would clearly prevail, as well as the general notion that combining classifiers can provide better predictions than individual models [5], lead us to believe that ensemble classifiers should be more effective than individual approaches.

This paper describes a process for choosing better-performing ensembles from a collection of candidates assembled from individual models. The objective is to build a classification model that can distinguish between highly-performing and poorly-performing ensembles, identify the ensembles that are more likely to be highly-

N.C. Oza et al. (Eds.): MCS 2005, LNCS 3541, pp. 186–195, 2005.
© Springer-Verlag Berlin Heidelberg 2005

performing ones, and produce a consensus result that is better than any individual classification model. The clear implication is that not all ensembles will perform better than individual models. Some ensembles will perform no better than an individual model, and some will even perform worse.

Our goal is to identify which specific groups of models will perform better based *a priori* on a specific set of identifiable characteristics of the models and the domain. Our study produced decision tree models that can identify better-performing ensembles based on certain situational characteristics, including the measured diversity of the ensembles as well as the performance of the ensembles' constituent models and the prevalence of the target group in the population at large. Starting from the assumption that ensemble performance is explained in part by the compensatory diversity of the ensemble's constituent models, the decision tree models identify which of the various diversity measures are most closely related to ensemble performance, and indicate specifically how the numerical values of those measures are indicative of either highly- or poorly-performing ensembles.

This application is representative of a more generic problem – i.e., a marketing problem that entails identifying a target audience and delivering customized advertising to that audience. The generic problem domain is characterized by two essential characteristics: 1) the target audience is a relatively small percentage of the overall population, and 2) the cost of incorrectly classifying a non-member of the target audience as a member (i.e., labeling a '0' as a '1') is much more costly than classifying a member as a non-member (i.e., labeling a '1' as a '0'). This is in turn distinguishes the underlying data set from the various candidate data sets in the public domain.

2 Measuring Performance

A classifier or ensemble might be considered to perform 'well' if it simply produces better predictions than random guessing [5]. Similarly, an ensemble might be considered accurate if it produces predictions that, overall, are better than the predictions of its constituents. Evidence suggests that ensembles indeed can be more accurate than individual models [6, 13] – but only when their predictions reflect some level of diversity – i.e., when they tend to disagree [1, 3, 4, 6]. Bagging and boosting methods, for example, improve performance because they produce diverse classifiers [2]. While the conceptual meaning of diversity is agreed upon – e.g., Dietterich defines diversity as the tendency of constituent models to produce different errors on new data points [5] – multiple ways have been proposed to measure it.

The way in which we choose to measure performance impacts significantly on the process of choosing an ensemble classifier for decision support. Because a number of criteria can be used to assess the performance of a classifier – either individual or ensemble – a decision maker has to determine which of those criteria are most important given the situation at hand.

Classification of television viewers is characterized by two measures of performance:

- *accuracy*: measures the percentage of observations predicted by a model to be members of a target group (i.e., predicted 1s) which actually are members of the group (i.e., actual 1s). Alternatively stated, it is the probability that an observation is a 1 given that it is predicted as a 1; i.e., *P(actual=1 | prediction=1)*.
- *sensitivity*: measures the percentage of actual members of the group that are predicted to be members of the group. In this case, it is the conditional probability of predicting that an observation is a 1 given that it is a 1; i.e., *P(prediction=1 | actual=1)*.

It is important to note that the accuracy and sensitivity performance are dependent measures, in that accuracy can be improved at the expense of sensitivity, and vice versa. For example, if a model is configured so that only the more likely group members are considered, the accuracy will improve – i.e., those predicted to be a member are more likely actually to be a member. However, constraining the number of observations under consideration by the model also means that the model will miss more of the actual members of the group, thereby degrading sensitivity (see [7] for a more detailed discussion of this issue).

When individual classifiers are collected into an ensemble, the consensus prediction of the ensemble decision problem involves three possible ensemble outcomes: 1) the ensemble performs better on all performance measures (i.e., on both accuracy and sensitivity), 2) the ensemble performs worse on all performance measures, or 3) the ensemble performs better on one performance measure but not on the other. The choice of ensemble, particularly in case 3, depends on the relative importance of the performance measures and the goals of the decision maker. For example, if an advertiser places more importance on identifying as many potential consumers as possible, then he or she might choose an ensemble that is better in sensitivity than in accuracy. Conversely, considering that a PVR is limited in the number of ads it can store physically, it becomes important to limit the ads delivered to the PVR only to those that are deemed potentially relevant to the viewer. In that case, accuracy is more important. The ideal solution of course is to find ensembles that are better than their constituents on both measures. That is the goal of this study.

3 Methodology and Experimental Design[1]

Our initial investigation of ensemble classification utilized generated data in an experimental context, which provided greater control over the large number of situational variables inherent in the actual viewing data. The process included the following steps: 1) identification of controllable experimental parameters, identified from the original (real world) data set, 2) generation of individual model and ensemble vectors, which simulate the output of multiple classifiers, and 3) generation of diver-

---

[1] The current study is an extension of our previous work. Because the methodology used in this study is similar, we provide an overview of the methodology and experimental design here, and refer the reader to the original study [8] for a more detailed explanation.

sity measures and decision tree models, to identify heuristics for identifying better performing ensembles. Each step is described below.

3.1 Experimental Parameters

Because we are using generated data, we were able to identify specific characteristics of the real world viewer data set and then manipulate those values in the context of 29 controlled experiments, each representing different values of selected parameters. The parameters and values used include:

Number of items classified (N): the number of individuals to be classified by each method. We used N=600, because this was the smallest number allowing for whole numbers in each cell of the individual classifiers' common confusion matrix.

Percent in the population (p): the fraction of the general population that belongs to the target group. In this experiment, we set p = 10, 20 and 30%, because in a television viewing application, those are typical values for a target audience.

Total number of models (c) from which an ensemble can be created. This and L determine the number of replications for each set of parameters, because we generate all $_cC_L$ ensembles of L items chosen from the c possible. We used c=20.

Number of models (L) that participate in the ensemble. We set L=3, because it avoids tie votes while also keeping the number of replications manageable. Thus there are $_{20}C_3 = 1140$ replications for each set of parameters.

Designed accuracy (ac) and sensitivity (se) of each individual model: We set the values of ac and se to 20, 30, 40 and 50%, depending on the value of p. As shown in Table 1, ac and se are set strictly better than p, based on the assumption that individual model accuracy and sensitivity should exceed that of random choice.

Voting policy: Currently, the consensus prediction of an ensemble is achieved through a simple majority (democratic) voting procedure, which is facilitated by having an odd number of voting models in each ensemble. While democratic voting is an effective and popular approach [12], other more complex voting schemes are potentially effective and could be employed based on a variety of criteria [9].

Table 1. Parameter values for the generation of individual classifiers

Experiment Number	p	ac	se
1-16	10	20, 30, 40, 50	20, 30, 40, 50
17-25	20	30, 40, 50	30, 40, 50
26-29	30	40, 50	40, 50

3.2 Individual and Ensemble Model Vectors

The data initialization phase of the experiment then generated performance and diversity measures in the context of the situational parameters defined for each of the experiments described above. This phase began with the generation of the actual group assignment vector, against which an ensemble's performance is assessed. In a real data set, this vector would indicate whether or not an individual belongs to the target class (i.e., either 1 or 0). In the experimental approach, the vector is populated with 1s and 0s depending on the value of the percent in the population (p) parameter. For example, if the value of p is 20 (percent) and the number of individuals (N) is 600, then 120 of the values in the vector would be '1', with the rest being '0'.

The next step is to generate the model prediction vectors that will represent the predictions of c different hypothetical models. The number and content of the vectors are based on the value of c defined in the database, along with the accuracy and sensitivity rates specified for each of the prediction vectors. Subsets of the ($c=20$) prediction vectors are then assembled into ensembles of ($L=3$) voting vectors, resulting in the generation of ($_cC_L = 1140$) ensemble predictions for each individual – achieved by tallying the votes of each of the participating voting vectors within each ensemble. The accuracy and sensitivity rates of each ensemble are calculated by comparing the consensus predictions of the ensemble with the actual values in the group assignment vector. The ensemble's performance is then determined by comparing it to the rates of the individual vectors/models within the ensemble.

3.3 Diversity Measures and Decision Tree Models

The use of diversity measures in this study builds on the work of Kuncheva and her colleagues [10, 11, 15, 16], as well as on our earlier explorations of diversity measures using neural networks [8]. Consistent with that approach, in this study we used twenty-two diversity measures for each ensemble, consisting of fifteen pairwise and seven non-pairwise measures. Each of these measures were used to calculate diversity between and among pairs and groups of the models in each ensemble across all observations.

The five pairwise measures are (1) Yule's Q-statistic (Q), (2) the correlation coefficient (ρ), (3) the disagreement measure (D), (4) the double-fault measure (DF), and (5) the chi-square ($\chi2$) value for deviation from independence for the two-way table induced by two models. Because each ensemble includes three models, each ensemble produces three pairwise values. Each of the five pairwise measures in turn consists of three separate measures – the average across the three values, as well as the minimum and the maximum – thus resulting in 15 pairwise measures. The minimum, maximum, and average are denoted by subscripts, i.e., Yule's-Q average is Q_{avg} and its minimum is Q_{min}.

The remaining seven diversity measures are derived from all of the models in the ensemble. The seven non-pairwise measures are: (1) the Kohavi-Wolpert variance (KW), (2) the interrater agreement (κ), (3) the entropy measure (E), (4) the measure of difficulty (θ), (5) the generalized diversity[2] (GD), (6) the coincident failure diversity (CFD), and (7) the chi-square value ($\chi2$) for deviation from independence for the table induced by all the models.

---

[2] This term is from Kuncheva, but also is referenced as Distinct Failure Diversity (DFD) [14].

The decision tree models in turn were generated using the diversity measures as independent variables – and in certain cases, the values of p, ac and se (described below) – and a binary measure of an ensemble's performance relative to its constituent models as the dependent variable. The value of the DV is 1 if the ensemble performed better on both accuracy and sensitivity; else, it is 0. Thus, the tree model attempts to predict an ensemble's relative performance (0 or 1) based on the values of the diversity measures.

The models were constructed using both the CART and C5 techniques available within Clementine version 8.5. We constructed decision tree models using two basic sets of input parameters: 1) the diversity measures and the fixed values of p, ac and se used to generate the individual classification models, and 2) the diversity measures only, based on the assumption that in many cases *a priori* knowledge of p, ac and/or se will not be available. Furthermore, for the C5 models, we varied the *minimum number of items in a child node*, setting the values to 125, 250, 375 and 500. For the CART models, we set both the *child node size minimum* and the *parent node size minimum* in the stopping criteria (again 125/250/375/500), and set the *pruning option* to 'off'. Other than these variations, we used the default options available for both the C5 and CART implementations within Clementine[3]. The result of these manipulations was 16 decision tree models: 8 using C5 and 8 using CART. The 8 trees from C5 and CART were each comprised of 2 sets of 4 trees (involving the 4 values of node size). In the first set, p, ac and se are included as additional situational parameters along with the diversity results; in the second set they are not included.

We should note that because this is a retrospective study, we did not either define a fixed test set or do cross-validation. In a purely retrospective study, there is an advantage in building a model using all of the data, because the resulting model may best represent the structure inherent in the data set. If the purpose of the model were to predict new observations, then proper validation methodology would have required either a fixed test set or cross-validation sufficient to verify the generalizability of the model to such new situations.

4   Results

The experimental results shed light on two essential questions. First, at a fundamental level, does a decision tree model assist a decision maker in choosing better-performing ensembles – i.e., is the decision tree approach viable? Second, assuming the approach is viable, how should decision trees be constructed – i.e., what situational parameters should be considered in the construction of decision tree models and what techniques should be used to build them? Answering the first question requires an assessment of the accuracy and sensitivity of each ensemble relative to its

---

[3] The default parameter values used in Clementine were as follows: symbolics not grouped, no boosting, no cross-validation, model favors accuracy over generality, 0% expected noise, pruning severity of 75, minimum of 2 cases in a child node, global pruning used, attributes are not winnowed, and equal misclassification costs.

constituent models, and a determination of whether the ensemble performs better on one or both of those measures. Notably, each of the generated ensembles produced an accuracy greater than any of its constituent models (i.e., 50%), which means that in the context of our experiments, sensitivity becomes the basis for assessing ensemble performance. A 'better' ensemble in the Pareto sense is one with a sensitivity greater than the *a priori* sensitivity value established for the constituent models, because that ensemble is at least as good in both measures and is strictly better in at least one.

A decision tree model in turn is judged based on how well it performs relative to a naïve model that simply predicts that all ensembles will perform better than their constituents. In that regard, 20% of the generated ensembles have a higher sensitivity value than their constituents, and thus are considered 'better'. Because the naïve model in these experiments will be correct in 20% of its predictions, the accuracy of any decision tree model should exceed that level to be considered viable.

Regarding the basic viability of the decision tree approach, the accuracy of both of the decision methods in identifying better-performing ensembles easily exceeded the actual number of better-performers (i.e., 20%). As shown in Table 2, the accuracy of the C5 models varied from 61.4% (min child nodes=500; p, ac and se unknown) to 69.55% (min. child nodes = 250; p, ac and se known). CART accuracy varied from 57.95% (all values of child/parent nodes; *p, ac* and *se* not available to the model) to 67.78% (min child nodes = 125; *p, ac* and *se* available to the model).

Table 2. Error and Accuracy Rates for CART and C5

	p, ac, and se not available				*p, ac, and se available*			
	CART							
min child nodes	125	250	375	500	125	250	375	500
Accuracy	0.6778	0.6468	0.6186	0.6125	0.5795	0.5795	0.5795	0.5795
	C5							
min child nodes	125	250	375	500	125	250	375	500
Accuracy	0.6740	0.6641	0.6439	0.6140	0.6821	0.6955	0.6736	0.6620

The answer to the second question – i.e., the structure and composition of the decision tree models – is somewhat more complex. Overall, C5 and CART perform differently depending on the parameters included in the model and the decision criteria being used. As suggested above, the overall accuracy of C5 was somewhat better than that of CART. When p, ac and se are available to the model, C5 is much more accurate: 67.83% vs. 57.95% on average across all values of *min. child nodes*. When p, ac and se are not known, C5 is marginally better: 64.89% vs. 63.89%. However, when a decision maker considers the sensitivity of the model – i.e., its ability to discover the better-performing ensembles – the performance of CART improves dramatically, particularly when p, ac and se are known. When *p, ac* and *se* are included in the model, CART's error rate in predicting actual 1s (i.e., better-performing ensembles) is much lower than C5 – for CART, P (predicted 0 I actual 1) = 10.28%

(avg); for C5, the average error is 31.71%. When *p, ac* and *se* are not available, the respective error rates are almost identical – CART = 36.64%, C5 = 36.62%.

The composition of the respective decision tree models is described in terms of the parameters included within the models (i.e., diversity measures, and p, ac and se), and the structure of the generated trees. Table 3 shows the parameters included within the 16 decision tree models described above.   The table is partitioned into whether the models had access to p, ac and se, and then for each of those, whether the models came from C5 or CART.   Thus, each cell in the table shows which of the diversity measures were included in the models across the four values of child node size. We considered the extent to which a parameters was included in the four models to be an indication of its contribution to the overall predictive power of the model. Thus, in the table, each cell lists the parameters that appeared in a) all four decision trees, b) a subset of the decision trees (i.e., [1], [2] or [3]), or c) none of the decision trees.

Several of the results are noteworthy. For example, Table 3 indicates that when model sensitivity is available, both C5 and CART include it in all models. CART also includes percent in population when that parameter is known. The CART models in particular rely on p and se to the extent that most of the diversity measures are not included at all. While C5 considers relatively more diversity measures, only 4 of those measures are included in all 4 of the C5 models. Only one of the measures – CFD – appears across all models for both C5 and CART, although chi-square appears in CART as a pairwise measure ($\chi2$(avg)) and in C5 as a non-pairwise measure. When *p, ac* and *se* are not available in the model construction, many more of the diversity measures are included by both C5 and CART. As shown, C5 includes 7 diversity measures in all 4 models; CART includes 8 measures. The double fault (average and minimum), correlation coefficient (average and minimum), and CFD measures appear in all 8 models. CFD is the only diversity measure included in all 16 decision tree models; i.e., regardless of whether p, ac and se are known.

5 Conclusions

This study suggests, in part, a contingency-based approach to the construction of decision tree models for predicting better-performing ensembles – based on *a priori* characteristics of the domain and preferences of the decision maker. When accuracy in identifying ensembles is most important, a decision maker would choose models constructed from C5, which clearly performed better than CART. However, when sensitivity of the decision tree model is most important, meaning that the objective is to find as many of the better-performing ensembles as possible, CART becomes the preferred technique. Its error rate in predicting actual 1s is at least as low as C5, and in some circumstances is much lower.

The differential performance of CART indicates the important role of situational characteristics such as percent of the target group in the population (*p*), as well as the accuracy (*ac*) and sensitivity (*se*) of the constituent models.   As hinted above, when those parameters are available and when sensitivity is the main decision criterion, CART performs better than C5. Furthermore, the overall model construction process also is governed by the availability of *p, ac* and *se*. With access to those parameters, the decision tree techniques are much less dependent on the diversity measures, and thus the potential need to calculate many of those measures is reduced. This is particularly true for CART, which consistently requires only two other diversity measures in order to build a model. Conversely, the diversity measures become much more important to the models when *p, ac* and *se* are *not* available. In that case, the results of this research provide a basis for identifying which of the diversity measures should be considered by a decision maker.

This research is an on-going activity, and in that respect it raises a number of questions for further investigation. First, our experimental design is set to either include or exclude p, ac and se as a group. In this and other domains, a decision maker might have knowledge of the percent in population of the target group, but not be able to ascertain the *a priori* accuracy and sensitivity of the individual decision models. Thus, a logical next step would be to allow the decision trees to include or exclude only the values for *p*. Second, the results do not shed light on the specific relationship

Table 3. Parameters included in the decision tree models ('*' = *p, ac* and *se* are available)

	C5*	CART*	C5	CART
Parameters included in all trees	se E $\chi 2$ D_{avg} CFD	*% in pop* *se* $\chi 2_{avg}$ CFD	$\rho_{avg}, \rho_{min},$ ρ_{max} DF_{avg} DF_{min} CFD GD	ρ_{avg} ρ_{min} DF_{avg} DF_{min} $\chi 2$ $\chi 2_{avg}$ E CFD
Parameters included in a subset of trees	$Q_{avg}[3]$ $DF_{avg}[3]$ $Q_{min}[1]$ $DF_{min}[1]$ $\rho_{avg}[1]$ $DF_{max}[2]$ $\chi 2_{avg}[2]$ $E[1]$ $D_{min}[2]$ $\kappa[2]$ $D_{max}[1]$ $GD[1]$ $\chi 2[3]$	$\chi 2[2]$	$\chi 2_{avg}[2]$ $DF_{min}[2]$ $D_{max}[3]$	$Q_{avg}[3]$ $D_{avg}[2]$ $D_{min}[1]$ $GD[1]$
Parameters excluded from all trees	$\chi 2_{min}$ Q_{max} ρ_{min}, ρ_{max} KW θ	Q_{avg} Q_{min} Q_{max} ρ_{avg}, ρ_{max} $\chi 2_{avg}$ $\chi 2_{min}$ DF_{avg} E DF_{min} κ DF_{max} GD D_{avg} $\chi 2$ D_{min} KW D_{max} θ	$\chi 2_{min}$ $\chi 2_{max}$ Q_{max} $\chi 2_{max}$ KW θ κ	Q_{min} Q_{max} D_{max} DF_{max} $\chi 2_{min}$ ρ_{max} κ KW θ

between diversity and performance. We have shown that knowledge of diversity measure values is useful to a decision tree model in identifying higher-performing ensembles, but further research is needed into the specific question of how diversity measures relate to diversity. For example, given that the value of CFD is highly indicative of ensemble performance, what are the specific elements of diversity measured by CFD that make it better at predicting performance? In other words, why is CFD a superior method? Answering this question requires a more detailed examination of the functionality of diversity measures in the context of this decision problem.

References

[1] Ali, K.M., Pazzani, M.J., Error Reduction through Learning Multiple Descriptions. Machine Learning, 24, 3, (1996), 173-202.

[2] Breiman, L., Bagging predictors. Machine Learning, 24, 2, (1996), 123-140.

[3] Chan, P.K., Stolfo, S.J., On the Accuracy of Meta-learning for Scalable Data Mining. Journal of Intelligent Information Systems, 8, (1997), 5-28.

[4] Davenport, T.H., Saving IT's Soul: Human-Centered Information Management. Harvard Business Review, March-April, (1994), 119-131.

[5] Dietterich, T.G., Machine Learning Research: Four Current Directions. AI Magazine, 18, 4, (1997), 97-136.

[6] Dietterich, T.G., An Experimental Comparison of Three Methods for Constructing Ensembles of Decision Trees: Bagging, Boosting, and Randomization. Machine Learning, 40, 2, (2000), 139-157.

[7] Gal-Or, E., Gal-Or, M., May, J.H., Spangler, W.E., Targeted Advertising Strategies on Television. (2005), University of Pittsburgh Working Paper.

[8] Gal-Or, M., May, J.H., Spangler, W.E., Assessing The Predictive Accuracy of Diversity Measures with Domain-Dependent, Asymmetric Misclassification Costs. Information Fusion, 6, 1, (2005), 37-48.

[9] Kittler, J., Hatef, M., Duin, R.P.W., Matas, J., On Combining Classifiers. IEEE Transactions on Pattern Analysis and Machine Intelligence, 20, 3, (1998), 226-239.

[10] Kuncheva, L.I., Whitaker, C.J., Measures of Diversity in Classifier Ensembles and Their Relationship with the Ensemble Accuracy. Machine Learning, 51, 2, (2003), 181-207.

[11] Kuncheva, L.I., Whitaker, C.J., Shipp, C.A., Duin, R.P.W., Limits on the majority vote accuracy in classifier fusion. Pattern Analysis Applications, 6, (2003), 22-31.

[12] Lam, L., Suen, C.Y., Application of Majority Voting to Pattern Recognition: An Analysis of Its Behavior and Performance. IEEE Transactions on Systems, Man and Cybernetics, 27, 5, (1997), 553-568.

[13] Opitz, D., Maclin, R., Popular Ensemble Methods: An Empirical Study. Journal of Artificial Intelligence Research, 11, (1999), 169-198.

[14] Partridge, D., Krzanowski, W., Software Diversity: Practical Statistics for its Measurement and Exploitation. Information and Software Technology, 39, (1997), 707-712.

[15] Shipp, C.A., Kuncheva, L.I., Relationships between combination methods and measures of diversity in combining classifiers. Information Fusion, 3, 2, (2002), 135-148.

[16] Whitaker, C.J., Kuncheva, L.I., Examining the relationship between majority vote accuracy and diversity in bagging and boosting. (2003), School of Informatics, University of Wales: Bangor.

Ensembles of Classifiers from Spatially Disjoint Data

Robert E. Banfield[1], Lawrence O. Hall[1], Kevin W. Bowyer[2],
and W. Philip Kegelmeyer[3]

[1] Department of Computer Science and Engineering, ENB118,
University of South Florida,
4202 E. Fowler Avenue, Tampa, FL 33620-9951, USA
{rbanfiel, hall}@csee.usf.edu
[2] Department of Computer Science and Engineering,
University of Notre Dame, South Bend, IN 46556, USA
kwb@cse.nd.edu
[3] Sandia National Laboratories,
Biosystems Research Department, P.O. Box 969, MS 9951
Livermore, CA 94551-0969, USA
wpk@ca.sandia.gov

Abstract. We describe an ensemble learning approach that accurately learns from data that has been partitioned according to the arbitrary spatial requirements of a large-scale simulation wherein classifiers may be trained only on the data local to a given partition. As a result, the class statistics can vary from partition to partition; some classes may even be missing from some partitions. In order to learn from such data, we combine a fast ensemble learning algorithm with Bayesian decision theory to generate an accurate predictive model of the simulation data. Results from a simulation of an impactor bar crushing a storage canister and from region recognition in face images show that regions of interest are successfully identified.

1 Introduction

We consider the problem of dealing with an amount of data too large to fit in the memory of any one computer node and too bandwidth-intensive to move around to neighboring nodes, a problem which has far-reaching implications [1]. Since the data cannot be moved around between nodes, there may exist no logical grouping other than that in which it was originally stored. Such a problem exists for the United States Department of Energy's Advanced Simulation and Computing program [2], wherein a supercomputer simulates a hypothetical real-world event. Data is stored on disks attached to compute nodes according to its spatial location within the 3D simulation. The concern is that the storage allocation for the simulation optimizes for balanced and efficient computation, without regard to conditions that might make it easy or difficult for a machine learning algorithm to use the resulting data.

In analyzing these simulations, developers and users want to spot anomalies which may take days to find in a massive simulation, especially if it is important to spot

N.C. Oza et al. (Eds.): MCS 2005, LNCS 3541, pp. 196–205, 2005.

every anomaly. So, marking some areas of interest and finding others in the same or similar types of simulations can greatly reduce the time to debug and analyze a simulation. Generally, experts will manually designate salient areas in the simulation as "interesting" according to personal, subjective criteria. This process would be markedly sped up by analyzing those points (examples) and suggesting new points across each compute node.

In this paper, we show examples from a simulation of a storage canister being crushed by an impactor bar from above at approximately 300 miles per hour. In order to illustrate how the complete simulation appears, a visualization of the partitions is provided below in Figure 1. The different shades of grey represent the partitioning of the simulation in a distributed environment. Note that pieces of the impactor bar crushing the canister are also broken up spatially according to the partition.

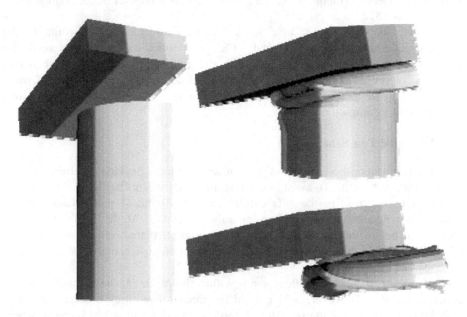

Fig. 1. A visualization of the data as distributed across compute nodes. There are four partitions shown in different gray levels as the storage canister is crushed

As a result of the partitioning, areas of saliency may be limited to only a few nodes. Salient points, being few in number, exhibit a pathological minority-class classification problem. In the case of a partition having zero salient points, a single-class "classifier" will be learned. Furthermore, a prominent event on one node is not necessarily indicative of saliency on another node experiencing a similar event.

We show that it is possible to obtain an accurate prediction of salient points even when the data is broken up arbitrarily in 3D space with no particular relation to feature space. Results on this data set indicate that experts working with much larger simulations can benefit from the predictive guidance obtained from only a small amount of relevant data.

2 Data Description

In this paper, we look at experiments in which a canister is rapidly crushed much like a person might crush a soda can. The walls of the canister buckle under the pressure and the top of the canister accelerates downward until it meets the bottom. In our experiments we observe 44 slices of time in which the above event was simulated and recorded.

2.1 Physical and Spatial Characteristics

Nine physical variables were stored for each of 10,088 nodes within each of 44 time steps. They are the displacement on the X, Y, and Z axes; velocity on the X, Y, and Z axes; and acceleration on the X, Y, and Z axes. The total number of data samples was 44•10088=443,872.

The data for each of the time steps was divided spatially according to the compute node to which it is assigned. The partitioning was performed vertically along the Y axis of the canister, dividing the canister into four disjoint spatial partitions of roughly equal size. Each compute node can see only one of these partitions, and we assume that it is too expensive in time or storage space to move data to another compute node.

2.2 Train and Test Sets

For every time step, those pieces of the canister that have buckled and been crushed were marked as salient. To assist in labeling, the "Equivalent Plastic Strain" (EQPS), a measure for the stress on the surface of the canister [3], has been calculated and was used as a general template in choosing salient points. At the beginning of the simulation, before the impactor bar has made contact, there were no salient nodes within the mesh. As time progresses and the canister collapses, more and more nodes were marked salient.

The process of marking salient nodes within the mesh can be as precise as the expert demands. However, a high level of precision requires a correspondingly high level of effort marking the data. In order to model a practical scenario where an expert is more interested in saving time than catering to the nuances of machine learning, we have allowed a fair amount of noise in the class labels by using tools that mark areas as salient rather than individual points—there are over 10,000 points per time step. Since the impactor bar and the canister are so close in proximity, it is quite reasonable to assume the bar will often have areas incorrectly marked as salient.

In each time step and in each partition, saliency was designated in the above fashion. For each partition, data present in the time steps was collapsed into two segments, a training set and a test set, according to the time step number: even time steps were combined into a training set, odd time steps were combined into a test set. Therefore our experiments used four partitions each having two data sets.

3 Classification System

For each training set developed on each compute node, we used Breiman's random forest algorithm to rapidly generate an ensemble of 25 classifiers. The motivation for using this ensemble technique stems from the inherent speed benefit of analyzing only a few possible attributes from which a test is selected at an internal tree node. A complete description of the random forest algorithm can be found in [4]. Its accuracy was evaluated in [5] and shown to be comparable with or better than other ensemble-generation techniques.

Classification of a test point within the simulation involves prediction by each partition's random forest. Because our algorithm was designed to work when only a few compute nodes have salient examples, a simple majority vote algorithm may fail to classify any salient points if the number of compute nodes trained with salient examples is less than half the number of compute nodes. In a large-scale simulation it is likely that there will be nodes which have no salient examples in training. Therefore we must consider the *priors*: the probability that any given node contained salient examples during training and so is capable of predicting an example as salient. A breakdown of our algorithm follows.

$p(w_1|x)$ = number of ensembles voting for class w1 for example x,
$P(w_1)$ = number of ensembles capable of predicting class w1
Classify as w_1 if: $p(w_1|x)/P(w_1) > p(w_2|x)/P(w_2)$
Classify as w_2 if: $p(w_1|x)/P(w_1) < p(w_2|x)/P(w_2)$
A tie, $p(w_1|x)/P(w_1) = p(w_2|x)/P(w_2)$, is broken randomly

Of course, this is nothing more than Bayesian decision theory applied to the majority vote for a two-class problem. Moving to an n-class problem is trivial:

$$\text{Classify as } w_n: \quad \text{argmax}_n \left(p(w_n|x)/P(w_n) \right) . \tag{1}$$

4 Experiments

The random forest of 25 trees for each partition returns a single prediction for a class. Those classifier predictions are combined into a single ensemble prediction for the example as outlined above, using the Bayesian majority vote with priors. Training is performed on the data contained in the even time steps. Predictions on odd time steps are compared to the marked saliency in the odd time steps on a point-by-point basis to obtain an estimate of the true error. We also obtain predictions on even time steps to evaluate the re-substitution error. Our results are compared with those of using a single classifier within each partition and a single classifier for the entire simulation.

5 Results

The goal of the prediction stage is to direct experts towards additional salient regions. Unfortunately, a suitable metric for the algorithm's usefulness in finding and classifying regions is non-trivial. For this reason, we provide figures to help illustrate the accuracy of our approach. Figures 2, 3, and 4 show the algorithm's predictive power while the canister is being crushed. In Figures 5, 6, and 7 we observe the re-

Fig. 2. *Left*: Ground truth as labeled in time step 3. *Right*: Predicted class labels

Fig. 3. *Left*: Ground truth as labeled in time step 19. *Right*: Predicted class labels

Fig. 4. *Left*: Ground truth as labeled in time step 37. *Right*: Predicted class labels

substitution error on the training data. Darker areas indicate regions that have been classified as salient. Ensemble predictions are provided to the right of the labeled data in each of the figures.

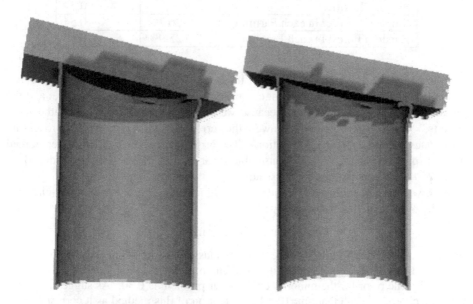

Fig. 5. *Left*: Training data as labeled in time step 4. *Right*: Predicted class labels

Fig. 6. *Left*: Training data as labeled in time step 20. *Right*: Predicted class labels

Fig. 7. *Left*: Training data as labeled in time step 38. *Right*: Predicted class labels

Table 1. Error percentage and m-estimates obtained in our experiments

Algorithm Used	Error Percentage	m-Estimate
Single Classifier	24.3%	0.59
Single Classifier in each Partition	26.7%	0.54
Random Forest in each Partition	25.9%	0.55

In Table 1, we provide an estimate of the true error for our experiments. Because this error is based on a point-to-point comparison between our labeled test set and the predictions upon the test set, and because we know "regions" are salient rather than "points," we could potentially lower the error by utilizing image processing techniques such as erosion and dilation. The error rate for a single classifier trained on each partition is 26.7%. The ensemble error rate of 25.9% was not reduced by using 250 classifiers per partition instead of 25.

As a way of calculating how accurate the algorithm was for the minority class we used the m-estimate [6] shown below:

$$P_m=(TP+mb)/(TP+FP+m) .\qquad(2)$$

In this equation b is the prior for the minority class, m is the parameter for controlling the shift towards b, and TP and FP represent number of True Positives and False Positives. The prior for the minority class in our problem is 0.30. As suggested in [7], we have chosen m such that bm=10. An evaluation of this method as it corresponds to decision trees is shown in [8]. In the preceding experiments, the forest of trees produced a slightly higher m-estimate, 0.55, than the single tree per partition, 0.54.

Partitioning the data spatially, while necessary for our large simulation, negatively affects the accuracy of the results. In a comparison with the performance of a single pruned decision tree, our multiple classifier spatially partitioned result is 1.6% less accurate. The m-estimate of the single pruned decision tree was 0.59. While such losses in accuracy are unfortunate, this result shows that the problem of having a spatially partitioned data set is non-trivial; even an ensemble created from a random disjoint partitioning often provides an increase in accuracy over a single classifier, especially so in the case of a large dataset [9].

6   Previous Work Revisited

In revisiting our previous work [1], we saw definite improvements in the classification accuracy of face images obtained from the FERET database [10] using the approach discussed here. In those experiments we employed a k-nearest centroid algorithm which lacked adequate speed for terascale data sets but achieved reasonable results given our assumption of spatially disjoint subsets. An example from the database is shown in Figure 8.

In previous experimentation with a k-nearest centroid algorithm we were able to identify salient regions though regions of noise were also labeled. These experiments did not use the Bayesian majority vote. We compare those results with a forest of 1,000 random forest trees trained on each of the eight partitions in combination with

Bayesian majority voting using priors. Many fewer pixels are labeled incorrectly using this later method. A comparison of the k-nearest centroid algorithm using eleven centroids to eight random forests of 1,000 decision trees is shown in Figure 9.

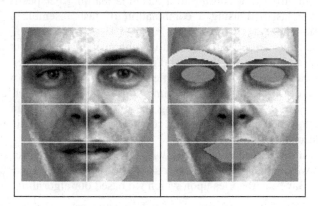

Fig. 8. Image from the FERET database showing marked saliency for both "Interesting" and "Somewhat Interesting" classes for eight partitions delineated by white lines. The "Interesting" class contains the eyes and mouth. The "Somewhat Interesting" class contains the eyebrows

Fig. 9. *Left*: Saliency predictions using KNC with 11 centroids. *Right*: Bayesian majority vote with priors using 1,000 random forest trees per partition

Though the random forest results are 5.2% more accurate than the KNC results for this image, neither provides for significant differentiation between the "interesting" and "somewhat interesting" classes, due to the weakness of the derived feature attributes. The random forest image contains fewer false positive regions than the one created with KNC, especially in the regions to the left and right of the mouth. Fewer false positives would guide researchers examining the data to fewer unimportant regions.

7 Summary and Discussion

Some simulations must be broken up across multiple processors in order to obtain results in a reasonable amount of time. The method of breaking data into pieces is not necessarily valuable, and possibly even harmful, to machine learning algorithms, as it violates the usual assumption that class statistics will be the same across all the training data and the test data. In this paper we have shown how large simulation data broken up non-intuitively (according to a machine learning perspective) into spatial regions may be classified using a combination of fast ensemble techniques and Bayesian decision theory.

Preliminary results on a relatively small problem indicate that our approach has merit. In our simulation of the crushing of the storage canister, the resultant predictions appear more accurately classified than the training data which has been labeled haphazardly in accordance with time constraints placed upon experts. This may signify that the algorithm is learning the underlying EQPS function that was generally used to label salient points. A comparison with our previous work using facial images also showed improvement.

In preparation for larger simulations with greater minority class problems, we conjecture that we might assign a bias, or risk ($R_n(w_n|x)$), to a particular class utilizing the same sound Bayesian theories upon which we based our algorithm:

$$\text{Classify as } w_n: \ \text{argmax}_n \ (R_n(w_n|x)/P(w_n)) . \tag{3}$$

It may also be possible to assign dynamic weights to the classifiers as shown in [11].

Of particular interest is the ability to classify regions rather than points since researchers examining these simulations will be looking at areas of interest within the simulation. An algorithm to perform such a task is currently being developed.

We believe the speed associated with the rapid generation of ensemble classifiers will enable the tractable prediction of saliency in much larger data sets. The general problem of creating an ensemble from data that was partitioned without regard to the simplicity of the machine learning algorithm is an important practical problem that merits additional attention.

Acknowledgments

This research was partially supported by the Department of Energy through the Advanced Strategic Computing Initiative (ASCI) Visual Interactive Environment for Weapons Simulation (VIEWS) Data Discovery Program Contract number: DE-AC04-76DO00789.

References

1. L. O. Hall, D. Bhadoria, and K. W. Bowyer. "Learning a model from spatially disjoint data," 2004 IEEE International Conference on Systems, Man and Cybernetics, October 2004.
2. National Nuclear Security Administration in collaboration with Sandia, Lawrence Livermore, and Los Alamos National Laboratories, "http://www.sandia.gov/NNSA/ASC/"
3. B.S. Lee, R.R. Snapp, R. Musick, "Toward a query language on simulation mesh data: an object oriented approach," Proceedings of the International Conference on Database Systems for Advanced Applications, Hong Kong, April 2001.
4. L. Breiman, "Random forests," *Machine Learning*, vol. 45, pp. 5-32, 2001.

5. R. E. Banfield, L. O. Hall, K. W. Bowyer, D. Bhadoria, W. P. Kegelmeyer and S. Eschrich, "A comparison of ensemble creation techniques", The Fifth International Conference on Multiple Classifier Systems, Cagliari, Italy, June, 2004.
6. J. Cussens, "Bayes and pseudo-Bayes estimates of conditional probabilities and their reliabilities", Proceedings of the European Conference on Machine Learning, 1993.
7. B. Zadrozny and C. Elkin, "Learning and making decisions when costs and probabilities are both unknown", Proceedings of the Seventh International Conference of Knowledge Discovery and Data Mining, 2001.
8. N. V. Chawla, "C4.5 and imbalanced data sets: investigating the effect of sampling method, probabilistic estimate, and decision tree structure, Workshop on Learning from Imbalanced Data Sets II, 2003.
9. N.V. Chawla, T.E. Moore, Jr., L.O. Hall, K.W. Bowyer, W.P. Kegelmeyer and C. Springer, "Distributed learning with bagging-like performance", Pattern Recognition Letters, Vol. 24 (1-3) pp. 455-471, 2003.
10. "The facial recognition technology (FERET) Database", http://www.itl.nist.gov/iad/humanid/feret/
11. M. Muhlbaier, A. Topalis, and R. Polikar, "Learn++.MT: A new approach to incremental learning," The Fifth International Conference on Multiple Classifier Systems, Cagliari, Italy, June, 2004.

Optimising Two-Stage Recognition Systems

Thomas Landgrebe, Pavel Paclík, David M.J. Tax,
and Robert P.W. Duin

Elect. Eng., Maths and Comp. Sc.,
Delft University of Technology, The Netherlands
{t.c.w.landgrebe, p.paclik, d.m.j.tax, r.p.w.duin}@ewi.tudelft.nl

Abstract. A typical recognition system consists of a sequential combination of two experts, called a detector and classifier respectively. The two stages are usually designed independently, but we show that this may be suboptimal due to interaction between the stages. In this paper we consider the two stages holistically, as components of a multiple classifier system. This allows for an optimal design that accounts for such interaction. An ROC-based analysis is developed that facilitates the study of the inter-stage interaction, and an analytic example is then used to compare independently designing each stage to a holistically optimised system, based on cost. The benefit of the proposed analysis is demonstrated practically via a number of experiments. The extension to any number of classes is discussed, highlighting the computational challenges, as well as its application in an imprecise environment.

1 Introduction

In this paper we view the sequential combination of two classifiers as a Multiple Classifier System (MCS). We illustrate that the independent design of individual classifiers in such sequential systems results in sub-optimal performance, since it ignores the interaction between stages. In this paper we demonstrate that optimality can be obtained by viewing such an MCS in a holistic manner. This research is targeted specifically at two-stage recognition systems, in which the first stage classifier attempts to detect *target* object distributed among a typically poorly sampled, or widely distributed *outlier* class. The second classifier then operates on objects selected by the first, and discriminates between sub-*target* classes. An example is image-based road-sign recognition [9], in which the first stage involves detecting road-signs that are distributed among an arbitrary background, and the second stage consists of a classifier to distinguish between different sign classes. Another application is fault diagnosis, such as [7], in which the first stage classifier is designed to detect a fault from normal operation, and the second stage to characterise the type of fault.

Considering the detector, since the *outlier* class is poorly defined, a two-class discrimination scheme is inappropriate, and other methods that are trained/ designed only on the *target* class are typically used, such as correlation. Recently One Class Classification (OCC) was introduced [12], consisting of a formal framework to train models in situations in which data from only a single

N.C. Oza et al. (Eds.): MCS 2005, LNCS 3541, pp. 206–215, 2005.

class is available. This allows a statistical pattern recognition methodology to be taken in designing the detector[1]. Thus we consider these recognition systems as a mixture of one-class and multi-class classifiers.

Evaluating the recognition system involves analysing the classification accuracy, and the rate of *outlier* false acceptances. Importantly, a poor detector that does not detect a large fraction of *target* objects results in poor classification performance. In the opposite case, a very sensitive detector may pass an unacceptably large fraction of *outlier* objects to the classifier, which may for example result in high manual processing costs or computational overload.

The paper is structured as follows: Section 2 presents an analytic example to demonstrate how the two classifiers interact. A cost-based approach using ROC analysis demonstrates how system optimisation can be performed in evaluating the entire system. In Section 3 the multiple-class extension is discussed briefly, highlighting some problems that exist in extending the analysis to a large number of *target* classes. In Section 4, some experiments on real data are performed, consisting of a simple problem with 2 *target* classes, and a 4-class problem involving hand-written digit recognition. In Section 5 we briefly consider the case in which priors or costs cannot be defined precisely, discussing how different system configurations can be chosen in these situations. Conclusions are given in Section 6.

2   The Dependence Between Classifiers

2.1   Two-Stage Recognition Systems

Consider a recognition task in which there are a number (n) *target* classes $\omega_{t1}, \omega_{t2}, \ldots, \omega_{tn}$, and an *outlier* class ω_o. A recognition system, as illustrated in Figure 1, has to classify these objects. A detector D_{DET} classifies incoming objects as either *target* (ω_t), or *outlier* via a detection threshold θ_d:

$$D_{DET}(\mathbf{x}) : \begin{cases} target & \text{if } f_{DET}(\mathbf{x}) > \theta_d \\ outlier & \text{otherwise} \end{cases} \qquad (1)$$

The detector selects objects from $\mathbf{x}$ such that the input to D_{CLF} is $\tilde{\mathbf{x}}$.

$$\tilde{\mathbf{x}} = \{\mathbf{x} | f_{DET}(\mathbf{x}) > \theta_d\} \qquad (2)$$

The classifier D_{CLF} then classifies incoming objects (according to $\tilde{\mathbf{x}}$) to any of the n *target* classes via the classification thresholds[2] $\theta_c^{t1}, \theta_c^{t2}, \ldots, \theta_c^{tn}$. The classifier

---

[1] Note that the MCS view on such a multi-stage system also holds for two-stage recognition systems that are constructed for computational reasons. In this case the first stage is typically designed for fast rejection of very abundant *outlier* objects, with a more complex second stage to discriminate between *target* classes.

[2] In an n-class situation, the classification thresholds can be considered to be the weighting applied to the output posterior density estimates together with priors.

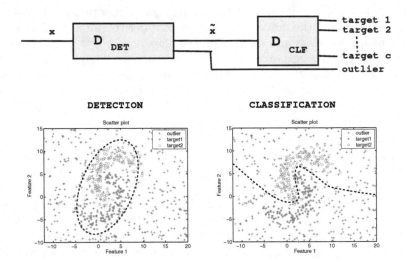

Fig. 1. Illustrating a typical recognition system on a synthetic example. The scatter plots show a 2-dimensional synthetic example with two *target* classes, illustrating the detector in the left plot, and the classifier in the right

outputs are weighted by classification thresholds and priors $p(\omega_{t1}), p(\omega_{t2}), \ldots,$ $p(\omega_{tn})$. The classifier outputs $f_{CLF}(\tilde{x})$ can then be written as:

$$[\theta_c^{t1}p(\omega_{t1})f_{CLF}(\omega_{t1}|\tilde{x}), \theta_c^{t2}p(\omega_{t2})f_{CLF}(\omega_{t2}|\tilde{x}), \ldots, \theta_c^{tn}p(\omega_{tn})f_{CLF}(\omega_{tn}|\tilde{x})] \quad (3)$$

Here $\sum_{i=1}^{n} \theta_c^{ti} = 1$. The final decision rule is then:

$$D_{CLF}(\tilde{x}) = \mathrm{argmax}_{i=1}^{n} \theta_c^{ti}p(\omega_{ti})f_{CLF}(\omega_{ti}|\tilde{x}) \quad (4)$$

The primary distinction between this two-stage system and a multi-class single-stage recognition system is that the input to the classification stage in the two-stage case is a subset of the system input, whereas in the single-stage case all data is processed. We are considering the dependence (in terms of overall system performance) of the 2 stages, and how the system should be optimised.

2.2   One-Dimensional Example

In this section a simple 1-dimensional analytical example is studied in order to illustrate how the detection and classification stages are related. Two Gaussian-distributed *target* classes ω_{t1} and ω_{t2} are to be detected from a uniformly-distributed *outlier* class ω_o, and subsequently discriminated. The *target* classes have means of -1.50 and 1.50 respectively, and variances of 1.50. The ω_o class has a density of 0.05 across the domain x. The class conditional densities for ω_{t1}, ω_{t2} and ω_o are denoted $p(x|\omega_{t1})$, $p(x|\omega_{t2})$, and $p(x|\omega_o)$ respectively, with priors $p(\omega_{t1})$, $p(\omega_{l2})$, and $p(\omega_o)$, which are assumed equal here. For the total probability distribution of x therefore holds:

$$p(x) = p(\omega_{t1})p(x|\omega_{t1}) + p(\omega_{t2})p(x|\omega_{t2}) + p(\omega_o)p(x|\omega_o) \quad (5)$$

For this 1-dimensional data, the classifier is defined consisting of only a single threshold, denoted θ_c. The position of θ_c determines the classification performance, and can be used to set an operating point to achieve a specified false-negative rate FN_r (with respect to ω_{t1}) or false-positive rate (FP_r). These two errors are known as the Error of Type I and II respectively (ϵ_I and ϵ_{II}). As θ_c varies, so do the respective ϵ_I and ϵ_{II}, resulting in the ROC (receiver-operator curve [8]) between ω_{t1} and ω_{t2}. In a typical discrimination problem (ignoring the detector) across domain x, we can define ϵ_I and ϵ_{II} in terms of θ_c as:

$$\epsilon_I = 1 - \int_{-\infty}^{\infty} p(x|\omega_{t1})I_1(x|\theta_c)dx, \quad \epsilon_{II} = 1 - \int_{-\infty}^{\infty} p(x|\omega_{t2})I_2(x|\theta_c)dx \quad (6)$$

The indicator functions $I_1(x|\theta)$ and $I_2(x|\theta)$ specify the relevant domain:

$$I_1(\mathbf{x}|\theta_c) = 1 \text{ if } p(\omega_{t1})p(\mathbf{x}|\omega_{t1}) - p(\omega_{t2})p(\mathbf{x}|\omega_{t2}) < \theta_c, \text{ 0 otherwise}$$
$$I_2(\mathbf{x}|\theta_c) = 1 \text{ if } p(\omega_{t1})p(\mathbf{x}|\omega_{t1}) - p(\omega_{t2})p(\mathbf{x}|\omega_{t2}) \geq \theta_c, \text{ 0 otherwise} \quad (7)$$

A two-stage recognition system consists of two sets of thresholds, namely a classification threshold θ_c (of which there are a number of thresholds according to the number of classes), and a detection threshold θ_d. Evaluating the recognition system involves estimating both classification performance (ϵ_I and ϵ_{II}), and the fraction of *outlier* objects incorrectly classified as *target*, denoted FP_r^o. Thus one axis of the evaluation is concerned with how well the system performs at detecting and discriminating *target* classes, and the other is concerned with the amount of false alarms that the system must deal with. Therefore the system must be evaluated with respect to ϵ_I, ϵ_{II}, and FP_r^o. In this simple example, we can write these as:

$$\epsilon_I = 1 - \int_{-\infty}^{\infty} p(x|\omega_{t1})I_1(x|\theta_c)I_R(x|\theta_d,\omega_{t1})dx$$
$$\epsilon_{II} = 1 - \int_{-\infty}^{\infty} p(x|\omega_{t2})I_2(x|\theta_c)I_R(x|\theta_d,\omega_{t2})dx \quad (8)$$
$$FP_r^o = \int_{-\infty}^{\infty} p(x|\omega_o)I_1(x|\theta_c)I_R(x|\theta_d,\omega_{t1}) + p(x|\omega_o)I_2(x|\theta_c)I_R(x|\theta_d,\omega_{t2})dx$$

$$I_R(\mathbf{x}|\theta_d,\omega) = 1 \text{ if } p(\mathbf{x}|\omega) > \theta_d, \text{ 0 otherwise} \quad (9)$$

Equation 8 yields the full operating characteristics of the system, shown in Figures 2 and 3 for the example. Referring first to Figure 2, this shows how the system operating characteristics vary for a number of fixed detection thresholds. The top row illustrates the position of the detection threshold, and the bottom row shows ϵ_I, ϵ_{II}, and FP_r^o for all classification thresholds (similar to standard ROC analysis, except an additional dimension is introduced to account for the detection threshold). In these plots, it is desirable for ϵ_I, ϵ_{II}, and FP_r^o to be minimal, indicating good classification and detection.

In Figure 2, as θ_d is increased, the plots show how FP_r^o progressively decreases. In the left-column, a very sensitive detector is used, with θ_d placed in the tails of the *target* distribution. It is clear that the classification performance is almost maximal for this threshold, but FP_r^o is very high i.e. the system will accept a very high percentage of *outlier* objects. The centre column plots show the case for which a higher detection threshold has been used ($\theta_d = 0.05$), resulting

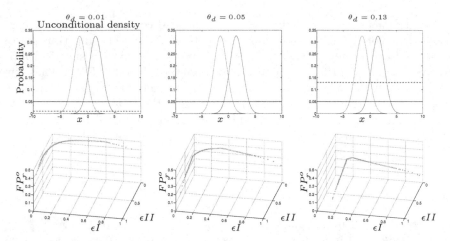

Fig. 2. Operating characteristics for a fixed θ_d, and varying θ_c. The left column is where $\theta_d = 0.01$, followed by $\theta_d = 0.05$ in the middle column, and $\theta_d = 0.13$ in the right column. The top row plots illustrate the distribution, with two Gaussian *target* classes, and a uniformly distributed *outlier* class. The position of the detection threshold is shown via the dotted line. The full operating characteristics for all possible θ_c are shown in the bottom row

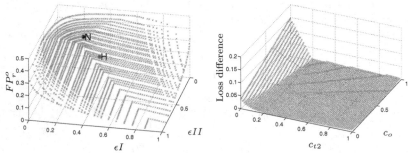

Fig. 3. Results of analytic experiment. The left plot shows the full operating characteristics, with ϵ_I plotted against ϵ_{II}, and FP_r^o. The right plot shows the loss difference between an independent and holistic design approach for all combinations of c_{t2}, and c_o over a $\{0,1\}$ range, where c_{t1} is fixed to 0.55

in a substantially lower FP_r^o, for a small sacrifice in classification performance. The third column shows a situation in which θ_d is again increased, resulting in a further decrease in classification performance. In this case the detector only accepts very probable *target* objects, reducing the volume of the *target* class decision space, at the expense of all *target* objects appearing outside the decision boundary. The left plot of Figure 3 shows the operating characteristics for all combinations of θ_c and θ_d. Next we show how using the full operating characteristic can be advantageous in system design.

2.3   Cost-Based Analysis

From the system perspective, the cost of misclassifying a ω_t object (as *outlier*) is c_t, and the cost of misclassifying a ω_o object (as *target*) is c_o. The individual *target* class misclassification costs can be written as $c_{t1}, c_{t2}, \ldots c_{t_n}$, which must sum to c_t together with the priors (note that we do not consider the entire loss matrix as defined in [2], but only consider the loss incurred due to misclassification, irrespective of the class to which it is assigned). The expected overall system loss L can be written as:

$$L = c_t p(\omega_t) FN_r + c_o p(\omega_o) FP_r^o, \; = \sum_{i=1}^{n} c_{t_i} p(\omega_{t_i}) FN_r^{t_i} + c_o p(\omega_o) FP_r^o, \; \sum_{i=1}^{n} c_{t_i} = c_t$$

(10)

The priors are denoted $p(\omega_t)$ and $p(\omega_o)$, and the false negative rate of ω_t is denoted FN_r. The *target* class misclassification costs are denoted c_{t_i} for *target* class ω_{t_i}. Cost-based classifier design involves minimising of L for the given costs, resulting in the optimal threshold values. The ROC is a tool that can be used to facilitate this minimisation, since it consists of performances for all possible threshold values (all FN_r and FP_r results). In a 2-class problem, the costs (and priors) specify the gradient of the cost line (also known as an *iso-performance* line as defined in [10]), and the intersection of the normal of this line with the ROC (plotting FN_r against FP_r) results in the optimal operating point[3]. We now demonstrate a cost-analysis for the example in order to emphasise the importance of designing the entire system holistically. Two different design approaches are compared, the first of which we refer to as the *independent* approach, and the second as the *holistic* approach. In the first case, we optimise the recognition and classification stages independently, and compare the expected system loss to the second case, in which the entire system is optimised holistically. We assume that the cost specification for the recognition system is such that misclassifying a ω_t object has a cost of 5, and the cost of classifying a ω_o object as *target* is 10. Among the two *target* classes ω_{t1} and ω_{t2}, these have misclassification costs of 2 and 3 respectively (summing to 5), i.e. ω_{t2} is favoured. From Equation 10, we can write the system loss (assuming equal priors) for the chosen θ_c and θ_d as $L(\theta_c, \theta_d) = 2\epsilon_I(\theta_c, \theta_d) + 3\epsilon_{II}(\theta_c, \theta_d) + 10 FP_r^o(\theta_c, \theta_d)$. In the *independent* approach, the detector is optimised using ω_t and ω_o data only (with operating characteristics generated for these classes only). The classifier is then optimised on ω_{t1} and ω_{t2}. The corresponding thresholds are indicated by the point marked **N** in the left plot of Figure 3. In the holistic approach, ω_{t1}, ω_{t2}, and ω_o are analysed simultaneously in the optimisation, resulting in the point marked **H**. The two points **N** and **H** are significantly apart on the operating characteristic. In the *independent* approach, the overall expected loss is thus **4.18**, and in the

---

[3] We deal with multi-dimensional ROC plots in this paper. Cost-based optimisation involves intersecting a plane (the gradient based on the cost associated with misclassifying each class) with the multi-dimensional ROC surface, resulting in optimised thresholds.

holistic approach, the loss is **4.02**. Thus independent approach is sub-optimal here. Depending on the problem and the costs, the *independent* approach may vary in the degree of sub-optimality. To assess how the holistic approach will improve performance in general, refer to the right plot of Figure 3. This plot shows the difference between the *independent* and *holistic* loss performances (where a positive score indicates superiority of the *holistic* approach) for all combinations of costs over a range. The cost c_{t1} is fixed to 0.55, and c_{t2} and c_o are varied for all combinations over the $\{0, 1\}$ range. It can be seen that for this artificial example, only imbalanced costs result in significant improvements. In the experiments, it will be shown models that do not fit the data well in real problems can benefit even more from this approach, including balanced cases.

3   Multiple Class Extension

The analytic example involved a recognition system with 2 *target* classes, resulting in a 3-dimensional ROC surface. As the number of *target* classes increase, the dimensionality of the ROC increases. The analysis extends to any number of classes [11]. However, as the number of dimensions increase, the computational burden becomes infeasible [5]. In this paper, experiments involved up to 3 *target* classes. In this case, the processing costs were already very high. and only a very sparsely sampled ROC could be generated. Extending this analysis to N classes would be infeasible. This is the topic of future work, exploring approaches that can be used to either approximate the full ROC, or to use search techniques in optimising the thresholds. Attention is drawn to [6], in which an initial set of thresholds is used, and a hill-climbing greedy-search is used.

4   Experiments

In this section a number of experiments are conducted on real data in order to demonstrate the holistic system design approach practically, and how model (or system configuration) selection can be performed. Two datasets are used, described as follows:

- *Banana*: A simple 2 dimensional problem with 2 *target* classes distributed non-linearly (the banana distribution [4]), in which there are 600 examples each of ω_{t1} and ω_{t2}, and 2400 *outlier* examples. The distribution is shown in Figure 1.
- *Mfeat*: This is a dataset consisting of examples of ten handwritten digits, originating from Dutch utility maps[4]. In this dataset, Fourier components have been extracted from the original images, resulting in a 76-dimensional representation of each digit. 200 examples of each digit are available. In these experiments, digits *3*, *4* and *8* are to be distinguished (i.e. 3 *target* classes ω_{t1}, ω_{t2}, and ω_{t3}), distributed among all other digit classes, which are considered to be *outlier*.

---

[4] Available at ftp://ftp.ics.uci.edu/pub/machine-learning-databases/mfeat/

We follow the same analysis approach as in Section 2. Classification and detection thresholds are generated across the full range. In the *Banana* case, 200 evenly sampled classification thresholds are used, and similarly 100 detection thresholds are used. For computational reasons, the *Mfeat* experiments only uses 10 detection thresholds, and 12 samples per classification threshold. Each experiment involves a 10-fold randomised hold-out procedure, with 80% of the data used in training, and the remainder for testing. The evaluation consists of evaluating the loss incurred for a number of chosen misclassification costs, using the ROC to find an optimal set of thresholds. In this evaluation it is assumed that the costs (and priors) are known beforehand, and as in Section 2, we only consider misclassification costs, applying Equation 10.

In the *Banana* experiments, 3 different system configurations are implemented, comparing the *independent* and *holistic* approaches for each case. The same detector is used for all 3 configurations, consisting of a Gaussian one class classifier (OCC) [12]. Three different classifier models are used, consisting of a Bayes linear, quadratic, and mixture of Gaussians classifier (with two mixtures per class), denoted LDC, QDC, and MOG respectively. In Table 1 the *Banana* experimental results are shown for 4 different system costs. These are shown in the four right-most columns, with the costs denoted $[c_{t1}, c_{t2}, c_o]$. For all 3 system configurations, the *holistic* design approach results in a lower overall expected loss than the *independent* approach. In some cases the difference in performance is not significant (see the MOG results for the case in which $c_{t1} = 3.0$, $c_{t2} = 1.0$, and $c_o = 4.0$). These experiments show that the benefit of an overall design approach can in many cases result in significant improvements in performance.

A similar set of experiments are conducted for the *Mfeat* problem, with costs denoted $[c_{t1}, c_{t2}, c_{t3}, c_o]$. Results are shown for four different cost specifications in the right-most columns of Table 1. Three different system configurations are considered, and in each case the *independent* and *holistic* design approaches are compared. The first configuration consists of a principal component analysis (PCA) mapping with 3 components and a Gaussian OCC as the detector, followed by a Fisher mapping and LDC as the classifier. The second configuration uses a 3-component PCA mapping Gaussian OCC for the detector, and a 3-component PCA LDC for the classifier. Finally the third system consists of a 5-component PCA with Gaussian OCC detector, and a 2-component PCA MOG classifier with 2 mixtures for the classifier. As before, the *holistic* approach consistently results in either a similar or lower overall loss compared to the *independent* approach. Once again, the improvement is dependent on the cost specification. For costs $[1, 8, 1, 10]$ (favouring ω_{t2}) and $[1, 1, 1, 12]$ (favouring ω_o), there is no significant improvement in using the *holistic* approach for all 3 systems. However, when the costs are in favour of ω_{t1}, the holistic approach leads to a significantly lower system loss. This suggests that the ω_{t1} threshold has more effect over the detection performance. In this case θ_d should be adjusted accordingly for optimal performance. The same observation is made for balanced costs $[1, 1, 1, 3]$. An interesting observation made in these experiments is models that do not fit the data well (e.g. the LDC in the *Banana* experiments, compared

Table 1. Results of cost-based analysis for the *Banana* and *Mfeat* datasets, comparing an *independent* (I) and *holistic* (H) design approach for a number of different system configurations (low scores are favourable). Standard deviations are shown

Detector	Classifier	Cost 1	Cost 2	Cost 3	Cost 4
Banana		$[5, 5, 10]$	$[3, 1, 4]$	$[1, 3, 4]$	$[1, 1, 4]$
Gauss	LDC I	0.081 ± 0.009	0.370 ± 0.049	0.233 ± 0.056	0.244 ± 0.046
Gauss	LDC H	0.067 ± 0.008	0.326 ± 0.039	0.171 ± 0.015	0.189 ± 0.027
Gauss	QDC I	0.089 ± 0.017	0.418 ± 0.051	0.260 ± 0.060	0.265 ± 0.053
Gauss	QDC H	0.072 ± 0.010	0.354 ± 0.036	0.179 ± 0.025	0.182 ± 0.030
Gauss	MOG I	0.059 ± 0.008	0.252 ± 0.033	0.206 ± 0.032	0.205 ± 0.030
Gauss	MOG H	0.049 ± 0.007	0.230 ± 0.035	0.170 ± 0.019	0.169 ± 0.021
Mfeat		$[1, 1, 1, 3]$	$[8, 1, 1, 10]$	$[1, 8, 1, 10]$	$[1, 1, 1, 12]$
PCA3 Gauss	Fisher LDC I	0.648 ± 0.050	0.212 ± 0.018	0.225 ± 0.017	1.385 ± 0.316
PCA3 Gauss	Fisher LDC H	0.547 ± 0.110	0.146 ± 0.014	0.223 ± 0.017	1.317 ± 0.435
PCA3 Gauss	PCA3 LDC I	0.654 ± 0.053	0.214 ± 0.018	0.225 ± 0.017	1.389 ± 0.316
PCA3 Gauss	PCA3 LDC H	0.551 ± 0.110	0.146 ± 0.015	0.224 ± 0.017	1.305 ± 0.432
PCA5 Gauss	PCA2 MOG2 I	0.442 ± 0.029	0.146 ± 0.011	0.154 ± 0.011	0.929 ± 0.202
PCA5 Gauss	PCA2 MOG2 H	0.380 ± 0.079	0.112 ± 0.024	0.148 ± 0.018	0.847 ± 0.124

to MOG), tend to benefit more from the holistic optimisation, suggesting that the interaction is more prominent for all costs.

5   Imprecise Environments

The approach taken thus far showed that, given both misclassification costs and priors, the optimal set of thresholds can be found. In many practical situations the costs or priors cannot be obtained or specified precisely [10]. In these situations we may still wish to choose the best system configuration, and have some idea of a good set of system thresholds that may, for example, be suitable for a range of operating conditions or costs (see [1] and [3]). We do not go into more detail here due to space constraints, but emphasise the fact that real problems are often within an imprecise setting, requiring an alternative evaluation to the cost-based approach. One strategy for this situation is to compute the AUC (Area Under the ROC curve) for a range operating points. An integrated error results that is useful for model selection. The next step is to choose thresholds, which may for example be specified by considering operating regions that are relatively insensitive to changes in cost or priors.

6   Conclusion

A two-stage recognition system was considered as an MCS, consisting of a detection and classification stage, with the objective of optimising the overall system. An analysis of a simple analytic problem was performed, in which the full operating characteristics were computed for all combinations of detection and classification thresholds. The holistic design approach was compared to the case in which the two stages are designed independently, showing that the holistic approach may result in a lower expected loss. The N-class extension was discussed, highlighting the computational difficulties in scaling the analysis to any number of classes. Some experiments with real data were then undertaken for a number of system configurations to demonstrate practical application of the analysis, consistently demonstrating the advantage of the holistic design approach. It was observed that the performance improvements vary according to the cost specification, and the respective degree of interference a class may impose on the detection stage. Models that fit the data well only seem to benefit for imbalanced costs/priors, whereas ill-fitting models can result in improvements for any costs. Finally, a short discussion on application of the methodology to imprecise environments was given. Future work includes exploring efficient multi-class ROC analysis, and application to an imprecise environment.

Acknowledgements. This research is/was supported by the Technology Foundation STW, applied science division of NWO and the technology programme of the Ministry of Economic Affairs.

References

[1] N.M. Adams and D.J. Hand. Comparing classifiers when misallocation costs are uncertain. *Pattern Recognition*, 32(7):1139–1147, 1999.

[2] C.M. Bishop. *Neural Networks for Pattern Recognition*. Oxford University Press Inc., New York, first edition, 1995.

[3] A.P. Bradley. The use of the area under the ROC curve in the evaluation of machine learning algorithms. *Pattern Recognition*, 30(7):1145–1159, 1997.

[4] R.P.W. Duin, P. Juszcak, P. Paclik, E. Pekalska, D. de Ridder, and D.M.J. Tax. Prtools, a matlab toolbox for pattern recognition, January 2004. version 4.0.

[5] C. Ferri, J. Hernndez-Orallo, and M.A. Salido. Volume under the roc surface for multi-class problems. *Proc. of 14th European Conference on Machine Learning*, pages 108–120, 2003.

[6] N. Lachiche and P. Flach. Improving accuracy and cost of two-class and multi-class probabilistic classifiers using ROC curves. *Proc. 20th International Conference on Machine Learning (ICML-2003), Washington DC*, pages 416–423, 2003.

[7] A. Lipnickas, J.S. da Costa, and C.D. Bocaniala. FDI based on two stage classifiers for fault diagnosis of valve actuators. *11th Int. Power Electronics and Motion Control Conference*, pages 3,147–153, September 2004.

[8] C. Metz. Basic principles of roc analysis. *Seminars in Nuclear Medicine*, 3(4), 1978.

[9] P. Paclík. Building road sign classifiers. *PhD thesis, CTU Prague, Czech Republic*, December 2004.

[10] F. Provost and T. Fawcett. Robust classification for imprecise environments. *Machine Learning*, 42:203–231, 2001.

[11] A. Srinivasan. Note on the location of optimal classifiers in N-dimensional ROC space. *Oxford University Computing Laboratory Technical report PRG-TR-2-99*, October 1999.

[12] D.M.J. Tax. One-class classification. *PhD thesis, TU Delft, The Netherlands*, June 2001.

Design of Multiple Classifier Systems for Time Series Data

Lei Chen and Mohamed S. Kamel

Pattern Analysis and Machine Intelligence Lab,
Electrical and Computer Engineering,
University of Waterloo, Ontario,
N2L 3G1, Canada

Abstract. In previous work, we showed that the use of Multiple Input Representation(MIR) for the classification of time series data provides complementary information that leads to better accuracy. [4]. In this paper, we introduce the Static Minimization-Maximization approach to build Multiple Classifier Systems(MCSs) using MIR. SMM consists of two steps. In the minimization step, a greedy algorithm is employed to iteratively select the classifiers from the knowledge space to minimize the training error of MCSs. In the maximization step, a modified version of Behavior Knowledge Space(BKS), Balanced Behavior Knowledge Space(BBKS), is used to maximize the expected accuracy of the whole system given that the training error is minimized. Several popular techniques including AdaBoost, Bagging and Random Subspace are used as the benchmark to evaluate the proposed approach on four time series data sets. The results obtained from our experiments show that the performance of the proposed approach is effective as well as robust for the classification of time series data. In addition, this approach could be further extended to other applications in our future research.

1   Introduction

Many real applications are interested in the knowledge varying over time. Currently, the temporal classification has been widely adopted in areas such as climate control research, medical diagnosis, economic forecast, sound recognition etc. However, while the classification of the non-temporal information has great achievement in recent years, temporal classification techniques are scarce. Temporal patterns contain dynamic information and are difficult to be represented by traditional approaches. Classifiers such as neural network, decision trees don't function well when applied to temporal data directly. Other solutions which employ temporal models are normally domain-dependent and could not be applied to general problems. In the current directions of the machine learning research, Multiple Classifier Systems(MCSs) have been proved to be an effective way to improve the classification performance and are widely used to achieve high pattern-recognition performances [11]. Currently, they have become one of the major focuses in this area. In this paper, we introduce the Static Minimization-Maximization approach to build MCSs. This approach is called *static* since we assume that the pool of classifiers available are explicitly specified in advance. In particular, for time series

N.C. Oza et al. (Eds.): MCS 2005, LNCS 3541, pp. 216–225, 2005.

data, the pool of classifiers is generated by MIR and other temporal information representation techniques [4].

This paper is organized as follows: Section 2 reviews the related work. In section 3, we model MCSs from the data mapping point of view. Section 4 presents the proposed approach. The experiments and discussions are presented in section 5. Section 6 concludes the work of this paper.

2   Related Works

In this section, we review several approaches for the classification of time series data. Bagging and boosting [5, 14] are two of the most popular classification techniques. In some situations, bagging could improve the pattern recognition for the unstable classifiers effectively. The boosting technique has been reported as the "best-off-shelf classifier in the world" [2]. Other techniques such as the random subspace, random forest and randomized C4.5[3, 7, 15] are also widely used. While these approaches focus on the general property of the data, they neglect some important information in time series data. Therefore, they may not be the best design for time series data. In [4], several designs of MCSs which focus on time series data have been reviewed. Sanchos et. al.[17] employ an ensemble of five base classifiers which are either Self-Organizing Mapping(SOM) or Multiple Layer Perceptron(MLP) for the classification of the time series data. Ghosh et. al.[8, 10] employ an ensemble of Artificial Neural Networks(ANNs) with the weighted average fusion technique to identify and classify the underwater acoustic signals. González et.al. [9] and Diez et.al. [6] propose interval based classification systems for time series data, in which the AdaBoost technique is adopted. Hsu et.al. [12] propose a hierarchical mixture model called specialist-moderator network for the time series classification. It combines recurrent ANN classifiers in a bottom-up architecture. Although these approaches give consideration to the property of time series data, their performances on time series data in general are not well demonstrated. In the following section, we introduce the SMM approach to design MCSs which can be effectively applied to general time series data.

3   Modelling Multiple Classifier Systems

We model MCSs from a data mapping point of view, in which the classification process with MCS is composed of two steps of data mappings. First, the input data X is mapped to the decision of the base classifiers, represented by the random variable D. In this situation, the input preprocessors and base classifiers are defined as a function which corresponds to a many-to-one mapping from X to D:

$$\phi : X \rightarrow D$$

Then, the decisions, D, are mapped to the label of the data, L. The combination approach of MCSs is thus defined as a function which corresponds to a many-to-one mapping from D to L:

$$\varphi : D \rightarrow L$$

Before we proceed further, we first provide the definitions of the error functions Θ_ϕ and Θ_φ for ϕ and φ respectively.

Suppose X_i represents the subset of X which has the same decision subsets for the base classifiers, D_i. Since the data in X_i may come from different categories, X_i could be further decomposed into a series of disjoint subsets $\{X_i^j\}$ ($j = 1..n$) such that for any $x \in X_i^j$, the category of x is L_j. Since each D_i is finally mapped to a unique category, it is impossible for all of the data in X_i to be correctly mapped to their corresponding categories if they are in different categories and mapped to the same D_i. For each X_i, only a certain subset X_i^j is finally mapped to the correct category. Therefore, the maximum likelihood estimation is adopted in which X_i is approximated by the subset set X_i^j with the most frequent occurrence. In this situation, the potential loss $\theta_\phi(X_i)$ in mapping from X_i to D_i is the sum of the probability of other subsets $\{X_i^k\}(k \neq j)$. Based on the above discussion, the error function Θ_ϕ is given as follows:

$$\Theta_\phi = \sum_i \theta_\phi(X_i)P(X_i) \tag{1}$$

Similarly, the loss function for $\varphi(D)$ is defined as follows:

$$\theta_\varphi(D_i) = \begin{cases} 0 & \varphi(D_i) = L_i; \\ 1 & \text{Otherwise.} \end{cases} \tag{2}$$

where L_i represents the actual label which is associated with D_i. Similarly, the function for φ_D is given as follows:

$$\Theta_\varphi = \sum_i \theta_\varphi(D_i)P(D_i) \tag{3}$$

Since the classification process of MCSs is composed of two independent steps of data mapping, the error function of MCSs Θ is decided by Θ_ϕ and Θ_φ. That is

$$\Theta = 1 - (1 - \Theta_\phi)(1 - \Theta_\varphi) \tag{4}$$

4   The Static Minimization-Maximization Approach

In this section, we introduce the proposed Static Minimization-Maximization(SMM) approach (Fig. 1) for the design of MCSs. First, we define the pool of classifiers available as the knowledge base Ω. In *Static* Minimization-Maximization(SMM), we assume that Ω is explicitly specified. Specially, for time series data, Ω is generated by MIR or other techniques which could effectively extract the temporal information.

The objective of SMM is to adaptively build an ensemble C ($C \subseteq \Omega$) such that the performance of C is effective and robust. In this paper, we find that SMM can be effectively applied to general time series data when Ω is built with MIR and other temporal information representation techniques. There are two steps in SMM. In the first step, SMM focuses on minimizing the training error. In the second step, SMM focuses on maximizing the expected testing accuracy given that the training error is minimized. In the following section, we discuss each step in detail.

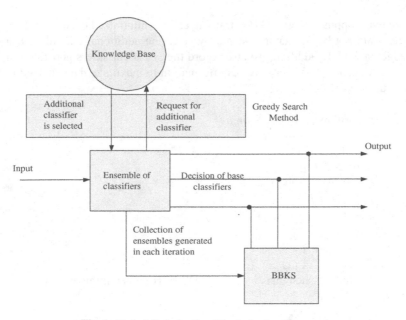

Fig. 1. Static Minimization-Maximization Approach

4.1   Minimization of Training Error

The underlying models vary for different data sets. Sometimes, the structure of the individual classifier in Ω is *complex* enough to represent the data while several classifiers need to be aggregated to achieve a satisfying performance in other situations. Therefore, one of the fundamental issues in the design of MCSs is how to build the ensemble adaptively. In SMM, the training error of MCSs is used to guide the generation of the ensemble. From Eq. 4,

$$\Theta^{train} = 1 - (1 - \Theta_\phi^{train})(1 - \Theta_\varphi^{train}) \tag{5}$$

In the second data mapping from D to L in the training process, SMM builds up a lookup table which describes the relation between each D_i and L_i. In this situation,

$$\Theta_\varphi^{train} = 0$$

From Eq.5, we get

$$\Theta^{train} = \Theta_\phi^{train}$$

Then, the objective in this step changes to minimizing Θ_ϕ^{train}. There are many ways to generate the ensemble to minimize Θ_ϕ^{train}. In this paper, we propose a greedy search method given the consideration of both the performance and time complexity.

In each round, the greedy search algorithm selects one classifier from the knowledge base Ω into the ensemble C by minimizing the training error of the current ensemble.

There are two stopping criteria: (1) the training error is minimized to zero (2) The training error could not be further minimized by selecting additional classifiers from the knowledge base Ω. In addition, we also record the set of classifiers generated in each round by a collection F which provides information to maximize the expected test accuracy in the second step.

Algorithm 1. *Greedy Search*

$\Omega = \{c_1, ...c_n\}$
$C(0) = NULL$
$\Theta_\phi^{train}(0) = 10000$
$F = NULL$
$k = 0$
do
$\quad k = k + 1$
$\quad C_k^j = C_{k-1} \cup c_j \quad (c_j \in \Omega)$
$\quad$find C_k^i such that $\qquad \Theta_\phi^{train}(C_k^i)$ is minimized
$\quad C_k = C_k^i$
$\quad F = F \cup C_k$
$\quad \Theta_\phi^{train}(k) = \qquad \Theta_\phi^{train}(C_k^i)$
while $(\Theta_\phi^{train}(k) > 0$ and $\qquad \Theta_\phi^{train}(k) < \Theta_\phi^{train}(k-1))$

4.2   Maximization of Expected Test Accuracy

In the first step, a greedy search algorithm is employed to generate the ensemble which is complex enough to represent the data. In this step, SMM focuses on how to maximize the expected test accuracy given the training error is minimized.

Since the ensemble has been decided in the first step, Θ_ϕ^{test} is also determined. Therefore, the key issue for the maximization of Θ^{test} is to maximize Θ_φ^{test}. We first consider one extreme condition: the data which is used to train the aggregation rules is sufficiently large. In this situation, we can always build a lookup table and record each mapping between D and L. Since the size of the validation data set is large enough, the estimated decision distribution converges to the real distribution. In this situation,

$$\Theta_\varphi^{test} = 0$$

It is easy to show that

$$\Theta^{test} = \Theta_\phi^{test}$$

Obviously, Behavior Knowledge Space(BKS) [13] is the best choice for the decision aggregation in this situation. However, this assumption is not always valid in real world. Therefore, the estimated distribution of the decision distribution may deviate from the real one significantly. The consequence is that the performance of MCSs tends to be *ad hoc* and significantly depends on various data sets, the classifiers generated etc. In order to overcome this difficulty, we propose the Balanced Behavior Knowledge

Space(BBKS) for the decision aggregation, which is a modification of the original BKS. Let A represents the event that the estimated probability is reliable. Then, the objective function for BBKS is given as follows:

$$\max_j P(\varphi(D_i) = L_j, A|D_i) \quad j = 1..n \qquad (6)$$

Here, we use the frequency as the probability measure. According to the Bayesian function, there is

$$P(\varphi(D_i) = L_j, A|D_i) = P(\varphi(D_i) = L_j|A, D_i)P(A|D_i)$$
$$= P(A|D_i)\frac{n(\varphi(D_i) = L_j)}{n(D_i)}$$

where $n(D_i)$ and $n(\varphi(D_i) = L_j)$ represent the number of data in X_i and X_i^j respectively. $P(\varphi(D_i) = L_j|A, D_i)$ could be approximated by the frequency that the decision D_i is assigned to the category L_j. Clearly, one of the key issues in BBKS is to decide $P(A|D_i)$. Let D represents the decisions of the classifiers and U_{ij} represents the event that decision D_i is assigned to the category L_j. Set $I_k(U_{ij})$ is the indicator function of U_{ij} on the kth trial.

$$I_k(U_{ij}) = \begin{cases} 1 & \varphi(D_i) = L_j,; \\ 0 & \text{Otherwise.} \end{cases} \qquad (7)$$

Let Z_{ij}^n represents average value of $I(U_{ij})$ in n independent and identical trials.

$$Z_{ij}^n = \frac{\sum_{k=1}^n I_k(U_{ij})}{n}$$

Suppose the data with the decision D_i is categorized to L_j. For any other category L_k, we want to find the probability $P(Z_{ij}^n > Z_{ik}^n)$ and use it to approximate $P(A|D_i)$. For the root of the maximum likelihood estimation, $\hat{\theta}_n$, there is $\hat{\theta}_n - \theta \rightarrow W \sim N(0, \frac{1}{J(\hat{\theta}_n)})$. Where $J(\hat{\theta}_n)$ is the fisher information Therefore, we could approximately assume that $Z_{ij}^n - E(Z_{ij}^n)$ and $Z_{ik}^n - E(Z_{ik}^n)$ are independent when the number of categories is more than 2. Suppose $d = E(Z_{ij}^n) - E(Z_{ik}^n)$, then

$$P(Z_{ij}^n > Z_{ik}^n)$$
$$= P(Z_{ij}^n - E(Z_{ij}^n) > Z_{ik}^n - E(Z_{ik}^n) - d)$$
$$\geq P(\bigcup_{0<x<d} (Z_{ij}^n - E(Z_{ij}^n) + d > x, Z_{ik}^n - E(Z_{ik}^n) < x))$$
$$\geq P(Z_{ij}^n - E(Z_{ij}^n) + d > \frac{d}{2}, Z_{ik}^n - E(Z_{ik}^n) < \frac{d}{2})$$

$$= P(Z_{ij}^n - E(Z_{ij}^n) + d > \frac{d}{2})P(Z_{ik}^n - E(Z_{ik}^n) < \frac{d}{2})$$

$$= P(E(Z_{ij}^n) - Z_{ij}^n < \frac{d}{2})P(Z_{ik}^n - E(Z_{ik}^n) < \frac{d}{2})$$

$$\geq (1 - \frac{Var(Z_{ij}^n)}{Var(Z_{ij}^n) + \frac{d^2}{4}})(1 - \frac{Var(Z_{ik}^n)}{Var(Z_{ik}^n) + \frac{d^2}{4}})$$

$$\geq (1 - \frac{1}{1 + n_i d^2})^2$$

The value of d is estimated as follows:

$$d = \hat{P}_{ij} - \hat{P}_{ik}$$
$$= \frac{n(\varphi(D_i) = L_j)}{n_i} - \frac{n(\varphi(D_i) = L_k)}{n_i}$$

Where $n(\varphi(D_i) = L_j)$ and $n(\varphi(D_i) = L_k)$ is the number of data which has the decision D_i and belongs to the category L_j and L_k respectively. n_i is the number of data with the decision D_i. L_j and L_k are the categories such that $\hat{P}_{ij}$ and $\hat{P}_{ik}$ are the largest and second largest respectively. Let $H = (1 - \frac{1}{1+n_i d^2})^2$. $P(Z_{ij}^n > Z_{ik}^n)$ is in the range [H,1]. Suppose the value of $P(Z_{ij}^n > Z_{ik}^n)$ is uniformly distributed in this range. Then, we can approximate $P(Z_{ij}^n > Z_{ik}^n)$ by $\frac{1+H}{2}$. Therefore, there is

$$P(A|D_i) = \frac{1 + H}{2}$$

The algorithm for BBKS is summarized as follows

Algorithm 2. *BBKS*

$F = \{C(1), ...C(k)\}$(Generated in the first step)
L_{max} = -1;
Temp = -1;
For i =1 to k
    Obtain the decision D_i based on the ensemble $C(i)$ for the input data
    Find L_j such that $P(\varphi(D_i) = L_j, A|D_i)$ is maximized over different categories
    if $P(\varphi(D_i) = L_j, A|D_i) >$ Temp
        Temp = $P(\varphi(D_i) = L_j, A|D_i)$
        $L_{max} = L_j$
    end
end
Label the input data with L_{max}

---

5   Experimental Results and Discussion

In this section, we use several popular time series data sets to demonstrate the feasibility of the proposed approach. These data sets are used by previous researchers and

Table 1. Characteristics of the Data Sets

Data Set	Source	Classes	Instances	Frames
CBF	[16]	3	600	200
Control Chart(CC)	UCI repository	6	600	60
Waveform(WF)	[1]	3	600	21
WF+Data Noise(WF+Data Noise)	[9]	3	600	40

available from the UCI repository or related references. The characteristics of the data are summarized in table 1.

We use Adaboost, Bagging, Random Subspace and single classifier as the benchmark for comparison. The Probabilistic Neural Network (PNNs) is employed as the base learner for all approaches, in which the gaussian width is set to 0.1. We use the classification toolbox version 2.0 of Matlab [5]. In all of the experiments, the data sets are randomly separated into 60% training and 40% testing. For the Bagging approach, we resample the data 12 times. For the Random Subspace approach, we conduct 12 rounds of selection, in each of which 50% of features are randomly chosen. For the Adaboost, we set the iteration times to 200. For the SMM approach, 66.7% of the training data are used to train the base classifiers and the remaining 33.3% used as a validation set to estimate the decision distribution of the base classifiers. In order to examine the effect of the knowledge base on SMM, we compare the performance of SMM under three different Ω. Let *Raw, DFT, DES+DG and RFS* represent those in which the base classifier takes the raw time series data, the data with the Discrete Fourier Transformation(DT), the data processed with the Double Exponential Smoothing and Differentiation Generation(DG) and the data with Random Feature Selection(RFS), respectively[4, 15]. Ω_1 is composed of 6 classifiers which take the 1 Raw, 1 DFT and 4 DES+DG as the input. Ω_2 contains 12 classifiers which is composed of the union of Ω_1 and 6 additional DES+DG. Ω_3 contains 18 classifiers which consist of the union of Ω_2 and 6 additional RFS. We use SMM^i to represent SMM which is build on Ω_i. The test results are shown in table 2, which summarizes the Mean of Correct Ratio(MCR) and Varaiance of Correct Ratio(VCR) of the different approaches from 10 continuous experiments. The entry is in the format of MCR%(VCR$\times 10^{-3}$).

From the test results in table 2, it is clear that the performance of the single PNN significantly depends on the data type. Bagging(Raw) doesn't improve the performance of individual classifiers significantly. Random subspace(Raw) outperforms the single classifier in CBF, WF and WF+DN data. In particular, its accuracy on WF is 96.6% which is the best over all methods. This indicates that RFS is an effective technique on Waveform Data. However, its performance on CC data is not impressive. Furthermore, although its improvement on CBF data is significant, which is around 7% more than the single classifier, its performance is still not very satisfying. AdaBoost(Raw) is similar with single classifier and Bagging(Raw) in WF and WF+DN. However, it is significantly better than the previous three approaches in CBF and CC data. In addition, the variation of its performance over various data sets is small. Therefore,

Table 2. Experimental Results: MCR(VCR$\times 10^{-3}$)

Methods	Data		Sets	
	CBF	CC	WF	WF+DN
Single(Raw)	72.5(1.0)	81.0(1.8)	93.7(0.3)	90.5(0.2)
Bagging(Raw)	71.6(0.3)	79.5(1.5)	93.7(0.3)	90.3(0.1)
Random Subspace(Raw)	79.3(1.3)	78.0(1.9)	96.6(0.1)	92.5(0.1)
AdaBoost(Raw)	90.6(0.3)	90.5(0.3)	92.4(0.1)	92.6(0.3)
AdaBoost(DFT)	93.4(0.3)	80.3(0.7)	85.3(0.2)	85.4(0.3)
AdaBoost(DES+DG)	79.3(0.7)	84.0(6.3)	93.1(0.3)	90.4(0.5)
SMM^1	90.2(1.5)	89.5(2.2)	92.6(0.5)	90.8(0.8)
SMM^2	92.7(0.9)	89.4(0.7)	92.5(0.3)	90.4(0.4)
SMM^3	92.8(0.5)	90.5(0.9)	94.4(0.3)	91.9(0.7)

AdaBoost(Raw) is a reliable technique, which could be applied to time series data in general. The performance of SMM is also reliable to various data sets. If we compare SMM^1, SMM^2 and SMM^3, we can find that the knowledge space has some impact on the performance of SMM. The SMM with larger Ω tends to perform better. For example, SMM^3 outperforms SMM^1 by 2.6% in CBF data. Furthermore SMM^3 also slightly outperforms SMM^1 in other data sets. Finally, we also compare the accuracy of SMM^3 and AdaBoost(Raw) statistically to show the possible advantage of SMM in the classification of time series data. We apply the t-test on the test accuracy with the confidence level of 95%. While the difference of their performances is not significant in CC and WF+DN data sets, SMM^3 significantly outperforms AdaBoost(Raw) in CBF and WF data sets. The possible reason may be that SMM allows the classifiers to be generated in various ways and it may have captured some important information in time series data while AdaBoost generates the classifiers only by changing the data distribution.

6   Conclusion and Future Work

In this paper, we proposed the SMM approach for classification of time series data in general. The basic idea of SMM is to first build an ensemble of classifiers which is complex enough to represent the data. Then, BBKS approach is applied to maximize the expected test accuracy. The experimental results show that SMM approach is a robust technique for time series data in general and it could be further extended to other applications. We also observed that SMM with large knowledge space tends to perform better. However, the time cost should also be taken into consideration when designing a specific MCS with the SMM approach since large knowledge space requires more searching time. In addition, the assumption that the knowledge space is given may not be practical for some applications in the real world.

References

1. Breiman, L., Friedman, J.H., Olshen, A., Stone, C.J.:Classification and regression trees. Chapman and Hall, New York, 1993. Previously published by Wadsworth and Books/Cole in 1984.
2. Breiman, L.:Bagging predictors. Machie Learning (1996) 26:123-140
3. Breiman, L.:Random forests. Machie Learning (2001) **45**(1):5–32
4. Chen, L., Kamel, M., Jiang, J.: A modular system for classification of time series data. MCS2004 (2004) LNCS **3077** 134–143 .
5. Duda, Richard O., Hart, Peter E., Stork, David G.: Pattern classification. 2nd Edition, Published by Wiely-Interscience, December 28,2000
6. Diez, J. J. R., González, C. J. A.: Applying boosting to similarity literals for time series classification. MCS2000 LNCS **1857** (2000) 210–219
7. Dietterich, T.G.: An experimental comparison of three methods of constructing ensembles of decision trees: bagging,boositing and randomization. Machine Learning, (2000) **40**(2) 139–157
8. Ghosh, J., Beck, S., Chu, C.C.: Evidence combination techniques for robust classification of short-duration oceanic signals. In SPIE Conf. on Adaptive and Learning Systems, SPIE Proc. **1706** (1992) 266–276
9. González, C. J. A., Diez, J, R.:Time series classification by boosting interval based literals. Inteligencia Artificial, Revista Iberoamericana de Inteligencia Artificial **11** (2000) 2–11
10. Ghosh, J., Deuser, L., Beck, S.: A neural network based hybrid system for detection,characterization and classification of short-duration oceanic signals. IEEE Journal of Ocean Engineering **17**(4) (1992) 351–363
11. Giancinto, G., Roli, F.: Dynamic classifier selection based on multiple classifier behaviour. Pattern Recognition **34**(9) (2001) 1879–1881
12. Hsu, William H., Ray, Sylvian R.: Construction of recurrent mixture models for time series classification. In Proceedings of the International Joint Conference on Neural Networks **3** (1999) 1574–1579
13. Huang, Y.S., Suen, C.Y.: A method of combining multiple experts for the recognition of unconstrained handwritten numerals. IEEE Transactions on Pattern Analysis and Machine Intelligence, Vol. **17** No. 1 (1995) 90–94
14. Hastie, T., Tibshirani, R., Friedman, J.: Elements of statistical learning: data mining, inference, and prediction. Published by Springer-Verlag Inc., 2001
15. Ho, T.K.: The random subspace method for constructing decision forests. IEEE Transactions on pattern analysis and machine in intelligence. Vol. **20** No. 8 (1998) 832–844
16. Saito, N.: Local feature extraction and its applications using a library of bases. Phd thesis, Department of Mathematics, Yale University, 1994
17. Sancho, Q. Isaac Moro, Alonso, C. , Rodrguez, J. J.: Applying simple combining techniques with artificial neural networks to some standard time series classification problems. In Juan M. Corchado, Luis Alonso, and Colin Fyfe, editors, Artificial Neural Networks in Pattern Recognition (2001) 43–50

Ensemble Learning with Biased Classifiers: The Triskel Algorithm

Andreas Heß, Rinat Khoussainov, and Nicholas Kushmerick

University College Dublin, Ireland
{andreas.hess, rinat, nick}@ucd.ie

Abstract. We propose a novel ensemble learning algorithm called Triskel, which has two interesting features. First, Triskel learns an ensemble of classifiers that are biased to have high precision (as opposed to, for example, boosting, where the ensemble members are biased to ignore portions of the instance space). Second, Triskel uses weighted voting like most ensemble methods, but the weights are assigned so that certain pairs of biased classifiers outweigh the rest of the ensemble, if their predictions agree. Our experiments on a variety of real-world tasks demonstrate that Triskel often outperforms boosting, in terms of both accuracy and training time.

1   Introduction

Ensemble techniques have been demonstrated to be an effective way to reduce the error a base learner across a wide variety of tasks. The basic idea is to vote together the predictions of a set of classifiers that have been trained slightly differently for the same task. There is a strong body of theory explaining why ensemble techniques work.

Nevertheless, it is straightforward to construct learning tasks that confound existing ensemble techniques. For example, consider a synthetic"layer cake" binary learning task shown in Fig. 1. SVM with a linear kernel learns a decision surface with a large error. Boosting SVM does not help: at each iteration, the classifier is unable to stop making mistakes on the middle two regions; these regions then get even more weight on the next iteration, and eventually boosting gives up because it can not find a classifier with error less than 0.5.

However, Fig. 1(b) shows that ensemble methods are in principle well suited to this task: when combined with a simple unweighted vote, the set of three linear decision surfaces yields an ensemble that has zero error.

Motivated by this sort of learning task, we propose a novel ensemble learning algorithm called Triskel, which has two interesting features. First, Triskel learns an ensemble of classifiers that are biased to have high precision for one particular class. For example, in Fig. 1(b), one of the "outer" classifiers is biased to (i.e. has high precision, albeit mediocre recall, for) the positive class, and the other classifier is biased for the negative class. In contrast, most existing ensemble techniques feature ensemble members that are biased to focus on various regions of the instance space. For example, at each round, boosting focuses on instances that were classified incorrectly in previous rounds; and bagging simply involves hiding some of the training data from each ensemble member.

N.C. Oza et al. (Eds.): MCS 2005, LNCS 3541, pp. 226–235, 2005.
© Springer-Verlag Berlin Heidelberg 2005

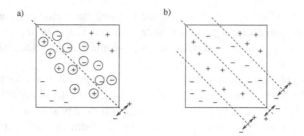

Fig. 1. The "layer cake" task: a) decision surface learned by a single SVM with linear kernel (circled instances are classified incorrectly); b) an ensemble of three linear SVMs that as zero training error when combined with a simple majority vote

The second interesting feature is the manner in which Triskel assigns weights to the ensemble members. Triskel uses weighted voting like most ensemble methods, but the weights are assigned so that certain pairs of biased classifiers outweigh the rest of the ensemble, if their predictions agree. For example, in Fig. 1(b), the two "outer" classifiers dominate the vote if they agree, but if they disagree then the "inner" classifier casts the deciding vote. Our algorithm is named Triskel after a Celtic spiral design with three branches. In its simplest incarnation, Triskel uses an ensemble of three classifiers: one classifier biased for the positive class, one classifier biased for the negative class, and one unbiased classifier to make predictions when the others disagree.

We make the following contributions. First, we motivate and describe Triskel, our novel approach to ensemble learning, and describe various ways to construct the biased classifiers on which Triskel relies. Second, we discuss how Triskel represents a middle ground between covering and ensemble techniques such as boosting. Finally, we evaluate Triskel on a variety of real-world tasks, and demonstrate that our method often outperforms boosting, in terms of both accuracy and training time.

2   Related Work

Various explanations for the success of ensemble methods have been proposed. For example, [1] presents two necessary and sufficient conditions for an ensemble to be more accurate than any of its member classifiers: the classifiers should be accurate (better than guessing randomly) and diverse (they make different—ideally, independent—mistakes on new data). A simple probabilistic argument shows that if the classifiers' errors are independent and their error rates are less than that of guessing randomly, then the probability that the majority of classifiers is wrong on a new instance is less than the error of any individual. Thus, combining the decisions using a majority vote always has lower error than any of the members.

Of course, these assumptions may not hold in practice, but [2] discusses three fundamental ways in which an ensemble can achieve better performance: statistical, computational and representational. The statistical analysis starts with the observation that any learning algorithm tries to find a hypothesis that has a good accuracy on the training data. When the amount of the training data is small, there may be many different hypotheses that all give the same accuracy on the training data. However, not all of these hypotheses may be correct for a given new data instance. Constructing an ensemble out of all these accurate classifiers can allow the algorithm to reduce the risk of choosing the wrong hypothesis.

The computational argument is that many learning algorithms perform some sort of local search in the hypotheses space that may get stuck in a local optimum. Examples include gradient-based search in neural networks and greedy search in decision trees. An ensemble constructed by running the local search from multiple different starting points may result in a better approximation to the true hypothesis. Finally, the representational analysis follows from the fact that a learning algorithm may not be capable of representing the true function either because it is outside of its hypothesis space or because it does not have sufficient training data to explore all of its hypothesis space to find it (e.g. the classifier would stop searching once it finds a hypothesis that fits the training data). By combining several different hypotheses (e.g. using a weighted sum) it may be possible to expand the space of representable functions.

Perhaps the best-known ensemble methods are bagging [3], and boosting [4, 5], in particular AdaBoost [6]. Bagging generates different training sets by drawing randomly with replacement from the original data set. The classifiers' decisions are combined using the majority vote. AdaBoost performs several learning iterations on the same training set. However, in each iteration it adjusts the weights of the training instances to emphasize the examples that were misclassified by the last learned classifier. The decisions of the classifiers in the ensemble are combined using weighted voting, where the weights depend on the error of the classifier on the training set.

Since bagging constructs its training sets (and, hence, its ensemble members) independently from the others, it mainly addresses the statistical and, to a lesser extent, computational problems. AdaBoost constructs each new hypothesis to eliminate remaining errors and, thus, is directly trying to address the representational problem. It has been shown that by focusing on incorrectly classified instances AdaBoost minimises a particular error function of the ensemble on the training data called the negative exponential of the margin [6, 2].

3   The Triskel Algorithm

Motivation. One of the problems with AdaBoost is that in each subsequent iteration the base learner is presented with more and more difficult problems. The redistribution of instance weights is based on the errors of the last learned hypothesis on the training data. Over multiple iterations, this can result in weight distributions that are too complex for the base learner to handle. For example, suppose we would like to boost a Support Vector Machine [7] with a linear kernel on a synthetic data set shown in Figure 1a. The Figure shows the decision surface that an SVM would learn on this data in the first iteration. We can see that the distribution of errors is such that a linear decision surface will do a poor job on such task. Specifically, the weight distribution will switch in this case between inner and outer instances after each boosting iteration without improvements to the resulting ensemble accuracy.

Nonetheless, the example in Figure 1a can be handled perfectly by an ensemble of three linear separators shown in Figure 1b combined using a majority vote. One classifier separates a part of the positive instances from the rest of positives and negatives, one classifier separates a part of the negative instances, and the remaining classifier handles the instances where the first two classifiers disagree.

An analogy between this approach and set covering can be drawn. Essentially, one classifiers covers the data instances that can be confidently classified as positive ("easy" positives), one classifier covers the data that can be confidently classified as negatives ("easy" negatives), and the last classifier is used to handle the remaining "hard" instances. Our Triskel algorithm is inspired by this idea of exploring a middle ground between ensemble and set covering methods.

In order to identify instances that can be confidently classified as positive or negative, we make use of biased classifiers. A classifier that is biased towards predicting positives will usually have a high precision on negative instances and vice versa. We train a biased classifier for each class. All instances where the biased classifiers agree are considered "easy", all other instances are "hard". The third classifier, the *arbiter*, is then trained only on those "hard" instances. The intuition is that the feature patterns among the "hard" instances may be different from those among the "easy" training examples. By separating away the "easy" instances and training the arbiter only on the "hard" ones, we make the learning problem for the arbiter easier since it only has to deal with a supposedly more regular subset of the data.

Like AdaBoost, we are trying to improve (boost) the classification accuracy of the base classifier on the training set by increasing the representational power using the ensemble. However, the expectation is that we can achieve better results by splitting one hard classification problem into a series of easier ones instead of progressively constructing more difficult problems as in AdaBoost.

The Algorithm. Consider first the Triskel algorithm for a binary classification problem. Assume that a classifier is a function mapping data instances onto a binary set of classes: $h : X \rightarrow \{-1, +1\}$. Similarly to AdaBoost, Triskel is an iterative algorithm. In each iteration, we train a pair of biased classifiers: one classifier biased towards the positive class, and one classifier biased towards the negative class. For a discussion of different ways of biasing classifiers, see section 3. Next, we evaluate the biased classifiers on the training data and obtain two sets of instances: "easy" examples, where the biased classifiers agree; and "hard" ones, where the biased classifiers disagree. To obtain the training set for the next iteration, the weights of the "easy" instances are reduced and the weights of the "hard" instances are increased. The training set obtained after the last iteration is used to train the *arbiter* classifier. Algorithm 1 shows the details.

To combine the decisions of the learned classifiers, we use a conventional weighted voting scheme, with the weights set in such a way that some ensemble members' votes can dominate the others. Specifically, we use a sequence of exponentially decreasing weights such that if two biased classifiers from a given iteration agree on the label of a new instance, then their combined vote outweighs the votes of the classifiers from all subsequent rounds. Essentially, in each iteration we classify and separate the "easy" instances and then use the ensemble members from subsequent iterations to handle the remaining "hard" instances in a recursive way.

Algorithm 1 Triskel

/* *To* _train_ *on* $\{\ldots,(x_i,y_i),\ldots\}$ $(y_i = \pm 1)$ */
Choose the method of weight adjustment:
$W_{easy} = 0; W_{hard} = 1$, or /* *"separation"* */
$W_{easy} = 1/2; W_{hard} = 2$ /* *"soft covering"* */
$D_0(i) = 1/N$ for each instance i
for $t = 1, 2, \ldots, K$ **do**
　　h_t^+ = Learn with weights D_{t-1}, biased for class +1
　　h_t^- = Learn with weights D_{t-1}, biased for class -1
　　$\alpha_t = 2^{K-t}$
　　for each instance i **do**
　　　$\Delta_{t,i} = \begin{cases} W_{easy}, & if\ h_t^+(x_i) = h_t^-(x_i) = y_i \\ W_{hard}, & otherwise \end{cases}$
　　　$D_t(i) = D_{t-1}(i) \cdot \Delta_{t,i}$ and normalise
　　end for
end for
h_{K+1} = Learn with weights D_K, unbiased
$\alpha_{K+1} = 1$
/* *To* _classify_ *instance* x */
return $y = \text{sign}\left[\sum_{t=1}^{K+1} \alpha_t h_t^*(x)\right]$, where $h_t^*(x) = h_t^+(x) + h_t^-(x)$ for $t \leq K$, and $h_t^*(x) = h_{K+1}(x)$ for $t = K + 1$.

There are two principle ways in which the instance weights can be adjusted during training. One way is to set the weights of the "easy" instances to zero, leaving the weights of the "hard" instances unchanged. In this case, the classifiers in each subsequent iteration are trained on a shrinking subset of the training data. This method is more similar to the set covering idea, since after each iteration (the covered) part of the training instances is completely removed from consideration. The problem with this method is that it may quickly "run out of instances". That is, the number of instances left in consideration may quickly become too small to train a sensible classifier.

Therefore, the second way to adjust the instance weights is more similar to boosting, when the weights of "easy" instances are reduced, while the weights of "hard" instances are increased. In our experiments, we increase or reduce the weights by the factor of 2 (see Algorithm 1).

Generating Biased Classifiers. Biasing techniques have been previously used for improving performance of neural net classifiers on imbalanced datasets [8] and for adaptive voting in the ensembles of classifiers for incremental learning [9].

Some machine learning algorithms have an inherent way of setting a bias. Bayesian classifiers, for example, output a probability distribution. The class with the highest posterior probability as calculated by the classifier is predicted. It is easy to bias a Bayesian classifier by either modifying the prior probabilities or to impose biased thresholds on the posterior probabilities. Support Vector Machines also use a confidence value threshold.

There are, however, more generic ways to bias classifiers. Resampling techniques have been used in literature to address the problem of imbalance in the training set. But resampling can of course also be used to create an imbalance, which is what we need for Triskel. Akbani et al. found in [10] that for imbalanced datasets undersampling the majority class to eliminate the bias leads to good performance, although some of the training examples are discarded.

In preliminary experiments, we tried over- and undersampling to create biased classifiers. We found that creating the bias through undersampling does not hurt the overall performance of Triskel, even if as little as 10% of the training instances of one class are kept. For some datasets, the performance was even slightly better than the approach with oversampling. Additionally, because we drop 90% of the instances for one class, training becomes faster. Therefore we decided to use undersampling with a 10% under-sampling rate for our final experiments.

Relation to Covering. There is a loose relationship between Triskel and rule covering algorithms (e.g. [11]). A covering algorithm tries to identify rules with high precision that cover a large number of (ideally uniformly positive or negative) training examples. These training examples are then removed from the training set, as they are covered by the rule, and rule learning continues until all examples are covered. In Triskel, identifying easy instances using biased classifiers could be seen as covering positive and negative instances, as these instances are then removed from the training set from which the arbiter is learned.

Comparison with Boosting. Shapire's original boosting algorithm [4] uses three classifiers: The first one is trained on the original dataset, the training set for the second classifier consists equally of instances that were classified correctly by the first classifier and instances that were incorrectly classified. A third classifier is trained on instances where the first two classifiers disagree. The predictions are combined by voting. In our algorithm we follow up on this idea, however the way we create the first two classifiers is fundamentally different. Also unlike the original boosting, we can use multiple iterations. This results in an ensemble containing more than three classifiers similar to AdaBoost.

Both AdaBoost [6] and Triskel try to enhance the decision surface of the ensemble by focusing on hard instances. The main difference between the two algorithms is, however, how the hard instances are defined. In AdaBoost, the hard instances are defined as the instances where the base classifier makes mistakes. In Triskel, the hard instances are defined as the instances that cannot be classified "confidently", where we assume that we can classify an instance "confidently", if the biased classifiers agree on its label.

4   Experimental Results

We evaluated Triskel on several multi-class datasets from the well-known UCI repository. Because of its very good accuracy, we chose AdaBoost as the benchmark ensemble algorithm for our experiments. We used SMO [12] as a base classifier, again because of its good performance. However, when comparing ensemble methods, accuracy is not the only important factor. The reduced error of ensemble algorithms comes at the price of a greater computational effort. Therefore, time and memory consumption has to be compared as well. Both are usually related to the ensemble size.

Algorithm 2 Comparison of Triskel (left) to AdaBoost (right)

/* To _train_ on $\{\ldots,(x_i,y_i),\ldots\}$ */   /* To _train_ on $\{\ldots,(x_i,y_i),\ldots\}$ */
$D_0(i) = 1/N$ for each instance i $D_0(i) = 1/N$ for each instance i
for $t = 1,2,\ldots,K$ **do**   **for** $t = 1,2,\ldots,K$ **do**
　$h_t^+ = $ Learn(weights D_{t-1}, biased +1)   　$h_t = $ Learn(weights D_{t-1}, unbiased)
　$h_t^- = $ Learn(weights D_{t-1}, biased -1)
　$\alpha_t = 2^{K-t}$ 　$\alpha_t = \frac{1}{2}\log\frac{1-\epsilon_t}{\epsilon_t},$
　　　　　　　　　　　　　　　　　where $\epsilon_t = \sum_i D_{t-1}(i)[\![y_i \neq h_t(x_i)]\!]$
　for each instance i **do**   　**for** each instance i **do**
　　$\Delta_{t,i} =$ 　　$\Delta_{t,i} =$
　　$= \begin{cases} W_{easy} & \text{if } h_t^+(x_i) = h_t^-(x_i) = y_i \\ W_{hard} & \text{otherwise} \end{cases}$ $= \begin{cases} \epsilon_t/(1-\epsilon_t) & \text{if } h_t(x_i) = y_i \\ 1 & \text{otherwise} \end{cases}$
　　$D_t(i) = D_{t-1}(i)\cdot\Delta_{t,i}$ and normalise   　　$D_t(i) = D_{t-1}(i)\cdot\Delta_{t,i}$ and normalise
　end for   　**end for**
end for   **end for**
$h_{K+1} = $ Learn(weights D_K, unbiased)
$\alpha_{K+1} = 1$
/* To _classify_ instance x */   /* To _classify_ instance x */
return $y = \text{sign}\left[\sum_{t=1}^{K+1}\alpha_t h_t^*(x)\right],$ return $y = \text{sign}\left[\sum_{t=1}^{K}\alpha_t h_t(x)\right]$

Because SMO can only handle binary problems, we had to choose a mode of splitting the multi-class problems into binary classification tasks. In all but one configurations we decided to use a one-against-one scheme: A binary classifier is contructed for all pairwise combinations of two classes. This means that for a dataset with k classes it is necessary to train $\frac{k(k-1)}{2}$ classifiers. Note that on datasets with more than 3 classes, this setup is computationally more expensive than a one-against-all scheme, but generally leads to a much better performance.

In conjunction with Triskel it is possible to use a compromise between one-vs-all and one-vs-one methods. We call this extension Triskel-M. For each class, a binary problem is created in order to separate this class ('positive instances') from all others ('negative instances'). These classifiers are biased towards high precision on the positive class and used similar as in binary Triskel: If exactly one of the biased classifiers predicts positive, this prediction is returned. If more than one or none of the biased classifiers predict positive, the prediction of the arbiter is returned. The arbiter is trained in one-vs-one mode to achieve a better accuracy. In our experiments, we used Triskel-M with $W_{easy} = 0$ and 1 round (denoted as Triskel-M1).

For AdaBoost, boosting the binary classifiers individually yielded a better performance than using AdaBoost-M1 [6].

We used a standard SMO as baseline. We used three different AdaBoost-ensembles with 3, 10 and 50 rounds. We compared these against standard Triskel with 1 round and discarding easy instances for the arbiter ($W_{easy} = 0$) (Triskel-1) and against Triskel with weighting ($W_{easy} = 1/2; W_{hard} = 2$) with 2 and 4 rounds (denoted as Triskel-W2 and Triskel-W4). Note that for a (binary) Triskel the actual ensemble size is twice the number of rounds plus one.

We used the Weka framework [13] to conduct our experiments. We evaluated all algorithms using 10-fold cross-validation with 10 randomized repetitions for statistical

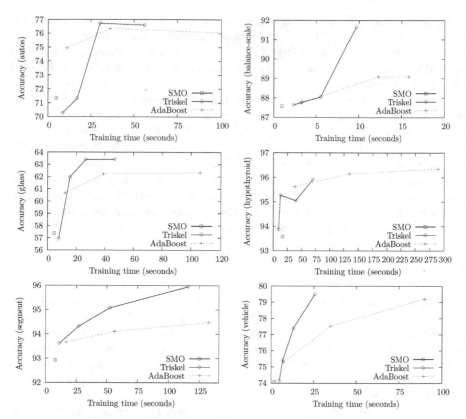

Fig. 2. Accuracy and training time for SMO, Triskel-M1, Triskel-1, -W2, -W4, AdaBoost-3, -10 and -50 on the (from left to right and top to bottom) "autos", "balance-scale", "glass", "hypothyroid", "segment" and "vehicle" datasets

significance testing, using a corrected resampled t-test as implemented in the Weka experimenter. [1]

The experiments show that AdaBoost with 50 rounds does not improve the accuracy over AdaBoost with 10 rounds when using SMO as a base classifier. Triskel-W4 outperforms AdaBoost with 3 significant wins out of the 15 datasets used. This quality improvement comes at the price of higher training cost when compared to AdaBoost-10. However, it is still faster than AdaBoost-50. Triskel-W2 (i.e. with an ensemble size of 5 classifiers) achieves a performance that is comparable to AdaBoost-10 (2 wins, 2 losses), but is significantly faster.

As expected, the M1 setup for Triskel is both the least accurate but also the fastest ensemble method. Although the biased classifiers are only trained in a one-against-

---

[1] Due to space restrictions we cannot present all our experimental results in this paper. Our WEKA-based implementation of Triskel and more experimental results are available from our website http://moguntia.ucd.ie/projects/triskel/

all mode, the ensemble can still sigificantly outperform the base SMO in one-against-one mode on the anneal.ORIG, hypothyroid and segment datasets. Because of its one-against-all nature, this setup of Triskel can even be faster than one-against-one SMO, especially on large datasets (here on the audiology, hypothyroid and soybean datasets), while not hurting accuracy.

Figure 2 illustrates the relation between training time and accuracy for the algorithms on four typical datasets. The data points on the Triskel line correspond to (from fastest to slowest) Triskel-M1, -1, -W2 and -W4, while the data points for AdaBoost show the setup for 3, 10 and 50 rounds. Note that in most cases the line for Triskel is above the AdaBoost line, indicating that Triskel offers a better trade-off between accuracy and speed. Triskel achieves greater accuracy in the same time, and the same accuracy can be reached faster. Furthermore, note that the highest accuracy for Triskel is usually above the highest accuracy for AdaBoost, indicating that, given enough time, Triskel can typically outperform any setting of AdaBoost.

5   Conclusion

Current and Future Work. We are currently researching many aspects of Triskel that we could only sketch shortly in this paper. For example, note that for the experiments presented in this paper, we have used undersampling as the only method of generating the biased classifiers. In future work we would like to explore the space of possible methods for generating bias, such as setting the bias of the classifier directly by means of thresholding, or to use oversampling with artificially created instances as used in the SMOTE algorithm [14].

We are currently working on a covering-inspired way of generating the biased classifiers. To train a classifier that is biased towards high precision on positive instances, we train multiple versions of a base classifier while iteratively removing instances from the training set that the base classifier predicts as negative (i.e. instances that are cov-

$D_0(i) = 1/N$ for each instance i
for $t = 1, 2, \ldots, K$ **do**
    $h_t = $ learn(instances weights D_{t-1})
    for each instance i **do**
        $D_t(i) = \begin{cases} 1 \text{ if } h_t(x_i) = 1 \\ 0 \text{ otherwise} \end{cases}$
    end for
end for
/* *To classify instance* x */
for $t = \overline{1, 2}, \ldots, K$ **do**
    if $h_t(x) = -1$ **then**
        halt and return -1
    end if
end for
return 1

Fig. 3. Cover Negatives Algorithm

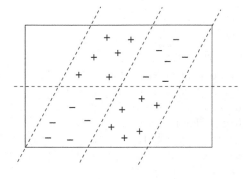

Fig. 4. "Slanted checkerboard" data set

ered). On classification time, an instance is predicted as positive only if all ensemble members classify it as positive. Achieving high precision on negative examples is symmetric, and the generalisation towards multi-class datasets is straightforward. Fig. 3 shows the covering-based biased classifier in pseudo-code.

This covering-like approach to biasing classifiers is more expressive than simple resampling approaches, because it is an ensemble itself. A Triskel classifier with covering-based biased classifiers is able to learn the correct hypothesis for a "slanted checkerboard" dataset (see Fig. 4), which is another example of a dataset that confounds many other algorithms. In preliminary experiments on real-world datasets, covering-like biasing improved classification accuracy slightly. On the other hand, this expressiveness is bought with the need for more ensemble members.

Summary. We have presented a novel ensemble learning algorithm called Triskel that makes use of biased classifiers to separate "easy" and "hard" instances. In its iterative nature, it is similar in style to Boosting methods, while the way Triskel separates easy and hard instances is loosely related to covering algorithms.

Empirical results suggest that, compared to AdaBoost, Triskel offers a better trade-off between accuracy and speed. Furthermore, the experiments show the maximum accuracy that can be achieved with Triskel is higher than the accuracy of AdaBoost.

References

1. Hansen, L.K., Salamon, P.: Neural Network Ensembles. IEEE Transactions on Pattern Analysis and Machine Intelligence **12** (1990) 993–1001
2. Dietterich, T.G.: Ensemble Methods in Machine Learning. In: First Int. Workshop on Multiple Classifier Systems, New York (2000)
3. Breiman, L.: Bagging predictors. Machine Learning **24** (1996) 123–140
4. Shapire, R.E.: The Strength of Weak Learnability. Machine Learning **5** (1990) 197–227
5. Freund, Y.: Boosting a Weak Learning Algorithm by Majority. Information and Computation **121** (1995) 256–285
6. Freund, Y., Shapire, R.E.: A Decision-Theoretic Generalization of On-Line Learning. Journal of Computer and System Sciences **55** (1997) 119–139
7. Vapnik, V.N.: Vosstanovlenije Zavisimostej po Empiricheskim Dannym. Nauka (1979) In Russian.
8. Murphey, Y.L., Guo, H., Feldkamp, L.A.: Neural learning from unbalanced data. Appl. Intell. **21** (2004) 117–128
9. Muhlbaier, M., Topalis, A., Polikar, R.: Learn++.MT: A New Approach to Incremental Learning. In: 5th Int. Workshop on Multiple Classifier Systems, Cagliari, Italy (2004)
10. Akbani, R., Kwek, S., Japkowicz, N.: Applying Support Vector Machines to Imabalanced Datasets. In: 15th European Conference on Machine Learning (ECML), Pisa (2004)
11. Fürnkranz, J.: Separate and Conquer Rule Learning. Art. Intell. Review **13** (1999) 3–54
12. Platt, J.C.: 12. In: Fast Training of Support Vector Machines using Sequential Minimal Optimization. MIT Press (1999) 185–208
13. Witten, I.H., Frank, E.: Data Mining: Practical Machine Learning Tools and Techniques with Java Implementations. Morgan Kaufmann (1999)
14. Chawla, N.V., Bowyer, K.W., Hall, L.O., Kegelmeyer, W.P.: SMOTE: Synthetic Minority Over-sampling TEchnique. Journal of Artificial Intelligence Research **16** (2002) 341–378

Cluster-Based Cumulative Ensembles

Hanan G. Ayad and Mohamed S. Kamel

Pattern Analysis and Machine Intelligence Lab,
Electrical and Computer Engineering, University of Waterloo,
Waterloo, Ontario N2L 3G1, Canada
{hanan, mkamel}@pami.uwaterloo.ca
http://pami.uwaterloo.ca/

Abstract. In this paper, we propose a cluster-based cumulative representation for cluster ensembles. Cluster labels are mapped to incrementally accumulated clusters, and a matching criterion based on maximum similarity is used. The ensemble method is investigated with bootstrap re-sampling, where the k-means algorithm is used to generate high granularity clusterings. For combining, group average hierarchical *meta-clustering* is applied and the Jaccard measure is used for cluster similarity computation. Patterns are assigned to combined meta-clusters based on estimated cluster assignment probabilities. The cluster-based cumulative ensembles are more compact than co-association-based ensembles. Experimental results on artificial and real data show reduction of the error rate across varying ensemble parameters and cluster structures.

1 Introduction

Motivated by the advances in classifier ensembles, which combine the predictions of multiple classifiers; cluster ensembles that combine multiple data partitionings have started to gain an increasing interest [1, 2, 3, 4, 5, 6, 7, 8].

Cluster ensembles can be illustrated by the schematic model in Figure 1. The model includes two main elements, the ensemble generation and the combination scheme. The ensemble generation takes as input a dataset of d-dimensional pattern vectors represented by an $N \times d$ matrix $\mathbf{X} = \{\mathbf{x}^{(i)}\}_{i=1}^{N}$, where N is the number of patterns and the row vector $\mathbf{x}^{(i)}$ represents the ith pattern. The ensemble generation generates multiple clusterings, represented here by cluster label vectors $\{\mathbf{y}^{(b)}\}_{b=1}^{B}$. The combining scheme (or the consensus function [1]), can be thought of as comprising two sub-elements. The first is the ensemble mapping which defines a representation $\mathbf{Z}$ of the ensemble outputs and an associated mapping method. The lack of direct correspondence between the labels generated by the individual clusterings leads to the need for this mapping component. For instance, the co-association (or co-occurrence) matrix [2] is an example of a representation generated by an ensemble mapping that side-steps the label correspondence problem, at a computational cost of $O(N^2)$. The maximum likelihood mapping [8] is another example of ensemble mapping in which the re-labelling problem is formulated as a weighted bipartite matching problem and is solved

N.C. Oza et al. (Eds.): MCS 2005, LNCS 3541, pp. 236–245, 2005.

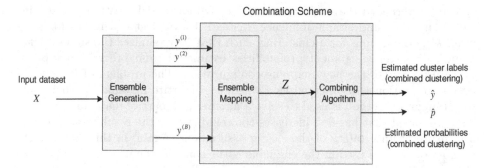

Fig. 1. Schematic model of cluster ensembles

using the Hungarian method [9] with a computational cost of $O(k^3)$ where k is the number of clusters.

The second sub-element of a combining scheme is the combining algorithm which uses $\mathbf{Z}$ to generate the combined clustering $\hat{\mathbf{y}}$. A potential derivative of the cluster ensemble is the estimation of the probabilities $\hat{p}$ with which data points belong to the combined clusters. The combining algorithm often lends itself to a clustering problem, where the data is given by the new representation $\mathbf{Z}$. It is noted that if the label correspondence problem is resolved and the number of clusters c in the base clusterings $\{\mathbf{y}^{(i)}\}_{i=1}^B$ is the same as the number of clusters k in the combined clustering $\hat{\mathbf{y}}$, majority voting [6] or maximum likelihood classification [8] can be readily applied. However, if $c \neq k$, co-association-based consensus functions are often applied [2, 3, 4]. While allowing arbitrary cluster structures to be discovered, co-association-based consensus functions are computationally expensive and hence not practical for large datasets.

Re-sampling methods are well established approaches for estimating improved data statistics [10]. In particular, bagging [11] has been introduced in regression and classification. In bagging, the training dataset of size N is perturbed using bootstrap re-sampling to generate learning datasets by randomly sampling N patterns with replacement. This yields duplicate patterns in a bootstrap dataset. The bootstrap re-sampling process is independently repeated B times and the B datasets are treated as independent learning sets.

Dudoit and Fridlyand [6] used bagging with the Partitioning Around Medoids (PAM) clustering method to improve the accuracy of clustering. They use two methods for combining multiple partitions. The first applies voting and the second creates a new dissimilarity matrix similar to the co-association matrix used in [2]. In the voting method, the same number of clusters is used for clustering and combining, and the input dataset is clustered once to create a reference clustering. The cluster labels of each bootstrap replication are permuted such that they fit best to the reference clustering. They reported that the bagged clustering were generally as accurate and often significantly more accurate than a single clustering. Fischer and Buhmann [8] applied bagging to improve the quality of the path-based clustering method. They critiqued the use of a reference clustering in the mapping method of Dudoit and Fridlyand [6], arguing that it imposes undesirable influence. Instead, they selected a re-labelling out of all $k!$ permutations for a clustering, such that it maximizes the sum over the empirical cluster assignment probabilities estimated from previous mappings, over all objects of the new mapping configuration. The problem of finding the best permutation is formulated as a weighted bipartite matching problem and the Hungarian method is used to solve a maximum bipartite matching problem. They reported that bagging increases the reliability of the results and provides a measure of uncertainty of the cluster assignment. Again, in this method, the number of clusters used in the ensemble is the same as the number of combined clusters. Minaei, Topchy and Punch [7] empirically investigated the effectiveness of bootstrapping with several consensus functions by examining the accuracy of the combined clustering for varied resolution of partitions (i.e., number of clusters) and ensemble size. They report that clustering of bootstrapping leads to improved consensus clustering of the data. They further conclude that the the best consensus function remains an open question, as different consensus functions seem to suit different cluster structures.

In this paper, we propose an ensemble mapping representation based on the generated clusters, as high-level data granules. Re-labelling of clusters is based on maximizing individual cluster similarity to incrementally-accumulated clusters. Based on this representation, different combining algorithms can be used such as hierarchical clustering algorithms, for instance. Here, group average (i.e. average link) hierarchical meta-clustering is applied. We experimentally investigate the effectiveness of the proposed consensus function, with bootstrap re-sampling, and the k-means as the underlying clustering algorithm.

2   Cluster-Based Cumulative Ensemble

2.1   Ensemble Mapping

The ensemble representation consists of a cumulative $c \times N$ matrix $\mathbf{Z}$ summarising the ensemble outputs, where c is a given number of clusters that is used in generating multiple clusterings, such that $k \leq c \ll N$ where k is the number of combined clusters. The data values in $\mathbf{Z}$ reflect the frequency of occurrence of each pattern in each of the accumulated clusters.

The k-means algorithm with the Euclidean distance is used to generate a clustering $\mathbf{y}^{(b)} = \pi(\mathbf{X}^{(b)}, c)$ of a bootstrapped learning set in $\{\mathbf{X}^{(b)}\}_{b=1}^{B}$, where B is the size of the ensemble, and $\mathbf{y}^{(b)}$ is an N-dimensional labeling vector. That is, π is a mapping function $\pi : \mathbf{X}^{(b)} \rightarrow \{0, \cdots, c\}$, where '0' label is assigned to patterns that didn't appear in the bootstrap learning set $\mathbf{X}^{(b)}$.

Each instance of the $c \times N$ matrix, denoted by $\mathbf{Z}^{(b)}$, is incrementally updated from the ensemble $\{\mathbf{y}^{(b)}\}_{b=1}^{B}$ as follows.

1. $\mathbf{Z}^{(1)}$ is initialized using $\mathbf{y}^{(1)}$, as given below. Re-labelling and accumulation start by processing clustering $\mathbf{y}^{(2)}$.

$$z_{ij}^{(1)} = \begin{cases} 1 & \text{if object } j \text{ is in cluster } i \text{ according to clustering } \mathbf{y}^{(1)} \\ 0 & \text{otherwise} \end{cases}$$

2. Let each cluster in a given clustering $\mathbf{y}^{(b+1)}$ be represented by a binary N-dimensional vector $\mathbf{v}$ with 1's in entries corresponding to the cluster members and 0's otherwise. Let each cluster extracted from the rows $\mathbf{z}_i^{(b)}$ of $\mathbf{Z}^{(b)}$ be represented by the binary N-dimensional vector $\mathbf{w}$ whose entries are 1's for non-zero columns of $\mathbf{z}_i^{(b)}$ and 0's otherwise. Compute the similarity between each pair of vectors $\mathbf{v}$ and $\mathbf{w}$ using the Jaccard measure given as $J(\mathbf{v}, \mathbf{w}) = \mathbf{v}\mathbf{w}/(\|\mathbf{v}\|^2 + \|\mathbf{w}\|^2 - \mathbf{v}\mathbf{w})$

3. Map each cluster label $i \in \{1, \cdots, c\}$ in clustering $\mathbf{y}^{(b+1)}$ to its most similar cluster labelled $j \in \{1, \cdots, c\}$ of the previously accumulated clusters represented by the rows of $\mathbf{Z}^{(b)}$. Hence, increment the entries of row j of $\mathbf{Z}^{(b)}$ corresponding to members of the cluster labelled i in clustering $\mathbf{y}^{(b+1)}$.

4. $\mathbf{Z}^{(b+1)} \leftarrow \mathbf{Z}^{(b)}$. The mapping process is repeated until $\mathbf{Z}^{(B)}$ is computed.

The cumulative cluster-based mapping of the ensemble culminates in the matrix $\mathbf{Z} = \mathbf{Z}^{(B)}$, as a voting structure that summarises the ensemble. While in the maximum likelihood mapping [8], the best cluster label permutation is found and $c = k$ is used, in this paper, each cluster is re-labelled to match its most similar cluster from the accumulated clusters. This is done for the following reasons. First, since the base clusterings represent high resolution partitions of non-identical bootstrap learning sets, this leads to highly diverse clusterings, such that finding the best permutation becomes less meaningful. For quantitative measures of diversity in cluster ensembles, the reader is referred to [5]. Second, since the accumulated clusters will be merged in a later stage by the combining algorithm, we are most concerned at this stage in a mapping which maximizes the similarities and hence minimizes the variance of the mapped clusters.

We found that this matching method can occasionally result in a cumulative cluster to become singled out when no subsequently added clusters are mapped to it. If a hierarchical clustering algorithm is used, this problem can lead to a degenerate dendrogram and empty cluster(s) in the combined clustering. Therefore, we detect this condition, and the corresponding solution is discarded. Usually, a good solution is reached in a few iterations. An alternative remedy is to match each of the cumulative clusters to its most similar cluster from each subsequently mapped clustering, instead of the reverse way. This ensures that the above mentioned condition does not occur, but it can introduce influence from earlier clusterings and less incorporation of the diversity in the ensemble.

An advantage of this representation is that it allows several alternative views (interpretations) to be considered by the combining algorithm. For instance, $\mathbf{Z}$ may be treated as a pattern matrix. This allows different distance/similarity measures and combining algorithms to be applied to generate the combined clustering. Alternatively, $\mathbf{Z}$ may be treated as the joint probability distribution of two discrete random variables indexing the rows and columns of $\mathbf{Z}$. This allows for information theoretic formulations for finding of the combined clusters.

Furthermore, the size of this representation is $c \times N$ versus N^2 for the co-association-based representation, where $c \ll N$. While, in the case of the co-association matrix, the hierarchical clustering algorithm runs on the $N \times N$

matrix, in the case of the cluster-based cumulative representation, it runs on a $c \times c$ distance matrix computed from the $c \times N$ matrix $\mathbf{Z}$.

2.2   Combining Using Hierarchical Group Average Meta-clustering

Motivated by what is believed to be a reasonable discriminating strategy based on the average of a chosen distance measure between clusters, the proposed algorithm is the group average hierarchical clustering. The combining algorithm starts by computing the distances between the rows of $\mathbf{Z}$ (i.e. the cumulative clusters). This is a total of $\binom{c}{2}$ distances, and one minus the binary Jaccard measure, given in Section 2.1, is used to compute the distances. The group-average hierarchical clustering is used to cluster the clusters, hence the name meta-clustering. In this algorithm, the distance between a pair of clusters $d(C_1, C_2)$ is defined as the average distance between the objects in each cluster, where the objects in this case are the cumulative clusters. It is computed as follows, $d(C_1, C_2) = mean_{(\mathbf{z}_1, \mathbf{z}_2) \in C_1 \times C_2} d(\mathbf{z}_1, \mathbf{z}_2)$, where $d(\mathbf{z}_1, \mathbf{z}_2) = 1 - J(\mathbf{z}_1, \mathbf{z}_2)$.

The dendrogram is cut to generate k meta-clusters $\{M_j\}_{j=1}^k$ representing a partitioning of the cumulative clusters $\{\mathbf{z}_i\}_{i=1}^c$. The merged clusters are averaged in a $k \times N$ matrix $\mathbf{M} = \{m_{ji}\}$ for $j \in \{1, \cdots, k\}$ and $i \in \{1, \cdots, N\}$. So far, only the binary version of the cumulative matrix has been used for distance computations. Now, in determining the final clustering, the frequency values accumulated in $\mathbf{Z}$ are averaged in the meta-cluster matrix $\mathbf{M}$ and used to compute the cluster assignment probabilities. Then, each object is assigned to its most likely meta-cluster. Let M be a random variable indexing the meta-clusters and taking values in $\{1, \cdots, k\}$, let X be a random variable indexing the patterns and taking values in $\{1, \cdots, N\}$, and let $\hat{p}(M = j | X = i)$ be the conditional probability of each of the k meta-clusters, given an object i, which we also write as $p(M_j | x_i)$. Here, we use x_i to denote the object index of the pattern $\mathbf{x}^{(i)}$, and we use M_j to denote a meta-cluster represented by the row j in $\mathbf{M}$. The probability estimates $\hat{p}(M_j | x_i)$ are computed as $\hat{p}(M_j | x_i) = \frac{m_{ji}}{\sum_{l=1}^k m_{li}}$.

3   Experimental Analysis

Performance is evaluated based on the error rates which are computed by solving the correspondence problem between the labels of a clustering solution and the true clustering using the Hungarian method.

3.1   Experiments with Artificial Data

The artificial datasets are shown in Figure 2. The first, called "Elongated-ellipses" consists of 1000 2D points in 2 equal clusters. The "Crescents" dataset consists of 1000 2D points in 2 equal clusters. The "Differing-ellipses" consists of 250 2D points in 2 clusters of sizes 50 and 200. The dataset called "8D5K" was generated and used in [1]. It consists of 1000 points from 8D Gaussian distributions (200 points each). For visualization, the "8D5K" data is projected onto the first two principal components.

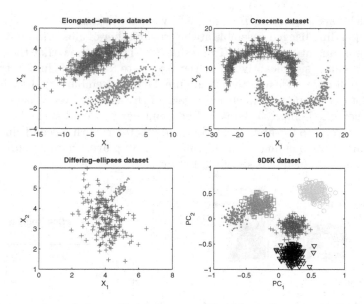

Fig. 2. Scatter plots of the artificial datasets. The last 8 dimensional dataset is projected on the first 2 principal components

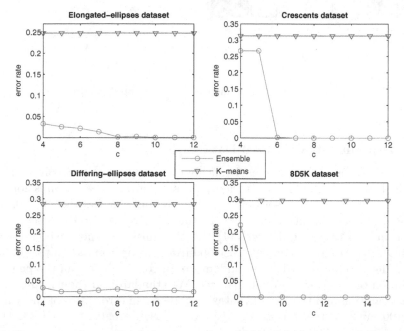

Fig. 3. Error rates for artificial datasets using the bagged cluster ensembles and the k-means algorithm at given k

For each dataset, we use $B = 100$, and vary c. We measure the error rate of the corresponding bagged ensemble at the true number of clusters k and compare it to the k-means at the same k. The results in Figure 3 show that the proposed bagging ensemble significantly lowers the error rate for varied cluster structures. In order to illustrate the cluster-based cumulative ensemble, we show in Figure 4 (a) a plot of the points frequencies in each of the accumulated clusters at $c = 4$ for the "elongated-ellipses" dataset. The points are ordered such that the first 500 points belong to the first cluster followed by 500 from the second cluster. The dendrogram corresponding to the hierarchical group average meta-clustering on the 4 cumulative clusters is shown in Figure 4 (b).

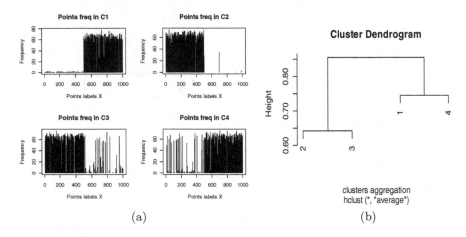

(a)   (b)

Fig. 4. (a) Accumulated clusters. (b) Generated dendrogram

3.2   Experiments with Real Data

We use six datasets from the UCI machine learning repository. Since the Euclidean distance is not scale invariant, we standardize the features for those datasets in which the scales widely vary for the different features. The datasets used are, (1) the iris plant dataset, (2) the wine recognition dataset, (3) the Wisconsin breast cancer dataset, (4) the Wisconsin diagnostic breast cancer (WDBC), (5) a random sample of size 500 from the optical recognition of handwritten digits dataset, and (6) a random sample of size 500 from the pen-based recognition of handwritten digits dataset. We standardized the features for the wine recognition and the WDBC datasets. The mean error rates of the k-means (over 100 runs), at the true k, for the above datasets are, 0.2007, 0.0378, 0.0395, 0.0923, 0.2808, 0.3298, respectively.

Figure 5 shows a comparison of the cluster-based cumulative ensembles with hierarchical group average (denoted in Figure 5 by cluster-based alink) to pattern co-association-based ensembles, when single, complete and average link variants of the hierarchical clustering are applied (denoted by pattern-based slink, clink,

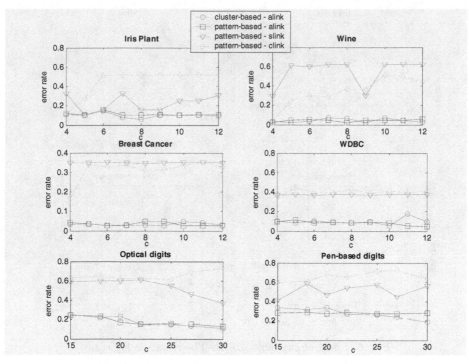

Fig. 5. Error rates on the real datasets for the proposed ensemble versus co-associations-based ensembles using single, complete and average link

and alink, respectively). In the experiments, we use $B = 100$ and k corresponding to the true number of clusters. The results show that the cluster-based alink ensembles perform competitively well compared to pattern-based alink ensembles. On the other hand, the co-association-based single and complete link ensembles showed poor performance.

3.3 Varying the Ensemble Size

We study the effect of the ensemble size B, for values of $B \leq 100$. Figure 6 shows the mean error rates on real and artificial datasets for $B = 5, 10, 25, 50$, and 100, and for varying number of base clusters c. Each ensemble at a given c and B is repeated $r = 5$ times and the mean is computed. There is a general trend of reduction in error rates as B increases. However, we observe that most gain in accuracy occurs for $B = 25$, and 50. We also observe that the differences between the error rates of ensembles of varying values of c tend to decrease as B increases, i.e., the variability of the error rates corresponding to different values of c is reduced when B is increased. However, in some cases, it is noted that that amount of reduction in the error depends on c. For instance, this can be observed for $c = 4$ in the crescents and differing-ellipses datasets.

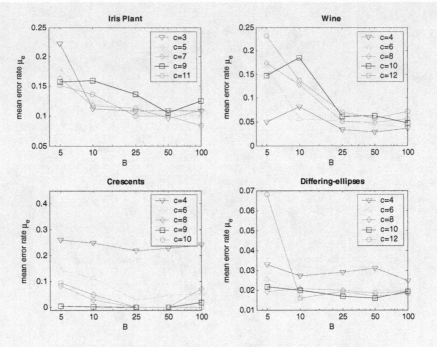

Fig. 6. Effect of ensemble size B. The X-axis is log scale

4   Conclusion

The proposed cluster-based cumulative representation is more compact than the co-association matrix. Experimental results on artificial datasets emphasised the potential of the proposed ensemble method in substantially lowering the error rate, and in finding arbitrary cluster structures. For the real datasets, the cluster-based cumulative ensembles, using group average hierarchical clustering, significantly outperformed co-association-based ensembles, using the single and complete link algorithms. They showed competitive performance compared to co-association-based ensembles, using the group average algorithm. In [12], the group average algorithm is shown to approximately minimize the maximum cluster variance. Such model seems to represent a better fit to the data summarised in **Z**. A further potential benefit of this paper is that co-association-based consensus functions other than hierarchical methods, such as [3, 4], can also be adapted to the cluster-based cumulative representation, rendering them more efficient. This will be investigated in future work.

Acknowledgment

This work was partially funded by an NSERC strategic grant.

References

1. A. Strehl and J. Ghosh. Cluster ensembles - a knowledge reuse framework for combining multiple partitions. *Journal on Machine Learning Research (JMLR)*, 3:583–617, December 2002.
2. A. Fred and A.K. Jain. Data clustering using evidence accumulation. In *Proceedings of the 16th International Conference on Pattern Recognition. ICPR 2002*, volume 4, pages 276–280, Quebec City, Quebec, Canada, August 2002.
3. H. Ayad and M. Kamel. Finding natural clusters using multi-clusterer combiner based on shared nearest neighbors. In *Multiple Classifier Systems: Fourth International Workshop, MCS 2003, UK, Proceedings.*, pages 166–175, 2003.
4. H. Ayad, O. Basir, and M. Kamel. A probabilistic model using information theoretic measures for cluster ensembles. In *Multiple Classifier Systems: Fifth International Workshop, MCS 2004, Cagliari, Italy, Proceedings*, pages 144–153, 2004.
5. L. I. Kuncheva and S.T. Hadjitodorov. Using diversity in cluster ensembles. In *IEEE International Conference on Systems, Man and Cybernetics, Proceedings*, The Hague, The Netherlands., 2004.
6. S. Dudoit and J. Fridlyand. Bagging to improve the accuracy of a clustering procedure. *Bioinformatics*, 19(9):1090–1099, 2003.
7. B. Minaei, A. Topchy, and W. Punch. Ensembles of partitions via data resampling. In *Intl. Conf. on Information Technology: Coding and Computing, ITCC04, Proceedings*, Las Vegas, April 2004.
8. B. Fischer and J.M. Buhmann. Bagging for path-based clustering. *IEEE Transactions on Pattern Analysis and Machine Intelligence*, 25(11):1411–1415, 2003.
9. H. Kuhn. The hungarian method for the assignment problem. *Naval Research Logistic Quarterly*, 2:83–97, 1955.
10. R.O. Duda, P.E. Hart, and D.G. Stork. *Pattern Classification*. John Wiley & Sons, 2001.
11. Leo Breiman. Bagging predictors. *Machine Learning*, 26(2):123–140, 1996.
12. S. Kamvar, D. Klein, and C. Manning. Interpreting and extending classical agglomerative clustering algorithms using a model-based approach. In *Proceedings of the 19th Int. Conf. Machine Learning*, pages 283–290, 2002.

Ensemble of SVMs for Incremental Learning

Zeki Erdem[1,4], Robi Polikar[2], Fikret Gurgen[3], and Nejat Yumusak[4]

[1] TUBITAK Marmara Research Center, Information Technologies Institute,
41470 Gebze - Kocaeli, Turkey
zeki.erdem@bte.mam.gov.tr
[2] Rowan University, Electrical and Computer Engineering Department,
210 Mullica Hill Rd., Glassboro, NJ 08028, USA
polikar@rowan.edu
[3] Bogazici University, Computer Engineering Department,
Bebek, 80815 Istanbul, Turkey
gurgen@boun.edu.tr
[4] Sakarya University, Computer Engineering Department,
Esentepe, 54187 Sakarya, Turkey
nyumusak@sakarya.edu.tr

Abstract. Support Vector Machines (SVMs) have been successfully applied to solve a large number of classification and regression problems. However, SVMs suffer from the *catastrophic forgetting* phenomenon, which results in loss of previously learned information. Learn[++] have recently been introduced as an incremental learning algorithm. The strength of Learn[++] lies in its ability to learn new data without forgetting previously acquired knowledge and without requiring access to any of the previously seen data, even when the new data introduce new classes. To address the *catastrophic forgetting* problem and to add the incremental learning capability to SVMs, we propose using an ensemble of SVMs trained with Learn[++]. Simulation results on real-world and benchmark datasets suggest that the proposed approach is promising.

1 Introduction

Support Vector Machines (SVMs) have enjoyed a remarkable success as effective and practical tools for a broad range of classification and regression applications [1-2]. As with any type of classifier, the performance and accuracy of SVMs rely on the availability of a representative set of training dataset. In many practical applications, however, acquisition of such a representative dataset is expensive and time consuming. Consequently, such data often become available in small and separate batches at different times. In such cases, a typical approach is combining new data with all previous data, and training a new classifier from scratch. In other words, such scenarios require a classifier to be trained and incrementally updated, where the classifier needs to learn the novel information provided by the new data without forgetting the knowledge previously acquired from the data seen earlier. Learning new information without forgetting previously acquired knowledge, however, raises the stability–plasticity dilemma [3]. A completely stable classifier can retain knowledge, but cannot learn

N.C. Oza et al. (Eds.): MCS 2005, LNCS 3541, pp. 246–256, 2005.
© Springer-Verlag Berlin Heidelberg 2005

new information, whereas a completely plastic classifier can instantly learn new information, but cannot retain previous knowledge. The approach generally followed for learning from new data involves discarding the existing classifier, combining the old and the new data and training a new classifier from scratch using the aggregate data. This approach, however, results in *catastrophic forgetting* (also called unlearning) [4], which can be defined as the inability of the system to learn new patterns without forgetting previously learned ones. Methods to adress this problem include retraining the classifier on a selection of past or new data points generated from the problem space. However, this approach is unfeasible if previous data are no longer available.

Such problems can be best addressed through incremental learning, defined as the process of extracting new information without losing prior knowledge from an additional dataset that later becomes available. Various definitions and interpretations of incremental learning can be found in [6] and references within. For the purposes of this paper, we define an incremental learning algorithm as one that meets the following demanding criteria [5,6]:

1. be able to learn additional information from new data.
2. not require access to the original data used to train the existing classifier.
3. preserve previously acquired knowledge (that is, it should not suffer from catastrophic forgetting).
4. be able to accommodate new classes that may be introduced with new data.

In this paper we describe an ensemble of classifiers approach: ensemble systems have attracted a great deal of attention over the last decade due to their empirical success over single classifier systems on a variety of applications. An ensemble of classifiers system is a set of classifiers whose individual decisions are combined in some way to obtain a meta classifier. One of the most active areas of research in supervised learning has been to study methods for constructing good ensembles of classifiers. The main discovery is that ensembles are often more accurate than the individual classifiers that make them up. A rich collection of algorithms have been developed using multiple classifiers, such as AdaBoost [7] and its many variations, with the general goal of improving the generalization performance of the classification system. Using multiple classifiers for incremental learning, however, has been largely unexplored. Learn^{++}, in part inspired by AdaBoost, was developed in response to recognizing the potential feasibility of ensemble of classifiers in solving the incremental learning problem. Learn^{++} was initially introduced in [5] as an incremental learning algorithm for MLP type networks. A more versatile form of the algorithm was presented in [6] for all supervised classifiers.

Since SVMs are stable classifiers and use the global partitioning (global learning) technique, they are also susceptible to the catastrophic forgetting problem [8]. The SVMs optimise the positioning of the hyperplanes to achieve maximum distance from all data samples on both sides of the hyperplane through learning. Therefore, SVMs are unable to learn incrementally from new data. Since training of SVMs is usually present as a quadratic programming problem, it is a challenging task for the large data sets due to the high memory requirements and slow convergence. To overcome these drawbacks, various methods have been proposed for incremental SVM learning in the literature [9-14]. On the other hand, some studies have also been presented to further improve classification performance and accuracy of SVMs with ensemble methods, such as boosting and bagging [15-18]. In this study, we consider the ensemble based incremental SVM approach. The purpose of this study was to investigate whether the incremental learning capability can be added to SVM classifiers through the Learn[++] algorithm, while avoiding the catastrophic forgetting problem.

2 Learn[++]

The strength of Learn[++] as an ensemble of classifiers approach lies in its ability to incrementally learn additional information from new data. Specifically, for each dataset that becomes available, Learn[++] generates an ensemble of classifiers, whose outputs are combined through weighted majority voting to obtain the final classification. Classifiers are trained based on a dynamically updated distribution over the training data instances, where the distribution is biased towards those novel instances that have not been properly learned or seen by the previous ensemble(s). The pseudocode for Learn[++] is provided in Figure 1.

For each dataset D_k, $k=1,...,K$ that is submitted to Learn[++], the inputs to the algorithm are (i) $S_k = \{(x_i, y_i)|i = 1,...,m_k\}$, a sequence of m_k training data instances x_i along with their correct labels y_i, (ii) a classification algorithm **BaseClassifier** to generate hypotheses, and (iii) an integer T_k specifying the number of classifiers (hypotheses) to be generated for that dataset. The only requirement on the **BaseClassifier** is that it obtains a 50% correct classification performance on its own training dataset. **BaseClassifier** can be any supervised classifier such as a multilayer perceptron, radial basis function, a decision tree, or of course, a SVM.

Learn[++] starts by initializing a set of weights for the training data, w, and a distribution D obtained from w, according to which a training subset TR_t and a test subset TE_t are drawn at the tth iteration of the algorithm. Unless a priori information indicates otherwise, this distribution is initially set to be uniform, giving equal probability to each instance to be selected into the first training subset.

At each iteration t, the weights adjusted at iteration t-1 are normalized to ensure that a legitimate distribution, D_t, is obtained (step 1). Training and test subsets are drawn according to D_t (step 2), and the base classifier is trained with the training subset (step 3). A hypothesis h_t is obtained as the tth classifier, whose error ε_t is computed on the entire (current) dataset $S_k = TR_t + TE_t$, simply by adding the distribution weights of the misclassified instances (step 4).

$$\varepsilon_t = \sum_{i:h_t(x_i) \neq y_i} D_t(i) \tag{1}$$

The error, as defined in Equation (1), is required to be less than ½ to ensure that a minimum reasonable performance can be expected from h_t. If this is the case, the hypothesis h_t is accepted and the error is normalized to obtain the normalized error

$$\beta_t = \varepsilon_t / (1 - \varepsilon_t), \quad 0 < \beta_t < 1 \tag{2}$$

If $\varepsilon_t \geq \frac{1}{2}$, then the current hypothesis is discarded, and a new training subset is selected by returning to step 2. All hypotheses generated so far are then combined using the weighted majority voting to obtain the composite hypothesis H_t (step 5).

$$H_t = \arg\max_{y \in Y} \sum_{t:h_t(x)=y} \log(1/\beta_t) \tag{3}$$

The weighted majority voting scheme allows the algorithm to choose the class receiving the highest vote from all hypotheses, where the voting weight for each hypothesis is inversely proportional to its normalized error. Therefore, those hypotheses with good performances are awarded a higher voting weight. The error of the composite hypothesis is then computed in a similar fashion as the sum of distribution weights of the instances that are misclassified by H_t (step 6):

$$E_t = \sum_{i:H_t(x_i) \neq y_i} D_t(i) = \sum_{i=1}^{m} D_t(i)[| H_t(x_i) \neq y_i |] \tag{4}$$

where $[|\cdot|]$ evaluates to 1, if the predicate holds true.

Input: For each dataset drawn from D_k $k=1,2,...,K$
- Sequence of m examples $S_k = \{(x_i, y_i) \mid i=1,...,m_k\}$.
- Learning algorithm **BaseClassifier**.
- Integer T_k, specifying the number of iterations.

Initialize $w_1(i) = D_1(i) = 1/m_k$, $\forall i$, $i = 1,2,\cdots,m_k$

Do for each $k=1,2,...,K$:
Do for $t = 1,2,...,T_k$:

1. Set $D_t = \mathbf{w}_t \Big/ \sum_{i=1}^{m} w_t(i)$ so that D_t is a distribution.

2. Choose training TR_t and testing TE_t subsets from D_t.

3. Call WeakLearn, providing it with TR_t.

4. Obtain a hypothesis $h_t : X \rightarrow Y$, and calculate the error of

    h_t: $\varepsilon_t = \sum_{i:h_t(x_i) \neq y_i} D_t(i)$ on $S_k = TR_t + TE_t$. If $\varepsilon_t > \frac{1}{2}$, set $t = t-1$,

    discard h_t and go to step 2. Otherwise, compute normalized error as $\beta_t = \varepsilon_t / (1-\varepsilon_t)$.

5. Call weighted majority voting and obtain the composite hypothesis

    $H_t = \arg\max_{y \in Y} \sum_{t:h_t(x)=y} \log(1/\beta_t)$

6. Compute the error of the composite hypothesis

    $E_t = \sum_{i:H_t(x_i) \neq y_i} D_t(i) = \sum_{i=1}^{m} D_t(i)[| H_t(x_i) \neq y_i |]$

7. Set $B_t = E_t/(1-E_t)$, and update the weights:

    $w_{t+1}(i) = w_t(i) \times \begin{cases} B_t, & if\ H_t(x_i) = y_i \\ 1, & otherwise \end{cases} = w_t(i) \times B_t^{1-[|H_t(x_i) \neq y_i|]}$

Call weighted majority voting and **Output** the final hypothesis:

$$H_{final}(x) = \arg\max_{y \in Y} \sum_{k=1}^{K} \sum_{t:h_t(x)=y} \log\frac{1}{\beta_t}$$

Fig. 1. The Learn^{++} Algorithm

The normalized composite error is then computed

$$B_t = E_t / (1 - E_t), \quad 0 < B_t < 1 \tag{5}$$

to be used in the weight update rule (step 7) of Equation (6). This rule reduces the weights of those instances that are correctly classified by the composite hypothesis H_t, lowering their probability of being selected into the next training subset.

$$w_{t+1}(i) \quad = w_t(i) \times \begin{cases} B_t, & \text{if } H_t(x_i) = y_i \\ 1, & \text{otherwise} \end{cases} = w_t(i) \times B_t^{1-[|H_t(x_i) \neq y_i|]} \tag{6}$$

In effect, the weights of misclassified instances are increased relative to the rest of the dataset. We emphasize that, unlike AdaBoost and its variations, the weight update rule in Learn[++] looks directly at the classification of the composite hypothesis (that is, the ensemble), not that of a specific hypothesis. This weight update procedure forces the algorithm to focus more and more on instances that have not been properly learned by the ensemble. When Learn[++] is learning incrementally, the instances introduced by the new dataset (and in particular from new classes, if applicable) are precisely those not learned by the ensemble, and hence the algorithm quickly focuses on these instances. At any point, a final hypothesis H_{final} can be obtained by combining all hypotheses that have been generated so far using the weighted majority voting rule.

$$H_{final}(x) = \arg \max_{y \in Y} \sum_{k=1}^{K} \sum_{t:h_t(x)=y} \log \frac{1}{\beta_t} \tag{7}$$

Simulation results of Learn[++] on incremental learning with MLPs used as base classifiers on a variety of datasets as well as comparisons to AdaBoost and other methods of incremental learning can be found in [6] and references within.

3 SVM Classifiers

Support vector machines (SVMs) have been successfully employed in a number of real world problems [1-2]. They directly implement the principle of structural risk minimization [1] and work by mapping the training points into a high dimensional feature space, where a separating hyperplane (w, b) is found by maximizing the distance from the closest data points (boundary-optimization). Given a set of training samples $S = \{(x_i, y_i) \mid i=1, \ldots, m\}$, where $x_i \in R^n$ are input patterns, $y_i \in \{+1, -1\}$ are class labels for a 2-class problem, SVMs attempt to find a classifier $h(x)$, which minimizes the expected misclassification rate. A linear classifier $h(x)$ is a hyperplane, and can be represented as $h(x) = \text{sign}(w^T x + b)$. The optimal SVM classifier can then be found by solving a convex quadratic optimization problem:

$$\max_{w,b} \frac{1}{2} \|w\|^2 + C \sum_{i=1}^{m} \xi_i \quad \text{subject to } y_i (\langle w, x_i \rangle + b) \geq 1 - \xi_i \text{ and } \xi_i \geq 0 \tag{8}$$

where b is the bias, w is weight vector, and C is the regularization parameter, used to balance the classifier's complexity and classification accuracy on the training set S. Simply replacing the involved vector inner-product with a non-linear kernel function converts linear SVM into a more flexible non-linear classifier, which is the essence of the famous *kernel trick*. In this case, the quadratic problem is generally solved through its dual formulation:

$$L(w,b,\alpha) = \sum_{i=1}^{m} \alpha_i - \frac{1}{2}\left(\sum_{i=1}^{m} y_i y_j \alpha_i \alpha_j K(x_i,x_j) \right) \text{ subject to } C \geq \alpha_i \geq 0 \text{ and } \sum_{i=1}^{m} \alpha_i y_i = 0 \qquad (9)$$

where α_i are the coefficients that are maximized by Lagrangian. For training samples x_i, for which the functional margin is one (and hence lie closest to the hyperplane), $\alpha_i > 0$. Only these instances are involved in the weight vector, and hence are called the *support vectors* [2]. The non-linear SVM classification function (optimum separating hyperplane) is then formulated in terms of these kernels as:

$$h(x) = sign\left(\sum_{i=1}^{m} \alpha_i y_i K(x_i,x_j) - b \right). \qquad (10)$$

As mentioned earlier in Learn^{++} algorithm, incremental learning of SVMs is based on the following intuition: The ensemble is obtained by retraining a single SVM using strategically updated distributions of the training dataset, which ensures that examples that are misclassified by the current ensemble have a high probability of being resampled. The examples that have a high probability of error are precisely those that are unknown or that have not yet been used to train the previous classifiers. Distribution update rule is optimized for incremental learning of new data, in particular when the new data introduce new classes. After T_k classifiers are generated for each D_k, the final ensemble of SVMs is obtained by the weighted majority of all composite SVMs:

$$H_{final}(x) = \arg\max_{y \in Y} \sum_{k=1}^{K} \sum_{t:h_t(x)=y} \log \frac{1}{\beta_t}. \qquad (11)$$

4   Simulation Results

Proposed incremental learning approach for SVMs using Learn^{++} has been tested on several datasets. For brevity, we will henceforth use the term SVMLearn^{++} for the proposed approach and present results on one benchmark dataset and one real-world application. The benchmark dataset is the Optical Character Recognition dataset from UCI machine learning repository, and the real world application is a gas identification problem for determining one of five volatile organic compounds based on chemical sensor data.

Two nonlinear SVM kernel functions were used in our experiments: Polynomial and Gaussian kernel functions.

Polynomial kernel: $K(x_i,x_j) = \left(\langle x_i,x_j \rangle + 1 \right)^d$ \qquad (12)

RBF kernel : $\qquad K(x_i, x_j) = \exp\left(-\|x_i - x_j\|^2 / 2\sigma^2\right)$ $\qquad$ (13)

SVM classifier parameters are the regularization constant C, and the polynomial degree d (for the polynomial kernel) or the RBF width σ, (for the RBF kernel function). The choice of classifier parameters is a form of model selection. Although the machine learning community has extensively considered model selection with SVMs, optimal model parameters are generally domain-specific [19]. Therefore, kernel and regularization parameters were selected jointly to evaluate the best model for each dataset. We used the cross-validation technique with 5-folds to assess SVMs with given kernel parameter and regularization constants.

4.1 Optical Character Recognition Dataset

The Optical Character Recognition (OCR) data has 10 classes with digits 0-9 and 64 attributes. The dataset was split into four to create three training (**DS1, DS2, DS3**) and a test subsets (**Test**), whose distribution is given in Table 1. We evaluated the performance and the incremental learning ability of SVMs using Learn^{++} on a fixed number of classifiers rather than determining the number of classifiers via a validation set. SVMLearn^{++} was allowed to create seven classifiers with the addition of each dataset using both polynomial kernel (PolySVM) and kernel (RBFSVM), for a total of classifiers in three training sessions. The data distribution was deliberately made rather challenging, specifically designed to test the ability of proposed approach to learn multiple new classes at once with each additional dataset while retaining the knowledge of previously learned classes. In this incremental learning problem, instances from only six of the ten classes are present in each subsequent dataset resulting in a rather difficult problem.

Table 1. OCR data distribution

Class	C1	C2	C3	C4	C5	C6	C7	C8	C9	C10
DS1	250	250	250	0	0	250	250	250	0	0
DS2	150	0	150	250	0	150	0	150	250	0
DS3	0	150	0	150	400	0	150	0	150	400
Test	110	114	111	114	113	111	111	113	110	112

Results from this test are shown in Tables 2 and 3 based on an average of 20 trials. The last two columns are the average overall generalization performance (**Gen.**) on test data, and the standard deviation (**Std.**) of the generalization performances.

Poly SVMLearn^{++} was able to learn the new classes, 4 and 9, only poorly after they were first introduced in **DS2** but able to learn them rather well, when further trained with these classes in **DS3**. However, it performs rather well on classes 5 and 10 after they are first introduced in **DS3**. RBF SVMLearn^{++} was able to learn the classes 4 and 9, only poorly when they were introduced in **DS2** but able to learn them rather well, when further trained with these classes in **DS3**. Similarly, it performs rather poorly on classes 5 and 10 after they are first introduced in **DS3**, though it is reasonable to expect that it would do well on these classes with additional training.

Table 2. SVMLearn[++] with polynomial kernel (*degree* = 3, *C* = 1) results on OCR dataset

	C1	C2	C3	C4	C5	C6	C7	C8	C9	C10	Gen.	Std.
DS1	99%	100%	99%	-	-	100%	100%	99%	-	-	60%	0.07%
DS2	99%	100%	99%	17%	-	100%	100%	99%	21%	-	63%	2.37%
DS3	99%	100%	99%	94%	84%	100%	100%	99%	91%	94%	78%	2.32%

Table 3. SVMLearn[++] with RBF kernel (σ = 0.1, C =1) results on OCR dataset

	C1	C2	C3	C4	C5	C6	C7	C8	C9	C10	Gen.	Std.
DS1	99%	100%	100%	-	-	98%	100%	99%	-	-	60%	0.03%
DS2	99%	73%	100%	44%	-	98%	68%	99%	47%	-	63%	1.54%
DS3	99%	100%	100%	93%	14%	97%	100%	99%	90%	13%	80%	4.17%

The generalization performance of Poly and RBF SVMLearn[++] is computed on the entire test data which included instances from all classes. This is why the generalization performance is only around 60% after the first training session, since the algorithms had seen only six of the 10 classes by that time. Both Poly and RBF SVMLean[++] exhibit the ability of learning incrementally with a final overall generalization performance of 78-80% after new datasets are introduced.

4.2 Volatile Organic Compounds Dataset

The Volatile Organic Compounds (VOC) dataset is from a real world application that consists of 5 classes (toluene, xylene, hectane, octane and ketone) with 6 attributes coming from six (quartz crystal microbalance type) chemical gas sensors. The dataset was divided into three training and a test dataset. The distribution of the data is given in Table 4, where a new class was introduced with each dataset.

Table 4. VOC data distribution

Class	C1	C2	C3	C4	C5
DS1	20	0	20	0	40
DS2	10	25	10	0	10
DS3	10	15	10	40	10
Test	24	24	24	40	52

Again, SVMLearn[++] was incrementally trained with three subsequent training datasets. In this experiment, Poly and RBF SVMLearn[++] was allowed to generate as many classifiers as necessary to obtain their maximum performance. The number of classifiers generated were 5, 10, 18 (a total of 33 classifiers to achieve their best performance) for SVM classifiers with polynomial kernel (PolySVM) and RBF kernel (RBFSVM) in three training sessions. Results from this test are shown in Tables 5 and 6 based on average of 30 trials.

Table 5. SVMLearn^{++} with polynomial kernel (*degree* = 3, C = 100) results on VOC dataset

	C1	C2	C3	C4	C5	Gen.	Std
DS1	92%	-	88%	-	100%	58%	1.21%
DS2	98%	91%	94%	-	97%	72%	1.29%
DS3	96%	96%	98%	78%	76%	85%	7.29%

Table 6. SVMLearn^{++} with RBF kernel (σ = 3, C =100) results on VOC dataset

	C1	C2	C3	C4	C5	Gen.	Std.
DS1	91%	-	95%	-	99%	58%	1.62%
DS2	97%	91%	81%	-	95%	70%	1.84%
DS3	93%	99%	94%	68%	76%	83%	8.19%

The generalization performance of Poly and RBF SVMLearn^{++} on the test dataset gradually improved from 58% to 83-85% as new data were introduced, demonstrating its incremental learning capability even when instances of new classes are introduced in subsequent training sessions.

5 Conclusions

In this paper, we have shown that the SVM classifiers can in fact be equipped with the incremental learning capability, to address the catastrophic forgetting problem. SVM ensembles generated with Learn^{++} learning rule (SVMLearn^{++}) are capable of learning new information provided by subsequent datasets, including new knowledge provided by instances of previously unseen classes. Some knowledge is indeed forgotten while new information is being learned; however, this appears to be mild, as indicated by the steady improvement in the generalization performance. SVMLearn^{++} with two different kernel functions has been tested on one real world dataset and one benchmark dataset. The results demonstrate that SVMLearn^{++} work rather well in a variety of applications.

Learn^{++} suffers from the inherent "out-voting" problem when asked to learn new classes, which causes it to generate an unnecessarily large number of classifiers [20]. Therefore, in future work, we will test the modified version of Learn^{++}, called Learn^{++}.MT that attempts to reduce the number of classifiers generated.

Acknowledgements

This work is supported in part by the National Science Foundation under Grant No. ECS-0239090, "CAREER: An Ensemble of Classifiers Approach for Incremental Learning." Z.E. would like to thank Mr. Apostolos Topalis and Mr. Michael Muhlbaier graduate students at Rowan University, NJ, for their invaluable suggestions and assistance.

References

1. V. Vapnik, Statistical Learning Theory. New York: Wiley, 1998.
2. N. Cristianini, J. Shawe-Taylor, An Introduction to Support Vector Machines and Other Kernel-based Learning Methods, Cambridge University Press, 2000.
3. S. Grossberg, "Nonlinear neural networks: principles, mechanisms and architectures," Neural Networks, Vol. 1, No. 1, pp. 17–61, 1988.
4. R. French, "Catastrophic forgetting in connectionist networks: Causes, Consequences and Solutions," Trends in Cognitive Sciences, vol. 3, no.4, pp. 128-135, 1999.
5. R. Polikar, L. Udpa, S. Udpa, V. Honavar, "Learn^{++}: An incremental learning algorithm for multilayer perceptrons." Proceedings of 25th. IEEE International Conference on Acoustics, Speech and Signal Processing, Vol. 6, pp: 3414-3417, Istanbul, Turkey, 2000.
6. R. Polikar, L. Udpa, S. Udpa, V. Honavar. "Learn^{++}: An incremental learning algorithm for supervised neural networks." IEEE Transactions on Systems, Man, and Cybernetics. Part C: Applications and Reviews, Vol. 31, No. 4, pp: 497-508, 2001.
7. Y. Freund, R. Schapire, "A decision theoretic generalization of on-line learning and an application to boosting," Computer and System Sciences, vol. 57, no. 1, pp. 119-139, 1997.
8. N. Kasabov, "Evolving Connectionist Systems: Methods and Applications in Bioinformatics, Brain Study and Intelligent Machines", Springer Verlag, 2002.
9. J. Platt, "Fast Training of Support Vector Machines using Sequential Minimal Optimization", Advances in Kernel Methods - Support Vector Learning, B. Schölkopf, C. Burges, and A. Smola, eds., MIT Press, 1998.
10. C. Domeniconi, D. Gunopulos, "Incremental Support Machine Construction", Proceedings of First IEEE Int. Conf. on Data Mining (ICDM 2001), pp. 589-592.
11. P. Mitra, C.A. Murthy, S.K. Pal, "Data condensation in large databases by incremental learning with support vector machines", Proceedings of 15th International Conference on Pattern Recognition, Vol.2, pp:708 – 711, 3-7 Sept 2000.
12. K. Li, H.-K. Huang, "Incremental learning proximal support vector machine classifiers", Proceedings of International Conference on Machine Learning and Cybernetics, vol. 3, pp:1635–1637, 4-5 November 2002.
13. J.-L. An, Z.-O. Wang, Z.-P. Ma, "An incremental learning algorithm for support vector machine", Proceedings of International Conference on Machine Learning and Cybernetics, Vol.2, pp:1153 – 1156, 2-5 November 2003.
14. Z.-W. Li; J.-P. Zhang, J. Yang, "A heuristic algorithm to incremental support vector machine learning", Proceedings of 2004 International Conference on Machine Learning and Cybernetics, Vol. 3, pp:1764–1767, 26-29 Aug. 2004.
15. D. Pavlov, J. Mao, and B. Dom, Scaling-up Support Vector Machines using The Boosting Algorithm, Proceedings of the International Conference on Pattern Recognition, Barcelona, Spain, September 3-7 2000, pp. 19-22.
16. G. Valentini, M. Muselli, and F. Ruffino, Cancer Recognition with Bagged Ensembles of Support Vector Machines, Neurocomputing 56(1), (2004), pp. 461-466.
17. G. Valentini, M. Muselli, F. Ruffino, Bagged Ensembles of SVMs for Gene Expression Data Analysis, Proceeding of the International Joint Conference on Neural Networks, Portland, OR, USA, July 20-24 2003, pp. 1844-1849.

18. H.-C. Kim, S. Pang, H.-M. Je, D. Kim, and S. Y. Bang, Constructing Support Vector Machine Ensemble, Pattern Recognition 36, (2003), pp. 2757-2767.
19. K. Duan, S.S. Keerthi, A.N. Poo, Evaluation of simple performance measures for tuning SVM hyperparameters, Neurocomputing, 51 (2003) 41-59.
20. M. Muhlbaier, A. Topalis, R. Polikar, Learn[++].MT: A New Approach to Incremental Learning, 5th Int. Workshop on Multiple Classifier Systems (MCS 2004), Springer LINS vol. 3077 , pp. 52-61, Cagliari, Italy, June 2004.

Design of a New Classifier Simulator[*]

Li-ying Yang[1] and Zheng Qin[1,2]

[1] Department of Computer Science and Technology,
Xi'an Jiaotong University, Xi'an 710049, China
yangliying1208@163.com
[2] School of Software, Tsinghua University, Beijing 100084, China
qingzh@mail.tsinghua.edu.cn

Abstract. Since standard data sets are not capable enough in evaluating classifier combination methods in multiple classifier systems, a new classifier simulator with sufficient diversity is proposed to generate artificial data sets. The
simulator can generate simulating data for a problem of any number of classes
and any classifier performance, and can also show pair wise dependency. It is
achieved via a three-step algorithm: firstly building the confusion matrices of
the classifiers on the basis of desired behavior, secondly generating the outputs
of one classifier based on its confusion matrix, and then producing the outputs
of other classifiers. The detailed generating algorithm is discussed. Experiments
on majority voting combination method shows that negative correlation could
improve the accuracy of multiple classifier systems, which indicates the validity
of the proposed simulator.

1 Introduction

In the field of pattern recognition, there has been a recent movement towards multiple
classifier systems, in which independence between classifiers is usually viewed as an
asset. However, it is not always possible to guarantee the independency. Kuncheva [1]
studied the limits on the majority vote accuracy when combining dependent classifiers. The research shows that, although the relationship between dependency and accuracy of the pool is ambivalent, better results are obtained indeed when there is negative dependency. Another problem in designing a multiple classifier system is the
choice of a suitable combination method among the available set. The standard practice for evaluation of classifier combination methods is using standard data sets with
known properties [2][3]. It is difficult to carry out controllable experiments since the
properties of the standard data sets cannot be specified in advance. In order to amend
to these cases, there is a new trend to use artificial outputs generated by a classifier
simulator to provide an underlying evaluation of classifier combination methods [4].

Lecce et al. [5] investigated the role of the a-priori knowledge in the process of
classifier combination. Given its recognition rate, the output of a classifier is simu-

---

[*] This work is supported by the Major State Basic Research Development Program of China
(973 Program), No.2004CB719401.

N.C. Oza et al. (Eds.): MCS 2005, LNCS 3541, pp. 257–266, 2005.

lated at abstract level and a similarity index is used to measure the agreement among classifiers. To generate its data is an enumeration process rather than an automatic procedure. Zouari et al. [6] proposed a classifier simulator for evaluating combination methods, which firstly built a confusion matrix based on the desired behavior and secondly generated the outputs. The simulator did not take the dependency between classifiers into account. Then they used distance measure to estimate the dependency [10], where the case of two classifiers was investigated and the case of three or more ones required further work. Kuncheva et al. [7] derived formulas according to how two classifiers can be generated with specified accuracies and dependencies between them. She proposed an algorithm for generating multiple dependent classifiers, and the outputs are binary vectors. That is, the outputs are not the class label of samples, but correct or incorrect classification. To this end, we designed a classifier simulator, which can not only show the dependency between classifiers, but also generate the class label as the output for the sample.

This paper is organized as follows. Section 2 describes the general simulation process, and the parameters used to define the desired behavior. Detailed algorithms for building confusion matrix and generating the outputs are presented in section 3 and section 4 respectively. Experiments and discussion are given in section 5. Conclusion is drawn in section 6.

2   The Proposed Method

2.1   Input Parameters

There exist many measures of dependency between classifiers while Q statistic is one of them [8]. Q statistic is a pair wise measure, which is used as the measure of dependency in this research due to its easy interpretation for independence,positive/negative dependences, and calculation. We carried out our work based on Q statistic.

Generally speaking, the output information that various classification algorithms supplying can be divided into three levels: the abstract level, the rank level and the measurement level [9]. A classifier outputs a unique class label for the sample in the abstract level, while it ranks all the labels in a queue with the label at the top being the first choice in the rank level. In the measurement level, a classifier attributes each label a measurement value to address the degree that the sample has the label. Outputs of the classifier simulator presented in this paper are of the abstract level. If other types are needed, they could be created from the confusion matrix of an abstract-level classifier [2]. An output of the simulator is as following:

$$(Original\_Class, Simulating\_Class)$$

where *Original_Class* denotes the correct classification of a given sample, and *Simulating_Class* denotes the decision of a simulated classifier.

The input parameters of the simulator, defining the classification problem and the desired behavior of the classifier, are: (1) the number of classes M; (2) the sample number of per class N; (3) l classifiers that need to be simulated $\{R_1, R_2, \cdots, R_l\}$ and their recognition rates $\{TL_1, TL_2, \cdots, TL_l\}$; (4) the desired dependency Q_{ij} between classifiers R_i and R_j, $i, j \in \{1, 2, \cdots, l\}$.

2.2 Simulating Process

Given the parameters, the classifier simulator is to generate the outputs. For each class of each classifier, it generates N outputs with the style (*Original_Class, Simulating_Class*). The generation of all outputs is achieved as follows. Firstly, to build confusion matrices for the classifiers ground to the input parameters. Secondly, to generate the outputs of one classifier from its confusion matrix. Finally, to generate the outputs of other classifiers based on the outputs obtained, the dependencies between classifiers and the confusion matrices.

3 Constructing of the Confusion Matrix

The confusion matrix of a classifier R_k is a $M \times M$ matrix CMN_k, if the rejection rate is not taken into account. The actual class under test is represented by the matrix row and the classification that R_k assigns to the sample is represented by the column. The element $CMN_k(i, j)$ gives the number of times that a class i sample is assigned to class j. The diagonal elements indicate correct classifications. If the matrix CMN_k is normalized, another $M \times M$ matrix CM_k can be obtained. The element $CM_k(i, j)$ gives the probability that a sample of class i will be assigned to class j. The diagonal elements of CM_k denote the recognition rate and the off-diagonal elements denote the confusion rate. For the sake of concision, we assume that all classes have the same recognition rate, then $CM_k(i, i) = TL_k$ holds, $i \in \{1, 2, \cdots, l\}$. When they are different, diagonal elements $CM_k(i, i)$ will be set to different values according to the recognition rate of per class, so long as the constraint is satisfied that total recognition rate of all classes is TL_k. In the row i of CM_k, the sum of all elements except column i is the confusion rate of class i, which is denoted by TC_k^i:

$$TC_k^i = \sum_{j=1, j \neq i}^{M} TC_k^{ij} = 100\% - TL_k, \tag{1}$$

in which TC_k^{ij} is the confusion probability that a class i sample will be assigned to class j ($i \neq j$). Based on the work above, the confusion matrix CM_k of classifier R_k can be constructed. Other l-1 confusion matrices can be built in the same way.

4 Generating the Outputs

4.1 Generating Algorithm for Two Classifiers

Consider two classifiers, R_i and R_j, and their respective recognition rates TL_i and TL_j. The dependency between them measured by Q statistic is Q_{ij}. The outputs of one classifier are generated firstly, and then the other classifier's outputs are obtained based on them. If classifier R_i decides incorrectly for a given sample, the output of R_i is alternated with probability $P_{F \to T}(i, j)$ to the proper classification in order to obtain the according output of classifier R_j. On the other hand, if classifier R_i decides correctly, the output of R_i is alternated with probability $P_{T \to F}(i, j)$ to the confusion class to obtain the output of classifier R_j, and the confusion class is decided by CM_j. $P_{F \to T}(i, j)$ and $P_{T \to F}(i, j)$ can be computed according to the input parameters as follows [7]:

If $Q_{ij} \neq 0$ holds, that is, R_i and R_j is dependent, then

$$P_{F \to T}(i, j) = \frac{-(1 - Q_{ij} + 2Q_{ij}(TL_i - TL_j)) \pm \sqrt{\Delta}}{4Q_{ij}(1 - TL_i)}, \tag{2}$$

where $\Delta = (1 - Q_{ij} + 2Q_{ij}(TL_i - TL_j))^2 - 8Q_{ij}(1 - TL_i)TL_j(Q_{ij} - 1)$.

$$P_{T \to F}(i, j) = 1 - P_{F \to T} + \frac{P_{F \to T} - TL_j}{TL_i}. \tag{3}$$

If $Q_{ij} = 0$ holds, that is, R_i and R_j is independent, then

$$P_{F \to T}(i, j) = TL_j. \tag{4}$$

$$P_{T \to F}(i, j) = 1 - TL_j. \tag{5}$$

In detail, the generating algorithm is accomplished in two steps: (1) building CM_i and from this confusion matrix, generating N outputs for each class. Thus the $M \times N$ outputs of classifier R_i are obtained; (2) generating the outputs of classifier R_j according to the outputs of R_i, CM_j, $P_{F \to T}(i, j)$ and $P_{T \to F}(i, j)$.

4.2 Generating Algorithm for Multiple Classifiers

In the generating algorithm for two classifiers, it is indifferent when different classifier is chosen to be the basic one. But this is not a trivial thing when there are three or more classifiers. For l classifiers $\{R_1, R_2, \cdots, R_l\}$, if we first generate R_1 and use it to obtain R_2 through the generating procedure described above, then use R_2 to produce R_3 and so on, there is no guarantee that non-adjoining classifiers will have the desired dependency. To tackle this problem, we followed the idea in reference [7]. For each output, a random permutation of $\{R_1, R_2, \cdots, R_l\}$ is generated. It is used to pick the order in which the classifiers will be selected as the basic and the subsequent ones. For example, when $\{R_{w_1}, R_{w_2}, \cdots, R_{w_l}\}$ is taken as the permutation for one output, R_{w_1} is nominated as the basic classifier. R_{w_2} is generated based on R_{w_1}, and so on, until R_{w_l} is obtained. If the sample number N is large enough, random nominations of l classifiers make every two classifiers have enough chances to be adjoining, so that the desired dependency between them is approached.

The pseudo-code for the generating algorithm of multiple classifiers is as follows:

```
Step1. Input parameters:{TL₁,TL₂,…,TL_l}; Q_ij, i,j
∈ {1,2,…,l}.

Step2. Generate CM_i, i ∈ {1,2,…,l}.

Step3. Compute P_{F→T}(i,j) and P_{T→F}(i,j), i,j∈ {1,2,···,l}.

Step4. For ii = 1 to M
  For jj = 1 to N

  (1) Choose a random permutation {R_{w_1},R_{w_2},···,R_{w_l}} of
      {R_1,R_2,···,R_l}.

  (2) Generate one output of R_{w_1} according to CM_{w_1}.

  (3) For kk = 2 to l
      ① Generate one output of R_{w_kk} based on the output
         of R_{w_{kk-1}}, P_{F→T}(w_{kk-1},w_kk) and P_{T→F}(w_{kk-1},w_kk).
      ② End kk.
  End jj.
End ii.

Step5. Return the total M×N×l outputs. Each one has
the form (Original Class, Simulating Class).
```

5 Experiments and Discussion

5.1 Experiments for the Proposed Simulator

In the following experiments, we assume the number of classes $M=10$ and the sample number of per class $N=1000$. Each algorithm was run 100 times and the average was calculated as the result. $\widetilde{X}$ denotes the simulating value of X.

Case 1. Two Classifiers
(1) Recognition rates are equal
Let there be two classifiers, R_i and R_j. They were of the same recognition rate and $TL \in \{0.5, 0.6, 0.7, 0.8, 0.9\}$. For each value of the recognition rate, a series of experiments were carried out with different dependency Q_{ij} with $Q_{ij} \in \{-1, -0.9, \cdots, -0.1, 0, 0.1, \cdots, 1\}$. The deviation of simulating results was given in Table 1.

Table 1. The deviation when two classifiers have equal recognition rates

Outputs	Recognition rate				
	0.5	0.6	0.7	0.8	0.9
$\widetilde{TL_i}$	±0.0011	±0.0009	±0.0011	±0.0010	±0.0006
$\widetilde{TL_j}$	±0.0011	±0.0012	±0.0007	±0.0009	±0.0008
$\widetilde{Q_{ij}}$	±0.0058	±0.0029	±0.0025	±0.0037	±0.0135

(2) Recognition rates are different
Given two classifiers R_i and R_j with different recognition rates. Let $TL_i = 0.6$ and $TL_j = 0.9$. A series of experiments were carried out with different dependency Q_{ij}, with $Q_{ij} \in \{-1, -0.9, \cdots, -0.1, 0, 0.1, \cdots, 1\}$. The outputs are given in Table 2.

Table 2. Simulating results when two classifiers have different recognition rates

$\widetilde{TL_i}$	$\widetilde{TL_j}$	$\widetilde{Q_{ij}}$
0.6±0.0011	0.9±0.0008	Q_{ij} ±0.0075

The results in Table 1 and Table 2 show that the generating algorithm for two classifiers can obtain accurate results in spite of what values the dependency and the recognition rate take.

Case 2. Multiple Classifiers

Without lose of generality, the experiments for multiple classifiers were carried out with $l=3$.

(1) Recognition rates and dependencies are both equal

Let there be three classifiers R_i, R_j and R_k, with the same recognition rate $TL \in \{0.6,0.7,0.8,0.9\}$ and the same dependency $Q \in \{-0.8, -0.5, -0.2,0.2,0.5,0.8\}$. Then there are 24 experiments. In each experiment, average simulating results of three recognition rates and three dependencies, denoted by $\overline{TL}$ and $\overline{Q}$, are listed in Table 3.

Table 3. Average simulating results when both desired values are equal

Depend ency	Recognition rate							
	0.6		0.7		0.8		0.9	
	$\overline{TL}$	$\overline{Q}$	$\overline{TL}$	$\overline{Q}$	$\overline{TL}$	$\overline{Q}$	$\overline{TL}$	$\overline{Q}$
-0.8	0.600	-0.4665	0.699	-0.4560	0.8002	-0.443	0.8999	-0.4289
-0.5	0.600	-0.3028	0.699	-0.2984	0.8001	-0.295	0.9001	-0.2913
-0.2	0.599	-0.1286	0.700	-0.1271	0.8000	-0.125	0.8999	-0.1278
0.2	0.599	0.1418	0.699	0.1412	0.8001	0.139	0.8998	0.1407
0.5	0.600	0.3895	0.700	0.3930	0.7999	0.390	0.8999	0.3935
0.8	0.600	0.7095	0.700	0.7118	0.8001	0.711	0.9001	0.7161

It is shown in Table 3 that the simulating results of recognition rates are accurate, and they are not influenced by the values of recognition rates and dependencies. Simulated Q is irrelevant with recognition rate, but the desired dependency has much impact on it.

The plot in Fig. 1 shows the relationship of the error for simulated Q (denoted by $|Q - Q_{Target}|$) and the desired Q for the case of the recognition rate being 0.8. From Fig. 1, that the error is less toward bigger Q can be indicated when the dependence is negative, and it is less toward bigger or smaller Q when the dependence is positive. As Q is irrelevant with recognition rate, this observation is common.

(2) Both of recognition rates and dependencies are different

Given three classifiers R_i, R_j and R_k, with different recognition rate and dependency. Let $(TL_i, TL_j, TL_k) = (0.6,0.7,0.8)$, and $(Q_{ij}, Q_{ik}, Q_{jk}) \in \{(0.2,0.3,0.4), (0.6,0.7,0.8), (-0.2,-0.3,-0.4), (-0.2,0.3,-0.4)\}$. The simulating results of recognition rates and dependencies are listed in Table 4.

From data in Table 4, three $|Q - Q_{Target}|$ values in each of the four dependencies groups could be calculated. It is shown that the largest error is obtained in the group with all negative dependencies. The error is less toward smaller absolute values of Q when dependencies are different in the group.

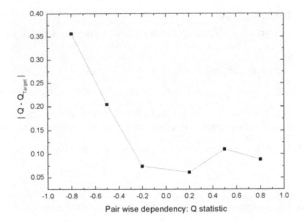

Fig. 1. Relationship between $\mid Q - Q_{T\,\arg et} \mid$ and the desired Q

Table 4. Simulated results when both desired values are different

(Q_{ij}, Q_{ik}, Q_{jk})	$\widetilde{TL_i}$	$\widetilde{TL_j}$	$\widetilde{TL_k}$	$\widetilde{Q_{ij}}$	$\widetilde{Q_{ik}}$	$\widetilde{Q_{jk}}$
(0.2,0.3,0.4)	0.6007	0.7001	0.8000	0.1506	0.2141	0.2908
(0.6,0.7,0.8)	0.6002	0.7000	0.8000	0.5099	0.5883	0.6658
(-0.2, -0.3, -0.4)	0.6002	0.6996	0.7998	-0.1221	-0.1911	-0.2518
(-0.2,0.3, -0.4)	0.5992	0.7002	0.8001	-0.1476	0.2176	-0.2741

Experiments in Case 1 and Case 2 demonstrate that desired recognition rates can be generated perfectly by simulating algorithms, but simulated dependencies are smaller than the targets when there are three or more classifiers. This is due to the generating procedure of multiple classifiers. In the generating algorithm for multiple classifiers, a random permutation is obtained for each output to determine the generating sequence of classifiers. Although the desired dependency could be approached when the number of samples is large enough, dependencies tend to be small since they are guaranteed only in a subset of all samples. A natural option to overcome the imperfect generation will be to set the dependency as a larger value.

5.2   The Effect of Correlation on Majority Voting Combination Method

In order to investigate the effect of correlation on the accuracy of majority voting combination method, experiments on simulated data sets, which were generated according to the algorithm proposed in this work, were carried out. The simulating algorithm for multiple classifiers was run with l=3, M=10, N=1000. We focus on using the same recognition rate ({0.6,0.7,0.8,0.9}) and correlation ({-0.9,-0.5,-0.2,0.2,0.5,0.9}) for classifiers. Thus 24 groups of simulated datasets were obtained. Majority voting combination method was run 100 times using the simulated datasets, and results were plotted in Figure 2, in which the values were calculated as averages of 100 experiments. The figure shows that variation of classification performance is obtained by varying the correlation in the ensemble. It indicates that there sustains a monotonous drop in accuracy when the correlation between classifiers increases, no matter how the single classifier performs. So negatively related classifiers are better than independent and positively related ones, which is in agreement with the observation in [1].

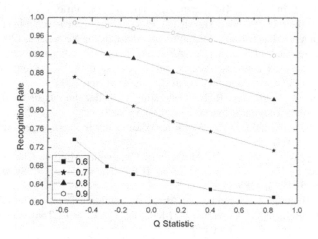

Fig. 2. Recognition rate versus Q Statistic in majority voting combination method for three classifiers based on the proposed simulator

6 Conclusion

In multiple classifier systems, evaluation of combination methods is the precondition of selecting a proper method for a given task. The standard practice for evaluation is to use standard data sets with known properties, so it is difficult to carry out controllable experiments. To solve this problem, it has recently been developed as a new trend to use artificial outputs generated by a classifier simulator to undertake the evaluation. Flexible control available to the experimenter using the simulation data makes it an extremely attractive solution. Research in this paper is dedicated to the new trend. We presented a classifier simulator, which could generate artificial data indicating dependencies between classifiers. Experimental evaluation of majority voting combination method based on the simulated datasets shows that negative correlation benefits the accuracy of multiple classifier systems, which is consistent with previous work. This suggests that the proposed algorithm is valid. Although some efforts have been done, the design of a classifier simulator is far from completely solved. The use of simulated classifiers requires further energy and study.

References

1. Kuncheva, L. I., Whitaker, C. J., Shipp, C. A., Duin, R. P. W.: Is independence good for combining classifiers, Proceedings of 15th International Conference on Pattern Recognition, Barcelona, Spain (2000) 168-171

2. Parker, J. R.: Rank and response combination from confusion matrix data. Information fusion, 2 (2001) 113-120
3. Kittler, J., Hatef, M., Duin, R. P. W., Matas, J.: On Combining Classifiers. IEEE Transactions On Pattern Analysis and Machine Intelligence, 3 (1998) 226-239
4. Parker, J. R.: Evaluating classifier combination using simulated classifiers. Department of Computer Science, University of Calgary, Research Report #2000/659/11
5. Lecce, V. D., Dimauro, G., Guerrierro, A., Impedovo, S., Pirlo, G., Salzo, A.: Classifier combination: the role of a-priori knowledge. Proceedings of the seventh international workshop on frontiers in handwriting recognition, Amsterdam, the Netherlands (2000) 143-152
6. Zouari, H., Heutte, L., Lecourtier, Y., Alimi, A.: A new classifier simulator for evaluating parallel combination methods. Proceedings of the seventh international conference on document analysis and recognition, IEEE Computer Society (2003)
7. Kuncheva, L. I., Kountchev, R. K.: Generating classifier outputs of fixed accuracy and diversity. Pattern recognition letters, 23 (2002) 593-600
8. Kuncheva, L. I., Whitaker, C. J.: Measures of diversity in classifier ensembles. Machine Learning, 51 (2003) 181-207
9. Xu, L., Krzyzak, A., Suen, C.Y.: Methods of Combining Multiple Classifiers and Their Applications to Handwriting Recognition. IEEE Transactions On Systems, Man and Cybernetics, 3 (1992) 418-435
10. Zouari, H., Heutte, L., Lecourtier, Y., Alimi, A.: Building Diverse Classifier Outputs to Evaluate the Behavior of Combination Methods: The Case of Two Classifiers. Lecture Notes in Computer Science, (2004) 273-282

Evaluation of Diversity Measures for Binary Classifier Ensembles

Anand Narasimhamurthy

Department of Computer Science and Engineering,
The Pennsylvania State University,
University Park, PA-16802,USA
narasimh@cse.psu.edu

Abstract. Diversity is an important consideration in classifier ensembles, it can be potentially exploited in order to obtain a higher classification accuracy. There is no widely accepted formal definition of diversity in classifier ensembles, thus making an objective evaluation of diversity measures difficult. We propose a set of properties and a linear program based framework for the analysis of diversity measures for ensembles of binary classifiers. Although we regard the question of what exactly defines diversity in a classifier ensemble as open, we show that the framework can be used effectively to evaluate diversity measures. We explore whether there is a useful relationship between the selected diversity measures and the ensemble accuracy. Our results cast doubt on the usefulness of diversity measures in designing a classifier ensemble, although the motivation for enforcing diversity in a classifier ensemble is justified.

1   Introduction

Diversity is defined in different ways in various fields [7–Chapter 10]. Rao [11] provides an axiomatic definition based on a comprehensive study on diversity in life sciences. In Software Engineering diversity is formulated in terms of coincident failure of different program (software) versions on a random input (e.g. Littlewood & Miller [8] and Partridge & Krzanowski [10]).

In the context of classification, one possible classification of diversity measures is pairwise and non-pairwise measures. In the case of pairwise measures, for a multiple classifier system (MCS) usually the average value of the measure (averaged over the number of pairs) is taken as a measure of diversity of the ensemble. Examples of pairwise diversity measures include the Q-Statistic [15], the Double Fault [3] and the Disagreement measure [13]. Non-pairwise measures are defined on the ensemble as a whole, examples of these are the Kohavi-Wolpert measure [5], the Entropy measure [1] and the measure of difficulty (θ) [4]. Another class of diversity measures arises from the bias-variance decomposition of the ensemble error. Examples of this class of measures include the Coincident Failure Diversity(CFD) and the Distinct Failure Diversity (DFD) due to Partridge & Krzanowski [10].

Kuncheva and Whitaker [6] list measures (both pairwise and non-pairwise) proposed in different contexts and examine how they can be adapted as diversity measures

N.C. Oza et al. (Eds.): MCS 2005, LNCS 3541, pp. 267–277, 2005.

for classifier ensembles. They also examine the relationship between the diversity measures and ensemble accuracy. They conclude that the relationship between the diversity measures and the combination methods is somewhat ambiguous.

Although diversity and complementarity are considered desirable characteristics of a classifier ensemble, a lack of a widely accepted formal definition of diversity renders the evaluation of diversity measures difficult. In [9] we show that the theoretical upper and lower bounds of majority voting performance for a binary classification problem are solutions of a linear program (LP). In this paper we propose a framework based on the linear programming formulation for evaluation of diversity measures for binary classifier ensembles. We also propose a set of properties for a diversity measure. Although we regard the question of what exactly defines diversity in a classifier ensemble as open, we show that the framework can be used effectively to evaluate whether diversity measures proposed in different contexts are suitable for classifier ensembles.

This paper is organized as follows. The framework is described in section 2. Diversity measures for classifier ensembles are discussed in section 3.1. An important motivation for enforcing diversity in an ensemble is to obtain an improvement in classification accuracy. The characterization of the role of "diversity" in majority voting (or classifier combination schemes in general) is not straightforward, owing to a lack of a widely accepted formal definition of classifier diversity. The proposed framework enables evaluating whether there is a useful correlation between a given "diversity" measure and majority voting accuracy. This is discussed in section 3.3. Conclusions are presented in section 4.

2   Description of the Framework and Proposed Properties

We introduce the notation used in the rest of the paper. Each binary classifier is represented by a bit (1 or 0) with 1 indicating that the classifier is correct and 0 indicating incorrect. The joint statistics can be represented by bit combinations. We follow the convention that if there are K classifiers $C1, C2, \ldots, CK$, $C1$ is the LSB (least significant bit) and CK corresponds to the MSB (most significant bit).

2.1   Notation and Definitions

Definition 1.   *1. Let $bit(i, K)$ represent the K bit binary expansion of i ($0 \leq i \leq 2^K - 1$). and*
   2. $N(b) =$ Number of 1s in b, where b is a binary string. (in vector form $N(b) = \mathbf{1}^T b$).

Definition 2.   *Let $x = [x_0, x_1, \ldots, x_{(2^K - 1)}]^T$ be the vector of probabilities of the joint correct/incorrect classifications (since there are 2^K possible combinations for K classifiers), where x_i ($0 \leq i \leq 2^K - 1$) is the probability of the correct/incorrect classification of the K classifiers represented by the bit combination $bit(i, K)$. For example if $K = 3$, $x = [x_0, x_1, \ldots, x_7]^T$; then $x_3 = P(bit(3,3)) = P(C3=0, C2=1, C1=1) = P(C3 incorrect, C2 correct, C1 correct)$.*

Definition 3. *We define a* **configuration** C *as a discrete probability distribution over the set* $\{0, 1, \ldots, 2^K - 1\}$ *where* K *is a parameter. i.e.* C *is a set of tuples of the form* $< i, x_i >$ *where* x_i *is the weight (probability) associated with* i, $0 \leq i \leq 2^K - 1$ *and* K *is a parameter.*

Definition 4. Complementary configuration
If $C = \{< i, x_i >\}$ $0 \leq i \leq 2^K - 1$ *is a configuration, the complementary configuration* $\bar{C}$ *is defined as follows:*

$$\bar{C} = \{< i, x_i^{(\bar{C})} >\} where \; x_i^{(\bar{C})} = x_{2^K-1-i}^{(C)}$$

2.2   Proposed Properties

Property 1. **The diversity measure must have a finite value for all configurations.**

We strongly recommend that a diversity measure satisfy Property 1. In addition we propose the following desirable properties. We do not claim that these are the most useful, rather this is one possible set of intuitive properties.

Property 2. A desirable property would be that the measure have a minimum and a maximum value.

Property 3. It is preferable that the diversity measure be capable of being expressed as an **easily computable closed form function of the joint probability vector x**. The minimum and maximum values of the measure for a particular ensemble can then be determined as solutions to the optimization problem in section 2.3.

Diversity measures may either be symmetrical or non-symmetrical with respect to correct and incorrect classifications (0 and 1) [12]. Although we list the symmetry property here, not satisfying the symmetry property is not necessarily undesirable or disadvantageous. We state the symmetry property formally below.

Property 4. **Symmetry property**
A diversity measure satisfies the symmetry property if it is symmetrical with respect to correct or incorrect decisions for the entire configuration. Mathematically this can be stated as : *"The diversity measure of a configuration and its complement (defined in section 2.1) is the same."*

2.3   Problem Formulation

For an ensemble of K binary classifiers with accuracies $p_1, p_2, \ldots, p_K$, if the diversity measure can be expressed as a closed form function g(x) of the joint probability vector x (Definition 2), the theoretical bounds may be derived as solutions to an optimization problem with linear constraints. g(x) is the objective function to be maximized/minimized subject to the constraints specified by equations (2-4). For the details the reader may refer [9] where we formulate the optimization problem to determine the theoretical bounds of majority vote accuracy for a given ensemble of classifiers (since the constraints are identical).

$$\max\ (\min)\ \ g(\mathbf{x}) \tag{1}$$

$$\textbf{s.t.}\quad A_{eq}\mathbf{x} = d \tag{2}$$

$$0 \le x_i \le 1 \quad 0 \le i \le 2^K - 1 \tag{3}$$

$$\mathbf{1}^T\mathbf{x} = 1 \tag{4}$$

where $d = [p_1, p_2, \ldots, p_K]^T$ (vector of classifier accuracies) $\tag{5}$

$$\mathbf{x} = [x_0, x_1, x_2, \ldots, x_{(2^K-1)}]^T \text{(vector of joint probabilities)}$$

and $A_{eq} = [b_1, b_2, \ldots, b_K]^T (K \times 2^K$ matrix of equality constraints,

row r corresponds to r th classifier.)

and $\boldsymbol{b_1}, \boldsymbol{b_2}, \ldots, \boldsymbol{b_K}$ are given by equation (6).

$$\boldsymbol{b_1} = [0\ 1, \ldots, 0\ 1]^T \tag{6}$$

$$\boldsymbol{b_2} = [0\ 0\ 1\ 1, \ldots, 0\ 0\ 1\ 1]^T$$

$$\vdots$$

$$\boldsymbol{b_K} = [\overbrace{0\ 0 \ldots 0\ 0}^{2^{(K-1)}}, \overbrace{1\ 1 \ldots 1\ 1}^{2^{(K-1)}}]^T$$

Some of the diversity measures discussed in [6] may be expressed as linear functions of x i.e. $g(\mathbf{x}) = \boldsymbol{f}^T\mathbf{x} + c$ where $\boldsymbol{f} = [f_0, f_1, \ldots, f_{(2^K-1)}]^T$. These are listed in Table 3. The derivation is omitted due to space constraints. In these cases, the optimization problem is a Linear Program (LP).

3   Results and Discussion

In this section we evaluate the measures discussed in [6] based on the framework described in section 2. We provide short definitions of some of the measures. For a more detailed overview the reader may refer [6–Sections 3,4 and Table 2]. We briefly discuss pairwise measures. Although we conducted similar experiments on pairwise measures, due to space constraints we only present sample results related to two non-pairwise measures, Cunningham measure [1] and measure of "difficulty" [4]. The analysis and experimental procedure are the same for the other measures and many of the discussions and conclusions also apply to them.

3.1   Pairwise vs Non-pairwise Diversity Measures

Pairwise classifier diversity measures: Four pairwise measures (for a pair of classifiers) are listed in Table 2. They are defined with respect to the confusion matrix shown in table 1. For multiple classifiers, the average value of the pairwise diversity measure (averaged over the total number of pairs) is taken as a measure of diversity of the ensemble. Kuncheva and Whitaker [6] suggest that pairwise measures may not be useful in the case of unequal pairwise distributions. We suggest other reasons why they may not be suitable and thus do not recommend their use for classifier ensembles.

Table 1. Confusion matrix for a pair of classifiers

	Classifier $D_2 \rightarrow$	
Classifier $D_1 \downarrow$	D_2 Incorrect	D_2 Correct
D_1 incorrect	N^{00}	N^{01}
D_1 correct	N^{10}	N^{11}

Table 2. Definitions of 4 selected pairwise diversity measures

Diversity measure	Definition
Q Statistic [15]	$Q = \frac{N^{11}N^{00} - N^{10}N^{01}}{N^{11}N^{00} + N^{10}N^{01}}$
Correlation coefficient [14]	$\rho = \frac{N^{11}N^{00} - N^{01}N^{10}}{\sqrt{(N^{11}+N^{10})(N^{01}+N^{00})(N^{11}+N^{01})(N^{10}+N^{00})}}$
Disagreement measure [13]	$\text{Dis} = \frac{N^{01}+N^{10}}{N^{00}+N^{01}+N^{10}+N^{11}}$
Double fault measure [3]	$\text{DF} = \frac{N^{00}}{N^{00}+N^{01}+N^{10}+N^{11}}$

- The Q-Statistic and the correlation coefficient do not satisfy the Property 1 listed in section 2.2. For example if both N^{00} and N^{10} are both 0 the Q-Statistic and correlation coefficient are undefined ($\frac{0}{0}$).
- The Disagreement measure,Q-Statistic and the correlation coefficient are symmetrical for a pair of classifiers, however they are not necessarily symmetrical with respect to the entire configuration i.e. the average Q-statistic (or correlation coefficient) for a configuration and its complement (defined in section 2.1) are not necessarily the same.
- Although the double-fault measure does not violate Properties 1 and 2, it may not capture the aspects of classifier diversity which may be regarded important. Consider for example configurations A_1 and A_2 as below.
  A_1:$x_0 = 0.5, x_1 = 0.3, x_2 = 0.2, x_3 = 0$; A_2:$x_0 = 0.5, x_1 = 0, x_2 = 0, x_3 = 0.5$
  Intuitively, A_1 is more diverse than A_2 (in A_2, there is total agreement with respect to all classifications), however the double fault value is the same for both cases.
- With pairwise measures, it is usually hard to express the diversity measure of a given ensemble as a simple closed form function of x. The objective function g(x) may be complicated, and hence it is difficult to determine the range of values for a given ensemble. Thus, they may not be amenable for analysis and evaluation.

Non-pairwise diversity measures:

1. **Cunningham (Entropy) measure [1]:** In [1] a diversity measure is proposed and is referred to as the Entropy measure. Since it is quite distinct from the entropy function in information theory, we refer to it as the Cunningham measure. In [6] it is defined as follows. Let z_j $j = 1, \ldots, N$ be examples classified by the classifiers and $l(z_j)$ the number of classifiers that correctly classify z_j. Let K be the number of classifiers. The Cunningham measure may be defined as :

$$E = \frac{1}{N} \sum_{j=1}^{N} \frac{1}{(\lfloor K/2 \rfloor)} min\{l(z_j), L - l(z_j)\} \tag{7}$$

In the limiting case the proportion of examples is the probability. With our notation the Cunningham measure may be defined as:

$$E = \frac{1}{\lfloor K/2 \rfloor} \sum_{i=0}^{2^K - 1} min(n, K - n)x_i \tag{8}$$

where $n = N(bit(i, K))$ i.e. n = Number of 1s in K bit binary expansion of i.

2. **Measure of "difficulty"** (θ): Hansen and Salamon [4] propose a measure as follows. Let the number of classifiers be K and let X be the random variable which denotes the fraction of classifiers that correctly classify a random input. Thus X is a discrete random variable which can take on the values $\{\frac{0}{K}, \frac{1}{K}, \ldots, \frac{K}{K}\}$. The variance of X ($\theta = \text{Var}(X)$) is proposed as the measure of diversity.

The Cunningham measure satisfies the symmetry property as defined in section 2.2 while Hansen's measure of difficulty does not.

3.2   Variation of Selected Diversity Measures with Classifier Accuracy

The results for the Cunningham measure and Hansen's measure of "difficulty" (θ) are shown in Figure 1. The Cunningham measure ranges from 0 (lowest diversity,complete agreement) to 1 (highest diversity). For the measure of difficulty, higher values correspond to lower diversity and vice versa. The curve in the middle corresponds to the value of the diversity measure, if the classifiers were statistically independent.

It is interesting to note that for statistically independent classifiers the value is on the side of higher "diversity". For the Cunningham measure it is much closer to the maximum while for the Hansen's measure of difficulty it is closer to the theoretical minimum (again note that for the Cunningham measure, higher values correspond to high diversity while for the measure of difficulty higher values correspond to lower diversity and vice versa). Although this seems to indicate that statistical independence bodes well for the classifier ensemble, it still leaves open the question of how to enforce statistical independence. For instance, Eckhardt and Lee [2] point out that software programs developed independently tended to fail on similar inputs, this being related to the difficulty of the specific inputs.

The absolute value of a diversity measure may have limited use even if the measure has a theoretical minimum and maximum value, since the range of values it can take depends on the particlular ensemble. Consider for example, ensembles E1 and E2 each consisting of three classifiers with the following accuracies:
E1 : $p_1 = p_2 = p_3 = 0.9$ and E2 : $p_1 = p_2 = p_3 = 0.6$
Although in general the theoretical minimum and maximum values of the Cunningham measure are 0 and 1 respectively, we can see from Figure 1(a) that the corresponding values for ensemble E1 are 0 and 0.3 and for E2 they are 0 and 1 respectively. Let the actual values of the Cunningham measure for E1 and E2 be 0.25 and 0.5 respectively. E1 is *relatively more diverse* than E2 even though the absolute value is smaller,

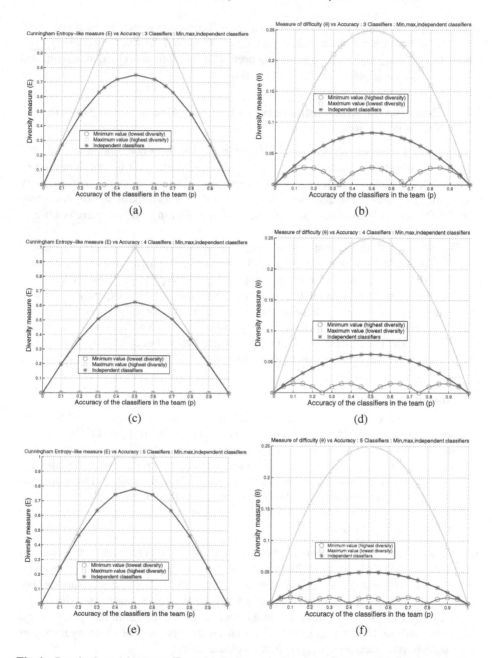

Fig. 1. Cunningham Measure (E) and Measure of difficulty (θ) vs classifier accuracy (p) : Lower,upper bounds and independent classifiers for 3 (a),(b) 4 (c),(d) 5 (e),(f) classifiers E vs p : Figures (a),(c),(e) θ vs p : Figures (b),(d),(f)

since the diversity value is relatively closer to its theoretical maximum. Thus it may be more useful to consider *relative diversity* as opposed to the absolute value of the diversity measure, especially if we wish to compare different ensembles. For a given set of classifier accuracies, we define the relative diversity (D_{rel}) as: $D_{rel} = \frac{D_{actual} - D_{min}}{D_{max} - D_{min}}$, where D_{min}, D_{max} and D_{actual} are the theoretical minimum, theoretical maximum and actual value of the given diversity measure, respectively.

3.3   Exploring the Relationship Between Diversity Measures and Majority Voting Performance

A motivation for designing a "diverse" ensemble of classifiers is to obtain an improvement in classification accuracy. Since there is no widely accepted formal definition of "diversity", the characterization of the relationship between "diversity" and majority voting (or classifier combination schemes in general) is not straightforward. Nevertheless, the framework formulated in the paper enables evaluating whether there is a useful correlation.

The main problem encountered in analyzing the relationship between a diversity measure and majority vote accuracy (p_{maj}) is to vary a given variable in a systematic manner over its full range in order to compute the corresponding value of the other variable. One could use a simulation scheme and an enumeration experiment such as in [6]. However this does not necessarily provide a means for varying a quantity in a systematic manner over its full range. The optimization problem framework addresses this problem. The experimental procedure is outlined below. For simplicity and purpose of illustration, all classifiers are assumed to have the same accuracy p. Let p_{maj} denote the majority vote accuracy.

Experimental procedure

1. Vary p in steps. For each p determine the majority vote theoretical upper and lower bounds p_{maj}^{max} and p_{maj}^{min} respectively by solving the linear program (LP) in [9] (constraints identical to the optimization problem in section 2.3).
2. Vary p_{maj} in steps from p_{maj}^{min} to p_{maj}^{max}. For each p_{maj} obtain a feasible solution i.e. a solution which satisfies the constraints given by Equations (2-4). Determine the value of the diversity measure (D) corresponding to the solution.
3. Find the coefficient of linear correlation between majority vote accuracy (p_{maj}) and the value of the diversity measure (D).

It is more useful to look at the overall trend instead of the actual values of the diversity measures (especially if the classifier accuracies are not the same). For the most part, the variation of the diversity measures was in line with their basic motivations. For example, the coefficient of linear correlation between Hansen's measure of "difficulty" (θ) and p_{maj} was mostly negative and that between the Cunningham measure (E) and p_{maj} was positive. However in general the relationship between the diversity measures and majority vote accuracy (p_{maj}) is hard to characterize.

We repeated the experiments by varying the Cunningham measure between its theoretical minimum and maximum values (which may be determined by solving the linear program in section 2.3 with g(x) given in table 3) and determining the corresponding majority vote accuracy (p_{maj}). The results are shown in Figure 2. As can be seen from figure 2 there may be no one-to-one correspondence between the diversity measure and majority vote accuracy. It is entirely possible that there is more than one solution x

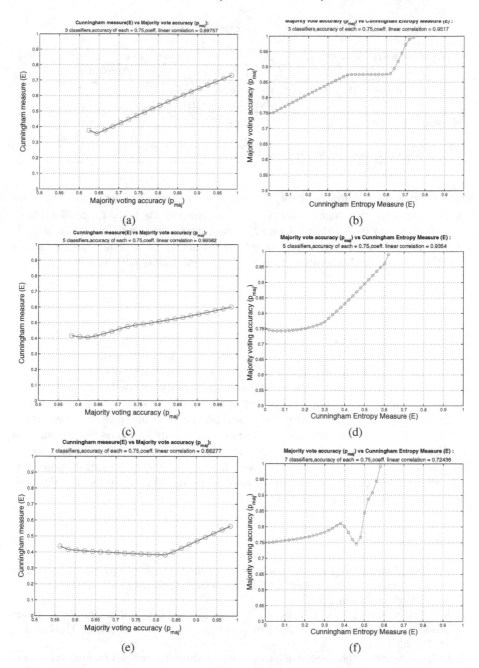

Fig. 2. Variation of Majority vote accuracy (p_{maj}) vs Cunningham (Entropy) measure (E) and vice versa : E vs p_{maj} : Figures (a),(c),(e) p_{maj} vs E : Figures (b),(d),(f). for 3 Classifiers (a),(b) 5 classifiers (c),(d) and 7 classifiers (e),(f); with equal accuracy p=0.75

Table 3. Diversity measures expressed as functions of x

Diversity measure	$g(x) = \boldsymbol{f}^T x + c$	
	$\boldsymbol{f} = [f_0, f_1, \ldots, f_{(2^K-1)}]^T$	c (constant)
Cunningham measure (E) [1]	$f_i = min(n, K-n)/\lfloor K/2 \rfloor$ where $n = N(bit(i,K))$	0
Measure of difficulty (θ) [4]	$f_i = \left(\frac{N(bit(i,K))}{K} \right)^2$	$-p_{mean}^2$ where $p_{mean}=$ Avg. classifier accuracy
Kohavi-Wolpert variance (KW) [5]	$f_i = \frac{N(bit(i,K))}{K} \frac{K-N(bit(i,K))}{K}$	0

which satisfies the constraints (2)-(4). For example in Figure 2(a) the values of E vary linearly with p_{maj}, the range of values of p_{maj} corresponding to the range [0.4:0.6] of E is approximately [0.7:0.85]. In Figure 2(b) there are multiple solutions where p_{maj} is very close to 0.85 while values of E range from 0.4 to 0.6. These results raise questions about the usefulness of diversity measures in designing a classifier ensemble.

4   Conclusions

In this paper we propose a linear program based framework for the analysis of diversity measures for ensembles of binary classifiers and also a set of properties for such a diversity measure. Although we regard the question of what exactly defines diversity in a classifier ensemble as open, we show that the framework can be used effectively to evaluate diversity measures for classifier ensembles. The framework was used for analyzing the relationship between selected diversity measures and accuracy of the classifier ensemble. Even though the motivation for enforcing diversity in a classifier ensemble is justified,the results cast doubt on whether diversity measures are useful in this regard. Based on our evaluation we suggest that although measures may be useful in the original context they were proposed, caution must be exercised in using them as diversity measures for classifier ensembles.

References

1. P. Cunningham and J. Carney. Diversity versus quality in classification ensembles based on feature selection. Technical Report TCD-CS-2000-02, Department of Computer Science, Trinity College, Dublin, 2000.
2. D.E. Eckhardt and L.D. Lee. A theoretical basis for the analysis of multiversion software subject of coincident errors. *IEEE Transactions on Software Engineering*, 11(12):1511–1517, 1985.
3. G. Giacinto and F. Roli. Design of effective neural network ensembles for image classification processes. *Image Vision and Computing Journal*, 19(9/10):699–707, 2001.
4. L. Hansen and P. Salamon. Neural network ensembles. *IEEE Transactions on Pattern Analysis and Machine Intelligence*, 12(10):993–1001, 1990.
5. R. Kohavi and D. H. Wolpert. Bias plus variance decomposition for zero-one loss functions. In L. Saitta, editor, *Machine Learning : 13th International Conference*, pages 275–283. Morgan Kaufmann, 1996.

6. L. I. Kuncheva and C. J. Whitaker. Measures of diversity in classifier ensembles and their relationship with the ensemble accuracy. *Machine Learning*, 51:181–207, 2003.
7. L.I. Kuncheva. *Combining Pattern Classifiers*. Wiley Interscience, 2004.
8. B. Littlewood and D.R. Miller. Conceptual modeling of coincident failures in multiversion software. *IEEE Transactions on Software Engineering*, 15(12):1596–1614, 1989.
9. A. Narasimhamurthy. A framework for the analysis of majority voting. In Josef Bigün and Tomas Gustavsson, editors, *SCIA*, volume 2749 of *Lecture Notes in Computer Science*, pages 268–274. Springer, 2003.
10. D. Partridge and W.J. Krzanowski. Software diversity:practical statistics for its measurement and exploitation. *Information & Software Technology*, 39:707–717, 1997.
11. C.R. Rao.   Diversity : Its measurement,decomposition,apportionment and analysis. *Sankya:The Indian Journal of Statistics*, 44(1):1–22, 1982.
12. D. Ruta and B. Gabrys. Application of the evolutionary algorithms for classifier selection in multiple classifier systems with majority voting. In *Proc. 2nd Multiple Classifier systems workshop (MCS)*, volume 2096 of *Lecture Notes in Computer Science*, pages 399–408, 2001.
13. D. Skalak. The sources of increased accuracy for two proposed boosting algorithms. In *Proc. American Association for Artificial Intelligence AAAI-96, Integrating Multiple Learned Models Workshop*, 1996.
14. P. Sneath and R. Sokal. *Numerical Taxonomy*. W.H. Freeman & Co., 1973.
15. G. U. Yule. On the association of attributes in statistics. *Philosophy Transactions*, 194:257–319, 1900.

Which Is the Best Multiclass SVM Method? An Empirical Study

Kai-Bo Duan[1] and S. Sathiya Keerthi[2]

[1] BioInformatics Research Centre,
Nanyang Technological University,
Nanyang Avenue, Singapore 639798
askbduan@ntu.edu.sg
[2] Yahoo! Research Labs,
210 S. DeLacey Street, Pasadena, CA-91105, USA
sathiya.keerthi@overture.com

Abstract. Multiclass SVMs are usually implemented by combining several two-class SVMs. The one-versus-all method using winner-takes-all strategy and the one-versus-one method implemented by max-wins voting are popularly used for this purpose. In this paper we give empirical evidence to show that these methods are inferior to another one-versus-one method: one that uses Platt's posterior probabilities together with the pairwise coupling idea of Hastie and Tibshirani. The evidence is particularly strong when the training dataset is sparse.

1 Introduction

Binary (two-class) classification using support vector machines (SVMs) is a very well developed technique [1] [11]. Due to various complexities, a direct solution of multiclass problems using a single SVM formulation is usually avoided. The better approach is to use a combination of several binary SVM classifiers to solve a given multiclass problem. Popular methods for doing this are: one-versus-all method using winner-takes-all strategy (WTA_SVM); one-versus-one method implemented by max-wins voting (MWV_SVM); DAGSVM [8]; and error-correcting codes [2].

Hastie and Tibshirani [4] proposed a good general strategy called *pairwise coupling* for combining posterior probabilities provided by individual binary classifiers in order to do multiclass classification. Since SVMs do not naturally give out posterior probabilities, they suggested a particular way of generating these probabilities from the binary SVM outputs and then used these probabilities together with pairwise coupling to do muticlass classification. Hastie and Tibshirani did a quick empirical evaluation of this method against MWV_SVM and found that the two methods give comparable generalization performances.

Platt [7] criticized Hastie and Tibshirani's method of generating posterior class probabilities for a binary SVM, and suggested the use of a properly designed sigmoid applied to the SVM output to form these probabilities. However, the

N.C. Oza et al. (Eds.): MCS 2005, LNCS 3541, pp. 278–285, 2005.

use of Platt's probabilities in combination with Hastie and Tibshirani's idea of pairwise coupling has not been carefully investigated thus far in the literature. The main aim of this paper is to fill this gap. We did an empirical study and were surprised to find that this method (we call it as PWC_PSVM) shows a clearly superior generalization performance over MWV_SVM and WTA_SVM; the superiority is particularly striking when the training dataset is sparse.

We also considered the use of binary kernel logistic regression classifiers[1] together with pairwise coupling. We found that even this method is somewhat inferior to PWC_PSVM, which clearly indicates the goodness of Platt's probabilities for SVMs. The results of this paper indicate that PWC_PSVM is the best single kernel discriminant method for solving multiclass problems.

The paper is organized as follows. In section 2, we briefly review the various implementations of one-versus-all and one-versus-one methods that are studied in this paper. In section 3, we describe the numerical experiments used to study the performances of these implementations. The results are analyzed and conclusions are made in section 4. The manuscript of this paper was prepared previously as a technical report [3].

2   Description of Multiclass Methods

In this section, we briefly review the implementations of the multiclass methods that will be studied in this paper. For a given multiclass problem, M will denote the number of classes and ω_i, $i = 1, \ldots, M$ will denote the M classes. For binary classification we will refer to the two classes as *positive* and *negative*; a binary classifier will be assumed to produce an output function that gives relatively large values for examples from the positive class and relatively small values for examples belonging to the negative class.

2.1   WTA_SVM

WTA_SVM constructs M binary classifiers. The ith classifier output function ρ_i is trained taking the examples from ω_i as positive and the examples from all other classes as negative. For a new example $\mathbf{x}$, WTA_SVM strategy assigns it to the class with the largest value of ρ_i.

2.2   MWV_SVM

This method constructs one binary classifier for every pair of distinct classes and so, all together $M(M-1)/2$ binary classifiers are constructed. The binary classifier C_{ij} is trained taking the examples from ω_i as positive and the examples from ω_j as negative. For a new example $\mathbf{x}$, if classifier C_{ij} says $\mathbf{x}$ is in class ω_i, then the vote for class ω_i is added by one. Otherwise, the vote for class ω_j is increased by one. After each of the $M(M-1)/2$ binary classifiers makes its vote, MWV strategy assigns $\mathbf{x}$ to the class with the largest number of votes.

---

[1] These classifiers provide natural posterior probabilities as part of their solution.

2.3   Pairwise Coupling

If the output of each binary classifier can be interpreted as the posterior probability of the positive class, Hastie and Tibshirani [4] suggested a *pairwise coupling* strategy for combining the probabilistic outputs of all the one-versus-one binary classifiers to obtain estimates of the posterior probabilities $p_i = \text{Prob}(\omega_i|\mathbf{x})$, $i = 1, \ldots, M$. After these are estimated, the PWC strategy assigns the example under consideration to the class with the largest p_i.

The actual problem formulation and procedure for doing this are as follows. Let C_{ij} be as in section 2.2. Let us denote the probabilistic output of C_{ij} as $r_{ij} = \text{Prob}(\omega_i|\omega_i \text{ or } \omega_j)$. To estimate the p_i's, $M(M-1)/2$ auxiliary variables μ_{ij}'s which relate to the p_i's are introduced: $\mu_{ij} = p_i/(p_i + p_j)$. p_i's are then determined so that μ_{ij}'s are close to r_{ij}'s in some sense. The Kullback-Leibler distance between r_{ij} and μ_{ij} is chosen as the measurement of closeness:

$$l(p) = \sum_{i<j} n_{ij} \left(r_{ij} \log \frac{r_{ij}}{\mu_{ij}} + (1 - r_{ij}) \log \frac{1 - r_{ij}}{1 - \mu_{ij}} \right) \tag{1}$$

where n_{ij} is the number of examples in $\omega_i \cup \omega_j$ in the training set.[2] The associated score equations are (see [4] for details):

$$\sum_{j \neq i} n_{ij} \mu_{ij} = \sum_{j \neq i} n_{ij} r_{ij}, \quad i = 1, \cdots, M, \quad \text{subject to} \quad \sum_{k=1}^{M} p_k = 1 \tag{2}$$

The p_i's are computed using the following iterative procedure:

1. Start from an initial guess of p_i's and corresponding μ_{ij}'s
2. Repeat $(i = 1, \ldots, M, 1, \ldots)$ until convergence:
   - $p_i \leftarrow p_i \cdot \dfrac{\sum_{j \neq i} n_{ij} r_{ij}}{\sum_{j \neq i} n_{ij} \mu_{ij}}$
   - renormalize the p_i's
   - recompute μ_{ij}'s

Let $\tilde{p}_i = 2 \sum_j r_{ij}/k(k-1)$. Hastie and Tibshirani [4] showed that the multicategory classification based on $\tilde{p}_i$'s is identical to that based on the p_i's obtained from pairwise coupling. However, $\tilde{p}_i$'s are inferior to the p_i's as estimates of posteriori probabilities. Also, log-likelihood values play an important role in the tuning of hyperparameters (see section 3). So, it is always better to use the p_i's as estimates of posteriori probabilities.

A recent paper [12] proposed two new pairwise coupling schemes for estimation of class probabilities. They are good alternatives for the pairwise coupling method of Hastie and Tibshirani.

---

[2] It is noted in [4] that, the weights n_{ij} in (1) can improve the efficiency of the estimates a little, but do not have much effect unless the class sizes are very different. In practice, for simplicity, equal weights ($n_{ij} = 1$) can be assumed.

Kernel logistic regression (KLR) [10] has a direct probabilistic interpretation built into its model and its output is the positive class posterior probability. Thus KLR can be directly used as the binary classification method in the PWC implementation. We will refer to this multiclass method as PWC_KLR.

The output of an SVM, however, is not a probabilistic value, but an uncalibrated distance measurement of an example to the separating hyperplane in the feature space. Platt [7] proposed a method to map the output of an SVM into the positive class posterior probability by applying a sigmoid function to the SVM output:

$$\text{Prob}(\omega_1|\mathbf{x}) = \frac{1}{1 + e^{Af+B}} \tag{3}$$

where f is the output of the SVM associated with example $\mathbf{x}$. The parameters A and B can be determined by minimizing the negative log-likelihood (NLL) function of the validation data. A pseudo-code for determining A and B is also given in [7]; see [6] for an improved pseudo-code. To distinguish from the usual SVM, we refer to the combination of SVM together with the sigmoid function mentioned above as PSVM. The multiclass method that uses Platt's probabilities together with PWC strategy will be referred to as PWC_PSVM.

3   Numerical Experiments

In this section, we numerically study the performance of the four methods discussed in the previous section, namely, WTA_SVM, MWV_SVM, PWC_PSVM and PWC_KLR. For all these kernel-based classification methods, the Gaussian kernel, $K(\mathbf{x}_i, \mathbf{x}_j) = e^{-\|\mathbf{x}_i - \mathbf{x}_j\|^2 / 2\sigma^2}$ is employed. Each binary classifier, whether it is SVM, PSVM or KLR, requires the selection of two hyperparameters: a regularization parameter C and a kernel parameter σ^2. Every multi-category classification method included in our study involves several binary classifiers. In line with the suggestion made by Hsu and Lin [5], we take the C and σ^2 of all the binary classifiers within a multiclass method to be the same.[3] The two hyperparameters are tuned using 5-fold cross-validation estimation of the multiclass generalization performance. We select the optimal hyperparameter pair by a two-step grid search. First we do a coarse grid search using the following sets of values: $C \in \{1.0e\text{-}3, \cdots, 1.0e\text{+}3\}$ and $\sigma^2 \in \{1.0e\text{-}3, \cdots, 1.0e\text{+}3\}$. Thus 49 combinations of C and σ^2 are tried in this step. An optimal pair (C_o, σ_o^2) is selected from this coarse grid search. In the second step, a fine grid search is conducted around (C_o, σ_o^2), with $C \in \{0.2C_o, 0.4C_o, 0.6C_o, 0.8C_o, C_o, 2C_o, 4C_o, 6C_o, 8C_o\}$ and $\sigma^2 \in \{0.2\sigma_o^2, 0.4\sigma_o^2, 0.6\sigma_o^2, 0.8\sigma_o^2, \sigma_o^2, 2\sigma_o^2, 4\sigma_o^2, 6\sigma_o^2, 8\sigma_o^2\}$. All together, 81 combinations of C and σ^2 are tried in this step. The final optimal hyperparameter pair is selected from this fine search. In each grid search, especially in the fine search step, it is quite often the case that there are several pairs of hyperparameters that give the same cross validational classification accuracy. In such

---

[3] An alternative is to choose the C and σ^2 of each binary classifier to minimize the generalization error of that binary classification problem.

Table 1. Basic information and training set sizes of the five datasets

Dataset	#Classes	#Total Examples	Training Set Sizes		
			Small	Medium	Large
ABE	3	2,323	280	560	1,120
DNA	3	3,186	300	500	1,000
SAT	6	6,435	1,000	1,500	2,000
SEG	7	2,310	250	500	1,000
WAV	3	5,000	150	300	600

a situation, we have found it worthwhile to follow some heuristic principles to select one pair of C and σ^2 from these short-listed combinations. For the methods with posteriori probability estimates, where a cross-validation estimate of error rate (cvErr) as well as a cross-validation estimate of negative log-likelihood (cvNLL) are available, the following strategies are applied sequentially until we find one unique parameter pair: (a) select the pair with smallest cvErr value; (b) select the pair with smallest cvNLL value; (c) select the pair with larger σ^2 value; (d) select the pair with smaller C value; (e) select the pair with smallest 8-neighbor average cvErr value; (f) select the pair with smallest C value. Usually step (b) yields a unique pair of hyperparameters. For the methods without posteriori probability estimates, step (b) is omitted.

The performance of the four methods are evaluated on the following datasets taken from the UCI collection: ABE, DNA, *Satellite Image* (SAT), *Image Segentation* (SEG) and *Waveform* (WAV). ABE is a dataset that we extracted from the dataset *Letter* by using only the classes corresponding to the characters "A", "B" and "E". Each continuous input variable of these datasets is normalized to have zero mean and unit standard deviation. For each dataset, we divide the whole data into a training set and a test set. When the training set size is large enough, all the methods perform equally very well. Differences between various methods can be clearly seen only when the training datasets are sparse. So, instead of using a single training set size (that is usually chosen to be reasonably large in most empirical studies), we use three different training set sizes: small, medium and large. For each dataset, the basic information together with the values of the three training set sizes are summarized in Table 1. For each dataset, at each training set size, the whole data is randomly partitioned into a training set and a test set 20 times by stratified sampling. For each such partition, after each multi-category classifier is designed using solely the training set, it is tested on the test set. The mean and standard deviation of the test set error rate (in percentage) are computed over the 20 runs. The results are reported in Table 2. Full details of all runs can be found at: *http://guppy.mpc.nus.edu.sg/~mpessk/multiclass.shtml*

Table 2. Mean and standard deviation of test set error (in percentage) over 20 divisions of training and test sets, for the five datasets, at the three training set sizes (small, medium and large)

Dataset	Training Set Size	Method WTA_SVM	MWV_SVM	PWC_PSVM	PWC_KLR
ABE	280	1.92±0.65	1.96±0.65	1.16±0.63	1.85±0.59
	560	0.96±0.36	1.06±0.42	0.58±0.29	1.02±0.43
	1,120	0.46±0.20	0.50±0.24	0.34±0.17	0.57±0.26
DNA	300	10.15±1.26	9.87±0.90	9.23±1.73	9.73±0.75
	500	7.84±0.79	7.67±0.93	7.41±1.14	7.80±0.71
	1,000	5.59±0.39	5.72±0.57	5.50±0.69	5.76±0.54
SAT	1,000	11.07±0.58	11.03±0.73	10.27±0.92	11.20±0.55
	1,500	10.08±0.49	10.20±0.51	10.05±0.60	10.23±0.42
	2,000	9.51±0.31	9.61±0.39	9.47±0.65	9.66±0.37
SEG	250	9.43±0.54	7.97±1.23	6.66±2.24	7.54±1.24
	500	6.51±0.99	5.40±1.04	5.19±0.74	4.83±0.68
	1,000	4.89±0.71	4.35±0.79	4.08±0.52	3.96±0.68
WAV	150	17.21±1.37	17.75±1.39	13.20±3.70	15.59±1.13
	300	15.43±0.97	15.96±0.98	12.97±2.02	14.71±0.72
	600	14.09±0.55	14.56±0.80	13.47±1.09	13.81±0.41

4   Results and Conclusions

Let us now analyze the results from our numerical study. From Table 2 we can see that, PWC_PSVM gives the best classification results and has significantly smaller mean values of test error. For WTA_SVM, MWV_SVM and PWC_KLR, it is hard to tell which one is better.

To give a more vivid presentation of the results from the numerical study, we draw, for each dataset and each training set size, a boxplot to show the 20 test errors of each method, obtained from the 20 partitions of training and test. The boxplots are shown in Figure 1. These boxplots clearly support the observation that PWC_PSVM is better than the other three methods. On some datasets, although the variances of PWC_PSVM error rates are larger than those of other methods, the corresponding median values of PWC_PSVM are much smaller than other three methods.

The boxplots also show that, as the training set size gets larger, the classification performances of all four methods get better and the performance differences between them become smaller. This re-emphasizes the need for using a range of training set sizes when comparing two methods. A good method should work well, even at small training set size. PWC_PSVM has this property.

We have also done a finer comparison of the methods by pairwise *t-test*. The results further consolidate the conclusions drawn from Table 2 and Figure 1. To

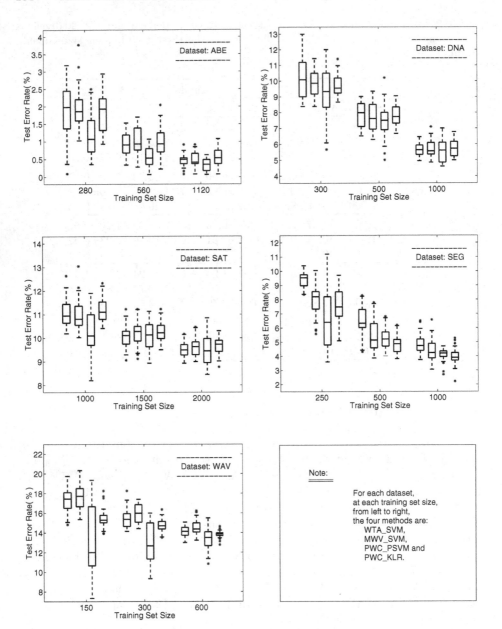

Fig. 1. The boxplots of the four methods for the five datasets, at the three training set sizes (small, medium and large). For easy comparison the boxplots of the four methods are put side by side

keep the paper short, we are not including the description of the pairwise *t-test* comparison and the p-values from the study. Interested readers may refer to our technical report [3] for details.

To conclude, we can say the following. WTA_SVM, MWV_SVM and PWC_KLR are competitive with each other and there is no clear superiority of one method over another. PWC_PSVM consistently outperforms the other three methods. The fact that the method is better than PWC_KLR indicates the goodness of Platt's posterior probabilities. PWC_PSVM using one of the pairwise coupling schemes in [4] and [12] is highly recommended as the best kernel discriminant method for solving multiclass problems.

References

1. Boser, B., Guyon, I., Vapnik, V.: An training algorithm for optimal margin classifiers. In: *Fifth Annual Workshop on Computational Learning Theory*, Pittsburgh, ACM (1992) 144–152
2. Dietterich, T., Bakiri, G.: Solving multiclass problem via error-correcting output code. *Journal of Artificial Intelligence Research*, Vol. 2 (1995) 263–286
3. Duan, K.-B., Keerthi, S.S.: Which is the best multiclass SVM method? An empirical study. Technical Report CD-03-12, Control Division, Department of Mechanical Engineering, National University of Singapore. (2003)
4. Hastie, T., Tibshirani, R.: Classification by pairwise coupling. In: Jordan, M.I., Kearns, M.J., Solla, A.S. (eds.): *Advances in Neural Information Processing Systems 10*. MIT Press (1998)
5. Hsu, C.-W., Lin, C.-J.: A comparison of methods for multi-class support vector machines. *IEEE Transactions on Neural Networks*, Vol. 13 (2002) 415–425
6. Lin, H.-T., Lin, C.-J., Weng, R.C.: A note on Platt's probabilistic outputs for support vector machines (2003). Available: *http://www.csie.ntu.edu.tw/~cjlin/papers/plattprob.ps*
7. Platt, J.: Probabilistic outputs for support vector machines and comparison to regularized likelihood methods. In: Smola, A.J., Bartlett, P., Schölkopf, B., Schuurmans, D. (eds.): *Advances in Large Margin Classifiers*. MIT Press (1999) 61–74
8. Platt, J., Cristanini, N., Shawe-Taylor, J.: Large margin DAGs for multiclass classification. *Advances in Neural Information Processing Systems 12*. MIT Press (2000) 543–557
9. Rifkin, R., Klautau, A.: In defence of one-versus-all classificaiton. *Journal of Machine Learning Research*, Vol. 5 (2004) 101–141
10. Roth, V.: Probabilistic discriminant kernel classifiers for multi-class problems. In: Radig, B., Florczyk, S. (eds.): *Pattern Recognition-DAGM'01*. Springer (2001) 246–253
11. Vapnik, V.: *Statistical Learning Theory*. Wiley Interscience (1998)
12. Wu, T.-F., Lin, C.-J., Weng, R.C.: Probability estimates for multi-class classification by pairwise coupling. *Journal of Machine Learning Research*, Vol. 5 (2004) 975–1005

Over-Fitting in Ensembles of Neural Network Classifiers Within ECOC Frameworks

Matthew Prior and Terry Windeatt

Centre for Vision, Speech and Signal Processing (CVSSP)
University of Surrey, Guildford, Surrey, GU2 5XH, UK
{m.prior, t.windeatt}@surrey.ac.uk

Abstract. We have investigated the performance of a generalisation error predictor, G_{est}, in the context of error correcting output coding ensembles based on multi-layer perceptrons. An experimental evaluation on benchmark datasets with added classification noise shows that over-fitting can be detected and a comparison is made with the Q measure of ensemble diversity. Each dichotomy associated with a column of an ECOC code matrix is presented with a bootstrap sample of the training set. G_{est} uses the out-of-bootstrap samples to efficiently estimate the mean column error for the independent test set and hence the test error. This estimate can then be used select a suitable complexity for the base classifiers in the ensemble.

1 Introduction

In many real world machine learning applications the available data is in short supply and is often corrupted by noise. Both of these attributes can encourage over-fitting. Avoiding this problem involves the selection of appropriately complex hypotheses to represent the problem behaviour. A desirable goal is to build learning systems that exhibit good generalisation – the ability to work well when presented with unseen data – and avoid over-fitting – the unintentional dependence of the learning hypothesis upon non representative features in the training sample.

To achieve good generalisation a strategy for limiting the power of the chosen model, in order to control over-fitting, is often employed. This can take a direct form, such as in regularisation, where a penalty term is introduced to limit the complexity of the solution or an indirect form, as in the case of multi-layer perceptrons (MLPs) subject to early stopping, weight sharing or network pruning [3]. MLPs provide general purpose functional approximators that are unstable. They can produce significantly different classifiers for small differences in initial conditions or distribution of training data. This diversity is highly desirable in multiple classifier systems that seek to reduce the variance of an ensemble by aggregating classifiers, such as Bagging or simple majority vote ensembles [11]. It is also relatively easy to adjust their complexity by modulating the amount of network training.

In the literature, tuning of the base classifier for ensemble systems has received relatively little attention [15], [16]. Motivated by work on the generalisation error of

N.C. Oza et al. (Eds.): MCS 2005, LNCS 3541, pp. 286–295, 2005.

two class datasets [5], this paper seeks to characterise the complexity of the base classifier and ensemble test error through the means of an out-of-bootstrap estimate of training column error within an error correcting output coding context (ECOC).

In an ECOC framework, diversity of base classifiers is not an obviously useful attribute as the learning problems are, in general, dissimilar. However, when the number of classes is small, the number of dichotomies available to the ECOC coding scheme, Table 1, can be significantly less than the desired length of the codeword. This leads to repeated instances of the same learning problems. Here the diversity of randomly initialised MLPs can help to de-correlate the column errors of replicated dichotomies and so utilise more of the error correcting capability available in the coding scheme.

Table 1. The number of supported dichotomies, D, for number of classes, N_k, in an ECOC framework, $D = 2^{N_k - 1} - 1$.

Classes, N_k	2	3	4	5	6	7	8	9	10	11
Number of dichotomies, D	1	3	7	15	31	63	127	255	511	1023

2 Estimating Generalisation Error

In the case of regression, the generalisation error, E_{Gen} , of a given hypothesis $h(x)$, which models an underlying process with additive, zero mean, Gaussian noise can be decomposed into three terms

$$E^2_{Gen} = \sigma^2 + \text{Bias}^2 (h(x)) + \text{Variance}(h(x)) \tag{1}$$

in (1) σ^2 is the irreducible error attributable to the variance of the underlying noise process, the second term is the error due to the bias of the hypothesis and the third term is the variance of the hypothesis [10]. In the context of 0/1 loss functions the decomposition of error into bias and variance terms is less clear [12]. No completely satisfactory definition exists for these quantities and the relationship between them and error rate is not clearly defined. In general, hypotheses with an underspecified degree of complexity exhibit high bias – evident as a systematic degree of error over all instances of the problem – whereas hypotheses with higher degrees of complexity show lower bias, but increased variance – evident as a variable amount of error on each instance of the problem. The best generalisation error occurs where the combined contributions from the bias and variance terms achieve a minimum.

Normally the desired power of the final hypotheses is not known beforehand, so the degree of regularisation, or complexity, that is appropriate for a given learning problem must be investigated empirically. To do this a good method of assessing the generalisation error and detecting over-fitting is required.

The most common estimate of the generalisation error is K-fold cross-validation. All the available data is separated into K equally sized folds and a classifier is trained on $K-1$ folds of the data and then tested on the remaining fold. This process is repeated for all the folds and the mean value is taken to be the generalisation error. As each fold contains different instances of the data it is necessary to re-train the classifier for each new fold requiring K times the number of hypotheses in the ensemble to be generated. For an ensemble of size B this requires $K*B$ classifiers.

Generally $K = 10$ is considered to be a good compromise between computational practicality and accurate error estimation. So computation times for generating all the required classifiers – a considerable portion of the whole when using MLPs – are multiplied by a factor of $K*(1+((K-1)/K)$ compared to an estimate gained using a 50/50 test/training split.

The bootstrap is an effective method for estimating any statistical quantity based on re-sampling, with replacement, of the available data [6]. It uses the idea that the relationship between the underlying distribution and a sample drawn from it is similar to the relationship between the empirical distribution and a secondary sample[14]. The bootstrap can be applied to estimate the generalisation error of an ensemble of B classifiers. However, the method requires that a new ensemble be trained for each bootstrap replicate of the data and a suggested practical value for the number of replicates to achieve a good estimates ranges from 50 to 200 [7], thus requiring a minimum of $50B$ hypotheses to be generated.

Both cross-validation and bootstrap estimation are computationally expensive procedures for predicting generalisation error. An alternative solution, proposed in [4], for bootstrapped ensembles is to take the data not represented in the bootstrap sample, approximately $1/e$ of the instances, and by using the in-sample hypotheses on the out-of-sample data to predict the generalisation error. This approach is much more efficient, as it avoids creating any new hypotheses. Unlike cross-validation and bootstrap estimation the hypotheses used to generate the estimate all form part of the final ensemble classifier and so exactly represent the final classifier performance. We propose combining bootstrap sampling within an ECOC framework to introduce a degree of beneficial randomness and allow the use of out-of-bootstrap error estimation to predict ensemble error via an estimator, G_{est}.

3 Error Correcting Output Coding

Error correcting output coding (ECOC) is a technique inspired by solutions to the problem of transmitting communication symbols over noisy channels [8]. In its original context symbols are typically represented by maximally separated code words in a suitably complex vector space; thus allowing errors in transmission to be corrected by exchanging corrupted code words for the closest neighbour from the original alphabet. In its application to machine learning problems the coding structure used by ECOC performs not just the task of error correction but also simultaneously imposes a binary output space decomposition onto the classes. A benefit of the output space decomposition is that it allows binary classifiers to be leveraged to the context of multi-class problems and provides a method of controlling individual classifier errors in a multi-classifier ensemble.

In Bagging, the out of bag estimate represents a sub-sampled version of the underlying distribution. In an ECOC ensemble employing bootstrapping, each bootstrap is seen by a (potentially unique) binary decomposition of the output space. As a result the variance of the out-of-bootstrap estimate may be comprised of a set of disparate estimates based on different learning problems and so if treated as a set of random variables the variance is the square root of the sum of the individual variances and twice the covariance terms [18].

To produce the set of dichotomies the classes of the problem domain are enunciated as a matrix. This contains rows which represent a codeword for each class. The columns of the matrix represent a specific binary decomposition of the learning problem. The ones and zeroes in the ith column are used to group the classes into two supersets, S_{0i} and S_{1i}.

ECOC coding schemes have been investigated in [9], [11], [12], [17]. The performance of the coding scheme is dependent on the problem and code length. Random codes were chosen on the grounds that they can form codes of arbitrary length, are easy to generate and generally give good performance.

4 Experimental Method

To investigate the behaviour of G_{est} on real world problems, a selection of datasets from the UCI repository was chosen, Table 2. To encourage over-fitting all the datasets were subject to 20% injected class noise. The noise was introduced by randomly selecting 20% of the samples from each class and flipping their class labels. The class distribution of the noise was shaped to be consistent with the original class distributions in the training set.

Table 2. Datasets, features and training and test set sizes

UCI Dataset	% Class Noise	No. Training Samples	No. Test Samples	Classes N_k	Categorical Features	Numerical Features
Iris	20	75	75	3	0	4
Glass	20	107	107	7	0	10
Segment	20	350	350	7	0	19
Soybean	20	23	24	4	35	0
Vehicle	20	423	423	4	0	18
Vowel	20	495	495	11	2	10

For this paper the following method was applied to each dataset in Table 2 to determine the empirical behaviour of the out-of-bootstrap estimator G_{est}. The method was repeated 10 times for each dataset with the complexity parameter, P_t, being varied to adjust the classifier complexity.

1. A code matrix, C, of length I and depth equal to N_k, the number of classes in the problem, and consisting of unique rows and random columns was generated. Where the number of dichotomies, D, supported by the classes was insufficient to achieve the codeword length, as is the case with the Iris, Soybean and Vehicle datasets, repeat random columns (dichotomies) were allowed.

2. The available data was divided randomly into equally sized test and training sets, T_r and T_s. For the ith column of the code matrix, C, a bootstrap sample B_r was taken from the training set, T_r, $B = \{ B_{r1}, B_{r2} \dots B_{rI} \}$.

3. The instances from the dataset which were not in each of the bootstrap samples were put aside to give the out of bootstrap samples, $B^* = \{ B_{r1}{}^*, B_{r2}{}^* \dots B_{rI}{}^* \}$.

4. Each of the datasets in B were then re-labelled into 2 super-classes, S_0 and S_1 with labels {0,1} defined by the values in the code matrix, C, to form a dichotomy on the problem space

$$B_{ri}^{`} = S_{0i} \cup S_{1i} \qquad\qquad i = 1..I$$
$$B^{`} = \{ B_{r1}^{`}, B_{r2}^{`} \dots B_{rI}^{`} \}$$

The same process is applied to the out of bootstrap samples and to the test set, T_s.

$$B^{`*} = \{ B_{r1}^{`*}, B_{r2}^{`*} \dots B_{rI}^{`*} \}, T_s^{`} = \{ T_{s1}^{`}, T_{s2}^{`} \dots T_{sI}^{`} \}$$

5. For the ith column in the code matrix a hypothesis, h_i, was trained from a randomly intialised multi-layer perceptron classifier, M_i, with architecture A, for a specified number of epochs, P_t on $B_{ri}^{`}$

$$h_i = h(C_i, B_{ri}^{`}, M_i, A, P_t) \qquad\qquad i = 1..I$$

6. The hypotheses are then applied to coded versions of the bootstrapped training sets, the out of bootstrap samples and the test sets to give the column outputs

$$O_{cB^{`}} = \{ h_1(B_{r1}^{`}), h_2(B_{r2}^{`}) \dots h_I(B_{rI}^{`})\}$$
$$O_{cB^{`*}} = \{ h_1(B_{r1}^{`*}), h_2(B_{r2}^{`*}) \dots h_I(B_{rI}^{`*})\}$$
$$O_{cT_s} = \{ h_1(T_{s1}^{`}), h_2(T_{s2}^{`}) \dots h_I(T_{sI}^{`})\}$$

7. The column outputs were compared to the original labelled datasets. $B^{`}$, $B^{`*}$ and $T_s^{`}$, to get the column errors for the hypothesis and these are averaged to get the mean column errors, E_c, for the bootstrapped training sets, the out of bootstrap samples and the test sets.

$$E_{c\chi_i} = \frac{1}{I} \sum_{i=1}^{I} |h_i(\chi_i) - Label(\chi_i)| \; ; \chi_i \in \{ B'_{ri}, B'^*_{ri}, T'_{si} \} \qquad (2)$$

In (2) $Label(k)$ returns the vector of superset class labels, $\{ l_1, l_2, \dots l_i \}$ $l \in \{ 0, 1 \}$, associated with dataset k. The mean of the out-of-bootstrap column error, $E_{cB^{`*}}$, forms the estimator for the generalisation error, G_{est}.

8. The column outputs were then decoded, via the ECOC matrix, to give the final classification for the datasets

$$O_{B^{`}} = L(O_{cB^{`}}, C) \, ; \, O_{B^{`*}} = L(O_{cB^{`*}}, C) \, ; \, O_{Ts} = L(O_{cTs}, C)$$

where $L(.)$ represents the decoding function, which returns the class represented by the closest code word to the column output using the L_1 norm as the distance metric.

9. Finally the ensemble errors, E_r and E_s, for the training set and test sets, T_r and T_s, were calculated from the original labels and the predictions, $O_{B^{`}}$ and O_{Ts}.

The code length was chosen to be in the range $[\log_2(\max(N_k)), \max(N_k)^2]$ and was set to be 48. Representing a sufficiently long code to support the number of dichotomies and achieve a balance between error gains due to code length and acceptable computation times [2],[9].

5   Experimental Evidence

In figure 1 the out-of-bootstrap estimate, G_{est}, is plotted against E_s and E_{cTs} for a range of values of base classifier complexity, measured in training epochs. G_{est} is clearly an optimistically biased estimator of E_s, but it does follow the trend of E_s closely and its minimum error rate corresponds well with that of the ensemble.

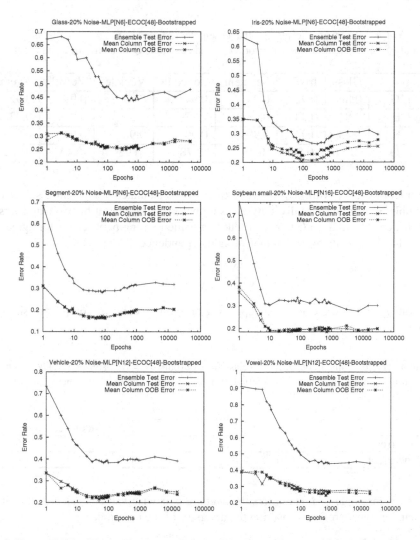

Fig. 1. Ensemble Test Error, E_s , Mean Column Test Error, E_{cTs} , and Mean Out-of-bootstrap Column error , G_{est} , against base classifier complexity, measured by log epochs, for five UCI datasets. [Nx] specifies the number of neurons in the hidden layer of the MLP

To verify the claim that G_{est} is a usable predictor of over-fitting, it is desirable to measure the relationship between the mean out-of-bag column error and the mean test column error. The correlation coefficients calculated for the six datasets shown in Table 3 confirm that G_{est} and E_{cTs} do indeed correlate well. This would be expected as they are essentially different sized random samples from the same distribution. Furthermore, G_{est} also correlates well with the ensemble test error, E_s, showing that there is a correlation between mean column test error and ensemble error.

Table 3. Correlation coefficents for the ensemble test error, E_s, mean column test error, E_{cTs}, out-of-bootstrap mean column error, G_{est} , and ensemble Q value for the training set

	Glass	Iris	Segment	Soybean	Vehicle	Vowel	Average
E_s / G_{est}	0.86	0.92	0.94	0.94	0.89	0.99	0.92
G_{est}/ E_{cTs}	0.84	0.93	0.95	0.97	0.93	0.94	0.93
E_s / E_{cTs}	0.93	0.99	0.99	0.99	0.98	0.94	0.97
E_s / Q	-0.51	-0.84	-0.85	-0.78	-0.92	-0.43	-0.72

For comparison with G_{est} the Q statistic was calculated for training set of each ensemble. Q is a pairwise diversity measure between the output of two classifiers, H_i and H_k , calculated as in (3), and produces a value ranging between +1 for agreement and -1 for disagreement, with 0 indicating independence.

$$Q_{i,k} = \frac{N^{11}N^{00} - N^{01}N^{10}}{N^{11}N^{00} + N^{01}N^{10}} \tag{3}$$

The values of N^{nm} are calculated depending on the two classifier outputs as shown in Table 4.

Table 4. The relationship between two classifiers outputs. $N = N^{00} + N^{11} + N^{01} + N^{10}$,where N is the total number of instances classified and N^{nm} is the number of instances for which the outputs are n and m

	H_k correct	H_k incorrect
H_i correct	N^{11}	N^{10}
H_i incorrect	N^{01}	N^{00}

For an ensemble of L classifiers the average pair-wise value is calculated as in (4) and can be considered as measuring the diversity of the ensemble

$$Q = \frac{2}{L(L-1)} \sum_{i=1}^{L-1} \sum_{k=i+1}^{L} Q_{i,k} \tag{4}$$

Q is highlighted in [13] as being the most useful measure of diversity for designing classifier committees that minimise error. Figure 2 show that Q achieves a maximum value that corresponds reasonably well with the test error minimum, but interestingly it is associated with a minimum in the diversity of the ECOC ensembles. This can be explained if we visualise a continuous vector space spanning base classifier accuracy and complexity. If we consider trajectories in this space representing identical deterministic base classifiers, such as identically initialised MLPs each of which can achieve Bayes optimality, they will all occupy the same paths. As the complexity of

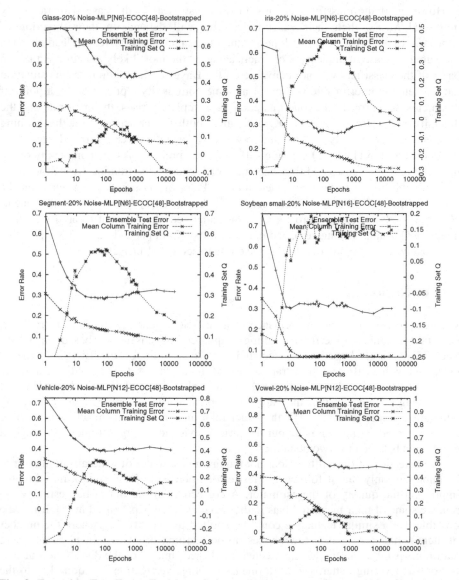

Fig. 2. Ensemble Test Error, E_s, Mean Column Training Error, E_{cB}, and the Q measure of ensemble diversity, Q_r, against base classifier complexity measured by log epochs for five UCI datasets. [Nx] specifies the number of neurons in the hidden layer of the MLP

each of these classifiers increases they will all arrive at the Bayes optimal point, where the classifier achieves the exact Bayes boundary, via the same trajectory. It is clear both that diversity will be non existent and the ensemble will also achieve the Bayes error rate. As the complexity of the base classifiers is increased further, over-fitting occurs and the error rate increases. As a result, the classifiers' paths through 'accuracy/complexity space' begin to move away from the Bayes optimal point. If the classifiers are deterministic, and identical, then their trajectories will also be identical.

However, if the classifiers are not identical, such as is the case with randomly initialised MLPs, then their exact trajectories will depend on their direction of approach to the Bayes optimal point and their paths will diverge, leading to a measured increase in diversity. For practical cases, the most likely situation is that the paths of the classifiers will not converge on the Bayes optimal point. In this situation the best ensemble error rate will occur at some complexity represented by a point of mean closest approach. Beyond this point, as complexity rises, the error rate and the diversity will increase. For ECOC ensembles both the classifiers and the learning problems are, potentially, distinct and so we can expect the diversity to be larger.

As observed in [1], the Q measure suffers from a problem. As the complexity of the base classifiers increases and they become more accurate the training error drops. It is then possible for Q to become indeterminate. Pairs of classifiers often agree on the correct outputs, N^{11}, but the double errors, N^{00}, drop to zero; requiring only that one of N^{01} or N^{10} also becomes zero for Q to be undefined. As it is not clear from which direction Q is approaching zero, and both the values from [1] and our own suggest that Q is positive in the region of interest, we chose to set $Q = 1$ in such cases.

6 Conclusion

We have investigated the performance of an efficient generalisation error predictor, G_{est}, in the context of error correcting output coding ensembles based on MLPs. Specifically, each hypothesis associated with a column of the ECOC matrix is presented with a different bootstrap sample of the training set. The predictor uses the out-of-bootstrap samples to estimate the mean column error for the independent test set, relying on the fact that they are both representative samples of the underlying population distribution. Though the exact relationship between mean column error and test error is not known, our empirical evidence suggests there is a good correlation between the two quantities.

The detection of over-fitting does not require an estimator of generalisation error to be unbiased, only that it follows the test error trend well. Future work may involve improving the quality of the estimator. A correction to the out-of-bag estimates to remove some of their measured bias in the two class case is proposed in [5]. It may be possible that a similar technique could be applied to improve G_{est} where the number of dichotomies are small – few classes in the learning problem – or in cases where additional parallel ensembles are created to allow estimates of the distribution of out-of-bootstrap voting patterns to be formed. Further investigation is required as to the effect of code word length and code choice on the estimator and their relationship to the underlying error rate.

Since G_{est} is independent of base classifier type it is our proposition that it shows good potential as a practical and efficient method of detecting over-fitting in ECOC ensembles regardless of base classifier type. Compared to cross-validation G_{est} is computationally efficient as it requires no additional classifiers to be trained. Our thanks to the reviewers of this paper for their helpful suggestions.

References

[1] Banfield, R et al. : A New Ensemble Diversity Measure Applied to Thinning Ensembles, Proc. MCS 4th International Workshop, Guildford, Springer-Verlag (2003)
[2] Berger, B. : Error-correcting output coding for text classification, IJCAI'99, Workshop on machine learning for information filtering, Stockholm, Sweden (1999)
[3] Bishop, C. : Neural Networks for Pattern Recognition, Oxford, Clarendon Press (1995)
[4] Breiman, L. : Out-of-bag estimation, Technical Report No. 421, University of California Berkeley (1994)
[5] Bylander, T. : Estimating Generalization Error on Two-Class Datasets Using Out-Of-Bag Estimates, Machine Learning, 48, (2002) 287-297
[6] Efron, B. : Bootstrap Methods: another look at the jackknife, Ann. Statistics 7 (1979) 1-26
[7] Efron, B. and Tibshirani, R.J. : An Introduction to the Bootstrap, Monographs on Statistics and Applied Probability 57, Chapman and Hall, (1993) 47
[8] Dietterich, T. and Bakiri, G. : Solving Multi-class Learning Problems via Error-Correcting Output Codes, Journal of Artificial Intelligence Research, 2 (1995) 236-286
[9] Ghani, R. : Using error-correcting codes for text classification, Proceedings of the 17th International Conference on Machine Learning, Morgan Kaufmann, San Francisco (2000) 303-310
[10] Hastie, T. , Tibshirani, R. , Friedman, J : The Elements of Statistical Learning, Springer-Verlag (2001)
[11] James, G. and Hastie, T. : The error coding method and PICTs, Computation and Graphical Statistics, 7 , (1998) 377-387
[12] James, G. : Majority Vote Classifiers - Theory and applications, PhD. Dissertation, Stanford University (1998)
[13] Kuncheva, L. and Whitaker, C. : Measures of Diversity in Classifier Ensembles and Their Relationship with the Ensemble Accuracy, Machine Learning 51, 2, Kluwer Academic Publishers (2002) 187-207
[14] Paass, G. : Assessing and Improving Neural Network Predictions by the Bootstrap Algorithm, Advances in Neural Information Processing Systems 5, Morgan Kaufman (1993) 196-203
[15] Rifkin, R. and Klautau, A. : In Defence of One-Vs-All Classification, Journal of Machine Learning Research 5 (2004) 101-141
[16] Windeatt, T. : Vote Counting Measures for Ensemble Classifiers: Pattern Recognition 36, Pergamon (2003) 2743-2756
[17] Windeatt, T. and Ghaderi, R. : Coding and Decoding Strategies for Multi-class Learning Problems : Information Fusion 4(1) (2003) 11-21
[18] Winston, W. : Operations Research – Applications and Algorithms 3rd Ed. , ITP (1994) 628

Between Two Extremes:
Examining Decompositions of the
Ensemble Objective Function

Gavin Brown[1], Jeremy Wyatt[2], and Ping Sun[2]

[1] School of Computer Science, University of Manchester,
Kilburn Building, Oxford Road, Manchester, M13 9PL
gavin.brown@manchester.ac.uk
http://www.cs.man.ac.uk/~gbrown/
[2] School of Computer Science, University of Birmingham,
Edgbaston Park Road, Birmingham, B15 2TT
{j.l.wyatt,p.sun}@cs.bham.ac.uk
http://www.cs.bham.ac.uk/~jlw/

Abstract. We study how the error of an ensemble regression estimator can be decomposed into two components: one accounting for the individual errors and the other accounting for the correlations within the ensemble. This is the well known Ambiguity decomposition; we show an alternative way to decompose the error, and show how both decompositions have been exploited in a learning scheme. Using a scaling parameter in the decomposition we can blend the gradient (and therefore the learning process) smoothly between two extremes, from concentrating on individual accuracies and ignoring diversity, up to a full non-linear optimization of all parameters, treating the ensemble as a single learning unit. We demonstrate how this also applies to ensembles using a soft combination of posterior probability estimates, so can be utilised for classifier ensembles.

1 Introduction

It is well recognised that for best performance, an ensemble of estimators should exhibit some kind of disagreement on certain datapoints. When estimators produce class labels and are combined by a majority vote, this is the often cited, but little understood notion of "diversity". When in a regression framework, using estimators combined by a simple averaging operation, the notion of disagreement between estimators is rigorously defined: with a single estimator, we have the well known bias-variance trade-off [5], and with an ensemble of estimators, we have a bias-variance-covariance trade-off [10]. The regression diversity issue can now be understood quite simply: in a single estimator we have a two way trade-off, and in a regression ensemble the optimal "diversity" is that which optimally balances the bias-variance-covariance *three way* trade-off.

The understanding of regression ensembles is therefore quite mature. The understanding of classification ensembles, using a majority vote combiner, is

N.C. Oza et al. (Eds.): MCS 2005, LNCS 3541, pp. 296–305, 2005.

substantially less well developed; see [1] for a recent survey of the field. However, this lack of understanding can be partially side-stepped considering that a classification problem can be reformulated as a regression problem by approximating the class posterior probabilities. In this case the theory is more well developed—Fumera and Roli [4] represent the current state of the art and Kuncheva [8] provides an excellent overview of the area.

Though the bias-variance-covariance decomposition fully quantifies the regression diversity issue, a more well known result is the *Ambiguity decomposition* [7]. This paper will summarise recent work explaining the link between these decompositions, and show an alternative new decomposition. We will see how these decompositions can be exploited in a learning procedure.

The structure of this paper is as follows. in section 2 we show two ways in which the ensemble error can be decomposed: one that has been seen in the literature before, and one new to the literature. In section 3 we illustrate how these can be used in a learning procedure. In section 4 we present a theoretical analysis of the new decomposition and learning procedure. In section 5 we show emprical results and finally conclude with observations on possible future work.

2   Decomposing the Ensemble Objective Function

2.1   The Ambiguity Decomposition

Let us assume that the ensemble combination function is a mean of the M ensemble member outputs, that is $\bar{f} = \frac{1}{M} \sum_i f_i$. For convenience of notation we have omitted dependence on any particular input $\mathbf{x}$; it can be assumed f_i is the output of estimator i for a single arbitary input. The quadratic loss of this estimator from its target d is:

$$e_{ens} = (\bar{f} - d)^2 \tag{1}$$

The Ambiguity Decomposition [7], states that the ensemble error is *guaranteed to be lower than the average individual error at an arbitrary datapoint*. Formally, this is:

$$e_{ens} = (\bar{f} - d)^2 = \frac{1}{M} \sum_i (f_i - d)^2 - \frac{1}{M} \sum_i (f_i - \bar{f})^2 \tag{2}$$

$$= \qquad \bar{e} \qquad - \qquad \bar{a}$$

This illustrates that the correlations between the members is a fundamental part of the quadratic error. If we take the expected value of eq (1) with respect to all possible training sets of fixed size, then we have the *mean squared error*. The *bias-variance-covariance decomposition* [10] shows that this can be broken down into three components:

$$E\{(\bar{f} - d)^2\} = \overline{bias}^2 + \frac{1}{M} \overline{var} + \left(1 - \frac{1}{M}\right) \overline{covar} \tag{3}$$

The relationship between these two decompositions has been found [2] to be:

$$E\{\frac{1}{M}\sum_i (f_i - d)^2\} = \overline{bias}^2 + \Omega \tag{4}$$

$$E\{\frac{1}{M}\sum_i (f_i - \bar{f})^2\} = \Omega - \frac{1}{M}\overline{var} - \left(1 - \frac{1}{M}\right)\overline{covar} \tag{5}$$

where the interaction between the expected average error and the expected Ambiguity is the Ω term:

$$\Omega = \frac{1}{M}\sum_i E\{(f_i - E\{\bar{f}\})^2\}$$

$$= \overline{var} + \frac{1}{M}\sum_i (E\{f_i\} - E\{\bar{f}\})^2 \tag{6}$$

The Ambiguity decomposition is useful for a number of reasons, the primary one being that since the Ambiguity is target-independent, it provides a way to estimate generalisation error of an ensemble from *unlabelled data* [7].

2.2   An Alternative Decomposition

We note that the ensemble objective can also be decomposed as so:

$$e_{ens} = (\bar{f} - d)^2$$

$$= (\frac{1}{M}\sum_i f_i - d)^2$$

$$= \frac{1}{M^2}\sum_i \left[(f_i - d)\sum_j (f_j - d)\right]$$

$$= \frac{1}{M^2}\sum_i (f_i - d)^2 + \frac{1}{M^2}\sum_i (f_i - d)\sum_{j\neq i} (f_j - d) \tag{7}$$

Regarding now eq (4), a simple deduction can be made:

$$E\{\frac{1}{M^2}\sum_i (f_i - d)^2\} = \frac{1}{M}\left[\overline{bias}^2 + \Omega\right] \tag{8}$$

and therefore:

$$E\{\frac{1}{M^2}\sum_i (f_i - d)\sum_{j\neq i} (f_j - d)\}$$

$$= \left(1 - \frac{1}{M}\right)\left[\overline{bias}^2 + \Omega\right] - \Omega + \frac{1}{M}\overline{var} + \left(1 - \frac{1}{M}\right)\overline{covar} \tag{9}$$

It can be seen that through this new decomposition, part of the $\overline{bias}^2$ and Ω has "moved over" to the second term of the decomposition. This new decompoistion obviously does not share the useful target-independence property of the

Ambiguity decomposition—however, the decompositions do share another property which makes them interesting to exploit in a learning scheme. This will be the focus of the next section.

3   Using the Decompositions for Learning

3.1   A Useful Property of the Decompositions

If we were to train a *single* estimator, the error and associated gradient are:

$$e_i = (f_i - d)^2 \qquad \frac{\partial e_i}{\partial f_i} = 2(f_i - d) \tag{10}$$

In the previous section we described two ways to decompose the ensemble error in (1) into *two* additive components. The decompositions share the property that the first component is directly proportional to the error gradient of a single estimator. By this we mean that if we calculate the gradient of the first term on the right hand side of eq (2), we have:

$$\frac{\partial \frac{1}{M} \sum_i (f_i - d)^2}{\partial f_i} = \frac{2}{M}(f_i - d) = \frac{1}{M} \frac{\partial e_i}{\partial f_i} \tag{11}$$

and the same applies to the new decomposition we have proposed, in eq (7), we have:

$$\frac{\partial \frac{1}{M^2} \sum_i (f_i - d)^2}{\partial f_i} = \frac{2}{M^2}(f_i - d) = \frac{1}{M^2} \frac{\partial e_i}{\partial f_i} \tag{12}$$

Imagine now that we take one of the decompositions as our error function to minimise, and place a scaling parameter in front of its second component. So for the Ambiguity decomposition we would have:

$$e_{amb} = \frac{1}{M} \sum_i (f_i - d)^2 - \gamma \frac{1}{M} \sum_i (f_i - \bar{f})^2 \tag{13}$$

where the γ is our scaling parameter. If we set $\gamma = 0$, the search landscape will be exactly equivalent (aside of a constant $\frac{1}{M}$ factor) to that of a single estimator, meaning all the minima will be in the same locations. If we set $\gamma = 1$ such that the two components are balanced, this will be equivalent to training the ensemble as a single unit, albeit a very complicated unit. This allows us to test a simple hypothesis– *"on a given dataset, which is better: a single complex machine, or an ensemble of separately trained simpler machines?"*. With γ, we blend between the extremes—sometimes a simple ensemble will have best performance ($\gamma = 0$), and sometimes a single, complex machine ($\gamma = 1$) will prevail. This could also be interpreted as varying the *fit of the model* from few up to many degrees of freedom.

3.2   An Existing Training Scheme That Exploits the Property

Negative Correlation (NC) Learning [9] adds penalty terms of a particular form to the error function of an individual estimator. In the original heuristic formulation of NC, the penalty term existed in several different forms:

$$e_i^{(1)} = \frac{1}{2}(f_i - d)^2 + \gamma(f_i - \bar{f})\sum_{j \neq i}(f_j - \bar{f}) \tag{14}$$

$$e_i^{(2)} = \frac{1}{2}(f_i - d)^2 + \gamma(f_i - d)\sum_{j \neq i}(f_j - d) \tag{15}$$

$$e_i^{(3)} = \frac{1}{2}(f_i - d)^2 + \gamma(f_i - 0.5)\sum_{j \neq i}(f_j - 0.5) \tag{16}$$

The training scheme is implemented as follows:

1. Let M be the final number of predictors required.
2. Take a training set $z = \{(\mathbf{x}_1, d_1), ..., (\mathbf{x}_N, d_N)\}$.
3. For each training pattern in z from $n = 1$ to N do :
   - (a) Calculate $\bar{f} = \frac{1}{M}\sum_i f_i(\mathbf{x}_n)$
   - (b) For each estimator from $i = 1$ to M,
     perform a *single* update for each weight w in estimator i according to one of error functions (14), (15), or (16).
4. Repeat from step 3 for a desired number of epochs.   ◇

After training, for any new testing point the output of the ensemble is given by the simple average combination. The γ parameter controls a trade-off between the objective and penalty terms. With $\gamma = 0$ we would have an ensemble with each estimator training with plain gradient descent exactly equivalent to training a set of estimators independently of one another. If γ is increased, more and more emphasis would be placed on the correlations by minimising the penalty.

The first form in (14) has been thoroughly investigated in a regresssion setting [2]. This can be summarised by noting that $(f_i - \bar{f}) = -\sum_{j \neq i}(f_j - \bar{f})$, and therefore:

$$e_i^{(1)} = \frac{1}{2}(f_i - d)^2 + \gamma(f_i - \bar{f})\sum_{j \neq i}(f_j - \bar{f})$$

$$= \frac{1}{2}(f_i - d)^2 - \gamma(f_i - \bar{f})^2 \tag{17}$$

The similarity to the Ambiguity decomposition can be seen immediately. This link to the Ambiguity and Bias-Variance-Covariance decompositions allowed a solid grounding, as well as a proven upper bound on the γ penalty coefficient entirely *independent* of all parameters except M, the size of the ensemble [2]. In benchmarks against other ensemble techniques such as Mixtures of Experts, Adaboost.R1 and Bagging, it was found to be a competitive technique. The remaining two forms were not as well understood. However, noting our new decomposition, a slight rearrangement shows:

$$e_{new} = \frac{1}{M^2} \sum_i \left[(f_i - d)^2 + (f_i - d) \sum_{j \neq i} (f_j - d) \right] \tag{18}$$

An immediate similarity to (15) can be seen, though the exact relationship is not yet clear. This form of NC was found [9] to sometimes be more successful on classification problems, than the original penalty. In the next section we proceed to analyze the decomposition, in an attempt to identify why this penalty may have outperformed the original.

4   Gradient Analysis of the New Decomposition

We have seen that the quadratic error of the simple average ensemble estimator can be decomposed in two ways: the Ambiguity decomposition [7] and our new decomposition in eq (7). Now that we know the ensemble error can be viewed in a composite form (1) and two decomposed forms, we can calculate the gradients either way. The composite form gives a simple result of:

$$\frac{\partial e_{ens}}{\partial f_i} = (\bar{f} - d) \cdot \frac{1}{M} \tag{19}$$

Performing this instead starting from our new decomposed form shows more interesting results. Before we begin the calculation, we first break it into two components, where the first term concerns estimator i, and the second concerns all the other estimators $k \neq i$:

$$e_{ens} = \frac{1}{M^2} \left[\frac{1}{2}(f_i - d)^2 - \frac{1}{2}(f_i - d) \sum_{j \neq i}(f_j - d) \right]$$
$$+ \frac{1}{M^2} \sum_{k \neq i} \left[\frac{1}{2}(f_k - d)^2 - \frac{1}{2}(f_k - d) \sum_{j \neq k}(f_j - d) \right]$$

It should be of course noted that we have multiplied through by a constant $\frac{1}{2}$, as is usual in gradient descent training of MLPs, which were the estimator used in this paper, but the analysis applies in general to any estimator. The partial derivative of this result with respect to f_i is:

$$\frac{\partial e_{ens}}{\partial f_i} = \frac{1}{M^2} \left[(f_i - d) + \frac{1}{2} \sum_{j \neq i}(f_j - d) \right]$$
$$+ \frac{1}{M^2} \sum_{k \neq i} \left[\frac{1}{2}(f_k - d) \right]$$

Or rearranged:

$$\frac{\partial e_{ens}}{\partial f_i} = \frac{1}{M^2}\left[(f_i - d) + \frac{1}{2}\sum_{j\neq i}(f_j - d) + \frac{1}{2}\sum_{k\neq i}(f_k - d)\right] \tag{20}$$

We have omitted details of this calculation for space considerations, though it is fairly involved and recommended that the reader attempt it to give assurance of the result and implications described in the remainder of the section. If we examine the final derivative, ignoring the constant scaling factor of $\frac{1}{M^2}$, we see the ensemble gradient has been broken into three components, which we will now label and make use of. Gradient component "A" is:

$$A = (f_i - d) \tag{21}$$

Noting that the second and third components are identical (apart from the indices j and k we have chosen), we have gradient components "B" and "C":

$$B = C = \frac{1}{2}\sum_{j\neq i}(f_j - d) \tag{22}$$

Though they are identical, it can be seen from the breakdown we have given that "B" is contributed by the ith estimator, whereas the "C" component is contributed by the sum of the other estimators. Remembering the NC error, using the second penalty term, eq (15), we have:

$$\frac{\partial e_i^{(2)}}{\partial f_i} = (f_i - d) + \gamma\sum_{j\neq i}(f_j - d)$$

$$= \quad A \quad + \gamma(B + C)$$

Reintroducing the $\frac{1}{M^2}$ scaling factor, we note that when $\gamma = 1$ we have:

$$\frac{\partial e_{ens}}{\partial f_i} = \frac{1}{M^2}\frac{\partial e_i^{(2)}}{\partial f_i} \tag{23}$$

or rearranged:

$$\frac{\partial e_i^{(2)}}{\partial f_i} = M^2 \cdot \frac{\partial e_{ens}}{\partial f_i} \tag{24}$$

The gradient of the ith estimator's error function when using NC and setting $\gamma = 1.0$ is proportional to, but M^2 times steeper than the ensemble error gradient. This means that the minima will all be in the same locations in the search space, but indicates that a much faster convergence down the landscape should be observed, with the obvious consequence of possibly overshooting the minimum. At $\gamma = 0.5$, it exactly models the individual estimator's contribution to the ensemble error. However, since the estimators' outputs are combined, the errors cannot be assumed to be independent of one another; with $\gamma = 1.0$, it "simulates" the gradients of the remaining estimators, only possible because $B = C$.

5   Empirical Results

In the original experiments on NC [9], the penalty term in (15) was found to be more successful on classification problems. With our new knowledge on where the penalty is derived from, and noting that training was performed over a fixed number of iterations, we hypothesize that in fact the steepness of the landscape simply allowed faster convergence. We therefore engage in a short empirical test to verify this, using a dataset that NC is known to perform well on, the *Phoneme*

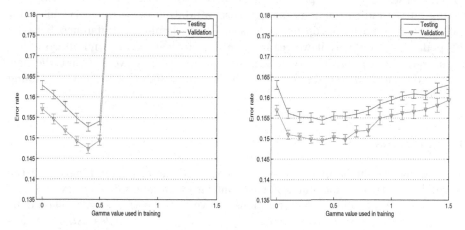

Fig. 1. Error using original penalty $(\bar{f})$ **Fig. 2.** Error using new penalty (d)

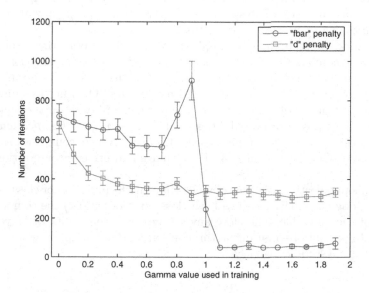

Fig. 3. Optimum number of training iterations

data [6]. A full empirical benchmarking of the new penalty is outside the scope of this paper.

We use an ensemble of 20 MLPs each with 6 hidden nodes. We perform a five-fold cross validation, using 1 fold for training, 1 fold as validation data for early stopping, and 3 folds as testing data. Training is stopped by monitoring validation data for a rise over a 500 epoch moving window, at this point weights are reset to the best point within the training period so far. Results are in figure 1 and 2, also indicating 95% confidence intervals. Results show statistically significant improvements in comparison to a simple ensemble, in both cases when γ is set optimally. The correlation between the validation and testing curves indicate it is possible to use validation error to select this γ for use on testing data. At optimal γ there is no significant difference between the penalties. However, if we regard figure 3, we can see the number of iterations required to converge to this minimum error: here we see that the new penalty does indeed converge much faster, in almost half the number of training iterations.

6   Conclusions

We examined what happens when we decompose the objective function of the ensemble into two components, one accounting for individual accuracy, and one accounting for the effect of correlations between the estimators. It should be noted *the decompositons in this paper applies only to ensembles using the simple average combination method, and a quadratic loss function.* We presented the Ambiguity decomposition [7], and a *new* alternative decomposition of the ensemble error. We showed how these decompositions have been exploited in a learning scheme, and used analysis of the error gradients to explain why one may outperform the other in certain situations.

In this work, we stated two assumptions which characterise the ensemble: a simple average combination function, and a quadratic loss error function. What happens when we use different assumptions? Are there decompositions when using other combiners, like the median and mode rules? Or other loss functions than quadratic? In classification, we are usually not interested in the quadratic loss from the true posterior probabilities - but more so in the *classification error rate*. This uses a *zero-one* loss function - are there analytic decompositions when this is the case? Current evidence [3] shows that an additive decomposition *does not exist.*

From this perspective, it seems obvious that any formulation of classification diversity will be intrinsically tied to 1) the loss function, and 2) the combination function, of the ensemble. Therefore any study citing the utility of "diversity" has a duty to present observations in this context, and not simply use "diversity" as if it were a mysterious panacea.

References

1. Gavin Brown, Jeremy Wyatt, Rachel Harris, and Xin Yao. Diversity creation methods: A survey and categorisation. *Journal of Information Fusion*, 6(1):5–20, March 2005.
2. Gavin Brown, Jeremy Wyatt, and Peter Tino. Managing diversity in regression ensembles. *Journal of Machine Learning Research*, 6, 2005.
3. J.H. Friedman. Bias, variance, 0-1 loss and the curse of dimensionality. Technical report, Stanford University, 1996.
4. Giorgio Fumera and Fabio Roli. Linear combiners for classifier fusion: Some theoretical and experimental results. In *Proc. Int. Workshop on Multiple Classifier Systems (LNCS 2709)*, pages 74–83, Guildford, Surrey, June 2003. Springer.
5. S. Geman, E. Bienenstock, and R. Doursat. Neural networks and the bias/variance dilemma. *Neural Computation*, 4(1):1–58, 1992.
6. University College London Neural Network Group. The Elena Project. http://www.dice.ucl.ac.be/neural-nets/Research/Projects/ELENA/elena.htm.
7. Anders Krogh and Jesper Vedelsby. Neural network ensembles, cross validation, and active learning. *NIPS*, 7:231–238, 1995.
8. Ludmila Kuncheva. *Combining Pattern Classifiers: Methods and Algorithms*. Wiley Press, 2004. ISBN 0-471-21078-1.
9. Yong Liu. *Negative Correlation Learning and Evolutionary Neural Network Ensembles*. PhD thesis, University College, The University of New South Wales, Australian Defence Force Academy, Canberra, Australia, 1998.
10. N. Ueda and R. Nakano. Generalization error of ensemble estimators. In *Proceedings of International Conference on Neural Networks*, pages 90–95, 1996.

Data Partitioning Evaluation Measures for Classifier Ensembles

Rozita A. Dara, Masoud Makrehchi, and Mohamed S. Kamel

Pattern Analysis and Machine Intelligence Laboratory,
University of Waterloo, Waterloo, Ont., Canada, N2L-3G1
{rdara, makrechi, mkamel}@pami.uwaterloo.ca

Abstract. Training data modification has shown to be a successful technique for the design of classifier ensemble. Current study is concerned with the analysis of different types of training set distribution and their impact on the generalization capability of multiple classifier systems. To provide a comparative study, several probabilistic measures have been proposed to assess data partitions with different characteristics and distributions. Based on these measures, a large number of disjoint training partitions were generated and used to construct classifier ensembles. Empirical assessment of the resulted ensembles and their performances have provided insights into the selection of appropriate evaluation measures as well as construction of efficient population of partitions.

1 Introduction

In the traditional pattern classification design strategies, experimental assessment of the performance of several classifiers, with the aim of selecting the best classifier, used to be considered. In a diversion from the traditional approach, the use of classifier ensemble has been proposed as an alternative technique to improve classification accuracy [1, 2]. The design of classifier ensemble can take place at four levels of data, feature, classifier and aggregation [3]. Most of the work in MCS has focused on developing new aggregation methods. In addition, the base classifiers and the architecture of the system have been the center of attention [4]. An alternative design methodology is based on training base classifiers using overlapped or disjoint feature subsets [5]. Moreover, another popular ensemble technique is accomplished by modifying input data (e.g. [6],[7]). There has been a lot of emphasis on this method, since it promotes diversity among individual classifiers [3].

The focus of this paper is on data level techniques. Data level partitioning strategies can be discussed from different perspectives. For example, from sharing point of view [8]. Majority of the methods use highly overlapped (shared) partitions to train the classifiers, while few others [9] apply disjoint subsets of the data. The latter approach is mostly used when dealing with large datasets. Another aspect of data level combining techniques is the type of information applied in the partitioning stage. Some methods, such as boosting and feature-

N.C. Oza et al. (Eds.): MCS 2005, LNCS 3541, pp. 306–315, 2005.
© Springer-Verlag Berlin Heidelberg 2005

based, use sort of a knowledge provided by the output of the classifiers to optimize the partitions. A key issue in this method is the computational effort required. Alternatively, some other techniques are based on random selection of data patterns, such as Bagging. Despite the significant number of theoretical and empirical studies on data partitioning methods, no criteria or guidelines for the use of different methods exist.

The present work introduces a novel direction in data level combining strategies. We suggest that a thorough understanding of the advantages and disadvantages of different data modification techniques will lead to more intelligent choices when designing MCS architectures. To achieve this goal, we first categorized data level combining techniques from a new perspective. Then, we proposed several correlation measures for training partitions, which will be discussed in the following sections. These measures were applied to estimate the degree and type of information provided by each partition. Through the splitting of the original training data using different class distributions and distances, we evaluated and compared the impact of different training partitions on the system performance. The main focus of this study was on the methods in which partitioning takes place independent of classifiers, filter approach, without a pass through training stage (Section 2). The empirical assessment of these measures has provided some insights into how training patterns are utilized in MCS system.

2   Categorization of Data Level Combining Techniques

Blum and Langley [10] have identified three types of feature selection methods: Embedded, Filter and Wrapper. We adopt the same terminologies for data and feature space partitioning in MCS. In this section, partitioning techniques are categorized into two groups: wrapper and filter approaches.

In the wrapper method, subsets are evaluated and partitioned based on the output of the base classifiers before making the final decision. Boosting and feature-based are methods that fall into this category. Boosting, proposed by Freund and Schapire, [6] is a popular method in which classifiers are built in sequence. At each step of boosting, training data for the next classifier is selected by assigning weights to data patterns that have been misclassified by the previous classifier. Kamel and Wanas [11] proposed an *evolving* training algorithm where base classifiers utilize the outcome of an aggregation method to rearrange the training subsets. Hierarchical Mixtures of Experts [12], and Learn++ [13] fit into the category of the wrapper approach, since partitioning depends on the output of the base classifiers. The wrapper approach has three drawbacks: *(i)* it is time demanding and expensive since the population of partitions has to be evaluated and optimized step by step before finalizing the training, *(ii)* decisions on base classifier and the MCS architecture have to be made in advance, and *(iii)* a powerful architecture and/or base classifiers may be traded off by the weakness of selected partitions.

In the filter method, however, subsets are partitioned before training. Bagging [7] is a well-recognized combining technique that partitions training data before constructing the base classifiers. Bagging presents each classifier with a set of data points sampled uniformly with replacement from the original data. The final classification decision is attained by taking the majority vote of the generated ensemble. K fold-corssvalidation is another example of filter approach. In this method, the training set is randomly divided into k subsets. Leaving one subset out, each classifier is presented with k-1 subsets for training. A more deterministic filter approach has been proposed in [14], where original training data is partitioned using clustering techniques. Each cluster is then used to train a new classifier. Filter method is less expensive and selection of the architecture and base classifiers does not have to be made in advance. However, the difficulty in this method is defining a cost function, which can estimate efficiency and capability of the generated partitions.

3   Data Partitioning Evaluation Measures

We developed and implemented several measures to evaluate partitions and their effects on MCS performance. These measures can be grouped into two main categories of feature-based and non-feature-based. In the non-feature-based measures, information provided by the feature space is not considered and only the class labels of training data are taken into account. While in feature-based methods, all measures are calculated based on the feature information. Non-feature-based measures have been previously discussed in [15]. The main focus of this paper is on feature-based measures. In addition to the mentioned categorization, we can apply the proposed measures at three levels of class, individual partition, and overall collection of partitions. We developed distance measures that utilized patterns from one class, *intraclass* distance, more than one class, *interclass* distance, one individual partition, *intra-partition* distance, and more than one partition, *inter-partition* distance. These categorizations are summarized in Table 1.

Table 1. Four Different Conditions for Location of Data Patterns

	same partitions	different partitions
same classes	intra-class intra-partition	intra-class inter-partition
different classes	inter-class intra-partition	inter-class inter-partition

3.1   Feature-Based Measures

Measure of distance can be used as a criterion to evaluate data partitioning schemes. Distance of the data patterns can be interpreted as *density*, within one class, or *correlation* between two classes or more. To calculate the distance of two sample points, the use of feature space of the data is inevitable. Therefore, all proposed measures in this section are addressed as feature-based. We employed Euclidean, Bhattacharyya, and Mahalanobis distance measures.

Euclidean Distance: The most popular and simple distance measure is Euclidean distance [16]. Defining a metric space, Euclidean measure is denoted as:

$$d_E = \sqrt{(\mathbf{x} - \mathbf{y})^T(\mathbf{x} - \mathbf{y})} \tag{1}$$

where $\mathbf{x}$ and $\mathbf{y}$ are feature vectors selected from spcific data populations. Each vector has n features, representing the dimension of the feature space.

Mahalanobis Distance: One drawback of Euclidean distance is that it does not consider the correlation between two features. Mahalanobis distance, on the other hand, takes into account the correlation of the features. The Mahalanobis distance between two feature vectors $\mathbf{x}$ and $\mathbf{y}$ are represented as:

$$d_M = \sqrt{(\mathbf{x} - \mathbf{y})^T \Sigma^{-1}(\mathbf{x} - \mathbf{y})} \tag{2}$$

where Σ is the within-group (pooled) covariance matrix of two samples. Σ is defined as

$$\Sigma = \frac{(n_x - 1)\Sigma_x + (n_y - 1)\Sigma_y}{n_x + n_y + 2} \tag{3}$$

where, n_x and n_y are the size of x and y samples, Σ_x and Σ_y are the covariance matrices of x and y accordingly.

Bhattacharyya Distance: Similar to Mahalanobis, Bhattacharyya distance measure is widely used as a measure of class separability, because of its precision and relation with the Bayes error [16].

$$d_B = \frac{1}{8}\sqrt{(x - y)^T (\frac{\Sigma_x + \Sigma_y}{2})^{-1}(x - y)} + \frac{1}{2}ln(\frac{|(\Sigma_x + \Sigma_y)/2|}{\sqrt{|\Sigma_x|.|\Sigma_y|}}). \tag{4}$$

Applying these distance measures, we can draw an overall evaluation value for a set of samples or partitions by averaging all pairwise distances in that population. Each population can belong to one of the following structures; *(i)* C_j^i, the jth class in the ith partition, *(ii)* P_i, the ith partition which consists of c classes, *(iii)* C_j, the jth class in the collection which is broken into m partitions, and *(iv)* the whole collection divided into m partitions. To calculate correlation of each of the mentioned structures, there are two options. We can either consider all patterns in the selected population and their distances from each other, or consider only center of that population. In the first approach, if a population consists of N samples, we need to calculate $\frac{N(N-1)}{2}$ distances. The second approach is much simpler, since instead of using pairwise measures, the distances of all samples from their own population center, or another population center, are calculated. This simplification reduces the number of operations to N distance measures.

The following notations are used through out the paper: μ_j^i or ν_j^i represent the mean (center) of the jth class in the ith partition and μ_j or ν_j the mean of the jth class. μ^i or ν^i is the mean of the ith partition, $x_{k,j}^i$ is considered as the feature vector of the kth sample of jth class in the ith partition, and $d(x, y)$ represent the distance between x and y. In addition, D_j^i is the correlation among the jth class in partition i, D_j is the correlation among class j, and finally, D^i is the correlation of ith partition. The number of partitions and classes are represented by m and c. n_{ij} is the number of samples in the jth class in i^{th} partition, M_i is the number of samples in partition i and N_j is the size of class j.

Intra-class, Intra-partition Distance: The population, in this category, consists of patterns from a specific type of class. Correlation is calculated as

$$D = \sum_{i=1}^{m} \sum_{j=1}^{c} p_{c_j} \sum_{k=1}^{n_{ij}} d(x_{k,j}^i, \mu_j^i), \quad p_{c_j} = \frac{n_{ij}}{M_i}. \tag{5}$$

Inter-class, Intra-partition Distance: Here, correlation among two or more classes in a partition is considered. We can either consider the actual patterns or their means. Their distances from the overall mean of partition can be considered as well.

$$D = \sum_{i=1}^{m} \sum_{j=1}^{c} p_{c_j} d(\mu^i, \mu_j^i), \quad p_{c_j} = \frac{n_{ij}}{M_i}. \tag{6}$$

Intra-class, Inter-partition Distance: Correlation of every class, which is broken down into m partitions, is the basis for evaluation. It is important to note that instead of the mean, μ, actual patterns can be used as well.

$$D = \sum_{j=1}^{c} \sum_{i=1}^{m} p_{p_i} d(\mu_j, \mu_j^i), \quad p_{p_i} = \frac{n_{ij}}{N_j}. \tag{7}$$

Inter-class, Inter-partition Distance: The overall correlation of a pool of partitions is calculated by considering the distances of $i)$ centers of all classes in the partition, or $ii)$ centers of all partitions from the overall mean.

$$D = \sum_{i=1}^{m} \sum_{j=1}^{c} d(\nu_j^i, \mu_j^i) \tag{8}$$

4   Experimental Setup

We carried out a set of experiments in order to assess the proposed evaluation measures and the impact of large set of partitions, generated with different distributions and distances, on generalization ability of the MCS. We considered all the previously discussed categories, including all three distance measure in four categories, either pairwise or non-pairwise, population center or actual patterns themselves, as well as all types of inter/intra class/partition measures. This section highlights a summary of the important observations.

We present the results for two of the benchmark datasets; both of them are available within the UCI Machine Learning Repository [18]. The first dataset is Pima Indians Diabetes, which contains 8 attributes and 2 classes. It includes 768 patterns with no missing values. The second one is again a real-world dataset, satimage, which contains 36 attributes, 6 classes and 6435 instances. Linear discriminant classifiers were used in the experiments. The use of stable classifiers was dictated by the need of obtaining consistent results by eliminating drastic fluctuation in the system performance caused by classifiers themselves. For the results presented in this paper, number of classifiers were set to 7 for diabetes and 9 for Satimage data. These selection of the ensemble sizes was based on the size and complexity of the data. The use of disjoint training subsets prohibited us from the use of larger ensembles. The product of the estimated posterior probabilities by the base classifiers was used as combining rule.

To examine our proposed measures, we considered disjoint subsets for training. Training subsets were obtained in a deterministic way, by opposing and controlling *bias* among partitions. Bias is defined as a fraction of a training data (%) that belongs to a specific group. In these experiments, bias was obtained by grouping training data based on the instances distances from the center of classes or training data itself. The initial set of partitions were obtained through opposing 100% bias to all partitions. Partitions with 100% bias was obtained by this procedure. We first sorted out the patterns based on their distance from center of the class or training data. We distributed the sorted patterns in such a way that first partition contained the largest distanced patterns, the second partition contained the second largest distanced patterns, and so on. It is important to note that the size of partitions has remained balanced through all the stages, as well as the type of class diversity. This set of partitions has remained the baseline for producing next sets of partitions by gradually reducing bias from 100% to 0% (Algo. 1).

Algorithm 1 Data Partitioning Evaluation Scheme

$b \leftarrow 10$
for $1 \leq b$,
  divide the data into training and test subsets, proportionally half and half
  determin the number of partitions, m
  initialize the first training partitions by forcing 100% bias (discussed above), p_0
  $bias \leftarrow 95\%$
  while *"bias is non-zero"*
   randomly select $(100 - bias)\%$ of the data, T_b
   construct new partitions based on the initial set of partitions p_0
   and distribute T_b among these subsets in such a way that there is no overlap
   $bias \leftarrow bias - step$; *step* is a predefined number
  end while
  calculate the correlation of all population of partitions using the measures discussed
  above train individual classifiers by partitioned training data and combine their
  outputs
end for

As discussed, we applied Euclidean, Mahalanobis, and Bhattacharyya distance measures to estimate correlation among training sets. Among all these measures, Euclidean distance has shown to have the largest inconsistency and fluctuations. The other two were more stable and demonstrated similar trends. Since feature-vectors do not have the same variance in each dimension, it is necessary to use a normalized distance measure. Mahalanobis, and Bhattacharyya have this property, as well as the fact that they are a good approximation of Bayes error.

The test error rates, y-axis, against correlation measures, x-axis, are summarized in Figures 1-3, for Pima and Satimage datasets. The presented results have been averaged over 10 different population sets. In addition, we evaluated the performance of generated partitions against bagging; presented as a straight line in all figures. Bagging was trained and tested with 20 classifiers and the same training and test sets that were used for the rest of the experiments. The average of 10 runs has been reported for bagging as well.

The effect of intra-class distance in each partition is depicted in Figures 1(a) and (b). As it is shown, the smaller the distance of instances get from their

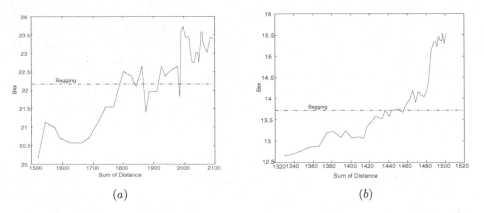

Fig. 1. Intra-class, Intra-partition Measure: a)Pima b)Satimage

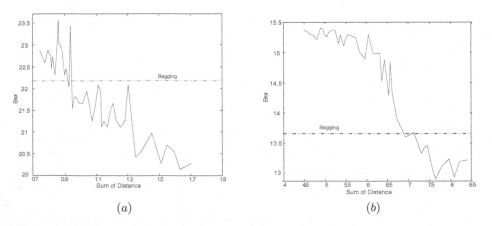

Fig. 2. Inter-class, Intra-partition Measure: a)Pima b)Satimage

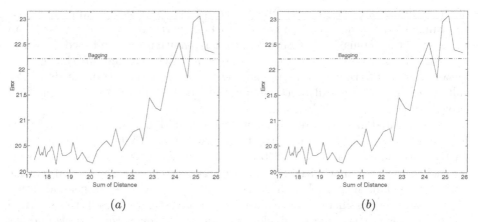

Fig. 3. a)Intra-class, Inter-partition Measure (Pima), b)Using Training Data Mean for Partitioning (Satimage)

mean (larger density), the more improvement can be seen in the accuracy. Similar investigation has been carried out among partitions, inter-partition measure. This time the mean of overall class in the training data has been considered, instead of the mean of the class in the partition (Fig. 3(a)). The error tends to increase with the increase of sum of the distances. This behaviour was expected in both cases, as it is well known in classical pattern recognition that larger class density increases the generalization ability. We also considered inter-class, intra-partition distance measures (Fig. 2 (a) and (b)). The overall trend in this case study was that larger inter-class distance resulted in lower error. This is due to the fact that by larger inter-class distance, the likelihood of having overlaps among classes decreases, which makes it easier for the system to distinguish different classes. As discussed before, patterns were forced to distribute either based on their distances from the mean of class or training data. By using the mean

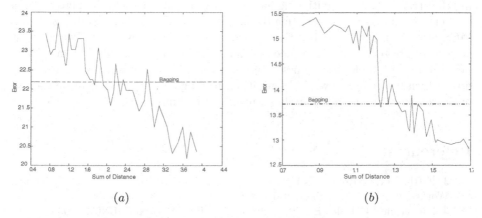

Fig. 4. Inter-partition Measure: a)Pima b) Satimage

of the training data (Fig. 3(a)), the pattern of change was the same, however, the range of difference between worst and best performance using class mean is larger, 2.6% versus 1.5%. Considering inter-partition feature-based measures (overall collection), we did not know what to expect when examining the distance between mean of training subsets and the mean of original training data. Results suggest that larger distances among the means improve MCS classification capability (Fig. 4(a) and (b)).

As illustrated in the figures, some of the generated disjoint partitions outperform bagging up to 2%. An important observation was that by examining each partition set individually, their distances, and their corresponding ensemble error, it became clear that initial partition set (generated with 100% bias) had the lowest error. This suggest that the larger the bias gets, the better generalization ability multiple classifiers obtain. More detailed investigation needs to be carried out to be able to make more reliable conclusions. However, the current findings promise to offer new design criteria for filter type partitioning strategy using feature-based measures.

5   Conclusion

In this paper, we proposed several feature-based distance measures, with which correlation among training partitions can be estimated. Using overall distance measures in different scopes of classes and partitions, large number of partitions were generated, and their impacts on classification accuracy were evaluated. It is important to note that we were not aiming at finding the best classification results. We were mostly searching for a linkage between data partitioning strategies, and performance of MCS. As a result, we used the simplest possible classification and aggregation algorithms to design ensemble members. The use of more sophisticated methods will be the focus of our future work.

The above observations support the notion that the proposed evaluation measures are beneficial in obtaining a nearly optimal partitioning solution, considering that training data partitioning based on these measures is less expensive than clustering and many other existing techniques. In addition, the results show that MCS error is a non-linear function of overall distance measure(s). Therefore, it is expected to be able to find some optimal or sub-optimal points in which MCS performance is at its best. These observations address an optimization procedure which is our future work. In addition, findings of this study can be used to optimize existing combining architectures and techniques.

References

1. J. Kittler and F. Roli, (Eds.), "Multiple Classifiers Systems", LNCS 3077, 5th Int. Workshop on MCS, Cagliari, Italy, 2004.
2. J. Kittler, and F. Roli, (Eds.), "Multiple Classifiers Systems", LNCS 2709, 4th Int. Workshop on MCS, Gambridge, UK, 2003.

3. L. Kuncheva, "Combining Pattern Classifiers: Methods and Algorithms", Wiley, 2004.
4. A. Sharkey, "Types of Multinet Systems," Third Int. Workshop on MCS, LNCS 2364 , Cagliari, Italy, , (2002) 108–117.
5. K. Tumer, and N. Oza, "Input Decimated Ensembles," Pattern Analysis and Applications, **6(1)**, (2003) 65-77.
6. Y. Freund, and R. Schapire, "Experiments with a New Boosting Algorithm," Proc. of the 13th Int. Conf. on Machine Learning, Bari Italy (1996) 148–156.
7. L. Breiman, Bagging Predictors. Machine Learning, **24(2)** (1996) 123–140.
8. R. Dara, and M. Kamel, "Effect of Sharing Training Patterns on the Performance of Classifier Ensemble," Proc. of Int. IEEE Conf. on System Man Cybernetics, The Hague, The Netherlands, (2004) 1220–1225.
9. N. Chawla, T. Moore, L. Hall, L. Bowyer, P. Kegelmeyer, and C. Springer, "Distributed Learning with Bagging-like Performance" Pattern Recognition Letters, 24 (2003) 455–471.
10. A. Blum, and P. Langley, "Selection of Relevant Features and Examples in Machine Learning", Artificial Intellignce, **97(1-2)**, (1997) 245–271.
11. M. Kamel, and N. Wanas, Data Dependence in Combining Classifiers. Fourth Int. Workshop on MCS, Guilford UK (2003) 1–14.
12. W. Jiang, and M. Tanner Hierarchical Mixtures of Experts for Generalized Linear Models. Neural Computation **11** (1999) 1183–1198.
13. D. Parikh, M. Kim, J. Oagaro , S. Mandayam and R. Polikar, "Combining classifiers for multisensor data fusion," Proc. of Int. IEEE Conf. on System Man Cybernetics, The Hague, The Netherlands, (2004), 1232–1237.
14. D. Frosyniotis, A. Stafylopatis, and A. Likas, "A Divide-and-Conquer Method for Mutli-Net Classifiers," Pattern Analysis and Applications, **6**, (2003) 32-40.
15. R. Dara, M. Makrehchi, and M. Kamel, " An Information-Theoretic Measure to Evaluate Data Partitions in Multiple Classifiers" Proc. of Int. IEEE Conf. on System Man Cybernetics, The Hague, The Netherlands, (2004) 4826–4831.
16. K. Fukunaga "Introduction to Statistical Pattern Recognition," Oxford University Press, 1990.
17. R. Duda, P. Hart, and D. Strok, "Pattern Recognition," John Wiley and Sons, 2000.
18. D. Blake, and C. Merz, UCI Repository of machine learning databases, [http://www.ics.uci.edu/ mlearn/MLRepository.html].

Dynamics of Variance Reduction in Bagging and Other Techniques Based on Randomisation

G. Fumera, F. Roli, and A. Serrau

Dept. of Electrical and Electronic Eng.,
University of Cagliari, Italy
{fumera, roli, serrau}@diee.unica.it

Abstract. In this paper the performance of bagging in classification problems is theoretically analysed, using a framework developed in works by Tumer and Ghosh and extended by the authors. A bias-variance decomposition is derived, which relates the expected misclassification probability attained by linearly combining classifiers trained on N bootstrap replicates of a *fixed* training set to that attained by a single bootstrap replicate of the same training set. Theoretical results show that the expected misclassification probability of bagging has the same bias component as a single bootstrap replicate, while the variance component is reduced by a factor N. Experimental results show that the performance of bagging as a function of the number of bootstrap replicates follows quite well our theoretical prediction. It is finally shown that theoretical results derived for bagging also apply to other methods for constructing multiple classifiers based on randomisation, such as the random subspace method and tree randomisation.

1 Introduction

Bagging [3] is the most popular method for constructing multiple classifier systems based on the "perturbing and combining" approach, which consists in combining multiple instances of the base classifier obtained introducing some randomness in the training phase. These methods seem to be effective in reducing the variance component of the expected misclassification probability of a classifier, and are thus believed to be effective especially for classifiers characterised by a high variance and a low bias, qualitatively defined by Breiman as "unstable", i.e. classifiers that undergo significant changes in response to small perturbations of the training set (or other training parameters). However it is not yet clear how exactly bagging affects the bias and variance of individual classifiers, and for what kind of problems and classifiers it is more effective. Theoretical investigations like [8, 4] focused only on regression problems, while analytical models for classification problems turned out to be more difficult to develop, especially because no additive bias-variance decomposition exists for them. Moreover, although several decompositions have been proposed so far [2, 5, 7, 14, 17], no general consensus exists about which one is more appropriate to analyse the behaviour of classification algorithms. Therefore, only experimental analyses of

N.C. Oza et al. (Eds.): MCS 2005, LNCS 3541, pp. 316–325, 2005.

bagging have been presented so far for classification problems [14, 16, 6, 10]. Empirical evidences seem to confirm that the main effect of bagging is to reduce the variance component of the expected misclassification probability, but some exceptions have been pointed out, for instance in [10]. Moreover, no clear definition of "instability" has been provided yet, directly related to the amount of variance reduction or to the performance improvement attainable by bagging, although some attempts have been made [16, 10].

In this paper we look at bagging from the perspective of the theoretical framework developed in works by Tumer and Ghosh [19, 20], and extended by Fumera and Roli in [9]. This model allows to evaluate the error reduction attainable by linearly combining the outputs of individual classifiers, and provides a particular bias-variance decomposition of the expected misclassification probability. Such decomposition accounts only for a fraction of the overall misclassification probability, and holds only under some assumptions. Nevertheless, we show that it can be exploited to analytically characterise the performance of bagging as a function of the number of bootstrap replicates N. This problem has not been considered so far in the literature. Indeed, bagging was proposed by Breiman as a method to approximate, using a single training set, an ideal "aggregated" predictor defined as the combination of the (possibly infinite) predictors obtained using all possible training sets of a fixed size. In practice, since there are m^m different and equiprobable bootstrap replicates of a given training set of size m, bagging itself is approximated using $N \ll m^m$ replicates. Bagging has been always analysed "asymptotically", i.e. for values of N sufficiently high to provide a good approximation of its theoretical definition. Empirical evidences showed that "asymptotic" values of N are between 10 and 50, depending on the particular data set and classifier used [3, 1, 16], that the performance of bagging tends to improve for increasing N until the "asymptotic" value is reached [16], and that such improvement is mainly due to variance reduction [3, 1]. However, the dynamics with which the performance of bagging reaches its "asymptotic" value has never been investigated. Under this viewpoint, we show that our theoretical framework provides a simple analytical relationship between the expected misclassification probability of bagging and that of an individual classifier trained on a single bootstrap replicate of a *fixed* training set. Such relationship shows that the performance of bagging improves as N increases, and this is entirely due to a reduction by a factor N of the variance of a single bootstrap replicate. We also show that our model theoretically supports the optimality of the simple average combining rule over the weighted average for classifiers generated by bagging. To the best of our knowledge, our model is the first to analytically characterise the dynamics of variance reduction attained by bagging as a function of the number N of combined classifers. Experiments carried out on the same data sets originally used in [3] support our theoretical predictions. The practical relevance of our results is that they provide a well grounded rule for choosing the number of bootstrap replicates N, which can be useful in applications characterised by strict requirements on computational complexity at operation time. Moreover, we show that our theoretical results are not limited to bagging, but hold for any method based on independently generating individual classifiers using the same randomisation process, like Ho's random subspace method [12] and Dietterich and Kong's tree randomisation [5].

2 Theoretical Analysis of Bagging

2.1 Expected Misclassification Probability of an Individual Classifier

Our analysis of bagging is based on the theoretical model developed in [19, 20], and extended in [9], which allows to analytically evaluate the reduction of the expected misclassification probability attainable by linearly combining the outputs of an ensemble of classifiers. This model considers classifiers that provide approximations $\hat{P}_k(\boldsymbol{x})$ of the class posterior probabilities $P_k(\boldsymbol{x})$ (where k denotes the class), and focuses on the expected value of the additional misclassification probability (from now on, added error) over Bayes error attained on a given boundary between any two classes i and j, in the case when the effect of using the approximated a posteriori probabilities is a shift of the ideal boundary. This situation is depicted in Fig. 1 for the case of a one-dimensional feature space. In the following we did not consider the case of multi-dimensional feature spaces, which is discussed in [18]. The approximation $\hat{P}_k(x)$ can be written as $P_k(x) + \epsilon_k(x)$, where $\epsilon_k(x)$ denotes the estimation error, which is assumed to be a random variable. One source of randomness in constructing a classifier (the one exploited by bagging) is the training set. Therefore, in the following we shall write the estimation errors by indicating explicitly their dependence on a training set t, as $\epsilon_i(x,t)$. However, we point out that all the following derivations hold also when other sources of randomness are considered (like the ones exploited by the random subspace method and by tree randomisation, or even random initial weights in neural networks). Under a first-order approximation of $P_i(x)$ and $P_j(x)$ around the ideal boundary x^*, and approximating the probability distribution $p(x)$ around the ideal boundary with $p(x^*)$, the additional misclassification probability for a given t turns out to be

$$z[\epsilon_i(x_b,t) - \epsilon_j(x_b,t)]^2 \ , \tag{1}$$

where x_b is the estimated class boundary (see Fig. 1), and z is a constant term equal to $\frac{p(x^*)}{2[P'_j(x)-P'_i(x)]}$ [19, 20, 13, 9]. It easily follows that the added error E_{add}, i.e. the expected value of eq. (1) over t, is

$$E_{\text{add}} = z[(\beta_i - \beta_j)^2 + \sigma_i^2 + \sigma_j^2 - 2\text{cov}_{ij}] \ , \tag{2}$$

where β_k and σ_k^2 denote the mean and variance (over t) of $\epsilon_k(x,t)$, $k = i,j$, while cov_{ij} denotes the covariance between $\epsilon_i(x,t)$ and $\epsilon_j(x,t)$, and it is assumed that such quantities do not depend on x around the considered class boundary.

We point out that eq. (2) can be viewed as a bias-variance decomposition, since it allows to express the added error as a function of the mean and variance

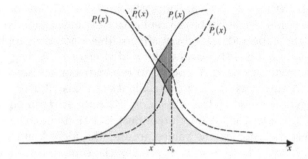

Fig. 1. True posterior probabilities around the ideal boundary x^* between classes i and j (solid lines), and estimated posteriors, leading to the boundary x_b, (dashed lines). Lightly and darkly shaded areas represent contribution of this class boundary to Bayes error and to additional misclassification error, respectively

over t of the estimated a posteriori probabilities provided by a classifier. Under this viewpoint, it is analogous to the decomposition given by Friedman for a fixed x in [7]. The difference between the decomposition (2) and others proposed in the literature [5, 2, 7, 17] is that it holds only under the assumptions explained above. Although these are quite strict assumptions as clearly explained in [13], they provide an additive decomposition which is not attainable in classification problems without any simplifying assumption, as shown in [7]. In the following we show how this decomposition can be exploited to analytically characterise the performance of bagging as a function of the number of bootstrap replicates.

2.2   Added Error of Linearly Combined Classifiers

Consider a linear combination $\hat{P}_k^{\text{ave}}(x)$ (by simple averaging) of the estimated a posteriori probabilities provided by N classifiers trained on different training sets $t_1, \ldots, t_N$, given by $\frac{1}{N} \sum_{m=1}^{N} \hat{P}_k^m(x) = P_k(x) + \frac{1}{N} \sum_{m=1}^{N} \epsilon_k(x, t_m)$. Under the same assumptions of Sect. 2.1, the additional misclassification probability on the same class boundary of Fig. 1 turns out to be

$$ z \left[\frac{1}{N} \sum_{m=1}^{N} \epsilon_i(x_{b^{\text{ave}}}, t_m) - \epsilon_j(x_{b^{\text{ave}}}, t_m) \right]^2 , \tag{3} $$

where z is the same as in eq. (1), while $x_{b^{\text{ave}}}$ is the estimated class boundary which can differ from that of a single classifier, x_b [19, 20, 13, 9].

We now focus on the case when the estimation errors of individual classifiers, $\epsilon_k(x, t_m)$, $m = 1, \ldots, N$, are i.i.d. random variables. This is the case of bagging: indeed, if $t_1, \ldots, t_N$ are bootstrap replicates of a *fixed* training set, then they are i.i.d. random variables since each one is made up of m samples drawn independently from the same distribution. This implies that also $\epsilon_k(x, t_m)$, $m = 1, \ldots, N$ are i.i.d. random variables. In this case, eq. (1) (which coincides to eq. (3) for $N = 1$) provides the misclassification probability of a classifier trained on a single bootstrap replicate t of the considered training set, and eq. (2) is the expected value over all possible bootstrap replicates, while the expected value of eq. (3) provides the added error of N bagged classifiers, over all possible realisations of N bootstrap replicates of the *same* training set. Since all the training sets $t_1, \ldots, t_N$ are identically distributed, also the estimation errors $\epsilon_k(x, t_m)$, $m = 1, \ldots, N$ in eq. 3 and $\epsilon_k(x, t)$ in eq. 1 are identically distributed. Under the assumption of Sect. 2.1 that the mean and variance of estimation errors are constant values around the ideal boundary x^*, it follows that each $\epsilon_k(x_{b^{\mathrm{ave}}}, t_m)$, $m = 1, \ldots, N$ has the same mean β_k and variance σ_k^2 as $\epsilon_k(x_b, t)$, while $\epsilon_i(x_{b^{\mathrm{ave}}}, t_m)$ and $\epsilon_j(x_{b^{\mathrm{ave}}}, t_m)$, $m = 1, \ldots, N$, have the same covariance cov_{ij} as $\epsilon_i(x_b, t)$ and $\epsilon_j(x_b, t)$, $m = 1, \ldots, N$. Moreover, since $\epsilon_k(x, t_m)$, $m = 1, \ldots, N$ are i.i.d., also $\epsilon_i(x_{b^{\mathrm{ave}}}, t_m) - \epsilon_j(x_{b^{\mathrm{ave}}}, t_m)$, $m = 1, \ldots, N$, are i.i.d. . It then follows that the added error $E_{\mathrm{add}}^{\mathrm{ave}}$ (the expected value of eq. (3)) with respect to the estimation errors is given by

$$E_{\mathrm{add}}^{\mathrm{ave}} = z \left[(\beta_i - \beta_j)^2 + \frac{1}{N}(\sigma_i^2 + \sigma_j^2 - 2\mathrm{cov}_{ij}) \right] . \tag{4}$$

It is worth noting that, according to the theoretical comparison between the simple and weighted average combining rules given in [9], based on the same theoretical framework considered here, the simple average is the optimal combining rule for classifiers generated by bagging, since the estimation errors of each classifier are i.i.d. .

2.3   Analysis of Bagging

In the previous section we obtained a bias-variance decomposition of the added error $E_{\mathrm{add}}^{\mathrm{ave}}$ of an ensemble of N classifiers trained on bootstrap replicates of a *fixed* training set (when the simple average combining rule is used), under the assumptions of Sect. 2.1. We showed that this decomposition relates the bias and variance components of N bagged classifiers to the ones of a classifier trained on a single bootstrap replicate. To the best of our knowledge, this is the first analytical model of the performance of bagging as a function of the number of bootstrap replicates N. Equations (2) and (4) show that the added error attained by N bagged classifiers has the same bias component of a classifier trained on a single bootstrap replicate, while its variance is reduced by a factor N. In other words our model states that, for a fixed training set, the expected performance of bagging always improves as N increases, and this is due only to variance reduction. This could seem an optimistic conclusion, since it is known that bagging does not always improve the performance of a classifier. However, we point out that the improvement predicted by our theoretical model does not refer to an individual classifier trained on the whole training set, but to an individual classifier trained on a single bootstrap replicate, where the expectation is taken over all possible bootstrap replicates of a fixed training set. In other words, the above result does not imply that bagging a given classifier always improves its performance, but only that, for any fixed training set, the expected performance of N bagged classifiers improves for increasing N. This qualitatively agrees with results like the ones in [16], where the performance of bagging was often found to improve for increasing N, even when an individual classifier (trained on the whole training set) outperformed bagging. Moreover, it also quantitatively agrees with the empirical observation that bagging more than 10 to 50 classifiers does not lead to significant performance improvements.

The above result can have a great practical relevance since it relates in a very simple way the performance improvement attainable by bagging to the number of bootstrap replicates N, and thus suggests a simple guideline to choose the value of N. Although the amount of the maximum reduction of the expected misclassification probability attainable by bagging is equal to the variance component, which is unknown in real applications, combining N bagged classifiers always provides an average reduction by a factor N of such component. This guideline can be useful in particular for applications characterised by strict requirements on the computational complexity at operation time, where it is necessary to find a trade-off between the potential performance improvement attainable by a combining method like bagging and the value of N. So far, this problem has been addressed through the development of techniques for selecting a subset of N classifiers out of an ensemble of $M > N$ classifiers generated by methods like bagging (see [16, 15, 11]). Selection techniques are aimed to keep the ensemble size small without worsening its performance [15, 11], or even to improve performance by discarding poor individual classifiers [16]. Under this viewpoint, our results do not directly allow to understand if selection techniques can be effective, since they provide only the *average* performance of an ensemble of N classifiers randomly generated by bagging. The improvement attainable by selection techniques depends instead on how much the performances of different ensembles of N classifiers change: the higher this difference, the higher the gain attainable by selecting a proper ensemble of N classifiers instead of a random ensemble.

2.4 Other Techniques Based on Randomisation

We point out that all the results discussed above do not apply only to bagging. Indeed, as pointed out in Sect. 2.2, the added error of N combined classifiers (3) is given by (4) whenever the estimation errors of different classifiers, $\epsilon_k(x)$, $k = 1, \ldots, N$ are i.i.d. random variables. Besides bagging, this is the case of any method for constructing classifier ensembles based on some randomisation process, in which the outputs of individual classifiers depends on i.i.d. random variables. For instance, this happens in the random subspace method [12], where each classifier is trained using a randomly selected feature subspace, in tree randomisation [5], where the split at each node is randomly selected among the k best splits, and even in the simple case of ensembles of neural networks trained using random initial weights. Therefore, the results of our analysis apply to all such techniques besides bagging. This opens an interesting perspective towards a unifying view of techniques for generating multiple classifiers based on randomisation.

3   Experimental Results

In this section we present an experimental evaluation on real data sets of the behaviour of bagging as a function of the number of bootstrap replicates N, and a comparison with the behaviour predicted by the theoretical model of Sect. 2. The experiments have been carried out on the same well known data sets used by Breiman in [3], i.e. Wisconsin breast cancer, Diabetes, Glass, Ionosphere, Soybean disease and Waveform. Decision trees have been used as base classifiers, and the linear combining rule (simple average) has been applied to the estimates of the a posteriori probabilities provided by individual trees. All data sets were randomly subdivided into a training and a test set of the same relative size as in [3]. To repeat the experiments, we constructed ten different training sets by randomly sampling without replacement a subset of the patterns from the original training set. Since we were interested in the expected error rate of bagging as a function of N, with respect to all possible realisations of N bootstrap replicates of a *fixed* training set, we estimated such value in each run by averaging over ten different sequences of N bootstrap replicates of the same training set, for $N = 1, \ldots, 50$ (where the value for $N = 1$ refers to a single bootstrap replicate). The values obtained in the ten runs were then averaged again.

In Figs. 2 and 3 we report the test set average misclassification rate and the standard deviation of bagging for $N = 1, \ldots, 50$, and of a single tree trained on the whole training set. We point out that the average misclassification rate of bagging as a function of N can not be directly compared to eq. (4), since the latter refers to a single class boundary, and is valid only under the assumptions of Sect. 2. However, as suggested by eq. (4), our aim was to investigate if the observed average overall misclassification rate of bagging as a function of N, $E(N)$, can be modeled as

$$E(N) = E_{\mathrm{B}} + \frac{1}{N} E_{\mathrm{V}} \ , \tag{5}$$

i.e. as the sum of a constant term and of a term decreasing as $1/N$, where $E_{\mathrm{B}} + E_{\mathrm{V}}$ is the average misclassification rate $E(1)$ of a single bootstrap replicate, E_{B} corresponds to the sum of the Bayes error and of the bias component, and E_{V} to the variance component. To verify this hypothesis, we fitted the curve of eq. 5 to the value of $E(1)$ for $N = 1$ (since we assume $E(1) = E_{\mathrm{B}} + E_{\mathrm{V}}$) and to the value of $E(50)$ for $N = 50$ (which should be the most "stable" value of $E(N)$), obtaining $E_{\mathrm{V}} = (1 - \frac{1}{50})[E(1) - E(50)]$, and thus $E_{\mathrm{B}} = E(1) - (1 - \frac{1}{50})[E(1) - E(50)]$. In Figs. 2 and 3 we report the curve $E_{\mathrm{B}} + \frac{1}{N} E_{\mathrm{V}}$ (dashed line), to be compared with the experimentally observed values of $E(N)$ (black circles), for $N = 2, \ldots, 49$.

From Figs. 2 and 3 we can see that, despite its simplicity, expression (5) fits quite well the average misclassification rate of bagging on five out of the six data sets considered, with the exception of Waveform for small N. On these five data sets, for values of N lower than 10, which are of great interest in practical applications, the deviation between the predicted and observed values of

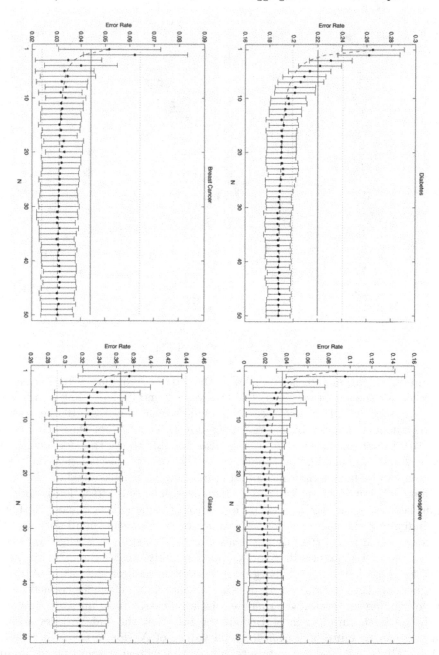

Fig. 2. Average test set misclassification rate of N bagged classifiers (black circles) for $N = 1, \ldots, 50$ (where $N = 1$ refers to a single bootstrap replicate), and standard deviation (shown as error bars). The dashed line represents the behaviour of the expected misclassification probability of bagging predicted by eq. 5. Horisontal lines represent the average misclassification rate (continuous line) and the standard deviation (dotted lines) of an individual classifier trained on the whole training set

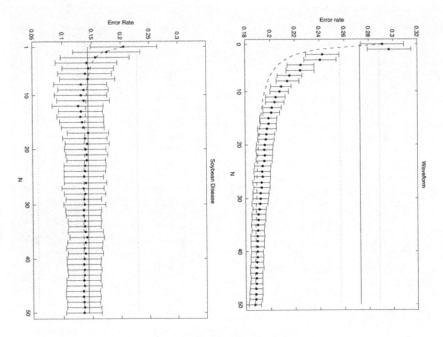

Fig. 3. See caption of Fig. 2

the misclassification rate is often lower than 0.01. A higher deviation can be observed for the smallest values of N (between 2 and 4, depending on the data set). Anyway, on all six data sets it is evident that for $N > 10$ the residual improvement attainable by bagging does not exceed 10% of that attained for $N = 10$, in agreement with eq. 5. It is also possible to see that for low N (between 2 and 5, depending on the data set) the average misclassification rate of bagging can be higher than that of an individual classifier trained on the whole training set, but becomes lower as N increases. The only exception is the Soybean data set, where the average performance of bagging is very close to that of the individual classifier even for high values of N. However, in all data sets the standard deviation of the misclassification rate of bagging is always lower than that of the individual classifier, for N approximately greater than 5. This means that, for a fixed training set, bagging N classifiers reduces the risk of obtaining a higher misclassification rate than using an individual classifier trained on the whole training set, even if the average misclassification rates are very similar as in the Soybean data set. In particular, the fact that the standard deviation of bagging can be quite high even for high values of N (for instance, it is about 0.04 on Glass and Soybean data sets) shows that classifier selection techniques could give a potential improvement, although no well grounded selection criteria has been proposed so far. Accordingly, the theoretically grounded guideline derived in this work can be considered as a contribution towards effective selection criteria.

References

1. Bauer, E., Kohavi, R.: An empirical comparison of voting classification algorithms: bagging, boosting, and variants. Machine Learning **36** (1999) 105–139
2. Breiman, L.: Bias, Variance, and arcing classifiers. Tech. Rep., Dept. of Statistics, Univ. of California (1995)
3. Breiman, L.: Bagging predictors. Machine Learning **24** (1996) 123–140
4. Buhlmann, P., Yu, B.: Analyzing bagging. Ann. Statist. **30** (2002) 927–961
5. Dietterich, T. G., Kong, E. B.: Machine Learning Bias, Statistical Bias, and Statistical Variance of Decision Tree Algorithms. Tech. Rep., Dept of Computer Science, Oregon State Univ. (1995)
6. Dietterich, T.G.: An experimental comparison of three methods for constructing ensembles of decision trees: bagging, boosting and randomization. Machine Learning **40** (1999) 1–22
7. Friedman, J.H.: On bias, variance, 0-1 - loss, and the curse-of-dimensionality. Data Mining and Knowledge Discovery **1** (1997) 55–77
8. Friedman, J.H., Hall, P.: On bagging and nonlinear estimation. Tech. Rep., Stanford University, Stanford, CA (2000)
9. Fumera, G., Roli, F.: A Theoretical and Experimental Analysis of Linear Combiners for Multiple Classifier Systems. IEEE Trans. Pattern Analysis Machine Intelligence, in press.
10. Grandvalet, Y.: Bagging can stabilize without reducing variance. In: Proc. Int. Conf. Artificial Neural Networks. LNCS, Springer (2001) 49–56
11. Banfield, H., Hall, L.O., Boweyer, K.W., Kegelmeyer, W.P.: A new ensemble diversity measure applied to thinning ensembles. In: Kittler, J., Roli, F. (eds.): Proc. Int. Workshop Multiple Classifier Systems. LNCS Vol. 2096, Spinger (2003) 306–316
12. Ho, T.K.: The random subspace method for constructing decision forests. IEEE Trans. Pattern Analysis Machine Intelligence **20** (1998) 832–844
13. Kuncheva, L.I.: Combining Pattern Classifiers: Methods and Algorithms. Hoboken, N.J., Wiley (2004)
14. Kohavi, R., Wolpert, D.H.: Bias plus variance decomposition for zero-one loss functions. In: Saitta, L. (ed.): Proc. Int. Conf. Machine Learning. Morgan Kaufmann (1996) 275–283
15. Latinne, P., Debeir, O., Decaestecker, C.: Limiting the number of trees in random forests. In: Kittler, J., Roli, F. (eds.): Proc. Int. Workshop Multiple Classifier Systems. LNCS Vol. 2096, Spinger (2001) 178–187
16. Skurichina, M., Duin, R.P.W.: Bagging for linear classifiers. Pattern Recognition **31** (1998) 909–930
17. Tibshirani, R.: Bias, variance and prediction error for classification rules. Tech. Rep., Dept. of Statistics, University of Toronto (1996)
18. Tumer, K.: Linear and order statistics combiners for reliable pattern classification. PhD dissertation, The University of Texas, Austin (1996)
19. Tumer, K., Ghosh, J.: Analysis of Decision Boundaries in Linearly Combined Neural Classifiers. Pattern Recognition **29** (1996) 341–348
20. Tumer, K., Ghosh, J.: Linear and order statistics combiners for pattern classification. In: Sharkey, A.J.C. (ed.): Combining Artificial Neural Nets. Springer (1999) 127–155

Ensemble Confidence Estimates Posterior Probability

Michael Muhlbaier, Apostolos Topalis, and Robi Polikar

Rowan University, Electrical and Computer Engineering,
201 Mullica Hill Rd., Glassboro, NJ 08028, USA
{muhlba60, topali50}@students.rowan.edu
polikar@rowan.edu

Abstract. We have previously introduced the Learn^{++} algorithm that provides surprisingly promising performance for incremental learning as well as data fusion applications. In this contribution we show that the algorithm can also be used to estimate the posterior probability, or the confidence of its decision on each test instance. On three increasingly difficult tests that are specifically designed to compare posterior probability estimates of the algorithm to that of the optimal Bayes classifier, we have observed that estimated posterior probability approaches to that of the Bayes classifier as the number of classifiers in the ensemble increase. This satisfying and intuitively expected outcome shows that ensemble systems can also be used to estimate confidence of their output.

1 Introduction

Ensemble / multiple classifier systems have enjoyed increasing attention and popularity over the last decade due to their favorable performances and/or other advantages over single classifier based systems. In particular, ensemble based systems have been shown, among other things, to successfully generate strong classifiers from weak classifiers, resist over-fitting problems [1, 2], provide an intuitive structure for data fusion [2-4], as well as incremental learning problems [5]. One area that has received somewhat less of an attention, however, is the confidence estimation potential of such systems. Due to their very character of generating multiple classifiers for a given database, ensemble systems provide a natural setting for estimating the confidence of the classification system on its generalization performance.

In this contribution, we show how our previously introduced algorithm Learn^{++} [5], inspired by AdaBoost but specifically modified for incremental learning applications, can also be used to determine its own confidence on any given specific test data instance. We estimate the posterior probability of the class chosen by the ensemble using a weighted softmax approach, and use that estimate as the confidence measure. We empirically show on three increasingly difficult datasets that as additional classifiers are added to the ensemble, the posterior probability of the class chosen by the ensemble approaches to that of the optimal Bayes classifier. It is important to note that the method of ensemble confidence estimation being proposed is not specific to Learn^{++}, but can be applied to any ensemble based system.

N.C. Oza et al. (Eds.): MCS 2005, LNCS 3541, pp. 326–335, 2005.

2 Learn^{++}

In ensemble approaches using a voting mechanism to combine classifier outputs, the individual classifiers vote on the class they predict. The final classification is then determined as the class that receives the highest total vote from all classifiers. Learn^{++} uses weighted majority voting, a rather non-democratic voting scheme, where each classifier receives a voting weight based on its training performance. One novelty of the Learn^{++} algorithm is its ability to incrementally learn from newly introduced data. For brevity, this feature of the algorithm is not discussed here and interested readers are referred to [4,5]. Instead, we briefly explain the algorithm and discuss how it can be used to determine its confidence – as an estimate of the posterior probability – on classifying test data.

For each dataset (D_k) that consecutively becomes available to Learn^{++}, the inputs to the algorithm are (i) a sequence of m training data instances $x_{k,i}$ along with their correct labels y_i, (ii) a classification algorithm **BaseClassifier**, and (iii) an integer T_k specifying the maximum number of classifiers to be generated using that database. If the algorithm is seeing its first database ($k=1$), a data distribution (D_t) – from which training instances will be drawn - is initialized to be uniform, making the probability of any instance being selected equal. If $k>1$, then a distribution initialization sequence, initializes the data distribution. The algorithm then adds T_k classifiers to the ensemble starting at $t=eT_k+1$ where eT_k denotes the number of classifiers that currently exist in the ensemble. The pseudocode of the algorithm is given in Figure 1.

For each iteration t, the instance weights, w_t, from the previous iteration are first normalized (step 1) to create a weight distribution D_t. A hypothesis, h_t, is generated using a subset of D_k drawn from D_t (step 2). The error, ε_t, of h_t is calculated: if $\varepsilon_t > \frac{1}{2}$, the algorithm deems the current classifier h_t to be too weak, discards it, and returns to step 2; otherwise, calculates the normalized error β_t (step 3). The weighted majority voting algorithm is called to obtain the composite hypothesis, H_t, of the ensemble (step 4). H_t represents the ensemble decision of the first t hypotheses generated thus far. The error E_t of H_t is then computed and normalized (step 5). The instance weights w_t are finally updated according to the performance of H_t (step 6), such that the weights of instances correctly classified by H_t are reduced and those that are misclassified are effectively increased. This ensures that the ensemble focus on those regions of the feature space that are yet to be learned. We note that H_t allows Learn^{++} to make its distribution update based on the ensemble decision, as opposed to AdaBoost which makes its update based on the current hypothesis h_t.

3 Confidence as an Estimate of Posterior Probability

In applications where the data distribution is known, an optimal Bayes classifier can be used for which the posterior probability of the chosen class can be calculated; a quantity which can then be interpreted as a measure of confidence [6]. The posterior probability of class ω_j given instance x is classically defined using the Bayes rule as:

Input: For each dataset D_k $k=1,2,...,K$
- Sequence of $i=1,...,m_k$ instances $\mathbf{x}_{k,i}$ with labels $y_i \in Y_k = \{1,...,c\}$
- Weak learning algorithm **BaseClassifier**.
- Integer T_k, specifying the number of iterations.

Do for $k=1,2,...,K$

    If k=1 **Initialize** $w_1 = D_1(i) = 1/m$, $eT_1 = 0$ for all i.

    Else Go to Step 5 to evaluate the current ensemble on new dataset D_k,

    update weights, and recall current number of classifiers $\rightarrow eT_k = \sum_{j=1}^{k-1} T_j$

Do for $t=eT_k+1,\ eT_k+2,...,\ eT_k+T_k$:

    1. Set $D_t = w_t \Big/ \sum_{i=1}^{m} w_t(i)$ so that D_t is a distribution.

    2. **Call BaseClassifier** with a subset of D_k randomly chosen using D_t.

    3. Obtain $h_t : X \rightarrow Y$, and calculate its error: $\varepsilon_t = \sum_{i:h_t(\mathbf{x}_i)\neq y_i} D_t(i)$

    If $\varepsilon_t > \frac{1}{2}$, discard h_t and go to step 2. Otherwise, compute

    normalized error as $\beta_t = \varepsilon_t / (1-\varepsilon_t)$.

    4. Call weighted majority voting to obtain the composite hypothesis
$$H_t = \arg\max_{y\in Y} \sum_{t:h_t(\mathbf{x}_i)=y_i} \log(1/\beta_t)$$

    5. Compute the error of the composite hypothesis
$$E_t = \sum_{i:H_t(\mathbf{x}_i)\neq y_i} D_t(i)$$

    6. Set $B_t=E_t/(1-E_t)$, $0<B_t<1$, and update the instance weights:
$$D_{t+1}(i) = D_t \times \begin{cases} B_t, & \text{if } H_t(\mathbf{x}_i) = y_i \\ 1, & \text{otherwise} \end{cases}$$

Call weighted majority voting to obtain the final hypothesis.
$$H_{final} = \arg\max_{y\in Y} \sum_{k=1}^{K} \sum_{t:h_t(\mathbf{x}_i)=y_i} \log(1/\beta_t)$$

Fig. 1. Learn^{++} Algorithm

$$P(\omega_j \mid \mathbf{x}) = \frac{P(\mathbf{x}\mid\omega_j)P(\omega_j)}{\sum_{k=1}^{N} P(\mathbf{x}\mid\omega_k)P(\omega_k)} \tag{1}$$

Since class distributions are rarely known in practice, posterior probabilities must be estimated. While there are several techniques for density estimation [7], such techniques are difficult to apply for large dimensional problems. A method that can estimate the Bayesian posterior probability would therefore prove to be a most valuable tool in evaluating classifier performance. Several methods have been proposed for this purpose [6-9]. One example is the softmax model [8], commonly used with classifiers whose outputs are binary encoded, as such outputs can be mapped into an estimate of the posterior class probability using

$$P(\omega_j \mid x) \approx C_j(x) = \frac{e^{A_j(x)}}{\sum_{k=1}^{N} e^{A_k(x)}} \tag{2}$$

where $A_j(x)$ represents the output for class j, and N is the number of classes. $C_j(x)$ is then the confidence of the classifier in predicting class ω_j for instance x, which is an estimate of the posterior probability $P(\omega_j|x)$. The softmax function essentially takes the exponential of the output and normalizes it to [0 1] range by summing over the exponentials of all outputs. This model is generally believed to provide good estimates if the classifier is well trained using sufficiently dense training data.

In an effort to generate a measure of confidence for an ensemble of classifiers in general, and for Learn++ in particular, we expand the softmax concept by using the individual classifier weights in place of a single expert's output. The ensemble confidence, estimating the posterior probability, can therefore be calculated as:

$$P(\omega_j \mid x) \approx C_j(x) = \frac{e^{F_j(x)}}{\sum_{k=1}^{N} e^{F_k(x)}} \tag{3}$$

where

$$F_j(x) = \sum_{t=1}^{N} \left(\begin{matrix} \log(1/\beta_t) & h_t(x) = \omega_j \\ 0 & otherwise \end{matrix} \right) \tag{4}$$

The confidence, $C_j(x)$, associated with class ω_j for instance x is therefore the exponential of the sum of classifier weights that selected class ω_j, divided by the sum of the aforementioned exponentials corresponding to each class. The significance of this confidence estimation scheme is in its consideration of the diversity in the classifier decisions: in calculating the confidence of class ω_j, the confidence will increase if the classifiers that did not choose class ω_j have varying decisions as opposed to having a common decision, that is, if the evidence against class ω_j is not strong. On the other hand, the confidence will decrease if the classifiers that did not choose class ω_j have a common decision, that is, there is strong evidence against class ω_j.

4 Simulation Results

In order to find out if and how well the Learn++ ensemble confidence approximates the Bayesian posterior probability, the modified softmax approach was analyzed on three increasingly difficult problems. In order to calculate the theoretical Bayesian posterior probabilities, and hence compare the Learn++ confidences to those of Bayesian probabilities, experimental data were generated from Gaussian distribution. For training, 100 random instances were selected from each class distribution, using which an ensemble of 30 MLP classifiers were generated with Learn[++]. The data and classifier generation process was then repeated and averaged 20 times with randomly selected data to ensure generality. For each simulation, we also benchmark the results by calculating a mean square error between Learn[++] and Bayes confidences over the entire grid of the feature space, with each added classifier to the ensemble.

4.1   Experiment 1

A two feature, three class problem, where each class has a known Gaussian distribution is seen in Fig. 2. In this experiment class 1, 2, and 3 have a variance of 0.5 and are centered at [-1, 0], [1, 1], and [1, -1], respectively. Since the distribution is known (and is Gaussian), the actual posterior probability can be calculated from Equation 1, given the known likelihood $P(x|\omega_j)$ that can be calculated as

$$P(x \mid \omega_j) = \frac{1}{(2\pi)^{d/2} |\Sigma_j|^{1/2}} e^{-\frac{1}{2}\left[(x-\mu_j)^T \Sigma_j^{-1}(x-\mu_j)\right]} \tag{5}$$

where d is the dimensionality, and μ_j and Σ_j are the mean and the covariance matrix of the distribution from which j^{th} class data are generated. Each class was equally likely, hence $P(\omega_j)=1/3$. For each instance, over the entire grid of the feature space shown in Fig.2, we calculated the posterior probability of the class chosen by the Bayes classifier, and plotted them as a confidence surface, as shown in Fig.3a. Calculating the confidences of Learn[++] decisions on the same feature space provided the plot in Fig 3b, indicating that the ensemble confidence surface closely approximates that of the Bayes classifier.

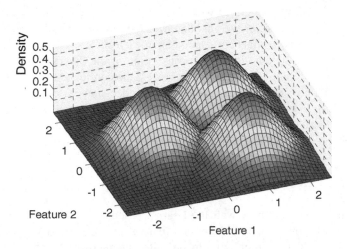

Fig. 2. Data distributions used in Experiment 1

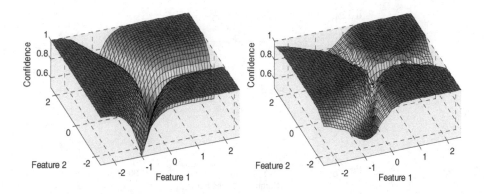

Fig. 3. (a) Bayesian and (b) Learn++ confidence surface for Experiment 1

It is interesting to note that the confidences in both cases plummet around the decision boundaries and approach 1 away from the decision boundary, an outcome that makes intuitive sense. To quantitatively determine how closely the Learn++ confidence approximates that of Bayes classifier, and how this approximation changes with each additional classifier, the mean squared error (MSE) was calculated between the ideal Bayesian confidence surface and the Learn++ confidence – over the entire grid of the feature space - for each additional classifier added to the ensemble. As seen in Fig.4, MSE between the two decreases as new classifiers are added to the ensemble, an expected, but nevertheless immensely satisfying outcome. Furthermore, the decrease in the error is exponential and rather monotonic, and does not appear to indicate any over-fitting, at least for as many as 30 classifiers added to the ensemble.

The ensemble confidence was then compared to that of a single MLP classifier, where the confidence was calculated using the MLP's raw output values. The mean squared error was calculated between the resulting confidence and the Bayesian confidence and has been plotted as a dotted line in Fig. 4 in comparison to the Learn++ confidence. The single MLP differs from classifiers generated using the Learn++ algorithm on two accounts. First, the single MLP is trained using all of the training data where each classifier in the Learn++ ensemble is trained on 2/3 of the training data. Also, Learn++ confidence is based on the discrete decision of each classifier. If there were only one classifier in the ensemble, "all" classifiers would "agree" resulting in a confidence of 1. Therefore, confidence of a single MLP can only be calculated based on the (softmax normalized) actual output values unlike Learn++ which uses a weighted vote of the discrete output labels.

4.2 Experiment 2

To further characterize the behavior of this confidence estimation scheme, Experiment 1 was repeated by increasing the variances of the class distributions from 0.5 to 0.75, resulting in a more overlapping distribution (Fig. 5) and a tougher classification problem.

Learn++ was trained with data generated from this distribution, its confidence calculated over the entire grid of the feature space and plotted in comparison to that of Bayes classifier in Fig. 6. We note that low confidence valleys around the decision boundaries are wider in this case, an expected outcome of the increased variance.

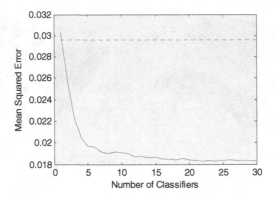

Fig. 4. Mean square error as a function of number of classifiers - Experiment 1

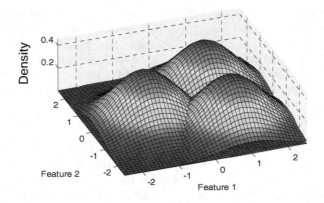

Fig. 5. Data distributions used in Experiment 2

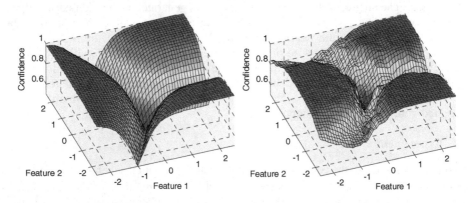

Fig. 6. (a) Bayesian and (b) Learn^{++} confidence surface for Experiment 2

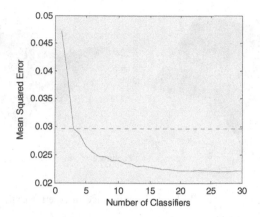

Fig. 7. Mean square error as a function of number of classifiers - Experiment 2

Fig.7 shows that the MSE between the Bayes and Learn^{++} confidences is once again decreasing as new classifiers are added to the ensemble. Fig. 7 also compares Learn^{++} performance to a single MLP, shown as the dotted line, as described above.

4.3 Experiment 3

Finally, an additional class was added to the distribution from Experiment 1 with a variance of 0.25 and mean at [0 0] (Fig. 8), making it an even more challenging classification problem due to additional overlap between classes.

Similar to the previous two experiments, an ensemble of 30 classifiers was generated by Learn^{++}, and trained with data drawn from the above distribution. The confidence of the ensemble over the entire feature space was calculated and plotted in comparison with the posterior probability based confidence of the Bayes classifier over the same feature space. Fig. 9 shows these confidence plots, where the Learn^{++} based ensemble confidence (Fig. 9b) closely approximates that of Bayes (Fig. 9a).

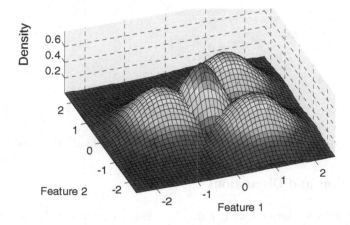

Fig. 8. Data distributions used in Experiment 3

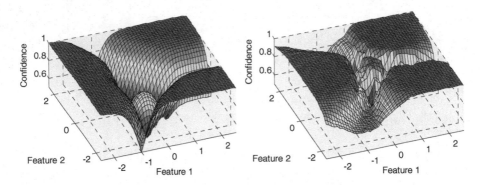

Fig. 9. (a) Bayesian and (b) Learn^{++} confidence surface for Experiment 3

Fig. 9 indicates that Learn^{++} assigns a larger peak confidence to the middle class than the Bayes classifier. Since the Learn^{++} confidence is based on the discrete decision of each classifier, when a test instance is presented from this portion of the space, most classifiers agree on the middle class resulting in a high confidence. However, the Bayesian confidence is based on the distribution of the particular class <u>and</u> the distribution overlap of the surrounding classes, thus lowering the confidence.

Finally, the MSE between the Learn^{++} confidence and the Bayesian confidence, plotted in Fig. 10, as a function of ensemble population, shows the now-familiar characteristic of decreasing error with each new classifier added to the ensemble. For comparison, a single MLP was also trained on the same data, and its mean squared error with respect to the Bayesian confidence is shown by a dotted line.

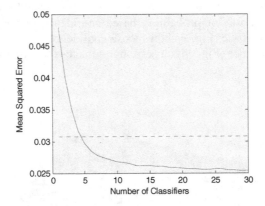

Fig. 10. Mean square error as a function of number of classifiers - Experiment 3

5   Conclusions and Discussions

In this contribution we have shown that the confidence of an ensemble based classification algorithm in its own decision can easily be calculated as an exponentially normalized ratio of the weights. Furthermore, we have shown - on three experiments of increasingly difficult Gaussian distribution - that the confidence calculated in this way approximates the posterior probability of the class chosen by the optimal Bayes classifier. In each case, we have observed that the confidences calculated by Learn^{++} approximated the Bayes posterior probabilities rather well. However, in order to quantitatively assess exactly how close the approximation was, we have also computed the mean square error between the two over the entire grid of the feature space on which the two classifiers were evaluated. We have plotted this error as a function of the number of classifiers in the ensemble, and noticed that the error decreased exponentially and monotonically as the number of classifiers increased; an intuitive, yet quite satisfying outcome. No over-fitting effects were observed after as many as 30 classifiers, and the final confidences estimated by Learn^{++} was typically within 2% of the posterior probabilities calculated for the Bayes classifier. While these results were obtained by using Learn^{++} as the ensemble algorithm, they should generalize well to other ensemble and/or boosting based algorithms.

Acknowledgement

This material is based upon work supported by the National Science Foundation under Grant No. ECS-0239090, "CAREER: An Ensemble of Classifiers Approach for Incremental Learning."

References

1. Kuncheva L.I. *Combining Pattern Classifiers, Methods and Algorithms*, Hoboken, NJ: Wiley Interscience, 2004.
2. Y. Freund and R. Schapire, "A decision theoretic generalization of on-line learning and an application to boosting," *Computer and System Sci.,* vol. 57, no. 1, pp. 119-139, 1997.
3. Kuncheva L.I., "A Theoretical Study on Six Classifier Fusion Strategies," *IEEE Trans. Pattern Analysis and Machine Intelligence*, vol. 24, no. 2, pp. 281–286, 2002.
4. Lewitt M. and Polikar R., "An ensemble approach for data fusion with Learn^{++}," *Proc. 4th Int. Work. on Multiple Classifier Systems*, (Windeatt T .and Roli F., eds.) LNCS vol. 2709, pp. 176-186, Berlin: Springer, 2003.
5. Polikar R., Udpa L., Udpa S., and Honavar V., "Learn^{++}: An incremental learning algorithm for supervised neural networks," *IEEE Trans. on System, Man and Cybernetics (C)*, vol. 31, no. 4, pp. 497-508, 2001.
6. Duin R.P., Tax M., "Classifier conditional posterior probabilities," *Lecture Notes in Computer Science*, LNCS vol. 1451, pp. 611-619, Berlin: Springer, 1998.
7. Duda R., Hart P., Stork D., In *Pattern Classification 2/e*, Chap. 3 &4, pp. 80-214, New York, NY: Wiley Interscience, 2001.
8. Alpaydin E. and Jordan M. "Local linear perceptrons for classification." *IEEE Transactions on Neural Networks* vol. 7, no. 3, pp. 788-792, 1996.
9. Wilson D., Martinez T., "Combining cross-validation and confidence to measure fitness," *IEEE Joint Conf. on Neural Networks*, vol. 2, pp. 1409-1414, 1999.

Using Domain Knowledge in the Random Subspace Method: Application to the Classification of Biomedical Spectra

Erinija Pranckeviciene[1,2], Richard Baumgartner[1] , and Ray Somorjai[1]

[1] Institute for Biodiagnostics, National Research Council Canada,
435 Ellice Avenue, Winnipeg ,Canada
{Erinija.Pranckevie, Richard.Baumgartner, Ray.Somorjai}
@nrc-cnrc.gc.ca
[2] Kaunas University of Technology, Studentu 50, Kaunas, Lithuania

Abstract. Spectra intrinsically possess domain knowledge, making possible a domain-based feature selection model. The random subspace method, in combination with domain-knowledge-based feature sets, leads to improved classification accuracies in real-life biomedical problems. Using such feature sets allows for an efficient reduction of dimensionality, while preserving interpretability of classification outcomes, important for the field expert. We demonstrate the utility of domain knowledge-based features for the random subspace method for the classification of three real-life high-dimensional biomedical magnetic resonance (MR) spectra.

Keywords: Random Subspace Method, biomedical spectra, feature selection, feature extraction, domain knowledge, PCA

1 Introduction

For complex classification problems, the use of multiple classifier systems (MCSs) usually leads to improved classification performance. An efficient method for building an MCS is the random subspace method (RSM) [1]. Even better classification accuracies can be achieved by introducing domain knowledge into the RSM, e.g., as discussed in a practical study of handwritten word recognition [2]. Recently, in a standard application of RSM to gene microarray data, a combination of RSM with feature selection was proposed as an area for further investigation [15].

Motivated by the ideas in [1] and [2], we investigate MCSs for classifying Magnetic Resonance (MR) spectra, while introducing domain knowledge into the RSM. The study on selection/extraction of informative spectral regions [3] also promotes the inclusion of domain knowledge into the spectral feature selection / classification rule. Domain knowledge distinguishes spectra from other types of data. A spectrum is a collection of peaks and valleys, whose positions and intensities carry discriminatory information because the physical / chemical basis of class separation is reflected in the peak / valley distribution and peak width. Correlation between adjacent spectral

N.C. Oza et al. (Eds.): MCS 2005, LNCS 3541, pp. 336–345, 2005.

features localizes the discriminatory information into spectral regions. We discover these spectral subregions through a Genetic-Algorithm (GA) -guided feature selection procedure [4]. The features are averages of spectral subregions. The objective of GA is to identify the optimal locations and sizes of these subregions that maximize the empirical classification accuracy provided by some classifier, such as Fisher's Linear Discriminant function. We shall call the set of discovered discriminatory patterns, comprised of the averaged spectral regions, the *domain feature (DF) set*.

The domain features obtained by GA generally exhibit *instability* because to the inherent randomness of initialization of the procedure: different GA runs produce different sets of domain features. These manifest as different discriminatory locations in the spectra. These unstable GA solutions are used to generate the input for the RSM. Preprocessing spectra by GA and assuming that the classification data model (LDA) applies, we expect significant reduction of dimensionality, accompanied by interpretable results, and without sacrificing classification accuracy. On three real-world datasets, we compare the spectral domain feature space in the RSM with 1) the feature space obtained from principal component analysis (PCA) and 2) the original, full-dimensional feature space.

The features obtained by PCA and by the genetic algorithm can be interpreted, using projections onto a lower dimensional linear subspace. For PCA, the subspace is spanned by the eigenvectors of the data covariance matrix. These eigenvectors give the directions of maximum variance and are obtained in an unsupervised way, i.e., independently of the class labeling. In the case of GA, for which the extracted features are averages of adjacent spectral intensities, the basis functions are boxcar functions. The width of the box corresponds to the segment of the spectrum to be averaged. Using GA for feature extraction is a realization of a best-basis algorithm for classification, utilizing domain knowledge. A similar interpretation of feature extraction was used in the related field of multi-spectral imaging [5]. Figure 1 illustrates the domain feature sets corresponding to the boxcar basis functions identified by GA.

Only a few publications discuss the applications of multiple classifier systems to the classification of MR spectra [6], [7], [8]. The current study is the first attempt to apply the RSM that incorporates spectral domain features for the classification of MR spectra. Section 2 introduces the data used in the study, section 3 provides details about the components of the MCS, section 4 contains the numerical results, and section 5 summarizes the outcomes of the investigation.

2 Data

Three real-world, two-class datasets were used. The datasets represent three levels of difficulty typically encountered in real-life biomedical data. D is the dimensionality of the data, N_1, N_2 are the total number of samples in class 1 and class 2, respectively. $Tr1+Tr2$ are the number of samples of class 1 and class 2 in the training set, and $Te1+Te2$ in the test set, respectively.

Dataset 1 consists of magnetic resonance (MR) spectra of pathogenic fungi (Candida albicans vs. Candida tropicalis). Dataset 1 was used in [9]. The characteristics of the dataset are: $D=1500$, $N_1=104$, $N_2=75$. $Tr1+Tr2=50+50$, and $Te1+Te2=54+25$.

Dataset 2 comprises MR spectra of biofluids obtained from normal subjects and cancer patients. Dataset 2 was used in [7] and [8]. The characteristics of the dataset are: $D=300$, $N_1=61$, $N_2=79$. $Tr1+Tr2=31+40$, and $Te1+Te2=30+39$.

Dataset 3 consists of MR spectra of biofluids obtained from patients with successful renal transplant vs. patients whose transplants were rejected. Dataset 3 was used in [10]. The characteristics of the dataset are: $D=3380$, $N_1=91$, $N_2=65$. $Tr1+Tr2=45+33$, and $Te1+Te2=46+32$. Dataset 3 represents a technically very difficult real-life problem.

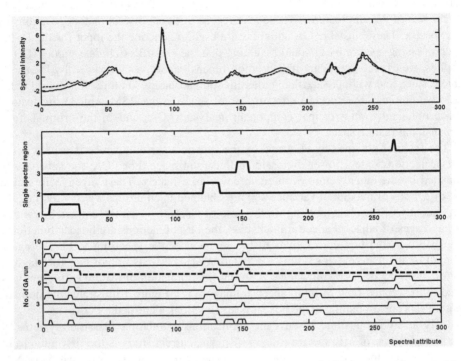

Fig. 1. Dataset 2. Representation of the correspondence of domain feature set with spectral locations. **Top panel**: The centroids of the spectral classes of Dataset 2 are represented by solid and dashed lines, respectively. **Middle panel:** The domain feature set obtained in one GA run is represented by the basis boxcar functions. **Bottom panel:** Feature sets are shown, obtained in 10 GA runs. The final feature set is a union of all single feature subsets found. Individual features are averages of the spectral attributes over the length of boxcar functions. The dashed line represents the combination of the four feature set basis functions of the middle panel

3 Methods

Different strategies exist for the design of a multiple classifier system for a particular problem. We investigate the Random Subspace method because of its simplicity and apparent effectiveness [1], [11].

3.1   Settings for the Random Subspace Method

The essence of the random subspace method is that feature subsets are selected randomly from the entire range of features. Then the base classifiers are trained on these randomly selected subsets. The procedure takes advantage of the randomness, thus inducing diversity in the ensemble of experts. The parameters of RSM are: the number of features in the subset, the number and type of base classifiers in the ensemble and the decision fusion rule. According to [1], increasing the number of experts is not very critical for the classification accuracies. However, the number of features is an important problem-dependent parameter. In our experiments we varied the number of features from 2 to 10, keeping the number of classifiers in the ensemble fixed at 31. Majority voting remains the most popular and effective among the fusion rules in the literature, particularly in a small sample size setting [11]. We used the majority voting fusion rule in our experiments. To avoid overoptimistic assessment of the classification methods under investigation due to selection bias, we used external crossvalidation [16].

3.2   Feature Spaces: PCA Features (FPCA) and Domain Feature (DF) Set

We considered the following feature spaces for the RSM: 1) the original features (full-dimensional data), 2) principal-components-based features, 3) the domain feature set.

PCA features are projections of the original feature vectors into the principal component space, spanned by the eigenvectors of the data covariance matrix. Feature extraction by PCA is the classical and established preprocessing method for data analysis [12]. We use as feature space (FPCA) only those projections corresponding to principal eigenvalues > 0.01. Total number of FPCA features used: Dataset 1 – 41, Dataset 2 – 55, Dataset 3 – 76.

The domain feature set is obtained by preprocessing the spectra by a genetic algorithm that identifies sets of discriminatory spectral regions. For each run of GA we request R discriminatory regions. We save the subset that provides the highest classification accuracy on the training set. The results of 10 runs are consolidated into a feature set containing $\leq 10R$ averaged spectral regions. This is our domain feature set. For the GA runs we used the following parameters: mutation rate 0.001, crossover rate 0.66, number of GA iterations 20.

3.3   Base Classifiers: 1-Nearest-Neighbor (1-NN) and L₂-Norm Linear SVM Classifier (L₂SVM)

The base classifiers (experts in the ensemble) were 1-nearest-neighbor classifiers and the L_2-norm linear SVM classifier. Nearest neighbor classifiers are amongst the simplest and yet quite powerful methods for classification problems for which the classes are not readily separable [12]. Support Vector Machines are currently considered the most successful state-of-the-art classifiers [13]. They use linear functions in the feature space. They are trained with a learning algorithm derived from a well-established optimization theory. They deal with the overfitting problem by using regularization during the training process. Only a small number of support vectors are involved in the classification. We used the SVM Matlab toolbox [14]. The diagram relating the basic blocks of the Multiple Classifier System is presented in Figure 2.

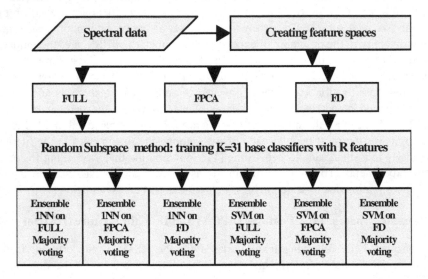

Fig. 2. Flowchart of the basic blocks of the Multiple Classifier System via the RSM. Spectral data are input to create three feature spaces: 1) the original features (full-dimensional data) **FULL**, 2) principal-components-based features **FPCA**, 3) the spectral domain feature set **FD**. These three feature spaces are used in the Random Subspace method for training the ensemble of classifiers. The base classifiers are 1-NN and L_2-norm linear SVM. Each of the K = 31 classifiers are trained by randomly selecting R features from the appropriate feature space. Outputs from the ensemble are combined using majority voting

4 Results

In this section we discuss the classification outcomes of the MCS. External crossvalidation was performed by 30 random partitioning of the samples into training and test sets. The baseline benchmark classification accuracy of the datasets is that of the L_2-norm linear SVM classifier on the original full dimensional data. Using external crossvalidation, the average benchmark test classification accuracies and their standard deviations are: **Dataset 1: 94.94% ± 2.21%; Dataset 2: 71.40% ± 4.25%; Dataset 3: 49.19% ± 5.70%.** The average classification accuracies for the three test sets, investigated via MCS using the RSM, are collected in Tables 1-3. For each R, the best results are in bold; bold italic is best overall.

Dataset 1 corresponds to two well-separable spectral classes. Increased classification accuracies were obtained by using the RSM with **L₂SVM** base classifiers on the FPCA and DF sets. When the base classifier is **1-NN**, increased accuracies were obtained with the FULL and DF sets. The classification accuracies achieved with MCS for Dataset 1 are comparable to the benchmark accuracy of L_2SVM without feature selection. For Dataset 1, even the PCA features performed well.

Table 1. Average classification accuracies and standard deviations for the test sets of Dataset 1

Ensemble: Average classification accuracies and standard deviations (%)								
Base classifier	Number of features R							
Feature Space	2	3	4	5	6	7	8	9	10
1-NN FULL	88.31 2.80	89.33 2.25	90.11 2.58	90.66 2.10	90.54 2.18	91.14 2.53	91.38 2.46	91.38 2.42	91.38 2.22
1-NN FPCA	87.64 2.19	88.97 2.86	89.63 2.461	89.75 2.46	90.17 2.50	90.60 2.73	90.72 2.60	90.72 2.72	90.72 2.51
1-NN FD	**89.87 3.69**	**92.59 2.95**	**92.28 3.12**	**92.04 3.23**	91.56 3.13	91.62 3.01	91.86 2.61	91.26 2.68	91.98 2.45
L₂SVM FULL	86.41 2.42	86.92 2.75	87.43 2.55	88.27 2.80	89.28 2.46	89.62 2.89	90.68 2.67	91.35 2.88	91.90 2.59
L₂SVM FPCA	87.05 2.48	89.71 2.44	90.51 2.27	91.27 2.36	**92.11 2.25**	**92.53 2.16**	**92.78 2.18**	**93.33 2.35**	93.59 2.23
L₂SVM FD	89.83 3.91	90.46 3.32	90.63 2.91	90.80 3.12	91.31 3.01	91.69 2.81	92.53 3.11	92.74 2.86	*93.80 2.79*

For Dataset 2, using the RSM with 1-NN and L₂SVM base classifiers on the FULL and DF sets, led to an increase of 1% to 3% in classification accuracy with respect to the benchmark. The L₂SVM base classifier performed better. FPCA features did not lead to improvement. The best classification accuracies achieved on Dataset 2 in other studies (without external crossvalidation) were: 81.2% [7] and 85.7% [8].

Table 2. Average classification accuracies and standard deviations for the test sets of Dataset 2

Ensemble: Average classification accuracies and standard deviations (%)								
Base classifier	Number of features R							
Feature Space	2	3	4	5	6	7	8	9	10
1-NN FULL	64.82 5.73	69.72 5.54	70.02 4.92	70.66 4.11	71.86 3.83	72.81 4.48	72.01 4.24	70.56 3.74	72.71 3.51
1-NN FPCA	63.37 6.17	66.92 5.94	67.87 5.17	67.17 3.86	68.12 4.57	67.92 5.19	67.87 5.35	68.62 5.33	67.87 5.14
1-NN FD	67.42 4.79	68.22 5.28	68.82 5.73	69.17 4.93	69.72 4.75	69.67 4.58	70.21 4.44	71.26 5.08	72.21 4.05
L₂SVM FULL	**71.45 4.38**	**74.01 3.75**	**74.25 4.61**	**74.20 3.68**	**74.20 3.70**	**74.11 4.25**	**73.86 3.56**	*74.40 4.21*	*74.40 3.87*
L₂SVM FPCA	63.91 6.62	65.90 4.91	68.41 4.91	69.61 4.21	69.08 3.74	70.00 3.49	70.39 3.89	70.34 3.40	70.72 3.56
L₂SVM FD	70.43 5.79	71.88 5.30	72.27 4.86	71.21 4.66	73.48 4.91	72.80 3.86	73.19 4.58	73.43 4.49	74.35 4.08

Dataset 3 represents a technically very difficult real-life problem. Using RSM with 1-NN and L_2SVM base classifiers on the FULL and DF sets led to an increase of 2% to 13% classification accuracy with respect to the benchmark. FPCA features failed again to produce an improvement. When using the domain feature set, we consistently observed an increase in classification accuracy. RSM with FD features was a clear winner in this classification problem, L_2SVM performing better for $R \leq 6$, 1-NN for R > 6. The best overall result was with two features, using L_2SVM (FD)

Table 3. Average classification accuracies and standard deviations for the test sets of Dataset 3

Ensemble: Average classification accuracies and standard deviations (%)									
Base Classifier	Number of features R								
Feature Space	2	3	4	5	6	7	8	9	10
1-NN FULL	51.32 5.77	51.67 5.51	53.08 4.98	50.94 5.95	51.84 4.41	53.42 5.53	50.94 5.58	52.74 6.35	51.84 5.74
1-NN FPCA	47.74 6.77	47.39 6.52	48.16 7.39	49.40 5.78	48.25 5.47	49.49 6.37	47.99 7.67	48.38 5.35	47.86 5.58
1-NN FD	56.71 5.45	54.96 5.77	57.09 5.42	54.91 4.97	54.91 5.83	**55.77** **5.79**	56.07 5.54	**56.07** **5.27**	**55.21** **5.46**
L_2SVM FULL	46.07 9.22	44.49 9.28	46.97 7.94	45.68 8.37	48.46 8.01	49.36 6.02	47.39 6.45	48.72 7.29	50.43 6.02
L_2SVM FPCA	41.79 8.47	41.11 8.72	40.85 7.78	41.79 8.62	41.20 8.16	41.88 7.42	41.62 7.87	42.22 7.24	42.27 7.91
L_2SVM FD	*63.21* *8.24*	**61.54** **7.77**	**57.48** **8.84**	**60.60** **6.42**	**56.45** **8.89**	54.74 7.87	**56.97** **9.11**	54.19 7.82	52.78 7.18

5   Conclusions

The aim of our study was to investigate the Random Subspace Method for classifying MR spectra, taking advantage of domain knowledge for feature selection, and applying MCS. We demonstrated on three real-world biomedical datasets that using domain features in the RSM leads to improved or comparable classification accuracies with respect to the benchmark. For difficult problems, features based on PCA are not efficient representations for spectral data, in agreement with [3]. We conclude that using domain feature sets in the RSM for MR spectra is beneficial because 1) the classification accuracies on domain features are as good or better than those obtained with the original features, 2) interpretability is preserved, very important for e.g., a clinician who is using spectral classification for prognosis/diagnosis, but would want to understand the biochemical causes of the disease. Neither principal component features nor the full-dimensional original data can provide the interpretable classification outputs that the domain features do.

We've tested the influence of using more classifiers in the ensemble. The results (not shown) suggest that there appears to be a positive correlation between the difficulty of classifying a dataset and the number of classifiers needed for improved MCS classification. Thus, for the easy Dataset 1 the best results are found with ≤ 35 classifiers, whereas the more difficult Dataset 2 typically requires a larger number of classifiers in the ensemble. This is true for the most difficult Dataset 3 as well (not shown). Similarly, increasing the number of features beyond the ten reported for Dataset 1, for five of the six feature space choices studied, the average classification accuracy does increase (not shown), and for both L_2SVM (Full) and L_2SVM (FD) even surpass the benchmark. In general, both the optimal number of features and the optimal number of classifiers in an ensemble are data-dependent, with a tendency towards requiring more classifiers for more difficult classification problems.

In this study, the L_2SVM base classifiers generally outperformed the 1-NN base classifiers in the ensembles.

Acknowledgment

The support of Natural Sciences and Engineering Research Council of Canada (NSERC) is gratefully acknowledged. We also thank the two reviewers for insightful suggestions that improved the manuscript.

References

1. Ho, T.K. The Random Subspace Method for Constructing Decision Forests. IEEE Transactions on Pattern Analysis and Machine Intelligence 1998; 20(8): 832-844.
2. Gunter S., Bunke H. Feature selection algorithms for the generation of multiple classifier systems and their application to handwritten word recognition. Pattern Recognition Letters 2004; (25): 1323-1336
3. Skurichina M., Paclik P., Duin R and et.al. Selection/extraction of spectral regions for autofluorescence spectra measured in the oral cavity. In: A. Fred et. al. (eds.) SSPR&SPR, 2004; LNCS 3138: 1096-1104
4. Nikulin A.E., Dolenko B., Bezabeh T. and Somorjai R. Near-optimal region selection for feature space reduction: novel preprocessing methods for classifying MR spectra. NMR in Biomedicine 1998; (11): 209-216.
5. Kumar S., Ghosh J. and Crawford M.M. Best–bases feature extraction algorithms for classification of hyperspectral data. IEEE Transactions on Geoscience and remote sensing 2001; 39(7):1368-1379.
6. Zhilkin P. and Somorjai R. Application of several methods of classification fusion to magnetic resonance spectra. Connection science 1996; (8) 3-4:427-424.
7. Raudys, S., Somorjai, R. and Baumgartner, R. Reducing the overconfidence of base classifiers when combining their decisions in: T. Windeatt and F. Roli (eds), MCS, 2003, LNCS 2709 : 65-73.
8. Somorjai R., Janeliunas A., Baumgartner R. and Raudys S. Comparison of two classification methodologies on a real-world biomedical problem. In T. Calli et. Al. (eds.) SSPR/SPR 2002 LNCS 2396: 433-441.

9. Himmelreich U., Somorjai R.L., Dolenko B., Lee O.C., Daniel H-M., Mountford C.E., et al. Rapid Identification of Candida Species Using Nuclear Magnetic Resonance Spectroscopy and a Statistical Classification Strategy. Appl Environ Microbiol 2003;(69):4566-74.
10. Somorjai R.L, Dolenko B., Nikulin A., Nickerson P., Rush D., Shaw A., Glogowski M., Rendell J. and Deslauriers R. Distinguishing Normal Allografts from Biopsy - Proven Rejections: Application of a Three - Stage Classification Strategy to Urine MR and IR Spectra. Vibrational Spectroscopy 2002; 28 (1): 97-102.
11. Skurichina M and Duin R.P.W. Bagging, boosting and the random subspace method for linear classifiers. Pattern Analysis and Applications 2002;(5):121-135.
12. Fukunaga K. Introduction to statistical pattern recognition . Academic Press, 1991.
13. Shawe-Taylor J. and Christianini N. Kernel Methods for pattern analysis. Cambridge university press, 2004.
14. http://www.igi.tugraz.at/aschwaig/software.html
15. 15 Bertoni A, Folgieri R, Valentini G. Bio-molecular cancer prediction problem with random subspace ensembles of support vector machines. Neurocomputing 2005, in press.
16. Ambroise C., McLachlan G.J. Selection bias in gene extraction on the basis of micrarray gene-expression data. Proc. Nat. Acad. Sci.USA 2002; 99(10):6562-6566.

Appendix: Formal Model for Domain Features and Search

Let N_1 and N_2 be the number of samples of *class 1* and 2, p: the original dimensionality of spectrum, i: the index of the ith spectrum, y_i: the class label of the ith sample, $y_i=\{+1,-1\}$, R: the number of components in the domain feature set, x_{iR}: the domain feature set, j: the class number. Let the vector x_{ij} denote the ith spectrum of the class j :

$$x_i^j = [x_{i1}^j,...,x_{ip}^j], \ j = \{1,2\}, \ p >> \max(N_1,N_2), \ i = 1,...,N_1 + N_2. \qquad (1)$$

A component of the domain feature set is computed as the average of an interval of spectral values:

$$x_{ir} = \frac{1}{r_2 - r_1 + 1} \sum_{k=r_1}^{r_2} x_{ik} \quad [r_1,r_2] \in [1,...,p], \ r_1 \leq r_2. \qquad (2)$$

The domain feature set for sample i is:

$$x_{iR} = [x_{i1},...,x_{ir}], \quad r < p, \ R < p, \ i = 1,...,N_1 + N_2. \qquad (3)$$

Our goal is to find x_R. We assume that adjacent attributes interact and that the class means are different. We model the domain feature set as a multivariate normal distribution. The two classes have a common covariance matrix. This model is known as the Gaussian Common Covariance Matrix model (GCCM). The class conditional distributions are:

$$p(x_R / class = 1) \sim N(m_1, \Sigma), \quad p(x_R / class = 2) \sim N(m_1, \Sigma). \qquad (4)$$

Fix the current domain feature set x_R at a particular iteration of the search procedure; then the *a posteriori* probability that sample i belongs to class j is:

$$p(class = j / x_{iR}) = \frac{q_j p(x_{iR} / class = j)}{\sum\limits_{j=1}^{2} q_j p(x_{iR} / class = j)}, \quad q_j = \frac{N_j}{N_1 + N_2}. \tag{5}$$

For a particular domain feature set, the sample means $\hat{m}_j$ and pooled covariance matrix $\hat{\Sigma}$ are estimated from the training data. These estimates are used to evaluate the class conditional probabilities of the domain features:

$$p(x_{iR} / class = j) = (2\pi)^{-\frac{1}{R}} \det(\hat{\Sigma})^{-\frac{1}{2}} \exp\!\left((x_{iR} - \hat{m}_j)\hat{\Sigma}^{-1}(x_{iR} - \hat{m}_j)^T\right). \tag{6}$$

Eq. (6) gives the *a priori* probability estimates for all samples and classes. These are used in estimating then *a posteriori* probabilities in Eq. (5). The objective function to be minimized during the search is the sum of squared differences between the *a posteriori* probability and the desired output:

$$J(x_R) = \sum\limits_{i=1}^{N_1+N_2} \left[(p(class = 1/x_{iR}) - y_i)^2 + (p(class = 2/x_{iR}) + y_i)^2 \right]. \tag{7}$$

The search procedure finds the optimal x_R among K candidates, based of the value of the objective function in Eq. (7):

$$x_R^* = \arg\min_{x_R} J(x_R^{\ k}), \quad k = [1,...,K]. \tag{8}$$

The number of candidates K and the stopping criterion T are parameters of the search procedure. The intervals $[r_1, r_2]$ of (2) are allowed to vary.

An Abnormal ECG Beat Detection Approach for Long-Term Monitoring of Heart Patients Based on Hybrid Kernel Machine Ensemble

Peng Li, Kap Luk Chan, Sheng Fu, and S.M. Krishnan

Biomedical Engineering Research Center,
Nanyang Technological University, Research Techno Plaza,
50 Nanyang Drive, XFrontiers Block, 6th Storey, 637553 Singapore
lipeng@pmail.ntu.edu.sg, {eklchan, msfu}@ntu.edu.sg

Abstract. In this paper, a novel hybrid kernel machine ensemble is proposed for abnormal ECG beat detection to facilitate long-term monitoring of heart patients. A binary SVM is trained using ECG beats from different patients to adapt to the reference values based on the general patient population. A one-class SVM is trained using only normal ECG beats from a specific patient to adapt to the specific reference value of the patient. Trained using different data sets, these two SVMs usually perform differently in classifying ECG beats of that specific patient. Therefore, integration of the two types of SVMs is expected to perform better than using either of them separately and that improving the generalization. Experimental results using MIT/BIH arrhythmia ECG database show good performance of our proposed ensemble and support its feasibility in practical clinical application.

1   Introduction

Electrocardiographic (ECG) signal is a recording of the cardiac activities, which is usually used by cardiologists to obtain information about the performance of heart function. Some typical ECG beats are illustrated in Figure 1. The analysis of heart beat cycles in ECG signal is very important for long-term monitoring of patients' heart conditions at patients' homes through a telemedicine network. However, it is very costly for the cardiologists to analyze the ECG recording beat by beat because the ECG recording may last for hours. Therefore, it is justified to develop a computer-assisted technique to examine and annotate the ECG recording, so to facilitate review by doctors. This computer annotation will assist doctors to select only the abnormal beats for further analysis.

Many algorithms have been applied to ECG beat cycle analysis, such as Kohonen self-organizing map [1, 2], learning vector quantization [2], multilayer perceptron [4], neural-fuzzy system [5] and Support Vector Machines (SVMs) [6, 7]. One of the major challenges faced by these ECG beat recognition algorithms is the large variation in the morphologies of ECG signals from patient to patient. The ranges of "normal beat" are different among the patients, which leads to the

N.C. Oza et al. (Eds.): MCS 2005, LNCS 3541, pp. 346–355, 2005.

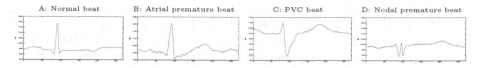

Fig. 1. Examples of ECG beats. A is a normal beat. The others are abnormal

so-called poor generalization problem, i.e., an ECG detector finely tuned to the training data from a large group of people may perform poorly when classifying the ECG beats of an individual patient. Hu et.al. attempted to solve this problem using a mixture of expert approach [2]. A mixture of expert structure was formed by combining the knowledge of a global expert trained using ECG data from a large database and a local expert trained using 3 to 5 minutes of ECG signals from a specific patient. The mixture of expert system was then used to classify the ECG beats from the specific patient, and the classification performance was improved over the global expert. However, the major drawback of such an approach is that a local expert has to be constructed for each patient, and the ECG recording of each patient has to be annotated by a doctor in order to train the local expert, even with only 5 minutes of a patient's ECG recording. Such annotation process is very costly and discourages the practical application of this approach [2, 3].

In this paper, a hybrid kernel machine ensemble approach is proposed to address such generalization problem. One-class Support Vector Classifier (νSVC) [8] is a one-class classifier whose goal is to find a decision region to include patterns from one class - called targets, and exclude the patterns from the other classes - called outliers. It is a non-discriminative recognition-based model. A particular advantage of νSVC is that it can be trained using data from one class only. In the context of long-term monitoring of some heart patients, the normal ECG beats usually dominate the ECG recordings, that is, the number of abnormal ECG beats is far less than that of the normal ones such as for patients suspected to suffer or suffering from asymptomatic heart failure, congestive heart failure, cardiac dysfunction etc. Furthermore, there are many kinds of abnormal ECG beats corresponding to different cardiac diseases, such as atrial premature beats, ventricular escape beats, fusion of ventricular and normal beats, supraventricular premature beats and premature ventricular contraction (PVC) beats, etc. Some of the typical abnormal beats and a normal ECG beat are illustrated in Figure 1. These abnormal ECG beats appear different in morphology. On the other hand, the normal ECG beats usually appear similar to each other and show less variation, which implies that the concept "normal" is more compact compared to that of the concept "abnormal" and thus easier to be learned using few samples. Since normal ECG beats can be easily obtained from patients, a νSVC can then be trained using only the normal ECG beats from each specific patient. Incorporated with the local information of the patient, such a trained νSVC can be used as a specific reference adapted to that patient. On the other hand, binary Support Vector Machines ($2SVC$) is known to be a powerful discriminative model [9]. It can be trained using a large database which consists of the ECG beats from a large group of people. Such a $2SVC$ incorporate the global information of the group of people, and thus it can be regarded as the reference values based on the general patient population. Due to different information learned by these two $SVMs$, they usually perform differently in classifying the ECG beats in the long-term ECG recording of the specific patient. Furthermore, νSVC is a non-discriminative recognition-based model and $2SVC$ is a discriminative model. Due to the complementary nature of such two types of $SVMs$, integration of the two types of kernel machines using an ensemble is expected to perform better than using either of them separately. Here Decision Template (DT) [10] is investigated as the fusion rule to integrate these two hybrid $SVMs$. Experimental results using MIT/BIH arrhythmia ECG database [11] show that our proposed patient-adaptable hybrid kernel machine ensemble outperforms both the local νSVC and the global $2SVC$. Compared to [2], such a hybrid kernel machine ensemble approach can relieve the doctors from annotating the ECG beats from each patient beat by beat and shows better or at least comparable performance to [2] and [3] in detecting the abnormal ECG beats of the specific patient without requiring annotated ECG from a specific patient, thus support its feasibility in practical clinical application.

2   Proposed Methodology

Figure 2 illustrates the flowchart of the proposed framework for ECG beat detection. The details are as follows.

2.1   Global Detector – Binary Support Vector Classifier

SVM is increasingly used in many medical applications and has been shown to achieve better performance than traditional classifiers [9]. SVM has good generalization ability by finding an optimal separating hyperplane which minimizes the classification errors made on the training set while maximize the "margin" between different classes. Given a two-class (labelled by $y_i = \pm 1$) training set

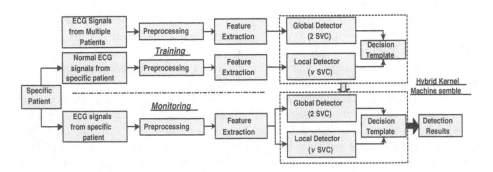

Fig. 2. Flowchart of the proposed framework for abnormal ECG beat detection

$X = \{x_i \in R^d | i = 1, 2, \cdots, N\}$ with N samples which are nonlinearly separable. The data are mapped to another feature space in which the data can be separated by an optimal separating hyperplane expressed as

$$f(x) = \sum_{i=1}^{N} y_i \beta_i K(x_i, x) + b \tag{1}$$

where b is a bias item, β_is $(i = 1, 2, \cdots, N)$ are the solution of a quadratic programming problem to find the maximum margin, $k(\cdot)$ is a kernel function, such as a Gaussian Radial Basis Function (RBF) kernel $k(x_i, x_j) = e^{\frac{-\|x_i - x_j\|^2}{\sigma}}$. There are only a few training samples whose β_is are non-zero, called the Support Vectors, which are either on or near to the separating hyperplane. The decision boundary, i.e. the separating hyperplane is along these support vectors, whose decision values $f(x)$ in (1) approach zero. Compared with the support vectors, the decision values of positive samples have larger positive values and those of negative samples have larger negative values. Therefore, the amplitude of the decision value can be regarded as the confidence of the SVM classifier. The larger the amplitude of $f(x)$, the more confident is the classification.

As a powerful discriminative model, $2SVC$ is very suitable as a global detector trained using ECG beats from a group of people. Recently, the application of SVM to ECG beat classification was investigated [6, 7]. These studies show that SVM can provide better classification performance than the other classifiers. In [7] only linear support vector machine was investigated. But the different classes of ECG beats may not be linearly separable. In [6] a multiple classifier network was introduced in which support vector machine was the basic classifier. But the selection of the hyperparameters was not investigated fully, which may limit the performance of SVMs. Therefore, there is still some scope to further improve the ECG beat classification using SVMs.

2.2   Local Detector – ν-Support Vector Classifier

ν–Support Vector Classifier (νSVC) is a kind of support vector machine [8] which can be used as an one-class classifier. Different from $2SVC$s, only data from one-class is used in the training of a νSVC, which makes it very suitable as a local detector to be trained using only "normal" ECG beats in the scenario of long-term monitoring of heart patients. νSVC is a recognition-based model rather than a discriminative model because it tries to estimate the support of the density of the target data [8]. Given a set of target data $X = \{x_i \in R^d | i = 1, 2, \cdots N\}$, the goal of νSVC is to find a decision function $f(x)$ such that most of the target data will have $f(x) \geq 0$ while most of the outliers will have $f(x) < 0$. The target data are mapped into a higher-dimensional space called feature space $\phi(x)$ in which the dot product can be computed using some kernel function, such as a RBF kernel. The mapped target data are separated from the origin corresponding the outliers with maximum margin using a hyperplane, which can be found by solving a quadratic programming problem [8]. The decision function corresponding to the hyperplane is

$$f(x) = \sum_{i=1}^{N} \beta_i K(x_i, x) + b \qquad (2)$$

Similar to $2SVC$s, the amplitude of the decision function of νSVC is proportional to the confidence of the classification.

There are two hyperparameters to be tuned in νSVC and $2SVC$ using RBF kernel, the width parameter of the RBF kernel and the regularization parameter where the latter is used to control the tradeoff of the errors. The hyperparameters of $2SVC$ can be optimized using cross validation on the training set. The values of the hyperparameters are chosen so that the error of both target class and outlier class on the validation set is minimized. As for νSVC, no information about the "abnormal" class is available. Such problem can be solved by generating artificial outliers [12]. Given a set of target samples, some outlier samples are generated randomly with the assumption that the outliers are uniformly distributed in a hypercube or hypersphere. The union of targets and generated outliers is used as a validation set. Some targets will be excluded by the decision boundary to make a tighter boundary. Therefore, the νSVC can be trained properly even if there are some abnormal ECG beats in the training samples.

2.3   Learning an Ensemble to Integrate Two Hybrid $SVMs$

Ensemble is often understood as mixture of experts, classifier fusion and combination of multiple classifiers, etc [10]. It is a mechanism to combine a set of classifiers so that the resulted ensemble has superior classification performance over the individual classifiers in the ensemble. The necessary condition to the success of the ensemble is that the outputs of individual classifiers to the same inputs must be diverse [13]. The diversity of the two classifiers can be evaluated using Plain Disagreement Measure (P) [14]:

- Plain Disagreement Measure (P): $P = \frac{N_{dis}}{N_{all}}$, where N_{dis} is the number of samples that two classifiers disagree and N_{all} is the number of all samples in the validation set. P varies from 0 to 1. The larger the value of P, the higher the diversity. This measure was recommended for ensemble feature selection in [14].

The diversity of the classifiers can be obtained by using different training set, feature subset, classifiers and ensemble rules. Since the νSVC and $2SVC$ are trained using local information and global information respectively, the training sets of such two kernel machines can be considered diverse. Furthermore, the different nature of the two $SVMs$ can help to increase the diversity further. Therefore, the ensemble of such two kernel machines is expected to improve the classification compared to either of the two $SVMs$.

Many fusion rules have been developed. In this study, Decision Template (DT) [10] was employed to integrate the two hybrid $SVMs$.

– Decision template: The decision template DT_j $(j = 1, 2)$ for class $y_j \in \{-1, +1\}$ is the average of the outputs of individual classifiers in the validation set to class y_j. The ensemble DT assigns an input x with the label given by the individual classifier whose Euclidean distance to the decision template DT_j is the smallest. The "normal" data from the specific patient and the generated artificial outliers can be used as a validation set so that the decision template of two $SVMs$ can be learned.

Oracle (ORA) is the optimal case or an upper bound which an ensemble can reach rather than a real ensemble. It assigns a correct class label to the pattern iff at least one individual SVM produces a correct class label [10]. Here it is used for comparison purpose only.

3 Experiments and Results

3.1 Data Preprocessing and Feature Extraction

The ECG signals come from 44 recordings of the original MIT/BIH ECG arrhythmia database [11]. The original signal consists of two leads sampled at $360Hz$. The data from lead 1 were used in this study. The signal was first processed using two averaging filters to suppress noises [15]. Then the baseline shift of the ECG signal can be obtained using two consecutive median filters whose widths are 200ms and 600ms respectively. The baseline was subtracted from the original signal and the resulted signal was then baseline-corrected [3]. The R-peak of the ECG signal can be detected using the first derivative of the ECG signal as in [15]. A window of 180 samples in length was taken to each ECG beats such that the window covers most of the information from a particular cardiac cycle, as shown in Figure 1. The signal in each window was then down-sampled uniformly to form a feature vector of 38-dimensions. It has been shown that R-R interval is useful in recognition of some abnormal ECG beats [2]. Therefore, it was also included in this study by appending it to the 38-dimensional feature vector. The length of the feature vector to represent the ECG beat is then 39. In order to deal with the variation of the amplitudes of ECG signals among the different patients, the feature vectors were divided by the mean value of R peaks in the training data of each patient, so that the maximum value of the each ECG window was around 1. The normalized ECG feature vectors were then used in the classification.

3.2 Training and Test Procedure

MIT/BIH arrhythmia ECG database consists of 48 annotated recordings from 47 subjects and each recording is about 30 minutes in length. The labels in the annotation file made by expert cardiologists are used as the ground truth in training and evaluating the classifiers. The ECG beats annotated as "normal" (NOR) are taken as the target class in the current research. All of the other

beats are regarded as outlier class or "abnormal" class, including atrial premature beats, nodal premature beats, premature ventricular contraction beats and
ventricular escape beats etc.

Four recordings (102, 104, 107, and 217) including paced beats of the MIT/BIH
arrhythmia database are excluded from the study. The ECG beats from the other
44 recordings were split into two parts. The training set of the global $2SVC$
beat detector consists of 4000 normal beats and 4000 abnormal beats from 22
recordings, which is called TN_G. Five-fold cross validation on TN_G was used to
select hyperparameters for $2SVC$. The ECG beats in each of the remaining 22
recordings were split into two subsets. The training sets of the local νSVC detectors were the normal beats from the first 5 minutes in each recording. Those
ECG beats of the remaining 25 minutes in each recording were used as the
test sets.

3.3   Evaluation Measures

Three measures are used to evaluate the performance of ECG beat classification, including sensitivity, specificity and balanced classification rate. *Sensitivity*
(SEN) is the fraction of abnormal ECG beats that are correctly detected among
all the abnormal ECG beats. *Specificity (SPE)* is the fraction of normal ECG
beats that are correctly classified among all the normal ECG beats. *Balanced*
Classification Rate (BCR) is the geometric mean of the SPE and SEN.
$BCR = \sqrt{SEN \cdot SPE}$. Only when both SEN and SPE have large value can
BCR has a large value. Therefore, the use of BCR can have a balanced performance in the evaluation of the classifiers which favors both higher SPE and
higher SEN. It is very suitable to this study since the data sets are imbalanced.

3.4   Experimental Results

The classification results of using global $2SVC$, local νSVC and the ensembles
are illustrated in Table 1, which are averaged over 22 test sets. The improved
$BCRs$ of the ensembles (DTs and $ORAs$) over the global $2SVC$ and local $\nu SVCs$
in the 22 test sets are illustrated in Figure 3. The relations between the improved
$BCRs$ of ensembles (DTs) over the global and local $SVMs$ and the plain disagreement measure are illustrated in Figure 4.

Table 1. Results (average ± standard deviation) of abnormal ECG beat detection

Classifiers	$2SVC$	νSVC	DT	ORA
BCR	0.774 ±0.280	0.881 ±0.146	0.912 ±0.132	0.971 ±0.048
SEN	0.808 ±0.287	0.819 ±0.210	0.876 ±0.195	0.964 ±0.075
SPE	0.819 ±0.252	0.972 ±0.051	0.967 ±0.055	0.980 ±0.044

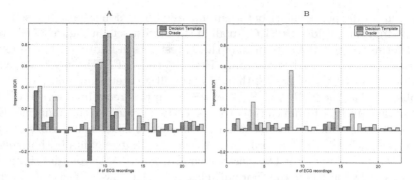

Fig. 3. The improved BCRs of the ensembles (DTs and ORAs) over the global $2SVC$ (A) and local νSVCs (B) of the 22 ECG recordings

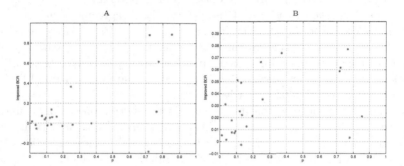

Fig. 4. The relation between the improved BCR of the ensembles (DTs) over the global $2SVC$ (A) and local νSVCs (B) and the plain disagreement measure

4   Discussions

It can be observed from Table 1 that the patient-adaptable kernel machine ensembles outperforms both the global $2SVC$ trained using large database TN_G after excluding the specific patients to be tested, and using the local νSVCs adapted to the specific patients. The improved average BCRs by the ensemble DT is 13.8% over the global $2SVC$ and 3.1% over the νSVCs. Furthermore, variance of the ensemble is less than either the global $2SVC$ or the local νSVC. This supports our claim that the hybrid kernel machine ensemble is superior than either the global $2SVC$ or the local νSVC in the abnormal ECG beat detection of the specific patients.

The local detector νSVCs outperform the global detector $2SVC$ in the abnormal ECG beat detection of the specific patients. The average BCR of the νSVC is 10.7% higher than that of the $2SVC$. It indicates that the local information is more important in the classification of the ECG beats from specific patient. Incorporation of such local information can help to deal with the difference between the distribution of training data and test data, hence help to improve the generalization.

The improved performance of the ensembles varies among the 22 test sets. The DT ensemble outperforms νSVCs in all of the 22 test sets in Figure 3 (B) and it outperforms the global $2SVC$ in 15 of the 22 test sets in Figure 3 (A). An exception is observed in the eighth recording. Here the BCR of DT is only 42.4% which is far less than 70.6% of $2SVC$, though it is still greater than 36.6% of νSVC. We observe that the SPE and SEN of νSVC in this recording were 100% and 13.4% respectively, which means that it correctly detected all the abnormal ECG beats but made a lot of false detection of the normal ECG beats. Since the performance of $2SVC$ in this recording is also not good, it may imply that there is a large overlap between the two class which prevents νSVC from discriminating the two class by modelling the "normal" class only. The low BCR of DT was then resulted from the low SEN of the local νSVC. Furthermore, there is a 6.0% gap in terms of BCR between the DT ensemble and the oracle which means there are still some space for further improvement of the DT ensemble.

It can be observed in Figure 4 that the plain disagreement measure is related to the improved BCRs. The larger the value of P, usually the more the improvement. However, there are only 22 test sets and the classification problem is different in each test set. Further testing is necessary to make the result more statistically reliable. This observation is roughly in agreement with [14] though it was used for ensemble feature selection purpose in [14].

Hu et.al. [2] concentrated on the classification between normal beats and ventricular ectopic beats using a mixture of two classifiers. The sensitivity and specificity achieved are 82.6% and 97.1%, which means it BCR is less than 90%. Philip et.al. [3] claimed to have achieved comparable performance to [2]. The BCR of our hybrid kernel machine ensemble is greater than 91% although only some "normal" ECG beats from each patient are used to train the local νSVCs. Therefore, our proposed method shows better or at least comparable performance compared to [2] and [3]. Another advantage of our method is that it can relieve the doctors from annotating the ECG beats one by one which is needed in [2].

5   Conclusion

In this paper, a new hybrid kernel machine ensemble is proposed to detect abnormal ECG beats for long-term monitoring of heart patients. A νSVC can be trained using only some "normal" ECG beats from a specific patient to obtain local information. A $2SVC$ can be trained using a large database which consists of ECG beats from many patients to obtain global information. Due to the different nature of two types of kernel machines, the ensemble of these two SVMs using decision template is able to outperform either of the two kernel machines in detecting the abnormal ECG beats from the specific patients. This approach can relieve the doctors from annotating the training ECG data beat by beat to train a local classifier and help improve the generalization. Experimental results using 44 ECG recordings of MIT/BIH arrhythmia database demonstrate the good performance of our proposed hybrid kernel machine ensemble and suggest its feasibility in practical clinical application.

Acknowledgements

The authors wish to acknowledge the support by Distributed Diagnosis and Home Healthcare project (D2H2) under Singapore-University of Washington Alliance (SUWA) Program in Bioengineering and Biomedical Engineering Research Center at Nanyang Technological University in Singapore. Also the first author would like to thank for the research scholarship from the School of Electrical and Electronic Engineering, Nanyang Technological University.

References

1. Vladutu, L., Papadimithou, S., Mavroudi, S., Bezerianos, A.: Ischemia detection using supervised learning for hierarchical neural networks based on kohonen-maps. Proceedings of the 23rd Ann. Inter. Con. of the IEEE EMBS. **2** (2001) 1688–1691
2. Hu Y. H., Palreddy S., Tompkins W. J.: A patient-adaptable ECG beat classifier using a mixture of experts approach. IEEE Trans. on Biomed. Eng. **44** (1997) 891–900
3. Philip de Chazal, O'Dwyer, M., Reilly, R.B.: Automatic classification of heartbeats using ECG morphology and heartbeat interval features. IEEE Trans. on Biomed. Eng. **51** (2004) 1196–1206
4. Guler I., Ubeyh E. D.: ECG beat classifier designed by combined neural network model. Pattern Recognition **38** (2005) 199–208
5. Engin M.: ECG beat classification using neuro-fuzzy network. Pattern Recognition Letters **25** (2004) 1715–1722
6. Osowski, S., Hoai, L.T., Markiewicz, T.: Support vector machine-based expert system for reliable heartbeat recognition. IEEE Trans. on Biomed. Eng. **51** (2004) 582–589
7. Millet-Roig, J., Ventura-Galiano, R., Chorro-Gasco, F.J., Cebrian, A.: Support Vector Machine for Arrhythmia Discrimination with Wavelet-Transform-Based Feature Selection. Computers in Cardiology (2000) 407–410
8. Scholkopf, B., Platt, J. C., Shawe-Taylor J., Smola, A. J., Williamson, R. C.: Estimating the support of a high-dimensional distribution. Neural Computation **13** (2001) 1443–1471
9. Cristianini, N., Shawe-Taylor, J. : An Introduction to Support Vector Machines. Cambridge University Press (2000)
10. Kuncheva, L., Bezdek, J., Duin, R.: Decision templates for multiple classifier fusion: an experimental comparison. Pattern Recognition. **34** (2001) 299–314
11. Massachusetts Institute of Technology: MIT-BIH Arrythmia ECG database. http://ecg.mit.edu/.
12. Tax, D. M. J., Duin R. P. W.: Uniform object generation for optimizing one-class classifiers. Journal of Machine Learning Research (2002) 155–173
13. Kuncheva, L. I., Whitaker, C. J.: Measures of diversity in classifier ensembles. Machine Learning**51** (2003) 181–207
14. Tsymbal A., Pechenizkiy M., Cunningham P.,: Diversity in search strategies for ensemble feature selection. Int. Journal on Information Fusion **6** (2004) 83–98
15. Christov, Ivaylo: Real time electrocardiogram QRS detection using combined adaptive threshold. BioMedical Engineering OnLine **3** (2004)

Speaker Verification Using Adapted User-Dependent Multilevel Fusion

Julian Fierrez-Aguilar, Daniel Garcia-Romero, Javier Ortega-Garcia,
and Joaquin Gonzalez-Rodriguez

Biometrics Research Lab./ATVS, Escuela Politecnica Superior,
Universidad Autonoma de Madrid, Campus de Cantoblanco,
C/ Francisco Tomas y Valiente 11, 28049 Madrid, Spain
{julian.fierrez, javier.ortega, joaquin.gonzalez}@uam.es

Abstract. In this paper we study the application of user-dependent score fusion to multilevel speaker recognition. After reviewing related works in multimodal biometric authentication, a new score fusion technique is described. The method is based on a form of Bayesian adaptation to derive the personalized fusion functions from prior user-independent data. Experimental results are reported using the MIT Lincoln Laboratory's multilevel speaker verification system. It is experimentally shown that the proposed adapted fusion method outperforms both user-independent and non-adapted user-dependent fusion approaches.

1 Introduction

The state of the art in speaker recognition has been widely dominated during the past decade by the Gaussian Mixture Model (GMM) approach working at the short-time spectral level [1]. Recently, new approaches based on Support Vector Machines (SVM) [2] are achieving similar performance, working also at the spectral level. These new techniques provide complementary information for the verification task, which has been exploited by the use of score fusion techniques [3].

On the other hand, higher levels of information conveyed in the speech signal have shown promising discriminative capabilities among speakers, and are a major goal of present speaker recognition research efforts. Some examples in this regard are the SuperSID project [4], and the MIT Lincoln Laboratory's (MIT-LL) speaker recognition system [5] applied to the 2004 NIST Speaker Recognition Evaluation (SRE) [6]. Since the inclusion of the extended data task in the 2002 NIST SRE, major advances have been done in finding, characterizing and modelling new high-level sources of speaker information. However, once the similarity scores from each individual system have been computed, little emphasis has been placed in developing new fusion approaches that take into account the speaker specificities [7].

Related works combining different sources of information for the person verification task are found in the multimodal biometric authentication literature [8].

N.C. Oza et al. (Eds.): MCS 2005, LNCS 3541, pp. 356–365, 2005.

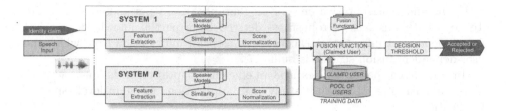

Fig. 1. System model of adapted user-dependent multilevel speaker verification

In this area, it has recently been shown [9, 10, 11, 12, 13] that using personalized fusion functions leads to improved verification performance, when some constraints on the number of training samples are considered. Motivated by the speaker specificities present in the speaker recognition problem [7], the present work is focused on studying user-dependent fusion techniques, and their application to multilevel speaker verification.

This paper is structured as follows. Related works on user-dependent fusion strategies found in the multimodal biometric authentication literature are reviewed in Sect. 2. A new adapted user-dependent score fusion strategy well suited to the common case of small training set size is described in Sect. 3 (see Fig. 1 for the system model). Experiments validating the proposed approach using the established multilevel speaker recognition system from MIT-LL on standard data from NIST SRE evaluations are reported in Sect. 4. Conclusions are finally drawn in Sect. 5.

2 User-Dependent Fusion in Biometric Authentication

The idea of user-dependent fusion in multiple classifier approaches for biometric authentication has probably been introduced in [9], and is receiving increasing attention in the multimodal biometric authentication literature [10, 11, 12, 13, 14, 15, 16].

In the preceding work [9], user-independent weighted linear combination of similarity scores was demonstrated to be improved by using user-dependent weights. A trained user-dependent scheme using support vector machines was subsequently presented in [10], also showing enhanced performance as compared to user-independent fusion. Other attempts to personalized fusion include: using the claimed identity index as a feature for Neural Network learning [14], computing user-dependent combination weights using lambness [7] metrics [15], learning user-dependent polynomial fusion functions [12], and using personalized score normalization techniques based on Fisher ratios [16] prior to user-independent fusion.

The use of general information in user-dependent fusion schemes has recently been introduced [11, 13]. The idea of adapted learning is based on the fact that the amount of available training data in user-dependent learning is usually not sufficient and representative enough to guarantee good parameter estimation. To cope with this lack of robustness derived from partial knowledge, general user-independent information is considered as prior information from which the user-dependent fusion scheme is built [17].

In the present paper, we describe an efficient adaptation technique based on Bayesian learning [13], and study its application to multilevel speaker verification.

3   Bayesian Adaptation for User-Dependent Fusion

Let the similarity scores $x \in \mathbb{R}$ provided by each one of the R individual systems be combined into a multilevel score $\mathbf{x} = [x_1, \dots, x_R]'$. Let the fusion training set be $X = (\mathbf{x}_i, y_i)_{i=1}^N$, where N is the number of multilevel scores in the training set, and $y_i \in \{\omega_0, \omega_1\} = \{\text{Impostor}, \text{Client}\}$. Impostor and client score distributions are modelled as the multivariate Gaussians $p(\mathbf{x}|\omega_0) = N(\mathbf{x}|\boldsymbol{\mu}_0, \boldsymbol{\sigma}_0^2)$ and $p(\mathbf{x}|\omega_1) = N(\mathbf{x}|\boldsymbol{\mu}_1, \boldsymbol{\sigma}_1^2)$, respectively[1]. The fused score s_T of a multilevel test $\mathbf{x}_T$ is defined as follows

$$s_T = f(\mathbf{x}_T) = \log p(\mathbf{x}_T|\omega_1) - \log p(\mathbf{x}_T|\omega_0) \tag{1}$$

which is known to be a Quadratic Discriminant function consistent with Bayes estimate for the case of equal impostor and client prior probabilities [18]. The score distributions are estimated using the available training data.

In the user-independent case, the global training set X_G includes scores from a pool of users, and the resulting global fusion rule, $f_G(\mathbf{x})$, is obtained by using the standard Maximum Likelihood criterion [18] for estimating $\{\boldsymbol{\mu}_{G,0}, \boldsymbol{\sigma}_{G,0}^2\}$ and $\{\boldsymbol{\mu}_{G,1}, \boldsymbol{\sigma}_{G,1}^2\}$. In the user-dependent case, a different local fusion function, $f_{j,L}(\mathbf{x})$, is obtained for each client enrolled in the system by using Maximum Likelihood estimates, $\{\boldsymbol{\mu}_{j,L,0}, \boldsymbol{\sigma}_{j,L,0}^2\}$ and $\{\boldsymbol{\mu}_{j,L,1}, \boldsymbol{\sigma}_{j,L,1}^2\}$, computed from a set of development scores X_j of the specific client j.

The proposed adapted fusion function, $f_{j,A}(\mathbf{x})$, trades off the general knowledge provided by X_G, and the user specificities provided by X_j, through Maximum a Posteriori density estimation [19]. This is done by adapting the sufficient statistics as follows [1]:

$$\begin{aligned}
\boldsymbol{\mu}_{j,A,i} &= \alpha_i \boldsymbol{\mu}_{j,L,i} + (1 - \alpha_i)\boldsymbol{\mu}_{G,i} \\
\boldsymbol{\sigma}_{j,A,i}^2 &= \alpha_i(\boldsymbol{\sigma}_{j,L,i}^2 + \boldsymbol{\mu}_{j,L,i}^2) + (1 - \alpha_i)(\boldsymbol{\sigma}_{G,i}^2 + \boldsymbol{\mu}_{G,i}^2) - \boldsymbol{\mu}_{j,A,i}^2
\end{aligned} \tag{2}$$

For each class $i = \{0 = \text{Impostor}, 1 = \text{Client}\}$, a data-dependent adaptation coefficient

$$\alpha_i = \frac{N_i}{N_i + r} \tag{3}$$

---

[1] We use diagonal covariance matrixes, so $\boldsymbol{\sigma}^2$ is shorthand for $\text{diag}(\boldsymbol{\Sigma})$. Similarly, $\boldsymbol{\mu}^2$ is shorthand for $\text{diag}(\boldsymbol{\mu\mu}')$.

is used [1], where N_i is the number of local training scores in class i, and r is a fixed relevance factor.

4 Experiments

4.1 Baseline Systems

In the present paper, the scores submitted by the MIT-LL [5] for the 2004 NIST SRE extended data task [6] are used. These scores were computed by using seven systems with speaker information from spectral level, pitch and duration prosodic behavior, and phoneme and word usage. These different types of information were modelled and classified using Gaussian Mixture Models (GMM), Support Vector Machines (SVM) and n-gram language models. In the following, a brief description of the main features of each individual system is presented:

MFCC_GMM. The system is based on a likelihood ratio detector with target and alternative probability distributions modeled by GMMs [1]. A Universal Background Model GMM is used as the alternative hypothesis model, and target models are derived using Bayesian adaptation. The techniques of feature mapping [20] and T-norm [21] are also used.

MFCC_SVM. The spectral SVM system uses a novel sequence kernel [2]. The sequence kernel compares entire utterances using a generalized linear discriminant. It uses the same front-end processing as the MFCC_GMM system.

PHONE_SVM. The SVM phone system uses a kernel for comparing conversation sides based upon methods from information retrieval. Sequences of phones are converted to a vector of probabilities of occurrences of terms, and co-occurrences of terms (bag of unigram, and bag of bigrams, respectively). A weighting based upon a linearization of likelihoods is then used to compare vectors for SVM training.

PHONE_NGM. A phone n-gram system was developed using the output of the MIT-LL phone recognizer. This system used the n-gram approach proposed in [22].

PROSODY_SLOPE. To capture prosodic differences in the realization of intonation, rhythm, and stress, the $F0$ and energy contours are converted into a sequence of tokens reflecting the joint state of the contours (rising or falling). A n-gram system is then used to model and classify distinctive token patterns from token sequences [23].

PROSODY_GMM. The aim of this system is to capture the characteristics of the $F0$ and short-term energy features distribution. This system is based on a likelihood ratio detector that uses adapted GMMs for estimating the likelihoods [24].

WORD_NGM. A word n-gram (idiolect) system was developed using the speech-to-text output from the BBN Byblos real-time system. This system used the idiolect word n-gram approach proposed in [22].

4.2   Database and Experimental Protocol

The experiments presented below were conducted on the 8sides-1side set of the 2004 NIST SRE corpus [6]. This database comprises conversational telephone speech in five different languages (English, Spanish, Russian, Arabic and Mandarin) over three different channels (cellular, cordless and landline), and four types of transducers (speaker-phone, head-mounted, ear-bud, and hand-held). Speaker models were trained with 8 single channel conversation sides of approximately five minutes total duration. Test segments consist of one side of the conversations. All trials were performed between two speakers of the same gender.

In order to provide a development set (DEV) for the experiments, data from Switchboard II phases $1-5$ were used to mimic the conditions in the 8sides-1side set of the 2004 NIST SRE corpus.

The following subsets of the 8sides-1side set were defined for the experiments:

ALL5. All speaker models with at least 5 genuine and 10 impostor attempts. In this way, ALL5 consists of 830 genuine and 4614 impostor attempts of 118 different speaker models.

COMMON5. All speaker models with > 75% of English enrollment, and at least 5 client and 10 impostor attempts. In this way, COMMON5 consists of 136 genuine and 378 impostor attempts of 19 different speaker models.

Three different types of experiments have been conducted:

User-Independent Fusion. Training on DEV data.

User-Dependent Fusion. For each user and each multilevel test score, 4 different genuine and 9 different impostor multilevel scores of the user at hand are randomly selected (different to the tested one). Local training is performed on the randomly selected multilevel scores. For each multilevel test score, 5 runs of the random sampling are performed.

Adapted User-Dependent Fusion. For each user and each multilevel test score, 4 different genuine and 9 different impostor multilevel scores of the user at hand are randomly selected (different to the tested one). Global training is performed on DEV data whereas local training is carried out on the randomly selected multilevel scores. For each multilevel test score, 5 runs of the random sampling are performed.

4.3   Results

Verification performance of the seven individual systems, along with various user-independent combinations, are given in Tables 1 and 2 for the ALL5 and COMMON5 datasets, respectively. Spectral level systems perform remarkably better than the other systems, and their combination with the high-level system WORD_NGM leads to enhanced performance. Worth noting, not all combinations provide improved performance over the best system, and the relative improvement between the best fused system and the best individual system is not

Table 1. Verification performance on **ALL5** dataset with **user-independent fusion** based on Quadratic Discriminant. EERs in %

information level	system label	individual performance	unilevel fusion	multilevel fusion		
				levels	best/level	all/level
1	MFCC_GMM	8.67		12	9.28	8.79
	MFCC_SVM	**7.70**	**7.39**	13	7.83	6.98
2	PHONE_SVM	16.90		14	7.46	**6.91**
	PHONE_NGM	22.16	18.21	123	9.05	8.07
3	PROSODY_SLOPE	20.86		124	8.98	8.25
	PROSODY_GMM	22.51	16.76	134	7.59	6.98
4	WORD_NGM	22.70		1234	9.19	7.96

Table 2. Verification performance on **COMMON5** dataset with **user-independent fusion** based on Quadratic Discriminant. EERs in %

information level	system label	individual performance	unilevel fusion	multilevel fusion		
				levels	best/level	all/level
1	MFCC_GMM	5.98		12	3.69	3.06
	MFCC_SVM	**3.06**	**3.56**	13	4.32	3.56
2	PHONE_SVM	10.31		14	3.56	**2.93**
	PHONE_NGM	18.32	10.94	123	3.56	3.56
3	PROSODY_SLOPE	22.14		124	4.32	**2.93**
	PROSODY_GMM	19.08	14.63	134	3.06	**2.93**
4	WORD_NGM	20.61		1234	3.56	3.19

very high (10% and 4% on ALL5 and COMMON5 respectively). Finally, performance on COMMON5 is remarkably better than performance on ALL5, specially for the spectral and phonetic systems (60% and 39% relative improvements in the best system of each level respectively).

Verification performance using non-adapted user-dependent fusion is given in Tables 3 and 4 for the ALL5 and COMMON5 datasets, respectively. The same behavior found in user-independent fusion is also observed here, obtaining similar performance figures. In particular, relative improvements between the best fused system and the best individual system are 9% and 12% for ALL5 and COMMON5 datasets, respectively.

Verification performance using the proposed adapted user-dependent fusion approach ($r = 1$) is given in Tables 5 and 6 for the ALL5 and COMMON5 datasets, respectively. In this case, all combinations are better than the best individual system, which is outperformed significantly by the best combination (i.e., spectral and lexical systems). In particular, relative improvement between the best fused system and the best individual system are 31% and 61% for ALL5 and COMMON5, respectively. Also worth noting, the unilevel combination of the two spectral level systems gives an interesting combination pair (31%

Table 3. Verification performance on **ALL5** dataset with **user-dependent fusion** based on Quadratic Discriminant. EERs in %

information level	system label	individual performance	unilevel fusion	multilevel fusion		
				levels	best/level	all/level
1	MFCC_GMM	8.67		12	7.86	7.22
	MFCC_SVM	**7.70**	**6.84**	13	8.27	8.15
2	PHONE_SVM	16.90		14	8.04	**6.98**
	PHONE_NGM	22.16	15.74	123	8.08	7.99
3	PROSODY_SLOPE	20.86		124	8.46	7.37
	PROSODY_GMM	22.51	18.46	134	8.57	8.04
4	WORD_NGM	22.70		1234	8.44	8.11

Table 4. Verification performance on **COMMON5** dataset with **user-dependent fusion** based on Quadratic Discriminant. EERs in %

information level	system label	individual performance	unilevel fusion	multilevel fusion		
				levels	best/level	all/level
1	MFCC_GMM	5.98		12	4.40	2.98
	MFCC_SVM	**3.06**	**2.95**	13	5.98	4.99
2	PHONE_SVM	10.31		14	5.42	**2.70**
	PHONE_NGM	18.32	11.60	123	5.60	4.43
3	PROSODY_SLOPE	22.14		124	5.04	2.77
	PROSODY_GMM	19.08	18.99	134	5.85	3.66
4	WORD_NGM	20.61		1234	5.60	3.66

Table 5. Verification performance on **ALL5** dataset with **adapted user-dependent fusion** based on Quadratic Discriminant ($r = 1$). EERs in %

information level	system label	individual performance	unilevel fusion	multilevel fusion		
				levels	best/level	all/level
1	MFCC_GMM	8.67		12	6.25	5.66
	MFCC_SVM	**7.70**	**5.35**	13	5.85	5.40
2	PHONE_SVM	16.90		14	6.14	**5.36**
	PHONE_NGM	22.16	13.61	123	5.92	5.39
3	PROSODY_SLOPE	20.86		124	6.72	5.61
	PROSODY_GMM	22.51	15.08	134	5.95	**5.32**
4	WORD_NGM	22.70		1234	6.16	5.37

and 34% relative improvement over the best system for ALL5 and COMMON5, respectively). The effect of varying the relevance factor of the adapted fusion scheme on the verification performance is shown in Fig. 2. A good working point is found at $r = 1$.

Table 6. Verification performance on **COMMON5** dataset with **adapted user-dependent fusion** based on Quadratic Discriminant ($r = 1$). EERs in %

information level	system label	individual performance	unilevel fusion	multilevel fusion levels	best/level	all/level
	MFCC_GMM	5.98		12	2.80	2.06
1	MFCC_SVM	**3.06**	**2.03**	13	2.37	2.27
	PHONE_SVM	10.31		14	2.49	**1.20**
2	PHONE_NGM	18.32	8.70	123	2.77	2.11
	PROSODY_SLOPE	22.14		124	2.92	1.68
3	PROSODY_GMM	19.08	15.65	134	1.91	1.66
4	WORD_NGM	20.61		1234	2.42	1.32

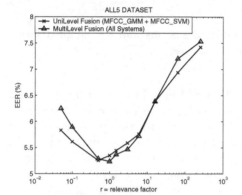 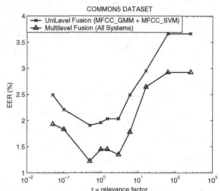

Fig. 2. Verification performance of the adapted fusion scheme on ALL5 (left) and COMMON5 (right) data sets for varying relevance factor

Verification performance results comparing the individual systems to the studied fusion strategies are summarized in Fig. 3 as DET plots [25].

5   Discussion and Conclusions

It can be argued against user-dependent fusion that training data scarcity is a major drawback for its success. In this paper, it has been demonstrated that the performance of multilevel speaker verification is improved in an standard evaluation scenario by considering user-dependent information at the fusion level. This has been achieved by using a novel user-dependent fusion technique based on Bayesian adaptation of the fusion functions and only a few training score samples from each user. Nevertheless, although we have used an un-biased cross-validation experimental procedure, it must be emphasized that we have used post-evaluation results for adapting to the user specificities. The study of the

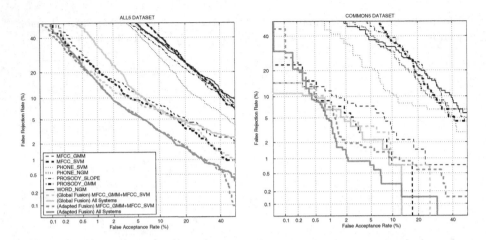

Fig. 3. Verification performance of the individual systems and the adapted fusion scheme on ALL5 (left) and COMMON5 (right) data sets

case of using only the available training data will be addressed in future work. In this regard, it is our belief that for the case of large training set size (such as the 8sides-1side or above scenarios defined by NIST), the use of resampling techniques (e.g., resubstitution, leave-one-out, bootstrap) [26] may result in a significant improvement. As a preliminary justification for this aim, we point out the related work [27], where resampling techniques were applied successfully in the related problem of training user-dependent score normalization techniques applied to signature verification. As a result, the present work is an encouraging starting and reference point for devising personalized fusion schemes with application to multilevel speaker recognition.

Acknowledgements

This work has been supported by the Spanish MCYT projects TIC2003-08382-C05-01 and TIC2003-09068-C01-01. J. F.-A. is also supported by a FPI scholarship from Comunidad de Madrid. The authors would like to thank MIT-LL for providing the speaker recognition scores used in this paper, and also for their substantive comments about the paper.

References

1. Reynolds, D.A., Quatieri, T.F., Dunn, R.B.: Speaker verification using adapted Gaussian mixture models. Digital Signal Processing **10** (2000) 19–41
2. Campbell, W.M.: A SVM/HMM system for speaker recognition. Proc. ICASSP (2003) 209–302

3. Campbell, W.M., Reynolds, D.A., Campbell, J.: Fusing discriminative and generative methods for speaker recognition: Experiments on Switchboard and NFI/TNO field data. Proc. ODYSSEY (2004) 41–44
4. Reynolds, D.A., et al.: The SuperSID project: Exploiting high-level information for high-accuracy speaker recognition. Proc. ICASSP (2003) 784–787
5. Reynolds, D.A., et al.: The 2004 MIT Lincoln Laboratory Speaker Recognition System. Proc. ICASSP (2005) (to appear)
6. NIST SRE Web (http://www.nist.gov/speech/tests/spk/2004/index.htm)
7. Doddington, G., et al.: Sheeps, goats, lambs and wolves: A statistical analysis of speaker performance in the NIST 1998 SRE. Proc. ICSLP (1998)
8. Bigun, E.S., Bigun, J., et al.: Expert conciliation for multi modal person authentication systems by Bayesian statistics. Springer LNCS-1206 (1997) 291–300
9. Jain, A.K., Ross, A.: Learning user-specific parameters in a multibiometric system. Proc. ICIP (2002) 57–60
10. Fierrez-Aguilar, J., et al.: A comparative evaluation of fusion strategies for multimodal biometric verification. Springer LNCS-2688 (2003) 830–837
11. Fierrez-Aguilar, J., et al.: Exploiting general knowledge in user-dependent fusion strategies for multimodal biometric verification. Proc. ICASSP (2004) 617–620
12. Toh, K.A., Jiang, X., Yau, W.Y.: Exploiting local and global decisions for multimodal biometrics verification. IEEE Trans. on SP **52** (2004) 3059–3072
13. Fierrez-Aguilar, J., et al.: Bayesian adaptation for user-dependent multimodal biometric authentication. Pattern Recognition (2005) (to appear)
14. Kumar, A., Zhang, D.: Integrating palmprint with face for user authentication. Proc. MMUA (2003) (available at http://mmua.cs.ucsb.edu/)
15. Snelick, R., et al.: Large scale evaluation of multimodal biometric authentication using state-of-the-art systems. IEEE Trans. PAMI **27** (2005) 450–455
16. Poh, N., Bengio, S.: An Investigation of F-ratio client-dependent normalisation on biometric authentication tasks. Proc. ICASSP (2005) (to appear)
17. Lee, C.H., Huo, Q.: On adaptive decision rules and decision parameter adaptation for automatic speech recognition. Proc. IEEE **88** (2000) 1241–1269
18. Duda, R.O., Hart, P.E., Stork, D.G.: Pattern Classification. Wiley (2001)
19. Gauvain, J.L., Lee, C.H.: Maximum a Posteriori estimation for multivariate Gaussian mixture observations of Markov chains. IEEE Trans. on SAP **2** (1994) 291–298
20. Reynolds, D.A.: Channel robust speaker verification via feature mapping. Proc. ICASSP (2003) 53–56
21. Auckenthaler, R., et al.: Score normalization for text-independent speaker verification systems. Digital Signal Processing **10** (2000) 42–54
22. Doddington, G.: Speaker recognition based on idiolectal differences between speakers. Proc. EUROSPEECH (2001) 2521–2524
23. Adami, A., Mihaescu, R., Reynolds, D.A., Godfrey, J.: Modeling prosodic dynamics for speaker recognition. Proc. ICASSP (2003) 788–791
24. Adami, A.G.: Modeling prosodic differences for speaker and language recognition. PhD thesis, OGI (2004)
25. Martin, A., Doddington, G., et al.: The DET curve in assessment of decision task performance. Proc. EUROSPEECH (1997) 1895–1898
26. Jain, A.K., Duin, R.P.W., Mao, J.: Statistical pattern recognition: A review. IEEE Trans. on PAMI **22** (2000) 4–37
27. Fierrez-Aguilar, J., Ortega-Garcia, J., Gonzalez-Rodriguez, J.: Target dependent score normalization techniques and their application to signature verification. IEEE Trans. on SMC-C **35** (2005) (to appear)

Multi-modal Person Recognition for Vehicular Applications

H. Erdoğan[1], A. Erçil[1], H.K. Ekenel[2], S.Y. Bilgin[1],
İ. Eden[3], M. Kirişçi[1], and H. Abut[1,4]

[1] Sabancı University, Istanbul, 34956, Turkey
[2] University of Karlsruhe, Karlsruhe, 76131, Germany
[3] Brown University, Providence, RI, 02912, USA
[4] San Diego State University, San Diego, CA 92182, USA
{haerdogan, aytulercil, abut}@sabanciuniv.edu.tr

Abstract. In this paper, we present biometric person recognition experiments in a real-world car environment using speech, face, and driving signals. We have performed experiments on a subset of the in-car corpus collected at the Nagoya University, Japan. We have used Mel-frequency cepstral coefficients (MFCC) for speaker recognition. For face recognition, we have reduced the feature dimension of each face image through principal component analysis (PCA). As for modeling the driving behavior, we have employed features based on the pressure readings of acceleration and brake pedals and their time-derivatives. For each modality, we use a Gaussian mixture model (GMM) to model each person's biometric data for classification. GMM is the most appropriate tool for audio and driving signals. For face, even though a nearest-neighbor-classifier is the preferred choice, we have experimented with a single mixture GMM as well. We use background models for each modality and also normalize each modality score using an appropriate sigmoid function. At the end, all modality scores are combined using a weighted sum rule. The weights are optimized using held-out data. Depending on the ultimate application, we consider three different recognition scenarios: verification, closed-set identification, and open-set identification. We show that each modality has a positive effect on improving the recognition performance.

1 Introduction

Biometric person identification is a new and exciting research area which finds application in many different problems related to authentication, access control, keyless entry, and secure communications. Application of person and behavior identification in a vehicular environment has also attracted interest recently. This paper presents experiments for recognizing people in moving vehicles.

Due to competition in automotive industry, it is not too far when we will have cameras, microphones and various other sensors inside a vehicle that will gather and process multimedia data with the purposes of safer driving, improved comfort of driver and the passengers, and secure communications. Recognizing people in a car will be important to achieve the following benefits [1]:

N.C. Oza et al. (Eds.): MCS 2005, LNCS 3541, pp. 366–375, 2005.
© Springer-Verlag Berlin Heidelberg 2005

1. Ensuring safety of the vehicle by requiring authorization before and/or during driving a car to make sure the current driver is an authorized driver,
2. Personalizing the vehicle suiting the driver's physical and behavioral characteristics, thereby, creating a comfortable, safe and efficient driving environment which minimizes distractions, and hence avoidance of many accidents attributed to driver distraction,
3. Providing safety to the vehicle, people, and goods in a commercial vehicle, via passive and active warning systems, even enabling authorities to disallow a driver who should not be or is not in a condition to be behind a wheel,
4. Opening opportunities to secure mobile transactions within a car, such as mobile banking, using biometric authentication.

There are serious challenges to person identification inside a car, especially if we are to assume no user cooperation. Over the past two decades, many algorithms, systems, and even technologies for speaker and face identification have been developed with varying degree of success (acceptable through excellent). Having been designed under idealized and controlled environments, however, both modalities suffer due to non-ideal conditions in real-world environments. In face recognition, for instance, change of illumination and pose, occlusions, facial expression, facial accessories, facial hair tend to deteriorate performance. For speaker recognition, external noise and channel effects, illnesses affecting the glottis and vocal tract, emotional speech may decrease performance. There are many studies to improve the performance of each modality within itself, such as to extract more robust features and to use more efficient normalization methods. Unfortunately, most of the methodologies under consideration are fairly mature and major breakthroughs are not forthcoming. Alternately, the research focus has shifted to the usage of multiple modalities together, so that when one of the modalities is not reliable or fails, other modalities can be relied upon.

In this paper, we attempt to use three different modalities, namely, speech, face and driving signals to recognize drivers of moving vehicles. We use MFCC features for speech, PCA features for face and the features extracted from the pressure readings of the acceleration and brake pedals and their derivatives. We combine information from each modality by computing a weighted sum of normalized modality scores. We determine the best weights by optimizing the verification performance on held-out[1] data. We consider three different types of person recognition: (*i*) verification, (*ii*) closed set identification, and (*iii*) open set identification, which will be explained in the next section.

We report our experimental results on a twenty people subset of the in-car corpus collected by the Center for Integrated Acoustic Information Research (CIAIR) [2]. We organize the paper in the following way. After introducing types of person recognition problems in section 2, we briefly introduce speaker and face recognition algorithms in sections 3 and 4. We explain how we used driving signals to recognize people in section 5. Next, we give details about our fusion algorithm. The experimental results are presented in section 7 and the conclusions are provided in section 8.

---

[1] The held-out data is a portion of available training data that is not used during training or testing, but used to adjust certain parameters of the recognition system. Sometimes held-out data is called validation data.

2 Problem Formulation

The task of recognizing people in vehicles is difficult for the following reasons:

- In vehicles, the subjects, especially the driver, are not expected to pose for the camera since their first priority is to operate the vehicle safely. Hence, there are large illumination and pose variations. In addition, partial occlusions and disguise are common.
- The quality of video is usually low, and due to the acquisition conditions and the physical constraints in positioning the camera, the face image sizes are smaller (sometimes much smaller) than the assumed sizes in most existing still image based face recognition systems.
- Speech acquisition in a car is prone to noise and channel distortions due to the engine and mechanical noise and reverberations in the vehicular chamber. For comfort and ease of use, far-talking microphones are employed instead of near-talking or head-set microphones, which decreases signal-to-noise ratio significantly and makes speaker recognition much more difficult.

Therefore, the use of multimodal biometrics becomes the most sensible route to follow for robust and reliable person identification inside a moving vehicle.

As in all other applications, the person recognition inside a car can be formulated as either a verification problem or an identification task. In the verification problem, a person's claimed identity is verified using her/his model in a known pool of subjects. On the other hand, one must be more careful in formulating an identification problem, which can be cast as either an open-set or a closed set identification problem. In the closed-set case, a reject scenario is not defined and an unknown subject is classified as one of the N-registered people. In the open-set case, the goal is to decide whether the person is among the registered people in the database or not. The system identifies the person if there is a match and otherwise rejects the claimed identity. Hence, the problem becomes an $N+1$-class identification problem, including a reject class. It is not difficult to see vehicle safety application can be addressed using an open-set identification scenario, while in-vehicle secure transactions application may be addressed under a verification task.

3 Speaker Recognition Mode

Speech signal is the most natural and non-invasive modality to identify a person in a vehicle. As in many other parametric speech processing applications, a set of features are extracted for each frame of speech over a short overlapping and advancing time window. It is worth noting that we preprocess speech signals to detect voice activity and extract features only from regions of audio where voice activity is present.

Features used for speaker recognition differ slightly from the ones used for speech recognition. In this study, we have used 12 coefficients of the Mel-frequency cepstral coefficients (MFCC) feature vector [3], i.e., in order to avoid dependence on acquired voice's energy, we have not included the energy coefficient. In this work, we did not use Δ and $\Delta\Delta$ features, which approximate first and second differences at the current frame respectively, as well, since their inclusion did not show noticeable improvement as reported in an earlier study [4].

MFCC features are obtained using a filterbank of overlapping triangular filters placed according to the critical bands of hearing [3]. The logarithms of filter output energies are computed. Then a DCT transform of these log-filterbank-energies is taken to de-correlate and reduce the dimension of the feature set as follows:

$$c_k = \sum_{j=1}^{N} m_j \cos\left(\frac{\pi k}{N}(j - 0.5)\right), \tag{1}$$

where $\{c_k\}$ represent MFCC features and $\{m_j\}$ stand for log-filterbank-energies. These speaker features are considered as independent identically distributed random vectors drawn from a parametric probability density function (pdf). To model the pdf, Gaussian mixture models (GMM) are commonly used in speech processing community:

$$f(\mathbf{x} \mid S_i) = \sum_{k=1}^{K} \gamma_k \, N(\mathbf{x}, \boldsymbol{\mu}_k, \boldsymbol{\Sigma}_k). \tag{2}$$

Here $\mathbf{x}$ represents the feature vector, γ_k are mixture coefficients and $N(\mathbf{x}, \boldsymbol{\mu}_k, \boldsymbol{\Sigma}_k)$ are individual Gaussians for representing a particular speaker S_i. For computational reasons, $\boldsymbol{\Sigma}_k$ are chosen to be diagonal matrices. GMMs have been used in text-independent speaker recognition with great success [5]. A popular way of using GMMs in speaker recognition is to train a large background speaker model (say with 1024 Gaussians) and adapt this model to each speaker using that particular speaker's data. GMM training is performed via the EM algorithm [6].

In this paper, we train a GMM for each speaker from scratch and we use eight mixtures, which nevertheless gives satisfactory performance in this application. We had compared the performance of eight and sixteen mixtures in an earlier study [4] and obtained a better result using eight mixtures. During the testing phase, the per-frame log-likelihood value of observed data $(\mathbf{x}_j)_{j=1}^{N}$ under the model of a particular speaker S_i can be computed as:

$$L_i = \frac{1}{N} \sum_{j=1}^{N} \log f(\mathbf{x}_j \mid S_i) = \frac{1}{N} \sum_{j=1}^{N} \left(\log \sum_{k=1}^{K} \gamma_k \, N(\mathbf{x}_j, \boldsymbol{\mu}_k, \boldsymbol{\Sigma}_k) \right). \tag{3}$$

We also train a background model, one more GMM, with twice the number of mixtures. Background GMM is required for normalization in likelihood ratio testing for speaker verification. The log-likelihood of the observed data under the background model, L_g can also be computed in a similar way. For verification task, the Bayesian decision amounts to the comparison of the log-likelihood-ratio, $L_i - L_g$ to a threshold.

Robustness against noise can be an important issue in speaker recognition, especially if the training and testing conditions are mismatched. In our case, we have had the training and testing conditions matched. Hence, we did not perform any specific robustness algorithm such as feature and score normalization. In our future studies, we plan to include algorithms for robustness against noise and channel effects.

4 Face Recognition Mode

Among the plethora of face recognition methods, the paradigm based on face appearance data, template-based algorithms and their concomitant subspace versions, such as PCA and LDA methods are the most popular (see [7] for a comprehensive review). Since number of pixels in a face image can be rather large, it is reasonable to reduce feature dimension by projecting to a lower dimensional subspace. Thus, subspace projection techniques perform well for face recognition. Principal component analysis (PCA) is the most popular subspace projection technique used for face recognition [8-10].

PCA computes a linear transformation that maximizes the total scatter of the face images in the projected space. PCA aims to determine a new orthogonal basis vector set that best reconstructs the face images in the mean-squared error sense. These orthogonal basis vectors, also called eigenfaces, are the eigenvectors of the covariance matrix of the face images, associated with the highest eigenvalues.

In this study, we have trained a single Gaussian model for each person's face. Since we are using video signals, it is feasible to obtain many face images of a single person and it is feasible to use a statistical model for recognition. The decision making process is identical to the speech case after the statistical model is built.

5 Person Recognition Using Driving Signals

Can drivers be identified from their driving behavior? or equivalently, is the driving behavior a biometric trait? To answer this question, researchers at CIAIR and the authors of this paper have studied driving signals as measured by different sensors in the vehicle. Driving signals that were analyzed include pressure readings from accelerator and brake pedals, as well as the vehicle speed variations [11]. After trying Fourier analysis and multi-dimensional linear prediction techniques with limited success, both groups have employed GMM method to model driving signal characteristics. GMMs are successfully used for modeling speech signals in speaker recognition and are well-suited for application to driving signals as well. We believe this can be attributed to the fact that temporal characteristics of driving signals exhibit quasi-stationary behavior like speech. Smoothed and sub-sampled driving signals (acceleration and brake pedal pressures) and their first derivatives were used as features for modeling driving behavior of the drivers. Driving signals can be obtained by frequent sampling in time, thus we can collect ample data from a single person to train a statistical model. After feature extraction, the statistical modeling (driver/impostor models) part is just like the speech case. Similarly, we construct a GMM to model the driving features of each person and also train a background model.

6 Fusion

In this work, fusion of information from different modalities is performed at the matching score level, which is often called "decision fusion". We have used the weighted sum rule to combine scores from different modalities. As reported in literature [12, 13], the weighted sum rule is more robust against noise and other disturbances as compared to several other score combination rules, such as product rule, max rule and min rule, and often outperforms them.

An important aspect of classifier combination at the score level is to carefully normalize scores from each modality before the actual combination. Typical likelihood ranges for genuine and impostors could differ largely among modalities. Thus, log-likelihood-ratio scores from different modalities cannot be directly superimposed. Therefore, it is logical to normalize scores to make them compatible. One way to normalize scores is to use the mean and standard deviation of likelihood scores obtained from held-out validation data. Normalization can be performed using a sigmoid function which will map the scores to the (0,1) range.

$$S'_k = \frac{1}{1 + \exp\left(-(S_k - \mu)/\sigma\right)}.$$ (4)

Here S_k denotes the old log-likelihood-ratio score for the kth modality, S_k' represents the new score. Furthermore, μ and σ are mean and standard deviation of old scores obtained on the validation set using all validation instances and all speaker models. In this work, we have used top $3N_t$ scores for N_t validation instances to compute the mean and standard deviation of scores, otherwise the mismatch scores (outnumbering genuine scores 19 to 1) would have dominated the statistics.

After normalization, we compute the weighted sum of new scores for each validation test case using the following formula:

$$S = \sum_{k=1}^{3} w_k S'_k.$$ (5)

We have chosen fixed weights w_k to minimize the verification equal error rate (EER)[2] on the validation data. The minimization is performed by exhaustively searching the weight space. After determining the optimal values for the weights on the validation data, we have employed them during testing phase for test data to compute overall final scores.

7 Experiments and Results

CIAIR at Nagoya University in Japan has been collecting an in-car speech database since 1999 with a data collection vehicle they have designed [2]. This vehicle supports synchronous recording of multi-channel audio data from 12 microphones that can be placed in flexible positions, multi-channel video data from 3 cameras and the vehicle related data such as the vehicle speed, the engine rpm, the steering wheel angle, acceleration and brake pedal pressures, where each channel is sampled at

---

[2] EER for verification is defined as the error rate when the false accept rate (FAR) is equal to the false reject rate (FRR) on the receiver operating characteristics curve which plots FRR versus FAR for different classification thresholds.

1.0 kHz. During the data collection stage, each subject has conversations with three types of dialogue systems. One is a human navigator, another is a Wizard of Oz system, and the last is a conversational system [2].

We have carried out person recognition experiments over a 20 person subset of the CIAIR database which consists of 812 drivers with well over a terabyte of data. We have used the camera facing the driver and the audio signal from the headset microphone for each person as video and audio sources, respectively. The faces were hand-cropped to 64x40 pixel size and non-silence audio sections were hand selected. We have smoothed and down-sampled the brake and acceleration pedal pressure readings by a factor of ten and their first derivatives to be the features for modeling the behavior of the driver. This resulted in four features at 100 Hz. Twelve static MFCC features (excluding c0) at 100 Hz were used as audio features. For faces, the PCA method was used to reduce the feature dimension to 20 for each image frame. The frame rate is 25 frames per second for the video.

From each driver, 50 image frames, 50 seconds of non-silence audio and around 600 seconds of driving signals were utilized. We extracted features from this dataset and divided all features into 20 equal length parts for each driver and modality and number the parts from one to 20. When we have formed the multimodal test-sets, we have assumed that each modality part was associated with the parts that have the same number in other modalities.

We have then performed a leave-one-out training procedure, where for each single testing part, seventeen parts were used for training and two parts were held-out for validation to optimize normalization parameters and fusion weights. This gave us 20 tests for each person (each time the training data is different although not independent), leading to 400 (20x20) genuine tests total. GMMs were used with eight, one and eight mixture components for speech, face and driving signals, respectively. Background GMM models were trained for each modality as well [6].

TRAINING:

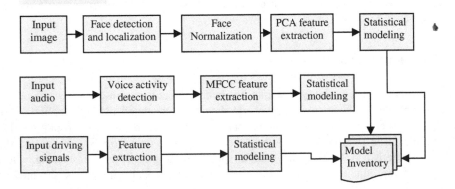

Fig. 1. System block diagram for training the multimodal driver recognition system

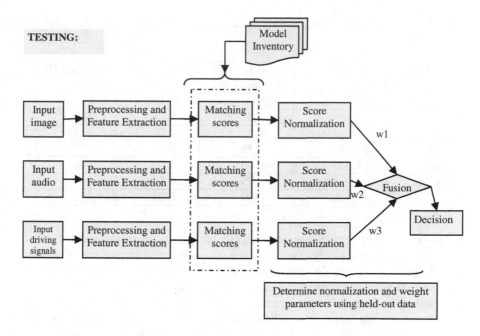

Fig. 2. System block diagram for testing the multimodal person recognition system

Block diagram of our training procedure is shown in Figure 1. Person recognition system is illustrated in Figure 2. We performed verification, closed set identification and open set identification tasks with the data. For verification, we have assumed each person's data as an impostor for the remaining 19 other drivers resulting at 7600 (19x20x20) impostor tests in total. For open-set identification tests, we leave one identity out at a time and perform open-set identification using the remaining 19 as genuine identities. We cycle through the set of identities to leave a different identity out each time to obtain 20 different testing setups for each test data. This procedure gives us 7600 genuine tests and 400 impostor tests. In this paper, we define EER for open-set scenario as the error rate when false-accept rate among the impostor attempts is equal to the sum of false-reject and false-classify rates among the genuine attempts.

The modalities were fused by the weighted score summation method mentioned earlier in section 6. Our findings from both the unimodal and multimodal performances are presented in Table 1.

The results from single-mode identification and verification are encouraging. As expected, audio-only yields the best performance since the speech samples were from the close-talking headset microphone. In a controlled lab environment face recognition algorithm has performed very successfully [1]. But in the CIAIR database, driver face segments were fairly small in comparison to other studies [4] and hence the results are expectedly not as good. We expect to get significantly higher results from face modality by using a custom-designed camera built-in to the visor which can be focused primarily on the face of the driver. The results based on analog driving signals are quite satisfactory and show improvement over an earlier study [11].

Table 1. Closed-set person identification, person verification and open-set person identification results

Modality	Weights	Closed-set ID (Accuracy %)	Verification (EER %)	Open-set ID (EER %)
A	Audio only	98.00	2.15	8.05
F	Face only	89.00	6.08	18.56
D	Driving only	88.25	4.00	21.06
A+D	(.62,.38)	99.25	0.83	3.75
F+D	(.43,.57)	98.00	1.62	8.86
A+F	(.63,.37)	99.75	0.50	1.75
A+F+D	(.47,.33,.20)	100.0	0.25	0.25

Pair-wise fusion scenarios result in significantly better performance over the face-only or driving-signals-only cases and even an incremental improvement is observed over the audio-only case. In many driver verification applications, an error rate of 0.5-1.62 percent would be satisfactory. For open-set identification, an EER rate of 1.75 percent, achieved by audio and face modalities, could be quite satisfactory as well.

As expected, the inclusion of all three modalities increases the performance of the person recognition system to an encouraging level. We believe that error rates of ¼ percent can bring most of the applications cited at the introduction section to reality and commercially viable systems can be built. Using multi-modal person recognition in a car is even more important than these results reveal, since any one of these modalities may fail or become impractical in certain cases, such as during driving at night or when there is presence of radio or other speakers in the vehicle.

However, we would like to point out that the results reported here are based on a relatively small data set and the investigators are experimenting with a much larger data set from the CIAIR corpus. We are also putting together a framework for a comprehensive and language/region-independent driver-specific data collection setup for the purposes of person recognition in a vehicle.

8 Conclusion

In this paper, we have introduced a multi-modal person recognition system that uses speech, face and driving signals for in-vehicle applications. It is interesting to note that, every modality has its own importance and improves the performance of the recognition system. Especially, it is interesting to see that driving signals are indicative of the person and those signals can be considered as a biometric trait which was not considered before.

We have obtained very encouraging results from a 20 person subset of the CIAIR database and have observed improvement in every multi-modal combination that we tried. These results show that, multimodal person recognition in a car is very promising. We conjecture that the improvement will be more important for adverse conditions when one of the modalities may become totally unreliable; nevertheless, it will still be possible to rely on the remaining modalities.

Acknowledgements

We would like to acknowledge Professor Kazuya Takeda of Nagoya University and his laboratory for providing the CIAIR database and Professor Fumitada Itakura of Meijo University, Nagoya, Japan for posing the original question and encouraging us to undertake the problem. Finally, we have been enjoying immensely our on-going collaboration with Professors A. Murat Tekalp, Engin Erzin, and Yücel Yemez of Koç University, Istanbul, Turkey.

References

[1] E. Erzin, Y. Yemez, A.M. Tekalp, A. Erçil, H. Erdogan, and H. Abut, "Multimodal Person Identification for Human Vehicle Interaction," accepted for publication in the IEEE Signal Processing Magazine Special Issue on Man-Machine Communication, to appear September 2005.

[2] N. Kawaguchi, S. Matsubara, I. Kishida, Y. Irie, H. Murao, Y. Yamaguchi, K. Takeda and F. Itakura, "Construction and Analysis of the Multi-layered In-car Spoken Dialogue Corpus," Chapter 1 in *DSP in Vehicular and Mobile Systems*, Springer, New York, NY, 2005.

[3] P. Mermelstein and S.B. Davis, "Comparison of parametric representations for monosyllabic word recognition in continuously spoken sentences," IEEE Trans. Acoustics, Speech and Signal Processing, vol. 28, pp. 357-366, August 1980.

[4] H.K. Ekenel, S.Y. Bilgin, I. Eden, M. Kirisçi, H. Erdogan and A. Erçil, "Multimodal Person Verification from Video Sequences," Proceedings, SWIM 2004, Maui, HI, January 2004.

[5] D.A. Reynolds, "Speaker identification and verification using Gaussian mixture speaker models," Speech Communications, 17, 91-108, 1995.

[6] A Dempster, N Laird, M Rubin, "Maximum Likelihood from Incomplete Data via the EM Algorithm", J. Royal Statistical Soc., 39, 1, 1978.

[7] W. Zhao, R. Chellappa, J. Phillips, and A. Rosenfeld "Face Recognition: A Literature Survey," ACM Computing Surveys, pp. 399-458, 2003.

[8] M. Turk and A. Pentland, "Eigenfaces for recognition," Journal of Cognitive Neuroscience, vol. 3, no. 1, pp. 586.591, September 1991.

[9] Y.Y.J. Zhang and M. Lades, "Face recognition: Eigenface, elastic matching, and neural nets," Proceedings of the IEEE, Vol. 85, no. 9, pp. 1423.1435, September 1997.

[10] W. Zhao, "Subspace Methods in Object/Face Recognition," in Proc. Int. Joint Conf. on Neural Networks, 1999.

[11] K. Igarashi, C. Miyajima, K. Itou, K. Takeda, H. Abut and F. Itakura, "Biometric Identification Using Driving Behavior," Proceedings IEEE ICME 2004, June 27-30, 2004, Taipei, Taiwan.

[12] J. Kittler, M. Hatef, R. Duin, and J. Matas, "On combining classifiers," *IEEE Trans. on Pattern Analysis and Machine Intelligence*, vol. 20, no. 3, pp. 226-239, 1998.

[13] A. K. Jain, A. Ross, and S. Prabhakar, "An Introduction to Biometric Recognition," IEEE Trans. On *Circuits and Systems for Video Technology, Special Issue on Image- and Video-Based Biometrics,* August 2003.

Using an Ensemble of Classifiers to Audit a Production Classifier

Piero Bonissone, Neil Eklund, and Kai Goebel

GE Global Research, One Research Circle, Niskayuna, NY 12309, USA
{bonissone, eklund, goebelk}@research.ge.com

Abstract. After deploying a classifier in production it is essential to support its lifecycle. This paper describes the application of an ensemble of classifiers to support two stages of the lifecycle of an on-line classifier used to underwrite life insurance applications: the *monitoring* of its decisions quality and the *updating* of the production classifier over time. All combinations of five classification methods and seven fusion methods were assessed from the perspective of accuracy and pairwise diversity of the classifiers, and accuracy, precision, and coverage of the fused classifiers. The proposed architecture consists of three off-line classifiers and a fusion module.

1 Introduction

The automation of a decision-making processes requires addressing each step in the lifecycle of the underlying decision engine. The development and deployment of such engine represent the first stage of its lifecycle. Once an engine has been placed in production, it is equally important to monitor its performance and probe the quality of its decisions. In previous papers we have described the design and optimization of two decision engines for underwriting insurance applications. Both engines, based on fuzzy constraints and fuzzy case-based reasoning [1,4], used an evolutionary algorithm to optimize their underlying parameters and minimize the cost of misclassification [6]. The core of this optimization was the generation of a set of Standard Reference Decisions (SRD). This set represents the ground truth against which every classifier is evaluated. In [4,18] we discussed the lifecycle of a classifier with an emphasis on its validation, verification, and knowledge-base maintenance. In this paper we focus on the final design and its validation with production data.

As discussed in [5], the design of a successful classifier fusion system consists of two important parts: design of the individual classifiers, selection of a set of classifiers [13, 21], and design of the classifier fusion mechanism [20]. Key to effective classifier fusion is the diversity of the individual classifiers. Strategies for boosting diversity include: 1) using different types of classifiers; 2) training individual classifiers with different data set (bagging and boosting); and 3) using different subsets of features. In our approach we follow the first and third strategies directly, and capitalize indirectly on the second strategy by employing the random forest classification method.

N.C. Oza et al. (Eds.): MCS 2005, LNCS 3541, pp. 376–386, 2005.

2   The Underwriting Problem and the Production Classifier

Insurance underwriting (UW) is a complex decision making task traditionally performed by individuals. UW can be formulated as a classical classification problem, consisting in assigning a given insurance application, described by its medical and demographic records, to one of a small set of rate classes. We define an insurance application as an input vector $\overline{X}$ containing discrete, continuous, and nominal (attribute) variables. These variables represent the applicant's medical and demographic information that has been identified by actuarial studies to be pertinent to the estimation of the applicant's claim risk. Similarly, we define the output space $\overline{Y}$, e.g. the underwriting decision space, as an ordered list of rate classes. Due to the intrinsic difficulty of representing risk as a real number on a scale, the output space $\overline{Y}$ is subdivided into rate classes containing similar risks. The underwriting process can be summarized as a discrete classifier that maps an input vector $\overline{X}$ into a decision space $\overline{Y}$, where: $|\overline{X}| = n$ and $|\overline{Y}| = T$.

The automation of this decision making process has strong accuracy, coverage and transparency requirements. The production classifier must satisfy several constraints: a) *high classification accuracy* in spite of highly non-linear boundaries of the rate classes; b) *consistency* in interpretation of actuarial guidelines; c) intrinsic *flexibility* to ensure a balance between *risk-tolerance*, necessary to maintain price competitiveness, and *risk-avoidance*, necessary to prevent overexposure to risk; d) *transparent* and *interpretable* decisions, to satisfy legal and compliance regulations.

Consequently, we face two main design tradeoffs: *1) Accuracy versus coverage -* requiring low misclassification rates for high volume of applications; *2) Accuracy versus interpretability -* requiring a transparent, traceable decision-making process. A fuzzy logic engine (FLE) was deployed for production. This classifier uses fuzzy rule sets to encode best underwriting standards. Each rule set represents a set of fuzzy constraints defining the boundaries between rate classes. These constraints were initialized from underwriting guidelines, refined through interviews with expert underwriters, and tuned by evolutionary algorithms. The goal of the FLE is to assign an applicant to the most competitive rate class, providing that the applicant's vital data meet all the constraints of that particular rate class to at least a minimum degree of satisfaction. The minimum degree of satisfaction of all relevant constraints determines the confidence measure in the decision. The FLE is described in [3] and [5].

3   Classification Ensembles and Fusion Approach Selection

The ensemble classification system was developed in three stages. First, five candidate classification methods were trained. Second, the diversity of the classifiers was assessed. Finally, the decision accuracy of all combinations of candidate classification methods under seven fusion methods plus single classifiers were evaluated using a leave-one-out approach. Although systems were developed for both smokers and non-smokers, only the results for non-smokers (for which there are both more cases and more rate classes) are presented here.

As discussed in [3], we created an indicator to encode the result of applying underwriters' domain knowledge. This indicator, referred to as TAG, defines the best available rate class for each applicant based on a set of hard-coded rules representing insurance standard policies. The use of this aggregated domain knowledge boosted most classifiers' performance, leading to an accuracy improvement of about 1-2% on average [3]. Moreover, it allowed us to drop nine of the 19 features, and use 10 features plus the indicator for training (except where noted in the random forest section).

3.1 Candidate Classification Methods

Feed-forward Neural Network Classifier Ensemble. An independent 12 input nodes, 5 hidden nodes, and 1 output node artificial neural network (NN) was trained for each class. For each network, the data was labeled one for the corresponding class, or zero for any of the other four classes. To classify an unknown case, each network evaluates the case, and the case is assigned the class corresponding to the network with the highest value of the activation function. This approach (rather than using a single NN with five output nodes) decomposes the complexity of the classification problem and reduces the overall training time. Activation functions for both hidden and output neurons are logistic sigmoid functions. The range of target values was scaled to [0.1 0.9] to prevent saturation during training process.

Multivariate Adaptive Regression Splines Classifier Ensemble. Multivariate Adaptive Regression Splines (MARS) [10] is an adaptive nonparametric regression technique, able to capture main and interaction effects in a hierarchical manner. Being a piecewise-linear adaptive regression procedure, MARS can approximates very well any non-linear structure, if present. However, global models cannot easily incorporate jumps in decision boundaries of a large number of variables in an extremely small bounded range. Two approaches were used to address this problem. First, the use of the TAG variable helps the MARS search algorithm in initializing spline knots in the right place. Second, we developed a *Parallel Network* arrangement of models. We created a collection of MARS models, each of which solves a two-class problem, and we collated their outputs in a manner similar to the one used for the NN classifiers.

Support Vector Machines Ensemble. Support Vector Machines (SVM) [22] are learning machines that non-linearly map an input feature space into a higher dimensional feature space. A linear classifier is then constructed in the higher dimensional feature space. Five SVM models (one for each class) were trained, and their outputs were resolved in a manner similar to the one used for the NN classifiers. The shape parameter for the radial basis function Kernel Gamma and the parameter for cost of constrain violation C were both set to 3. The overall SVM classification was resolved in the same as the NN classifiers.

Random Forests. Random Forests (RF) [8] is a classification method that applies bagging [7] to a variation of classification trees [9]. A standard classification tree is constructed by splitting the data on the best feature of all possible features at each node. For RF, only a randomly selected subset (chosen always from the full set) of features are eligible to split each node. Moreover, in contrast to standard classification trees, the individual RF trees are not pruned; rather they are grown to 100% node purity. Although typically hundreds of trees are developed, RF's are very quick to train (e.g., much faster than neural networks for a given data set and computer). Within our application, the performance of RF was superior to that of the other classification algorithms, including NN and SVM. While RF's contained 1000 trees, NN's and SVM's were much smaller ensembles, containing only five binary classifiers each.

Two RF classifiers were developed. The first RF was trained on the regular set of features (including TAG). The second (referred to as RFA) was trained on a larger set of features, comprised of the regular set (*excluding* TAG) and the features used to create the TAG variable. Although the performance of the RFA suffered slightly (though much less than any other classification method tried on the RFA dataset), the results were not surprisingly quite diverse from the other classifiers (see below). The results presented here for both RF and RFA are based on 1000 trees per forest, and six variables eligible to be split at each node.

3.2 Classification Accuracy

The single classifier classification accuracy was evaluated using five fold cross validation (using the same folds for each method). Table 1 shows the performance of the individual classifiers and the production classifier (FLE) as expressed by the true positive rate. While their accuracies are roughly comparables, their pairwise diversities are not, as shown in the next subsection.

Table 1. Five fold cross validation classification accuracy

Method	Accuracy	Method	Accuracy
MARS	92.71%	RF	93.30%
NN	92.87%	RFA	91.26%
SVM	92.23%	FLE	93.41%

3.3 Classifier Diversity

We assessed pairwise classifier diversity using four measures described in [14], Q, *rho*, *disagreement*, and *double fault*. Results were comparable across all four measures. Only results for Yule's Q are presented here because of its more transparent interpretation.

Q ranges from -1 to 1. For statistically independent classifiers, Q is 0. Correlated classifiers have positive values of Q, while uncorrelated classifiers (i.e., classifiers that make mistakes on different cases) have negative values of Q. Q is only used for two classifiers at a time (Table 2) and is calculated

$$Q = \frac{ad - bc}{ad + bc} \ . \tag{1}$$

The values of the Q statistic for all five classifiers and the production classifier (fuzzy logic engine or FLE) are reported in Table 3, and reveal several interesting things about the classifiers for these data. First, all classification methods that use the TAG variable are highly correlated (i.e., they tend to misclassify the same cases). Both MARS and SVM show a moderate degree of positive correlation with the FLE, while the RFA is the only classifier to have a negative correlation with the FLE.

Table 2. Probabilities for two classifiers, C1 and C2. Note that $a + b + c + d = 1$

	C1 correct	C1 wrong
C2 correct	a	b
C2 wrong	c	d

Table 3. Q statistic for all five classifiers and the PC

	FLE	MARS	NN	SVM	RF	RFA
FLE	1.000	0.412	0.225	0.416	0.383	-0.308
MARS	0.412	1.000	0.873	0.915	0.925	0.021
NN	0.225	0.873	1.000	0.937	0.776	-0.142
SVM	0.416	0.915	0.937	1.000	0.820	-0.059
RF	0.383	0.925	0.776	0.820	1.000	0.411
RFA	-0.308	0.021	-0.142	-0.059	0.411	1.000

3.4 Fusion Methods

Seven fusion methods were evaluated using each of the 26 unique combinations of two or more of the five classifiers (excluding the FLE), along with the performance of each single classifier method. The fusion methods used are described below.

Majority Vote. Each classifier has one vote and the case is assigned the winning class. Ties are broken randomly.

Averaging. The normalized output of each classifier is averaged for each class, and the case is assigned the class with the highest average. Ties are broken randomly.

Borda Count. The case is assigned to the class with the maximum sum of the rank of the negative class weights (within each classifier). Ties are broken randomly.

N of All. Under the N of All (NOA) fusion scheme, if the number of classifiers voting for a particular class is greater than N (where N is > 1 and ≤ the number of classifiers), a case is assigned that class; otherwise, the case is assigned "no decision".

Behavior Knowledge Space (BKS). This fusion method [12] treats every possible combination of output from different classifiers as a cell in a lookup table (the BKS table). During training, training samples associated with a particular call are partitioned by actual class and the most representative class (the majority class) is selected for each cell. This equates in essence to setting up the classifier output probability distribution. For test patterns, the classification is accomplished using the class label of the BKS cell indexed by the classifiers output. In our implementation, the BKS assigns "no decision" to novel patterns.

Naïve Bayes. The naïve Bayes (NB) fusion approach makes the assumption that the decisions of the individual classifiers are independent. While this assumption is almost certainly invalid, this approach works quite well in practice [15]. Using n features f (individual classifier decisions) that pick a particular class c of a set of classes C, the NB decision rule is

$$classify(f_1,...,f_n) = \text{argmax}_c \, p(C = c)\prod_{i=1}^{n} p(F_i = f_i \mid C = c) \cdot \tag{2}$$

Meta-SVM. The Meta-SVM (MSVM) uses the normalized output of each classifier as a feature space to train a new SVM classifier. The output of the MSVM classifier assigns the five classes to some region of one dimension; thus, there is a further problem of dividing that dimension into five separate regions. To automate this process, a classification tree [9] was trained on the MSVM output, and the smallest tree with exactly five leaf classes was used to determine the class boundaries. The use of a classification tree to automate determining class boundaries is both faster and more accurate than hand tuning.

3.5 Fusion Accuracy

Of the 1866 cases, there were 188 where the result of at least one combination of fusion method and classifier method (FMCM) differed from the ground truth, i.e., the standard reference decision (SRD) set. The leave-one-out accuracy (LA) for each FMCM is plotted in the lower set of axes in Figure 1 (for the 188 cases). The upper set of axes is on a different scale, showing only the best performing combinations, and revealing there are three FMCMs that have the same maximum accuracy. FMCM details, Precision [$TP/(TP+FP)$] and Recall [$(TP/(TP+FN)$)] scores (with respect to the FLE) of the three most accurate FMCMs are listed in Table 4.

Across all combinations of classification method, majority vote, averaging, Borda count, and NB do better than individual classifiers. However, NOA, BKS and MSVM do on average worse than a single classifier. The shortcomings of NOA and BKS arise from a common explanation: both methods allow "no decision". While this

Table 4. Classification method, fusion method, precision and recall scores of the three most accurate FMCMs. One reprenents inclusion of a classification method, zero exclusion

MARS	NN	RFA	RF	SVM	Method	Precision	Recall
0	1	1	1	0	Borda count	55.8%	71.7%
0	1	1	1	0	Majority vote	55.6%	75.0%
1	1	1	1	0	Naïve Bayes	55.6%	75.0%

option may be a desirable behavior in many circumstances, nonetheless it does not count toward total correct decisions. The failure of MSVM is probably related to the size of the feature space: MSVM is the only classifier trained on the raw output of the other classifiers. This suggests that some intelligent preprocessing of the data before-hand might have improved performance.

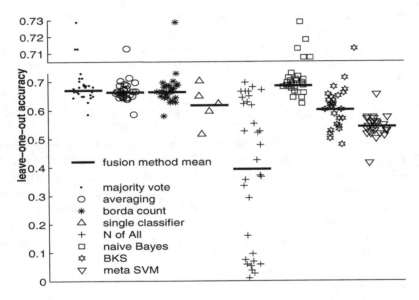

Fig. 1. Fraction of correct calls for each FMCM. Note the upper set of axes is on a different scale to highlight detail. Each point represents a unique combination of classification methods

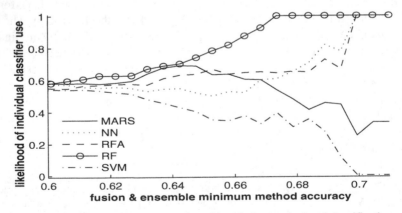

Fig. 2. The likelihood that a classifier is employed in a fusion method and classification method combination of a given or greater accuracy

The likelihood that a classifier of a given or greater accuracy is included in a FMCM (e.g., out of all of the fusion method and classification method combinations with an accuracy ≥ 0.68, about 41% used MARS, 65% used NN, etc.) is plotted in

Figure 2. SVM is particularly unlikely to appear in highly accurate classifiers, while RF is particularly likely (occurring in all of the 28 most accurate FMCMs).

We speculate the RF is included in the most accurate FMCMs because it is the single most accurate individual classifier. The RFA has the worst single classifier accuracy, but it is the least correlated with other classification methods (Table 3) and somewhat uncorrelated with the FCM (which is important in catching errors in the FCM), so its diversity outweighs its poor performance. Of the remaining three classifiers, SVM and MARS are highly correlated with RF (Table 3); NN is both the least correlated and most accurate of the three, so is employed at high accuracy.

4   Quality Assurance Architecture

Based on the results above, the NN, RFA, RF ensemble using the majority vote fusion scheme was adopted to monitor the performance of the FLE and assure the quality of the production engine decisions. In addition, this fusion will identify the best cases that could be used to tune the production engine in future releases, as well as controversial or unusual cases that should be highlighted for manual audit by senior underwriters, as part of the Quality Assurance system. Figure 3 is a diagram of the system.

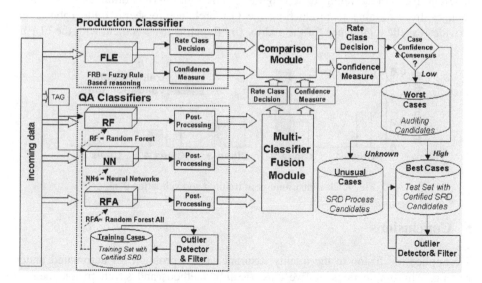

Fig. 3. The Production classifier and QA system

Initially, each classifier in the system was forced to commit to a particular rate class. The results reported in this paper reflect this constraint. If preferred, we can modify this specific tradeoff of coverage versus accuracy by implementing post-processing filters prior to the fusion process. We can treat each classifier's output as a discrete membership distribution over the rate classes considered, and compute four features to summarize such memberships: cardinality, entropy, difference and rank order separation between the highest and the second highest values of the outputs.

Then we can impose a set of thresholds (lower or upper bounds) on these features to identify the cases with weak decisions. For such cases, we change their final conclusions to "unknown". In our experiments, the values of the threshold were obtained using local search, looking for different tradeoffs with better accuracy at the expense of coverage.

4.1 Validation Results Using Production Data

The QA system was validated using 3292 cases, of which 393 showed disagreement between the FLE and the classifier fusion. Of those cases, 131 were randomly selected for evaluation by a human underwriter. Of the 131 cases, the FLE was correct in 77 of them, i.e., false positives (in the sense that the QA classifier incorrectly identified them as being incorrectly classified by the FLE). The fusion was right in 43 cases, implying a correction to the automated FLE. Neither was correct in 11 cases, which is still a good call by the QA system insofar as it will entail a correction of the FLE decision by a human underwriter. Note that this analysis gives no insight into false negatives (false negatives is defined here as both the fusion and the FLE are wrong).

The precision of the QA system was 44.2%, down over 11 percentage points from the training data. However, the distribution of the validation data was substantially different from the training data (Figure 4). In light of the dramatic distribution changes from training to production, the QA architecture seems quite robust, and provides excellent guidance for the auditor (by flagging disagreement with the FLE).

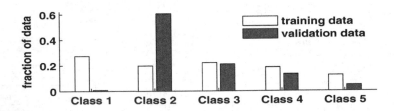

Fig. 4. Class distribution of training and validation data

5 Conclusions

We applied the fusion to the quality assurance (QA) problem for automated underwriting. All combinations of five classification methods and seven fusion methods (plus single classifier) were assessed from the perspective of accuracy and pairwise diversity of the classifiers, and accuracy, precision, and coverage of the fused classifiers. The final classifier ensemble and fusion method performed well, despite considerable differences in the distribution of the training and validation data. This QA system can be used to monitor the performance of the automated decision making system, identifying cases that might be suspect, and should be examined by a human. Moreover, these cases can be incorporated into the standard reference decision set, to further tune the performance of both the automated decision maker (the FLE) and the QA system.

One of the most interesting results is the insight into the tradeoff between accuracy and diversity (Figure 2). We intend to exploit this behavior and plan some future experiments to further explore this tradeoff.

References

[1] Aggour, K., Pavese M., Bonissone, P. and. Cheetham W.   SOFT-CBR: A Self-Optimizing Fuzzy Tool for Case-Based Reasoning, *5th Int. Conf. on Case-Based Reasoning (ICCBR)*, pp. 5-19, Springer-Verlag, Trondheim, Norway, 2003.

[2] Bonissone, P. The life cycle of a Fuzzy Knowledge-based Classifier, *North American Fuzzy Information Processing Society (NAFIPS 2003)*, pp. 488-494, Chicago, IL, Aug. 2003.

[3] Bonissone, P. Automating the Quality Assurance of an On-line Knowledge-Based Classifier By Fusing Multiple Off-line Classifiers, *Proc. IPMU 2004*, 309-316, Perugia, Italy, 2004.

[4] Bonissone, P. and. Cheetham W. Fuzzy Case-based Reasoning for Decision Making, *IEEE Int. Conf. on Fuzzy Systems*, pp. 995-998, Melbourne, Australia, 2001.

[5] Bonissone, P., Goebel, K, and Yan, W. Classifier Fusion using Triangular Norms, *Proc. 2004 Multi Classifier Systems (MCS'04)*, pp. 154-163, Cagliari, Italy, 2004.

[6] Bonissone, P., Subbu, R., and Aggour , K. Evolutionary Optimization of Fuzzy Decision Systems for Automated Insurance Underwriting, *IEEE Int. Conf. on Fuzzy Systems (FUZZ-IEEE '02)*, pp 1003-1008, Honolulu, Hawaii, USA,2002.

[7] Breiman, L. Bagging predictors. *Machine Learning*, 24(2), 123–140, 1996.

[8] Breiman, L. Random forests. *Machine Learning*, 45(1), 5–32, 2001.

[9] Breiman, L., Friedman, J., Olshen, R. and Stone, C. *Classification and Regression Trees*. Wadsworth, Belmont, CA, 1984.

[10] Friedman, J. Multivariate Adaptive Regression Splines. *Annals of Statistics*, 19: 1-141, 1991.

[11] Ho, T., Hull, J., and Srihari, S. Decision Combination in Multiple Classifier Systems, *IEEE Trans. on Pattern Analysis and Machine Intelligence*, Vol. 16, No.1, pp.66-75, 1994.

[12] Huang, Y. and Suen, C. A method of combining multiple experts for the recognition of unconstrained handwritten numerals. In *Trans. IEEE Pattern Analysis and Machine Intelligence* 17(1), pages 90-94, 1995.

[13] Kuncheva L. Switching between selection and fusion in combining classifiers: An experiment, *IEEE Transactions on SMC, Part B*, 32 (2), 2002, 146-156.

[14] Kuncheva, L., and Whitaker C. Ten measures of diversity in classifier ensembles: Limits for two classifiers, *Proceedings of IEE Workshop on Intelligent Sensor Processing*, Birmingham, February, 2001, 10/1-10/6, 2001.

[15] Langley, P., Iba, W., and Thomson, K. An analysis of Bayesian classifiers. *Proceeding of National Conference on Artificial Intelligence* (AAAI-92), pp. 223-228, 1992.

[16] Niyogi, P Pierrot, J-B, and Siohan.O. On decorrelating classifiers and combining them, MIT AI Lab., September 2001

[17] Partridge, D., Yates, W. Engineering multiversion neural-net systems. *Neural Computation*, 8:869-893, 1996.

[18] Patterson, A., Bonissone, P. and Pavese, M. Six Sigma Quality Applied Throughout the Lifecycle of and Automated Decision System, *Journal of Quality and Reliability International* (2005, to appear).

[19] Petrakos, M., Kannelopoulos, I., Benediktsson, J., and Pesaresi, M. The Effect of Correlation on the Accuracy of the Combined Classifier in Decision Level Fusion, *Proceedings of IEEE 2000 International Geo-science and Remote Sensing Symposium*, Vol. 6, 2000.

[20] Roli, F., Giacinto, G., and Vernazza, G. Methods for Designing Multiple Classifier Systems, *MCS 200, LNCS 2096*, 78-87, 2001

[21] Tumer, K.& Ghosh, J. Error correlation and error reduction in ensemble classifiers, *Connection Science*, 8:385-404, 1996.

[22] Vapnik, V.N., *The Nature of Statistical Learning Theory*, Springer-Verlag, New York, 1995.

Analysis and Modelling of Diversity Contribution to Ensemble-Based Texture Recognition Performance

Samuel Chindaro, Konstantinos Sirlantzis, and Michael Fairhurst

Department of Electronics, University of Kent,
Canterbury, Kent CT2 7NT
http://www.ee.kent.ac.uk/
{S.Chindaro, K.Sirlantzis, M.C.Fairhurst}@kent.ac.uk

Abstract. The RGB colour space is prominent as a colour representation and display scheme, although a number of other colour spaces have been developed over the years each with its own advantages and shortcomings with regard to its usefulness for colour/texture recognition. However, the recent advent of multiple classifier systems provides the unique opportunity to exploit the diverse information encapsulated in the different colour representations in a systematic fashion. In this paper we propose the use of classifier combination schemes which utilise information from different colour domains. We subsequently use suitable measures to investigate the diversity of the information infused by the different colour spaces. Experiments with two 40-class colour/texture datasets show the benefit of our multiple classifier approach, and reveal the existence of strong correlations between the accuracy achieved and the diversity measures. Finally, we illustrate, using quadratic regression, that there is significant scope to build and explore further (potentially causal) models of the observed relations between ensemble performance and diversity metrics. Our results point towards the use of diversity along with other statistical measures as possible predictors of the ensemble behaviour.

1 Introduction

Colour and texture are basic features used in many visual processing applications, including scene analysis, computer vision and image retrieval in databases or video sequences. Texture plays an important role in human visual perception and provides vital information for recognition and interpretation [1]. Whilst recently researchers have started to investigate the combination of colour and texture for various applications [2, 3], there has been no consensus on the best colour space to use. The advent of multiple classifier systems presents us with the unique opportunity to exploit the diverse information encapsulated in the different colour representations in a systematic fashion.

The last decade has witnessed extensive research on the problem of combining classification data supplied by various experts with the aim of improving the generalisation and hence the overall performance of the system [1,4,5]. The approach is based on the fundamental assumption that more successful classifiers can be built by com-

N.C. Oza et al. (Eds.): MCS 2005, LNCS 3541, pp. 387–396, 2005.

bining a pool of classifiers who make different but complementary decisions. Empirical observations and specific machine learning applications confirm that a given algorithm outperforms all others for a specific problem or for a specific subset of the input data, but it is unusual to find a single expert achieving the best results on the overall problem domain. This has been the case with methods applied to colour processing, with researchers advocating for different colour spaces for different applications [2,3].

For multiple classifier systems to be efficient, it has been established that members should produce uncorrelated errors. Thus the issue of addressing how different (or *diverse*) the pool members are has become important in designing successful multiple classifier systems[4,5,6,7]. In this paper, we focus on analysis of the *diversity* of the information supplied by these colour spaces and how we can use that information in the design of multiple classifier systems. Despite the different notions that exist on the concept of diversity, there is a consistent approach to the measures that are used by various authors to describe it [4,5,6,7]. Here we use some of them to show that diversity is an important attribute introduced by using different colour spaces for texture classification. The approach adopted in this paper is not based on finding the best colour space for texture classification, but on combining the different strengths and weaknesses of these colour representations to achieve improved results.

A pixel-based texture classifier based on ensemble methods, which integrates different families of texture feature extraction methods is presented in [1], with reported significant improvements over single feature extraction method-based approaches. In this paper we focus on extracting the same family of features from a diverse range of colour spaces and then use this in an ensemble. We are thus effectively combining different colour representation methods to achieve improvements in colour texture classification. In this paper, we refer to an expert as a classifier obtained from considering features obtained using a particular colour space.

Almost all colour image acquisition devices produce vector valued output images in RGB (Red, Green, Blue) space. However, the difficulty of using the RGB space has already been well documented [1,2]. In this work we use other colour spaces in addition to the RGB and its derivative, the normalised RGB (nrgb), and explore their contribution to the classification of 2 sets of different colour texture classes, from two different databases. We use the CIEL*a*b and CIEL*u*v* developed to overcome the problem of non-perceptual uniformity of the RGB colour space [8]. Experiments in this work are also carried out using the HSV colour model and two other colour spaces, YIQ and YUV [8]. These colour spaces are finding their way into the image processing community most essentially because of their ability to be broken down into their luminance and chromaticity components.

Various textural feature extraction techniques have been developed and more are still emerging. The texture classification experiments carried out in this paper are based on second order colour Gaussian Markov Random Fields (GMRFs). The GMRFs are a special case of the MRFs [9] and have been shown to provide an accurate compact representation for a range of textures [9,10]. Extensive discussion of MRFs can be found in [9].

Colour texture feature extraction methods have mainly followed two approaches; a multi-channel approach and a single channel approach. In a multi-channel approach two or more channels are handled simultaneously [10]. The single channel approach treats each channel separately and has the advantage of being able to utilise well established gray-scale texture analysis methods. This approach has been used successfully in a number of reported works [2, 3]. We adopt the single channel approach in our experiments, extending the grey scale concept of GMRFs to colour textures.

In the following section descriptions of the feature extraction and classification methods are given. In Section 3, we present the diversity measures that we used. Section 4 describes the experimental set-up and evaluation of the results obtained. The conclusions drawn from our observations are presented in Section 5.

2   Feature Extraction and Classification

Markov Random Field (MRF) methods characterise the statistical relationship between a pixel and its neighbours. The idea of MRF in image processing is to represent an image by capturing local characteristics in terms of conditional probability distribution. If the structural form for the local conditional probability distribution is assumed to be Gaussian, the model is called Gaussian Markov Random Field (GMRF) [9]. The model parameters can be used as texture features by assuming that parameter differences among different textures facilitate texture discrimination. In this paper, we obtain six features from each of the colour channels. The experiments described henceforth are based on classifications involving a total of 18 variables from each colour space. A detailed explanation of the feature extraction method is presented in [11]. For classification in the individual colour spaces, we used two classifiers, namely, the Fisher linear discriminant (FLD) and the k nearest neighbour classifier (knn). For the nearest neighbour classifier, initial investigations showed that the best performance is obtained using $k = 7$ neighbours.

The accuracy of classification has been shown by recent research to be improved in many cases when multiple classifiers are used and the overall decision obtained by combining the individual classifier outputs. To this end after training each one of the above classifiers separately on the different colour spaces and sub-spaces we attempt combinations of their outputs according to a variety of fusion rules. We have implemented the *product, mean, median,* and *majority voting* rules [12].

3   The Diversity Measures

In our experiments we used 6 diversity measures proposed in various studies. These measures which are based on the oracle outputs of the classifiers can be divided into pairwise and non-pairwise measures. *Pairwise measures* are calculated for the different pairings of classifiers in the pool. These estimates are then averaged to give the overall measure for the pool of classifiers. We have included 3 such measures in our study; the Q statistic [13], the correlation coefficient [14] and the double fault measure [15]. For pairwise measures C_{11} as means both classifiers correct, C_{00} indicates both classifiers wrong and C_{10} and C_{01} represent one of the classifiers is correct and one is wrong. The total number of decisions *(T)* is obtained by adding up all four conditions; $T = C_{11} + C_{00} + C_{10} + C_{01}$.

Three *non-pairwise measures,* i.e. the entropy [16], the interrater agreement [17], and the coincidence failure diversity [18] were also used. In the table, for the non-pairwise measures, M represents the total number of classifiers and S is the number of cases in labelled dataset z_j. $m(z_j)$ is the number of classifiers that correctly classify z_j. If K is random variable expressing the proportion of classifiers from S, that fail on a randomly drawn sample x, we can denote by p_i the probability $K = i/S$.

Table 1. Diversity Measures

Diversity Measure	Formula
	Pairwise Measures
Q-Statistic	$Q = \dfrac{C_{11}C_{00} - C_{10}C_{01}}{C_{11}C_{00} + C_{01}C_{10}}$
Correlation Coefficient	$\rho = \dfrac{C_{11}C_{00} - C_{10}C_{01}}{\sqrt{(C_{11}+C_{10})(C_{01}+C_{00})(C_{11}+C_{01})(C_{10}+C_{00})}}$
Double Fault Measure	$DF = \dfrac{C_{00}}{T}$
	Non- Pairwise Measures
Entropy Measure (E)	$E = \dfrac{1}{S}\sum_{j=1}^{S}\dfrac{1}{M-[M/2]}\min\{m(z_j), M-m(z_j)\}$
Interrater Agreement	$\kappa = 1 - \dfrac{\dfrac{1}{M}\sum_{j=1}^{S}m(z_j)(M-m(z_j))}{S(M-1)\varpi(1-\varpi)}$ Where; $\varpi = \dfrac{1}{SM}S\sum_{j=1}^{S}\sum_{i=1}^{M}y_{j,i}$
Coincidence Failure Diversity	$CFD = \begin{cases} 0, & p_0 = 1 \\ \dfrac{1}{1-p_0}\sum_{i=1}^{M}\dfrac{M-i}{M-1}p_i, & p_0 < 1 \end{cases}$

The success of an ensemble of classifiers has often been judged by how much improvement it brings over the performance of the *best (Bst)* member or the *mean (Mn)* of the ensemble team. Since the accuracy of the team members is also a factor governing the resultant performance of the ensemble, the mean accuracy of the team members and the best performance from the team can therefore be incorporated into factors that govern its performance. Besides these two performance indicators, the influence of the *worst (Wst)* team member has also been included in the investigations. We have also included the *standard deviation (Std)* of all the runs from all team members in the classifier team which gives an indication of the stability among the members of the ensemble.

4   Experimental Set-up and Evaluation

For the classification experiments we used a set of 40 RGB colour images of size 128 x 128 which are a part of the VisTex database[19] (Dataset 1). The textures consist of images, which include grass, water, bricks, buildings, and clouds, etc, obtained under various conditions Another set of 40 colour texture images of various sizes, were extracted from the Texture Library database (Dataset 2) and reduced to sizes of 128 x 128 [20] . The Texture Library database was chosen for use here because of its diversity, as it contains natural textures obtained from various sources. Each texture class contained 150 samples. These samples were divided into equal training and test samples per class (75 samples each). The approach used involved random partitioning of the available dataset into training and test sets for a ten-fold cross validation experiment. In each trial therefore, we have different sets of training, validation and test data. The recognition performance presented in the tables is averaged across all trials.

Table 2. Classification results for individual colour spaces (the figures in brackets refer to the accuracy rankings) and classification results using a multi-expert approach which combined the 6 colour spaces features (figures in brackets refer to the % accuracy improvement over the best individual colour space results)

	Dataset 1 Classification Rate (%)		Dataset 2 Classification Rate (%)	
Colour Space	**knn**	**FLD**	**knn**	**FLD**
Colour. Space				
RGB	55.4 *(5)*	58.1 *(5)*	45.3 *(6)*	60.7 *(6)*
nrgb	52.8 *(6)*	50.4 *(6)*	62.2 *(4)*	61.0 *(5)*
YUV	63.3 *(4)*	63.3 *(3)*	59.4 *(5)*	**70.4** *(1)*
YIQ	72.7 *(2)*	**66.6** *(1)*	74.8 *(2)*	69.7 *(2)*
lAB	72.1 *(3)*	58.6 *(4)*	67.6 *(3)*	69.4 *(3)*
HSV	**76.3** *(1)*	64.1 *(2)*	**81.8** *(1)*	66.9 *(4)*
All Features	*49.5*	*90.1*	*49.1*	*90.3*
Combiner				
Prod	97.2 *(20.8)*	93.8 *(27.2)*	93.4*(11.6)*	92.2 *(21.9)*
Mean	96.8 *(20.4)*	87.2 *(20.6)*	93.0*(11.1)*	88.1 *(17.7)*
Med	95.8 *(19.4)*	91.5 *(24.9)*	92.7*(10.9)*	91.9 *(21.6)*
Maj	89.3 *(13.0)*	83.0 *(16.4)*	87.2 *(5.4)*	85.7 *(15.4)*

The results for both the knn and the FLD show no classifier producing significant overall better results than the other classifier, with the mean classification rate for all cases between 60 and 66% (Table2). However the distribution of the individual colour space classification rates is different for the two classification methods, for the same datasets. Individual colour spaces have different accuracies for the two classification methods. The accuracy rankings in brackets clearly show that there is no overall best colour space, indicating that accuracy is dependent on both the data and the classification method used. However, what is clear from the results in Table 2 is that the overall classification results are significantly improved by using the multiple expert approach which combines individual colour space results. The gains in accuracy are not less than 10% and are as high as 27.2% for the *product* rule. Similar high gains in accuracy are achieved by the *mean* and *median* rule.

The results labelled '*all features*' are that of classification using all features from the six different colour spaces (18 x 6 = 108 features). This does not only bring computational increased complexity but also a large deterioration in performance in the case of the knn classifier.

4.1 Diversity Calculation

The aim of this part of the experiment was to establish whether different colour spaces introduce useful diversity for the ensemble methods in colour texture classification. Using the diversity measures obtained in the training set, we also aimed at observing whether correlation existed between these diversity measures and the test set performance of the multi-classifier systems. In doing so, we formed the basis for construction of a model, which incorporates the diversity measures and combination results as independent and dependant variables respectively (Section 4.2).

The individual colour space training sets outputs were placed into pools of 3 and all possible combinations of pools of 3 were generated, resulting in 20 different pools. The 6 diversity measures as well as the test combination results of the corresponding groups were calculated. An intermediate table was created incorporating the error rates obtained from the combinations in the test sets and diversity measures estimated from the training sets. The pools of individually trained colour space classifiers were then sampled with replacement into 10 randomly selected groups of 12. The correlation coefficients were calculated for each group, and the results averaged.

Table 2. The correlation coefficients between the error results from the combination methods and the diversity measures for Dataset 1 using the FLD classifier

	Q	CR	D F	Entr	Int	GD
Prod	0.36	0.45	**0.86**	0.33	0.43	**0.79**
Mean	0.37	0.46	**0.87**	0.32	0.43	**0.80**
Med	0.37	0.45	**0.86**	0.36	0.40	**0.80**
Maj	**0.61**	**0.68**	**0.98**	0.22	**0.61**	**0.96**

Table 3. The correlation coefficients between the error results from the combination methods and the diversity measures for Dataset 2 using the FLD classifier

	Q	CR	D F	Entr	Int	GD
Prod	0.27	0.12	**0.97**	**0.64**	0.14	**0.89**
Mean	0.27	0.12	**0.97**	**0.64**	0.14	**0.89**
Med	0.27	0.12	**0.94**	**0.63**	0.14	**0.88**
Maj	0.46	0.32	**0.97**	**0.80**	0.36	**0.75**

A number of observations can be made from these tables. The double fault (DF) and the generalised diversity (GD) measures have high correlation values in both databases and both types of classifiers. The entropy measure (Entr) also has high values in all cases except for Database 1 using the FLD. Besides these three measures, no single measure had low correlations in all cases. High correlations for all measures were only obtained in one case (Dataset 1, knn classifier, Table 4). For the same type of classifier, the correlation levels are different for each database, and they are also different for the same database using different classifiers.

Table 4. The correlation coefficients between the error results from the combination methods and the diversity measures for Dataset 1 using the knn classifier

	Q	CR	D F	Entr	Int	GD
Prod	0.67	0.85	0.95	0.76	0.86	0.96
Mean	0.66	0.85	0.95	0.76	0.86	0.96
Med	0.64	0.84	0.95	0.77	0.84	0.96
Maj	0.60	0.81	0.99	0.89	0.78	0.98

Table 5. The correlation coefficients between the error results from the combination methods and the diversity measures for Dataset 2 using the knn classifier

	Q	CR	D F	Entr	Int	GD
Prod	0.01	0.36	0.98	0.71	0.45	0.95
Mean	0.04	0.28	0.91	0.88	0.15	0.83
Med	0.07	0.44	0.99	0.71	0.48	0.98
Maj	0.03	0.35	0.99	0.81	0.37	0.96

From these observations it can be noted that for a number of measures, there is significant correlation between the diversity of the members of the classifier ensembles and the performance metric. This is particularly true for the DF and the GD measures, and in three out of four cases; the Entr measure. Considering the improvement in performance achieved by combining colour spaces, we can conclude that this diversity is useful for the ensemble. The fact that the correlation was calculated between the diversity in the training set and the accuracy in the test set lays the basis for forming a predictive model, whereby the performance of an ensemble can be deduced from diversity measures estimated from training set results. This formed the basis of the modelling experiments.

4.2 Modelling Experiments

Having established that there are at least noticeable correlations between achieved results and individual diversity measures, we took the next step of investigating whether a dependent variable (y), the ensemble gain, is related to *more* than one independent variable (e.g. x_1, x_2, x_3) in our case a number of ensemble characteristics and diversity measures. Multiple regression [21] allows the simultaneous testing and modelling of multiple independent variables. The model for a multiple regression takes the form: $y = \beta_0 + \beta_1 x_1 + \beta_2 x_2 + \beta_3 x_3 + \ldots + \varepsilon$; and we wish to estimate the $\beta_0, \beta_1, \beta_2$, etc.

by obtaining: $\hat{y} = b_0 + b_1 x_1 + b_2 x_2 + b_3 x_3 + \dots$; where the b's are the regression coefficients. In this paper we implement the quadratic model based initially on all 10 measures. We then implemented stepwise regression [20]. For modeling purposes we used only results from the training set.

To investigate ensembles characteristics a variety of ensemble teams have to be created. Creation of a diverse range of classifier teams is a difficult task, due to the various measures and definitions applied to diversity. Without a standardized procedure for creation of ensemble teams, we have chosen a classifier team size of 5 and enumerated all possible teams from the 12 available participant classifiers (2 classifiers, each applied to the six colour spaces) resulting in 792 different ensembles. The majority voting combination strategy was applied to each of the groups and the absolute gain obtained by this strategy over the best result of each group was used in the modelling experiments as the dependent variable. The table below shows the model statistics for the model containing all 10 measures.

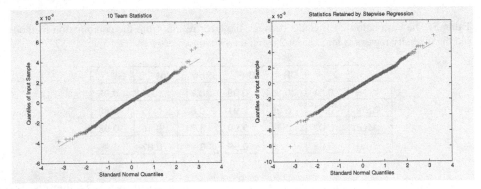

Fig. 1. Q-Q plot of residuals from a) 10-variable model b) the stepwise regression mode

Table 6. Statistics +from the training model

	Std	Mn	Wst	Bst	Q	CR	DF	Ent	Int	CF
Pr	-0.0003	-0.0292	0.0004	0.0099	0.0017	-0.0179	0.0172	0.0162	0.0216	-0.0320
Pr^2	0.0177	0.0103	-0.0005	-0.0007	0.0034	0.0205	0.0173	-0.0027	0.0047	0.0255
mse = 6.70E-06;					**R-Sq =0.99660**					

Figure 1.a shows a Q-Q plot of the residuals obtained from the training model. Despite the existence of a few outliers, the residuals for the models approximate well the assumption of normality on which this model is based. The model is improved when stepwise regression is used (Figure 1.b). The mse of the model (6.7E-O6) R-Squared value (0.9966) indicate an excellent fit. The *R-square* value from the model indicates that this model accounts for almost all the variability with the specified variables. In this model the CF variable has the most significant contribution followed by the mean, and CF squared measures respectively. It is interesting to note the significant contribution of the mean accuracy (M) of the base classifiers.

The model was tested by using the beta values obtained from the training set and the statistics obtained from the test set. The mean squared error for the residuals (difference between predicted gains by the model and actual gains in the test set) was 1.273 and 0.004 for the 10 variable regression model and the model obtained by using stepwise regression respectively. The stepwise regression model resulted in 4 independent variables being removed (DF, and the *squared* Best, Q and CR) using a minimum *p-value*[1] of 0.1 for a predictor variable to be removed. The predictive power of this model is indicated by the low mean square error (0.004) of the residuals between the predicted classification gain and the actual gain, in particular for the stepwise regression model.

5 Conclusion

In this paper we set out to investigate whether different colour space representation introduce useful diversity for the ensemble methods in colour texture classification. We did this by exploring whether there was any correlation between the diversity and the accuracy of ensembles, based on combining information from different colour domains. This we did by computing the correlation between the error rates of the different ensemble methods and the diversity measures using data from two different databases. Our results have supported the use of different colour spaces as a diversity inducement method based on the diversity measures investigated. Strong correlation was found between the accuracy and the diversity measures in the majority of the ensembles cases investigated.

We have constructed and analyzed a diversity-based predictive model which uses multiple regression. Even though the model used was a simple quadratic based one, it has shown encouraging predictive qualities and can be used to form the basis of more complex and accurate meta-models for ensemble creation, which forms the basis for further investigations.

A novel approach to integration of colour information from different colour spaces, have shown that it leads to significant improvements on results from individual colour spaces. We deviated from the general concern of most investigators on finding the 'best' colour space, and instead advocated for a colour space combination strategy. The accuracy of classification has been shown to improve when multiple classifiers utilising the diverse information contained in individual colour spaces are used and the overall decision is obtained by combining the individual classifier outputs. Our results for the individual classifiers trained on the different colour spaces also indicate that the performance is not only dependent on the colour space used but also on the classifiers used.

Acknowledgements

We acknowledge the support of the UK Engineering and Physical Sciences Research Council (EPSRC) in carrying out this research.

---

[1] Refer to the 'stepwisefit' function from the Matlab Statistics Toolbox.

References

1. Garcia M.A. and Puig D.: Improving Texture Pattern Recognition by Integration of Multiple Texture Feature Extraction Methods, Proc. 16 th International Conference on Pattern Recognition (ICPR'02) Volume 3, Quebec City, QC, Canada(2002).
2. Singh M, Markou M and Singh S.: Colour Image Texture Analysis: Dependence on Colour Spaces, Proc. 15th Int. Conf. on Pat. Recog. (ICPR'02), Canada (2002).
3. Chindaro S. and Deravi F.: Directional Properties of Colour Co-occurrence Matrices for Lip Location and Segmentation. Lect. Notes in Comp. Sc., Aug.17, (2001) 84-85,
4. Kuncheva L.I. and Whitaker C.J.: Measures of diversity in classifier ensembles, Machine Learning, 51 , (2003) 181-207
5. Tumer, K and Ghosh, J.: Error correlation and reduction in ensemble classifiers, Connection Science, 8:3/4, London:Springer-Verlag, (1996) 127-161,.
6. Cunningham, P and Carney, J.: Diversity versus quality in classification ensembles based on feature selection. Technical Report TCD-CS-200-02, Department of Computer Science, Trinity College Dublin (2000).
7. Patridge, D. and Krazanowski, W,J.: Software Diversity: Practical Statistics for its measurement and exploitation. Inf. and Software Techn., Vol 39, (1997) 707-717.
8. Foely, J., Van Dam, A., Feiner, S. and Hughes, J.: Computer Graphics: Principals and Practice Addison Wesley, Reading, MA, (1990).
9. Cross, R., G. and Jain, A., K.: Markov Random Fields Texture Models. IEEE Trans. On Patt. An. and Mach. Intelligence, Vol. PAMI-5, No. 1, January (1983) 25-39.
10. Panjwani, D., K and Healey, G.: Markov Random fields for Unsupervised Segmentation of Textured Colour Images. IEEE Trans. On Pattern Analysis and Machine Intelligence, Vol. 17, No. 10, October (1995).
11. Chindaro, S., Sirlantzis, K and Deravi, F.:Colour Space Fusion for Texture Recognition. Proc. of the 4th EURASIP Conf. on Video/Image Processing and Multimedia Communications (EC-VIP-MC 2003), Zagreb, Croatia, July (2003), 181-186.
12. Kittler, J.: Combining Classifiers: a Theoretical Framework. Pattern Analysis and Application, 1, (1998) 18-27.
13. Yule, G.: On the association of attributes in statistics. Phil. Transaction, A, 194, (1900) 257-319,
14. Sneath, P and Sokal, R.: Numerical Taxonomy. W.H. Freeman and Company, 1973.
15. Giacinto G. and Roli F.: Design of effective neural network ensembles for image classification processes. Image and Vision Computing , 19:9/10, 2001) 699-707.
16. Cunningham P. and Carney J.: Diversity versus quality in classification ensembles based on feature selection. *TCD-CS-200-02*, Trinity College Dublin.(2000)
17. Dietterich T.:. An experimental comparison of 3 methods for constructing ensembles of decision trees: Bagging, boosting and randomization. Machine Learning, 40:2, (2000) 139-157
18. Patridge D and Krazanowski W.J.: Software Diversity: Practical Statistics for its measurement and exploitation. *Inf. and Software Tech.*, Vol 39, (1997) 707-717.
19. VisTex, 2000. Colour Image Database: http://www.white.media.mit.edu/vismod/imagery/VisionTexture
20. Texture Library Database: http://textures.forrest.cz
21. Kleinbaum D.G and Kupper LL.: Applied Regression Analysis and other Multivariable methods. Duxberry Press, North Scituate, Masssachusetts, ISBN 0-87872-139-8.

Combining Audio-Based and Video-Based Shot Classification Systems for News Videos Segmentation

M. De Santo[1], G. Percannella[1], C. Sansone[2], and M. Vento[1]

[1] Dip. di Ingegn. dell'Informazione ed Ingegn. Elettrica,
Università degli Studi di Salerno,
Via Ponte Don Melillo, I, I-84084, Fisciano (SA), Italy
{desanto, pergen, mvento}@unisa.it
[2] Dipartimento di Informatica e Sistemistica,
Università degli Studi di Napoli "Federico II"
Via Claudio 21, I-80125 Napoli, Italy
carlo.sansone@unina.it

Abstract. In this paper we propose an innovative combination strategy for a system using video and audio stream of a news video to automatically segment it into stories. In our approach, the segmentation is performed in two steps: first, shots are classified by combining three different anchor shot detection algorithms using video information only. Then, the shot classification is improved by using a novel anchor shot detection method based on features extracted from the audio track.

Experimental results demonstrate that the combined use of audio and video allows our system to perform better than approaches based only on video information in terms of both shot classification and news story segmentation.

1 Introduction

The segmentation of a news video into stories implies, at a first stage, the partition of the video into *shots*, i.e. sequences of frames, obtained by detecting transitions that are typically associated to camera changes. Once shots have been individuated, they can be classified on the basis of their content. Two different classes are typically considered: *anchor shots* and *news-report shots*. Successively, the given news video can be segmented into stories. This is obtained by linking each anchor shot with all successive news report shots until another anchor shot, or the end of the news video, occurs. Using this model for the stories, the news boundaries typically correspond to a transition from a news report shot to an anchor shot.

In the following, we address the shot classification problem as the basic step for segmenting a news video into stories. Up to now, existing approaches have been mainly based on the extraction of information from the video frames by using image analysis techniques. Namely, they usually try to classify shots by detecting the presence or the absence of an anchorperson inside each considered shot. Anchor shot detection is typically performed either by defining a model of the anchor and using

N.C. Oza et al. (Eds.): MCS 2005, LNCS 3541, pp. 397–406, 2005.
© Springer-Verlag Berlin Heidelberg 2005

some sort of template matching technique [1] or by searching shots with similar visual content that repeatedly occur during the whole news video [2,3].

On the other hand, in the last years the use of audio as an additional source of information for video segmentation has been rapidly raised up. Most of the presented proposals use audio features for directly individuating news boundaries, in order to strengthen or to weaken the boundaries provided from the analysis based on video techniques. They typically implement a silence detection module [4], assuming that the separation between a story and the successive one is given by a significant pause of the speaker.

In this paper, we propose a novel strategy for combining two shot classification systems that respectively analyze the video and the audio tracks of a news video. In more detail, the proposed approach performs shot classification by means of a two steps process: a first classification is obtained by using the Multi-Expert System presented in [5] that employs just video information. Then, the classification is refined by using a novel anchor shot detection method based only on audio data. The aim of this second step is that of trying to recover errors made by the video-based approach.

The system has been tested on a database that is comparable with those reported until now in the scientific literature [2]. In order to obtain more robust results from a statistical point of view, a k-fold cross validation has been also acted upon the used database. Executed tests show that the proposed system improves the performance of the multi-expert approach based on the video information only and performs significantly better of each single expert.

The organization of the paper is as follows: in Section 2 the architecture of our system is presented. In Section 3 the tests carried out in order to assess the performance of the proposed system are reported. Finally, some conclusions are drawn in Section 4.

2 System Architecture

As stated in the introduction, most of the systems that integrate audio and video data for news segmentation use audio features for directly individuating news boundaries, in order to strengthen or to weaken the boundaries provided from video-based techniques. Our proposal is instead to use two shot classification systems (*experts*) that separately try to classify each shots by respectively using video data (*video-based expert*) and audio data (*audio-based expert*). As regards the strategy for combining these two systems, we propose the use of the audio-based expert for trying to recover some of the missed anchor shot detections and/or some of the false alarms produced by the video-based expert. In other words, audio information is used after a video-based expert has furnished its decision and only in a limited number of cases. The rationale of this two stages approach lies in the fact that a typical combination of experts based on video features and experts based on audio features (by using, for example, them in a parallel combination scheme) is rather difficult. In fact, a shot classification system based only on audio features typically performs worse than a video-based system: hence, a parallel combination of the experts based on video and audio data could lead to a poor performance. Moreover, the combination of the outputs of audio and video anchor shot detection systems is not trivial: in a news video there are some cases in which the images of a news-report flow on the screen, while the voice of the anchorman, not visible on the screen, comments on them. In this case, the analysis based only on the visual content should consider the shot as a news-report shot. On the contrary, a system that analyzes the audio track should attribute the shot to the anchor shot class. So the two systems disagree, but they both take the correct decision based on their own information. By limiting the use of audio information in the whole classification process to a selected number of cases, the above described problem should become much less critical.

Once the strategy of combining audio and video information has been defined, it remains the problem of deciding when audio features should be used for trying to improve the performance of a video-based classification system. This could be difficult, since the output of a typical video-based expert is made only by a label indicating if the shot under analysis is attributed to the anchor class or to the news-report class [6]. However, we have recently proposed a video-based Multi-Expert System (MES) for shot classification [5,6]. The obtained results demonstrate the validity of this approach in improving the performance of each single video-based expert. On the other hand, various papers [7,8] have shown how to measure the classification reliability of a MES. Starting from these considerations, we propose the following criterion for deciding when using audio information: a video-based MES is first used for classifying a shot, then if its classification reliability is lower than a suitably fixed threshold, audio information is employed. The optimal value of the threshold can be computed by following the approach proposed in [8].

It is worth noticing that the importance of a video-based MES is twofold: on one hand, it permits to achieve a better performance than that obtainable with a single shot classification system; on the other hand, it allows us to obtain a reliability measure of each video-based shot classification, as required for combining audio and video data within our approach. In order to take advantage of a MES approach, the audio-based expert can be realized by using a multi-expert approach, too.

The proposed system architecture is then as follows: a first shot classification is performed by a parallel MES composed by video-experts. Each of the video-experts receives in input the list of all the shot boundaries of a news video together with the video itself and provides its own classification for each shot. Then, the combination module of the MES classifies each shot on the basis of the outputs of the video-experts and of the chosen combining rule.

The decision of the video-based MES, say C_V, together with its associated reliability R_V is then entered into a decision engine (*decisor*). If the value of R_V is lower than a suitably fixed threshold Th_V, the decisor activates a second MES composed by experts based on the audio track, otherwise the final decision of the system is that taken by the video-based MES. Note that also the proposed audio-based MES provides the reliability R_A of the performed classification.

All summarized, we have the following decisional path: when the audio-based MES is activated, if its classification shows a reliability value R_A higher than a given threshold Th_A, the final decision of the system agrees with that of the audio-based MES, let us call it C_A. Otherwise, the system assumes the decision of the video-based MES, i.e. C_V. The rational of this choice lies in the fact that when both MES's provide a low reliable classification, it is better to trust the video-based MES, given that its absolute performances are typically better than those obtainable by the audio-based MES, as it will be confirmed by the tests made in the next Section.

Let us note that the video-experts are based on three anchor shot detection algorithms presented in the literature, while the audio-based MES is composed by three brand new anchor shot detection algorithms based on features extracted from the audio track of the news videos.

In the following, we will first briefly describe the video-based MES, specifying how the chosen combining rule can be used within our approach. Then the algorithms proposed to perform the audio-based shot classification will be presented. Note that they all operate on the same feature vectors extracted from the audio track as described in [9].

2.1 Video-Based MES

The experts employed in the video-based MES implement the shot classification algorithms proposed by Bertini et *al.* in [3], Gao and Tang in [2] and Hanjalic et *al.* in [1]. See [5] for a description of their main features and for details about the rationale inspiring their choice. Hereinafter, for the sake of simplicity, we will refer to these experts with the terms BER, GAO and HAN, according to the first three letters of the first author's name.

As regards the combining rule, it is important to outline that the output of selected experts is made only by a "crisp" label indicating if the shot under analysis is attributed to the anchor class or to the news-report class. Thus, only three combining rules can be suitably used in this case: the majority voting rule [8], the Naïve Bayes Rule [10] and the Behavior Knowledge Space (BKS) Rule [7]. Among them, the BKS rule was chosen, since it does not explicitly require the classifier independence assumption. This characteristic is important because even if the selected shot classification techniques adopt complementary features, they all work on the same input source, i.e. a video shot.

Moreover, it is worth noting that the BKS rule is able to provide a reliability of the performed classification (see [7] for details), as required by our system architecture.

2.2 Audio-Based MES

The three audio-experts perform classification in an unsupervised way, in the sense that no information about the number or the identity of the speakers is required. However, they use information provided from the video-based MES about the guess class of the feature vectors. Since the video-experts are all unsupervised, the whole audio-video system can be seen as unsupervised too.

Generally speaking, the proposed algorithms try to detect the part of the feature space where vectors belonging to the voice of the anchorman lie. In particular, they use the Rival Penalized Competitive Learning (*RPCL*) [11] algorithm, a learning algorithm typically used for training competitive neural networks. In a competitive neural network, after the training phase, each neural unit (or *prototype*, hereinafter denoted as w_k) represents the centroid of one of the regions which the feature space has been partitioned into. In other words, a net with k prototypes partitions the feature space into k regions. The RPCL algorithm is able to allocate an appropriate number of prototypes for a given input set of data, so overcoming the problem of the correct preselection of k. This is an important characteristic, since in our case we cannot *a priori* know the number of different speakers within a news video and then cannot establish a suitable value for k. All the audio-experts described below have been trained by using 30 prototypes. This number is surely sufficient to model the different number of speakers which can appear throughout a single news video edition. In order to perform the classification of a whole shot, each audio-expert uses a majority voting approach. All the classification results (votes) on the single feature vectors relative to the audio frames composing the shot are first collected; then the expert attributes the shot to the class which has obtained the higher number of votes.

We also implemented the computation of a reliability measure of each classification. For each sample to be classified, the reliability R is measured as follows:

$$R = 1 - N_2/N_1 \tag{1}$$

where N_1 is the number of feature vectors attributed to the most likely class and N_2 is the number of feature vectors attributed to the other class. The value of R ranges from 0 (completely unreliable) to 1 (very reliable).

In the following some further details are given about the three different classification strategies adopted and the rule used for combining them. In particular, for each expert, the classification function $C: A_i \rightarrow \{Anchor, News\text{-}report\}$ used for assigning an audio sample A_i to one of the two possible classes will be reported.

2.2.1 Audio-Expert A

Among all the feature vectors generated from the audio track, only those belonging to audio frames that occur within shots classified as anchor shots by all the experts of the video-based MES are selected. These vectors are used to train a competitive network with the RPCL algorithm. Once the training phase ends, the network prototypes w_k should represent the centroids of the regions where the majority of samples describing audio frames of the anchorman are concentrated. Therefore, it is possible to assume that vectors that are sufficiently far from each prototype should describe audio frames belonging to the voice of a speaker different from the anchorman. In order to take into account this consideration, the maximum distance (say, *MaxDist*) among all the distances of a vector of the training set from its nearest prototype is evaluated and used in the classification phase. In this phase an audio sample A is attributed to the anchor shot class if its distance from the nearest prototype is smaller than $MaxDist*\alpha$ (where α is a suitably chosen threshold greater than one), otherwise it is attributed to the news-report shot class. So, the class attributed to each audio sample A_i is:

$$C(A_i) = \begin{cases} Anchor & if \; d(A_i, w_j) < MaxDist * \alpha; where \; j = \underset{k}{\arg\min} \, d(A_i, w_k) \\ News - report & otherwise \end{cases} \tag{2}$$

being $d(A_i, w_k)$ the distance of A_i from the k-th prototype.

The value of α can be chosen as the one that maximizes the classification performance on a suitable set of audio samples.

2.2.2 Audio-Expert B

The training is performed in the same way as the previous expert. The difference is that, after the training phase, a different value *MaxDist(k)* is calculated for each of the *k* prototypes. This value represents the maximum distance between an input sample and the *k*-th prototype evaluated among all the cases in which the *k*-th prototype resulted to be the nearest one to the input sample. So, in the classification phase, if the *j*-th prototype is the nearest to the sample to be classified, the sample *A* is attributed to the anchor shot class if its distance is smaller than *MaxDist(j)*β* (where *β* is again a suitably chosen threshold greater than one), otherwise it is attributed to the news-report shot class. In this way, a more accurate estimation of the regions where the audio samples of the anchorman are gathered should be obtained. In this case the class *C* attributed to the audio sample *A* is:

$$C(A_i) = \begin{cases} Anchor & if\ d(A_i, w_j) < MaxDist(j) * \beta;\ j = \arg\min_k d(A_i, w_k) \\ News - report & otherwise \end{cases} \tag{3}$$

being again $d(A_i, w_j)$ the distance of A_i from the *k*-th prototype.

Also in this case the value of *β* can be chosen as the one that maximizes the classification performance on a suitable set of audio samples.

2.2.3 Audio-Expert C

Differently from the previous two, this expert is trained by using all the feature vectors computed from the audio track. Indeed, for reducing the computational cost of the training, only a part of the available data can be used, by sub-sampling the whole data set. Once the training phase ends, some of the training vectors are used to label a *posteriori* the obtained prototypes. As in the previous cases, these vectors belong to audio frames occurring within shots classified as anchor shots by the video-based MES. Here the basic idea is that of trying to individuate also the region of the feature space where samples belonging to other speakers (different from the anchorman) are present. The labeling is performed by first associating a counter *count(w_k)* to each prototype w_k, which evaluates the number of times it results to be the nearest one to the vectors selected for the labeling phase. Then, the prototypes whose associated counter is greater than a suitable chosen threshold γ are attributed to the anchor class, while the others are attributed to the news-report class. In this case, since all the prototypes w_k are attributed to a class, say $C(w_k)$, the classification is performed by simply evaluating for each sample to be classified the nearest prototypes and by attributing to it the class of that prototype. More concisely:

$$C(A_i) = C(w_j) \qquad where\ j = \arg\min_k d(A_i, w_k) \tag{4}$$

The value of γ is chosen as in the two previous cases.

2.2.4 The Combining Rule

As regards the combining rule, since in this case each expert provides a reliability value together with its decision, a different rule with respect to the video-based MES is used. In particular, a dynamic selection criterion is adopted. For each shot S_i to be classified, the class C^k attributed to it by each single expert E^k is collected. The reliability of each expert R^k is also computed by using eq. (1) and weighted by the probability P^k ($C^k(S_i)$= correct class $|$ $C^k(S_i)$ = guess class) that this expert takes the right decision when it decides for the class $C^k(S_i)$. This probability is estimated by adopting the method proposed in [10], which uses the so-called confusion matrix, i.e. the classification results of the expert on a reference set of samples. Then, the final decision of the audio-based MES, together with the associated reliability R_A, coincides with that supplied by the audio expert that maximizes the value $R^k * P^k$.

In formulas, the audio-based MES attributes each shot S_i to the class C such that:

$$C(S_i) = \underset{k}{\mathrm{argmax}}\ P^k\ (C^k(S_i) = \text{correct class} \mid C^k(S_i) = \text{guess class})* R^k \qquad (5)$$

3 Experimental Results

Some efforts have been spent in the recent past by other researchers in building video databases for benchmarking purposes; in particular in [12] a database was built in order to characterize the performance of shot change detection algorithms. This database, however, is not adequate for our aims, since it is made up not only of news video but also of sport events and sitcom videos, and the duration of news videos is only 20 minutes. A bigger database, composed of about 70 hours of video captured by the Linguistic Data Consortium during the last half of 1998 from CNN Headline News and ABC World News Tonight, has been made available to the participants to the TREC Video Retrieval Evaluation contest in 2004 (TRECVID 2004). Videos are in MPEG-1 format and are estimated to take up about 80 gigabytes. Unfortunately, these data are not publicly available outside the TRECVID contest.

So, we have built a new video database. The acquisition was performed by means of a digital satellite decoder. We encoded the videos in the MPEG-1 format using the TMPGEnc encoder (ver. 2.01). The video is coded at 2 Mbit/s with a 704x576 frame size. As regards the audio signal, it has been extracted from the MPEG-1 stream by using the TMPGEnc, so obtaining data into the MP2 format. Then, the MP2 files were converted into the wave format at 44.1 kHz rate and 16 bits per sample, by using the Winamp2 waveOut plug-in.

The database used in this paper (over six hours) is composed by nineteen news videos from the main Italian public network (namely, RAI 1). Particular care was taken in order to include in the database different news editions from this TV-network. It is worth noting that the database used here is part of a bigger one (over nine hours) employed for testing the MES proposed in [6]. From that database we removed all the editions shorter than seven minutes. In those editions, in fact, almost all the stories were commented by the anchorperson himself. Then, the audio information cannot be useful employed within our approach, since the hypotheses made by the proposed audio-experts are no longer valid. However, all the stories of the short editions are typically included (and expanded) within the long editions of the same day, so this does not appear as a limitation of our approach in real cases.

In order to obtain a more realistic estimate of the performance of the proposed system, a four-fold cross validation was performed. Therefore, we divided the nineteen videos of the database in four subsets. Then, we performed four tests: in each one, three subsets of the database were used as training set and one subset for testing. In each fold, the training set was used to calculate the Behavior-Knowledge Space matrix (see [7]) needed by the BKS rule and the threshold Th_V on the reliability of the video-base MES. Moreover, it was used for choosing the thresholds (α, β and γ) needed by the three audio-based experts, for estimating the probabilities P^k needed by the dynamic selection rule and for calculating the threshold Th_A on the reliability of the audio-based MES. The test set was instead used to test the single experts, the video-based and the audio-based MES and the proposed system. Hence, all the reported results were obtained as the average of the performance on the four test sets.

When dealing with unbalanced data sets, the system performance is typically reported in terms of *Precision* and *Recall* [12,13]. Moreover, we will characterize the system performance by using also a unique figure of merits F [13] that combines *Precision* and *Recall* as reported in the following equation:

$$F = (2 \cdot Precision \cdot Recall) / (Precision + Recall) \tag{6}$$

As a first step of our tests, we evaluate the performance obtained by the three video-experts and by the three audio-based experts. Table 1 reports the global performance of each expert: as it could be expected, the audio-based experts perform sensibly worse than the video-based experts. The best audio-expert, in fact, exhibits a performance that is only comparable with the worst video-based expert (HAN). This poor performance is mainly due to the Precision value exhibited by these experts that instead give rise to a quite acceptable Recall.

Table 1. The performance of the considered video-based and audio-based experts averaged on the four test sets. Standard deviations are reported in parenthesis

Expert	Recall	Precision	F
GAO	0.929 (3.645E-02)	0.817 (9.057E-02)	0.867 (4.609E-02)
BER	0.845 (8.677E-02)	0.988 (8.164E-03)	0.909 (5.009E-02)
HAN	0.644 (9.320E-02)	0.686 (7.265E-02)	0.664 (8.176E-02)
Audio-expert A	0.581 (8.949E-02)	0.459 (6.056E-02)	0.507 (3.876E-02)
Audio-expert B	0.774 (1.182E-01)	0.591 (1.096E-01)	0.669 (1.070E-01)
Audio-expert C	0.695 (1,960E-01)	0.804 (9.299E-02)	0.736 (1.408E-01)

When dealing with the evaluation of a MES, it is important to consider the performance of the so-called *oracle*. The *oracle* is the theoretic MES that correctly classifies a shot as anchor shot or as news-report shot if at least one of the employed experts is able to provide the correct classification. It is evident that for a defined set of experts, the performance of the oracle is the upper bound of all the MES's obtainable from the same set of experts by using any combining rule.

In table 2, the performance of the *oracle*, of the proposed system and of the video-based and the audio-based MES is reported. From the table it is possible to notice how the proposed video-based MES outperforms the best video-expert (BER) in terms of the both *Precision* and *Recall*, so giving rise to a better value of F. On the other hand, the audio-based MES outperforms the three audio-based experts in terms of both *Precision* and F, but performs considerably worse than the video-based MES. As regards the comparison of the audio-based MES with the single video-based experts, it can be noted that the former is able to outperform the HAN expert. Finally, it is worth noting that the proposed audio-video system is able to further increase the *Recall* of the video-based MES. This is paid by an only slightly worse performance in terms of *Precision*, so giving rise to a better *F* value.

Table 2. The performance of the oracle, of the proposed system, and of the video-based and of the audio-based MES. Standard deviations are reported in parenthesis

	Recall	Precision	F
Oracle	0.955 *(3.972E-02)*	1.000 *(0.000E+00)*	0.977 *(2.111E-02)*
Proposed audio-video system	0.914 *(2.177E-02)*	0.990 *(1.923E-02)*	0.950 *(1.208E-02)*
Video-based MES	0.885 *(3.095E-02)*	1.000 *(0.000E+00)*	0.939 *(1.731E-02)*
Audio-based MES	0.728 *(1.288E-01)*	0.750 *(3.170E-02)*	0.735 *(7.271E-02)*

To better understand the reasons of the obtained improvement, it is interesting to investigate which type of errors of the video-based MES is recovered by the proposed system. As illustrated in Section 2, the audio-based MES is activated when a video-based MES classification does not reach the reliability threshold Th_V. For each fold, this occurs when BER and HAN provide the same decision while GAO disagrees with them. In particular, it has been verified that the proposed system is able to recover, by using audio data, situations in which BER and HAN miss the detection of an anchor-person, while GAO does not.

Another very interesting way to examine the obtained results is showed by considering the data reported in table 3. Here, the performance of the proposed architecture is expressed in terms of the relative improvement with respect to the performance of the oracle. Such improvement has been calculated as:

$$RI_{par} = \frac{par_{proposedSystem} - par_{Exp}}{par_{oracle} - par_{Exp}} \qquad (7)$$

being par $\in \{Recall, Precision, F\}$ one of the parameters defined for evaluating the performance and *Exp* a single expert or even a MES.

Table 3. The relative improvement introduced by the proposed audio-video architecture with respect to the performance that can be obtained by using the *oracle*

	RI_{Recall}	$RI_{Precision}$	RI_F
Video-based MES	41.4%	--	28.9%
Best video-based expert	62.7%	16.7%	60.3%
Audio-based MES	81.9%	96.0%	88.8%

The results reported in table 3 show that the proposed audio-video architecture is able to achieve an improvement of the *F* value obtained by the video-based MES that is about the 29% of the maximum possible improvement.

4 Conclusions

Integrating audio and video data for performing story detection in news videos is not a trivial task. In this paper, we proposed a novel system for segmenting news videos into stories where three shot classification techniques based on audio features are combined and specifically used for recovering the errors of a video-based Multi-Expert System that occur when it classifies shots with a low reliability.

Experimental results on six hours of news videos demonstrated that the proposed audio-video system performs better than approaches based on video information only.

References

1. A. Hanjalic, R. L. Lagendijk, J. Biemond, "Semi-Automatic News Analysis, Indexing, and Classification System Based on Topics Preselection", Proc. of SPIE: Electronic Imaging: Storage and Retrieval of Image and Video Databases, San Jose (CA), 1999.
2. X. Gao, X. Tang, "Unsupervised Video-Shot Segmentation and Model-Free Anchorperson Detection for News Video Story Parsing", IEEE Transactions on Circuits and Systems for Video Technology, Vol. 12, No. 9, pp. 765 776, 2002.
3. M. Bertini, A. Del Bimbo, P. Pala, "Content-based indexing and retrieval of TV News", Pattern Recognition Letters, vol. 22, pp. 503-516, 2001.
4. W. Wei, W. Gao, Automatic Segmentation of News Items Based on Video and Audio Features, Journal of Computer Science and Technology 17 (2), pp. 189-195, 2002.
5. M. De Santo, G. Percannella, C. Sansone, M. Vento, "Combining experts for anchorperson shot detection in news videos", Pattern Analysis and Applications, vol. 7 no. 4, Springer, Berlin, 2004 (*in press* – online first: DOI: 10.1007/s10044-004-0227-0).
6. M. De Santo, G. Percannella, C. Sansone, M. Vento, "A Multi-Expert Approach for Shot Classification in News Videos", Lecture Notes in Computer Science vol. 3211, pp. 564-571, 2004.
7. Y. S. Huang and C. Y. Suen, "A Method of Combining Multiple Experts for the Recognition of Unconstrained Handwritten Numerals", IEEE Transactions on Pattern Analysis and Machine Intelligence, Vol. 17, no. 1, pp. 90-94, 1995.
8. C. Sansone, F. Tortorella, M.Vento, "A Classification Reliability Driven Reject Rule for Multi-Expert Systems", International Journal of Pattern Recognition and Artificial Intelligence, vol. 15, no. 6, pp. 885-904, 2001.
9. L.P. Cordella, P. Foggia, C. Sansone, M. Vento, "A Real-Time Text-Independent Speaker Identification System", Proceedings of the 12th International Conference on Image Analysis and Processing, Mantova, September 17 19, pp. 632-637, 2003.
10. L. Xu, A. Krzyzak and C.Y. Suen, "Methods of Combining Multiple Classifiers and Their Application to Handwritten Numeral Recognition", IEEE Trans. on Systems, Man and Cybernetics, 22(3), (1992), 418-435.
11. L. Xu, A. Krzyzak, and E. Oja, "Rival Penalized Competitive Learning for Clustering Analysis, RBF net and Curve Detection", IEEE Trans. on Neural Networks, vol. 4, pp. 636-649, 1993.
12. U. Gargi, R. Kasturi, S.H. Strayer, "Performance Characterization of Video-Shot-Change Detection Methods", IEEE Trans. on Circuits and Systems for Video Technology, Vol. 10, No. 1, pp. 1-13, 2000.
13. L. Chaisorn, T.-S. Chua, C.-H. Lee, "A Multi-Modal Approach to Story Segmentation for News Video", World Wide Web, vol. 6, pp. 187–208, 2003.

Designing Multiple Classifier Systems for Face Recognition

Nitesh V. Chawla and Kevin W. Bowyer

Department of Computer Science and Engineering,
University of Notre Dame, IN 46556, USA
{nchawla, kwb}@cse.nd.edu

Abstract. Face recognition systems often use different images of a subject for training and enrollment. Typically, one may use LDA using all the image samples or train a nearest neighbor classifier for each (separate) set of images. The latter can require that information about lighting or expression about each testing point be available. In this paper, we propose usage of different images in a multiple classifier systems setting. Our main goals are to see (1) what is the preferred use of different images? And (2) can the multiple classifiers generalize well enough across different kinds of images in the testing set, thus mitigating the need of the meta-information? We show that an ensemble of classifiers outperforms the single classifier versions without any tuning, and is as good as a single classifier trained on all the images and tuned on the test set.

1 Introduction

Face recognition is becoming an increasing popular and relevant area of study. The Face Recognition Grand Challenge (FRGC) sponsored by various US Government agencies is a prime example of the growing importance of improving or benchmarking face recognition techniques [1, 2]. In this paper we focus on 2-D face recognition, which has been a subject of significant study [3, 4]. Two dimensional face images are usually represented as high-dimensional pixel matrices, where in each matrix cell is a gray-level intensity value. These raw feature vectors can be very large and highly correlated. Moreover, the size of the training data is usually small. To combat these issues of very high feature correlation, small sample size and computational complexity, the face images are often transformed into a lower dimensional manifold. One of the most popular techniques for linear transformation in feature space is Principal Component Analysis (PCA) [5, 6]. PCA reduces the dimensions by rotating feature vectors from a large highly correlated feature space *(image space)* to a smaller feature space *(face space)* that has no sample covariance between the features. After applying PCA to reduce the face space to a lower dimensional manifold, a single nearest neighbor classifier or a linear discriminant classifier is typically used.

We will now introduce some terms and notation from biometrics that will be used throughout the paper. **Subject**: A person or a subject in the training

N.C. Oza et al. (Eds.): MCS 2005, LNCS 3541, pp. 407–416, 2005.

set is similar to a class or concept in data. This person can be associated with multiple images in the training set; **Training set**: The training set is defined to be all the images of subjects that are available for constructing the face space; **Gallery set**: Gallery is the set of subjects enrolled in the database and can either be the same as the training set or different. Due to a lack of enough data, the gallery images are often used as the training set for constructing the face space. However, gallery images in this paper comprise of the same subjects (but images captured on a different date) and completely new subjects; **Probe set**: Probe set is the "testing" set. The images in the probe set are typically of the same subjects who are in the gallery set, but are taken at a later point in time. The goal is to project the probe set into the trained face space and correctly match it with the projected representative in the gallery.

Two dimensional face recognition presents a multitude of challenges when applied to conditions (including subjects) that weren't part of the training set. An example of this is a face space trained on a neutral expression if presented with a smiling expression face space. Ideally, the face recognition algorithm should be fairly insensitive to changes in the lighting direction and intensity or facial expression. In addition, even if we try to control the face space of the training session and the testing session to have the identical lighting and expression conditions, there still can be differences between the two caused by errors in normalization, slight pose changes, illumination variations etc. Even if the same controlled lighting environment is used, it can still cause illumination variations if the testing set image is captured on a different day, for example.

One may construct a single classifier by combining possible variations in the lighting direction and facial expression for constructing a face space. However, PCA can potentially retain the variation in lighting direction, illumination, and expression that is not relevant for recognition. The covariance matrix constructed will capture both inter-class and intra-class variance. To maximize the inter-class distance (across subjects) and minimize the intra-class distance (within subjects), Linear Discriminant Analysis [7, 8] (LDA) can be used. But LDA suffers from the small-sample size problem, and requires "enough" images of a subject [9, 7]. Typically, researchers have proposed using at least 10 images of each subject [10]. The goal is to correctly recognize a face, and not essentially distinguish between different variations of a face. Also another challenge in 2-D face recognition is that the subjects used in the testing or the probe set may not be present in the training set. So, essentially, we need a classifier that can generalize well enough, without overtraining on a specific face space.

We propose to utilize multiple classifier systems or ensembles in the biometric problem of 2-D face recognition. We randomly sample from the acquired images of a subject to construct face spaces. We construct 50 such face spaces for an ensemble. Given 4 images (different expression and lighting conditions) of each subject, we randomly sample 1, 2 and 3 images 50 times. We explain the data in the subsequent sections. In the sections that follow, we will compare different ways of defining the training set for using a classifier or a set of classifiers. We can formalize the objective of this paper as follows:

1. What is the best use of available multiple training images of a subject?
2. Can we construct a classifier or a set of classifiers that can be applied across probe images with different expressions and/or lighting conditions? The goal is to do as well if not better than the different single classifiers constructed specifically to represent particular lighting and expression conditions.

2   Classifiers

In this section, we discuss in brief the PCA methodology, the MahCosine distance metric as implemented in the CSU code [11], and the linear discriminant analysis classifier or LDA. For both nearest neighbor and LDA, PCA methodology is applied first. All the images are first normalized such that the pixel values have a zero mean and unit variance.

2.1   PCA

The raw feature vectors are a concatenation of the gray-level pixel values from the images. Let us assume there are m images and n pixel values per image. Let Z be a matrix of (m,n), where m is the number of images and n is the number of pixels (raw feature vector). The mean image of Z is then subtracted from each of the images in the training set, $\Delta Z_i = Z_i - E[Z_i]$. Let the matrix M represent the resulting "centered" images; $M = (\Delta Z_1, \Delta Z_2, ..\Delta Z_m)^T$. The covariance matrix can then be represented as: $\Omega = M.M^T$. Ω is symmetric and can be expressed in terms of the singular value decomposition $\Omega = U.\Lambda.U^T$, where U is an m x m unitary matrix and $\Lambda = diag(\lambda_1, ..., \lambda_m)$. The vectors $U_1, ..., U_m$ are a basis for the m-dimensional subspace. The covariance matrix can now be re-written as

$$\Omega = \sum_{i=1}^{m} \zeta_i.U_i$$

The coordinate ζ_i, $i \in 1, 2, ...m$, is called the ζ_i^{th} principal component. It represents the projection of ΔZ onto the basis vector U. The basis vectors, U_i, are the principal components of the training set. Once the subspace is constructed, recognition is done by projecting a centered probe image into the subspace, and the closest gallery image to the probe image is selected as the match.

Before applying PCA, the images are normalized and cropped resulting in an image size of 130x150. Unwrapping the image results in a vector of size 19,500. PCA reduces this to a basis vector count of $m - 1$, where m is the number of images. PCA approaches to face recognition typically drop some vectors to form the face space. A small number from the beginning and a larger number from the end.

2.2   Distance Measure

A popular and simple classification technique in 2-D face recognition is the nearest neighbor classifier. An image in the probe set is assigned the label that is closest in the gallery set. Various distance measures have been evaluated in the realm of face recognition [12, 13]. For our experiments, we utilized the Mah-Cosine distance metric [11]. Our initial experiments showed that MahCosine significantly outperformed the other distance measures, such as Euclidean or Mahalanobis distance measures.

The MahCosine measure is the cosine of the angle between the images after they have been transformed to the Mahalanobis space [11]. Formally, the MahCosine measure between the images i and j with projections a and b in the Mahalanobis space is computed as:

$$MahCosine(i,j) = cos(\theta_{ij}) = \frac{|a||b|cos(\theta_{ij})}{|a||b|}$$

2.3   Linear Discriminant Analysis (LDA)

LDA tries to achieve a projection that best discriminates between the the different subjects. PCA can be used to reduce the dimensionality before applying LDA. The *Fisherface* is constructed by defining a d dimensional subspace in the first d principal components [14]. Fisher's method finds the projecting vectors W, such that the basis vectors in W maximize the ratio of the determinant of the inter-class scatter matrix S_b and the determinant of the intra-class scatter matrix S_w.

$$W = argmax \frac{|W^T S_b W|}{|W^T S_w W|}$$

Let us define the number of subjects to be m and the number of images (samples) per subject available for training to be s_i, where i is the subject index. Then S_b and S_w can be defined as:

$$S_w = \sum_{i=1}^{m} \sum_{x_k \in X_i} (x_k - \mu_i)(x_k - \mu_i)^T$$

$$S_b = \sum_{i=1}^{m} s_i(\mu_i - \mu)(\mu_i - \mu)^T$$

and where μ_i is the mean of vector of samples belonging to the class (or subject) i, μ is the mean vector of all the samples. S_w may not be well estimated if the number of samples is too small.

3   Data Collection

The data for this paper was acquired from that available from the University of Notre Dame[1] [2]. The subjects participate in the acquisition at week intervals

---

[1] http://www.cse.nd.edu/~cvrl

FA-LF   FA-LM   FB-LF   FB-LM

Fig. 1. Sample images of a subject in the training data

over a period of time. For the experiments in this paper, images were captured either with two side lights on (LF) or with two side lights and a center light on (LM). In addition, subjects were asked to have either a neutral expression (FA) or a smile expression (FB). The nomenclature is as used by FERET [15]. The data was acquired during Spring 2002, Fall 2002, and Spring 2003. Figure 1 shows sample images of a subject captured under the four conditions.

We divided the data into training, gallery, and probe sets. To run multiple trials, we randomly selected 10 times 121 subjects from an available pool of 484 subjects. For each of the 10 random runs, we utilized the same probe and gallery sets. We report the mean and standard deviation in the rank-one recognition rates on the probe and gallery sets. Each selected subject had four images for *FA-LF*, *FB-LF*, *FA-LM* and *FB-LM*. The training set images were captured at the first acquisition session. Then we took all the subjects that had at least three acqusition sessions. The 2nd session of acquisition became the gallery set and the last session became the probe set. This gave us 381 subjects for testing. This ensured that only a small subset of subjects in the probe set was used in the training set, and moreover there was a time-lapse element introduced in testing. The probe sets, however, comprised of completely different images (even if of same subjects) than the training set. There was no overlap whatsoever in the images between the training and probe sets. We tried to mimic a setting that may be used in a 2-D face recognition system — the subjects in the gallery may not always be in the training data. Our probe sets always had different images than the training set.

4   Multiple Classifier System

The applications of multiple classifier systems are becoming relevant in face recognition. Beveridge et al. [14] used bagging without replacement; they randomly sampled without replacement from their population of 160 subjects. They showed that replicates produced by sampling with replacement can cause problems with the scoring methodology. We also sample without replacement, albeit from the four different images available for each subject, thus always having at least one representative of each subject in the training set. Lu and Jain [10] randomly sampled within each class (or subject) to construct a set of the LDA classifiers. However, they had 10 images for each class. Wang and Tang [16] recently used random subspaces to improve the performance of LDA classifier. Lemieux and Parizeau [17] utilized a multi-classifier architecture also, but they used four different classifiers: HMM, DCT, EigenFaces and EigenObjects. We randomly sample from the set of images for each subject, and construct a set of one nearest neighbor classifiers using the MahCosine measure. To establish the generality of the classifiers, we evaluate on a varying set of expressions, lighting conditions, and subjects.

We included LDA as a comparison benchmark, even though we had a smaller set of images per subject than is typically used with LDA. We compared four techniques. Please note that the number of basis vectors after the PCA was $m - 1$, where m is the number of images considered as part of each of the techniques. For example, if there are 121 images in the training set, then the basis vector count is 120. (1) Single *specialized* face space: This is the face space trained on a particular expression and lighting combination. In this type, a single face space was constructed for each of the FA-LF, FA-LM, FB-LF, and FB-LM. Thus, it is called *specialized* as each one is representative of a particular lighting and expression combination. (2) *Complete* face space (*All-1NN*): This is constructed using a 1-nearest neighbor classifier on a training set of size 484 (121x4), where each subject has four representative images in the training set. We concatenated all the four images available of a subject and constructed a single training set. The face-space was then constructed on all the concatenated 484 images. (3) *All-LDA* classifier using the four images per subject. Again, for LDA we considered all the available images for each subject, giving us 121 classes (or subjects) with four images (or examples) each. (4) *Ensemble*: We randomly sampled (*num =*) one, two, and three images (from the four images) per subject and constructed multiple classifiers. These will be referred to as *Ensemble-1, Ensemble-2, Ensemble-3*. While we varied the number of images for each ensemble, we maintained the same size of 50 classifiers. Each of the aforementioned Ensembles had a different number of (randomly selected) training set images for each subject. Given 121 subjects, *Ensemble-1* had 121 images; *Ensemble-2* had 242 images; and *Ensemble-3* had 363 images. We can summarize our procedure as follows:

1. For each k=1,2,..,K (where K is the number of classifiers, set as 50 in our case.)
   (a) Randomly select without replacement *num* images for each subject.
   (b) Construct a face space, X^k. As we mentioned before, the number of basis vectors after PCA is $m - 1$. Thus, the number of basis vectors for *Ensemble-1* is 120; for *Ensemble-2* is 241; and for *Ensemble-3* is 362.
   (c) For each probe image, find the closest gallery image with X^k using the MahCosine measure. Each individual classifier (k) assigns a distance measure to the probe image.
2. Aggregate the distances assigned to each probe image by each X^k.
3. Rank order the images and compute the rank-one recognition rate. This is the final rank-one recognition rate of the ensemble.

5   Experiments

To test the suitability of multiple classifiers in this domain, we compare to classifiers specialized for the lighting and expression condition, and to classifiers that use all the available training images. In the specialized comparisons, our probe and gallery sets were used separately for each expression and lighting combination (FA-LF, FA-LM, FB-LF, and FB-LM). Thus, each classifier was tested four times and performances are shown in Table 1. The rows are the training face spaces and the columns are the probe face spaces. Besides each specialized classifier, we also indicate the performance obtained by All-1NN and All-LDA in Table 2.

We did not tune the individual classifiers by dropping eigen vectors either from "front" or "back" of the face space. Typically, the first couple of vectors are assumed to carry the illumination variation [13]. One can also drop some low variance eigen vectors from behind to further improve the individual classifiers. However, to maintain the same performance benchmark across all classifiers we retained all the eigen vectors. As part of our future work we propose to utlize a validation set to tune the face spaces before applying them to the testing (probe) sets. This is similar to the wrapper techniques deployed in feature selection wherein a validation scheme is introduced for selecting the appropriate subset of features. If the face space is tuned on the probe set, it can lead to overestimated accuracies; a bias is introduced in developing the nearest neighbor classifier.

As evident by Table 1, the specialized classifier usually performs better if the testing set comes from the corresponding set of conditions. However, we notice that the classifiers trained on the LF lighting condition tend to perform better on the LM lighting condition (than the corresponding LF lighting condition). It could be that the LF classifiers are potentially overfitting on their space, thus leading to a reduced accuracy. In addition, there can be implicit illumination variations in the probe set that were unaccounted for. Similar results were noted by Chang et al. [18]. Moreover, making a complete face space of all the available images performs better than the specialized classifier across the board. It is perhaps not surprising that *All-1NN* does better than any *Specialized* classifier, across all 4 conditions, since it has more representatives for each subject under varying conditions. It is very much possible that the images captured under exactly the same controlled environment, still have an implicit element of illumination and pose variation. Having a diverse set of images in the training set can help in such scenario. However, we expect that as the number of images in the training set increases, the face-space can be overfit. This can require tuning to get rid of the low variance vectors, as we are more interested in distinguishing between subjects than between different variations of a subject. Surprisingly, LDA does not perform as well as 1-NN with all the images. LDA's performance can be hurt by small-sample size in high dimensional spaces [7, 9]. We only have four samples per class. Not having enough images per subject, we also run into the curse of dimensionality problem. One may drop eigen vectors to improve the performance of the LDA classifiers.

Table 1. The rank-one recognition rates and the standard deviation for the *Specialized* classifiers. The columns are the probe and gallery sets, and the rows are the training sets

	FA-LF	FA-LM	FB-LF	FB-LM
FA-LF (Specialized)	0.660 ± 0.025	0.712 ± 0.01	0.649 ± 0.012	0.666 ± 0.017
FA-LM (Specialized)	0.649 ± 0.018	0.716 ± 0.009	0.637 ± 0.017	0.66 ± 0.014
FB-LF (Specialized)	0.603 ± 0.014	0.659 ± 0.014	0.711 ± 0.012	0.725 ± 0.007
FB-LM (Specialized)	0.583 ± 0.017	0.648 ± 0.015	0.699 ± 0.01	0.729 ± 0.015

Table 2. The rank-one recognition rates and the standard deviations of the *Ensemble* methods, *All-1NN*, and *All-LDA* across the probe sets with varying lighting and expression combinations (columns). The entries in bold indicate the best performances

	FA-LF	FA-LM	FB-LF	FB-LM
Ensemble-1	0.653 ± 0.017	0.717 ± 0.012	0.714 ± 0.013	0.738 ± 0.01
Ensemble-2	0.697 ± 0.014	0.739 ± 0.011	0.748 ± 0.011	0.76 ± 0.006
Ensemble-3	**0.707 ± 0.009**	**0.743 ± 0.012**	**0.756 ± 0.009**	**0.769 ± 0.01**
All-1NN	0.69 ± 0.01	0.73 ± 0.015	0.734 ± 0.0137	0.754 ± 0.01
All-LDA	0.569 ± 0.024	0.615 ± 0.021	0.604 ± 0.026	0.6601 ± 0.022

Table 2 shows the results of different sample sizes on the four different probe sets. Due to a lack of space, we only include the performance obtained at the iteration where the performance plateaued for the ensemble methods. Typically, that was by the 10th iteration. We notice a consistent trend in the Table: *Ensemble-2* and *Ensemble-3* are fairly comparable and outperforming the other classifiers. Moreover, both *Ensemble-2* and *Ensemble-3* generalize very well across different sets of images, and exceed the accuracy obtained by both the *Specialized* and *All-1NN* classifiers. *Ensemble-3* is statistically significantly better at 95% than *All-1NN* for FA-LM and FB-LF. And both the *Ensemble-2* and *Ensemble-3* methods are statistically significantly better (at 95%) than the *Specialized* classifiers tested on their corresponding face spaces. Ensemble power with fewer images exceeds the single classifier with all the images. This is in agreement with what is typically observed by the MCS community.

We note that *Ensemble-1* is consistently lower than the classifiers with more images, but (almost) always above the *Specialized* case. The FA-LF classifier is slightly better than *Ensemble-1*. Constructing multiple classifiers of one image for each subject may not be representative enough for each of the subsequent spaces, as the training set size will be small. Typically, a learning curve can be plotted to identify the "critical" amount of data for different domains as applicable for a classifier. Also, we believe that randomly sampled images for each subject are adding the "diversity" element in the ensemble. Various studies have shown that different classifiers follow a learning curve that typically grows with the amount of data and eventually plateaus [19, 20, 21]. Skurichina et al. show that bagging with linear classifiers does not work for very small datasets or large datasets [20].

6   Conclusions

We empirically evaluated various training set sizes by randomly sampling from the available images for each subject. We showed that the multiple classifier system of randomly sampled images achieves good performances across the different probe sets. We constructed our training and testing such that the testing set not only contained images that were captured at a different time than the training set images but also a set of unique subjects. This maintained the difficulty of testing sets. Moreover, we tested the set of classifiers across four different expressions and lighting conditions combinations. The changing environment of the new images is a very important problem. We quote from a recent article from the Government Security Newsletter: "It turns out that uncooperative subjects, poor lighting and the difficulty of capturing comparable images often make it difficult for face recognition systems to achieve the accuracy that government officials might seek in large-scale anti-terrorism applications. [22]" Hence, we tried to imitate that setting in our paper. Our results are indeed interesting in this scenario, as we show that multiple classifier systems generalize better across different kinds of images, without any explicit assumption, thus mitigating the need of specialized and tuned classifiers.

As part of future work, we plan to extend our study to include increasing number of subjects and study the effect of that on the face space as we resample. We believe that as the number of subjects increase the face space constructed from all the images might overfit, requiring a tuning by dropping eigen vectors from the front or back. We also aim to introduce diversity metrics in our system to understand the behavior of different classifiers in the ensemble. However, we would like to utilize a separate validation set for any tuning to make the results as generalizable as possible. We also propose to utilize more images of a subject and implement a resampling framework for LDA as by Lu and Jain [10]. We believe that multiple classifier systems will be generally applicable to the recognition task due to an improved generalization on out-of-time and out-of-sample data.

Acknowledgments

This work is supported by National Science Foundation grant EIA 01-20839 and Department of Justice grant 2004-DD-BX-1224.

References

1. "Face recognition grand challenge and the biometrics experimentation environment." available at http://bee-biometrics.org.
2. P. J. Flynn, K. W. Bowyer, and P. J. Phillips, "Assessment of time dependency in face recognition: An initial study," in *International Conference on Audio and Video Based Biometric Person Authentication*, pp. 44–51, 2003.
3. R. Chellappa, C. Wilson, and S. Sirohey, "Human and machine recognition of faces: A survey," *Proceedings of hte IEEE*, vol. 83, no. 5, pp. 705 – 740, 1995.

4. A. Samal and P. Iyengar, "Automatic recognition and analysis of human faces and facial expressions: A survey," *Pattern Recognition*, vol. 25, no. 1, pp. 65 – 77, 1992.
5. M. Turk and A. Pentland, "Eigenfaces for recognition," *Journal of Cognitive Neuroscience*, vol. 3, no. 1, pp. 71–86, 1991.
6. G. Shakhnarovich and G. Moghaddam, *Handbook of Face Recognition*, ch. Face recognition in subspaces. Springer-Verlag, 2004.
7. K. Fukunaga, *Introduction to Statistical Pattern Recognition*. New York: Academic Press, 1990.
8. R. O. Duda, P. E. Hart, and D. G. Stork, *Pattern Classification*. New York: Wiley, 2nd ed., 2000.
9. A. M. Martinez and A. C. Kak, "Pca versus lda," *IEEE Transactions on Pattern Analysis and Machine Intelligence*, vol. 23, no. 2, pp. 228–233, 2001.
10. X. Lu and A. K. Jain, "Resampling for face recognition," in *International Conference on Audio and Video Based Biometric Person Authentication*, pp. 869 – 877, 2003.
11. D. Beveridge and B. Draper, "Evaluation of face recognition algorithms (release version 4.0)." available at http://www.cs.colostate.edu/evalfacerec/index.html.
12. V. Perlibakas, "Distance measures for pca-based face recognition," *Pattern Recognition Letters*, vol. 25, no. 6, pp. 711–724, 2004.
13. W. Yambor, B. Draper, and R. Beveridge, "Analyzing PCA-based face recognition algorithms: Eigenvector selection and distance measures," July 2000.
14. J. R. Beveridge, K. She, B. Draper, and G. Givens, "A nonparametric statistical comparison of principal component and linear discriminant subspaces for face recognition," in *IEEE Conference on Computer Vision and Pattern Recognition*, pp. 535 – 542, 2001.
15. P. J. Phillips, H. Moon, S. A. Rizvi, and P. J. Rauss, "The FERET evaluation methodology for face-recognition algorithms," *IEEE Transactions on Pattern Analysis and Machine Intelligence*, vol. 22, no. 10, pp. 1090–1104, 2000.
16. X. Wang and X. Tang, "Random sampling LDA for face recognition," in *IEEE International Conference on Computer Vision and Pattern Recognition*, pp. 259–265, 2004.
17. A. Lemieux and M. Parizeau, "Flexible multi-classifier architecture for face recognition systems," *Vision Interface*, 2003.
18. K. Chang, K. W. Bowyer, and P. Flynn, "An evaluation of multi-modal 2d+3d face biometrics," *IEEE Transactions on Pattern Analysis and Machine Intelligence*, 2005.
19. F. Provost, D. Jensen, and T. Oates, "Efficient progressive sampling," in *Fifth International of Knowledge Discovery and Databases*, pp. 23–32, 1999.
20. M. Skurichina, L. Kuncheva, and R. P. W. Duin, "Bagging and boosting for the nearest mean classifier: Effects of sample size on diversity and accuracy," in *Third International Workshop on Multiple Classifier Systems*, pp. 62 – 71, 2002.
21. N. V. Chawla, L. O. Hall, K. W. Bowyer, and W. P. Kegelmeyer, "Learning ensembles from bites: A scalable and accurate approach," *Journal of Machine Learning Research*, vol. 5, pp. 421 – 451, 2004.
22. "GSN Perspectives –Grand challenge sets critical biometric face-off." available at http://www.gsnmagazine.com/dec_04/grand_challenge.html.

Exploiting Class Hierarchies for Knowledge Transfer in Hyperspectral Data

Suju Rajan and Joydeep Ghosh

Dept. of Electrical and Computer Engineering,
University of Texas at Austin, Austin TX 78712, USA
{rsuju, ghosh}@lans.ece.utexas.edu

Abstract. Obtaining ground truth for hyperspectral data is an expensive task. In addition, a number of factors cause the spectral signatures of the same class to vary with location and/or time. Therefore, adapting a classifier designed from available labeled data to classify new hyperspectral images is difficult, but invaluable to the remote sensing community. In this paper, we use the Binary Hierarchical Classifier to propose a knowledge transfer framework that leverages the information gathered from existing labeled data to classify the data obtained from a spatially separate test area. Experimental results show that in the absence of any labeled data in the new area, our approach is better than a direct application of the old classifier on the new data. Moreover, when small amounts of labeled data are available from the new area, our framework offers further improvements through semi-supervised learning mechanisms.

1 Introduction

The deployment of hyperspectral sensors on-board the earth observing satellites has generated large amounts of remotely sensed data, providing detailed hyperspectral images over extensive regions of the earth. A typical application is to determine the land cover types corresponding to the spectral signatures in the hyperspectral image, which can then be used, for example, to monitor changes in the ecosystem over large geographic areas. However, while large quantities of hyperspectral data are now available, obtaining reliable and accurate class labels for each 'pixel' is a non-trivial task, involving either expensive field campaigns or time-consuming manual interpretation of the hyperspectral images. Currently, researchers obtain the class labels for a few pixels in an image (which typically have 100,000+ pixels) and then attempt to label some other pixels in that same image. Characterizing a new image is treated as a separate, independent classification problem. Note that factors such as atmospheric and light conditions, topographic variations, etc., alter the spectral signatures corresponding to the same land cover type over images acquired at different times and/or different regions. Hence, naïve use of a classifier trained on data from one area to either spatially or temporally different data without accounting for the variability of the class signatures results in poor classification accuracies [2] [4]. Theoretically,

N.C. Oza et al. (Eds.): MCS 2005, LNCS 3541, pp. 417–427, 2005.

an ideal approach would be to pool all images of interest and then extract training data sampled uniformly at random from this pool to form a classifier that works on all these images. But a host of real-life issues such as non-availability of all the data at a given time, ownership, poor performance due to spatial variability of class signatures, size of data, etc., currently prevent researchers from being able to follow this path.

In this paper, we study a more feasible middle ground of how to exploit the knowledge inherent in a classifier trained over one area to help classify the data obtained (perhaps at a later time) from a spatially separate area. Our framework exploits additional knowledge from existing classifiers. Specifically, we use a multi-classifier system called Binary Hierarchical Classifier (BHC) [8] for this purpose. The BHC automatically derives a hierarchy of the target classes based on their mutual affinities. This hierarchy, along with the knowledge of the features extracted at each node of the BHC tree, can be used to facilitate the unsupervised classification of new data from the *spatially separate* area. Besides the unsupervised setting, the framework presented can also be employed in a semi-supervised scenario when very small quantities of labeled data are available from the spatially separate area. We present results of experiments that demonstrate the advantages of our proposed framework over other powerful multi-classifier systems, such as the ECOC [3], for the purposes of knowledge transfer for hyperspectral data.

2   Related Work

Given that obtaining labeled data, especially for remote-sensing applications is difficult and time-consuming especially for remote areas, any scheme that can leverage existing labeled data even from an area other than the one under consideration, is very desirable. The advantages of using unlabeled data in a semi-supervised setting to mitigate the sample size problems for hyperspectral data was first studied in [16]. In this work both the labeled and the unlabeled data samples came from the same image, i.e. from a common underlying distribution.

A related problem was addressed in the context of temporally varying remote sensing images in [2]. Given an image t_1 of a certain land area with a labeled training set, the problem was to classify another image t_2 of the same land area obtained at a different time. A maximum likelihood classifier was first trained on the labeled data from t_1, assuming normal distribution of the class-conditional density functions. The mean vector and the covariance matrix of the classes from t_1 were used as initial approximations to the parameter values of the same classes from t_2. These initial estimates to the classes from t_2 were then improved via EM using the corresponding unlabeled data. Experimental results on a couple of multispectral images acquired at different times showed that utilizing the labeled data from t_1 yielded comparable classification accuracy with that of a maximum likelihood classifier trained on the labeled data from t_2.

Several online-learning algorithms [1] have also been proposed to deal with the problem of temporally varying data distributions. Various possibilities of applying such online techniques in a multi-classifier setting are outlined in [9]. Most approaches to the problem of population drift design the classifier as a feedback system, in which it is assumed that there is a steady stream of objects whose true labels are revealed immediately after classification by the existing classifier. This additional knowledge of the true class labels may then cause a change in the existing classifier [6]. While hyperspectral data obtained over extensive regions (or different times) also faces a similar problem of 'population drift', unlike the on-line frameworks, one does not have access to a streaming set of labeled data samples.

While [2] demonstrates the advantage of using previously acquired knowledge in classifying a novel image, the amount of knowledge transferred was restricted by the classifier under consideration, namely the maximum likelihood classifier. The only knowledge from the training data that was transferred in that framework, were the estimates of the distributions of the class density functions in the original feature space. Using other classifier systems might enable one to extract and transfer more information from the available training data. It is in this context that we propose using the BHC as the classifier in our knowledge transfer framework.

2.1   Binary Hierarchical Classifier

The BHC [8] is a multi-classifier system that was developed primarily to deal with multi-class hyperspectral data. The BHC involves recursively decomposing a multi-class (C-classes) problem into (C-1) binary meta-class problems, resulting in (C-1) classifiers arranged as a binary tree. The given set of classes is first partitioned into two disjoint meta-classes, and each meta-class thus obtained is partitioned recursively until it contains only one of the original classes. The number of leaf nodes in the tree is, thus, equal to the number of classes in the output space. The partitioning of a parent set of classes into two-meta-classes is not arbitrary, but is obtained through a deterministic annealing process, which encourages similar classes to remain in the same partition. Thus, as a direct consequence of the BHC algorithm, classes that are similar in the input feature space are lumped into the same meta-class higher in the tree. Interested readers are referred to [8] for details of the algorithm. Each internal node of the BHC utilizes a Fisher discriminant and a Bayesian classifier. To combat the small sample size problems, the dimensionality of the feature space is reduced by recursively combining highly, correlated adjacent hyperspectral bands [7]. This best-bases method of feature extraction makes use of class information, as the correlation between bands varies among the classes, thereby yielding an interpretable feature space.

Recent empirical evaluations have shown that the BHC offers comparable classification accuracies with that of other multi-classifier systems such as the ECOC [15]. Moreover, the BHC also reveals a lot of knowledge inherent in the training data. The hierarchy of classes, for instance, might be useful as the relationships between classes in one area might still hold in another new area. Further, since the best-bases feature extraction method makes use of class-specific information in deciding the set of adjacent bands that are to be merged, this information can also be exploited in the new area. Finally, the Fisher discriminant makes use of both within-class and between-class covariances, which can also be helpful as we might expect similar correlations between the classes in the new area.

3   Knowledge Transfer Framework

Let us assume that we have hyperspectral data from two spatially separate areas, area 1 and 2. Let us also suppose that for area 1, there is an adequate amount of labeled data to build a supervised classifier. We first consider the situation where all the data from area 2 is unlabeled (unsupervised case). Subsequently, the impact on design and performance of the proposed framework is studied when labels are provided for a small part of the data from area 2 (semi-supervised case).

3.1   Unsupervised Case

In the absence of any labeled data from area 2, the first step in the knowledge transfer framework is to use the training data from area 1 to generate the corresponding BHC tree. We then attempt to transfer the knowledge in this BHC to area 2.

The first approach was to use the hierarchy of classes and the best bases feature extractors of the area 1 solution, but modify the binary classifiers in this multiclassifier system to account for the changed statistics of the spatially separate data. This was achieved via the EM framework [14] in which the training data was used to initialize the EM algorithm and the spatially separate data from area 2 was treated as the unlabeled data. Mixtures of Gaussians were used at each node of the BHC tree, with the number of Gaussians corresponding to the number of classes at each node. Each Gaussian was initialized with the mean and the covariance of the corresponding class in the training data. The initial estimates were then used to determine the posterior probabilities of the corresponding classes in the spatially separate area. EM iterations were performed until the average change in the posteriors between two iterations fell below a threshold [2] [14]. Thus, an updated Fisher-m feature extractor was computed at each node based on the statistics of the meta-classes at that iteration.

An analysis of the results showed that, while this approach was somewhat better than a direct application of the old classifier, the errors were mostly concentrated in a few classes. A closer inspection revealed that the spectral signatures of these classes had changed sufficiently enough for them to be grouped differently in the BHC hierarchies if there had been adequate amounts of labeled data from area 2. This suggested that we should have obtained multiple trees from area 1 so that some of them would be more suitable for the new area.

Thus our second approach was to introduce different randomizations into the training data and generate a BHC tree for each such randomization. The design space for the BHC tree also offers a lot of possibilities for randomizing its tree generation process. Some of the factors that were varied are the percentage of available training data, the number of features available at each node and also the process of generating meta-classes (top-down versus bottom-up) [8]. To account for the possibility of changing priors of classes, another set of BHC trees was generated by randomly altering the priors of the classes in the training data. Bagging - a popular method for generating classifier ensembles was also used to generate a set of BHC trees. Finally, in an attempt to account for the changes in class spectral signatures, a fourth set of classifiers was generated by randomly switching the labels of a small percentage of the data-points for each class. Note that in the absence of any labeled data from area 2, there is no way of evaluating which of the randomly generated BHC trees best suits the spatially separate data. Hence, we can only generate an ensemble of classifiers using the training data, hoping that the ensemble contains some classifiers that are better suited to area 2.

The Q-diversity measure [10], which indicates the degree of correlation between a pair of classifiers, was used to ensure the diversity of our classifier ensemble. Each tree in the classifier ensemble was made to label the data from area 2 and these labels were then used to obtain the Q- diversity measure between each pair of classifiers. The classification results of a smaller set of classifiers with the lowest average pairwise Q-measure (i.e., higher diversity) were then combined via simple majority voting.

3.2   Semi-supervised Case

If there are adequate amounts of labeled data from area 2, one can just train a classifier using the available labeled data. But for small amounts of labeled data, we would expect the two knowledge transfer mechanisms discussed earlier to be superior especially if they exploit this added information. In this section, we generalize both knowledge transfer methods in order to leverage the labeled data, and also determine how much labeled data is required from the spatially separate area before the advantages of transferring information from the old solution disappear.

The EM-based method was modified to perform constrained EM instead. Simply stated, in this technique, the E step only updates the posterior probabilities (memberships) for the unlabeled data, while fixing the memberships of the labeled instances according to the known class assignments.

The ensemble based approach was modified in two stages. First, after the set of classifiers was pruned to improve the diversity of the ensemble by using the Q-diversity measure, we went through another round of pruning to include only those classifiers with higher classification accuracies on the labeled data. A scheme similar to the on-line weighted majority algorithm as detailed in [11] was used to weight the different classifiers. In the weighted majority algorithm, all classifiers are assigned a weight. Prior to learning, the weights of all the classifiers are the same, and then as each data sample is presented to the ensemble, a classifier's weight is reduced if it misclassifies that example. At the end of this learning, all those classifiers that have better classification accuracies on the incoming data will have higher weights. Then for each new example, the ensemble returns the class that gets the maximum total weighted vote over all the classifiers. This weighted majority scheme ensures that the performance of the ensemble is not much worse than that of the best individual predictor, regardless of the dependence between the members of the ensemble [11].

The labeled data was also used to initialize the mean vectors and the covariance matrices of the meta-classes, at the nodes of the binary trees in the Q-diversity measure pruned ensemble. The labeled and the unlabeled data from area 2 were then used for constrained EM in each of the binary trees. The classification results of the resulting ensemble were then combined using the weighted majority algorithm as detailed above.

4   Experimental Evaluation

In this section, we provide empirical evidence that in the absence of labeled data from the spatially separate area, using knowledge transfer is better than the direct application of existing classifiers to this new area. We also present results showing that with small amounts of labeled data from the new area, our framework performs better than the current state-of-the-art ECOC multiclassifier system [3] with SVMs [5] as the binary classifiers.

4.1   Datasets

The knowledge transfer approaches described above were tested on hyperspectral datasets obtained from two sites: NASA's John F. Kennedy Space Center (KSC), Florida [12] and the Okavango Delta, Botswana [4]. In both these datasets, the labeled data (area 1) was subsampled such that 75% of the data was used for training and 25% as the test set. For both cases, a second test set was also acquired from a spatially separate region (area 2). Since the spatially separate test set comes from a different geographic location, various factors such as the sun angle, shadow and other temporal factors cause a natural variation of the hyperspectral signatures. This variation in spectral signatures along with the changes in the apriori probabilities of the landcover classes offers an ideal setting to test the knowledge transfer framework. While the numbers of classes in the two regions vary, we restrict ourselves to those classes that are present in both regions.

4.2   Experimental Methodology

For our experiments, we used a BHC based on the Fisher-m feature extractor and the posterior probabilities were obtained by soft combining. Adjacent hyperspectral bands that were highly correlated were merged using the best bases feature extraction technique [7] prior to applying the Fisher feature extractor. Adjacent bands were merged until the ratio of the training samples to the number of dimensions was at least five at each node of the classifier tree [13]. For

Table 1. Average unsupervised classification accuracies for the spatially separate test sets

Name	Baselines			Knowledge Transfer Approaches	
	Old BHC	Old ECOC +SVM	Ensemble BHC +Maj. Vote	Old BHC + EM	Ensemble BHC +EM +Maj. Vote
KSC	61.84 (0.60)	64.27 (0.27)	64.4 (0.10)	65.82 (2.86)	65.12(1.97)
Botswana	73.04 (2.25)	75.22(0.65)	74.82(0.75)	79.13 (1.96)	79.8 (1.8)

both the unsupervised and the semi-supervised cases, the classification accuracies were obtained by averaging over 5 different samples of the training data (from area 1) or the labeled spatially separate data (from area 2) as the case may be.

The ensemble of BHC trees was generated by varying the percentages of available training data (5 different rates), the number of features available at each node (10 different subsets), the top-down and bottom-up generation of the BHC tree, by randomly altering the priors of the classes in the training data (40 such randomizations), bagging (40 samplings with replacement) and by randomly switching the labels of a small percentage (10%) of the data-points for each class (40 such randomizations). Thus, a total of 220 different randomizations of the BHC were generated from the original training data. The Q-diversity measure was then used to prune the existing ensemble such that the final ensemble contained the 10 classifiers with the lowest average pairwise Q-measure.

For the ECOC system, the code matrix was generated using the technique proposed in [3]. SVMs with Gaussian kernels were trained for each binary problem induced by the code matrix. The The implementation and the tuning of the SVM classifiers followed the same method as in [15] with 40% of the available labeled data as the validation data.

4.3   Results and Discussion

Unsupervised Case: First, the BHC, the ECOC-SVM and the BHC-Ensemble built on the training data from area 1 were used without any modification to classify the data from the spatially separate area 2. Table 1 shows the classification accuracies obtained by the baseline and the knowledge transfer approaches on the area 2 data. As a frame of reference, the classification accuracies on the area 1 test set for the BHC and the ECOC-SVM are 93.05%(±1.17) and 93%(±1.03) for the KSC dataset. For the Botswana dataset the corresponding classification accuracies are and 94.52%(±0.79) and 95.63%(±0.95) respectively.

It can be seen from Table 1 that when the unlabeled data from area 2 is used via EM to update the statistics of the meta-classes in the BHC tree, the resulting BHC tree performs better than the old BHC. However, updating the BHC ensemble via semi-supervised learning does not provide any additional gains.

The Botswana dataset benefits a lot more from the information in area 1 than the KSC. While the area 1 and area 2 data of the Botswana dataset were

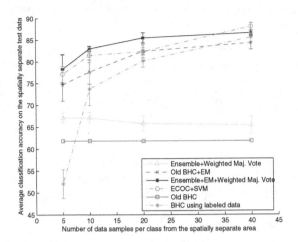

Fig. 1. Average semi-supervised classification accuracies for the KSC dataset

obtained from the same flightline [4], the area 2 data for the KSC was obtained from a different subset of the flightline [12]. Therefore, the greater disparity in the spectral signatures of the classes between the two areas in the KSC dataset limits the amount of knowledge that can be transferred from one area to another.

Semi-supervised Case: Fig. 1 and Fig. 2 show the learning curves for the KSC and the Botswana dataset when labeled data is available from area 2. It can be observed from Fig.1 and Fig.2 that the ensemble with the weighted majority vote does not offer any advantage over the other classification systems, especially when there is an adequate amount of labeled data. For both the KSC and the Botswana datasets, an examination of the weights assigned to the classifiers of the ensemble showed that when the number of labeled samples per class (> 10) was high, the classifiers in the ensemble had almost equal weights. Hence, the accuracy of the ensemble was limited by the classification accuracies of its constituent classifiers.

Similar to the unsupervised scenario, using the data (labeled and unlabeled) from area 2 with EM to update the statistics of the classifiers improved the classification accuracy of the old BHC for the KSC dataset (Fig. 1). For the Botswana dataset the old BHC with EM showed an improvement only when a sufficient number of labeled samples per class (> 10) were available from the spatially separate area. This may be due to the complexity of the classification problem (14 classes as opposed to 10 in the KSC) or due to a poor choice of the labeled data samples. The high values of standard deviation seem to hint at the latter reason.

By adapting the BHC ensemble components via constrained EM some of them became more effective for the new area. The weighted majority algorithm was then able to exploit this differentiation to produce a knowledge transfer

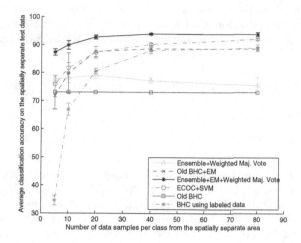

Fig. 2. Average semi-supervised classification accuracies for the Botswana dataset

framework that proved a clear winner for small amounts of labeled data. As more labeled data becomes available from area 2, classifiers trained on that data will perform at least as well if not better than the updated classifiers from area 1. The amount of labeled data from area 2 required for this cross-over is surprisingly a lot especially for the Botswana dataset where knowledge transfer is more effective because of the reason mentioned earlier.

5   Summary and Conclusions

We initially thought that the BHC would be particularly well-suited for knowledge transfer since it provides not only a class hierarchy but also the feature extractors that are suitable for resolving the dichotomies involved at the different stages of the hierarchy. In particular, it would be more effective than alternative classifiers, including the maximum likelihood based approach investigated earlier. However, in this application the data characteristics change fairly substantially from area to area, demanding more elaborate adjustments. The best suited class hierarchies as well as the most appropriate feature extractors change at least incrementally as one moves to a new area. We were able to cater to both these needs by (i) using the weighted majority combining approach on an ensemble of trees so that trees more suitable for the new area get higher weights, and (ii) using constrained, semi-supervised EM that can adjust the feature spaces as well as classification boundaries based on both labeled/unlabeled data acquired from the new area. Against this combination, the alternative of building a new classifier from scratch using a powerful and suitable method (ECOC-SVM) was advantageous only when over 30 labeled samples/class were available from the new area for KSC. For Botswana, where the two areas are more similar, the composite knowledge transfer approach was superior even when

80 labeled samples/class were available from the new area. In addition, our approaches provide computational advantages since fewer iterations are required for model parameters to converge because of good initialization based on prior knowledge.

Acknowledgements. This research was supported by NSF (Grant IIS-0312471).

References

1. A. Blum. On-line algorithms in machine learning. In Fiat and Woeginger, editors, *Online Algorithms: The State of the Art.* LNCS Vol.1442, Springer, 1998.
2. L. Bruzzone and D. F. Prieto. Unsupervised retraining of a maximum likelihood classifier for the analysis of multitemporal remote sensing images. *IEEE Trans. Geoscience and Remote Sensing*, 39:456–460, 2001.
3. T. G. Dietterich and G. Bakiri. Solving multiclass learning problems via error-correcting output codes. *Journal of Artificial Intelligence Research*, 2:263–286, 1995.
4. J. Ham, Y. Chen, M. M. Crawford, and J. Ghosh. Investigation of the random forest framework for classification of hyperspectral data. *IEEE Trans. Geoscience and Remote Sensing*, page to appear, 2005.
5. T. Joachims. Making large-scale SVM learning practical. In C. Burges B. Scholkopf and A. Smola, editors, *Advances in Kernel Methods: Support Vector Learning*, pages 169–184. MIT Press, Cambridge, USA, 1999.
6. M. G. Kelly, D. J. Hand, and M. N. Adams. The impact of changing populations on classifier performance. In *The Fifth ACM SIGKDD International Conference on Knowledge Discovery and Data Mining*, pages 67–371, 1999.
7. S. Kumar, J. Ghosh, and M. M. Crawford. Best-bases feature extraction algorithms for classification of hyperspectral data. *IEEE Trans. Geoscience and Remote Sensing*, 39(7):1368–79, 2001.
8. S. Kumar, J. Ghosh, and M. M. Crawford. Hierarchical fusion of multiple classifiers for hyperspectral data analysis. *Pattern Analysis and Applications, spl. Issue on Fusion of Multiple Classifiers*, 5(2):210–220, 2002.
9. L. I. Kuncheva. Classifier ensembles for changing environments. In J. Kittler and F. Roli, editors, *Multiple Classifier Systems*, pages 1–15. LNCS Vol. 3077, Springer, 2004.
10. L. I. Kuncheva and C. J. Whitaker. Measures of diversity in classifier ensembles. *Machine Learning*, 51:181–207, 2003.
11. N. Littlestone and M. K. Warmuth. The weighted majority algorithm. *Information and Computation*, 108:212–261, 1994.
12. J. T. Morgan. *Adaptive Hierarchical Classifier with Limited Training Data.* PhD thesis, Dept. of Mech. Eng., Univ. of Texas at Austin, 2002.
13. J. T. Morgan, A. Henneguelle, J. Ham, M. M. Crawford, and J. Ghosh. Adaptive feature spaces for land cover classification with limited ground truth data". *International Journal of Pattern Recognition and Artificial Intelligence (IJPRAI)*, 18:777–800, 2004.
14. K. Nigam, A. K. Mccallum, S. Thrun, and T. Mitchell. Text classification from labeled and unlabeled documents using EM. *Machine Learning*, 39(2/3):103–134, 2000.

15. S. Rajan and J. Ghosh. An empirical comparison of hierarchical vs. two-level approaches to multiclass problems. In F. Roli, J. Kittler, and T. Windeatt, editors, *Multiple Classifier Systems*, pages 283–292. LNCS Vol. 3077, Springer, 2004.
16. B. M. Shahshahani and D. A. Landgrebe. The effect of unlabeled samples in reducing the small sample size problem and mitigating the hughes phenomenon. *IEEE Trans. Geoscience and Remote Sensing*, 32:1087–1095, 1994.

Author Index

Lecture Notes in Computer Science

For information about Vols. 1–3442

please contact your bookseller or Springer

Vol. 3556: H. Baumeister, M. Marchesi, M. Holcombe (Eds.), Extreme Programming and Agile Processes in Software Engineering. XIV, 332 pages. 2005.

Vol. 3555: T. Vardanega, A. Wellings (Eds.), Reliable Software Technology – Ada-Europe 2005. XV, 273 pages. 2005.

Vol. 3552: H. de Meer, N. Bhatti (Eds.), Quality of Service – IWQoS 2005. XV, 273 pages. 2005.

Vol. 3543: L. Kutvonen, N. Alonistioti (Eds.), Distributed Applications and Interoperable Systems. XI, 235 pages. 2005.

Vol. 3541: N.C. Oza, R. Polikar, J. Kittler, F. Roli (Eds.), Multiple Classifier Systems. XII, 430 pages. 2005.

Vol. 3537: A. Apostolico, M. Crochemore, K. Park (Eds.), Combinatorial Pattern Matching. XI, 444 pages. 2005.

Vol. 3535: M. Steffen, G. Zavattaro (Eds.), Formal Methods for Open Object-Based Distributed Systems. X, 323 pages. 2005.

Vol. 3532: A. Gómez-Pérez, J. Euzenat (Eds.), The Semantic Web: Research and Applications. XV, 728 pages. 2005.

Vol. 3531: J. Ioannidis, A. Keromytis, M. Yung (Eds.), Applied Cryptography and Network Security. XI, 530 pages. 2005.

Vol. 3528: P.S. Szczepaniak, J. Kacprzyk, A. Niewiadomski (Eds.), Advances in Web Intelligence. XVII, 513 pages. 2005. (Subseries LNAI).

Vol. 3527: R. Morrison, F. Oquendo (Eds.), Software Architecture. XII, 263 pages. 2005.

Vol. 3526: S.B. Cooper, B. Löwe, L. Torenvliet (Eds.), New Computational Paradigms. XVII, 574 pages. 2005.

Vol. 3525: A.E. Abdallah, C.B. Jones, J.W. Sanders (Eds.), Communicating Sequential Processes. XIV, 321 pages. 2005.

Vol. 3524: R. Barták, M. Milano (Eds.), Integration of AI and OR Techniques in Constraint Programming for Combinatorial Optimization Problems. XI, 320 pages. 2005.

Vol. 3523: J.S. Marques, N.P. de la Blanca, P. Pina (Eds.), Pattern Recognition and Image Analysis, Part II. XXVI, 733 pages. 2005.

Vol. 3522: J.S. Marques, N.P. de la Blanca, P. Pina (Eds.), Pattern Recognition and Image Analysis, Part I. XXVI, 703 pages. 2005.

Vol. 3521: N. Megiddo, Y. Xu, B. Zhu (Eds.), Algorithmic Applications in Management. XIII, 484 pages. 2005.

Vol. 3520: O. Pastor, J. Falcão e Cunha (Eds.), Advanced Information Systems Engineering. XVI, 584 pages. 2005.

Vol. 3519: H. Li, P. J. Olver, G. Sommer (Eds.), Computer Algebra and Geometric Algebra with Applications. IX, 449 pages. 2005.

Vol. 3518: T.B. Ho, D. Cheung, H. Li (Eds.), Advances in Knowledge Discovery and Data Mining. XXI, 864 pages. 2005. (Subseries LNAI).

Vol. 3517: H.S. Baird, D.P. Lopresti (Eds.), Human Interactive Proofs. IX, 143 pages. 2005.

Vol. 3516: V.S. Sunderam, G.D.v. Albada, P.M.A. Sloot, J.J. Dongarra (Eds.), Computational Science – ICCS 2005, Part III. LXIII, 1143 pages. 2005.

Vol. 3515: V.S. Sunderam, G.D.v. Albada, P.M.A. Sloot, J.J. Dongarra (Eds.), Computational Science – ICCS 2005, Part II. LXIII, 1101 pages. 2005.

Vol. 3514: V.S. Sunderam, G.D.v. Albada, P.M.A. Sloot, J.J. Dongarra (Eds.), Computational Science – ICCS 2005, Part I. LXIII, 1089 pages. 2005.

Vol. 3513: A. Montoyo, R. Muñoz, E. Métais (Eds.), Natural Language Processing and Information Systems. XII, 408 pages. 2005.

Vol. 3512: J. Cabestany, A. Prieto, F. Sandoval (Eds.), Computational Intelligence and Bioinspired Systems. XXV, 1260 pages. 2005.

Vol. 3510: T. Braun, G. Carle, Y. Koucheryavy, V. Tsaoussidis (Eds.), Wired/Wireless Internet Communications. XIV, 366 pages. 2005.

Vol. 3509: M. Jünger, V. Kaibel (Eds.), Integer Programming and Combinatorial Optimization. XI, 484 pages. 2005.

Vol. 3508: P. Bresciani, P. Giorgini, B. Henderson-Sellers, G. Low, M. Winikoff (Eds.), Agent-Oriented Information Systems II. X, 227 pages. 2005. (Subseries LNAI).

Vol. 3507: F. Crestani, I. Ruthven (Eds.), Information Context: Nature, Impact, and Role. XIII, 253 pages. 2005.

Vol. 3506: C. Park, S. Chee (Eds.), Information Security and Cryptology – ICISC 2004. XIV, 490 pages. 2005.

Vol. 3505: V. Gorodetsky, J. Liu, V. A. Skormin (Eds.), Autonomous Intelligent Systems: Agents and Data Mining. XIII, 303 pages. 2005. (Subseries LNAI).

Vol. 3504: A.F. Frangi, P.I. Radeva, A. Santos, M. Hernandez (Eds.), Functional Imaging and Modeling of the Heart. XV, 489 pages. 2005.

Vol. 3503: S.E. Nikoletseas (Ed.), Experimental and Efficient Algorithms. XV, 624 pages. 2005.

Vol. 3502: F. Khendek, R. Dssouli (Eds.), Testing of Communicating Systems. X, 381 pages. 2005.

Vol. 3501: B. Kégl, G. Lapalme (Eds.), Advances in Artificial Intelligence. XV, 458 pages. 2005. (Subseries LNAI).

Vol. 3500: S. Miyano, J. Mesirov, S. Kasif, S. Istrail, P. Pevzner, M. Waterman (Eds.), Research in Computational Molecular Biology. XVII, 632 pages. 2005. (Subseries LNBI).

Vol. 3499: A. Pelc, M. Raynal (Eds.), Structural Information and Communication Complexity. X, 323 pages. 2005.

Vol. 3498: J. Wang, X. Liao, Z. Yi (Eds.), Advances in Neural Networks – ISNN 2005, Part III. L, 1077 pages. 2005.

Vol. 3497: J. Wang, X. Liao, Z. Yi (Eds.), Advances in Neural Networks – ISNN 2005, Part II. L, 947 pages. 2005.

Vol. 3496: J. Wang, X. Liao, Z. Yi (Eds.), Advances in Neural Networks – ISNN 2005, Part II. L, 1055 pages. 2005.

Vol. 3495: P. Kantor, G. Muresan, F. Roberts, D.D. Zeng, F.-Y. Wang, H. Chen, R.C. Merkle (Eds.), Intelligence and Security Informatics. XVIII, 674 pages. 2005.

Vol. 3494: R. Cramer (Ed.), Advances in Cryptology – EUROCRYPT 2005. XIV, 576 pages. 2005.

Vol. 3493: N. Fuhr, M. Lalmas, S. Malik, Z. Szlávik (Eds.), Advances in XML Information Retrieval. XI, 438 pages. 2005.

Vol. 3492: P. Blache, E. Stabler, J. Busquets, R. Moot (Eds.), Logical Aspects of Computational Linguistics. X, 363 pages. 2005. (Subseries LNAI).

Vol. 3489: G.T. Heineman, I. Crnkovic, H.W. Schmidt, J.A. Stafford, C. Szyperski, K. Wallnau (Eds.), Component-Based Software Engineering. XI, 358 pages. 2005.

Vol. 3488: M.-S. Hacid, N.V. Murray, Z.W. Raś, S. Tsumoto (Eds.), Foundations of Intelligent Systems. XIII, 700 pages. 2005. (Subseries LNAI).

Vol. 3486: T. Helleseth, D. Sarwate, H.-Y. Song, K. Yang (Eds.), Sequences and Their Applications - SETA 2004. XII, 451 pages. 2005.

Vol. 3483: O. Gervasi, M.L. Gavrilova, V. Kumar, A. Laganà, H.P. Lee, Y. Mun, D. Taniar, C.J.K. Tan (Eds.), Computational Science and Its Applications – ICCSA 2005, Part IV. XXVII, 1362 pages. 2005.

Vol. 3482: O. Gervasi, M.L. Gavrilova, V. Kumar, A. Laganà, H.P. Lee, Y. Mun, D. Taniar, C.J.K. Tan (Eds.), Computational Science and Its Applications – ICCSA 2005, Part III. LXVI, 1340 pages. 2005.

Vol. 3481: O. Gervasi, M.L. Gavrilova, V. Kumar, A. Laganà, H.P. Lee, Y. Mun, D. Taniar, C.J.K. Tan (Eds.), Computational Science and Its Applications – ICCSA 2005, Part II. LXIV, 1316 pages. 2005.

Vol. 3480: O. Gervasi, M.L. Gavrilova, V. Kumar, A. Laganà, H.P. Lee, Y. Mun, D. Taniar, C.J.K. Tan (Eds.), Computational Science and Its Applications – ICCSA 2005, Part I. LXV, 1234 pages. 2005.

Vol. 3479: T. Strang, C. Linnhoff-Popien (Eds.), Location- and Context-Awareness. XII, 378 pages. 2005.

Vol. 3478: C. Jermann, A. Neumaier, D. Sam (Eds.), Global Optimization and Constraint Satisfaction. XIII, 193 pages. 2005.

Vol. 3477: P. Herrmann, V. Issarny, S. Shiu (Eds.), Trust Management. XII, 426 pages. 2005.

Vol. 3476: J. Leite, A. Omicini, P. Torroni, P. Yolum (Eds.), Declarative Agent Languages and Technologies. XII, 289 pages. 2005.

Vol. 3475: N. Guelfi (Ed.), Rapid Integration of Software Engineering Techniques. X, 145 pages. 2005.

Vol. 3474: C. Grelck, F. Huch, G.J. Michaelson, P. Trinder (Eds.), Implementation and Application of Functional Languages. X, 227 pages. 2005.

Vol. 3468: H.W. Gellersen, R. Want, A. Schmidt (Eds.), Pervasive Computing. XIII, 347 pages. 2005.

Vol. 3467: J. Giesl (Ed.), Term Rewriting and Applications. XIII, 517 pages. 2005.

Vol. 3465: M. Bernardo, A. Bogliolo (Eds.), Formal Methods for Mobile Computing. VII, 271 pages. 2005.

Vol. 3464: S.A. Brueckner, G.D.M. Serugendo, A. Karageorgos, R. Nagpal (Eds.), Engineering Self-Organising Systems. XIII, 299 pages. 2005. (Subseries LNAI).

Vol. 3463: M. Dal Cin, M. Kaâniche, A. Pataricza (Eds.), Dependable Computing - EDCC 2005. XVI, 472 pages. 2005.

Vol. 3462: R. Boutaba, K.C. Almeroth, R. Puigjaner, S. Shen, J.P. Black (Eds.), NETWORKING 2005. XXX, 1483 pages. 2005.

Vol. 3461: P. Urzyczyn (Ed.), Typed Lambda Calculi and Applications. XI, 433 pages. 2005.

Vol. 3460: Ö. Babaoglu, M. Jelasity, A. Montresor, C. Fetzer, S. Leonardi, A. van Moorsel, M. van Steen (Eds.), Self-star Properties in Complex Information Systems. IX, 447 pages. 2005.

Vol. 3459: R. Kimmel, N.A. Sochen, J. Weickert (Eds.), Scale Space and PDE Methods in Computer Vision. XI, 634 pages. 2005.

Vol. 3458: P. Herrero, M.S. Pérez, V. Robles (Eds.), Scientific Applications of Grid Computing. X, 208 pages. 2005.

Vol. 3456: H. Rust, Operational Semantics for Timed Systems. XII, 223 pages. 2005.

Vol. 3455: H. Treharne, S. King, M. Henson, S. Schneider (Eds.), ZB 2005: Formal Specification and Development in Z and B. XV, 493 pages. 2005.

Vol. 3454: J.-M. Jacquet, G.P. Picco (Eds.), Coordination Models and Languages. X, 299 pages. 2005.

Vol. 3453: L. Zhou, B.C. Ooi, X. Meng (Eds.), Database Systems for Advanced Applications. XXVII, 929 pages. 2005.

Vol. 3452: F. Baader, A. Voronkov (Eds.), Logic for Programming, Artificial Intelligence, and Reasoning. XI, 562 pages. 2005. (Subseries LNAI).

Vol. 3450: D. Hutter, M. Ullmann (Eds.), Security in Pervasive Computing. XI, 239 pages. 2005.

Vol. 3449: F. Rothlauf, J. Branke, S. Cagnoni, D.W. Corne, R. Drechsler, Y. Jin, P. Machado, E. Marchiori, J. Romero, G.D. Smith, G. Squillero (Eds.), Applications of Evolutionary Computing. XX, 631 pages. 2005.

Vol. 3448: G.R. Raidl, J. Gottlieb (Eds.), Evolutionary Computation in Combinatorial Optimization. XI, 271 pages. 2005.

Vol. 3447: M. Keijzer, A. Tettamanzi, P. Collet, J.v. Hemert, M. Tomassini (Eds.), Genetic Programming. XIII, 382 pages. 2005.

Vol. 3444: M. Sagiv (Ed.), Programming Languages and Systems. XIII, 439 pages. 2005.

Vol. 3443: R. Bodik (Ed.), Compiler Construction. XI, 305 pages. 2005.